# WORKING CAPITAL

## Life and Labour in Contemporary London

To the memory of

**MICHAEL YOUNG**
1915–2002

**ROY PORTER**
1946–2002

*Fellow Researchers into*
*London Life and Labour*

# WORKING CAPITAL

## Life and Labour in Contemporary London

NICK BUCK
IAN GORDON
PETER HALL
MICHAEL HARLOE
MARK KLEINMAN

*In association with*

Belinda Brown
Karen O'Reilly
Gareth Potts
Laura Smethurst
Jo Sparkes

Routledge
Taylor & Francis Group

LONDON AND NEW YORK

First published 2002 by Routledge
11 New Fetter Lane, London EC4P 4EE

Simultaneously published in the USA and Canada
by Routledge, 29 West 35th Street, New York, NY 10001

Routledge is an imprint of the Taylor & Francis Group

Typeset in Humanist and Palatino by PNR Design, Didcot, Oxfordshire
Printed and bound in Great Britain by TJ International Ltd, Padstow, Cornwall

This book was commissioned and edited by Alexandrine Press, Oxford

British Library Cataloguing in Publication Data

*A catalogue record for this book is available from the British Library*

Library of Congress Cataloging in Publication Data

Working capital: life and labour in contemporary London/Nick Buck ... [et al.]
    p. cm.
  Includes bibliographical references and index.
  ISBN 0–415–27931–3 — ISBN 0–415–27932–1 (pbk.)
     1. London (Eng.)—Social conditions. 2. London (Eng.)—Economic conditions.
  3. London (Eng.)—Politics and government. 4. Social classes—England—London.
  5. Labor—England—London. I. Buck, N. H., 1953–

HN398.L7 W67 2002
306'.09421—dc21

                                                        2002026940


ISBN 0  415  27931–3 (hb)  0–415–27932–1 (pb)

# Contents

# List of Figures

# List of Abbreviations

| | | | | |
|---|---|---|---|---|
| BAA | British Airports Authority | IT | Information Technology |
| BCS | British Crime Survey | JIT | Just in Time |
| BHPS | British Household Panel Study | LCC | London County Council |
| CBD | Central Business District | LDA | London Development Agency |
| CTRL | Channel Tunnel Rail Link | LDDC | London Docklands Development Corporation |
| DETR | Department of Environment, Transport and the Regions | LEA | Local Education Authority |
| DfEE | Department for Education and Employment | LES | London Employer Survey |
| DFES | Department of Education and Science | LFS | Labour Force Survey |
| DTLR | Department of Transport, Local Government and the Regions | LRC | London Research Centre |
| | | LSE | London School of Economics |
| EEDA | East of England Development Agency | LTB | London Tourist Board |
| EC | European Community | MOT | Ministry of Transport (vehicle test) |
| EU | European Union | NES | New Earnings Survey |
| FE | Further Education | NOMIS | National Online Manpower Information System |
| FTE | Full-Time Equivalent | OECD | Organisation for Economic Co-operation and Development |
| FUR | Functional Urban Region | | |
| GB | Great Britain | OFSTED | Office for Standards in Education |
| GCSE | General Certificate of Secondary Education | ODPM | Office of the Deputy Prime Minister |
| | | OMA | Outer Metropolitan Area |
| GDP | Gross Domestic Product | R&D | Research and Development |
| GLA | Greater London Authority | RAE | Research Assessment Exercise |
| GLC | Greater London Council | RDA | Regional Development Agency |
| GM | Grant Maintained (school) | ROSE | Rest Of the South East |
| GOL | Government Office for London | SEEDA | South East England Development Agency |
| GWR | Great Western Railway | | |
| HESA | Higher Education Statistics Agency | SEG | Socio-Economic Group |
| HQ | Headquarters | SRB | Single Regeneration Budget |
| ICT | Information and Communications Technologies | UK | United Kingdom |
| | | US | United States |
| ILEA | Inner London Education Authority | VAT | Value Added Tax |
| IMD2000 | Index of Multiple Deprivation for 2000 | | |

# The Authors

Nick Buck is Professor, Director of the ESRC UK Longitudinal Studies Centre and Acting Director of the Institute for Social and Economic Research at the University of Essex, where he has particular responsibility for the British Household Panel Study. His personal research interests involve the causes and consequences of household and territorial inequality; labour market marginality and multiple deprivation; neighbourhood effects on social exclusion; and methodological aspects of longitudinal data. Among his previous publications are: *The London Employment Problem* (with Gordon and Young), *Changing Households* and *Understanding Panel Data*. He was a major contributor to *Divided Cities: London* and *New York in the contemporary world* (ed. Fainstein, Gordon and Harloe) and was a co-author of the Socio-economic Appraisal of London for the EU/Association of London Government's 1997 'London Study' (with Crookston, Gordon and Hall).

Ian Gordon is Professor of Human Geography at the London School of Economics, and Director of LSE London. His main research interests are in urban economic development, spatial labour markets, migration, and urban policy, particularly in the context of the London region and comparable metropoles. Previous publications include: *The London Employment Problem* (with Buck and Young, 1986); *Unemployment, Regions and Labour Markets*; *Divided Cities: London and New York in the contemporary world* (co-edited with Fainstein and Harloe); and *Territorial Competition in an Integrating Europe* (co-edited with Cheshire). Contributions to published reports on the region include co-authorship of the *Socio-economic Appraisal of London* (with Buck, Crookston and Hall) and *The Place of London in the UK Economy* (with Travers and Whitehead).

Peter Hall is Professor of Planning at the Bartlett School of Architecture and Planning, University College London, and Director of the Institute of Community Studies. He is author or editor of over thirty books on cities, planning and economic geography, including *The Industries of London since 1861*, *London 2000*, *The World Cities, Cities of Tomorrow, London 2001*, *Technopoles of the World*, *Cities in Civilization* and *Urban Future 21*. Major advisory roles have included: Special Adviser on Strategic Planning to the Secretary of State for the Environment (1991–94); member of the Deputy Prime Minister's Urban Task Force (chaired by Richard Rogers, 1998–89); chair of the (US) SSRC's Research Committee on the Urban Underclass (1992–94); and convenor of the World Commission on 21st-Century Urbanization (Urban21, reporting in 2000). He is a Fellow of the British Academy and was knighted in 1998 for services to the Town and Country Planning Association.

Michael Harloe is Vice Chancellor and Professor of Sociology at the University of Salford. He is the author of many books and papers on urban social theory, housing and urban development, including comparative studies involving Western and Eastern Europe and the USA. He was the founder editor of the International Journal of Urban and Regional Research. His first major book, published in 1974, was on housing in London and he jointly edited *Divided Cities: New York and London in the contemporary world* (with Fainstein and Gordon, 1992). He is a Member of the Academy of Learned Societies in the Social Sciences. In the 1970s he was a member of the Greater London Council Housing Development Committee. Currently he chairs an urban regeneration partnership in inner Salford, is Chair of the North West University Association and a member of the North West Regional Assembly.

Mark Kleinman is Professor of International Social Policy at the University of Bristol and a member of the Public Policy Group at the London School of Economics. His research interests include comparative urban governance; citizenship and welfare in the European Union; and international migration and urban labour markets. His publications include: *A European Welfare State? European social policy in context* (2001); and *Housing, Welfare and the State in Europe: a comparative analysis of Britain, France and Germany* (1996) as well as a forthcoming book with Tony Travers – *Governing London: power and politics in a global city*. He has been a member of advisory panels for the Minister for Local Government and for HM Treasury, and has acted as a consultant for, among others, the European Commission, the Department for Education and Skills, the National Audit Office and several local authorities. He is currently on secondment to the UK Cabinet Office Strategy Unit.

# Preface

This is not the first time any of us has written about London. Far from it: we seem to have been studying it, and trying to get to grips with its daunting richness and complexity, for most of our academic lives. But this book is different from anything we have done before, in three important ways.

First, in it we attempt to make sense of what has happened to London over a period of some 20 years, from the early 1980s, during which its experience – like that of cities generally, and indeed the ways we talk about cities worldwide – seems to have turned some kind of corner. Secondly, we try to understand how broad trends, evident at the metropolitan level, relate down to life and business as they are carried on in the very different localities of the region. Thirdly, we approach this by drawing on an extensive range of interviews with households, business people, educators and public sector actors, as well as detailed analyses of a body of survey and statistical sources on the region, much of which was unavailable for our earlier work on the city region.

London is in different ways both a particularly difficult and a relatively easy city to write about. On the one hand, its sheer scale and complexity are challenging, particularly if you take the view – as we do – that it needs to be viewed from a city-regional perspective. On the other hand, new work stands on the shoulders of a mass of existing literature, some of very high quality, and in the midst of a very strong research community (both of Londoners and overseas scholars) currently working on aspects of its socio-economic and political development. While we were completing this book, this research community lost two of its most distinguished members: Michael Young and Roy Porter, to whom we dedicate this book.

Practically our work was made possible by a substantial grant (L130 25 1027) from the ESRC *Cities: Competitiveness and Cohesion* programme, as one of four 'integrative city studies' whose brief was to examine how a wide range of processes affecting these concerns interacted in particular places. This grant supported a strong interdisciplinary team of researchers who worked together with us, researching and writing and meeting, monthly and sometimes more frequently, for three years. Within this team Karen O'Reilly was responsible in the first year for much of the quantitative sociological work, particularly on issues of social capital, before moving on to a lectureship at the other end of the country. The other four members of the research team – Belinda Brown, Gareth Potts, Laura Smethurst, and Jo Sparkes – were responsible for the area-based fieldwork which was the focus of later phases of the project. Each was responsible for scoping studies and then for interviews in a particular pair of areas, while each of them also took the lead in generating information on one sub-set of themes, designing relevant parts of the semi-structured interview programme, and feeding through information for writing up the main findings in relation to these: Belinda took primary responsibility for issues of community and crime; Gareth for business and employment issues; Laura for services, social exclusion and social capital; and Jo for education and governance. Jo also did further work on London-wide governance issues under a related project, part of ESRC's *Devolution and Constitutional Change* programme, supported by grant L220 25 2003, jointly directed by Mark Kleinman and Peter Hall. Within the main project a number of supplementary interviews were carried out by Henrietta Owusu Ansah in Southwark and by Tad Heuer in the City. Tad also carried out some London governance interviews. Completion of this book has taken a further twelve months since the grant (and employment contracts) expired, but we were fortunate that Belinda and Laura were able to continue playing an active role in meetings and discussions through a long sequence of drafts of chapters. This book depends totally on their work.

Among other members of London's research community we want particularly to acknowledge our debt to those who participated in the ESRC-sponsored 'London' research seminar which we convened through the four-year period preceding this study. We benefited particularly from discussions with a core group of continuing participants including Irene Bruegel, Les Budd, Tim Butler, John Davis, Michael Edwards, Dan Graham, John Hall, Chris Hamnett, Michael Hebbert, Michael Keith, Michal Lyons, Ann Page, Judith Ryser, and Andy Thornley. During this period we also gained valuable insights, which fed directly into this book, from our work with Llewelyn Davies Planning on the ALG-sponsored London study, *A Socio-Economic Assessment of London*, which was published in 1997.

We have also had valuable interchanges with our counterparts on other projects within the ESRC *Cities: Competitiveness and Cohesion* programme, particularly the other 'integrative city studies' – Martin Boddy in Bristol, Alan Harding in Liverpool-Manchester and Ivan Turok in Glasgow – and also with researchers from 'thematic' projects working on aspects of development in the region, including Sophie Bowlby, Tim Butler, Jo Foord, Norman Ginsburg, Geoff Meen and James Simmie. We also recognize the contributions made by discussions with collaborators on related projects – Nick Banks, Paul Cheshire, Martin Crookston, Christian Lefevre, Ray Pahl, Tony Travers and Christine Whitehead – and with members of the Global Cities Working Group – John Mollenkopf, Pierre Bekouche, Toshio Kamo, Takashi Machimura, Edmond Preteceille, Masayuki Sasaki and Barney Warf.

On a number of occasions we also benefited substantially from the presence and contributions of Paul Barker as 'our journalist in (intermittent) residence' and from Susan Fainstein as our one-person 'international (occasionally visiting) advisory committee'. The Programme Director, Michael Parkinson, actively supported the work with stimuli of various kinds, and some indulgence regarding deadlines.

We thank Stephen Sheppard for data from his project on Higher Education flows, and Marian Fitzgerald for data from Policing London.

Most of all we are very grateful to the several hundred Londoners who gave their time for extended interviews, providing us with rich insights into the circumstances, often difficult, in which people in different parts of the city region live and labour.

Finally we owe a special debt of thanks to Ann Rudkin, who played an unusual triple role as our commissioning editor, manuscript editor and general amanuensis during the production of the book.

While we were writing this book two major external events occurred, with uncertain implications for the future life of this city. Our study was conceived, and the proposal for support written, just before Tony Blair's New Labour government came to power. In consequence, after a long interregnum, Greater London regained a political authority in May 2000, though of a very new kind, with a directly elected Mayor charged formally with developing a wide range of strategies for London; he moved into his new offices on London's South Bank as this book went to press. So far however, most of his energies have been devoted to fighting with central government for effective local control over the London Underground. But he or his agencies have developed a series of strategies – for London's economy, its environment, its transport – culminating in the spatial development strategy – the London Plan – also published as we went to press. It offers an expansive vision of London's future, with an emphasis on competitiveness and cohesion very close to the concerns of this book – on which we comment in a postscript.

The other, much more traumatic, development was the attack on the World Trade Center in New York, London's main counterpart and competitor as an international financial centre, on September 11th 2001. Initially this seemed to raise very great uncertainties both about prospects for the international economy and about the continuing attraction of very densely built office centres. In the ten months which have followed none of the worst fears has yet materialized. But we have stood by a decision, which we took last autumn, not to speculate about these issues; instead we present an analysis based on the hard evidence available from our research, virtually all of which pre-dates September 11th. In addition, London's history as well as economic theory suggests that its long-term development is unlikely to be seriously affected by short-term events, however dramatic and shocking.

## Copyright acknowledgements

All Census, NOMIS and Labour Force Survey data used for maps and tables are Crown Copyright. All maps use boundary data which are copyright of the Crown and the ED-LINE Consortium. Both Census and boundary data were provided with the support of the ESRC and JISC. Labour Force Survey data, originally collected by the Office for National Statistics, and British Household Panel Survey data, originally collected by the Institute for Social and Economic Research, University of Essex, and funded by the ESRC, were obtained through the UK Data Archive. The Land Registry house price data used in Figure 2.9 come from the Experian Limited Postal Sector Data Set distributed by the JISC supported MIMAS service, University of Manchester. The Indices of deprivation used in Figures 2.15, 5.1, 6.2, 7.1, 7.2, and 7.3, and referred to in the text as IMD2000, are taken from the Department of Transport, Local Government and the Regions, *Indices of Deprivation 2000*. Other Crown Copyright materials are reproduced with the permission of the Controller of HMSO. The mapping of 1991 Census commuter flows in Figure 2.1 is courtesy of Mike Coombes and Simon Raybould of the Centre for Urban and Regional Development Studies, University of Newcastle upon Tyne. Needless to say, in all cases the original owners of these data bear no responsibility for our analyses and uses of them.

Chapter 1

# Competition, Cohesion, Governance:
# The Urban Triangle

But what is to be the fate of the great wen? The monster, called . . . 'the metropolis of the empire'?
William Cobbett, *Rural Rides*, 1830

At the dawn of the twenty-first century, big cities are again big news. They always were – long before Corbett wrote. But over the last 30 years the news has changed and changed again. In the crisis-ridden 1970s, the city was seen as the problem. In the Reagan-Thatcherite neo-liberal boom of the late 1980s, it became the global solution. Now, paradoxically, it is both. In a globalized economy, big cities present themselves as paramount centres of competitive business, culture and creativity. Yet they are widely perceived as lacking social cohesion and marred by social exclusion – thus generating a vicious triangle that threatens their continued competitive success.

This paradox has an important political consequence: everywhere, a central urban policy objective is now to reconcile economic competitiveness with social cohesion. And this is to be achieved through an institutional shift: from traditional local government to a responsive, highly networked, system of local and regional governance. As so often before, academic social science helps shape the real-world political agenda.

London is in many ways the epitome of these processes and these debates. In this book, which analyses change and transformation in the London region in the 1980s and 1990s, we shall explore the twin themes of competitiveness and cohesion, so as to understand how they help shape its present fortunes and future prospects. We shall find that they are complex processes, whose causes and effects are far less simple and certain than policy-makers often suppose. This will cause us to question the third concept, governance, as the policy precept. And in doing this, we shall need to challenge some of the ways in which our academic colleagues have analysed these changes.

First, then, we need to highlight some of the key factors which lie behind the recent *volte face* in attitudes to cities and how these have affected London. Then we have to cast a critical light on these key concepts – *competitiveness, cohesion* and network *governance* – which dominate contemporary thinking about cities and form the key themes of this book. And finally, we turn to the study itself: the key research questions and methodologies and an outline of the subsequent chapters.

## London and the New Urban Agenda

Three major changes lie behind the contemporary re-evaluation of big cities. First, there is growing concern about the social costs of unrestrained free market competition: a new worry about social exclusion, perhaps reflecting a deeper fear about social conflict. Second, there is a new academic insight: that internationalization and new modes of competition are increasing the significance of *urban* structures and processes for competitiveness and cohesion, and for the relations between them. And third, there has been a startling shift in the fortunes of some cities, from slow decline to vibrant growth. London, as we were studying it, was well into its second economic boom in 15 years; there had been continuous employment growth for 8 years, and the population was growing for the first time in half a century. And similar trends have been reported across European and North American cities.

In parallel, there has been a major shift in the way that economists see cities: they have rediscovered agglomeration economies and their significance for competitiveness, thus becoming interested in how urban economies work, and they have belatedly recognized that economic processes may be embedded in social networks, including local ones (Fujita and Krugman, 1995; Venables, 1995; Granovetter, 1995). They have thus come to appreciate that – even in a global and electronic era – face-to-face relations can be vital in facilitating business, above all in the most dynamic sectors, characterized by innovation, flexible specialization and turbulence (Amin and Graham, 1997). An influential version of this argument is the 'global cities thesis' in its many variants (Cohen, 1981; Friedmann and Wolff, 1982); most notably, Saskia Sassen's study of the three pre-eminent 'global cities', Tokyo, London and New York, based on their complementary roles in driving the new globalized financial system that has emerged since the mid-1980s (Sassen, 1991). Sassen and others conclude that these economic changes lead to new social divisions, though their nature is disputed: some argue that a dual social structure is emerging, with an increasingly separate 'underclass' or 'socially excluded' group; some think that this is over-simplified and misleading, and this will be our thesis.

These debates have particular resonance for London. Here is an undisputed and highly successful global city, yet one that seems to exhibit poverty and affluence side by side, provoking an obvious comparison with the worlds of Henry Mayhew and Charles Booth, a century and more ago (Mayhew, 1862; Booth, 1902–1903). This reminds us of London's long history as a 'global city' (King, 1990; Abu-Lughod, 1999).

Over the last 40 years a succession of London studies, to be discussed in Chapter 2, have charted successive waves of de-industrialization and decentralization, recently giving way to what we can only call insecure growth. And nearly all these works have found intensifying inequalities and social divisions. The last such major study, focusing on change up to the early 1990s, found that 'economic revival and urban renaissance had been accompanied by accelerating economic and social polarization' (Fainstein, Gordon and Harloe, 1992): in the 1980s, aided by Thatcherite policies, London's economy became more internationally competitive but also more unequal, as many people failed to share in the new prosperity.

This research, and much else besides, raised questions which are now central both to urban politics and policy-making, and to the urban research agenda. First, can economic success only be maintained at the cost of social cohesion? Second, would such success be sustainable – or would it self-destruct, by creating a social maelstrom that would repel potential investors and a mobile, highly-skilled workforce? Third, could a new kind of network governance, with regulatory systems operating across the conventional public-private 'third sector' divisions, deliver the requirements for *both* urban competitiveness and cohesion? These are the three key questions which our study, and this book, address.

Again, these are not just academic questions. The growing concern with competitiveness *and* cohesion has shaped urban policy. Starting in the Major years of the early and mid-1990s, government came to accept a direct role in fostering competitiveness and – to mitigate the downside – new area-based initiatives to combat urban deprivation. London, without metropolitan level government since the Greater London Council was abolished in 1986, spawned new organizations: a Government Office for London, a Minister for London, and an array of public-private sector bodies whose main remit was to supply the missing ingredients of strategic thinking and lobbying for London.

But the 1997 election of a 'New Labour' government injected a much stronger concern with social exclusion into the competitiveness agenda (Hill, 2000). These twin themes were central to the new government's programme, alongside devolution for Scotland and Wales, the establishment of Regional Development Agencies and, in London, the re-establishment of metropolitan government with Britain's first directly elected Mayor. Despite the best efforts of the government (or possibly because of them) the new Mayor, taking office with the members of a newly elected Greater London Authority (GLA) in summer 2000, was Ken Livingstone, the reputedly 'Old Labour' last Leader of the GLC, whose pursuit of a socialist alternative then had precipitated its abolition by Margaret Thatcher. But that was long in the past: now the broad political and policy agenda for the new Mayor and Authority was close to that of the national government, and that which had previously been set out in a series of influential reports. The last of these, the Association of London Government's *London Study* (1997), was endorsed by the body set up to pave the way for the new GLA. It defined the overall objectives for the Authority and the Mayor as the fostering of 'economic efficiency and business competitiveness, environmental responsibility and equal opportunity for all' (London Development Partnership, 1998, 3).

In summer 2000 these objectives were taken up in the Mayor's first report on *The State of London*, which links national concerns about economic competitiveness 'in the new globalized economy' with London's role 'as the main gateway to its economy'. It stresses the need for investment to improve London's competitive edge, especially in relation to European capitals such as Paris and Berlin. Globalization has to 'be built into the very foundations of the city and our thinking' as 'the prosperity of every Londoner is completely tied up with the city's role in the international economy'. However, there must also be a drive to address 'London's extremes of poverty, alongside great affluence' which 'undermine social cohesion and waste the talents of tens of thousands of citizens'. Echoing the language of the national government, the Mayor sees this not only as unjust but also a source of economic inefficiency: a hindrance to competitiveness.

So there is a clear resonance between London's new urban agenda and the wider political and academic concern with competitiveness and cohesion. These issues are important to cities across the world. Our concern is to understand how they impact distinctively on one such city, London.

A key part of London's distinctiveness is its economic diversity. This has a long history; but by the late nineteenth century the London economy was already diverse. It offered a long-established market for luxury goods and personal services, requiring proximity and flexibility from suppliers and a pool of highly skilled labour. It had the Port of London, with its key role in national trade, and with attendant import processing activities, and financial and associated business services. It had a vast supply of casual labour, especially through immigration, supplying small workshops making cheap consumer goods. It had also a growing regional market for mass-produced consumer products, served by an expanding array of factories on London's periphery. Finally, it had a mass of services and activities linked to its role as the national and imperial, economic and political capital.

A century later each of these factors, updated (for example, with Heathrow replacing the Port of London) and modified (for example, through changing communications and transport costs), has continuing relevance for London's competitiveness. And, it has been suggested, London may superficially at least have returned to some late-Victorian patterns: the economy is again internationalized; many small firms fulfil specialist roles in highly competitive markets; and fluctuations in demand again create unstable labour markets. But this is superficial. Underlying the most recent changes in London's economy is a more general shift in the cities of the developed world: away from what some call the 'Fordist' city, with large-scale manufacturing for mass consumer markets, low unemployment and rising affluence across a broad swathe of the class structure and extensive cross-class state welfare provision, and towards a very different model. This new model includes three key elements: first, de-industrialization and a switch from goods-handling to information-handling; second, internationalization – specifically, the growth of control, marketing and servicing activities associated with increasingly integrated global and continental economies; third and finally, the spread of 'flexible specialization' based on smaller plants serving smaller-scale markets for 'customized' products with relatively unstable demand.

London has played a key role in these changes. Most of the growth sectors of the UK economy, in output and/or employment, are over-represented in the London region. These include almost all the fastest-growing informational, cultural and consumer services. London's population, already the most diverse in the nation, has become even more so as a result of new immigrant flows. And the economic geography and socio-spatial structure of London has changed: by the late 1980s the effective London region was the Greater South East, stretching out to the coast on the south and east, up to 100 miles north and west, and encompassing numerous substantial existing centres as well as some emergent 'fringe cities' (which our study also encompasses), many of which have become dynamic centres within a complex regional space economy.

## Competitiveness, Cohesion and Governance: Issues and Debates

The new urban policy agenda, built around competitiveness, cohesion and governance, has been strongly influenced by recent research. So key ideas from this research have led a double life: academically, as topics for debate and research, where many questions still remain unresolved; and in policy-making, where they have been selectively and incautiously appropriated as cornerstones of new urban and social policies. Importantly, these policies do not just draw on theory and research on competitiveness, cohesion and associated social relationships; they also assume strong links between them. Throughout this book we want to examine closely these concepts, hypotheses and links, and their uses in policy formation, confronting theory with evidence. First though we need to provide the essential background for this analysis, starting with competitiveness.

### Cities and Competitiveness

There are major difficulties in pinning down the notion of urban competitiveness, and we will return to them in Chapter 3. But one starting point is to consider the various markets in which 'cities' might be in competition with each other: product markets, inward private investment, public sector funding, and desirable residents (Gordon, 1999a). Such competition is not new, but now it is more intense and it extends more widely, because of the growing internationalization of trade and capital flows; the shift into high value-added service activities which seek a high-quality urban environment; the need to access potentially-mobile high-quality labour; and pro-competitive government investment policies. And thus we see the rise of overt policies which accompany territorial competition: so-called 'city marketing' and central government interest in urban strategies as a means of pursuing national competitiveness.

But there is a controversial question: is it appropriate to conceive of cities in competition (rather than the businesses they contain) and to encourage public agencies to pursue competitive policies on behalf of their cities? Here, the biggest influence on the public policy agenda has been Michael Porter's *Competitive Advantage of Nations* (1990), which popularized the view that in a world of quality-based competition, successful companies will draw on particular attributes of their home city-regions: no longer the classical ones (resource availability, labour costs and macro-economic context) but qualitative aspects of the environment, intensified through clustering. The argument, for which there is some evidence, is that by agglomerating in cities (and less easily outside them), some kinds of firm can enjoy 'increasing returns' and therefore enhanced competitiveness. Cities thus have a new significance for competitiveness – a view shared by other theorists besides Porter.

Porter later drew some policy lessons (Porter, 1995) that policy-makers have taken on board, not least in the agenda-setting studies for the new London government, earlier described. They include adopting a focused strategy to identify and build on competitive advantage; investing in institutions that have a strong knowledge-base and a positive business-oriented culture; improving the efficiency of business-related infrastructure; making the city an inviting place for people and enterprises to concentrate; eliminating obstacles to productivity growth; and developing the skills and attitudes of the workforce.

This approach has influential critics – notably Paul Krugman, who attacks the idea that we can meaningfully describe territorial entities, such as nations or cities, as competing; firms compete, not nations. But this argument is somewhat blunted by his own earlier emphasis on urban agglomeration economies as a source of increasing returns (Krugman, 1995, 1996). His real point seems to be not theoretical but practical: policies to promote competitiveness, whether at national or local level, are likely to be ineffective or protectionist.

Krugman and Porter are both mainstream economists, but the radically different approach of the political economy school (in its many variants) shares the same starting point: the importance of internationalization, new forms of flexible production, and the salience of agglomeration economies (Amin, 1994; Soja, 2000). These theorists, from a very different perspective, share an explanation which emphasizes the search for 'competitiveness' in an increasingly internationalized economy, the adoption of new production techniques, and changes in regional/local as well as national governance (Jessop, 1994). So they lead to the same conclusion: fostering competitiveness is an imperative for governments, and a key role is played by sub-national units.

Reports of the death of the nation state – or even its 'hollowing out' – have, however, been much exaggerated: 'globalization is not dissolving the state and bureaucratism in general any more than it is unravelling capitalism. Contemporary changes in governance are far more 'subtle and complex' (Scholte, 2000, 158). Nations and nation states remain key players in the new world of 'multi-level governance'. But they now have to share power and sovereignty with other levels of governance (including the supra-national) and with the market: 'Large national supervisory organizations and institutions have lost their arrogance. The state itself has faced up to serious challenges and has had to adapt' (Le Gales, 1998, 485).

Thus, as so often, policy developments reflect academic debates. But many unanswered questions remain. For example, just how important are new forms of agglomeration for competitiveness, and for which branches of economic activity are they important? Equally important, but lacking a firm base in evidence, are the 'more political questions as to how meaningful is the notion of a collective economic interests; whether in particular instances local integration ensures that gains to key sectors benefit all; and how the priorities of competitive strategies are actually constructed' (Gordon, 1999a, 1002). These questions, involving politics and economics, are largely glossed over in recent policy documents, including those related to London.

## Cohesion, Exclusion and Social Capital

'Social cohesion' is a much-discussed term, particularly by policy-makers worried about its absence or fragility. It harks back to some very old sociological questions about social order, a century and a half ago, in the age of rapid urbanization in Western Europe and North America. It conflates three quite separate concerns: about social inequality; about social connectedness and 'community'; and about social order. Between these three there *may* be various linkages. But the language of 'social cohesion' frequently obscures such issues, for example mixing ethical concerns over levels of inequality (or poverty) with functional questions of social order in relation to competitiveness. Nonetheless, we will take 'cohesion' to embrace all three of the dimensions noted above; we will emphasize issues of inequality and connectedness as well as issues of order, since all may affect individuals' and businesses' capacity to function successfully in London and its region.

Recent academic literature, taken up by policy-makers, has used other terms as well: social exclusion and social capital. New Labour's key early policy statements, in particular, wove together ideas of cohesion, exclusion and social capital and made explicit links with competitiveness. Tony Blair (1997a) signalled the new approach, in his first speech as Prime Minister, at the Aylesbury public housing estate in Southwark: a potent symbol of urban decay and social exclusion, not far from one of our case study areas. Blair stated:

> For 18 years the poorest people in our country have been forgotten by government. They have been left out of growing prosperity . . . I want that to change.

But the problem was not simply poverty or inequality (Old Labour terms): it involved the growth of 'an underclass of people cut off from society's mainstream, without any sense of shared purpose'. And the central message was that:

> (We should reject the rootless morality whose symptom is a false choice between bleeding hearts and couldn't care less, what we need is one grounded in the core of British values, the sense of fairness and a balance between rights and duties. The basis of this modern civic society is an ethic of mutual responsibility or duty. It is something for something. You only take out if you put in. That's the bargain.

These sentiments were close to American 'communitarianism', which laid responsibility on individual citizens and communities to fight their own way out of exclusion and the culture of fatalism (Etzioni, 1995, 1997, 2000), albeit with government help.

In a second speech, some months later, the Prime Minister set out the key assumptions and conclusions embodied in this concern with exclusion (Blair, 1997*b*). First, he made an explicit link between national competitiveness and prosperity and having a 'strong and active community of citizens': this was the 'civic engagement' agenda, again, based on the idea that a socially cohesive society (however understood) is desirable. Second, and more alarmist, there was an argument that contemporary economic transformations threaten cohesion:

> (T)he public knows only too well the dangers of a society that is falling apart. They know that worsening inequality, hopelessness, crime and poverty undermine the decency on which any good society rests. They know how easily shared values and rules can unravel.

Implicit here is a view that only through a common set of values and rules, which almost all agree to follow, can we prevent society falling apart. As much sociological research has shown, this is simply not the case. Not only can society continue with considerable disagreement about these matters; other factors, such as economic and social ties, bind it together.

However, for Blair, social exclusion affects more than just the excluded, and this is more than a matter of poverty:

> (S)ocial exclusion is about income but it is about more. It is about prospects and networks and life chances. It's a very modern problem, and one that is more harmful to the individual, more damaging to self-esteem, more corrosive for society as a whole, more likely to be passed down from generation to generation than material poverty.

Here Blair was using sociological language (networks and life chances) to touch on a further key idea: that social exclusion involves absence or deficiency of 'social capital', the involvement in social networks and relationships that facilitates access to life chances. But the references to social order owed relatively little to recent social science: they stemmed from an idealized traditional community, based on co-operative interaction and shared values, as a foil to current causes of concern, including crime, lone parenthood and street poverty. As Vertovec (1997) contends, in current political discourse it is not cohesion but its absence or threatened loss that is paramount. But the implicit alternative is couched in terms far too simplistic for a modern urban society, where the reality is one of more heterogeneous forms of interdependence and even forms of conflict which actually hold people and society together, for example by reducing sources of more serious conflict; democratic party politics is a good example (Coser, 1976; Sennett, 1999).

The social exclusion debate does, however, relate in one way to newer social science, which questions the old class-based social categories, eroded by changes in economic and occupational structures and labour markets (Erikson and Goldthorpe, 1993). It develops an alternative approach that incorporates other divisions – gender, citizenship, ethnicity and age – which relate to labour market position less directly, or even not at all; it denies the significance of clear or simple social divisions, and espouses a more pluralistic structure. And there is yet another account, politically very influential, which suggests a new and even simpler segmentation between insiders and outsiders and which thus has close affinities with the social exclusion literature. Examples include the much debated idea of an 'underclass', the German notion of a 'two-thirds: one-third society' and Will Hutton's (1996) notion of the '30:30:40 society'.

To a large degree, British thinking on social exclusion has come from European social policy – particularly from France, where exclusion is defined in the context of republican notions of citizenship involving 'solidarity' and 'inclusion', leading recently to policies to '(re)insert' those who are marginalized from the economic and social mainstream (Silver, 1996; Castel, 1998; Body-Gendrot, 2000). Even more influential, however, has been the looser European Union use of the language of 'solidarity', 'inclusion' and (by extension) 'exclusion' to find a common basis for discussion of European social policy issues. Despite its lack of clear definition (frequently exclusion is merely defined in terms of observable social and economic effects), the term goes beyond traditional concepts of poverty and deprivation in three important respects. First, it suggests a multi-dimensional approach to the causes and consequences of disadvantage. Second, through its emphasis on persistent disadvantage, it directs attention not only to processes which generate disadvantage but also to those that lead to its persistence. Finally, it implies agency: exclusion, partly at least, is something that is done to people by others. This gets us beyond simply 'blaming the victim' and involves examining the processes by which individuals may be shut out from opportunities; for example, by forms of racial or other discrimination (Akinson, 1998).

But there are dangers in the use of the concept. One is the possible implication that the 'excluded' are disconnected from the wider society. In fact, they are still very much connected: first, because exclusion is generated by overall processes of social and economic change, and policy development needs to be aware of the fact; second, as recent research shows, exclusion is not normally a lifetime phenomenon. Finally, the 'excluded' are not necessarily shut out of the social networks of the non-excluded, and these networks may be an important basis for re-inclusion: getting a job, for instance.

There is also a danger – especially in the UK but to some degree across Europe – in focusing only on labour market exclusion (Levitas, 1998). This focus has had important policy implications: for instance, its impact on British educational policy, with its concern to improve educational outcomes to help improve competitiveness and promote social cohesion. Theories of both 'human' and 'social' capital development (OECD, 2001), though much questioned, underpin these policies. In London, educational outcomes are widely seen as defective in both respects, although – as we show in Chapter 5 – the reality is somewhat different, particularly if we consider the whole of Greater London or the London Region.

In fact, there are several bases for social exclusion, operating at the individual, household or community level. Individuals may be excluded from households (young vagrants) or be excluded as households (lone mothers). The form of exclusion may be in terms of employment, housing, access to welfare services and benefits, social attachments or communal solidarities. Social exclusion may be transient (lone parents with pre-school children), endemic (low-skilled workers moving in and out of an insecure sector of the labour market) or, perhaps, permanent (isolated old people).

Our study of London therefore needed to operate with a concept of social exclusion that could encompass its three main aspects, as already discussed, but that went beyond the purely descriptive definitions – which effectively are not definitions at all – of exclusion found in official discussions. (These, in effect, try to explain the *causes* of exclusion by referring to its empirically observable *consequences*.) The need, then, is to provide an adequate definition or theory of exclusion, which links it to those social, economic and political changes that cause it to occur. These matters are discussed in Chapter 7.

'Social capital', like exclusion, is a topic that has excited intense political discussion: a discussion that is closely linked to the developing social science literature on the topic, but in a very selective way. In general terms, social capital refers to the resources which are obtained through membership of social networks; it is an economistic formalization of the old sociological observation that 'involvement and participation in groups can have positive consequences for the individual and the community' (Portes, 1998, 2). However, as Portes also notes, the contemporary political discussion shows a marked focus 'on the positive consequences of sociability while putting aside its less attractive features'. And, by focusing on social capital as a source of non-monetary resources, presumed to be generated by individuals and 'communities', it 'engages the attention of policy-makers seeking less costly, non-economic solutions to social problems'.

The academic literature, however, reveals substantial ambiguities in the concept. One is whether social capital is essentially an *individual* asset – used by people to 'get on' or 'get by', with unintended social spillovers which may be positive and/or negative – or whether it is an intrinsically *social* good. Our preference – following the French sociologist Pierre Bourdieu – is to treat it as an individual resource. Of course, wider social benefits or disadvantages may follow from the fact that individuals with various levels of social capital concentrate in different localities or social groupings – but this demands investigation in each particular circumstance. From this perspective, what is 'social' about the asset is that it is based in 'possession of a durable network of . . . relationships of mutual acquaintance and recognition providing entitlement to "credit", in the various senses of the word' (Bourdieu, 1985, 248–249). It is thus distinct from alienable forms of economic capital (money, goods and saleable claims) and embodied human capital (Coleman, 1990). To the extent that relationships are still facilitated by propinquity, social capital may have a more explicitly spatial dimension than more mobile forms of economic and human capital. But how far social capital is in fact tied to particular locations is also an open question for empirical research.

A second confusion, in some literature and more pervasively in the policy discourse, involves equating social capital with other things: the resources obtained through it; the values which some forms of social capital may promote; and/or the social preconditions necessary to produce certain kinds of social capital. Again, as with exclusion, there is the same confusion: between the causes of a social phenomenon, and its social consequences (OECD, 2001; Portes, 1998; Foley and Edwards, 1999).

Disregarding these theoretical limitations (indeed, often ignoring them), numerous studies have sought to measure it and to demonstrate the consequences that flow from its presence or absence. 'Social capital' is treated as an independent variable, affecting many outcomes: school dropouts and academic performance, employment and occupational attainment, crime and juvenile delinquency, immigrant and ethnic performance, indices of health, local economic development, neighbourhood stability and government-community relations (Foley and Edwards, 1999). So, given the current political emphasis on cohesion, exclusion and competitiveness, it is easy to see why social capital should loom so large.

Several writers have stressed the importance of reciprocity in the social networks involved in social capital: high levels of trust and shared expectations, norms or values. These are central to Robert Putnam's hugely influential account of social capital (Putnam 1993, 1995, and 2000). He defines it as '. . . connections among individuals – social networks and the norms of reciprocity and trustworthiness that arise from them' (2000, 19). In his celebrated article (1995) and his subsequent book, he argues that in the United States, a decline in social cohesion (especially relating to trust and civic and political engagement) is linked to a decline in social capital, produced by contemporary political and social change. It follows that the absence of social capital may be a significant element in social exclusion.

Putnam's analysis has been enthusiastically taken up by New Labour. It has echoes of an earlier era, notably nineteenth-century critiques of the socially fragmenting effects of urbanization and fears about threats to social order. But it also links to contemporary hypotheses: about the role of urban agglomerations in enabling trust-based business networks, widely seen as necessary for competitive success in more fragmented and rapidly changing economic conditions. As with both of these, the Putnam hypothesis needs both greater theoretical clarification and empirical testing: what consequences may (or may not) follow from stronger relations between individuals or businesses, and what has geographical proximity to do with it? And are these effects positive for social order or social inclusion? (Counter-examples would be organized crime networks and closure of labour market opportunities against outsiders). These issues are taken up in Chapter 8.

## Policy Issues and Urban Governance

In Britain there is a long history of concern with – and responses to – 'urban problems'. This engagement has been double-edged: first, with conditions in working-class, inner-city areas, seen as a threat to all classes and to the urban economy; second, with the spread of urban development and urban population into rural areas, and their effects on the environment and the quality of rural life. Over the last century, urban policy has shifted between these two priorities, but from the mid-1970s, as the major cities de-industrialized, there has been a major focus on attempting to reverse urban economic and population decline.

Initially, the public sector (especially the local authorities) aimed directly and indirectly to create new jobs, so mitigating the impact of international competition and national recession on the worst-affected areas. This economic orientation survives, but from the early 1980s successive Thatcher administrations began to blame urban economic decline and unemployment on what they saw as the profligacy, anti-business sentiment, bureaucracy, and dependency-inducing housing policies of Labour local authorities in the major cities. Their answer was for central government to intervene directly (by establishing Urban Development Corporations in London's Docklands and elsewhere), to shift power away from town halls (to school governors, housing trusts, training and enterprise councils and the like), to cap budgets, to involve business in decision-making through public-private partnerships, and – in the major conurbations including Greater London – to abolish the 'recalcitrant' and 'redundant' metropolitan authorities.

The New Labour government that came to power in 1997 has demonstrated important differences from its Conservative predecessors – but also continuities with them. Tony Blair – unlike John Major – had never been a local councillor, had no sentimental attachment to local government, and saw New Labour's key task as one of 'modernization'. A striking feature of the Blair government's approach to these issues is its multi-dimensionality, embracing physical, social, economic and political/institutional dimensions, and its emphasis on 'joined-up' thinking and government. Some key themes – competitiveness, self-reliance and partnership – were inherited from the Conservatives, but they were complemented with a strong emphasis on work as the main route out of poverty and exclusion, on education (with strong pressure on schools to improve standards), and a somewhat vague (and later diluted) notion of community. In urban policy, a Cities White Paper (GB Department of Environment, Transport and the Regions, 2000) announced a shift back into the cities as the answer to urban-rural, global-environmental and intra-urban problems. But by and large the urban agenda was driven not by specifically urban initiatives, but rather by New Labour's overall approach, which emphasized modernization, competitiveness and entrepreneurialism and (particularly in the second term in office after 2001) improvements in the delivery of public services.

A key aspect of this programme has been its recognition of the need to address the problems of those who do not benefit from the successful economy – both as a moral duty and because, as Peter Mandelson, the Minister first responsible for the government's Social Exclusion Unit stated at a Fabian Society Symposium in 1997, 'a permanently excluded underclass hinders flexibility rather than enhancing it', acting as a drag on competitiveness. This approach has resulted in a set of national programmes to tackle social exclusion. As summarized in the *National Strategy for Neighbourhood Renewal* (Social Exclusion Unit, 1998) they include a range of 'New Deal' programmes, targeted at key groups of the unemployed and economically inactive such as young people and single mothers (a British version of American workfare, which reflects the influence of Clinton's New Democrats on New Labour; Giddens, 2000); child care and tax incentives for the non-employed to take jobs; initiatives to 'crack down' on crime and drugs; spatially targeted 'zones' to improve health, education and employment; and regional development agencies to promote regeneration and competitiveness. In addition, a 'New Deal for Communities' channels substantial funds into regeneration of some of the most deprived localities. Such area programmes are not new, but they have had a problematic history in Britain because of their time-limited, 'one-off' nature. So now there is an intention of linking them closely to mainstream programmes relating to employment, welfare, health, education and so on.

London figures strongly in these initiatives since, as we shall see in Chapter 2 and later, it has a disproportionate share of the most deprived areas in the nation. But the one London-specific development has been the establishment of the elected Greater London Assembly and Mayor who also appoints a London Development Agency (LDA), the economic development agency. This reflected the view of Blair and the other modernizers at the top of the New Labour hierarchy: that London in the later 1970s and 1980s had been a key setting for Labour's disastrous turn to the politics of the New Left, with its idea of permanent municipal revolution. Significantly, as we discuss in Chapter 10, the new agencies are lean in staffing and executive responsibilities, while appointment criteria for the LDA, with a quota of business representatives and other arrangements, are intended to secure involvement of a broader range of interests in policy-making. One influence is the government's desire to revitalize local democracy, using London as a trial area to generate pressure for 'modernization' of 'failing' local administrations. But it would be wrong to portray the shifts in local governance in London as being an entirely top-down process. Modernization has also happened at borough level, where some of the most radical New Left boroughs of the 1980s have reshaped themselves as model New Labour authorities in the 1990s – Blairite *avant la lettre*.

These changes are part of a shift towards urban 'governance', that is towards a way of managing the urban system in the interests of competitiveness and cohesion, achieved through networking a set of agencies and interests that traditionally have not been directly included in local government. This entails weakening the public-private divide and promoting partnerships in which constellations of local authorities, community and business representatives combine to pursue major projects and initiatives. 'Governance' is thus part of the same lexicography as 'competitiveness' and 'cohesion'.

This new form of governance has been the subject of much recent urban political research and theorizing – in both North America and Europe. At first it concentrated on public-private 'growth coalitions' and 'regimes' concerned with business-led regeneration in certain US cities (Elkin, 1987; Logan and Molotch, 1987; Stone, 1989). Since then, it has broadened to consider emergent forms of network governance in the very different political circumstances of European cities, where urban policy-making has been concerned with cohesion as much as competitiveness (Harding, 1994, 1997, Stewart and Stoker, 1994). And the political shift from government to governance has been associated with the economic transition from a 'Fordist' to a 'Post-Fordist' regime (Stoker and Mossberger, 1994). Recently too, work has suggested that the new governing coalitions, involving the public, private and voluntary sectors, are replacing traditional local authority government in London. We return to this issue of 'regime governance' in Chapter 10 (Dowding *et al.*, 1999).

These new academic developments have tended to track the emergence of local network governance, not to shape it. But national government has significantly supported such research and drawn on its findings – for example in formulating policies to establish regional government, including the GLA (Harding *et al.*, 1998).

This research leads us to expect that – at the very least – there should be some connection between success in pursuing the competitiveness-cohesion agenda and the emergence of forms of local network governance. In Chapter 10 we examine whether this is so. However, *local* network governance raises an issue of special importance for London: how to combine strategic integration on the one hand, and effective, flexible, locally appropriate initiatives on the other. London's unique size, complexity and significance – both nationally and internationally – clearly exacerbate the need for strategic management of externalities, in economic and social development as much as in transport or sewerage systems. Over a century and more, they have generated endless conflict over the appropriate role for metropolitan-wide institutions.

This argument includes both efficiency and equity aspects – or, in today's language, it contains dimensions of both competitiveness and cohesion. In efficiency terms, the argument for metropolitan government has always been about better delivery of urban services, through economies of scale and scope. Ranged against metropolitan reformers have been advocates from the public choice school, who, following the abstract analysis of Tiebout (1956), saw merit in more locally-based units of government, the counterpart to market processes, which would allow households to migrate across political jurisdictions in search of the tax/service bundle which most closely met their individual preferences. In equity terms, the issue was whether metropolitan government was needed to redistribute costs and benefits across a socially and economically mixed territory. Better-off, mainly suburban communities notoriously tend to resist the fiscal and other forms of burden-sharing implied by metropolitan government. Thus abolition of the GLC was apparently a defeat for the metropolitan reformers and a victory for localist conservatives. But it also brought about a period of experiment, with new ways of achieving co-ordination without an overarching authority, to fill some of the vacuum left by abolition. So, rather than the collapse of metropolitan governance, local politicians began to be absorbed into new forms of network governance that went beyond their immediate localities. Nor did abolition of the GLC make suburban voters less conscious that they were part of London, as evidenced by their positive vote for the establishment of the GLA.

## Conclusion: From Theory to Research

At this point there is a problem. Social scientists do their best to develop and test concepts that are both theoretically and empirically well-grounded. Our trilogy – competitiveness, cohesion and governance – is no exception. But policy-makers and politicians have used them selectively and sometimes misleadingly. So we need to understand how this has happened.

A key part of this misreading was that politicians saw the three concepts as connected, but in a curiously optimistic way: cohesion, competitiveness and more broadly-based forms of community governance were presented as mutually supportive targets. Social exclusion was potentially or actually reducing competitiveness and disrupting social order. So, conversely, social inclusion, connectedness and order were all seen as enhancing competitiveness. Additionally, social capital provided resources that supported enhanced competitiveness, social integration and the avoidance of exclusion. Finally, network governance, linking government, business and community organizations across all levels – from neighbourhood to metropolis – would enhance and extend the impact of social capital, and sustain conditions for the achievement of competitiveness and cohesion. Thus there was a choice: between a virtuous triangle of urban competitiveness, cohesion and effective governance, or a vicious triangle of economic failure, social disintegration and incoherent/ unresponsive government.

In practice, the academic literature suggests a different interpretation: while all these aspects of urban life may be inter-connected, the links are unlikely to be as simple and unproblematic as this vision suggests. This was our starting-point. It led to a set of basic research questions, which the remaining chapters of the book seek to address:

• What do competitiveness, social cohesion and social exclusion actually mean for the residential and business communities of London?

• Which processes within the city are key to the achievement of a more economically competitive and socially cohesive future? Which processes may work against either or both of these?

• How substantially have these processes changed as a result of internationalization and intensified competition since the early 1980s?

• How important are different aspects of social cohesion, social exclusion and social capital (and policies for these) for sustaining economic success in this new context? And are there causal links in the other direction too?

• What role does urban governance play in relation to achieving competitiveness, reducing exclusion, fostering social capital or, to put it more generally, economic progress, social integration and an enhanced quality of life for London's workers and residents?

Thus, we had to look at processes and outcomes that impact on households, localities, firms, housing and labour market areas, public agencies, local government territories and so on. These would be complex anywhere, but especially in a large metropolitan area such as London. So our research project had to operate at a number of different levels and to employ both quantitative and qualitative methods, localized and London-wide studies and analyses. In Chapter 2 we describe how we go about this; notably, we present our geographical definition of 'London' – an area that runs out beyond the boundaries of the Greater London Authority – and our choice of eight residential areas, with linked local employment areas, for closer study.

The structure of the book follows a logic dictated by the basic research questions. Chapter 2 discusses the problem of defining London, outlines the main changes in the social, economic and political geography of London in the last half century, and shows how they impacted on our eight localities.

Chapter 3 considers London's economy and its competitiveness: how it may be measured, how and why it has changed so significantly within the past two decades and what role networks and other forms of agglomeration economies have played in this. Chapter 4 seeks to relate economic outcomes to social structure, in particular London's labour force. We ask how economic change has affected the social structure of 'global cities' such as London, in particular how far it is responsible for the sharp changes in inequality and class structure that have occurred. Chapter 5 concentrates on education and its contribution to competitiveness and cohesion. It looks critically at the conventional view that London's educational system is defective both in promoting competitiveness and fostering cohesion, and finds a more complex and varied story: unequal outcomes, with implications for cohesion and competition, which involve complex social, economic and institutional factors. Against this background, Chapter 6 looks at the labour market, identifying major changes and their outcomes for different sections of the population.

Together these chapters establish a paradox: alongside competitive success, there has been a seemingly irreversible upward trend in poverty and social exclusion. Chapter 7 draws on recent theories concerning social exclusion and our empirical work to explore this phenomenon and explain its growth. It also looks forward to Chapter 8 which focuses on social capital, looking at the empirical evidence for its presence or absence, and for the economic and social outcomes – both negative and positive – that theory and policy assume.

Chapter 9 is in some respects a counterpart to Chapter 2. Here the focus returns to our eight neighbourhoods, looking at the effects of change on the localities in which individuals and groups live. It seeks to understand the quality of life across neighbourhoods and its effects on the residents. Some recent research has begun the systematic exploration and explanation of these effects. Our more modest aim in Chapter 9 is to link some broad variations in neighbourhood quality of life to the wider processes of social and economic transformation in London.

Chapter 10 focuses on our third major theme: governance. We examine just what is the current reality of network governance in London. How pervasive is it, how is it constituted, and how far does it seem to be adequate for pursuing the dominant urban agenda which we have described in this Introduction?

In the concluding chapter we bring together the main findings of our work and its implications, providing some answers to the five key questions outlined above. Many aspects of London life and labour have been transformed in the past two decades, as well as the physical face of the city. Current theories of competitiveness, cohesion, governance and their possible links have proved to be a useful – though imperfect – means of helping us to understand this new situation and its outcomes. So we also consider some of the implications of our research for these theories and, finally, what are the lessons of this book for London, for other big cities and for current and future urban policies more generally.

Chapter 2

# Spaces and People: Changing Geographies of the Region

For the city and the book are opposed forms: to force the city's spread, contingency and aimless motion into the tight progression of a narrative is to risk a total falsehood. There is no single point of view from which one can grasp the city as a whole. That indeed is the central distinction between the city and the small town. For each citizen, the city is a unique and private reality; and the novelist, planner or sociologist (whose aims have more in common than each is often willing to admit) finds himself dealing with an impossibly intricate tessellation of personal routes, spoors and histories within the labyrinth of the city . . . Writing a book one pretends to an omniscience and a command of logic which the experience of living in a city continuously contradicts.

Jonathan Raban, *Soft City: What Cities Do to Us, and How they Change the Way we Live, Think and Feel*, 1973, p. 222.

So far we have mostly talked about London as though it was a single, clearly demarcated area, with widely shared economic and social characteristics, and with a single focus of government in the Mayor and Assembly of Greater London. But none of this is actually the case. The administrative boundaries of Greater London, established in 1963–1965, do correspond to a remarkable degree with the physical bounds of its continuously built up area, set by the Green Belt which Patrick Abercrombie's 1944 Greater London Plan devised as a means of stopping London's growth. But as one of us put it, 40 years ago:

> London has never taken kindly to attempts at delimitation, whether by people who wanted to govern it, or by those who wanted to fix it statistically; every time this was done, London promptly outgrew its administration or its figures. (Hall, 1963, 17)

And the Green Belt did not actually stop the city growing. Instead it produced a discontinuous form of growth, leap-frogging the belt and stretching into areas which not only retain their own entirely independent governments, but now also fall under separate regional administrations (for the South Eastern or Eastern regions, rather than that of the Greater London Authority and Government Office for London).

Functionally, these new growth areas 'belong' with London, *both* on the basis that they are linked to the core city and each other by strong commuting flows, *and* in terms of widely-shared economic assets. In technical terms, many of the agglomeration economies arising from the concentration of high-level activities and skills in the metropolis are readily available to businesses across a much broader region. And increasingly, over the past 40 years, the activities and skills of this surrounding region have themselves become major contributors to these agglomeration economies. To focus only on Greater London thus means getting only a partial view of the scale and strength of the metropolitan economy. And it also produces a quite biased view of its characteristics, since the people, activities and physical developments that locate in the outer parts of the region are significantly different from those found in London's centre or its suburbs. In particular, developments that need extensive space are inevitably more likely to be found in the outer rings.

Though patterns of development are discontinuous beyond the Greater London border, transport links are not. Most tube lines and bus routes do stop there, but the main line commuter services do not; nor do the motorways and trunk roads. The rail lines in particular provide more rapid access to the centre than can be achieved by other modes from many areas within Greater London. Along these arteries there flow very large volumes of traffic, including daily travel to work. In 2000, according to the Labour Force Survey, 21 per cent of Greater London's workforce commuted in from outside, while 7 per cent of employed residents of Greater London worked outside. Between the mid-1960s and 1981, London's commuting area increased substantially, with both old towns and New Towns in the OMA becoming much less self-contained in commuting terms (Breheny, 1990, 9.18). This trend has not been evident since then, and there has been some growth of reverse commuting, particularly on the west side of London. Commuting flows into London are naturally greater from areas which are closer in, but they are also clearly larger from places on the east side of London, where the local employment base is weaker, than from areas to the west. Census data from 1991 showed that from areas close to London on the eastern side, such as Dartford, Broxbourne and Brentwood, about 40 per cent of employed residents worked in London – representing the main elements in their economic bases – whereas in Slough, Runnymede or Chiltern on the west the figure was about 20 per cent. Nearer the outer edge of the OMA, around 15 per cent of employed residents in Maidstone, Southend, Tonbridge and Rochester (to the east) worked in London, whereas equivalent figures for Reading, Crawley and Aylesbury (on the west side) were around 5 per cent.

How these patterns have changed during the last decade is less clear, both because the last available detailed information dates from the 1991 Census, and because during the 1990s there seem to have been some very sharp fluctuations in the balance of commuting, paralleling the bust and subsequent boom in London employment. Overall, however, there seems to be no clear trend of increasing or decreasing commuting into London, though the counterflow out of the city has clearly become more important. Almost without doubt, however, the commuter belt has encroached still further into the Home Counties during this period, extending the bounds of the functional region. But the complication is that these places are a confusing mixture: they are partly self-contained, partly dormitory towns for London. And trends can move in opposite directions: between 1981 and 1991, Essex and Kent and Hertfordshire (on the east side of the region), became more dependent on commuting into London, especially into the City, while Berkshire and Buckinghamshire (on the west) remained more self-contained as their economies grew (Arup, 1996, 42). So the areas revealingly identified as the Rest of the South East (or ROSE), especially the nearer parts of it, form a confusing half-world, part dependent on London for work, part independent, and with effective boundaries being both fuzzy and fluid.

Attempts to define the functional urban region in spatial terms almost always rely on analyses of commuting patterns, which are the only generally available indicator of economic linkages between areas. The most recent exercise of this kind, applying a methodology close to that of the American SMSA definition to derive a consistent set of functional region boundaries for major cities in north-west Europe, produces a version of the London Functional Urban Region (FUR) about 100 miles across with a 1991 Census population of 12.5 million: about 10 times larger than the comparably defined Paris region and 5 or 6 times the next largest British FURs, Manchester and Glasgow. In this study, we have chosen to work with a rather similar unit: the London Metropolitan Region first defined by official statisticians in the early 1960s – including a hinterland around Greater London identified as the Outer Metropolitan Area (or OMA). Its population was some 11 million at the 1991 Census, and is estimated to have reached 12.8 million by 2000. Adopting this unit has the merit of consistency both with some historic statistical sources and with a number of earlier studies (Hall, 1963; Young and Willmott, 1973). As indicated in Figure 2.1, it incorporates most of the web of commuter links to London, stretching from Reading in the Thames Valley growth area into the west, to the eastern Thames Estuary towns of Southend and Medway; to the north it reaches Stevenage in the post-war belt of London New Towns; while in the south it encompasses another New Town, Crawley, adjoining London Gatwick airport.

From some perspectives this might be seen as a rather conservative definition of the current functional region, since the metropolitan 'growth frontier' on the north and west sides of the region has now clearly moved further out into margins of the Greater South East – including areas outside the South East standard statistical region, in Wiltshire, Northamptonshire, and Cambridgeshire (Hall, 1989; Gordon, 1999b). But while growth here is strongly linked to the assets of the London region that is much less true of older-established activities, and these areas are by no means yet fully integrated into the metropolitan region. There is a trade-off: between achieving an inclusive definition of the functional region and avoiding a dilution of its distinctive characteristics, which we resolve by excluding these fringe areas from

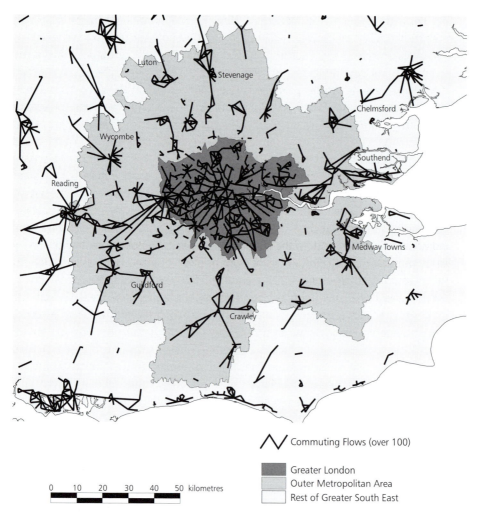

Commuting Flows (over 100)

Greater London
Outer Metropolitan Area
Rest of Greater South East

0   10   20   30   40   50 kilometres

**Figure 2.1.** London Metropolitan Region and 1991 commuting flows. (*Source:* 1991 Census; flows mapped by M. Coombes and S. Raybould, CURDS, Newcastle University)

the core of our work, while recognizing the particular roles which they have been assuming in relation to, for example, high-technology growth sectors. From the basic standpoint of defining a region that is sufficiently self-contained to include areas of residence for the vast majority of those working within it (and *vice versa*), the metropolitan region is inclusive enough: in 1991 its resident workforce almost equalled the numbers who worked there.

In later chapters we will argue strongly that this functional region – or even the Greater South East – operates in many ways as a single unit. It is clearly not a unit which many people, or even many businesses, see as directly relevant to their lives and operations. Yet it is significant, because in principle many activities could be effectively undertaken from any place within it, and because the overlapping of local housing, labour and service markets leads to their effective integration. It is clearly not because any very large proportion of people would actively consider switching their workplace, residence or service supplier outside a much more local area – or because many firms would actually consider moving beyond such an area. And some types of people and business – including the less highly-skilled, the poor, part-time workers, the economically inactive, small firms and some ethnic minorities – are likely to operate within especially localized environments, or 'action spaces'. Partly because of this, rather small areas can develop and maintain quite distinct characteristics and roles, all within the context of the regional economy. And many of the problems which individuals face will occur within these particular areas, demanding responses from equally local governmental bodies – even when these problems may stem from processes and structural shifts operating across much wider scales. One of the central challenges for this book is to seek to relate things which are happening (and are experienced) at these different spatial scales, from the region down to the individual neighbourhood. In the chapters that follow, we follow the trail of inquiry all the way down, on to the streets of eight of these localities. Here, as a preliminary guide to what follows, we first trace some of the main patterns of variation in London's economic and social geographies; then, we introduce the eight selected localities which we are going to use as our windows on to street-level experiences and processes in the region.

## Structures and Processes: London and Its Region since 1950

First, though, we need to understand just how economic and social forces worked to transform London's geography in the second half of the twentieth century. For these changes have been drastic. A Londoner of 1950, transported forward 50 years, would recognize some familiar landscapes, but would be amazed even by the extent of superficial physical change: the new central offices, the transformation of docklands, the rebuilding of huge tracts of east and south London – and the upsurge of business parks and new housing developments across the outer metropolitan area. And such a time-traveller would be even more staggered by the deeper changes in the social and economic map of the region. A Londoner of 1975 would be less taken by surprise, because some parts of this transformation, especially the regionalization of London, were substantially complete by that date. But others affecting more central areas – the creation of the new Docklands and the second rebuild of much of central and inner London – had scarcely begun: they were a product of 20 hectic years, the 1980s and 1990s.

### The London of 1950

In 1950 London had a fairly clearly demarcated geographical structure, some of it reflecting old and long-continued processes, some more recent developments. This geography reflected its emergence as the first great world trading and financial city, as long ago as the sixteenth and seventeenth centuries, its growth as the world's greatest port, its development as Britain's largest single centre of manufacturing (though not always recognized as such), and its huge nineteenth- and twentieth-century physical expansion, the result of new transport technologies and new modes of housing finance.

This structure was dominated by the ten-square-mile Central area, first officially recognized by the 1951 Census. It stretched from the museum quarter of Kensington in the west to Aldgate in the east, and from the northern terminal stations to the South Bank (then housing the Festival of Britain) and the Elephant and Castle. Ever since the Middle Ages, this had been a dual centre: the trading and financial City of London balanced by the governmental and courtly City of Westminster. By 1939, these two cores had been surrounded and overlaid by multiple other functions in other districts: law and the print media in the Inns of Court, Fleet Street and Bloomsbury; advertising and corporate headquarters in Mayfair; entertainment in the West End; shopping in Oxford Street and Regent Street and Knightsbridge; museums and concert halls and higher education in Bloomsbury and Kensington, and many others. But in general, this central area still had the same boundaries as 40 or 50 years earlier, on the eve of World War One – and near the end of London's era as an Imperial City.

Around it to the north and east and south was a tight horseshoe of warehouses and factories and houses converted into workshops, interspersed with railways and canals and by the river Thames, which broadened below Tower Bridge into an unbridgeable barrier. This was London's original zone of industry, nearly all of it organized into small workshops which were intensely networked into what economists now call an economy of flexible specialization. Such an organization demanded that the units cluster tightly into specialized industrial districts, a fact first recognized around 1890 by Charles Booth in his survey of *Life and Labour of the People in London* (1902–1903) and by Alfred Marshall in his *Principles of Economics* (1920, 1890). Thus Camden Town meant musical instruments, Clerkenwell and Hatton Garden meant watches and clocks and jewellery, Shoreditch and Bethnal Green meant furniture, and Whitechapel meant ready-made clothing (Hall, 1962; Martin, 1966). Some of these trades required high levels of skill and training; others were the province of poor casual labour, including large enclaves of recent immigrants, who worked in or very close to their congested homes.

On the east side, where wharves bordered the Thames, this area overlapped with London's Docklands, which in fact bisected it. The product of the growth of international trade in the eighteenth and nineteenth centuries, Docklands – stretching for more than 8 miles below Tower Bridge – had a dual physical structure. First in time were the wharves themselves, created to unload and load goods directly from ships moored in the river, through a system of small lighters. Second were the enclosed wet docks, constructed from 1800 onwards in the alluvial floodplain bordering the river. Each piece of construction resulted in progressively larger basins, culminating in the huge Royal Docks system at the extreme eastern end. On the river and dock fronts, interspersed with the warehouses, were large factories processing some of the bulk goods brought through the port: gasworks, sugar refineries, oil crushing plants. And, just beyond the boundary of the old London Country Council, in what is now Newham, noxious or polluting industries set themselves up to escape LCC regulation. Here too, on both sides of the river, were found the giant nineteenth-century sewage outfalls, which further lowered the desirability of the area as a place in which to live or work.

Outside these specific zones, and especially on the slightly higher ground which had a reputation for being healthier, Inner London's residential zones had spread under the influence of the steam commuter railway, the horse bus and horse tram, and then, from 1900, the electric tram, motor bus, electric train and tube. But, with the exception of the commuter train, down to 1914 none gave a fast or a convenient ride, so their impact was limited to a radius of about 6 miles; the development that resulted was quite dense and compact, in the form of high-density row housing, much of it subdivided from the start into apartments. The social structure of this area, roughly corresponding to that of the London County Council which provided higher-level government services for it between 1889 and 1965, was quite mixed and fine-grained. Though there was a familiar distinction between a rich west and a poor east, there were plenty of exceptions – artisan cottages in Chelsea and Notting Hill, subdivided Georgian and Victorian houses for blue-collar workers in Camden Town, Islington and Stockwell, grand squares in Southwark and in Bromley-by-Bow.

Wartime bombing, though limited compared with the destruction wrought on German cities, had major effects in Docklands and on key strategic targets, such as railways, in Inner London. Ironically, these were the slum areas which planners had already designated for comprehensive reconstruction. The great wartime plans were made, but post-war shortages and economic crises made it impossible to realize them. Not until the mid-1950s would the rebuilding of blitzed and blighted east and south-east London begin in earnest.

Beyond that were the broad tracts of Outer London, nearly four times the area of Inner London yet with less than twice the population. They had been developed at extraordinary speed between the two world wars, the product of above-ground tube extensions and electrification of the commuter lines south of the river, coupled with the affluence of a new white-collar salariat and the availability of cheap mortgage finance. Stockbroker's Tudor was followed by By-Pass Variegated in Metroland and its countless imitations. Many of the people who bought these houses new in the 1920s and 1930s, young and newly-married, were still living in them in 1950, approaching retirement.

These suburbs were lower-density and more homogeneous than their equivalents in Inner London. Large uniform residential areas, built as detached or (much more commonly) semi-detached housing at twelve houses to the acre or less, were broken only by the parades of shops around the Underground or Southern Electric train stations, together with the obligatory Post Office, public library and Odeon or ABC cinema. Quite often, as in Ealing, Harrow, Ilford, Croydon or Kingston, these centres were old villages or small market towns that had been swallowed up in the suburban flood. Sometimes, as at Rayners Lane, Hendon Central or Gants Hill, they were brand-new constructions around stations or junctions on the new arterial roads (Jackson, 1991; Weightman and Humphries, 1983).

By the 1920s and 1930s, town planning powers were already affecting the pattern of London's growth: manufacturing industry did not invade these residential enclaves, but instead occupied broad swathes of land along the arterial roads, especially on the less attractive lower-lying land. As Young and Willmott (1973) observed, the distribution of these industrial areas took the form of a giant cross with four arms: one, by far the most important, westwards along the Great West Road, Western Avenue, and Edgware Road; a second, more discontinuously, running eastwards along the north of the river, culminating in the giant Ford factory at Dagenham; a third northwards up the Lea Valley in east London, from Stratford to Enfield Lock; and a fourth southwards along the river Wandle in south-west London, from Wandsworth through Merton and Mitcham (Hall, 1962; Martin, 1966). This also marked out a social geography, with areas of working-class housing in the lower-lying areas along the arms of this industrial cross (as well as around the centre), while the most desirable upper-middle-class housing was found on higher land between these arms (Young and Willmott, 1973).

Already, London stopped with remarkable suddenness. Abercrombie's Green Belt was widely recognized as the basis for planning and was just receiving statutory expression in the first-generation county development plans. And in any case, post-war shortages and licensing of new building had reduced development to a minimum. Eight new towns had been designated in the ring immediately beyond, the first (Stevenage) in 1946, the last (Bracknell) in 1949, but there was precious little to see on the ground. The landscape here was essentially that of 1938: rural towns, some of them, especially south of the river, served by commuter services, and a few (Luton, Slough) with larger concentrations of the new industries (including inward investment by US businesses); nearer London, some ribbon development along the main transport corridors, punctuating the newly-established Green Belt; beyond that, wide stretches of open countryside with less insistent new development. Most of these places, with the exception of stops along the (recently-nationalized) southern commuter lines, were still quite independent and quite rural.

## An Intermediate Geography: London in 1975

A quarter of a century on, an enormous amount had changed, stimulating a new urban sociological literature on the city and its region. One side of this literature told a story of loss, decline in London's established economic base, and social polarization – in ways which shocked, coming so soon after its 1960s era as the archetypal swinging city, home to Carnaby Street, Mary Quant and (by adoption) the Beatles. In particular, Donnison and Eversley's (1973) edited volume charted the onset and consequences of de-industrialization, involving the progressive loss of the economic base of large areas of the conurbation. Already, half the Port of London had shut down, a victim of vicious industrial relations and competition from more efficient container ports. All around, old workshop areas, the home of staple industries like clothing and furniture, were closing down, and the old multi-storey factories were being occupied by a new generation of young artists. And the first signs were appearing of trouble further out, in the great industrial areas along the arterial roads: some firms, unable to find the space they needed for expansion and for efficient assembly line production, were moving out to the Home Counties and beyond; others were rationalizing their production processes and shedding workers; but, as Gripaios (1977) showed in an early path-breaking study, many others were simply giving up the ghost. In Donnison and Eversley's analysis the consequent loss of employment was linked with a continuing fall in Greater London's population, as part of a spiral of decline which left London with an increasingly weak economy, growing concentrations of social disadvantage among its population (as the more affluent moved out) and a range of threats to social cohesion.

In social terms, these observers provided an early version of what has been called the theory of the disappearing middle. The middle ranks of the London labour force, comprising the skilled and semi-skilled manual workers and even junior non-manual workers, were seen as being gradually squeezed out of existence through firm closures and relocations. On the other hand, the ranks of the top people, the highly-educated and the highly-qualified managerial and professional workers, were growing. So too, it was suggested, was an army of unskilled casual workers who performed the most menial service jobs, recalling the patterns of the London of the 1880s and 1890s (Buck et al., 1986). Actually, in terms of the distribution of jobs by earnings or social status, it is questionable whether the middle was actually disappearing (even if attention is confined to the Greater London population). But clearly a whole set of processes that had created an entire structure of employment in London during the long period from 1900 to 1970 – including the Fordist system of manufacturing and the development of a white-collar salariat – was beginning to unravel (Donnison and Eversley, 1973). Within Greater London during this period this unravelling was largely a consequence of space constraints and a loss of comparative advantage for routine and/or goods handling activities, rather than either international competition or more general crises of profitability (Buck et al., 1986).

But in any event this was a partial picture, and a rather different view emerges from Young and Willmott's (1973) classic sociological study of life and family relationships across the London region, which focused on the impacts of growing service employment, population decentralization and the progressive incorporation of women into the workforce. The picture here is much more one of change, both social and spatial, with positive as well as negative features, than simply one of decline and loss. In large part this is because Young and Willmott take the whole metropolitan region as their frame of reference, rather than Greater London alone, which was becoming an increasingly unrealistic unit of analysis in the face of a rapid regionalization of London population and activities during the previous quarter of a century.

In the 1950s and 1960s, government policies had encouraged the de-centralization of people and jobs from London into the surrounding region. But they were pushing at an open door. Employers – first in manufacturing, then in more routine office employment – had been only too enthusiastic in responding to official blandishments and inducements. Industrial location policies had tried to steer manufacturing to the development areas of Northern England, South Wales and Central Scotland, or failing that the New Towns. But they had been only partially successful: fast-growing high-technology industries, especially those ministering to defence needs in this Cold War era, remained locked in a tight agglomeration around the Defence Research Establishments in the Thames Valley, and, as the resulting cluster of firms attracted inward market-led investment, these firms logically located themselves in the same area, further attracted by proximity to Heathrow airport. Then, responding to the government's Location of Offices Bureau, routine back-office activities likewise began to decentralize to towns in the Outer Metropolitan Area, where a well-educated labour force was readily available. Reading was already on the way to becoming the third major office centre in the South East (after central London and Croydon, in outer south London), boosted by completion of the M4 motorway in 1971 and the opening of Europe's first high-speed rail system in 1976. But almost every centre in the outer metropolitan ring was also beginning to spawn a cluster of office towers. And, once the process was set in train, it appeared almost unstoppable: from this point, the London region was turning into something else, a polycentric mega-city region extending over progressively wider areas of South East England.

Similarly, while planned population decentralization to New and Expanded Towns was a major plank in the post-war strategy to relieve pressure on housing in London, the large-scale out-movement of households from the mid-1950s on (peaking in the decade between the mid-1960s and mid-1970s when there was a net outflow of a million people to other areas in the South East) was predominantly a matter of individual initiative within the burgeoning owner-occupied sector. The first generation of New Towns was already essentially complete by the mid-1970s; Bracknell, next to Reading, was the slowest, but even it had acquired a major new town centre. And a second generation, farther out – Milton Keynes, Northampton and Peterborough – was by now under construction.

In addition, following the prescription in the Abercrombie plan, a whole series of towns had undergone planned expansion, both within the South East region and beyond its boundaries; many were small East Anglian market towns, but a few – Basingstoke, Andover, Swindon, Wellingborough – were big expansions, almost indistinguishable from New Towns. However, impressive as these achievements might seem to planners, they paled into statistical insignificance compared with the general processes of market-led growth. In common with much of the outward shift of employment, much of this movement was driven by demand for lower densities, and hence more space than could be found inside Greater London. Every town in the South East had one or more extensions of almost identical red brick boxes, laid out along the cul-de-sac closes that by then had become the planning norm for new developments. Often the results were condemned by the cognoscenti: the largest such development, Lower Earley south of Reading, was memorably labelled 'Berkshire's new slurb' by the planning correspondent of *The Guardian*. But they catered for a market, and they sold.

All this was planned, after a fashion. The government's South East Study of 1964 had been followed by the Regional Economic Planning Council's Strategy of 1967 and finally by the South East Strategic Plan of 1970. An elaborate and expensive enterprise, product of central-local government partnership, it was hailed as the logical successor to the Abercrombie plan. But its proposals for huge new planned conurbations – around Reading, between Southampton and Portsmouth, between Crawley and Gatwick, in South Essex – fell foul of local Nimbyism, whereby each proposed development evoked passionate opposition. The irony was that in the area where passions ran highest of all, the Thames Valley, these constraints had the effect of enhancing local quality of life, thus making the area even more attractive to inward investment by multi-national high-technology firms (Hall *et al.*, 1987). And inevitably, the difficulties simply pushed the development pressures even farther out, to the very boundaries of the region, thus progressively increasing the size and complexity of this vast multi-centred urban region.

By the mid-1970s then, the region was already beginning to exhibit the complexity of form and function that we noted at the start of this chapter. But within Greater London, the immediate political reaction was (almost inevitably) to deny reality and seek to halt change. In London Docklands, during the mid-1970s, bitter battles were fought over the pattern of future development. In 1973, when consultants suggested that one scenario might involve attracting new international business, the result was a howl of protest and a demand to find a new future for the old docks and the old industries. The government set up a Docklands Joint Committee, which wrangled and did little; the area succumbed to dereliction. It was hard indeed for local communities and Labour-led local councils, whose entire life had been based on the old manufacturing and goods-handling economy, to accept the fact that it might have died. From a more strategic perspective, both the GLC and national government (in the Inner Cities White Paper of 1977) came to see all the emergent social problems of the city in terms of decline, symbolized by falling population and employment in the core areas, and to fix much of the blame on decentralization policies. Thus, New and Expanded Town programmes were frozen and the brief of the Location of Offices Bureau was changed to one of facilitating local moves within London.

## The Changed Geography of London 2000

Despite such policy shifts, in the following quarter century these processes have continued to operate, intensified in many cases by the impacts of 'globalization' and increasingly competitive forms of economic organization. London seeks to maintain and expand its role as provider of high-level specialized services to the world, ranging from banking and finance to entertainment, culture and tourism. But, in the process what manufacturing employment remained in the mid-1970s has now very largely gone, while the port has been reduced to a shadow of its former importance, located well outside Greater London's boundaries at Tilbury. Gentrification (already underway in the 1960s) has spread its way across a large proportion of Inner London's traditional working-class residential areas, and has begun to affect the outer suburbs too. Huge public housing programmes continued into the early 1980s to replace other working-class areas with planners' visions, some of which themselves deteriorated into unloved social ghettos. And, since then, new waves of immigration from an increasing variety of origins (not just the West Indies and India/Pakistan as in the previous period) have created ethnically-distinct areas with their own shops, social networks and places of worship.

In consequence, each piece of the 1950 geography has been changed more or less radically. In the OMA this largely involved a consolidation and extension of the processes and patterns laid down in the previous period, with further development in successful areas starting to meet more Nimbyist resistance. But within inner parts of London change clearly accelerated and started to shift direction. New service functions, and the growth of older ones, extended the old central area into a wide east-west corridor, with the western end in the White City and Hammersmith, and the eastern end in Docklands, currently in the Isle of Dogs but expanding to reach the Royal Docks, and soon Stratford. As well as the two traditional cores, the City and Westminster/West End, this expanded central area has a third at Canary Wharf in the east, employing close on 50,000 but likely soon to expand to 100,000 and to embrace the Royals and Stratford, as well as subsidiary centres at White City (television and radio), and Hammersmith (consultancy) in the west and on the South Bank (culture, entertainment and tourism). Areas, that in 1950 were still primarily residential, have become largely or partly commercial or governmental: hotels in South Kensington, embassies in Belgravia, offices in Mayfair and St James's. Covent Garden has lost its market to the fringe of the central area in Nine Elms, Billingsgate to Docklands, Spitalfields Market to Leyton. Fleet Street has almost entirely lost its newspaper industry to Docklands and locations even wider afield.

Around it, the warehouse-workshop ring has been similarly transformed. Though some specialized industry survives, particularly printing and photographic processing, the traditional trades have either disappeared or have been transformed in the hands of new immigrant groups (as in Whitechapel, where the old Jewish clothing trade has been taken over by Bengali arrivals of the 1950s and 1960s and their children). In Camden Town and Clerkenwell and Hoxton and Spitalfields, a few of the old warehouses have been converted to craft workshops or artists' studios, but most have become new loft apartments, attracting a predominantly younger clientele who seek a cosmopolitan lifestyle close to central jobs, with easily available restaurants and wine bars and boutique shops.

The inner parts of Docklands, which cut through this zone and in effect form part of it, have been similarly transformed: witness Wapping, London Bridge, Bermondsey and the old Surrey Docks. On the south bank of the Thames below London Bridge, a whole line of warehouses has been transformed to accommodate boutique shops, restaurants and bars and tourist attractions, and luxury apartments. Farther out, the picture is more complex: new homes wrap around Canary Wharf and Heron Quay, all along the river front of the Isle of Dogs, but eastwards, so far, they form only isolated islands of development. The future of the Royal Docks seems to be emerging in the form of big space-using complexes: a major exhibition centre (eventually perhaps the country's largest), a business park, a university campus, and an airport.

Inner London's dense terraces of Georgian and Victorian housing have been profoundly affected by five decades of gentrification. Artisan housing in the back streets of Chelsea, Victorian terraces in Barnsbury and North Kensington, late Victorian and Edwardian semis in Palmers Green and Muswell Hill have all progressively met the same fate. Latterly, the same process has been washing into what estate agents call the leafy outliers: the late Victorian and Edwardian villa suburbs of the middle ring, the zone that lies between the dense core and the looser outer suburbs, along the underground and commuter rail lines of south-west and west London – Putney, Wimbledon, Barnes, Richmond, Bedford Park and Ealing. In this spreading middle-class professional and managerial mass, corresponding to the transformations of London's economy, sit increasingly anomalous areas of public housing, the product of the great rebuilding of the 1950s and 1960s. The more desirable among them, meaning especially the low-rise LCC cottage estates, have largely been transformed into owner-occupier enclaves, especially attractive as starter homes for the aspiring middle-class, as have some of the better-designed high-rise blocks; but other estates, perceived as less attractive aesthetically or socially, have descended into a downward spiral of outward exodus and desperate refilling by the least fortunate and most desperate: the homeless, the refugees and asylum-seekers, the people turned out from the mental hospitals into community care, the problem families expelled from more desirable accommodation. Some London boroughs, at the beginning of the new century, see the answer in eliminating these housing ghettos, decanting their populations and recolonizing them with middle-class arrivals.

London's outer industrial areas have suffered a similar fate to its inner workshop zone. Many of the companies which established themselves here in the 1920s and 1930s, the high-tech industries of their day, have gone: they, or their successors or spin-offs, have migrated outside London, into parts of the Western Crescent on the M3, M4 and M40 motorways. Typically, therefore, these areas employ no more than a third of the people they employed in 1950, and many of these are no longer engaged in traditional manufacturing jobs. Local planning authorities have reacted to the situation, and to resulting redevelopment pressures, by flexible rezoning: old factory areas house back offices, superstores and retail parks, and multiplex cinemas.

But, although this is happening everywhere, there are differential impacts. Because of their access to Heathrow – which has become a really key element in the capital's economy during the last two decades, with huge spin-offs in air-related activities and businesses with intense business travel requirements – West London's industrial zones are booming in new guises (albeit with sharply-reduced employment). The Wandle Valley has been transformed into a vast retail park, as has the North Circular at Neasden; symbolically, they house London's two branches of IKEA. Despite similar adaptations, the Lea Valley has been less successful in recycling itself, and unemployment is locally higher here; and even more so along the old A13 in Barking and Dagenham, where car production has now ended in the vast Ford factory.

Between these industrial or ex-industrial corridors, the interwar residential suburbs have continued to age. As the new century begins, they are between 60 and

80 years old. They have experienced only marginal rebuilding – a new apartment block here, a piece of higher-density infilling there – and a great deal of minor tinkering to the house stock: new double-glazing, small extensions and conservatories. Generally, the areas that were higher-quality have retained their quality; the lower-quality areas have remained so, and even deteriorated. Often, travelling through them, one guesses that the grandchildren and great-grandchildren of the original inhabitants have long since located themselves elsewhere, many in residential areas that were in turn new when they bought, farther out along the train lines and the motorways. So, quite often, there is a sense of ageing and of decay; some of these suburbs are not wearing well. And that is compounded by the impact of mass motorization, with second and third cars spilling out of garages into front gardens and on to overcrowded roads.

Some of these suburbs have also clearly experienced social and ethnic change. Originally, of course, they were almost without exception occupied by native-born white Britons. Now, some have become new ethnic enclaves: Gujerati Indians in Wembley and Kenton, Armenians in Chiswick, Pakistanis in Gants Hill, and many others. In places, one senses quite sharp ethnic borders, accompanied perhaps by delicate ethnic tensions.

The shopping centres of the outer suburbs, which were so perfect a realization of their time, have suffered competition from different places: from the new superstores that have so often sprouted on ex-industrial sites or railway sidings, from the West End, from new regional centres like Brent Cross within London and from Lakeside and Bluewater beyond its boundaries, and from centres on the other side of the Green Belt. Though generalization is difficult, it seems that the bigger among them have tended to meet the competition by extensive rebuilding: Kingston, Harrow, Ilford are in reasonably good heart and trading well. Far more problematic are the second- and third-level centres, especially those serving less-affluent populations; here, too often, there is clear evidence of decay in the form of boarded-up shops and low-grade uses.

These are massive generalizations largely based on a single dimension, central-inner-outer. Such a simplistic taxonomy is bound to prove inadequate because it fails to take account of other geographical dimensions: west versus east, north versus south. Since the sixteenth century, at least, London has divided itself into an upmarket west and a downmarket east. That division further deepened in the nineteenth century, when noxious industries and effluents made tracts of east London highly undesirable and even unhealthy places in which to live and work. But even that generalization fails to work perfectly: whole areas of west London, close to industry and railways, look and feel like east London, while east London has its leafy high-quality suburbs too. Nonetheless, it remains true that over the last half-century west London, the aristocratic and *haut-bourgeois* quarter of the capital, has retained that quality and has effectively spread outward, across the Green Belt, into the neighbouring Western Crescent. Paradoxically, tight planning restrictions may have had the effect of making this area appear even more desirable, so stimulating in-migration and attracting inward investment. And the decision to locate Heathrow Airport here, taken in secret in the middle of World War Two, only added to the area's attractiveness – despite the impacts of plane noise and traffic congestion which now afflict so much of the area. In contrast, the eastern side remains the poor relation, despite recent gentrification of parts of the waterfront, and the emergence of much-publicised artists' colonies in some of these areas, where property is relatively cheap. Various social characteristics of the East End have also diffused into Essex and Kent, since (as elsewhere in London) people have tended to move out along radial axes, to the nearest parts of Outer London, and then the nearest segments of the Outer Metropolitan Area. Docklands and then Thames Gateway, the great planned linear development following the route of the Channel Tunnel high-speed train link, are bold attempts to reverse this polarity over a long time span. This thrust is also central to the Mayor's draft London Plan. It is too early to say whether or how far they will prove successful.

## Mapping London's Geographies

Against that broad-brush picture, we can better start to understand the micro-processes of economic and social change in London and its surrounding ring by looking at spatial patterns of specialization, change and segregation across the region. For the broad-brush analysis, the basic geographical framework we shall employ is the one we have described earlier: the London Metropolitan Area, embracing Greater London and the so-called Outer Metropolitan Area (OMA), extending somewhat irregularly to a line roughly 40 miles (70 kilometres) from central London (Figure. 2.1). The time frame is the period since 1981 centred around the 1991 Census of Population. The spatial level of analysis used here is that of the neighbourhood, represented either by electoral wards or postal sectors, each of which divide the region up into some 1800 units, with typical populations of around 7,000 people – and spatial extents which are more extensive in the low-density fringes than close to urban cores. Mapping socio-economic indicators at this scale serves both to reveal some of the broad patterns and contrasts which we have been discussing, and to show how much or how little local variation there is within these broad patterns. In some cases, as we shall see, there is a very great deal, reflecting perhaps the effects of chance factors, local physical geography or the details of route networks, but also local spatial structures nested within the broader structures of region and sub-region.

### The Changing Geography of Employment

A starting point is to look at the distribution of economic activity across the region, in terms of employment densities. As Figure. 2.2, shows, this pattern is still dominated by a sharp peak at the centre, showing just how monocentric the London economy remains; outside Central London, there are just local concentrations of activity in OMA towns like Reading, Slough, Luton or Southend. Large-scale decentralization of activity over the past 40 years has produced neither continuous sprawl nor the emergence of major counter-magnets, but growth at and around most of the existing urban centres, especially those on the western side. Little of this is evident, however, in the map of rates of employment change during the 1990s (Figure. 2.3). Some local changes here are exaggerated by applying to a small base. And this period (for which we have comparable local data) is dominated by the long upswing since 1993, including only part of the preceding recession. But what is evident is that there has been no systematic decentralization of employment over these years, suggesting that much of the growth has taken place more or less *in situ*. It is evident that performance has tended to be less positive around Outer London than in either

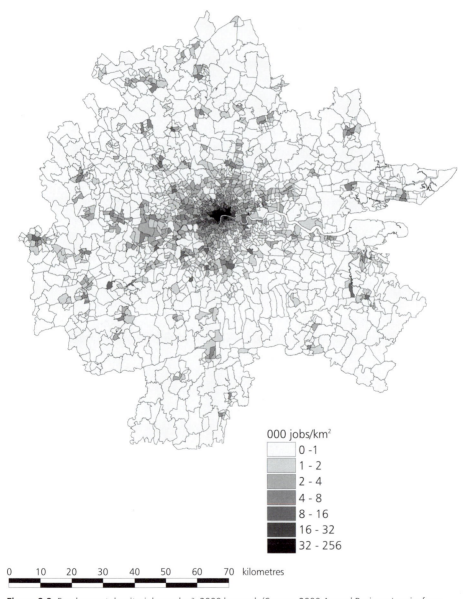

000 jobs/km²

- 0 - 1
- 1 - 2
- 2 - 4
- 4 - 8
- 8 - 16
- 16 - 32
- 32 - 256

0  10  20  30  40  50  60  70  kilometres

**Figure 2.2.** Employment density: jobs per km², 2000 by ward. (*Source:* 2000 Annual Business Inquiry from NOMIS)

the inner areas or the OMA. There is also a west-east contrast: areas in the west tend to have increasing employment, whereas east London and south-east London display widespread decline. In fact, on the west side of the capital there is a huge 'wedge' of areas with employment growth, with the strongest growth rates of all in the sector between the M3 and M4 motorways. In sharp contrast, the eastern side of the OMA appears as a zone of declining employment density or at best slow growth, with a few exceptions in places like Basildon-Southend and the Medway towns. As compared with the past, however, what is remarkable is the employment growth in the inner areas – most conspicuously in the loop of the river which includes Canary Wharf, though not confined either to Docklands or the traditional CBD.

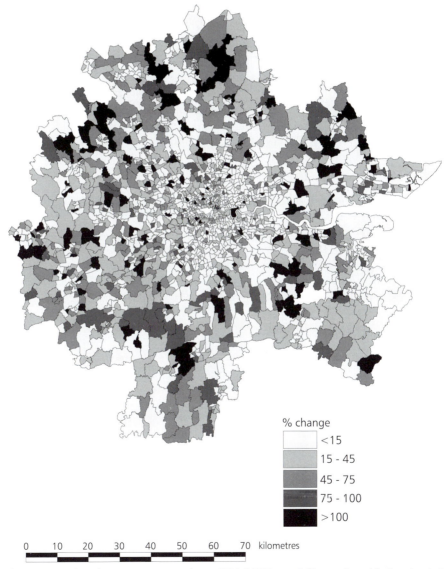

% change

☐ <15

▨ 15 - 45

▨ 45 - 75

▨ 75 - 100

■ >100

0   10   20   30   40   50   60   70   kilometres

**Figure 2.3.** Total employment: percentage change 1991–2000 by ward. (*Source:* Annual Business Inquiry/ AES from NOMIS)

Figures 2.4 and 2.5, which show the distribution of employment in sectors representing the region's old and new economic bases, suggest some reasons for the differences in performance which are evident. In the first case, production industries are weakly represented within London itself and strongest in a few key manufacturing towns in the outer ring, such as Luton, Harlow or the Medway towns – but with a general bias to the east (Figure 2.4). Within London the old Lea Valley concentration is still visible, while there are fewer industrial areas on the western side of London or in the adjoining Surrey and Thames Valley areas. Business services employment

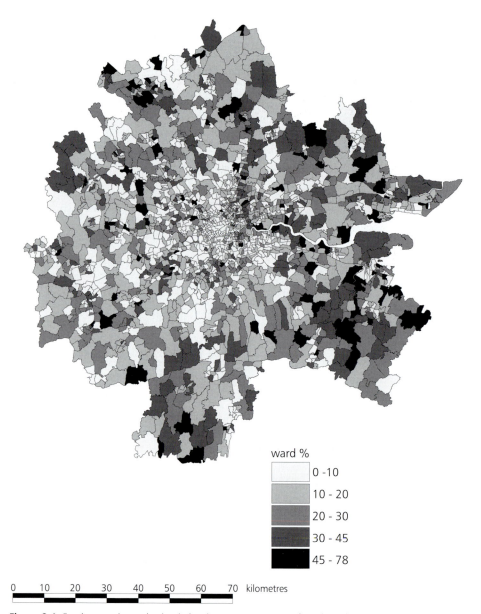

**Figure 2.4.** Employment in production industries as a percentage of total employment, 2000 by ward. (*Source:* 2000 Annual Business Inquiry from NOMIS)

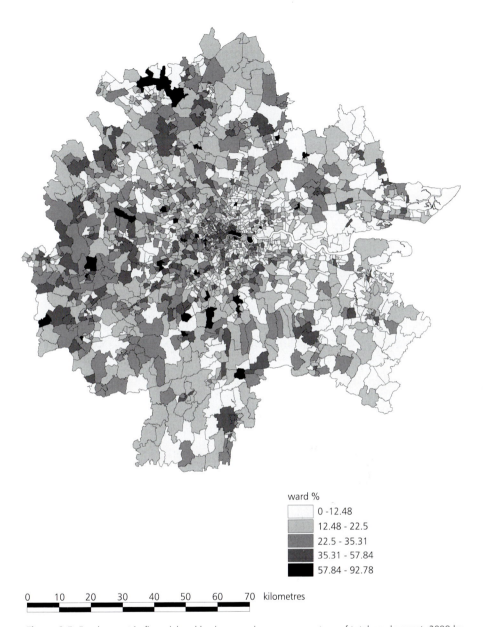

ward %

| | |
|---|---|
| | 0 -12.48 |
| | 12.48 - 22.5 |
| | 22.5 - 35.31 |
| | 35.31 - 57.84 |
| | 57.84 - 92.78 |

0    10    20    30    40    50    60    70   kilometres

**Figure 2.5.** Employment in financial and business services as a percentage of total employment, 2000 by ward. (*Source*: 2000 Annual Business Inquiry from NOMIS)

(including finance and IT among other activities) in contrast is heavily concentrated in the core of London, and exhibits a strong westward bias in its distribution (Figure 2.5). Since this has been the major drivers of growth in the 1990s (as in the 1980s), while production employment has continued to shrink, it is not surprising that they should produce the pattern observed in Figure 2.3: growth at the centre and in west London; fairly strong growth across the western wedge; moderate growth throughout the outer ring; and decline in outer east London.

## Social Structure

Employment by sector is linked to social structure through the occupational balance in different industries. But local social structures reflect nearby employment only in part: the influence is reduced by commuting, and also affected by the character of local housing stocks, the scale of desirability versus affordability. This last is also a crucial factor for the non-employed segment of the working age population. Over the post-war years the social geography of the region has been dominated by sharp inner-outer and east-west contrasts – with higher status groups in outer and western areas, reflecting selective patterns of population decentralization. At the top end, professionals and managers have been highly concentrated in the western half of the OMA, in a wide horseshoe that extended from Hertfordshire through Buckinghamshire, Berkshire and Surrey, down to West Sussex. Within London they were more strongly represented in the west and south-west, with localized concentrations in the north and north-west, and were particularly lacking on the east side from Hackney to Barking and back to Southwark.

Skilled manual workers were initially more concentrated inside London but they also decentralized, while their numbers there were also depleted through rapid de-industrialization. The main concentrations then came to be found in a few traditional industrial centres and areas: Luton and Dunstable in Bedfordshire, Broxbourne in Hertfordshire, Harlow in Essex, south Essex, Dartford-Gravesham and the Medway Towns in Kent. For semi- and unskilled workers, many of them in public sector housing, decentralization had been a less feasible option and they remained in Inner London, especially in the east London boroughs from Hackney to Barking & Dagenham, further downstream in Thurrock, and in isolated outliers like Slough, Luton, Harlow and Crawley. Within the OMA generally they have been more strongly represented on the eastern than on the western side of London. For similar reasons, and because these groups were most at risk of unemployment, the non-employed showed a rather similar distribution to the less skilled manual groups.

Within the last 20 years, patterns have changed quite significantly, although we can only illustrate this at present for first decade, between the 1981 and 1991 Censuses. At the top end of the distribution, the *professional and managerial* group showed a general and substantial increase in numbers, which on its own tends to reinforce their existing concentrations. But, as Figure 2.6 shows, not only did the share of this group increase particularly in its western OMA heartland from mid-Hertfordshire to mid-Surrey, but there were also above-average gains in a belt of south-western London boroughs from Richmond inward to Lambeth, Hammersmith & Fulham and Kensington & Chelsea. Within this broad social grouping some differences were evident as between the professionals and managerial elements, though the distinction is not a clear-cut one. Broadly employers and managers continued to show a strong preference for the western side of the OMA, including the small towns and villages of Berkshire and Buckinghamshire, whereas the professionals have made stronger inroads into the belt of London areas running diagonally from Haringey in the inner north-east and Tower Hamlets in the inner east to Richmond and Kingston in the outer south-west. This is indicative of a difference in tastes as well as residential preferences, in part associated with higher levels of education among the professionals, and a stronger taste for more 'urban' leisure pursuits as well as for closeness to work. This professionally-led colonization of the middle and inner-western London boroughs does not seem to be parallelled in any of the other urban centres except perhaps in Reading, where employment grew very rapidly in this period.

At the other end of the occupational distribution, numbers of manual workers contracted drastically as de-industrialization continued to take its toll. Naturally this produced the biggest losses where the group had previously been strongest, but the concentration of shrinkage in areas of east London is particularly striking (Figure 2.7). Within Inner London, the main exception to this pattern was in a few areas of the inner west. In areas where manual representation declined most, the effect was not,

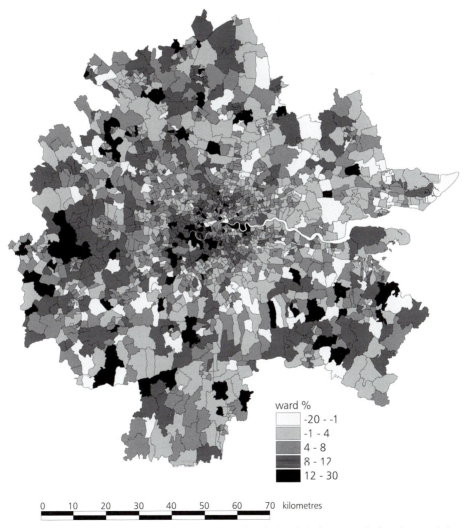

ward %

-20 - -1
-1 - 4
4 - 8
8 - 12
12 - 30

0    10    20    30    40    50    60    70    kilometres

**Figure 2.6.** Percentage of employers, managers and professionals in the economically active population: change 1981–1991 by ward. (*Source:* 1981 and 1991 Censuses: converted to a consistent ward basis by Dorling *et al.*, 2001)

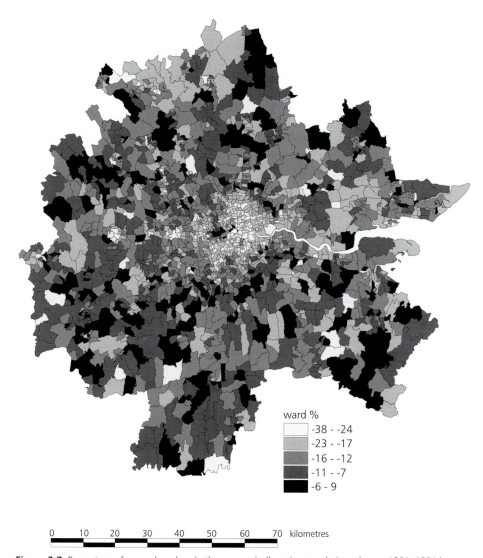

ward %

| | |
|---|---|
| ☐ | -38 - -24 |
| ☐ | -23 - -17 |
| ☐ | -16 - -12 |
| ☐ | -11 - -7 |
| ■ | -6 - 9 |

0   10   20   30   40   50   60   70   kilometres

**Figure 2.7.** Percentage of manual workers in the economically active population: change 1981–1991 by ward. (*Source:* 1981 and 1991 Censuses: converted to a consistent ward basis by Dorling *et al.*, 2001)

however, simply one of an upward shift in social status, as the third main element in shifting local social structures over this decade was the rise of the non-employed as a group. They are not entirely independent of the manual worker group, but the geography of their change is quite different. We can indicate this here by looking at the change in unemployment rates (Figure 2.8) though lone parents, who we discuss below, were another growing group with a not dissimilar distribution. At one level, the pattern of change in unemployment over the decade between the 1981 and 1991 Censuses is quite simple: little change over the greater part of the region, especially around the Western Crescent, but sharp increases in inner areas on the eastern side of Greater London. But within this clear pattern, slightly closer inspection reveals considerable variations at a local scale, with separate concentrations around

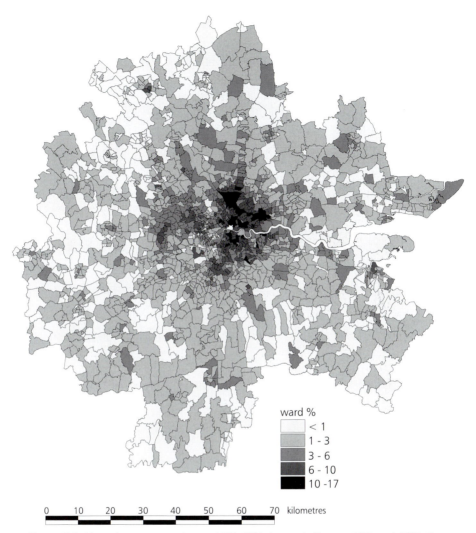

**Figure 2.8.** Unemployment rate: change 1981–1991 by ward. (*Source:* 1981 and 1991 Censuses: converted to a consistent ward basis by Dorling *et al.*, 20001)

Tottenham on the northern side of Inner London, the old East End near the river, near Stratford to the east, and in north Southwark, as well as more local islands also experiencing large increases. It should be emphasized that this is a particular reflection of developments during the 1980s, and we should not expect the 2001 Census to reveal a continuation of this during the last decade. But nor is it likely to show a complete reversal: effects of the changes shown here will continue to mark London for some time to come – and require clear explanation.

## House Prices: An Index of Social Change

Within the region there are very large variations in house prices, reflecting a combination of the differential desirability of particular areas and varying elasticities of local housing supply. In the second half of the 1990s, prices (simply adjusted to reflect different mixes of flats, terraced, detached and semi-detached houses) showed an astonishing eight-fold variation between neighbourhoods in the region (Figure 2.9). The broad geography of this is quite simple, and consistent over time, with the highest values in a few inner western boroughs – Camden, Westminster, Kensington & Chelsea – and a belt of high values extending south-westwards through Richmond into Surrey, with an outlier near Ascot. The lowest values were found along the Thames from outer eastern London out to north Kent and south Essex, along the Lea Valley in east London, and around both Heathrow and Gatwick airports. Most other parts of the OMA had moderately high values. This is one of the simplest patterns evident in any of the maps, reflecting in a clear way the pervasive role of market forces in shaping the social geography of the region.

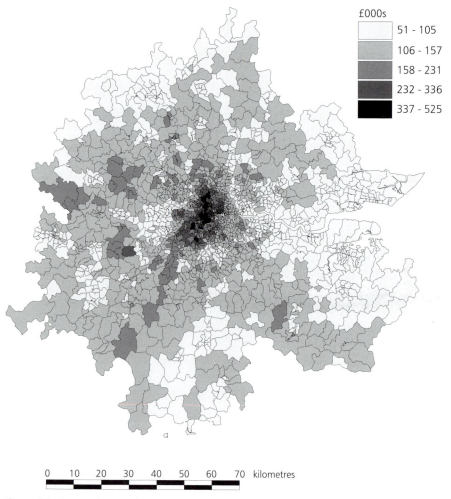

**Figure 2.9.** Average house prices 1995–2000 by postcode sector. (*Source:* Land Registry data from Experian database)

In important respects the house price pattern reflects the pattern of growth of professionals and managers that we have just shown for the 1980s, and that seems to have continued through the following decade. Gentrification has continued to drive up prices in a favoured belt of London boroughs, but it has also begun to affect inner eastern boroughs: not merely Tower Hamlets, where the regeneration of Docklands has had a continuing effect, but also in the neighbouring borough of Hackney. A new sociological divide seemed to be appearing in London: the professional middle-classes were colonizing eastwards, with the frontier now along the Lea Valley.

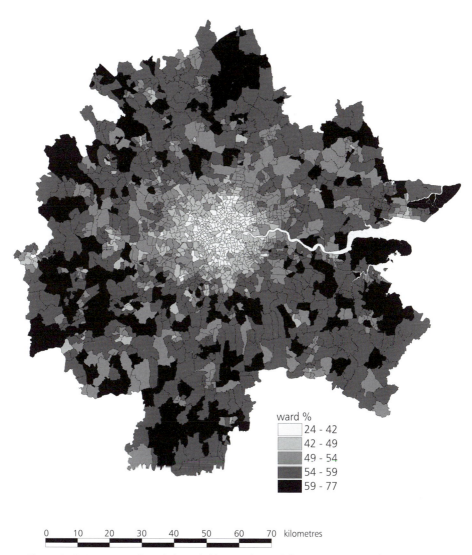

ward %
24 - 42
42 - 49
49 - 54
54 - 59
59 - 77

0  10  20  30  40  50  60  70  kilometres

**Figure 2.10.** Percentage of couple households, 1991 by ward. (*Source:* 1991 Census)

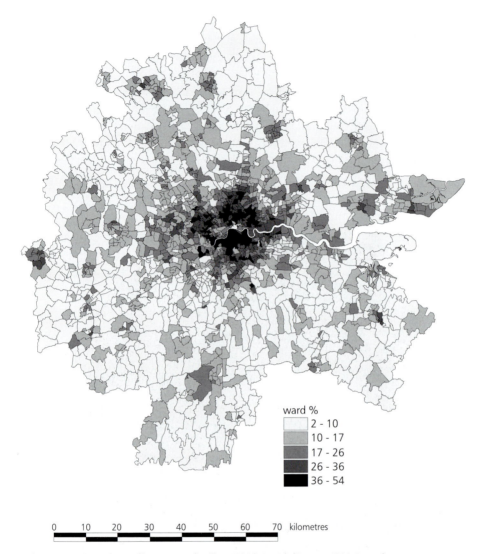

ward %

2 - 10
10 - 17
17 - 26
26 - 36
36 - 54

0    10    20    30    40    50    60    70   kilometres

**Figure 2.11.** Percentage of lone parent families, 1991 by ward. (*Source:* 1991 Census)

## Social Patterns across the Region: Households, Ethnicity and Deprivation

This analysis helps explain some key features of economic and social change in the region, but the social geography of the region is not simply a matter of class and purchasing power; it also involves differences in household composition and ethnicity, to which we turn now. In the first case, the main distinction is between couple-based and other household types, with a remarkable pattern of variation by 1991: couples predominated in the OMA, but were much weaker within London and especially Inner London (Figure 2.10). One of the other household types, lone parent families, strongly associated with child poverty, came to represent an extraordinarily high proportion of all families in a belt of wards in inner north-east, east and south London, with a small outlier in north-west London (Figure 2.11). Both of these are patterns which markedly intensified during the 1980s, making the inner-outer dimension of difference in the region increasingly one of household structure more than one of social class. Growing concentrations of non-working lone parents, alongside those of the unemployed, in parts of Inner London contributed to an increasing physical separation of employed from non-employed groups.

In terms of ethnicity there are also important inner-outer differences. At a broad level there are evident parallels between the distribution of household types and of white versus non-white ethnic groups, with most of the OMA remaining an area of predominantly white residents (Figure 2.12), as well as of couple-based

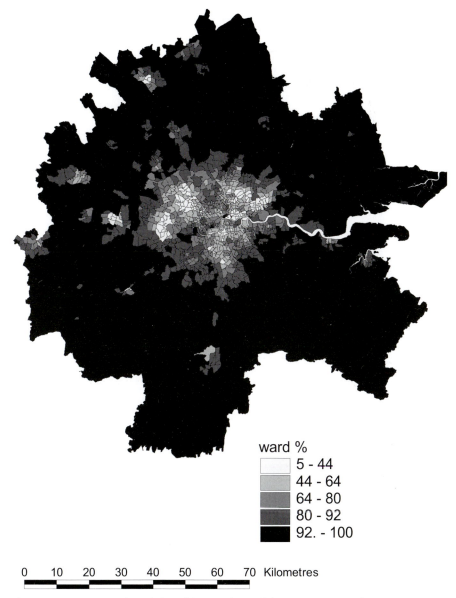

ward %

| | |
|---|---|
| | 5 - 44 |
| | 44 - 64 |
| | 64 - 80 |
| | 80 - 92 |
| | 92. - 100 |

0    10    20    30    40    50    60    70   Kilometres

**Figure 2.12.** Percentage of population white, 1991 by ward. (*Source:* 1991 Census)

households. On the other hand, in parts of west, inner south, and north-east London, by 1991 all other groups taken together represented a majority of the population, which would also be true by now of other nearby areas. In south-east and outer east London, on the other hand, many more areas remain predominantly white in their ethnic composition. Within these broad patterns, there are considerable local variations, especially as regards particular groups within the non-white population. As pointed out by Peach (1996) black population groups do not generally show very high degrees of local concentration, and by comparison with American cities London appears to be quite highly integrated in spatial terms. Despite a few well

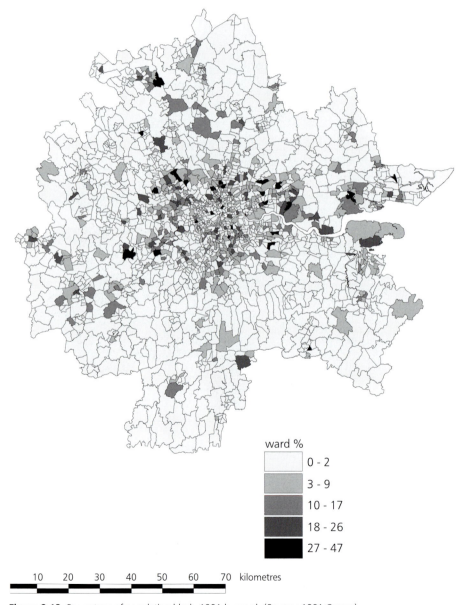

ward %

| | |
|---|---|
| | 0 - 2 |
| | 3 - 9 |
| | 10 - 17 |
| | 18 - 26 |
| | 27 - 47 |

10   20   30   40   50   60   70   kilometres

**Figure 2.13.** Percentage of population black, 1991 by ward. (*Source:* 1991 Census)

known concentrations, as in Brixton or Harlesden, Figure 2.13 shows these groups to be quite widely distributed across London (with variable mixes of Africans and Afro-Caribbeans) and in scattered locations in the OMA, mainly in industrial centres like Reading or Luton. Within this group, the African population is more localized than the Afro-Caribbean, reflecting more recent arrival. As compared with blacks, population groups from the Indian subcontinent are rather more highly concentrated in a few locations in London, especially in west and north-west and in a few wards in east London, and some industrial centres outside (Figure 2.14). In particular, the smaller Pakistani and Bangladeshi communities appear strongly concentrated in a

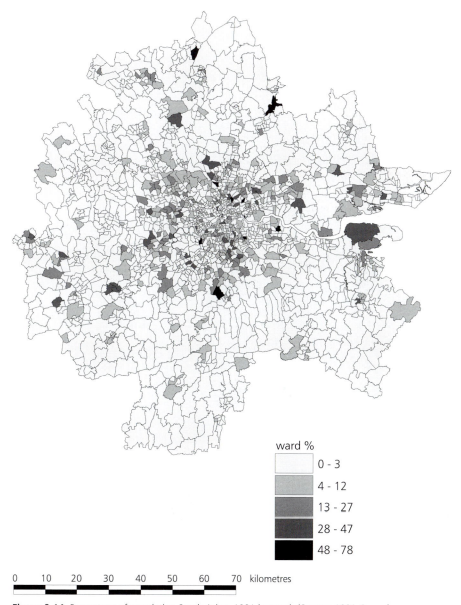

ward %

0 - 3
4 - 12
13 - 27
28 - 47
48 - 78

0    10    20    30    40    50    60    70   kilometres

**Figure 2.14.** Percentage of population South Asian, 1991 by ward. (*Source:* 1991 Census)

few London wards, especially in east London, and (for Pakistanis) selected locations outside it, apparently reflecting particular employment opportunities. But again the concentrations are local, rather than bunched together in particular parts of the city.

DTLR's year 2000 composite index of multiple deprivation (GB DTLR, 2000) provides a new and contemporary picture of the spatial distribution of disadvantage across London and its region (Figure 2.15). It is built up from separate indicators for several domains, including income, employment, housing, health, education and access to services, several of which we shall discuss in later chapters. But with the exception of the service accessibility map, which unsurprisingly shows urban areas to be less disadvantaged than their suburban and rural hinterlands, some key patterns recur across the domains with depressing regularity, highlighted in the overall composite map of multiple deprivation. In particular, this shows a concentration

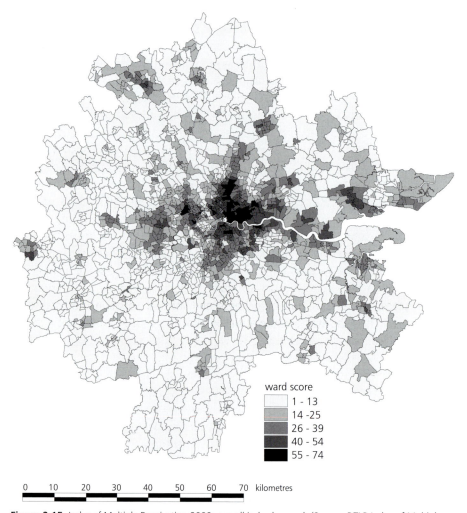

ward score

| | |
|---|---|
| | 1 - 13 |
| | 14 -25 |
| | 26 - 39 |
| | 40 - 54 |
| | 55 - 74 |

0    10    20    30    40    50    60    70   kilometres

**Figure 2.15.** Index of Multiple Deprivation 2000: overall index by ward. (Source: DTLR Index of Multiple Deprivation 2000)

of the highest levels of disadvantage in a tightly defined group of central and inner north-east London wards, stretching from the centre northwards into Haringey and eastwards into Newham, with small outliers across the river in inner south London. More broadly it reveals the two spatial dimensions to the incidence of deprivation in the London region: an inner-outer one and an east-west one. Deprived people are far more likely to be found in Inner London than in Outer London, and least likely in the OMA; they are somewhat more likely to be found in east London than in west London, though the measure of housing deprivation in particular shows important west London concentrations as well as those in the east.

## The Eight Localities

For our detailed investigations into life and work in contemporary London, we need to go into the localities in which people live their lives, in which businesses strive to operate, and in which local governments provide them with services. We go there for two reasons. The first is to exploit qualitative information, especially household interviews, which might allow us to interpret region-wide processes in local contexts. The other is to understand better how these local contexts influence the quality of people's lives, the performance of businesses and the quality of governance, and how these interact locally – which means that we must compare different localities. For the first, we need to find areas which will give us a representative sample of people, businesses and service providers.[1] For the second, we must encapsulate the almost infinite richness and variation of this huge city region within a few small neighbourhoods – an impossible task, perhaps, but we had to try.

We approached this problem in two ways. Firstly, we used Census data on population characteristics at ward level to pinpoint variations and identify clusters of wards with distinctive combinations of characteristics. Some results are discussed in Chapter 4. Though we used these to inform our choices – and also used some of the specific indicators to ensure representativeness across the set of areas – the choice was not based on any rigorous statistical technique: these eight areas are typical pieces of London, full of richness and internal variation, not statistical archetypes. In part this was because at this level of aggregation it becomes a rather arbitrary procedure, but also because we were interested in some features of areas beyond the immediate residential locality, including the economic base of nearby centres and characteristics of the local political regime. The second approach thus drew on a combination of past London research and our own direct knowledge of London's streets and spaces, to identify combinations of residential wards, related employment centres and boroughs/districts, which would best meet our needs for representativeness and significant comparisons. To simplify this process slightly, and in the knowledge that the major lines of contrast within the region were between inner/outer and eastern/western areas, we focused attention on a broad belt (12 miles deep) running from west to east (through central London), ignoring areas north and south of this belt.

Of the eight areas eventually selected (Figure 2.16), two are located outside

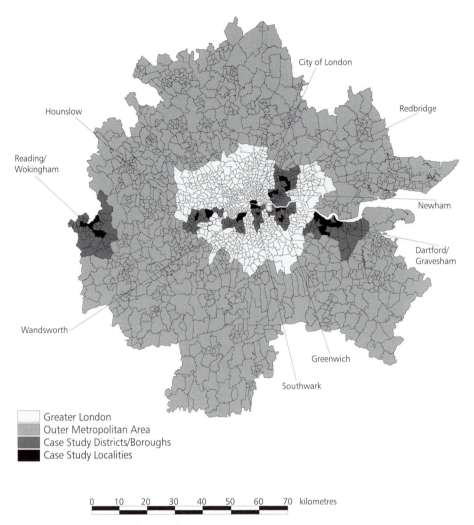

**Figure 2.16.** Sub-regions and case study areas.

London, at the extremes of the belt: Reading and Wokingham in the west, Dartford and Gravesham in the east. These were chosen to illustrate the contrast between the dynamic high-technology and advanced-service economy of the western sector, and the Thames Gateway region in the east where projected growth depends on planning initiatives. The other six are within Greater London: three in Inner London – Battersea-Clapham (in north Wandsworth), Bankside-Bermondsey-Peckham (in north Southwark), Stratford-Upton Park (in Newham) – and three in Outer London – Heston-Great West Road (in Hounslow), Gants Hill-Ilford (in Redbridge) and Charlton-Eltham (in Greenwich). In each case, a socially distinct residential area – or in Greater Reading and Southwark two contrasting areas – and a local employment centre were selected, and defined in terms of one or two Census wards. For the business interviews (used in Chapters 3 and 6) the financial district of the City of London was used as an additional study area but without any related work on residents or public services. For the school and governance interviews (used in Chapters 5 and 10) in the Dartford/Gravesham case study area we confined our attention to Dartford district. The full set of districts and localities used for the case study, and the names by which we refer to them in later chapters, are summarized in Table 2.1.

**Table 2.1.** The case study areas: local authority area, residential neighbourhood and employment centre identifiers.

| Local Authority Areas | Residential Neighbourhoods | Employment Centres |
|---|---|---|
| Reading/Wokingham | East Reading and Earley | Central and East Reading |
| Hounslow | Heston | Great West Road |
| Wandsworth | Battersea | Battersea and Clapham |
| City of London | – | City of London |
| Southwark | Bermondsey and Peckham | Bankside and Bermondsey |
| Newham | Upton Park | Stratford |
| Greenwich | Eltham | Charlton |
| Redbridge | Gants Hill | Ilford |
| Dartford/Gravesham | Dartford | Kent Thames-side |

In the remainder of this chapter, however, we focus on the eight full study areas, outlining the history and distinctive features of each,[2] in a traverse from Reading in the west to Dartford in the east.

## Reading/Wokingham (East and Central Reading and Earley)

Unlike the study areas within Greater London, or even Dartford/Gravesham to the east, Reading is really a free-standing town, with a quarter of a million residents. In this respect it is typical of settlements within the OMA. In local government terms, however, it is split between several districts, principally between Reading borough and Wokingham district, which actually includes much of the continuously built-up area of south-east Reading (as well as the separate town of Wokingham). Our study areas include residential neighbourhoods and employment nodes on both sides of this border in east/south-east Reading. This is clearly the most prosperous and economically dynamic of our case study areas, epitomizing the strength of the Thames Valley and the broader 'Western Crescent' during the past 20 years. Unlike some of the other towns in this sub-region, however, it is quite socially and ethnically mixed, by no means genteel, and has (in Reading borough) a local council which is solidly Labour.

### *Development*

Reading was historically the county town of Berkshire, remaining so until the mid-1990s when the county was dissolved into a set of distinct unitary authorities. Founded by the Saxons at the confluence of the Thames and Kennet rivers, it long performed the traditional roles of any such town: local government, justice, agricultural marketing and processing, and retailing. At the intersection of major highways – London to Bath and Bristol, Basingstoke to Oxford – it became an important eighteenth-century mail coach town. Then came the Kennet and Avon canal, linking the Thames westwards to Bristol, soon followed (in 1840) by Brunel's Great Western Railway on which Reading became an important junction. Later it gained a small university (the only one founded between the two world wars), but until the 1950s it was very much a sleepy county town.

Logically, the Reading economy of those days was dominated by the 'Three Bs' – Beer, Biscuits, Bulbs, all typical agricultural processing industries – together with brick manufacture. The most important of these, both as an employer and a truly global exporter, was represented by the firm of Huntley and Palmers, with vast factories in the town, employing some 6,000 workers in production both of biscuits and their decorated tins. By the end of the 1970s, however, all of these industries had either closed or relocated (though the brewery remained nearby on the M4), and Reading's industrial history is now just that. The town has become an archetype of the 'post-industrial' economy: with wholesale/retail, business services, finance, and transport/communications all over-represented, though none dominates the economy. In this process, transport links have again played a major role, with Reading benefiting greatly in the 1970s from the arrival both of the M4 London-Bristol motorway, passing south of the town, and of high-speed train services, with Reading as the first stop west of London. The growing importance of international air services through London Heathrow airport (just 25 miles east along the M4) has also reinforced the town's status as a highly accessible business location. Partly for these reasons, the Reading/Aldershot/Basingstoke area was designated for major growth in plans of the 1970s (GB South East Joint Planning Team, 1970) – although this now seems more a recognition of existing market dynamics than as something which significantly altered those trends.

In the town centre, these trends, boosted by the decentralization of London engineering and insurance offices in the 1970s, have transformed the skyline and the town's image. By the turn of the century the property consultants Healey and Baker judged it the top English city for office quality of life of office workers. In many ways, however, the heart of the new Reading economy is to be found in the series of new campus-style business parks which have grown up at the edge of the town and beyond, on sites with good access to the M4, notably in Wokingham district. Much of the activity in these parks reflects the leading role of the Western Crescent/M4 Corridor sub-region within the British IT industry, although they also host other business services. Thus in the riverside Thames Valley Business Park tenants include Microsoft, Oracle and J.D. Edwards but also the headquarters of British Gas's exploration division. Not far away, in Winnersh Triangle hi-tech firms include the inward investors: US Robotics, Mars Electronics, Hewlett Packard, and Symbol Technology. In the latest developments at Green Park (claimed as the largest such park in Europe) and the nearby Reading International Business Park, new tenants include Cisco Systems and the ill-starred MCI Worldcom – while an older industrial estate on the edge of Whitley nearby houses a major Compaq (formerly Digital) establishment. As in comparable developments in nearby centres such as Bracknell or Basingstoke, many of the larger operations on these sites are actually UK (or European) headquarters for non-British multi-national businesses.

These new business developments have generally been welcomed by the local community as well as by the two councils involved, particularly following the shock of the early 1990s recession. But finding sites to house the associated population growth has become much more problematic. The last major housing developments date from the 1970s, in the contiguous suburbs of Woodley, Earley and Lower Earley (within Wokingham district), and were then said to be the largest private housing development in Europe. But since then resistance to greenfield development for housing has become strong, as in most of the pressurized areas of the South East, with particular conflict over schemes which would effectively extend Reading beyond the M4, towards Basingstoke. Two effects have been to further raise (already high) local house prices – with those for semi-detached properties averaging £158,000 by summer 2001 (against £124,000 nationally) – and to promote infill development and higher density redevelopment (including on commercial sites) within Reading.

### Economic structure

Across Greater Reading the largest elements in the employment structure are – as just about everywhere – business services and distribution, but the main specialization is in business services (accounting for 27 per cent of employment in 1999), and there is also an above-average share in financial services. Within these broad headings, IT, engineering services and insurance stand out, but Reading does now have a quite broadly-based producer service sector. Its overall balance between the manual and non-manual sectors of employment (i.e. production industries, transport and wholesaling versus the rest) is much the same as in most of our other case study areas, with just a quarter of jobs in the former. During the 1990s, however, it has shown the strongest growth performance among these areas, with a net addition of 19 per cent to employment between 1991 and 1998, mostly in business services, including an extra 5,000 jobs in ICT activities. Total employment in the manual sectors stayed more or less constant, but in the non-manual sectors the rate of growth in Reading/Wokingham (27 per cent) was much faster than in any other of the case study districts apart from Hounslow. This is also the most self-contained of the case study areas, with as many jobs as resident workers and just 24 per cent of employed residents working outside the area in 1991.

### Social and ethnic composition

Because a large part of Reading's middle-class suburbs, both old and new, actually lie outside the borough (principally in Wokingham district), while most of its public sector estates as well as inner areas of less desirable housing are inside the borough, we need to combine the two districts to see the town's overall population profile. On this basis it has the strongest representation of professionals and managers among our case study areas (with 29 per cent of household heads engaged in such jobs in 1991), and one of the lowest proportions of manual workers (28 per cent). The proportion of households with inactive household heads is very low (28 per cent), reflecting both the strength of the local economy and a relatively low proportion of residents over retirement age. Another contributory factor is a rather low proportion of lone parent households (just 10 per cent of those with dependent children in 1991). Conversely, it is one of the only two case study areas (with Dartford/Gravesham) where couple-based households were in the majority in 1991. In these respects it is much closer to the national average than are the areas within Greater London. It is more extreme, however, in the rate of owner-occupation (76 per cent), which was exceeded only in Redbridge among our sample areas. With a much smaller rented sector than in London, but house prices approaching London levels in recent years, the problem is that lower-income workers find it hard to get by and employers have difficulty recruiting.

In terms of ethnic composition, it is again closer to Dartford/Gravesham (the other OMA case) than to the inner areas, having just 6 per cent of its Census population from non-white origins. As elsewhere, minorities are more significant within the school population, but even here they accounted for only 14 per cent of pupils in 1999. Among the minorities, there were almost equal numbers of Afro-Caribbeans, Pakistanis and Indians, so no one group is of any great size. This is a key respect in which Reading differs from Wokingham: it has proportionately many more of these groups (especially the first two), with the largest Bajan population outside Barbados, and it has a firmly multi-cultural policy stance.

Other significant differences between the districts are in social composition and housing tenure, Wokingham having a lot more white collar workers and owner-occupiers (85 per cent of households against 8 per cent in social housing). This contrast is reflected in an exaggerated way in political representation, with Reading council having a very large Labour majority and a Liberal Democrat opposition, while on Wokingham council the Liberal Democrats exercise control with the barest of majorities over the Conservatives, and there are no Labour members.

### Social conditions and deprivation

Greater Reading is the most generally affluent of the case study districts. In common with other parts of the Western Crescent, it has for long enjoyed employment rates well above the national average, or those experienced within Greater London and the OMA. After 8 years of falling unemployment, the claimant count unemployment rate (adjusted to a residence basis) was just 1.3 per cent in October 2001, and though, as elsewhere, the real level of unemployment among those wanting jobs might be twice as high, there is effectively full employment in the area. And on the extended measures of non-employment used to compute the DTLR's 2000 Index of Deprivation, Reading/Wokingham together come about 300th out 354 English local authorities (GB Department of Transport, Local Government and the Regions, 2000). As far as the case study areas are concerned, this is in a class of its own.

In terms of measures of income deprivation, based on the proportion of the population within various 'poor' groups, the picture is very similar. However, if attention is focused solely on average earnings among tax-payers (i.e. the non-poor), Greater Reading comes in second place, some way behind Wandsworth. Given that Wandsworth house prices are about three times as high as in Reading, however, it is not clear in which area average taxpayers enjoy the higher level of disposable income.

Within Reading (if not Wokingham), there are still islands of deprivation, notably in Whitley, an overwhelmingly white working-class area dominated by a large council estate, at the southern end of the town next to the motorway. Whitley is a rather stigmatized area, with relatively high unemployment and a concentration of social problems, but even this area falls outside the worst 10 per cent of wards nationally (at which neighbourhood initiatives are particularly targeted). This is partly because employment rates are quite high by national standards. In two of the domains covered by the Indices of Deprivation, education and housing, Whitley does appear to have serious problems even by national standards – and so, to a lesser degree do a number of other areas within Reading borough. On the index of educational deprivation (which covers adult qualification levels as well as school exams and university entrance), Whitley actually figures amongst the 1 per cent worst areas nationally, while the area as a whole has its quota of wards in the worst 10 per cent. On the housing index, the area's performance looks worse, with twice its 'fair share' of areas in the worst 10 per cent, including Whitley, but with higher levels of deprivation indicated for the inner-city wards. Since for both housing and education Greater Reading also has twice its share of areas in the best 10 per cent, it is evident that local variations are particularly strong in these fields.

In terms of crime risks, Greater Reading appears to be a relatively safe area, with rates of recorded violent crime which are much lower than in the case study areas within Greater London (and below the national average), though rates of property crime (other than robbery) are closer to the London norm (and above the national average).

### Neighbourhood profiles

For our studies of residential neighbourhoods we chose a strip on the eastern side of Greater Reading, running from the edge of the inner city through to outer suburbia. The first half of this strip lies within the borough of Reading and the second half within Reading district, with significant differences between these two halves. Inside Reading the strip includes both an area of high-density terraced housing in New Town and much larger Edwardian housing on the university fringes. New Town, on the south bank of the river Kennet, retains quite a strong sense of community, although as in the nearby areas its population mix now includes substantial proportions of both students and Pakistani families. Within Wokingham district the strip includes both the older suburbs of Earley and a large part of the less characterful Lower Earley estate, which is archetypal 1970s suburbia. Both ends of the strip are preponderantly owner-occupied and middle-class, but in East Reading about a quarter of the households are private renters, and there is a significant minority of less-skilled manual workers, whereas in (Lower) Earley 94 per cent of households were owner-occupiers in 1991, and the social composition is more strongly managerial. There are also significant differences in ethnic mix, with the non-white groups forming about 25 per cent of the East Reading population (in 1991), compared with just 5 per cent in (Lower) Earley. Average property prices in summer 2001 varied between £163,000 in Lower Earley and £125,000 in East Reading.

For the related employment areas in which business interviews were undertaken, we took both Reading town centre – including the new Oracle retail/leisure complex as well as the established CBD – and the two high-tech parks on the eastern side of the town, Thames Valley Business Park (lying across the Reading-Wokingham border), and the Winnersh Triangle (which is wholly in Wokingham). As we have already seen, both of these include strong concentrations of IT firms, including many multi-nationals – Information Technology firms including Microsoft and Oracle; and Winnersh ward in Wokingham borough, with the Winnersh triangle, another major high-technology concentration including Hewlett Packard and US Robotics.

## Hounslow (Heston and Great West Road)

Hounslow, some 25 miles down the Thames from Reading, is an Outer London borough – but by no means simply a residential suburb. With Slough, a few miles to the west in the OMA, it was one of the major centres of (Fordist) industrial development in the inter-war period – now mostly replaced by offices and by ICT activities, which link it to Thames Valley centres such as Reading. But the key influence on its recent development, both economically and environmentally, has been the dramatic growth of Heathrow airport, straddling the north-west corner of the borough and parts of Hillingdon to its north. This is the core of the major employment node outside Greater London, generating large amounts of traffic by all modes, and contributing to a much more cosmopolitan population than is found in Western Crescent areas beyond Slough.

### *Development*

Like Reading, Hounslow grew up as a mail coach town on the main Bath Road, at a point where it crosses a flat and extremely fertile plain of river gravels. As London grew, the wheat fields increasingly gave way to fruit gardens, and then to suburban development. Hounslow was also a significant industrial centre, with traditional agricultural processing – mills, maltings, breweries – as well as Pears Soap, sword-making, gunpowder, potteries, brickworks and turpentine. The nineteenth century saw the extension of the Grand Union canal to the Midlands, the building of gas and water works, the GWR transhipment dock, and boat-building around Brentford Docks.

The key agent in transforming Hounslow was the railways, with a line to Waterloo arriving in 1849–1850 and a second 20 years later, followed in 1883 by the Metropolitan District Railway (later integrated into London Underground). In each case, house-building quickly followed, with the Metro line serving as the trigger for the first large-scale suburban development at Bedford Park, with more sporadic building at Osterley and around Hounslow. However, really large-scale suburbanization had to await the Piccadilly line extension of 1933, which provided an express service to Hammersmith, and was integrated with local bus feeders. To this day, the distribution of good-quality residential property follows these rail lines: it is concentrated around Chiswick in the extreme east – especially in Hounslow's half of the Bedford Park garden suburb, where prices now rival Notting Hill. Turnham Green offers a variety of restored cottages, and in Osterley homes are to be found alongside green fields, conveying a distinctly rural feel. By contrast, areas of more working-class housing along the old Bath Road through Brentford and Isleworth to Hounslow reflect the influence of the electric tram route established there in 1901. Across the borough as a whole, average prices for semi-detached properties averaged £236,000 in autumn 2001; this is about 45 per cent above those in Greater Reading, and well above prices in comparable suburbs on the east side of London. In relation to its immediate neighbours, Hounslow house prices tended to be significantly above those in Hillingdon to the north, but were about 40 per cent below those of high-status Richmond to the south.

From the mid-nineteenth century, metropolitan expansion and the development of transport links of all kinds replaced the older Hounslow industries with larger-scale activities, including a very large railway goods yard at Feltham, an early aircraft industry and tram-building. The major industrial developments followed from construction of the Great West Road in 1925, with Gillette, Martini and Firestone Tyres (the borough's major private employer up to the mid-1970s) as early arrivals in what became the largest industrial complex in West London. This is still evident along the 'Golden Mile' from western Chiswick through Brentford and Isleworth, which in the early 1990s had no less than twelve trading estates or business parks. With other significant industrial concentrations in Brentford, Hanworth and Feltham, up to the mid-1970s half of the borough's male labour force and a third of the women worked in manufacturing, particularly electrical engineering, although office development was already occurring around the major shopping centres and the Great West Road.

One consequence was that the borough was particularly heavily exposed to the job losses which hit London manufacturing, including the inter-war industries, during the 1970s and 1980s. Between 1973 and 1988 over 23,000 jobs were lost, reflecting both growth constraints on local firms and closure of several major manufacturers, including Firestone and United Biscuits on the Golden Mile. On the other side of the picture, however, first Heathrow airport (just over the north-west edge of the borough) and then the M4 and M25 motorways (intersecting nearby) have given the borough enormous new locational advantages, especially for headquarter functions of international businesses. The current Chiswick Park development in Gunnersbury is claimed to be the largest in London since Canary Wharf.

### Economic structure

Hounslow is now predominantly a service economy, though with a third of employment in manual activities, it remains more dependent on these than any of the other case study districts, except for Dartford/Gravesham on the Thames estuary. Its transition toward a post-industrial structure of activity (such as that in Reading) reflects both very strong growth in business service employment and continuing heavy job losses in manufacturing. During the 1990s these job losses spread to a newer range of industries, including defence-related activities where numbers employed fell by about 4,000 between 1990 and 1996, attracting European aid for the borough from the KONVER (defence restructuring) fund. Now there are only 9,000 jobs left in this sector (7 per cent of total employment), with even less actually involved in making things, as distinct from managing, servicing or selling. However, the scale of manual job loss in recent years has been substantially exceeded by that of expansion in non-manual activities, where an employment growth rate of 31 per cent between 1991 and 1998 exceeded that in any other of our case study districts – thanks particularly to the addition of 5,000 jobs in ICT activities. As a consequence the overall rate of employment growth (16 per cent) approached that in Reading/Wokingham.

Even with a high degree of commuting to Heathrow airport – with some 83,000 jobs on/off-site according to BAA estimates, almost all credited statistically to the neighbouring borough of Hillingdon – Hounslow is a net importer of labour, with 100,000 inward commuters, two-thirds of them from elsewhere in West London. Local employment includes an increasingly large element in company headquarters, with 200 in all, notably on old factory sites along the Golden Mile, and including many multi-nationals, for whom rapid airport access has been a key location factor. Major corporations represented here include particular concentrations of airlines, computer manufacturers and private mail services, together with a range of other industrial headquarters. Since the mid-1990s, high profile developments have included Samsung's European HQ, Kvaerner (the Norwegian-based multi-national) and a new headquarters for SmithKlineBeecham (actually on the site vacated by Samsung after the Far East economic downturn).

### Social and ethnic composition

In social terms the Hounslow population is quite mixed, with 19 per cent of heads of households in professional/managerial jobs, 26 per cent in manual work and 33 per cent inactive, according to the 1991 Census. Compared with neighbouring boroughs such as Hillingdon or (especially) Richmond, there are many fewer Hounslow residents in managerial occupations. This reflects modest levels of educational or vocational qualification among the local workforce, which limit their ability to take advantage of growing concentrations of managerial and high-tech activity in the area. The socially mixed character of the borough is also reflected in housing tenure (with 61 per cent of owner-occupier households and 27 per cent in social housing in 1991).

Hounslow, like much of West London (and its near neighbour Slough in the OMA), has a substantial Asian population, reflected in an above average share of households with three or more adults. Overall the London Research Centre estimated 32 per cent of the population as coming from non-white ethnic minorities in 1998, with the majority of these from Indian origins and sizeable numbers also from Pakistani and other Asian descent. This compares with just 16 per cent in 1981 (Peach,

1996), since when the white population appears to have fallen by about 25,000, while the number of non-whites has increased by about 35,000. One element in this growth has been an inflow of asylum seekers and refugees who were estimated to comprise about 3 per cent of the resident population by 1997 (actually a little below the London average, despite the closeness of Heathrow as a point of entry). Thus whereas at the time of the 1991 Census, a quarter of the wards in the borough had between 40 per cent and 50 per cent of their populations from non-white ethnic origins, all of these are now likely to have a non-white majority – although rarely with more than 30 per cent from any other single origin. As elsewhere, ethnic minorities are more strongly represented within the school-age population: 48 per cent of those in the borough's schools were non-white by 1999, while for 39 per cent English was a second language; twelve primary and two secondary schools had over 80 per cent of their pupils from minority ethnic groups. Politically, Indians are now strongly represented within the Labour group on the borough council, with about a third of the seats.

### Social conditions and deprivation

Unemployment rates in Hounslow are not quite as low as in Reading, but still very modest by national and regional standards. In October 2001, the claimant count unemployment rate (adjusted to a residence basis) was just 2 per cent – under half the Greater London average and also well below that elsewhere in Outer London. Average incomes among taxpayers are rather lower than in Reading, but close to those in most of the other case study districts. As this might suggest, Hounslow is not one of the more deprived London boroughs, and lies in the middle of a ranking of boroughs on the IMD2000 index, apparently less comfortable than Hillingdon or Richmond, its neighbours to north and south, but with less evidence of social disadvantage than Ealing to its north-east. The one domain in which there is some real evidence of weakness is housing, where 18 of the 21 wards figure among the 10 per cent most deprived in England, and all are within the bottom quartile. On other domains no local wards figure among the most deprived areas nationally – the nearest being Hanworth, an uncharacteristically white area with a large proportion of social housing in the south-east corner of the borough. Despite its suburban character, Hounslow has rates of violent crime which are considerably higher than in Reading, and twice the national average. This is the case also for robbery, though for this offence rates are still much lower than in some of the inner areas. For property crimes, however, though rates are above the national average, they differ little from those in Reading.

### Neighbourhood profiles

The residential area chosen for study spans the Great West Road, just east of Heathrow airport, including central Heston, to the north and Hounslow Heath to the south. Both socially and in terms of housing tenure, this area is close to the regional average, with a somewhat middle-class population and a majority of owner-occupied properties, alongside smaller public and private rented sectors. However, like several other areas in the borough it now has a majority of non-white residents, including a large proportion of people of Indian ethnic origin. All of the local councillors are also of Indian origin. Only in housing terms does this appear to be an area with any serious deprivation (to judge by the IMD2000 indicators), and there is evidence of some overcrowding. This primarily reflects larger family sizes, rather than generally high densities, however, and access to open space is good, notably on the large Hounslow Heath, which is the site of a Nature Reserve. Average property prices here in summer 2001 were around £188,000.

The related employment area selected for business interviews was focused on the 'Golden Mile' a couple of miles to the east along the Great West Road. As we have already seen, this is the base for national and international headquarters of many companies, including Gillette, Data-General and Carillon, and the site of a cluster of stylish high-rise office developments.

## Wandsworth (Battersea and Clapham)

Battersea, situated on the south bank of the Thames in the inner west London borough of Wandsworth, has a complex socio-economic geography, which reflects both its location and its particular history. Cheap land (on what has traditionally been the 'wrong' side of the river) facilitated nineteenth-century suburban housing, some of very good quality which provided an obvious target for gentrification a century and more later. But a basic division – between a physically more elevated, higher-class south Battersea and a riverside, working-class north Battersea – was massively underlined by nineteenth-century railway building and riverside industrialization. These brought large-scale public housing schemes to the northern areas, many of which still survive. Though some of these contrasts remain, during the 1980s and 1990s the population and tenure structure of the area (as of other parts of Wandsworth) has been transformed through the social (and political) engineering efforts of a radical Conservative borough council, which has greatly accelerated the gentrification process.

### *Development*

South Battersea, on the higher and healthier ground away from the river, early began to develop as a salubrious rural suburb, with first Clapham and then Stockwell becoming select residential areas in the nineteenth century for commuters to the city. But, except on the perimeter of Battersea Park, they did not move on to the lower ground of north Battersea: here, the railways, which brought the working classes in, blighted the land and kept the middle classes out. In fact, until the second half of the nineteenth century lower Battersea remained predominantly agricultural, although a wide range of industries grew up on the riverside – some using the Thames for transport or its tributary, the Wandle, for power, others simply because the land was cheap upstream of the port. With the coming of the railways, which by the late

1860s had brought a great 'tangle' of interconnecting tracks to Battersea, more substantial industries followed, employing working-class people displaced from the centre of London by railway development and rising rents.

Only with the arrival in the 1900s of the LCC's electric trams, with their substantially cheaper workmen's fares, did much working-class housing follow. This was provided by a mixture of speculators, philanthropic trusts, and (from 1901) Battersea Borough Council, which under Labour control prioritized house building, together with an ambitious range of social services (Rudder, 1993). While its estates attracted the skilled artisan and upper-working-class families, poorer people went into inferior developments, on damp, low-lying, polluted land, with growing multi-occupancy. Slums developed which the LCC started to replace with walk-up flats from the 1920s, increasing the concentration of public housing in north Battersea. A heavy incidence of bomb damage during World War Two added to housing needs, which were met by LCC/GLC and borough council construction of tower blocks. Built at lower densities, these meant export of population from Battersea, while by cutting across established community areas and destroying traditional settings for social life, they also served to weaken community life. This process was accentuated when the borough was swallowed up by Wandsworth in the London government reorganization of 1965.

Under Labour control, Wandsworth's response to continuing housing need involved a mix of municipalizing repairable rented properties, housing improvement initiatives, and support for owner-occupation – rather than further redevelopment. But, as smog clearance, increasing transport problems/costs, and new service jobs made areas more attractive to middle-class residents, properties from the private rental sector were increasingly bought up by a new wave of gentrifiers, for (re)conversion to larger family homes. By 1978 it was reported that in north Battersea

> An increasing number of young professional people have moved into the area. A whole range of shops and services have sprung up to serve them, like wine bars, specialist and antique shops, which also have the effect of squeezing out those that previously met the needs of the existing population. (Beresford and Beresford, 1978, 24–25)

With Conservative control of the council from 1978, this process was more actively supported, as was the Thatcher government's promotion of council house sales, both to sitting tenants and on the open market. Improvement grants were now targeted at pre-1919 houses needing substantial repairs, with the consequence that by late 1983 80 per cent of grants were going to owner-occupiers, rather than for rented properties. The council house sales policy was advanced by ploughing back proceeds into improvement of council estates, increasing the attractiveness of purchasing flats (at substantial discounts) – and introducing Conservative voters to areas of the borough dominated by council housing, such as Battersea. The process was accelerated through sale of whole blocks to developers, with the effect that owner-occupation in the borough rose to 54 per cent in 1991, the highest level in Inner London, while the proportion of local authority renters fell to 21 per cent (from 35 per cent in 1981). These processes were operated in a way which led to a much less even spread of local authority housing across areas of Battersea. In some wards the sector has virtually disappeared, while estates in north Battersea seem to have been allowed to remain so as to take on 'problem' tenants from other areas, on an increasing scale as older-established tenants are provoked to leave.

Further changes in tenure patterns are under way, with luxury apartment conversions in former industrial areas on the riverside and the reappearance of large-scale private renting. These are taking a stage further the transformation of Battersea from the working-class community which it was in 1950 (and even 1975) into what is in 2000 more of a haven for young middle-class couples and singles wanting easy access to City work and ample local restaurants and bars in which to relax (*Wandsworth Borough News*, 13 August 1999). This is reflected in house prices, which though much lower than in Hammersmith or Chelsea across the river, are well above the London average (e.g. a borough average of £497,000 for a semi-detached property in summer 2001). But in north Battersea these affluent incomers are still juxtaposed with a residual group of disadvantaged tower block residents who have no real choice over their location.

## Economic structure

Across Wandsworth as a whole, there are now very few jobs in manufacturing (about 5 per cent) but the bulk of employment is spread across a wide range of service activities. Almost all of these, apart from finance, are more heavily represented here than in the national employment profile, but the degree of specialization is generally low – being strongest in business services and in health. Wandsworth has one of the lowest proportion of jobs in the manual sectors of activity among our case study districts (one-fifth). Uniquely, however, this proportion actually grew during the 1990s, since the borough combined one of the slowest rates of growth in non-manual activities with the only substantial net growth of manual sector employment. This was thanks to expansion in both transport and wholesale distribution (including the relocated New Covent Garden food markets), which are considerably more important here than are the production sectors. In the producer service sector strong growth during the 1990s included the emergence of a significant ICT sector. But growth in business services generally was offset by public sector job losses, in both education and health services. Overall growth was consequently much slower than in either Reading or Hounslow: just 4 per cent between 1991 and 1998.

## Social and ethnic composition

Socially, the balance of the borough's population has decisively switched toward groups in white-collar employment: in 1991 fewer households here were headed by manual workers than in any of the other case study areas (19 per cent). The proportion in professional and managerial jobs was still a lot less than in Reading, however, and what was distinctive was the proportion in junior or (especially) intermediate level non-manual jobs. This suggests that it occupies a niche somewhere below the core areas of gentrification, presumably because of the mix of properties which has been on offer, notably those transferred from the council sector. This, and the age structure – with an above average proportion between 20 and 35 – are also presumably related to the tenure mix, which is distinguished (from the other case study areas) by a higher proportion in private rented property, especially furnished lets.

The proportions of single parent families and of households comprising a single working-age adult were also quite high. Those in the former group (representing 23 per cent of local families in 1991) tend to be educationally disadvantaged, and could have benefited from the knock-on effects of gentrification if the newcomers had patronized local schools and pushed for higher standards. However, gentrifying families have actually tended to respond to school quality problems in 'exit' rather than 'voice' terms, by withdrawing their children from the state system. One consequence was that in 2000, despite strong but ineffectual local protest, two primary schools in north Battersea were closed, after a negative Ofsted report on one and falling rolls in both.

The ethnic composition of the borough population is quite mixed, with 22 per cent from non-white origins in 1998, of whom half were black. By 1999 there was a majority (53 per cent) from non-white ethnic origins within local maintained schools, though the proportion with English as a second language (30 per cent) was significantly lower than in most Inner London boroughs. Local ethnic geographies vary a lot, and have changed as the tenure transition proceeded. All ethnic groups have shown a shift from private and council tenancies into owner-occupation, if rather more among whites than for Afro-Caribbeans. But in the process, ethnic minorities have become more and more concentrated in particular wards, reversing the trend of the 1970s. The process is not simply one of segregation, however; some significant ethnic pockets (with 30 to 40 per cent minority population in a ward) seem to have all but disappeared during the 1980s as these areas became solidly owner-occupied. The actual pattern of variation suggests that while white gentrifiers have been buying up Victorian cottages, ethnic minorities were more commonly purchasing flats on council estates.

The area as a whole is steadily becoming more middle-class: every year, thousands of affluent young private tenants or owner-occupiers move in, while a roughly equivalent number – including, it is thought, less-affluent pensioners – move out. So there are increasing divisions between long-term residents, restricted to the council estates, and highly-mobile newcomers who can afford to buy.

### Social conditions and deprivation

In terms of average incomes among taxpayers, Wandsworth seems to be easily the most affluent of the case study districts – though the relation between mean and median incomes reported by the Inland Revenue for 1999/2000 suggests a rather uneven distribution (if less so than in Kensington & Chelsea or Westminster across the river). This impression of substantial inequality is reinforced by the fact that the claimant unemployment rate (adjusted to a residence basis) of 3.5 per cent in October 2001, though well below that in Southwark or Newham, was above that in a majority of the case study districts. Overall, Wandsworth appears somewhere near the middle of national rankings of area deprivation from IMD2000 – except in relation to the housing domain, where a majority of Wandsworth wards appear in the worst 10 per cent nationally (and all are in the worst 20 per cent). This largely reflects a region-wide pressure on housing availability, generally translated into lower levels of consumption than would be acceptable elsewhere. But there are also some wards which come into the worst 10 per cent (or close to it) on the core income and employment domains – though none quite get there on the overall index. In particular, there is evidence of a concentration of child poverty in four wards which still have a large proportion of social housing, including three in north Battersea and Roehampton in the west of the borough. This reflects the incidence of lone parenthood. Other child-related problem indicators are the rates of inclusion of children and young people on the child protection register, and of secondary school pupil exclusion which (at 0.5 per cent and 1 per cent respectively in 1998/99) are among the highest in London. Crime rates are high by national standards, but very close to the London average, and similar to Hounslow except for a significantly higher robbery rate.

### Neighbourhood profiles

For our residential interviews we focused on a group of three wards in north Battersea: Latchmere, containing some of the borough's most deprived public housing; St Mary's Park, with a mixture of council estates, terraced houses and new luxury apartments; and Shaftesbury, comprising an old-established Peabody trust estate, together with some gentrified terraces. In the 1998 borough elections, the first of these returned three of the eleven Labour councillors in the borough, while the other two wards both have Conservative councillors. Taken together, they contain a mix of tenures, although with a proportion of residents in social housing which is well above average. Average property prices here in summer 2001 were around £295,000, reflecting a location advertised as 'only minutes from the Kings Road'. The population mix is preponderantly white, but with a significant black minority (especially in the first sub-area where it represented about 30 per cent of the population in 1991). Socially, the most distinctive feature is a relatively high proportion of lone parents (about 30 per cent of all families with dependent children).

For the related employment and business studies we chose two areas. The first was in Nine Elms area, which is the main employment centre, with the New Covent Garden market, complementary transport activities and some industry on former railway land, and growing food-related activities. Nearby, the former Battersea Power station is beginning development as a leisure centre, after substantial delays. As a complementary location we used the Clapham Junction area, including Wandsworth's main shopping centre and some adjacent industrial sites.

### Southwark (Bankside, Bermondsey and Peckham)

Southwark, the borough in which our next study areas lie, presents an intriguing comparison with Wandsworth borough and with Battersea. Four miles farther north-east along the south bank of the river, its early development had many similarities, although it has always been closer to the economic heart of the city. Its recent political evolution has shown quite distinctive twists and turns, however: with control shifting from Old Labour in the 1960s to militant Labour in the 1970s and 1980s, and then to very New Labour in the 1990s – now actively encouraging gentrification like the radical Conservatives in Wandsworth. However, three in five of its residents still live in social housing, much of it substandard, the borough continues to suffer the full range of 'inner-city' problems, and, while new jobs are arriving, many locals lack the qualifications needed to fill them.

## Development

These problems have deep roots. Southwark has always been the poor neighbour of the City of London across the river. Developing first along the Borough High Street that led south from London Bridge – the only river crossing up to the mid-eighteenth century – it became a place of intense traffic of goods and people. It was a seat of markets, including the surviving Borough Market, while the wharves which lined the 'Pool of London', for a mile or more below the bridge, concentrated much of London's port activity until enclosed docks started to be built on clear land further east in the nineteenth century.

By then, packed into the intervening space was a mixture of industry, including noxious activities such as leather tanning, and one of the worst slums in London. Above the bridge, Bankside was traditionally London's red light district, a place of theatres, bear pits, taverns and brothels. The High Street was also a centre for coaching inns until the first rail terminus was built nearby at London Bridge. Two major commuter railways, serving the City of London across the river, then produced a huge complex of east-west railway tracks on high arches, effectively severing the area in two. Below the tracks, was a tangled mass of slum housing, warehousing and industry, including trades ancillary to the City, such as printing and food processing, as well as heavier industry – including a gasworks on Bankside, replaced in the 1950s by London's last power station, itself just transmogrified into the Tate Modern gallery.

Slowly, from the mid-nineteenth century, charitable trusts and then municipal endeavour began to replace the worst of the slums, squeezing new housing into the limited spaces between the viaducts. This development accelerated in the twentieth century, with Southwark and Bermondsey councils building up to the limit of their powers and finances, and being joined in this effort by the LCC from 1934, when the Labour administration switched emphasis from peripheral out-county estates to denser inner-London renewal schemes. Then as later, an effect of reconstruction was to lower residential densities, and with the arrival first of LCC tram termini and then of tube services, out-movement of population started in the 1890s, initially to new LCC cottage homes. This process continued, accelerated by the Blitz, taking the combined population of the (pre-1965) Southwark and Bermondsey boroughs from a peak of 337,000 in 1901 to just 158,000 by 1951 (Cherry and Pevsner, 1983, 560–561). Initiation of a comprehensive renewal strategy in the 1950s brought huge new public estates both in Bermondsey and North Peckham, but again housing and area improvements entailed reduced densities and substantial population overspill from these areas.

The riverside area of wharves and warehouses was left more or less untouched, until competition from more entrepreneurial container ports on the east coast led to the unexpected contraction and eventual closure of the Port of London between 1967 and 1981, leaving a vast stretch of derelict land along 8 miles of riverfront. During the 1970s there were successive redevelopment schemes, involving much paper and much talk but very little action. To remedy this situation, in 1981 the Thatcher government removed both initiative and veto powers from the local authorities, and imposed a London Docklands Development Corporation to single-mindedly secure redevelopment of the entire dockland area, including the Southwark waterfront. This proposal was fought all the way up to the High Court, delaying the LDDC's inauguration for a year. Even after this, Southwark council – whose traditional working-class trade-union leadership was displaced by a group of left-wing activists – pursued a bitter guerrilla war against the government, producing a rival development plan which had to be struck down in the High Court, and rejecting any collaboration with the LDDC (Hall, 1998, chapter 28). Beyond simple issues of power, there was a fundamental conflict about the kind of area that this should be. The council's priorities were to preserve traditional land uses and activities employing the existing working-class population; LDDC, however, saw the future in terms of an informational economy and was determined to attract jobs in activities serving this and to build homes for the predominantly middle-class people who would work in it.

The main impact of the LDDC was in the areas of enclosed docks, both on the north bank and further east in the Surrey Docks. But its territory also included the line of river-side warehouses stretching up to London Bridge, most of which were converted into shops, restaurants, bars and luxury apartments, through two major developments in the 1980s: Hay's Galleria near London Bridge and Butler's Wharf just below Tower Bridge. The early 1990s collapse of the property market delayed a third major scheme, London Bridge City, beyond the LDDC's winding-up in 1998. By then, however, the Southwark riverside (like that opposite in Tower Hamlets) displayed two starkly dissimilar landscapes, that of public-sector rebuilding (from 1934 to 1981), and that of commercial redevelopment under public-private partnership (from 1982 to 1998) – separated by a kind of invisible Berlin Wall.

Initiative has now passed back to the local authority, itself transformed in the meantime into a model of Blairite New Labour. Southwark council now accepts the revolution that the LDDC wrought, and is pushing towards its logical conclusion through pursuit of both private investment and a more affluent population. To this end, extensive development and regeneration are underway across the northern half of Southwark, especially in five areas: the riverine areas of Bankside and London Bridge (home to the new GLA); North Peckham; the Aylesbury Estate; and the Elephant and Castle. The entrepreneurial strategy – promoted by Southwark's then Director of Development, Fred Manson, in conjunction with a Cross-River Partnership – involves linking Southwark as a whole into the City and Westminster economies, with Bankside being seen as the crucial bridgehead for this. This is an area which since the 1970s has attracted overspill business service development from the City during boom spells. But the key to its recent and planned-for transformation is incorporation into an extended cultural quarter, with the rebuilt Globe Theatre (1996), the new Tate Modern (2000) and associated development (including Vinopolis and smaller galleries) now linked along the riverside to the post-war South Bank arts complex, just to the west. There is some evidence of effects of this in terms of house prices which have risen faster than in most other parts of London since the mid-1990s, with average prices for semi-detached properties in Southwark reaching £334,000 in summer 2001 (putting it in about eighth place among London boroughs).

### Economic structure

Since 1970 there have been vast changes in Southwark's employment structure with the closure of the docks, and most manufacturing industry either shutting down or moving away. Between 1991 and 1998 a further 4,000 manufacturing jobs were lost. What survives is mostly printing activity, which retains its traditional advantages of proximity to CBD customers, and now operates alongside newspaper publishing, television and video production. Another set of activities which have long been over-represented in the area are (or were) public services, including railway transport, post, telecommunications and public administration. These have been subject to substantial reorganization/privatization, which make the detail of local employment trends hard to disentangle. Overall, however, employment in this group of activities has remained fairly stable through the 1990s, although rail employment actually seems to have grown quite substantially. Elsewhere within the public sector, educational employment also seems to have expanded significantly (within existing institutions).

But now, most of the area's employment is in offices, especially in finance and business, which together account for a third of all employment. The employment structure is now one that is favourable to growth, although within the producer service sector growth rates in Southwark have been no more than average during the 1990s. The other cluster of activities where regeneration policies are expected to generate large numbers of additional jobs involves the creative, cultural and tourist activities on Bankside. The extent to which these expectations have been realized is not easy to measure, however, both because these activity groupings cut across conventional sectoral divisions and because some of the growth stimuli (particularly those linked to millennium celebrations) are very recent. Even before the arrival of the Globe Theatre and the Tate Modern, there was an important local cluster of creative industries, and it can now boast some sixteen art galleries and many advertising and design companies, as well as media operations. During the 1990s, borough employment in recreational and cultural services more than doubled, though this part of the cluster still only employed 6,000 people in 1999. A similar number are employed in catering and hotel services, where there has also been substantial growth, though this sector remains under-represented in the borough as a whole, and its growth probably owes as much to expanding local demand as to that from tourists.

Overall, there has been clear evidence of employment growth in Southwark during the 1990s – of about 8 per cent between 1991 and 1998, faster than in Wandsworth, though much slower than in Hounslow or Reading. Even in the manual sectors, the rate of job loss over this period has been modest (about 3 per cent), while in non-manual activities the rate of growth has been in the middle group among the case study districts. This reflects a substantial improvement as compared with the area's economic situation in the 1970s and early 1980s.

### Social and ethnic structure

In social terms, the most striking feature of Southwark's population structure – at least relative to the three more westerly case study areas – is the high proportion of households with economically inactive heads (including many lone parents). Among those who are economically active, the largest group still are manual workers, now followed by intermediate and junior non-manual workers, while the proportion of professional and managerial workers is low (13 per cent of all household heads in 1991) – certainly much lower than in nearby Wandsworth. As this implies, the better-paid of the new local jobs in financial and business services tend to be filled by commuters from outside the borough.

The contrast with Wandsworth is even stronger in terms of housing tenure: in 1998 no less than 58 per cent of Southwark households remained in social housing – against 47 per cent in the next highest among the case study boroughs – while the Census recorded just 27 per cent in owner-occupation. In terms of household composition, however, the pattern is quite similar to Wandsworth's, with many small households and relatively few couples. The one significant difference is in relation to lone parent families, who though still a small part of the population (9 or 10 per cent of households in 1991) represent a large proportion of the families with dependent children in Southwark (33 per cent or 38 per cent if households with multiple adults of the same sex are counted).

Southwark's population as of 1998 included (according to LRC estimates) a significantly larger proportion of those of black ethnic origins than other case study areas (21 per cent), including more or less equal numbers from Afro-Caribbean and African origins. A further 8 per cent were split between a variety of other non-white groups. The relatively large black population provides part of the explanation for the high proportion of lone parents. In 1981 the ethnic minority population of the borough was just 18 per cent (Peach, 1996) and subsequent growth – including a relatively large element of refugees and asylum seekers (estimated at around 4 per cent of the resident population by 1997) – has effectively reversed the long-term pattern of population decline in the borough. The change is highlighted within the school population, where by 1999 55 per cent were from ethnic minorities (including 15 per cent Afro-Caribbean and 26 per cent African) and 36 per cent had English as a second language.

### Social conditions and deprivation

Unsurprisingly, Southwark emerges from area-based assessments of deprivation levels among the four London boroughs with the greatest concentration of deprivation, and fourteenth among English local authority areas on the DTLR's IMD2000 rankings. Average incomes of taxpayers in the borough are actually on a par with those in most of the case study districts. But there is a severe problem of unemployment: in terms of numbers of claimants the rate (adjusted to a residence basis) was still 8 per cent in October 2001, having come down from 22 per cent in the depths of the last recession 8 years previously. In addition there is a great deal of concealed unemployment, and of inactivity among the high proportion of lone parents, with an actual working age employment rate of only 66 per cent in 1999, against an average for the region of 75 per cent, according to the Labour Force Survey (LFS). As elsewhere in London, the level of housing deprivation is particularly severe, with 13 per cent of households being defined as in housing need, and with all but one ward appearing among the worst 10 per cent in England on the IMD2000 rankings. This ward – in Dulwich at the south end of the borough – is also the only one which is clearly outside the worst quartile of wards on the overall area deprivation index. The most deprived areas still appear to be around Peckham – with three wards in the worst 3 per cent – despite the huge investment pumped into the area in recent years. Other indicators of deprivation include a quarter of the primary school population being designated as having special education needs, and relatively high rates of child protection registration (0.4 per cent) and secondary school exclusion (1 per cent). Crime rates for almost all types of offence are the highest among the case study districts, most notably for drug offences, where they are more than twice the London average.

### Neighbourhood profiles

For the residential studies we chose two distinct neighbourhoods: Bermondsey, along the river east of Tower Bridge, and the North Peckham estate, about a mile inland. Of the two areas, Bermondsey is the more mixed in housing terms, including both a large council housing area, and (a clearly separated) area of new owner-occupied apartments, including some converted warehouses. This is the area most closely identified with former port functions and it remains essentially a white working-class community, with local internal divisions stemming from the physical fragmentation of the area (cut by road and rail routes) and through the family linkage policies of local housing associations, typified by the father-son tenancies of the Peabody Estate. These can produce quite inward-looking and even reactionary tendencies among communities that increasingly feel squeezed out of their own borough, both because of their inability to access the office jobs that have replaced port employment as the area's mainstay, and because their local amenities have been replaced either by these offices or tourist facilities. With average property prices here reaching £273,000 in summer 2001, the new developments are also seen as raising rents beyond the budgets of local residents. At London Bridge City these concerns and cynicism about past experience have brought strong opposition to redevelopment plans from the Tooley Street Residents Association. A particular problem is the shortage of secondary school places in the north of the borough, so that many children have to travel long distances to school while others stay at home.

In North Peckham the huge council estates have recently been rebuilt, under the aegis of the Peckham Partnership, on a mixed-tenure lower-density basis, with an accompanying upgrading of the town centre (including an award-winning public library). For many old residents of this very deprived area, this provided a welcome opportunity to move out of a claustrophobic and crime-ridden estate. Those who remain have benefited both from housing standards higher than in many private developments, and falling crime rates. Property prices remain low, averaging just £111,000 in summer 2001. But there have also been many teething problems, with delays to construction of social facilities, and bureaucratic problems in resettling families, while steeply declining registers have threatened school viability. The most vulnerable were the hardest hit; elderly residents, in particular, sometimes did not survive the move. Most recently the area achieved notoriety for gang activity, with the much-publicised murder of a ten-year-old Nigerian child, Damilola Taylor.

The related employment area, chosen for business interviews, includes the heart of Bankside, and Borough High Street, which include most of Southwark's major employers, notably in publishing, finance and tourism, together with the local teaching hospital (Guy's Hospital). Regeneration of this area, which had severe problems of dereliction, environmental decay and obsolescent commercial premises, has brought jobs, notably in business services, including the relocation of two Fleet Street papers, but also in tourism. There are problems, however, in linking these to the needs and potential of an under-skilled, and currently under-employed, local population. Hopes to remedy this situation rest on a combination of training projects and better transport links (as with the 1999 Jubilee Line extension and the planned Thameslink 2000 scheme), but many employers prefer to recruit outside the area, which is made easier as transport links improve.

### Newham (Stratford and Upton Park)

Stratford lies at the lower end of the Lea Valley within the inner north-east London borough of Newham, twenty minutes across the Thames from Southwark stations along the Jubilee Line. This is the most modern piece of the London underground, and passes under the largest piece of urban regeneration in Europe, in Docklands, before reaching its terminus in (yet to be regenerated) Stratford. As the train emerges from the tunnel at Canning Town, the passenger can see Canary Wharf on one side, and the huge new ExCel exhibition centre on the other. But from there, the scene is less prepossessing as the line runs up the Lower Lea Valley, the most intensive of the surviving industrial areas in London, including a chaotic sequence of tin sheds, sewerage outfalls, and old mills. This has long been one of London's main dumping grounds, becoming so particularly after the formation of the LCC, when West Ham (of which Stratford forms the north-western corner) became home to a range of noxious activities, exiled from the LCC area. Now it is an area with clear evidence both of decline and deprivation, but at a nodal location which is strategic for current plans to shift the balance of London development eastward.

## Development

Stratford started life as a small market town at a bridgehead on the river Lea, at the junction of roads out to Cambridge and Colchester. It was already an industrial area before the nineteenth century, with a range of activities including mills, gunpowder manufacture, distilling, and oil and timber milling, calico and silk weaving, and a pottery. With the coming of the railways, Stratford occupied a junction position, leading to the establishment of locomotive works, and the growth of a vast complex of railway yards, with a new town built to house the workers. When an extension was built involving the demolition of local housing in the 1860s, the Great Eastern railway was required to offer cheap early-morning workers' trains, a requirement later extended but most enthusiastically pursued here. The result was the rapid spread during the last 30 years of the nineteenth century of cheap working-class housing along the lines north and east of Stratford, with a mass of uniform terraced streets across the nearby areas of Leyton, Leytonstone, Maryland, Forest Gate, and Manor Park. Other developments followed along the lines to the south of the borough.

Lying downwind of the Lea Valley's industries, these eastern suburbs of London never had the social cachet of their western counterparts and were built quickly and cheaply by speculative builders, as standard by-law minimal housing, without overmuch charm or character, to house junior city clerks and respectable artisans. Immediately to the south, the terrace streets of Canning Town were built to house casual workers from the Port of London's new Royal Docks.

When the area was incorporated in the new Greater London in 1965, East Ham and West Ham were combined as the London Borough of Newham. They had always been working-class districts and even areas of poverty and deprivation, but their situation was soon to change, with a new set of problems emerging as a consequence of dock closure, with its attendant de-industrialization, and of immigration.

The dock closures came later here than elsewhere, because these were the latest and largest docks in the entire system, built to accommodate seagoing vessels; but they were all derelict by 1981. On top of that, from the 1970s both large and small industrial undertakings alike were buffeted by huge structural forces: overseas competition, technical changes (such as the replacement of coal gas by North Sea gas, which brought the closure of huge gasworks at Bow and Beckton), and the struggle for greater efficiency which led to mass redundancies. Industrial employment in the borough contracted by two-thirds between 1960 and 2000.

Substantial parts of the south of the borough were included in the LDDC area, but development has been much slower to proceed here than in the western end of Docklands, closer to the CBD. Housing prices are now just about the lowest in London, with Newham semi-detached house prices averaging just £143,000 in summer 2001, somewhere between our two OMA case study areas, despite Newham's much more central location.

## Economic structure

The economy that has survived de-industrialization is dominated by small service firms: in Newham as a whole in 1999 only 25 per cent of employment was in establishments with 200 or more workers, compared with 33 per cent across the region as a whole. This is a characteristic shared with our two other east London case study areas, reflecting not the vitality of small business, but a failure to replace those large establishments which had been key to the local economy in the past. Current local businesses tend to cater for local demand, but to use non-local suppliers. Ethnic minority businesses are common in distribution and catering, but tend to have a small turnover. Manufacturing actually continues to employ a greater proportion of workers than in most parts of London (12 per cent in 1999), with some evidence of specialization in chemicals, food industries (in Forest Gate) and clothing production. The biggest Newham employers are in the public sector, however, and the borough has above-average shares of employment both in public administration and education – as well as in transport and storage. Other significant employers include the new exhibition centre, and insurance company headquarters in Forest Gate.

This is the only one of the case study districts in which the manual sectors as a group (i.e. production industries, wholesaling and transport) continued to experience large-scale and widespread job losses through the 1990s. The net employment reduction in this group between 1991 and 1998 amounted to 5,000 jobs (23 per cent). Within the non-manual sectors on the other hand, the pattern of change in Newham was fairly average – similar, for example, to that in Southwark – but job gains in business services only served to counterbalance the losses in local manufacturing, energy and transport activities. Overall, borough employment declined very slightly between 1991 and 1998.

### Social and ethnic composition

This is the most uniformly working-class of our case study boroughs, with much the lowest proportion of professional and managerial workers among heads of households (9 per cent in 1991), the highest proportion of manual workers (31 per cent) and one of the highest proportion of economically inactive household heads (42 per cent). This is despite having many more owner-occupiers than Southwark (50 per cent in 1991). It differs also in the proportion of families with children, which is the highest among the case study areas (34 per cent) – including a moderately high proportion of lone parents but also many families with multiple adult members.

This mixture of family structures seems to be linked to ethnic diversity, which is particularly strong in Newham. Overall (in 1998) 52 per cent of the borough population is estimated to have ethnic minority backgrounds – compared with just 31 per cent in 1981. The largest group are Indians (13 per cent), but there are also sizeable numbers of Afro-Caribbeans, Africans, Pakistanis and Bangladeshis. Some of these communities arose from outward movement from areas of original immigrant settlement, particularly as members of the second generation sought affordable owner-occupation. In particular, Pakistanis/Bangladeshis moved from Whitechapel to the Upton Park area of East Ham, and Afro-Caribbeans from Dalston and Hackney to Stratford. Others communities reflect the new waves of immigration, notably of refugees and asylum-seekers, since the mid-1980s. By 1997 refugees and asylum seekers numbered over 15,000 – the largest number received by any borough, representing 7 or 8 per cent of the resident population – mainly from Asia and Africa, but also including notable populations of Polish, Vietnamese, and Russians. The borough schools have more than 400 refugee children on the rolls.

As elsewhere, proportions from immigrant and minority groups are larger among the school-age population: in 1999, only 30 per cent of Newham school children were white, while the majority were bilingual, and 42 per cent needed help with English. It is tempting to link these characteristics with poor educational outcomes (e.g. 80 per cent of primary schools failing to achieve national average performance levels, with worse results still in maths and science). But within the borough there is no clear relation between school results and the ethnic mix of their pupils, and generally low performances may have more to do with a high incidence of family poverty. Indeed, it is notable that the Education Action Zone established to deal with serious schooling problems in the south-west of the borough, including alienation of schools from the community, covers an area with a majority white British intake.

### Social conditions and deprivation

This is probably the most deprived of the case study districts, with an unemployment rate of 8.1 per cent in October 2001 (down from 22 per cent in 1993), marginally above that in Southwark, and average incomes among taxpayers in 1999 which were significantly lower – reflecting much more limited gentrification. Among working age people, only just over half (55 per cent) were in work in 1999, a strikingly low proportion – 11 per cent below Southwark's – which is only marginally attributable to low participation rates of Pakistani/Bangladeshi women. On the IMD2000 index of area deprivation it stands sixth among the 354 English districts, a position which reflects the pervasiveness of poverty across the borough, with all but one ward appearing among the worst 10 per cent in the country. Housing conditions are generally poor, with much poor quality housing in the private rented sector, and the wards on the north-east side of the borough almost all figure among the worst 1 per cent in England on the housing deprivation indicator. In terms of social disorganization, however, problems appear less intense than in Southwark – partly perhaps because of the different ethnic mix: in particular, the rates of lone parenthood, child protection registration and (particularly) school exclusion are less high. This is also true for most categories of crime (though not for assault), where rates are closer to the London average, though still high by national standards.

### Neighbourhood profiles

Upton Park, the residential neighbourhood which we chose for household interviews, lies south-east of Stratford, and is composed primarily of Victorian/Edwardian terraced housing, some quite substantial, together with a couple of council estates, parts of which (including one high-rise block) are currently being refurbished by a council/housing association partnership, and some infill areas of small, new terraced houses. Most of the housing is either owner-occupied or privately rented (with many of the more substantial houses subdivided into very small flats, or one-room lets with shared facilities). Dwelling conditions and forms of occupancy vary from street to street, but in some parts of the area both over-crowding and poor/unsafe housing conditions have led to council prosecution of private landlords and/or compulsory purchase. Housing here is generally cheap by London standards, with average prices in summer 2001 around £110,000 (similar to those in Peckham), but – as in Newham generally – price increases have accelerated in the past two years. This reflects its positioning within Newham's 'Arc of Opportunity', recently improved rail access to central London, and the future opening of a Channel Tunnel Rail Link station.

The local population is fairly poor, with an unemployment rate of 16 per cent in winter 1999 and some 20 per cent receiving income support: the area figures within the 5 per cent most deprived small areas in the country according to the government's IMD2000 index. There is a large and diverse ethnic minority population, including many of Pakistani origin, the remains of a local Sikh population (others having prospered and moved further out in the 1990s), a growing Bangladeshi population (including outward movers from Tower Hamlets), some Africans and the newer waves of migrants from areas such as Somalia, Eastern Europe, Kosovo and Afghanistan. The last group tend to be living in particularly poor and overcrowded housing, with a significant element of unregistered refugees in the worst position.

In addition to a normal range of local shops, the area has a widely known Asian shopping area in Green Street, supported by a very active Green Street Partnership, undertaking education, environmental and health related projects as well as promoting local business. Community support is also provided by a very wide range of religious establishments, including mosques, temples, a synagogue and various types of church (from both English and minority traditions) – whose activities extend into education and (in some cases) even business advice – together with a great array of voluntary and statutory organizations.

Stratford centre was taken as the focus for our employment and business studies. This is Newham's main shopping centre, a major transport node – for local, regional and (from 2007) international services – and also the focus of redevelopment and regeneration in the borough. Currently it suffers from abandoned premises on the main street, in parts of the surrounding industrial area, and even in 1970s and 1980s office blocks vacated by former back-office operations. Various forms of redevelopment are already underway, including small workshop construction, conversion of an office tower to affordable housing for public sector professionals, one substantial factory (for a local family business) and a major film/TV production facility. Larger-scale regeneration plans envisage development of a cultural quarter around a new arts centre and the refurbished Theatre Royal.

### Redbridge (Gants Hill and Ilford)

The borough of Redbridge lies to the east of Newham in Outer London, and is traditionally an area of higher social status, consisting of twentieth-century suburbs. The area on which we focus, Gants Hill and the nearby centre of Ilford, are some

4 miles north-east of Stratford. Though less prosperous than their counterparts to the west, these have been areas, typical of Jackson's (1991) *Semi-detached London,* whose comfortable respectability made them a magnet for upwardly mobile households from inner areas. The security of this reputation has, however, recently been challenged by a much publicised recent report, arguing that under-investment in such older suburban areas was bringing signs of incipient decline and decay – with Gants Hill offered as the prime example. The report highlighted its position as a major transport focus with strong road, tube and bus links, but argued that the priority assumed by motor traffic was a threat to pedestrian safety and producing an 'unattractive, highly congested and polluted environment'. Together with inadequate parking and competition from three neighbouring centres, these failings were undermining Gants Hill's viability as a retail centre, with under-investment in recent years now signalled by vacant properties and conversion of shops to night-time uses (Gwilliam *et al.*, 1998).

As we will see, older local residents have a sense of other kinds of social decline in the area, which at least suggest new instabilities. In these respects also Gants Hill may perhaps be the harbinger of ways in which metropolitan change will come to affect the hundreds of other suburbs of that vintage. But, like all the others, it has subtle features that make it slightly individual, and may help account for current sources of concern.

### Development

Until the nineteenth century, what is now Redbridge was very largely agricultural land, with a number of gentlemen's residences in the north of the borough, some of which survive as listed buildings and public open space. The pattern of land ownership also influenced the subsequent form of residential development, where large properties were developed as private housing estates. Ilford itself started as an agricultural village, with working-class and artisan housing being added to the south-west when brick works and lime fields were developed there in the early nineteenth century. However, large-scale development in the form of dense rows of terraced housing only dates from the 1890s, following the main railway line through Stratford to Chelmsford and Colchester (White, 1963, 170–171, 179). Very rapid growth in traffic at the end of this decade brought large-scale private residential development, carried out by speculative builders, acting together with the Great Eastern Railway where new stations were required to service developments. These dwellings were bought by clerks, skilled workers and officials, and a few better-paid shopworkers, most of whom commuted on the frequent trains to Liverpool Street. However, papermaking and printing were significant local industries, including Ilford Photographic which was established in 1879, and rose to international prominence (though the local site closed in 1983).

In the early twentieth century, small villa estates were built for the professional classes, to the north and west, in Woodford and Wanstead. Some of the new electronics and engineering industries also moved east into the area, including Plesseys which had a large factory there from the 1920s. However, residential growth was relatively slow, partly because the rail journey into central London on steam-hauled trains was slow and uncomfortable (White, 1963, 184). Nevertheless, from the 1920s arterial road-building round London – often followed by bus services – opened up new areas for development, including Gants Hill, just north of Ilford, where two key roads crossed. Even without a rail connection, estates of semi-detached and detached properties sprang up, stimulated particularly by demand from the upwardly-mobile children of the Jewish refugees who had settled in Whitechapel during the 1890s. Whether progressing through inheritance of businesses built up by their parents, or by passage to professional careers via the great East End grammar schools, this group rejected the dense slum streets, and sought middle-class homes in nearby areas such as Gants Hill. These places soon had the standard appurtenances of the new suburb – the Odeon, the shopping parade with its kosher shops – but they suffered from poor transport, until the Central Line eventually reached there in the late 1940s. This was a rare example where transport followed rather than guided London's spread (Barker and Robbins, 1974, 289; Barker, 1990, 103–104, 106). Subsequent residential expansion in the borough was largely in the form of council estates to meet local housing needs, though many of these houses were later bought under the 1980s right-to-buy scheme.

### Economic structure

Since the early 1980s the borough has experienced a number of negative economic developments, losing major employers (including Plessey) and back-office branches of City firms, while weakness in the small firm economy also is suggested by high rates of VAT de-registration. By the end of the 1990s, manufacturing represented only 7 per cent of local jobs, and the three main sectors of employment had become distribution, business services and education/health, each somewhat over-represented in the borough, and each accounting for about 20 per cent of jobs. The relatively high proportion of public sector employment is typical of east London and reflects competitive weakness in the local private sector – as does a concentration on activities with fairly local markets, and a low proportion of employment in larger establishments. The council's economic development strategy explains this relative weakness primarily in terms of the lack of suitable sites for new development, combined with poor public transport links between north and south of the borough inhibiting the travel to work and links with Dockland or Thames Gateway developments. Given environmental constraints on site release, the council's vision for the future is one of 'enhanc[ing] the Quality of Life for all' as a route to promoting economic growth, and/or securing a more affluent population as a market for services in the borough.

In terms of overall employment structure, Redbridge is comparable with Wandsworth in its low proportion of jobs in the manual sectors (about one-fifth in 1998). Employment in these sectors has remained stable during the 1990s, with substantial growth in wholesaling balancing losses elsewhere – while the rate of job growth in the non-manual activities has been in the middle range of the case study districts (10 per cent between 1991 and 1998). Growth in the 'other business services' grouping (excluding IT and professional services) has proceeded as fast as in Reading, adding some 5,000 jobs over this period.

### Social and ethnic composition

In class terms, the area remains what it has been ever since its original development: middle-middle class – although there are some pockets of severe deprivation (notably in South Ilford) with characteristics similar to the adjoining Inner London borough of Newham. In the borough as a whole there is an extremely high proportion of owner-occupation (78 per cent of households in 1991) and very little social housing (12 per cent). The social composition of the population is very similar, however, to that of Hounslow, which has a much larger rental sector – perhaps reflecting the greater affordability of house purchase in east London – and the proportion of professionals/managers is significantly lower than in (Inner London) Wandsworth. In terms of household composition also Redbridge is rather like Hounslow, with an above average share of large households, and an even lower proportion of lone parent families (11 per cent).

This reflects similarities in their ethnic composition. In 1998 30 per cent of the Redbridge population was from non-white ethnic origins, with half of these being Indian. In local schools, no less than 47 per cent of pupils come from ethnic minority backgrounds (with 36 per cent having English as a second language). This shows a substantial change since 1981 (when ethnic minorities formed just 12 per cent of the local population). Social class composition has changed much less, however, since population change has largely taken the form of suburbanizing movement by a middle-class second generation from the large Asian communities immediately to the south, in Forest Gate and Upton Park – following the trail set by the East End Jewish community 50 years before. In response the older Jewish community has tended to move on, though concentrations remain, particularly in Gants Hill. Refugees and asylum seekers have been much less significant here than in inner boroughs such as Newham, representing only about 2 per cent of residents in 1997 – though numbers supported by the council increased from 250 to 1,600 (including 200 unaccompanied children) in the following four years.

The area remains pleasant; there is a large number of parks and much open space, while the borough's schools – including a range of independent, grant maintained, single-sex and faith-based secondary schools, as well as mainstream coeducational comprehensives – enjoy a high reputation both locally and more widely across East London. In 1999, the borough's secondary schools as a whole achieved the fifth best GCSE results among English LEAs. Unsurprisingly, the borough population is quite highly skilled. But this is much less true of those actually working in the borough, and the better-qualified figure strongly among the sizeable number of out-commuters (including the 17 per cent travelling to the City and Westminster).

### Social conditions and deprivation

Except for a small area in the south-west of the borough, adjoining some of the poorer areas of Newham, this is a borough with rather low levels of deprivation, consistently figuring in the middle ranges of national deprivation rankings. Unemployment across the borough as a whole was down to 3.3 per cent in October 2001 (on a residence adjusted claimant count basis) from a peak of 10.6 per cent in 1993. Average earnings among taxpayers are similar to those in most of the case study areas, but a median value close to that in Greater Reading indicates that there are few residents on low earnings. As elsewhere in London, housing conditions appear less good by national standards, but only to be problematic in the south-west area already referred to. This is a borough with generally low rates of lone parenthood (13 per cent), low absenteeism from school, and rates of violent crime which are low by London standards, if still above the national average (and those prevailing in Reading or Dartford). Robbery rates are twice the national average, but those for burglary are not. Overall this still appears to be a rather comfortable area.

## Neighbourhood profiles

Within Gants Hill, which covers four wards, our residential study focused on Barkingside, which is rather better than average on deprivation indices, and had just 6 per cent of its population on income support in 1998, below the borough average of 8 per cent. The majority of housing is owner-occupied, with house prices averaging about £123,000 in summer 2001, slightly higher than in some other parts of Redbridge, but still clearly lower than in western suburbs. There are variations in housing character within the area, however, with one neighbourhood of substantial pre-war semi-detached houses or bungalows, some more modern blocks of private flats, a small council estate, and another neighbourhood of smaller post-war semi-detached housing with some more recent terraced housing.

The area still has a predominantly white middle-class population, although with an increasing number of middle-class Asian families. A significant Jewish population remains, though the more affluent have moved north-west to Woodford Green or out into Essex. Although there are some younger families, the majority of residents are in their late 30s and 40s or older, including many over retirement age. Most residents work outside the borough, commuting on the Central Line from Gants Hill.

Until the mid to late 1970s, Gants Hill Cross was a thriving local shopping area, providing a wide range of services. However, it is at the intersection of two very busy dual carriageways, requiring access via a subway system, which is widely regarded as unsafe, due to a series of attacks on pedestrians in recent years. This seems to have affected the commercial viability of the local service centre, which has suffered closure of all the banks bar one, and the post office, together with the clothes and shoe shops, and many food stores. What remains is a small convenience store, newsagents, estate agents, two furniture stores and the cinema. The area looks run-down, though encouragement of 'night-time' uses has brought a number of new restaurants and a small night club. Two large office blocks remain occupied but the council is concerned about redundant office space.

For studies of employment and local business, the area chosen was central Ilford, which is the borough's major shopping and administrative centre. This has been partially pedestrianized, and there has been significant commercial investment, with redevelopment of The Exchange (despite some difficulty in letting units) and a major new development of leisure facilities currently underway. Other firms are typically small/micro business service operations, although outside the town centre there is a small enterprise park housing some manufacturing micro-businesses, such as jewellery and computer design. Elsewhere in the area a few medium-sized manufacturing firms remain, together with specialist construction firms. But most, like the large firms that located their back-office functions here (such as the Prudential), have relocated outside the borough. The largest firm in the area now is a home shopping company. There is understandable concern about over-reliance on jobs in the public sector and small service firms, and also about Ilford's continuing viability as a retail centre, with the huge Thurrock Lakeside Centre 14 miles away and the even bigger Bluewater retail development at Dartford 19 miles away across the Dartford Bridge. But a key policy issue, locally, is the balance to be struck between securing job opportunities (for less-qualified workers who require local employment) and maintaining a quality suburban living environment (particularly for out-commuters with a choice as to where they live).

## Greenwich (Charlton and Eltham)

Woolwich and Eltham lie within the borough of Greenwich, on the margins of Inner London, about 5 miles downstream from Bermondsey and Peckham on the south side of the Thames. Woolwich occupies the middle of the north of the borough, while Eltham is to the south. Technically they are now within Outer London, though Greenwich as a whole was included in the old LCC area and its social characteristics remain rather closer to the inner boroughs. This ambiguous position was highlighted during the late 1990s, when Eltham's Well Hall estate – originally built as a model garden suburb for First War munitions workers from Woolwich Arsenal, and now largely owner-occupied – became notorious as the place where Stephen Lawrence, a promising young black student, was murdered by a gang of white racists, so far not brought to justice (Cathcart, 1999). Indeed Greenwich is a very mixed borough, both socially and environmentally, with areas of very desirable middle-class housing (for example, near the royal parkland further south in Eltham) and other working-class areas (for example, in Woolwich near the river) which are physically rather squalid. Unlike the inner areas, and indeed most of London, this is also an area where large, stable employers (notably the Royal Arsenal) once provided the social base for the development of labour organizations – including the Royal Arsenal Co-operative Society, Woolwich Council (a flagship socialist borough in the 1920s) – as well as the strong community spirit which had typified Well Hall. This economic base has now gone. But, further west, on the Greenwich peninsula, the now empty Millennium Dome is a (visible if not auspicious) marker of the ongoing efforts to regenerate eastern Thames-side areas through massive physical investment.

## Development

This part of south-east London developed through a combination of heavy industrial development on the banks of the Thames, and suburban expansion along the three commuter railway lines passing through the borough. These lines initially brought high-class suburban development, including clusters of villas and developments such as the Eltham Park Estate whose substantial houses had servant annexes (White, 1963, 5–8; Jackson, 1991, 182–183).

On the waterfront, in contrast, the Royal Arsenal grew from the seventeenth century to encompass large industrial buildings, and an artillery testing ground, which was both noisy and grossly contaminating. The Arsenal workers constituted effectively a separate, isolated community, in some ways like the dockland communities across the river in Silvertown. They lived within walking distance of their work, historically in sordid housing. From the mid-nineteenth century, Woolwich also became the first seat in Britain of the new electrical engineering industry, with the Berlin firm of Siemens establishing a factory to exploit the growing market for undersea telegraph cables, with heavy materials and products being shipped in and out by water. Thames-side became the national centre for the industry, remaining so into the 1950s (Hall, 1962, 151; Martin, 1966, 17). All sorts of other basic, often polluting, industries set up along the waterfront – including paint, plaster, glass, chemicals, tanning, and milling (White, 1963, 46). These firms also were typically large, and at its peak the local manufacturing base employed some 150,000 workers. As in the Lea Valley, this was generally industry that the rest of London did not want.

When the London County Council was established in 1888, these were among its outermost areas, and Eltham in particular was among the new housing areas built on electric tram routes to accommodate the working-class poor who the LCC sought to move out from inner-city slums. This compromised private developers' vision of the area as a series of superior bourgeois suburbs, leading in the inter-war years to an uneasy relationship between areas of speculative semi-detached housing which spread along the railway lines, and the LCC/municipal estates built along the tramway lines. To complete this set of juxtapositions, in the late 1960s a new Greater London Council built the Ferrier estate at Kidbrooke in North Eltham:

> Grim grey concrete . . . an extreme example of the stark geometry produced by industrialized building methods. (Cherry and Pevsner, 1983, 278)

It was instantly unpopular, deteriorated rapidly and came to be used only for the most desperate and uncomplaining tenants – most recently refugees and asylum-seekers; as we went to press, it was about to be demolished.

The balance between these elements in the area's role has shifted substantially in the last few decades and Greenwich as a whole is now more a residential suburb than an employment centre, with 56 per cent of residents working outside the borough in 1991. Public transport connections to the centre have speeded up from the west side at least with the Docklands Light Railway and Jubilee Line extension, but most of the borough is less well connected, and house prices (averaging

£178,000 for a semi-detached property in summer 2001) remain below those in western suburbs, or more central areas.

### Economic structure

As an industrial suburb, Woolwich has suffered particularly badly from the pervasive de-industrialization of London over the past 40 years, which left it with high unemployment, isolation, and environmental contamination. Between 1960 and 1990 the area's manufacturing base simply collapsed, a process highlighted by the closure of both the Arsenal's Royal Ordnance factory and Siemens (then the dominant employer) in 1967/68. In fact total employment in Greenwich continued to decline right through to the 1990s.

Today, the local economy is dominated by the service sector, as elsewhere in London. Just 9 per cent of jobs were in manufacturing in 1999. But the borough has not really developed a compensating strength in financial or business services, and to an even greater extent than in other parts of east London, there is a high dependence on the public sector: 35 per cent of employment in the borough is in health, education or public administration. Indeed, these are the only sectors apart from construction which are substantially over-represented in Greenwich. Most jobs are concentrated in the Greenwich waterfront area. As in Newham and Redbridge, there is now a lack of employment in larger establishments (with 27 per cent in those with 200 workers or more), while less than a quarter of businesses have main markets outside the region. And one-third of firms, interviewed in the early 1990s, said they were likely to move out.

This generally negative picture is reflected in employment trends during the 1990s. Employment in the manual sectors continued to decline (by about 7 per cent between 1991 and 1998), while there were net job losses also in non-manual activities – against the trend in all the other case study districts. However, the contraction in the latter sectors seems to have been entirely the result of major reductions in public sector jobs (in public administration, education and health), and strong growth was evident in private producer and consumer services. Whatever the cause, however, the overall outcome was to produce the only significant employment reduction (of about 3 per cent between 1991 and 1998) in any of the case study districts. Following efforts to revive the old waterfront industrial area, with major development projects at North Greenwich and the Royal Arsenal, the borough now pins its hopes of substantial job growth over the next 7 years on retailing, leisure, tourism, and construction, with administrative, service and light industrial employment following in the longer term.

### Social and ethnic composition

Greenwich is predominantly a working-class borough. At the 1991 Census, it had one of the highest proportions of economically inactive heads of households among our case study areas (41 per cent), but of the remainder almost half (26 per cent) were in manual occupations. The closest comparison is with Newham, the main difference being that Greenwich has some more professional/managerial workers (13 per cent). Rates of owner-occupation are also similar to Newham (47 per cent in 1991), but Greenwich has a significantly larger social housing sector (including 43 per cent of households). Educational achievements reflect the social class profile, with just 8 per cent qualified to degree level or above, while Greenwich school results are also conspicuously below the London average. In terms of household composition, the significant features of the Greenwich population are a relatively high proportion (16 per cent) of elderly single person households and a fairly high incidence of lone parent families (23 per cent), which is again comparable with Newham.

Where Greenwich notably differs from Newham is in its ethnic composition, having a proportion of non-white residents (17 per cent in 1998) which is well below our other Greater London case study areas. In this respect, it reflects a broader characteristic of lower Thames-side and outer south-east London – though many other boroughs around here are even more strikingly white. And in Greenwich no single minority group is particularly important: those of Indian origin, Afro-Caribbeans and Africans each represent 3–4 per cent of the population. Some of these established groups appear relatively successful, notably Indians who account for 6 per cent of those in the highest social category, and perform well in the education system. Within local maintained schools 29 per cent of pupils in 1999 came from ethnic minority backgrounds, with 19 per cent having English as a second language. But, as in Newham, the general perception is that it is young white males from poor backgrounds who are the under-achieving group, with problems not only of school performance but also of motivation and self-esteem.

The various groups of recently arrived asylum seekers have a distinct set of problems. By 1997, LRC estimates indicate that these formed about 3 per cent of the borough population. They come from a wide variety of origins, including many Vietnamese and Somalis, but also Iranians, Tamils, Ugandans, Kurds and Eritreans. A local survey reveals a high level of isolation and exclusion among younger refugees, with few feeling their home culture was valued, a majority (particularly of girls) experiencing bullying, 80 per cent reporting that they felt unsafe in their local area after dark, and a quarter saying that they or a family member had been physically attacked. Some groups with high proportions of women and children (such as the Eritreans concentrated in Kidbrooke, including the Ferrier estate) seem to be living in near-total unemployment, experiencing severe poverty and isolation – while others (such as the Tamils) with more family units and mobile single men, and better education, have good networks of community support and little unemployment. In the case of the two largest groups, the Somalis and Vietnamese, there is evidence of entrepreneurial potential, though currently they seem to experience barriers in realizing this.

### Social conditions and deprivation

The IMD2000 index of local conditions indicates that Greenwich is the eighth most deprived borough in London and among the worst 50 districts in England. Unemployment has fallen steadily since 1993, reaching 5.3 per cent in October

2001, but remains well above the Greater London average (if not as high as in Southwark or Newham). Local studies indicate that among the young long-term unemployed, many have never worked while others have occupied only a series of short-term jobs, with many still being mentally oriented toward the lost industrial economy of the waterfront. However, average earnings among taxpayers are on a par with those in most of the case study areas. In fact conditions vary greatly between different parts of the borough: about 15 per cent of the population (in the east of Eltham) are in areas figuring in the bottom (good) half of the national (IMD2000) ranking of area deprivation, while another 30 per cent (in a line of wards running north-south through the centre of the borough) figure among the worst 10 per cent of wards in England.

Indicators of social problems also convey a rather mixed impression. The rate of lone parenthood (28 per cent) is above the London average and there is a rather high incidence of child protection registrations (0.4 per cent), and unauthorized school absences, but the proportion of school exclusions is amongst the lowest in London. In terms of crime, the rate of robbery is well below the London average, but that of personal assaults is substantially higher (and 2.5 times the national rate). Data on racist incidents (from the Policing London project) indicate that the risks of victimization among the local black and Asian population are a good deal higher than in most parts of London – though this is a characteristic shared by other boroughs with a relatively small ethnic minority presence.

### Neighbourhood profiles

For the residential studies we chose an area in North Eltham, about 2 miles south of the river, in the middle of the borough, comprising two wards with somewhat different characters: Well Hall (to which we have already referred) and Sherard. Except for local shopping parades both are entirely residential, and the general feeling is rather suburban, with lower densities than by the river and plenty of green open space, including public parks like Well Hall Pleasances as well as playing fields. There is some local community infrastructure but the majority of services are delivered from outside the area. Well Hall has the higher quality housing, which is popular and now mostly owner-occupied, with a small proportion of housing association-sheltered housing. Unemployment is low and residents appear to be relatively prosperous, often commuting into other parts of London to work. In Sherard by contrast most of the housing is less attractive 1920s brick-built houses, on the Page Estate still owned and managed by the local authority, and cut into four by major roads. Here and on other local cottage estates, adjustment to the post-industrial economy has been slow and there are clear signs of deprivation. Currently Sherard is amongst the most deprived 10 per cent of wards nationally. Rates of unemployment and teenage pregnancy are higher than for London as a whole, and participation in formal education, training and work among 17 and 18 year olds is among the lowest in the capital. These are among the North Eltham wards with particularly low proportions of non-white residents (about 5 per cent in 1991), and among the areas which Hewitt (1997) in his study of racism among local adolescents described as 'at the front line of the white hinterland'. Like Bermondsey, this is an area where kith-and-kin housing allocation policies have maintained rather inward-looking local communities, although here there is a much stronger tradition of upward mobility (Cathcart, 1999). House prices here are significantly higher than in Woolwich, averaging £153,000 in summer 2001.

For the studies of a related employment centre, we focused on a riverside area just east of the Greenwich peninsula (and the Dome), which was at the heart of Greenwich's industrial economy, and still represents the backbone of local employment, providing 40 per cent of jobs in the borough. Streets of housing are interwoven with various commercial uses, with Woolwich town centre as the major focus for both shopping and office jobs (particularly in the public sector). This centre went into spiralling decline after the loss of local industrial jobs, but regeneration investment now seems to have halted this, at least along the High Street. To the west a number of more recent industrial estates house a range of different industries including printing and other types of manufacture, small retail parks and the Valley, Charlton Athletic's Football Ground. Transport links by road include the South Circular, and just to the south the A2 London-Dover route, while links across the river include foot tunnels, the Woolwich Ferry and the notoriously congested Blackwall Tunnel.

## Dartford/Gravesham (Kent Thames-side)

The last of our eight localities is in some ways the most distinctive. The 22 square-mile area known as Kent Thames-side lies between the Thames and the A2 London-Dover road, about 10 miles downstream from Woolwich. It stretches from the Greater London boundary in the west to the North Kent Marshes in the east, in the weakest segment of the London Green Belt. It encompasses half a dozen communities (with a combined population of about 180,000), together with large tracts of land around these residential areas. Its entire development has been dominated by the river, by the parallel lines of road and rail that followed its south bank, and by the industries that grew up around these two great lines of movement. Its economic story is one of growth, decline and now resurgence.

This then is an area in the throes of major transition, where the visitor today experiences a real sense of shock at the juxtaposition of opposites. The brand new elements – the retail park, the new warehouses, the hotel, the executive housing – contrast starkly with the surviving chalk quarries and industrial plants and with small-scale pieces of industrial urbanism, recalling the Black Country or Yorkshire much more than the 'garden' county of Kent. And these superficial signs reflect a deeper economic and social reality: this is an area of heavy industry, which is being rapidly transformed into a new and special part of South East England.

### *Development*

The Thames is key to everything here, where it widens to half a mile or more across.

As well as the passing stream of trade into what was for long the greatest port in the world, there were regular passenger services along and across the river, while Gravesend functioned as a key landing point for barges carrying goods for markets in London and beyond. This area was also the training ground for sailors and officers in the Merchant Navy, with an extensive naval college complex in Greenhithe and training ships moored just off shore.

On land, the area's position on the London-Dover road (the Roman Watling Street) was also crucial, and as a river bridging point on this route Dartford developed into an important market town by Tudor times. From the eighteenth century, however, this was transformed into an area of heavy industry, with the river used to ship materials both in and products out. The country's first commercial paper and iron splitting mills were built here, while Portland cement production from local lime and clay was also pioneered in the area, to serve the London market. During the early nineteenth century, paper making and cement manufacture in particular expanded along the shores of the Thames, receiving a further boost with the coming of the railways. Their noxious character discouraged residential development in the area, however, while prospective commuters were also put off by the slowness of the rail link to London (then as now). Nonetheless, local employment growth brought rapid population expansion, with Dartford growing eight-fold during the nineteenth century. Despite construction of new suburbs, and some better quality building by paternalistic employers (as in our residential study area), living conditions suffered from bad sanitation in town and airborne pollution (including thick cement dust) in the industrial areas.

Although there was some ribbon development in the inter-war period, the local towns and villages remained small and quite isolated, little related to the wider London economy only 20 miles away, separated from each other by the huge chalk quarries, and lacking any direct link to the Essex side of the estuary (until 1963). However, as the local heavy industries started to shut down in the 1970s, with large job losses, local people increasingly had to find work in London. Unemployment rates rose nevertheless (peaking at 10.7 per cent in 1993), while the area was also left with a large number of derelict sites, both on the river front and in the cement industry's vast chalk pits. Much of the land was owned by the Blue Circle Cement Company who first exploited it for infilling, with rubbish lorries converging on the area from across London – an image that those trying to attract inward investment into the area have had to work hard to overcome.

The corner was turned with the coming of the M25 London orbital motorway in the 1980s, leading via first a doubling of the Dartford tunnel and then (in 1991) the Queen Elizabeth Bridge to a four-fold increase in capacity of the Thames crossing. As the point of intersection between the M25 and the main freight route to the continent, the area now became particularly attractive for distribution and logistics activities – notably in the new Crossways Business Park, which attracted £30 million investment (Cluttons/Kent County Council, 2000) – and a viable location for decentralized back-office functions, especially from financial services, including Woolwich PLC.

Construction of the bridge also gave the area a very much larger potential market area as a service centre, with some 10 million people within 60 minutes drive time. This was capitalized on with the development during the 1990s of Europe's largest regional shopping and leisure centre in a 300 acre chalk pit at Bluewater near the interchange. Because of its major incursion into the Green Belt, government approval required over-ruling the conclusion of a major public enquiry, but the centre now attracts 80,000 shoppers per day. Local worries about the likely impact of Bluewater, and the similar Lakeside development across the estuary, on existing town centres led to an SRB-funded town-centre management initiative funded by the government's Single Regeneration Budget (SRB), for which Gravesham has been accorded 'beacon' status by the government as a town centre regenerator (along with Reading). The success of these strategies and the overall effect of Bluewater on the towns are as yet unclear, however.

Furthermore, massive development should follow from the 1991 government decision to route the fast Channel Tunnel Rail Link through the area – rather than to the south as British Rail proposed – thus acting as an instrument of regeneration for the East Thames Corridor downstream of London Docklands. This idea emanated from a Kent county planner, Martin Simmons (Simmons, 1987) and was enthusiastically adopted by Michael Heseltine, Secretary of State for the Environment, in 1991 as a central element in his vast Thames Gateway regeneration scheme. In particular, a passenger station at Ebbsfleet (due in 2007), cutting the time of rail travel to central London from an hour to just 15 minutes, and putting both Paris and Brussels within two hours reach, is seen as the crucial catalyst for the area (Kent Thames-side, 1999, 16–18, 39). In addition to a huge mixed-use development already approved for the station site, dense city-scale development is planned for the surrounding area. In reaction to the negative effects of earlier road-based regeneration on the quality of life of residents, approval of this growth is conditional on the bulk of the associated journeys being made on a new public transport system, Fastrack, not by car. Uncertainties remain, however, and there is considerable local grass roots activity around these issues.

The Thames Gateway Planning Framework (GB Thames Gateway Task Force, 1995) envisaged 50,000 new jobs and 30,000 new homes being created in the area by 2021 from a combination of the station development with other ongoing projects – including a new University of Greenwich campus and science park; a new privately funded hospital; further development of the Crossways Business Park; a new urban village in the Eastern Quarry; environmental improvement on the Swanscombe peninsula; and redevelopment of industrial sites on the Gravesend waterfront. Lead responsibility has been given to a public-private partnership, Kent Thames-side Association, encompassing county and district authorities, property developers, the CTRL rail company and the University of Greenwich – rather than a single centralized structure as was used in Docklands. With the benefit of concentrated land ownership and active support from Kent County Council, anxious to divert development pressures from the neighbouring 'Garden of England', by the millennium there was a master plan, encompassing a major new town and business park. Actual housing and highway developments are also underway.

Though generally welcome, development is creating new patterns of inequality.

While house prices remain low by London standards (averaging £134,000 for a semi-detached property in summer 2001), there are fears that a stronger economy will raise rental levels and hurt residents on low and fixed incomes, including the long-term unemployed, sick and elderly (Chambers *et al.*, 1999). Local authorities are committed to securing affordable housing through planning gain, but it is unclear how far this is achievable here given the high costs associated of developing brownfield sites.

### Economic structure

The current structure of the local economy still includes a substantial manufacturing element, with 17 per cent of employment in 1999, one of the highest proportions in the London region. This is still concentrated around traditional heavy industries, including substantial employment in chemicals, though 1,500 jobs have been lost here since 1999 through closure of Wellcome's manufacturing operations in Dartford following mergers with Glaxo and SmithKlineBeecham.

The most distinctive feature of the local employment structure, however, when measured against the national pattern, is the concentration of transport and storage activity, employing some 8,000 workers (12 per cent of the total). For obvious reasons the area also currently has an above average share of construction jobs. The balance of employment is thus still quite strongly toward sectors offering manual employment (representing 37 per cent of jobs in 1998), much more so than in the other case study areas. And other private services, such as finance, business services or catering are relatively under-represented. Local concerns about high labour turnover and poor management, communication and IT skills (Learning and Business Link Company, 1998) may be particularly relevant to growth prospects for these activities.

Growth performance during the 1990s has been in the middle range among the case study districts – comparable for example with Southwark or Redbridge, though with much less evidence of dynamism than in the Thames Valley areas (Reading and Hounslow). Among the manual sectors, there were only modest job losses, as a result of quite strong growth in road transport activities, compensating for decline in manufacturing and public utilities. On the non-manual side there was a very healthy rate of growth in business services from a rather low base. The overall outcome between 1991 and 1998 was a net growth of 8 per cent in total employment.

### Social and ethnic composition

Like Greenwich this is a largely working-class area, with Labour-controlled local councils. Taking the two districts together, the proportion of households with an economically inactive head is less high than in Greenwich (34 per cent). But of those attached to the labour market almost half (32 per cent) were in manual occupations, while the proportion of professionals and managers (17 per cent) was much lower than in our western OMA area (i.e. Greater Reading). This was despite a quite similar rate of owner-occupation (72 per cent in 1991). Again the explanation seems to be that with a lower pressure of demand access to owner-occupation is easier on the eastern side of London. In terms of household composition, the distinctive features of Dartford/Gravesham area are a high proportion of couple-based households with few working-age single person households and a low rate of lone parent families (just 10 per cent as in Reading/Wokingham). Representation of non-white ethnic minorities is also close to that in the western OMA area (6 per cent in 1991), almost all of them Indians, including members of the very old-established Gravesham Sikh community – and as in Reading their numbers do not seem to have been growing very rapidly (by just 25 per cent between 1981 and 1991 on Peach's (1996) estimates).

In social class terms, then, Dartford/Gravesham is clearly identifiable with the eastern rather than the western side of the region, but in most other respects it clearly embodies characteristics of the OMA, rather than typical areas within Greater London. In part, this reflects the fact that it has long been an important dormitory for people working in London, and that there is self-selection of those who choose to live outside Greater London. They trade-off long journeys to work for the combination of high London wages and more affordable living space outside the city. Typically, the out-commuters from this area are secretarial, clerical occupations and other junior non-manual workers – while those commuting in from further east in Kent tend to be manual workers.

As in other parts of the OMA, formal educational attainment is strong in the area, with above average rates of GCSE success. Under Kent County Council's (Conservative) control, there is a selective school system in North Kent including six grammar schools, which are popular with parents both locally and in the neighbouring London boroughs, that export significant numbers of pupils there.

### Social conditions and deprivation

Though this is one of our OMA case study areas, levels of affluence and deprivation in Dartford/Gravesham are more comparable with those in Hounslow than in Greater Reading, the western OMA case study area. In October 2001 the (residence-adjusted) claimant unemployment rate here was just 2.2 per cent, down from 10 per cent in 1993. As elsewhere, falling unemployment brought an even larger reduction in long-term unemployment, but more persists here than in Hounslow, with one in six of the unemployed having been out of work for a year or more – though this proportion is still lower than in any of the other case study areas within Greater London. Average earnings of taxpayers here are lower than in most of the other case study areas (including Hounslow), although this has to be seen in relation to lower housing costs.

On the IMD2000 deprivation indices, Dartford/Gravesham was in the middle of the range of local authorities or below, with just one Dartford ward figuring in the worst 10 per cent overall – though on the education domain the area has its share in this band. Local crime reports suggest that race relations are harmonious with very low levels of reported race related crime, although stories in the local press give a different impression. Overall crime levels are low by national as well as London standards, particular for violent offences, though rates of car crime are above the national average.

### Neighbourhood profiles

For our residential studies we focused on a group of wards in the coastal belt between Dartford and Gravesham. Socially these span the mid-range of local wards, although including some of the areas of educational deprivation, and having a somewhat greater proportion both of council tenants and lone parents. The distinctive feature of these neighbourhoods, compared with our other case study areas is, however, that they are on the cutting edge of residential development – including one ward in which population rose by 12 per cent between 1991and 1997. Here new luxury riverside houses have been built on former factory sites, in close proximity to – but relatively segregated from – an older Victorian housing stock and newer social housing built in the 1950s. It is unclear how these communities relate to one another. In some areas new development has limited public access to the river-front and this seems to have caused resentment among local people.

Our choice of a related employment zone also focused on areas of major change near the motorway interchange, including both Bluewater and Crossways Business Park which we discussed earlier. On its opening Bluewater created over 6,000 new retail jobs, although many were part time and appear to have been occupied predominantly by women. Jobs in Crossways, by contrast, are more geared to male employment.

## Conclusion: Unpicking the London Puzzle

From this tour through time and space, we already learn some important facts about London, which need to inform the whole of our subsequent inquiry.

First, there is more than one London. One could say that there are as many Londons as there are Londoners, but that would not be helpful – both because it would be impractical, and because nonetheless it avoids the question of who is a Londoner. Individuals, certainly, have their own sense of what is London, and this sense differs hugely from one to another: from the poor child of an ethnic minority who may know only the streets between home and school and shops, to the taxi driver who has painstakingly acquired the Knowledge; from the unemployed single mother whose daily path follows the needs of her children, to the cosmopolitan professional whose work – whether as architect, television producer or entrepreneur – ranges across London. But even the most sophisticated Londoner can never know more than a part of this enormous whole.

There is also an official London: the London of the Greater London Authority, over which London's Mayor holds sway, and the thirty-two London boroughs plus the ancient City of London. It has a measure of coherence, rather rare among the world's great cities: it approximates fairly closely to the built-up area, barely changed since World War Two because it is bounded by the Metropolitan Green Belt, and it is neatly marked by the M25 Orbital Motorway which bisects that belt. But, as seen, even here there is a major problem: in a functional sense London has continued to grow, leapfrogging to the towns beyond, but the story there is a complex one: these places do have ties – of commuting, of information exchange – to London, but they also have a high degree of independence: you could call them half-London, half-Buckinghamshire or Kent. And the story becomes even more tangled when it emerges that many places in Outer London are rather like that too.

In fact, perhaps the most important lesson to take forward is that as a functioning mechanism London has progressively become exceedingly complex both economically and geographically. At its core is still a dense and highly interlinked complex of firms and jobs, fulfilling functions that are national and even international in scale. But around that core, and extending far beyond the formal physical or administrative limits of London, is an immensely complicated and interconnected series of markets, producers, consumers, firms both large and small, which enjoy special advantages from their co-location within the privileged space that is South East England. London is now far bigger than London: it is a region that has no clear boundaries, and in which therefore all attempts to draw such boundaries – the Outer Metropolitan Area, the South East and Eastern England Standard Regions – are arbitrary, perhaps too wide in some senses, too narrow in others.

One key question therefore is the nature of these special ties and linkages, and of the locational advantages that firms and people get from them. To try to answer this question will be a first task of the chapter that follows.

## NOTES

1. However, we deliberately restricted our coverage of the top 20 per cent of the social class distribution, because we believed that local contexts would prove much less important for them.

2. These profiles draw largely on local materials from 'scoping' studies carried out in each area, but for presentational purposes we have included references to some common statistical indicators. The main sources for these are as follows: household structures, demography, socio-economic composition and detailed ethnic/tenure mixes in 1991 all come from Census Small Area statistics; more recent ethnic composition estimates for London boroughs derive from the London Research Centre, and for the school population from DfEE School Censuses, while summary tenure figures come from the ONS Regions in Figures volumes. Deprivation indicators, produced by an Oxford University group in 2000, come from the DETR (now OPDM) website, and house prices from the Land Registry website. Employment change estimates from the Annual Business Enquiry/Employment Survey are from the NOMIS data base. This also is the source for the claimant count unemployment figures, although the denominators used to convert these into rates on a consistent residence basis are estimates of the economically active population from the Labour Force Survey, rather than traditional combinations of workplace-based employment and residence-based unemployment. Estimates of average incomes among taxpayers come from the Inland Revenue website, and crime rates from the Home Office website – except for figures on racially motivated crime in London boroughs which derive from the Metropolitan Police via the website of the Policing London project at South Bank University. This site is also the immediate source for borough data on the child protection register and school exclusions.

Chapter 3

# Complex Business: Growth and Volatility in London's Economies

A co-evolving system gets itself to the edge of chaos . . . and the edge of chaos is a favored place to be, because . . . the system optimises sustained fitness there.

Roger Lewin, *Complexity*, 1993, p. 186.

Dull, inert cities . . . contain the seeds of their own destruction and little else. But lively, diverse, intense cities contain the seeds of their own regeneration, with energy enough to carry over for problems and needs outside themselves.

Jane Jacobs, *The Death and Life of Great American Cities*, 1961, p. 444.

The closure of the region's two car-making plants – Vauxhall's at Luton and Ford at Dagenham – in the early months of 2002 drew a line under an era of large-scale manufacturing in the London region. Decline in this sector, and in goods handling activities, represents one side of a radical transformation of the metropolitan economy over the past 40 years. In broad sectoral terms London can now seem a rather one-dimensional 'service economy'. In fact, however, this label hides an extraordinarily diverse range of specialist activities in which London can claim a competitive advantage. In spatial terms too there is great variety. Important groups of businesses serve markets ranging in area from the global to the local. And their sites include not only the dense, high-rent urban core, but also poorly connected inner-city ex-industrial areas, established suburban centres, and edge-city type business parks near motorway exits well out in the OMA. This extraordinary scale and diversity (now also evident in cultural terms) represents huge economic assets. But they make it hard to assess London's competitive strengths and weaknesses, or to say how radically these have been recently altered by broader economic and social forces. As we shall see later, in considering issues of governance, they are also hard to do justice to in policy arenas, against the appealing simplicity of assertions that some particularly distinctive activity is fundamental to competitive success and economic welfare.

Beyond sheer diversity, the London economy is complex because of the high degree of inter-connection among its many parts. This is more than a matter of the supply and demand chains of some core activities, or of the conglomeration of local economic clusters. If these were all, London would long ago have lost out to smaller and more specialized centres, which could offer the same interlinkages without the attendant overhead costs – high rents, high wages, and super-congestion. London competes because these evident disadvantages are outweighed by what are familiarly known as 'agglomeration economies'. But though familiar, these are not simple: they consist of a highly-dynamic, spatially structured field of markets, rivals, potential partners and information sources.

London businesses tend not to be conscious of these. Rightly, they think that their own prospects depend much more on company-specific or macroeconomic influences than on where they happen to be located. Yet if we look at aggregate patterns of growth and decline, or at cyclical or structural changes, or at outcomes in the labour and property market, all suggest that interlinked region-wide influences and processes play a major role. The problem is to tease out their effects.

In this chapter, we start from the hypothesis, developed by economic geographers in the 1990s, that specifically 'urban assets' have become critical to the success of many activities, and underlie an economic revival of cities such as London. Our investigation of how this applies to London's situation starts with an assessment of its current competitiveness and the dynamics of change in the metropolitan economy using aggregative data, before drilling down to examine in more depth developments in key sectors, and in the localities where we undertook our case studies. This will involve several different time frames: from the broad sweep of change over the past century, through the structural changes of recent decades, to the short-term dynamics of boom and bust during the 1980s and 1990s. Then, we start the process of trying to identify causal links between economic competitiveness and social cohesion (i.e. equality, connectedness and social order). In this chapter this involves identifying aspects of London's economic performance which may be significant for cohesion, and those which may be influenced by London's social conditions and relations, and then drawing on qualitative material from the local case studies for evidence about some of the immediate links with economic performance.

Several of these issues have been the subject of vigorous debate in the territory between academic research and policy analysis, including (as we saw in Chapter 1) the question of how much cities really matter for competitiveness. On one side, Paul Krugman has been widely quoted as asserting that cities (unlike firms) 'don't compete' in any meaningful sense (Krugman, 1996). But Krugman is not saying that what cities offer to business is economically unimportant – his own research contradicts that – nor that urban economic strategies are irrelevant to competitiveness. Rather, his target is one-eyed competitiveness-boosters who equate a place's interests with that of a specific activity, promoting interventions actually likely to reduce overall levels of welfare in the area concerned. Obviously places do compete, and always have, at least in the sense that uneven market processes differentially reward stakeholders in particular areas, partly on the basis of more or less favourable attributes of those places. Most basically this operates through the performance of local firms in product market competition, but areas also compete for investment, for residents with economic assets, and for political favours from above (Gordon, 1999a). The issue is whether the nature of this territorial competition has radically changed in the past 20 years or so, in ways requiring stronger local interventions. This depends particularly on the answers to three questions, each of which we shall address in this book:

◆ whether the local business environment has become significantly more important as a source of competitive advantage;

◆ whether the types of place-attribute that matter have also changed, toward more qualitative aspects; and

◆ whether evolving local governance systems have the capacity to manipulate these attributes to the general benefit of local residents.

A starting point in approaching these is to think about firms as drawing on three broad sets of asset. The first set is associated essentially with the *company* (its financial, technological and organizational capital) and is available to it almost irrespective of where its operations are located. Those in the second set (including access to the material inputs, space, labour and markets required for routine business) involve matters of *location*, and vary in importance according to the costs of overcoming distance for particular, more or less predictable kinds of transaction. A third set also varies across space, but more discontinuously, reflecting the contributions of *proximity* to various kinds of specific and differentiated local resource, including the potential availability of customers, collaborators, skill and information sources in unforeseen circumstances. This last set represents what are currently referred to as *urban* assets, in contrast to company and locational assets.

Within this simplified framework, there are basically two sorts of process which are believed to be increasing the importance of the 'urban' assets. The first of these, in operation for a century and more, involves the diminished significance of locational assets, relative to urban and company assets, as a result of continuously falling costs of overcoming distance. This is the familiar process of distance-compression, with globalization as an ultimate outcome, driven largely by technological change, both in transport/communications, and in production (with the shift towards a 'weightless economy'). But, to an extent which has accelerated in the post World War Two era, it has also been promoted by developments in management 'technology' and business organization, facilitating co-ordination at a distance, and shifting the balance of importance from locational toward company assets. In the circumstances of steady post-war growth, and tight labour markets, which encouraged 'Fordist' companies to internalize transactions, and engage in longer-term planning to exploit (internal) economies of scale and scope, another effect of these developments was to shift the balance from urban assets toward company assets – since proximity no longer seemed to matter so much. Since the economic crises of the late 1970s, however, this process is believed to have gone into reverse, with new emphases on flexibility, risk-shifting and qualitatively differentiated production inducing another shift in balance, back from company to urban assets. This would then provide a second reason for the heightened importance of this class of assets.

Of course, theory as well as real life is a good deal more complicated than this sketch allows, but it is realistic at least in conveying the idea that there is more than one broad process affecting the competitive position of cities – and that these processes are likely to be operating over quite different time scales. One problem, however, with the line of argument is that, while consultants as well as academics emphasize the new types of urban asset (see, for example Netherlands Economic Institute with Ernst and Young, 1992), surveys of business attitudes still give centre stage to what seem to be classic kinds of locational asset. This is exemplified by Cheshire and Gordon's (1995) TeCSEM survey of firms in Greater London, Reading (in the OMA), and Swindon (near the edge of the Greater South East). The survey highlights the continuing importance to businesses with various functional roles of accessibility, together with availability/cost of premises and relevant kinds of labour, rather than more qualitative factors such as service availability, as Table 3.1 shows. One possible qualification to this finding is that many firms emphasized 'access to London', which might be taken as standing for a whole range of (unidentified) urban assets. Another more fundamental reservation is that such questions about the importance of such place-based characteristics attract answers in relation to potential site choices, which may be quite different from the more crucial question of what influences the performance of firms in given locations. Most firm mobility is actually local, and for premises reasons, not raising questions about the advantages and disadvantages of the region as a whole: in the 1999 London Employers Survey (LES) firms representing just 5 per cent of employment were planning a move beyond Greater London (mostly to other parts of the South East). And for firms in London and Reading (though not those outside the South East) analysis of the TeCSEM survey data does suggest that actual performance (in terms of growth and international competitiveness) was more strongly associated with factors such as (perceived) service availability and proximity to competitors (Gordon, 1996a).

Conceptually, urban assets represent forms of public (or quasi-public) good, available only, or preferentially, to economic actors based in a particular area – with a value reflected in local rent levels. Key examples include both connection to external transport or informational networks, and the existence value of marketed local services, suppliers and skill pools (as distinct from the price paid for their routine use). Where such assets are available, firms have the choice of substituting external economies of agglomeration for internal economies of scale – acquiring close access (on a face-to-face basis) to sources of business intelligence, skilled labour, components and support services which they find impractical or uneconomic to provide on their own account. This option is likely to be particularly attractive to: small firms (both new ones, and those serving niche markets); businesses operating in uncertain environments (whether because of the novelty of their products or more

COMPLEX BUSINESS: GROWTH AND VOLATILITY IN LONDON'S ECONOMIES | **93**

**Table 3.1.** Importance of location factors by establishment function: Greater South East.

| | Administration | Distribution | Manufacturing | R&D | Sales/Marketing | Services | TOTAL |
|---|---|---|---|---|---|---|---|
| | | | **Percentage of Respondents Citing as Important** | | | | |
| Cost of labour | 27 | 15 | 14 | 14 | 9 | 13 | 13 |
| Availability of white collar labour | 33 | 35 | 21 | 26 | 39 | 22 | 29 |
| Availability of manual labour | 7 | 25 | 39 | 14 | 3 | 7 | 14 |
| Availability of general business services | 0 | 5 | 0 | 3 | 0 | 5 | 2 |
| Availability of specialized business services | 0 | 5 | 0 | 4 | 3 | 5 | 4 |
| Availability of premises | 0 | 10 | 21 | 15 | 9 | 16 | 14 |
| Cost of premises | 20 | 25 | 29 | 32 | 33 | 35 | 31 |
| Proximity of customers | 7 | 25 | 18 | 28 | 30 | 36 | 28 |
| Proximity of suppliers | 7 | 20 | 18 | 7 | 9 | 4 | 9 |
| Proximity of competitors | 7 | 10 | 0 | 8 | 6 | 15 | 7 |
| Availability of adequate housing | 7 | 5 | 0 | 3 | 6 | 5 | 5 |
| Traffic congestion | 13 | 15 | 11 | 10 | 6 | 11 | 9 |
| Access to London | 27 | 25 | 11 | 22 | 24 | 33 | 26 |
| Good rail connections | 33 | 25 | 21 | 22 | 15 | 36 | 26 |
| Access to national road network | 40 | 60 | 50 | 56 | 48 | 51 | 54 |
| Access to major airport | 40 | 30 | 25 | 22 | 33 | 22 | 28 |
| N | 15 | 20 | 28 | 18 | 33 | 55 | 163 |

*Source:* Gordon (1996).

Notes:
1. Data relate to 'locationally sensitive' businesses in London, Reading and Swindon.
2. Columns relate to the main activity/activities undertaken at particular establishments.

general market turbulence); and those whose production processes are non-routine. And it ought to prove particularly significant in times (such as the present) of more rapid product innovation, market turbulence, and/or swings of demand away from standardized products. But, since as Granovetter (1985) contended, economic activities are 'embedded' in social relations, for urban assets to be an effective substitute for company assets there has to be some basis for 'trust' relations among local businesses. This is especially so in novel situations with a high degree of risk and uncertainty. Hence the networks and institutions which can underpin such trust – Putnam's (1993) 'social capital' – may also be increasingly relevant urban assets.

Some key evidence for the significance of urban assets in a world shifting to quality-based competition has come from Porter's (1990) finding that internationally successful firms in many countries tend to be spatially clustered alongside successful firms in related activities. But there are some distinctive aspects of Porter's work with particular relevance to this book. The first is that he finds such clusters occurring typically at the scale of a city-region, rather than either nationally or very locally. Second is his emphasis on the importance of local rivalry and of demanding local consumers in raising firms' competitive game, rather than simply trust-based mutual support. And, third is his recognition, in relation to the London region, that 'advanced demand for many goods and services', with a variety of skilled labour pools and other agglomeration factors, can secure competitive advantage across a broad range of activities, rather than simply one or a few specialized clusters (Porter, 1990, 158).

Another quite specific reason why the quality of London's urban assets has become increasingly important follows from the progress of internationalization (another stage in the devaluation of locational assets), both within Europe and globally. What is new about this in the past two decades or so – over and above the longer term expansion of trade in goods – has been emergence of substantial trade in advanced services, and very rapid growth in capital flows and in transnational businesses. In order to cope with the inherent uncertainties of international operations, these require support through a new hierarchy of international command/control and service centres offering immediate face-to-face access to a wide range of specialist internationally-oriented skill and information sources (Friedmann and Wolff, 1982; Friedmann, 1995; Sassen, 1991; Amin and Thrift, 1992).

Though much else has changed over the past century – notably the much reduced importance of locational assets – the current emphasis on urban assets as critical both in meeting the need for flexibility in a context of unstable market demands, and in articulating an internationalized economy, has echoes of London's role before World War One (as we noted in Chapter 1), though such parallels should not be pushed too far. For much of the intervening period the combination of Fordist production methods with relatively high transport costs for finished goods brought a quite different role (and set of social relations) to the city. The return of a more competitive, 'flexible' economy and of internationalization seems, however, to play to the more traditional strengths of a sophisticated metropolitan economy. To assess how far this has been true in practice, we now need to examine the empirical evidence for a significant change in London's competitive position over the last two decades of the twentieth century, before considering what role these processes may have played in any observed change.

## Assessing London's Recent Competitive Performance

The most basic test of competitiveness is how far a city's firms can successfully sell their products in contested markets. But how to assess this is not clear. Porter (1990) focuses on overseas sales, though taking account not only of a firm's direct exports, but also of indirect sales achieved via investment in overseas production – which he attributes to the quality of strategic, sales and design functions in the 'home base'. Applying this approach in an urban context presents two problems, however. First, interest is typically in the amount of activity generated locally, and in how local conditions affect the competitiveness of establishments, whether or not these have 'home bases' in the area. And, secondly, export-based measures may be unduly biased by an area's degree of specialization in activities, such as manufacturing or international finance, with inherently higher trade ratios.

For a more comprehensive view, the measure of competitiveness could be taken as the whole income stream that local activities and factors of production are able to generate, represented by some overall indicator of productivity (Krugman, 1996). But, at an urban scale, there are problems with this approach also. The first is that productivity levels may be inflated in areas able to draw in higher quality factors of production from elsewhere, as with London's tendency to 'cream off' young workers with high natural potential from other areas. Secondly, where (as in London) there are physical constraints on expansion, these may tend to squeeze out activities gaining less from agglomeration economies, and so also tend to inflate measured productivity levels. And, most fundamentally, there are problems in making fair comparisons over time, and as between places, when various markets assign shifting values to output and to some factor inputs, especially in a service economy where physical measures of these are lacking.

As indicators of competitiveness, which is an inherently dynamic idea, both of these approaches probably reflect too strongly the effects of past achievements and inherited market positions. To off-set this we need also to look at areas' growth performance. To some degree this will, of course, reflect areas' competitive success in markets for mobile investment as well as that for products, but comparative evidence from a range of European cities (including Greater London) indicates that rates of *in situ* growth/decline of established businesses are the predominant influence on growth performance (Cheshire and Gordon, 1998). A more seriously biasing factor is that, whatever the competitive strength of their individual businesses, constrained city-regions tend to have slower growth rates because any major expansion gets squeezed outside their boundaries. This is an issue even with our broad definition of the London region, which still excludes the areas of most rapid growth on the fringes of the Greater South East.

There thus appears to be no single obvious approach to measuring a city-region's competitiveness: the three obvious measures – trade, productivity and growth – all have their merits and limitations. So we shall need to look at all three in turn for indications of London's overall competitive strength, or changes in it. For reasons of data availability and reliability we shall discuss growth performance first, in terms of employment changes, then productivity and exports.


**Employment Change**

Our theoretical sketch has suggested a key distinction: between trends associated with major structural changes (including de-industrialization and decentralization) more or less continuously over the decades since 1960, and others (including internationalization and flexible specialization) which appear to have come to the fore in the 1980s and 1990s. So it is appropriate to start off with a longer-term view, which is only really possible with employment data.

Over the past 40 years, overall employment levels in the London region have grown by 10 per cent, closely in line with national trends, adding some 0.6 million jobs overall. But trends have been very different in particular parts of the regional economy:

- Greater London has lost some 0.5 million jobs (12 per cent) while the OMA has added 1.2 million (76 per cent).

- Manufacturing has lost 1.6 million jobs (73 per cent) while services have added 2.3 million (61 per cent).

- Men have lost 0.3 million jobs (8 per cent) while women have added 0.9 million (41 per cent).

All three of these shifts – decentralization, de-industrialization and feminization – were evident across the UK as a whole, but they started earlier in the London region, and (for the first two at least) had proportionately much greater effects here. In fact, de-industrialization and decentralization were quite closely linked in London, since much of the manual job loss concentrated in its core areas, thus contributing disproportionately to the outward shift of employment to the OMA and beyond. In 1960 Greater London had three-quarters of the region's manufacturing jobs; by 2000 this was down to a half. A major factor in the high rate of job loss in the goods-related sectors of this region was their comparative disadvantage in competing for extra space requirements against expanding activities with a need for more frequent face-to-face interaction with others in London (Buck et al., 1986; Buck and Drennan, 1992). The competition has mostly been indirect, however. Relatively few manufacturing jobs have been lost through the transfer of industrial sites to office use (Graham and Spence, 1997). But manufacturing businesses in Greater London have not been able to secure any of the vast increases in industrial land area which would have been needed to sustain employment levels, given steadily rising labour productivity over this period (Fothergill et al., 1988). Space costs, reflecting constrained supply and the competitive success of other sectors, were thus key to the rapid loss of London manufacturing jobs, rather than any intensified version of the relatively high labour costs and fading competitive advantage underlying de-industrialization in the UK as a whole.

Each of these broad employment trends has continued to operate throughout the past four decades. Identifying how they have been modified in the last two, and the extent to which internationalization and flexible specialization were responsible, is complicated by extended cyclical fluctuations during the latter period (discussed in the next section). In order to try to control for this cyclicality and focus on the longer-term trends, we have adopted several strategies. The most straightforward is to concentrate on changes between particular years (near the start and end of the period) which seem to represent more or less comparable points in the economic cycle. We have chosen 1978 and 2000, between which there seem to have been two full cycles. And, since both part-time employment and multiple job-holding became increasingly important for some places and activities during this time, comparisons are made in terms of full-time equivalent (FTE) jobs, equating two part-time jobs with one full-time position.

Estimates of total employment on this basis show overall growth for the region, in contrast to the two previous decades, with even Greater London experiencing some net growth (see Table 3.2). An alternative approach to controlling for cyclicality, relating annual data (including self-employed numbers) to GDP fluctuations, suggests a flat trend in Greater London through the 1980s/90s. On either basis, however, the significant point is that Greater London employment is no longer trending downward at the rates experienced in the 1960s/70s. Trends in the OMA seem to have changed less. Though there is an improvement (see Figure 3.2 later in this chapter), growth rates here now lag behind those in the fringe areas of the Greater South East region, notably in the arc between Peterborough, Swindon and South Hampshire (65–90 miles out), where employment growth rates averaged 2 per cent per annum over the last decade. Within the London region, rates of employment change over the

**Table 3.2.** Employment change in the London region, 1978–2000.

| Sector | Greater London | | Outer Metropolitan Area | | London Region | | Great Britain |
|---|---|---|---|---|---|---|---|
| | 000s | % | 000s | % | 000s | % | % |
| Manufacturing | −432 | −63% | −283 | −48% | −716 | −56% | -44% |
| Other manual sectors | −183 | −24% | 144 | 35% | −34 | −3% | 6% |
| Business services | 582 | 81% | 385 | 166% | 967 | 101% | 79% |
| Health education and government | −68 | −9% | 36 | 8% | −30 | −2% | 17% |
| Consumer services | 171 | 28% | 182 | 56% | 351 | 37% | 31% |
| Total | 70 | 2% | 466 | 23% | 536 | 10% | 4% |

*Source:* NOMIS.

*Notes:*
1. Data relate to employees only, and are expressed as full-time equivalent jobs.
2. Other manual sectors include extraction, energy, construction, transport and wholesaling; business services includes finance, IT, and other business services; consumer services includes retail, catering and other community, social and personal activities.

two decades are a little above those for the country as a whole, though the margin is modest considering the heavy job losses sustained by older manufacturing areas during the 1980s.

In sectoral terms, there were substantial job losses in virtually all the manual employing sectors (i.e. the production industries plus transport and wholesaling), with total losses over the period of some 750,000 jobs, representing a steeper rate of decline than in the country as a whole. This was also the case in public administration/defence, reflecting both continuing dispersal of administrative jobs from London, and the impact of cuts in defence activity, an important activity in parts of the OMA. All private sector service activities, plus education and health, recorded significant growth in employment, at slightly above national average rates. But most of the net growth in the non-manual sectors was concentrated in business services. Contrary to some preconceptions, this growth did not come from financial services, but rather from a wide range of other professional and producer services. In fact, the fastest percentage rates of growth were in IT and telecommunications-related services, though these accounted for only a minor part of overall growth in the sector. The net effect of these sectoral shifts has been to produce an employment structure which is even more distinctively weighted toward activities with a majority of non-manual jobs. This reflects both the region's comparative advantage in (generally) growing sectors, and the squeezing out of activities in which it has a comparative disadvantage.

Geographically (see Table 3.3), the pattern of change over the two decades involved a heavy concentration of growth in the western and southern parts of the OMA, with some net increase in Greater London's own western sectors, and substantial decline in east London (both inner and outer). The established Central

**Table 3.3.** Employment change in sub-divisions of the London region, 1978–2000.

| Sub-division | Manual sectors | | Non-manual sectors | | TOTAL | |
|---|---|---|---|---|---|---|
| | 000s | % | 000s | % | 000s | % |
| Centre | -128 | -62% | 178 | 30% | 50 | 6% |
| Inner West | -107 | -42% | 173 | 48% | 66 | 11% |
| Inner East | -173 | -53% | 136 | 34% | -37 | -5% |
| **Inner London** | **-408** | **-52%** | **487** | **36%** | **79** | **4%** |
| Outer West | -78 | -31% | 112 | 61% | 34 | 8% |
| Outer South | -55 | -30% | 62 | 29% | 7 | 2% |
| Outer East | -87 | -57% | 30 | 25% | -57 | -21% |
| **Outer London** | **-220** | **-38%** | **204** | **39%** | **-16** | **-1%** |
| OMA North | -57 | -22% | 100 | 55% | 43 | 10% |
| OMA West | -27 | -14% | 174 | 101% | 147 | 41% |
| OMA South | 29 | 14% | 203 | 97% | 232 | 56% |
| OMA Essex | -48 | -29% | 81 | 64% | 33 | 11% |
| OMA Kent | -34 | -24% | 54 | 44% | 20 | 8% |
| **Outer Metropolitan Area** | **-137** | **-14%** | **612** | **75%** | **475** | **27%** |

*Source and notes:* See Table 3.2.

area (defined here as the Cities of London and Westminster) also showed a modest expansion in employment, despite reductions in some core locations. But faster growth occurred all round its fringes, producing an extended CBD, running some 10 miles west-east, from Hammersmith to Canary Wharf in Docklands. Throughout all parts of Inner London, however, and to a lesser degree in Outer London too, growth in office-based activities has been heavily off-set by losses in other traditional inner-city trades. For activities making significant use of freight transport, this seems to reflect a real weakening of the areas' locational advantages. But for other activities, it essentially reflects an inelastic supply of space in the inner areas – which is also the major reason for inner-outer differentials in growth within the non-manual sectors. Space constraints cannot explain the very sharp east-west divide in growth rates, however, which does seem to reflect a real, and possibly increasing, differential in competitive advantage, with locations on the west/south-west sides of the conurbation in a substantially stronger position.

In terms of employment trends, then, evidence of the region's competitive success is rather equivocal, even by British standards. But some new factors during the last two decades do seem to have brought the long-term decline of Greater London employment to a halt. In the OMA change has been less, but its growth also seems to have received a significant boost. Extending the frame of reference to other European cities, relevant comparisons can be made in relation to population growth rates for comparable functional urban regions in north-west Europe. During the 1990s period of general expansion these show the London region keeping pace with Amsterdam, Brussels, Düsseldorf, Edinburgh, Frankfurt and Paris in terms of population change, with only Dublin doing significantly better (Cheshire and Gornostaeva, 2001).

## Productivity

In terms of productivity and earnings, the region's competitive success seems more clear-cut, but there are considerable problems in evaluating trends. One reason for this is practical: there are serious doubts about the consistency of official measures of GDP and employment, which form the numerator and denominator of productivity estimates, but are separately compiled. It is clear that levels of productivity in the London region significantly exceed those in any other part of the UK – but both the margin of difference, and how it has been changing, are much less clear. For Greater London, published official estimates for 1998 indicate levels of output per worker and per hour worked which are respectively 18 per cent and 17 per cent above the national average (Daffin, 2001). With alternative measures of numbers employed (based on the Labour Force Survey rather than the Census of Employment), the gap widens to 27 per cent, while earnings data (free of consistency problems) points to a differential of 30 per cent (in 2000). Applying the LFS-based approach to the region as a whole suggests a level of GDP per head in 1998 22 per cent above the national average, while also pointing to substantial sub-regional variations.[1] For the Outer Metropolitan Area as a whole GDP per worker is estimated to have been 15 per cent above the national average, but within this area there was a large range. On the western side, in Berkshire and Surrey, the estimated level of productivity was 29 per cent above the national average, whereas in the areas to the east of London it was about 4 per cent below. Within London the variation is even greater, between 50 per cent above the national average in the Inner West sub-region (here including the two central 'cities'), via about 15 per cent above that average in the Inner East (including Docklands) and Outer West (including Heathrow), to about 10 per cent *below* average in Outer East London.

In looking at possible shifts in London's relative productivity over the past two decades, these data problems are compounded. In particular, there is clear evidence of inconsistencies affecting the GDP series (i.e. the numerator for productivity measures) before 1995, when compared with any alternative indicator of income (Cameron and Muellbauer, 2000). In this case, the only solution is to focus on measures of average earnings derived from employer surveys (the annual New Earnings Survey) as a proxy for value-added per head. Although only directly covering about 63 per cent of value added, these have the virtue of consistency, both between areas and over time, and cannot move too far away from productivity levels except in the short run. These data show that the earnings gap between the London region and the UK as a whole widened considerably within the past couple of decades, but that this development was effectively confined to the years 1979–1990. Over this period, all the spatial differentials more or less doubled. Thus, estimated average earnings for the region as a whole rose from 11 per cent to 21 per cent above the national average; for Greater London from 15 per cent to 28 per cent above; for the OMA from 4 per cent to 7 per cent above, and for the City and Westminster from 28 per cent to 50 per cent above.[2]

This looks like a once-for-all shift, sandwiched between decades (the 1970s and 1990s) in which the differentials seem to have remained pretty stable (see Figure 3.1). It also closely coincides with the period in which the UK experienced a general widening of earnings differentials – between occupations, industries and individuals – apparently reflecting a more competitive pattern of wage determination and reduced union power (Machin, 1999; Gosling and Lemieux, 2002; Pencavel, 2002).[3] However, whereas at the individual level earnings differentials seem to have increased by 40–50 per cent, the spatial differentials affecting the London region widened by around 100 per cent. The upward shift in earnings levels, especially in core areas of the region (and particularly at the top of the occupational spectrum) cannot therefore simply be explained in terms of increased inequality in individuals' rewards. But this is a significant part of the picture, to which should be added the effects of a shift away from national bargaining and national pay norms during this period. In terms of the region's competitiveness, all that this would imply is that London businesses were able either to absorb or pass on the additional labour costs arising from these shifts in differentials. This would have been comparatively easy in those cases where competing activities elsewhere in the UK were similarly affected or in high level service functions where London businesses enjoyed a degree of monopoly.

Beyond this, more dynamic London businesses may well have gained market share as service markets were opened up to competition during the 1980s – but this is impossible to quantify. Two more specific factors could be London's substantial protection from the severe rationalization in older manufacturing industries during the 1979–1983 recession, and/or the rapid growth in international financial operations around 1985–1987. But the continuity of growth in the London earnings premium during the 1979–1990 period suggests that more pervasive structural influences predominated, with the regional economy benefiting from the combined effects of increasing competitive pressures and increasing inequality in the allocation of rewards. The much more modest changes experienced since the start of the 1990s (both in earnings and, we infer, in productivity), despite sharp fluctuations in regional employment, are also consistent with the hypothesis of a major structural break during the 1980s having substantially boosted the region's competitive position.

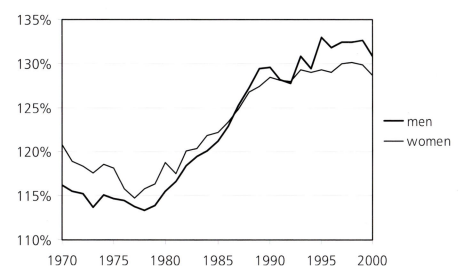

**Figure 3.1.** Average weekly earnings of full-time men and women workers: Greater London relative to Great Britain, 1970–2000.

A side-effect of rising earnings in sectors which are particularly competitive in London or able to pass on higher costs without loss of market share is to push up labour costs in some other sectors which lack these advantages. These spill-over effects would be likely to lead to some squeezing out of less productive businesses, activities and jobs. And there is econometric evidence that rising relative wages during the 1980s did have a significant effect in diverting employment growth to areas outside the South East (Dignan et al., 1996). Assuming that the diverted jobs would typically have lower productivity levels this would have tended to raise average productivity levels within the region, for purely compositional reasons, even if nothing changed within those establishments that remained.

Again, it is arguable that the most relevant comparisons are with other leading European cities, rather than with the rest of the UK. These have additional complications in terms of the exchange rates to be used for comparison, and because of national differences in the timing of cyclical fluctuations. However, in terms of GDP per head (on a Purchasing Power Parity basis), over the years from 1991 to 1997, much the same generalization seems to hold as for population growth, namely that the London Functional Urban Region's (FUR) performance is in line with most other leading city-regions in north-west Europe: slightly ahead of four, and behind three others, including Dublin which is in a league of its own in terms of GDP growth. In terms of levels of GDP per head, the London FUR in 1997 was nevertheless 12 per cent behind Düsseldorf, 18 per cent behind Paris, and 44 per cent behind Frankfurt (Cheshire and Gornostaeva, 2001).

## International Markets

There are complications also in assessing London's competitiveness in relation to international markets. Official estimates of regional trade in goods, derived from Customs records, suggest that Greater London alone accounted for 15 per cent of UK goods exports in 1999 (and 21 per cent of those beyond the EU), roughly double its (7 per cent) share of manufacturing employment. This is a particularly striking statistic, although on this basis London's share of goods imports seems even higher (20 per cent overall and 24 per cent for areas beyond the EU). However, it is clear that the export figure does not simply relate to goods produced by manufacturers in London, since this would require over 40 per cent of their gross output to be exported, as compared with the (employment weighted) average of 26 per cent recorded in the 1997 London Employers Survey (LES). Much of this trade must either reflect attribution of production elsewhere to London office addresses, or else (as Customs statisticians suggest) reflect London's role in precious goods and fine art dealing.

Taking the LES (with data from 3,800 establishments located in Greater London) as a basis, and comparing businesses' responses on the proportion of turnover exported with data from the 1997 UK Input-Output Tables, it appears that the proportion of *goods* sold overseas was close to the national average, except for printing and publishing where it was almost three times as high. In almost every *service* sector, however, overseas sales by London businesses look substantially higher, averaging 18 per cent of turnover compared with 8 per cent for (private) services nationally. In financial services, hotels/restaurants and transport/communications the London proportion is about 30 per cent. Overall it seems that something like 60 per cent of UK service exports may come from London establishments, as compared with about 6 per cent of goods exports. Nevertheless, because trade in goods is still about three times that in services, London's total dependence on export markets is only slightly above the national average (representing about 19 per cent of turnover as against 15 per cent). It is therefore an enormous exaggeration to claim, as some have, that during recent decades the London economy has become substantially detached from that of the UK.

For the areas in our region outside Greater London, data are more fragmentary,[4] but suggest a pattern of exporting similar to that of Outer London businesses. In fact, the main differences within the region appear to lie between central London (i.e. the City plus Westminster) and the rest, with substantially higher export sales in the central area, averaging 25 per cent of turnover on an employment weighted basis, as compared with 11 per cent in the rest of London. The difference is especially marked for financial services, retailing and hotels/restaurants, where exporting is especially concentrated among central London businesses. Even in the OMA, however, it appears that the incidence of producer service and publishing exports is about double that outside the region.

## Overall Competitive Performance

Putting together these three perspectives, we find a strong London competitive performance by UK standards, except in relation to growth where that of our London region (as opposed to its extension in the Greater South East) is no more than average. On the two indicators for which we have time series data, there is also evidence of an upgrading of the region's performance in changed circumstances since the start of the 1980s – although earnings/productivity growth was a feature of the 1980s, whereas the stabilization of employment trends (after a period of long decline) has been more evident in the 1990s. Both of these are consistent with a revaluation of the city's assets in a more competitive and international economic context, though other factors may have played a role, labour market deregulation in the first case, and accelerated immigration in the second (this is discussed in the next chapter). But by European standards, London's performance looks rather less good: in fact, as we have seen from the comparisons of growth and GDP levels with other north-west European FURs, it was only average. And, in terms of growth and productivity at least, another conspicuous feature is the much weaker performance of the eastern part of the region as compared with the west, both inside and outside Greater London.

For firms within Greater London, aspects of this picture can be corroborated by evidence from the 1999 LES on businesses' own perception of how their products relate to those of competitors. Overall, this showed a majority of private sector employment (54 per cent) in establishments claiming a general competitive advantage for their products and services, while those claiming this for some part of their output represented a further 25 per cent, and hardly any (1 per cent) admitted a competitive disadvantage. This positive pattern was evident in almost all sectors: at its strongest in ICT services and the hotel industry (with 70 per cent of employment in generally advantaged establishments), followed by education, health and publishing (around 60 per cent); and with the share of activity in 'competitive' businesses falling only to around 40 per cent in financial services and recreation/culture. On this indicator, multivariate analyses suggest that the most competitive businesses were the larger ones (with over 200 employees), with main markets outside the region, higher proportions of professional and managerial workers, and in product markets where overall demand was perceived to be growing. Even when these factors were controlled for, businesses owned by members of non-white ethnic minorities were significantly less likely to claim a competitive advantage for their products. Spatially, within London there were proportionately more 'competitive' businesses in the central and western areas (i.e. around the corridor from the CBD to Heathrow), and fewest in outer east London. There was also some evidence of an association with the period in which businesses were founded: businesses from the early twentieth century more often claimed competitive advantage than those from the interwar years or the 1970s, perhaps implying that firms from the Fordist era of London development were faring less well than others in the new competitive environment.

## Instability and Volatility in the Regional Economy

There is a downside to this success story: the same processes that boosted the region's overall competitive performance from the 1980s seem also to have added to its instability and to a more uneven distribution of the resultant gains. The distributional issue will be extensively treated in following chapters. Here, we simply note that gains in competitiveness have been heavily concentrated among sectors employing non-manual workers and have given a further boost to the continuing shift in employment away from goods-related sectors, particularly towards those with a large proportion of professional workers. Partly for this reason, the geographic pattern of growth has been skewed more strongly toward the already advantaged western side of the region. And rising relative earnings/productivity have principally been associated with parts of the economy which already offered the highest rewards.

But in addition to this social-sectoral-spatial unevenness, temporal change has also become increasingly uneven. Increasing volatility, particularly in employment, has been a national feature since the late 1970s. But it has been particularly notable in the London region, which had earlier been relatively protected from the effects of macroeconomic fluctuations – both because of its limited employment in export and investment-oriented manufacturing activities, and because lack of space restricted expansion possibilities during growth phases of the business cycle (Buck et al., 1986). Indeed up to the mid-1980s cyclical fluctuations in London employment tended to be only on half the scale experienced elsewhere. Since then, however, the London region has actually shown a greater volatility in employment terms than most other parts of the UK, experiencing a strong boom in the mid to late 1980s, followed by a sharp bust, and then another more prolonged boom (see Figure 3.2).

This is despite the fact that generally manufacturing has remained much more cyclically sensitive than other activities, and that the region's exposure to this source of fluctuations has continued to reduce. What has happened is that the service sector in the London region has become much more volatile, both absolutely and relative to other parts of the country. A simple measure of cyclicality over the last cycle can be derived by averaging employment in 1989 and 2000 (as representative of near peak activity) and expressing this as a ratio of employment at the trough in 1993. On this measure, a range of private consumer and producer services appear about three times as volatile in the London region as in the rest of the country. Financial services

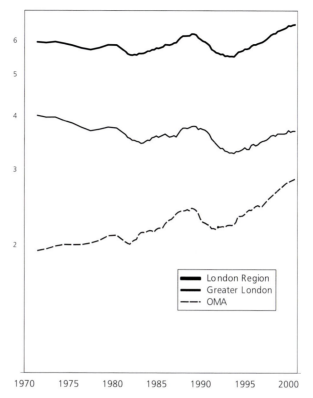

**Figure 3.2.** London region employment, 1970–2000, millions full-time equivalent (log scale).

and law/accountancy are notable cases, since they appear cyclically stable in the rest of the country. But in terms of excess cyclical swings, most financial and business service groups, together with catering show similar differentials, around 15 per cent of 1993 employment levels. In retail and recreational services there are differentials about half this size.

Four main factors acting together seem to have produced this new volatility. Two of these are permissive, rather than directly causative. One of these relates to aspects of the new flexible economy which allow firms to adjust their expenditure on services and labour more closely to their current needs and expectations. A second, similar factor is financial deregulation which has greatly reduced financing constraints both for property developers (as with the international flows funding major commercial projects in boom years) and private individuals (with greater freedom to borrow against financial assets, whether for housing or consumption). Taken together these have enabled the expectations of various groups about prospective changes in the regional economy to be translated into speculative behaviour of various kinds. Examples from the 'bubble economy' of the late 1980s and subsequently include:

• the growth strategies of finance houses in the City during the mid-1980s, predicated on the assumption that opening up of competition for market functions previously restricted to one group of actors would allow each to increase their market share;

◆ high levels of office development stimulated by prevailing rent levels close to the peak of the boom, despite the likelihood that by the time buildings were completed, higher supply and lower demand (from occupiers shifting part of their demand elsewhere) would undermine expected gains;

◆ increasing treatment of housing as an investment asset, responding to and reinforcing a differentially sharp upward movement in the region's house prices (see Figure 4.1 in next chapter), exaggerated by an inelastic supply, but ultimately dependent on expectations of economic growth;

◆ upward adjustments to consumption levels, beyond the level justified by earnings growth, on the basis of the perceived wealth embodied in increasing expensive houses.

The third crucial set of factors has been events or developments triggering belief in above average growth prospects. In the 1980s boom, the Big Bang deregulation of City financial markets (discussed in the next section) was a specific example, linked to more generally exaggerated belief in the economic gains flowing from a 'world city' role. In the 1990s, after the recession, this has continued to play a role, together with more general excitements about dot.com business and high-tech stocks, contributing to climbing stock market values up to the end of 1999. A final factor amplifying the effects of these is the high proportion of employment now represented by service jobs sensitive to swings in local incomes and spending. Within Greater London, for example, the 1999 LES indicated that over 60 per cent of employment was now in establishments mainly serving the regional market – and the proportion in the OMA (housing many commuters to London jobs) would be even higher. Though comparative data are lacking, these proportions must have grown significantly in recent decades, both because of growing demand for services, which are still much less likely to be traded than are goods, and because of slower productivity growth in service activities.

Over these two decades London experience supports the view that a more flexible economy, more reliant on urban assets, will tend to be a more volatile economy, especially in the case of a leading region with an inelastic supply of space. In more open and competitive markets, with internationally-mobile capital flows pursuing profitable development opportunities, the scope for sharp changes of course is greater. And the more that perceptions of intangible urban assets become important, the more speculative can urban growth become. Our interpretation of trends in the London economy is not wholly shared by local actors, however, many of whom (including the GLA leadership) see the 'bust' episode of the early 1990s as anomalous, and recent growth as more sustainable than that of the 1980s, given the more 'prudent' macroeconomic regime established by the Major/Blair governments. However, it is fair to note that virtually no-one in the London economy foresaw the 1989 recession either. We have found it reasonable to work on the basis that the present boom will also be followed by a downturn, and that trends should be assessed in relation to previous years of peak activity, rather than the onset of this boom.

## Key Sectors and Clusters

### The Economic Base of the Regional Economy

We take the view (following Krugman) that the performance of all businesses (and public sector activities) in the London region matters for the overall competitiveness of the region and the living standards which its residents enjoy. However, clearly there are activities which function as key drivers of change: they generate most of the external income on which demand for other activities depends; they embody the main elements of competitive advantage which the region possesses; and they are most directly exposed to competitive challenge from outside the region. We can try to identify them in two ways. First, we can look at the extent to which particular activities are over-represented in the region's employment structure, relative to their share in national employment, treating the 'excess' employment in each activity as its contribution to the 'economic base'. Secondly, for Greater London at least, we can identify those establishments, within a representative sample of London businesses, whose main market area is somewhere outside the region, and count them as comprising the economic base. Both approaches are pursued here.

In terms of employment to population ratios, almost all extractive and manufacturing activities are under-represented in the region, the important exceptions being publishing and pharmaceuticals, and to a lesser degree printing and measurement instruments. In the service sector, on the other hand, most tradable services are significantly over-represented in the region, the main exceptions being those which support agricultural functions. Overall, at 4 digit SIC level, 16 per cent of manufacturing and extractive industries are substantially over-represented in the region (by more than 10 per cent) and 77 per cent substantially under-represented; for services the corresponding proportions are 58 per cent and 15 per cent. In a few cases the bias towards particular services reflects a particularly strong demand in the region – as for cleaning and employment agencies, taxis, catering, and perhaps restaurants. For the great majority, however, it clearly reflects some competitive advantage. Following this approach it is possible to identify three large groupings of activities within the economic base, and a series of smaller ones. The first comprise financial services (accounting for 17 per cent of basic employment, predominantly within central London), commercial services (including real estate, consultancy, law and accountancy, with 24 per cent, mostly within Greater London), and high-tech services (II, telecoms and research, with 13 per cent, mostly in the OMA). Other significant groupings include publishing and cultural services (11 per cent, mostly in Greater London), transport (9 per cent), and retail/catering (9 per cent).

Although only available for Greater London, the more direct measures of external market orientation show some similarities in terms of the sectoral distribution of jobs contributing to the region's economic base (Table 3.4). But there are also significant differences. Even without the OMA, manufacturing activities emerge as especially oriented to external markets (and thus a significant part of the base) despite their general under-representation in the region. A number of service activities (education, health, government and hotels), which are only averagely represented in the region's employment structure, also turn out to have a substantial element oriented to external markets. In these cases the explanation may not just be that they include some specific elements which are more widely traded, but also that supply constraints and higher prices lead to the displacement of some domestic demand. However in market terms the economic base of the region emerges as even more diversified than estimates of the 'excess' component in sectors' employment would suggest. Nor is it the case that there is a dominant complex of activities serving 'global' markets, which might be vulnerable to particular kinds of instability. From evidence in the table, this does not appear to be the case even within the 'basic' element of financial services, and is clearly not for other business services. On the other hand, for almost all activities (except hotels and catering), external demand does tend to be dominated by the national UK market.

## Global City Functions

### Finance

The City of London – representing the advanced, 'wholesale' sector of London's financial services, not all now actually within the Square Mile – is not the largest financial centre in the world, nor the most efficient for routine transactions. But it is the most international of the leading centres and also probably the most sophisticated. In terms of the volume of share trading, for example, the US NASDAQ is about four times the scale of the London Stock Exchange, while the New York Stock Exchange is at least twice as large – and Paris only slightly smaller than London. Tokyo and Frankfurt's (more restricted) measures of turnover suggest current activity levels only half that in London – though Tokyo had twice as much up to the early 1990s. In terms of trading in foreign stocks, however, London appears to be the leading player, and is the only exchange in the World Federation of Exchange data (WFE, 2002) (apart from Bermuda!) where this represented the majority of trading. Relative sophistication is exemplified in the derivatives market (growing up during the past 20 years), where London accounted in 2000 for only 8 per cent of the contracts going through organized exchanges (such as LIFFE), but 36 per cent of all the customized 'Over The Counter' business (International Financial Services London, 2001).

Financial services are the activity which has come closest to effective globalization over the past 30 years. This has been encouraged by structural economic changes, including the growing share of international trade in world GDP, and the rapid growth of Foreign Direct Investment, linked particularly to the expansion of trans-national corporations (Drennan, 1996), with explosive growth of flows to emerging markets since 1989. But technical and legal changes have also

**Table 3.4.** Distribution of Greater London employment (in thousands) by sector and main market area, 1999.

| | Local/ Borough | Greater London | South East | Rest of UK | European Union | Rest of World | % of all with markets outside the South East |
|---|---|---|---|---|---|---|---|
| Agriculture, quarrying etc. | 4 | 1 | 1 | 1 | | | 0% |
| Paper and printing | 11 | 32 | 13 | 32 | 3 | 12 | 3% |
| Other manufacturing | 11 | 38 | 26 | 87 | 18 | 12 | 7% |
| Construction | 18 | 53 | 27 | 28 | 2 | 5 | 2% |
| Wholesale distribution | 37 | 38 | 31 | 65 | 10 | 11 | 5% |
| Retailing | 150 | 100 | 14 | 179 | 2 | 2 | 10% |
| Hotels | 1 | 5 | 2 | 11 | 7 | 24 | 2% |
| Restaurants & catering | 133 | 64 | 25 | 4 | | | 0% |
| Air transport | | 13 | 3 | 3 | | 20 | 1% |
| Other transport | 35 | 56 | 15 | 61 | 8 | 32 | 6% |
| Financial services | 16 | 46 | 12 | 140 | 42 | 84 | 15% |
| Professions | 14 | 63 | 25 | 69 | 11 | 17 | 5% |
| IT, R&D, telecoms. | 7 | 29 | 10 | 64 | 26 | 33 | 7% |
| Other business services | 93 | 185 | 55 | 187 | 30 | 50 | 15% |
| Government | 130 | 29 | | 64 | | 5 | 4% |
| Education | 112 | 58 | 17 | 57 | 2 | 5 | 4% |
| Health | 133 | 50 | 18 | 89 | | 17 | 6% |
| Recreation and culture | 26 | 38 | 7 | 66 | | 19 | 5% |
| Other community services | 17 | 14 | 9 | 56 | 2 | 3 | 3% |
| TOTAL | 948 | 912 | 310 | 1263 | 163 | 351 | 100% |

*Source*: London Employer Survey.

*Note*:
Sample responses from 5,600 establishments, grossed up using employment figures (by area, sector and sizeband) from the 1999 Annual Business Inquiry.

played a major role in facilitating international movements of capital and credits. In addition, there have been conjunctural developments at particular times, creating large imbalances as between the distribution of investable funds and opportunities for profitable investment (as with the US deficit and the Japanese surplus in the 1980s), or affecting the perceived rates of return in different markets. As significant as the growing scale of international financial transactions, however, was the change in their routing during the 1980s:

> . . . financial markets, rather than banks, have become the key locations for intermediation functions. While banks are a simple mechanism of intermediation, the financial markets are complex, competitive, innovative and risky. (Sassen, 1991, 84)

In the 1990s this continued with a five-fold growth in international equity trading (accounting for 23 per cent of all equity trading in 1998, according to data from Cross-Border Trading). There have been two important implications. It has given renewed importance to the agglomeration economies available in the largest, most sophisticated, and best serviced centres. And, by enlarging the scope for speculation, it has added greatly to the volatility of business in those markets, and in the major cities involved.

Within the 'club' of major financial centres there are big differences in role, both in degrees of internationalization and in particular specialist strengths. A simple indicator of internationalization is the share of business in a centre which is cross-national, on which basis London emerges as the most international of centres, partly because its main rivals, New York and Tokyo, serve much larger domestic markets. Beyond this, however, there is a distinction between cross-national transactions which are integral to the operations of domestic business, and those which are servicing international demands on a third party basis. This is especially important given that most 'multi-national corporations' actually retain very strong roots in one or other of the major national economies. In these terms London stands out from all the other leading centres:

> While a substantial proportion of New York and Tokyo's business is domestic in origin, London is pre-eminently an international centre and can be regarded as the only true world centre. It is among other things the world's largest centre for foreign exchange trading, international bank lending to non-residents, marine and aviation insurance, international bond underwriting and trading, cross-border fund management, metals future trading, and ship broking. (City Research Project, 1995, xviii)

Hence it has been observed that more Japanese banks are represented in London than in Tokyo and more American banks than in New York. The distinction is underwritten by Sassen (1991) who shows that Tokyo's importance in the 1980s was essentially as a base for the export of capital (with very little inward investment, or trade in foreign shares), while New York was heavily involved in the inflow of capital into the US – leaving London (in a country with both large inflows and outflows) to play more of an entrepôt role. This puts it in an especially competitive situation, with its share of the international market dependent on sustaining quality, product innovation, and specialization. Some of its specializations are well-established and relatively secure, notably in currency dealing, where it handled 31 per cent of global transactions in 2001, with only 13 per cent of its business involving sterling. In other cases, however, it is involved in niche markets, where potential competitive threats may come from minor centres, such as Luxembourg or Dublin in off-shore fund management, Bermuda in insurance, or Piraeus in ship-broking (City Research Project, 1995).

Deregulation has played a fundamental part in facilitating this change, as well as in enhancing the competitive attractions of particular centres. Indeed the re-emergence of London as an international financial centre in the 1960s, via the development of euro-markets, reflected a relaxing of exchange controls in the UK coupled with tighter taxation and regulation in the US (City Research Project, 1995). In the 1980s, the Thatcher government's removal of exchange controls, and the subsequent 1986 'Big Bang', opening up the City to foreign finance houses (in this case following deregulation in New York), was partly aimed at boosting or at least sustaining London's competitive position. Indeed this is probably the most significant competitive initiative which has been taken to date on London's behalf, reflecting the City's unusual capacity for collective action, and direct links to the centres of power (cf. Gordon, 1995). A particular fear was that, 'unless foreign firms were given easy access to the City they would set up a rival market elsewhere' (Augar, 2000). But deregulation was also intended to restore competitive advantage for City firms, sapped by previous restrictive practices, by exposing them to invigorating open competition.

Its first profound effects, however, were on the operations of monetary institutions in the domestic market, increasing the potential for speculative behaviour (now involving individual home-owners) and further destabilizing the regional economy, as we have seen in relation to the 1980s boom. This had wide-ranging effects, but within financial services itself the combination of Big Bang and external developments brought an 80 per cent growth in exports between 1984 and 1987, supporting a substantial expansion in City employment. Both exports and employment fell back again over the following four years, but the episode encouraged belief that globalization would provide the basis for more sustained expansion in this sector. However, analyses relating employment trends to fluctuations in financial service trade and in the sector's employment outside the South East (where international business is minimal) indicate that, while the international sector was responsible for the sharp fluctuation in London's financial and business service employment from 1984 to 1989 (after which domestic factors took over), the strong upward trend through the 1980s and early 1990s was very largely due to growing domestic demand (Gordon, 2000). Much of this growth was itself stimulated by deregulation and by the Thatcher government's strong encouragement of personal rather than state provision in health insurance, pensions, housing and education. One indicator of this was a doubling of the share of consumer expenditure going on purchase of financial services between 1979 and 1990. An increasing role for private business in public service delivery also played a part – eventually including an export business for London consultants as advisors on PPP, especially in relation to transport (International Financial Services London, 2001)!

Removal of traditional barriers was insufficient to invigorate rather conservative British finance houses, however (Kynaston, 2001). The initial consequence was a loss of market share (within London) to branches of overseas firms, especially from New York. Then, with gathering speed through the 1990s, British firms were actually taken over, with about a third of City employment now in such branches. Whether this matters so long as trading activity continues to be based in London, generating large numbers of very high salaries, is a matter of vigorous debate. On the one hand, greater dynamism among foreign firms and the inflow of American expatriates to the City should add to the competitive advantage of the London market and bring a new multi-cultural strength. Interestingly, the 1999 LES showed that British-owned firms were now substantially more innovative. On the other hand, Augar (2000) and others take the view that loss of domestic control, alongside the ending of face-to-face trading, inevitably weakens London's long-term ability to hold on to business. In particular he foresees a major rationalization within the London branches of New York-based investment banks when the next major downturn arrives.

During the 1990s much discussion focused on the challenge which Frankfurt might pose to London's dominance as a European financial centre. For the stock exchange, however, the reality was simply one of growth rates falling behind those of other leading exchanges, apart from Tokyo, hard hit by the Japanese economic crisis (International Financial Services London, 2001). Toward the end of the decade all traditional exchanges started to come under pressure from new digital trading systems allowing remote dealing across Europe or the US. A response has been first the transformation of exchanges into public companies and then waves of merger and attempted merger activity. Among other City institutions, LIFFE and Lloyds both faced particular crises, surviving through radical reorganization. Despite these shocks and the removal of trading floors as physical foci for interaction, the view remains strong in the City that face to face contact is still a crucial underpinning for time-sensitive transactions in uncertain environments – and that its scale, expertise and international links make it a uniquely effective site for such contacts. In our interviews these points were emphasized both by established City firms, and by an analyst from the small London office of a European investment bank. He made the point that not only was the City the best location in which to acquire information, from brokers and overseas visitors, about less well known stocks, but:

> There is an argument at the moment that brokers' income has been very much derived from IPOs, and people say that what they write in reports is not actually what they mean! And it's easier to get their (honest) outlook if you meet them than if you talk to them on the phone – because they're often very careful about what they write in their reports!

Larger scale evidence from the 1996 LES confirms the value that American, Japanese or European finance houses in the City attach to the access to shared intelligence which it affords. Among this group, respondents representing 88 per cent of employment reported significant advantages from location close to related businesses, compared with 45 per cent for other City firms (and 39 per cent outside the City). As well as intelligence they also emphasized competition and bringing business in as advantages, while British firms gave more emphasis to the labour pool.

### Other global activities

International financial services (like their domestic counterparts) generate substantial demands from supporting services (including significant parts of the hospitality industry). Their quality, particularly in dealing with the complexities of trans-national business is widely recognized as one of the pre-requisites for successful financial and control centres (cf. Friedman and Wolff, 1982; Sassen, 1991; City Research Project, 1995). But many service activities also contribute independently to London's global city role. Among these are establishments carrying out co-ordinating or strategic sales functions for businesses with main markets outside the UK. Together these accounted for some 35,000 jobs in 1999 according to the LES, with 50 per cent in business services, 30 per cent in distribution, and 10 per cent in manufacturing firms. More important than these, however, is direct provision of services to such markets – notably in law/accountancy/architecture, ICT and other business services (including marketing and consultancies of various kinds) with a combined employment of 82,000 (similar to that in financial services).

Among these, law and accountancy are particularly interesting both because of their rapidly growing international business, and because of the role of institutional factors. In each case there is a small number of large international businesses responsible for much of the global trade, with multi-nationals preferring to use the same firms in each of their locations. As far as law is concerned, the pattern of commercial business is substantially shaped by the fact that it is conventional to specify *either* English *or* New York law as governing international financial contracts, and by the fact that disputes involving one or other of these systems have ultimately to be resolved in the London or New York courts (London Economics Limited, 1994). Of the twenty leading firms, six are London-based, and larger London firms are more export-oriented, though specialist international firms tend to be small, and the one large, truly international practice operates from Chicago. One or other system tends to predominate in different regions, as can be seen from the different patterns of representation of London- and US-based law firms across international centres (Taylor and Walker, 2001). In accountancy the internationally dominant Big Five straddle the North Atlantic and have increased their hegemony as the evolution of internationalization has promoted the development of common business (e.g. through the EU's Business Law Directives), leading to the rapid growth of an audit market favouring Anglo-Saxon accounting styles (London Economics Limited, 1994). In this case, more of the professional work is actually undertaken on site, either through branches or peripatetic staff, rather than remotely, since there is no counterpart to the role of courts as a locational attractor. In this case branch structures reveal little distinction between UK- and US-based firms – though London offices tend to take the lead in European work – but there are regions, particularly Eastern Europe and Pacific Asia, where international firms have only a very weak presence (Taylor and Walker, 2001).

London based offices of the Big Five tend to play a leading role in their European networks, although each practice is largely independent. Links with financial services are much weaker than in the case of law, and much more accounting work is actually undertaken by London based firms in the areas where demand arises (London Economics Limited, 1994; City Research Project, 1995). Both of these activities are heavily concentrated in the City and Westminster, but this less true of the international segment of other business services, much of which is in other parts of Inner London, and some (including engineering consultancies) in the Thames Valley.

## Tourism

The other major component of the 'global city' complex is tourism. The core of this is found in the hotel sector, where there were some 57,000 Greater London jobs in establishments primarily serving overseas markets in 1999. These are heavily concentrated in the boroughs of Westminster and Camden where about 60 per cent of hotel employment and 15–20 per cent of retail, restaurant and theatre employment are export dependent (according to the 1996 LES). Across Greater London as a whole in the hospitality, retailing and recreation sectors, there appear to be some 70,000 jobs directly dependent on overseas visitors, representing about 25 per cent of the international sector of the economy in employment terms in 1999. In income terms the share would be substantially less, given pay rates in these sectors are about 40 per cent of those in business services. These figures probably under-estimate demands generated by the half of overseas visitors who do not stay in hotels (30 per cent with friends). But, on the other hand they do include the 20 per cent of business visitors associated with other international business activities. In British terms, London is clearly a very competitive destination, attracting more than half of all overseas visitors, and nearer two-thirds of those from outside Europe. The number of overseas visitors to the city is similar to the number visiting Paris, though from a different mix of destinations (more Americans, fewer Japanese), significantly more than New York and accounts for around 2 per cent of worldwide tourism (Llewelyn-Davies et al., 1996). Growth in overseas visitor numbers has been strong (+78 per cent between 1983 and 1998), though its share of the national total has fluctuated, depending on shifts in the balance of short- to long-haul visitors – but in the 1990s it held its own. Key factors in its competitive strength include the global diffusion of English as a medium of business, and of cultural products including British theatre, television and rock music – together with the 'buzz' of a 'global city', especially for young visitors. There are weaknesses, however, in overcrowded transport and the perceived dirtiness of public spaces. And, despite the self-confidence noted earlier, core hospitality sectors do not appear competitively strong: not only do London Tourist Board surveys of overseas visitors reveal concerns about value for money (partly due to an overvalued currency) but also views about indifferent service and accommodation quality. Recognition in London, during the 1990s, of more intense competitive relations with other international cities (notably in Coopers and Lybrand Deloitte, 1991) has given a higher profile to tourism planning and marketing, but not yet major steps toward quality control.

## Capital City Functions

London's capital city functions generally parallel its global/European city role, though on a significantly larger scale, as we have seen in Table 3.4. Most importantly, it is the principal national supplier of high-order specialist services of all kinds, achieving clearly higher levels of competitiveness in quality terms in fields such as business services than provincial centres (Hitchens *et al.*, 1992). Here, however, we concentrate on its command and control functions in relation to the management of economic assets and social relations within the UK. Their institutional centres are parliament in Westminster and the money markets of the City. But the complex also includes arrays of representative organizations, lobbyists, support services, the media and those cultural facilities whose *raison d'être* for being in London is proximity to powerful groups within UK society. Broadly defined this could include other key sectors which we will discuss separately, but there are some specific questions which need to be discussed here about how changes over the past two decades have affected London's capital city role.

First we should establish the scale of some key elements. Within the private sector, these include headquarters operations within firms whose main markets are national (not regional or international). In 1999, according to the LES, these employed some 152,000 workers in Greater London, three-quarters in Inner London, though proportionately less in the centre than for more international businesses. There are no comparable figures for the OMA, but in the particular case of holding company headquarters we know there are now as many jobs there as within Greater London. In the public sector the core is represented by the policy and central administrative units of the civil service and related executive agencies, together employing some 80,000 people in London – while headquarters of representative organizations involve another 15,000 or so.

In the public sector the scale of these capital city functions was significantly cut back during the 1980s/90s through step-by-step devolution of executive responsibility to semi-independent agencies. This is a form of vertical disintegration intended to promote more business-like patterns of management. Similar shifts within the private sector are expected to heighten the importance of face-to-face contacts and hence promote agglomeration. In the public sector, however, reorganization has been accompanied by decentralization of jobs to provincial locations, not just for reasons of economy and regional devolution, but largely because the new agencies are not answerable to parliament. A key nexus of face-to-face communication thus no longer has the same force. Taken together with an overall decline in civil service numbers, the effect has been to reduce non-industrial civil service employment in London by 63,000 (42 per cent) since 1976, with above average losses also recorded for the South East government office region, including much of the OMA.

In the private sector, there is little evidence that capital city functions have actually reduced in importance, despite continued decentralization of back office functions. In the case of holding company employment, growth between 1991 and 2000 was almost entirely outside Greater London, and though the OMA (with 63 per cent growth) kept pace with other regions the metropolitan region as a whole fell well behind. But recent rounds of the LES suggest that the growth performance of domestically oriented headquarters (in Greater London) has been no less good than that for companies with international markets, or establishments involved in direct service provision. Nor are they significantly more likely to be considering moves out of London.

## Innovative and Knowledge-based Activities

A large and growing part of the London economy is knowledge-oriented in the sense that it depends on a superior access and processing ability in relation to novel, specialized and non-local forms of information, whether this relates to technologies, markets or cultural developments. In this sense, advanced financial, business and policy-related activities within the global and capital city functions are clearly knowledge-based, as are large parts of the cultural sectors (discussed below). Here, however, the focus is on two more specific questions: about the role within the regional economy of activities dependent on advanced scientific knowledge; and about the economy's performance in relation to product innovation.

### *High-technology industry*

The London region as a whole, together with the adjoining counties of the Greater South East, contain the main centres of R&D activity in the UK. By European standards, however, it is more distinguished for its scientific output than for applied industrial activity. Comparing functional urban regions across Europe Blatt and Gollain (2000) show the London region to be slightly ahead of the Île-de-France in terms of volume of scientific publications, with 7 per cent of the EU total, about twice that of any other European region, and with a particular strength in biological and (especially) medical sciences. In common with the other leading regions, however, output appeared to have fallen between 1990 and 1996 – and more so than in the Île-de-France – whereas it grew in Milan, Madrid and (especially) Barcelona. The region's performance was substantially weaker in relation to industrial research, with only 3 per cent of EU patent applications in 1996, under half that in the Île-de-France or Rhine-Ruhr regions, and behind two other German regions. The London region's relative performance was strongest in pharmaceuticals, electronics and instrumentation, although in each case this only put it in fourth place in the European league table. Between 1990 and 1996 the rate of patenting in the London region was more or less static, whereas there was a significant fall in the Île-de-France and Rhine-Ruhr, and rapid growth in Scandinavian and Spanish centres, plus Brussels. Within the London region growth was strongest in pharmaceuticals and weakest in electronics. These findings tend to bear out Porter's (1990) cluster analyses which suggest that health care goods are the one science-based sector in the region with real competitive advantage by international standards. National analyses for the government (Trends Business Research, 2001), however, suggest a wider range of such sectors in the region, including information and communications technologies. We shall focus on this example since it is much more heavily represented within employment in the region – notably in Reading and Hounslow among our case study areas, but also in the City.

### Information and communications technology

The scale of ICT employment, relative to pharmaceuticals for example, reflects both the fact that the sector tends to be labour-intensive and the generic nature of their technologies, which are of central importance to many activities in the region. Skill requirements in the industry are high, but only a small proportion of the work actually involves major innovations or close links with research activity. Within our set of business interviews the range of establishments spanned: (relatively large) branches of major American software and hardware producers – most of whom have UK/European headquarters in the Thames Valley; an (independent) low-cost national distribution centre for hardware; smaller producers/integrators of customized or original equipment, subsidiaries of European-owned IT consultancies; a (US-owned) disaster recovery centre; and one producer of original software for risk management in financial services. Among the thirteen businesses just one was involved in patentable activities and recruiting at PhD level, while three others appeared to be producing original products. Together these accounted for just over 200 employees out of 2,250 in the responding establishments.

Ownership was a key differentiating factor, with all substantial product and software development for the US-owned companies being carried out there, while their Thames Valley operations concentrated on customization, integration, and product support in conjunction with sales. The element of originality was greatest among the independent British establishments. In the Thames Valley, this pattern of differentiation had been evident from the early 1980s, when most of the innovative work was in defence-related activities (Hall *et al.*, 1987). Since then the defence element has shrunk, the US-owned branches have grown considerably in number and scale, and the independent producers (who were the third element) have remained a minor part of the picture.

For the American businesses, the three significant location factors are: proximity to the established pool of IT professionals in the 'Western Crescent'; access to Heathrow airport for links with HQ and European branches; and closeness to users with particularly complex requirements, notably multinational HQs, and City firms:

> *If you're providing to stock-broking firms you've got to be in central London. It's pretty much mission-critical – if their data's not accessible and their system crashes, then they're losing millions of pounds. The software we provide for such cases is different to what we'd provide for companies where it's less mission critical. To go in there and sell to them you've got to show them what it's all about – and part of that is having a drink!*
>
> US software house, Reading

Explicit comparisons were drawn by interviewees between the advantages, despite housing costs, of recruiting appropriate staff in the (west) London area as opposed to Manchester or even Swindon (40 miles west of Reading):

*I guess they see also that, if they work for us and it doesn't work out, they can go somewhere else relatively easily. Whereas if they move to the South West, you know, there aren't that many opportunities.*

US-owned IT services, Hounslow

From this perspective, Cambridge was suggested as the only comparable UK location.

For independent businesses the crucial reason for a Thames Valley location was founders living locally, but in the one case where a partner came from elsewhere, there was 'a very strong steer' from their American venture capitalist financier that:

*'The Thames Valley is where the hi-tech business in the UK is.' They recognized that we would need to grow the business very rapidly and therefore we'd need to draw on a very large pool of talent.*

3 year-old start-up, Reading

In the case of the two City-based firms, labour market factors were also very important, in terms of transport access from where staff lived, as was the atmosphere, characterized as having:

*A real buzz to it, it's young, it's trendy, it's funky, it's where people want to be – like-minded people.*

European-owned IT solutions and skills transfer business

None of our other case study areas was described in these terms, nor did financial service or legal interviewees in the City describe it this way. It seems specifically related to a concentration of advertising firms shifting to work on the web and of dot.com businesses (booming at the time). Even within this dot.com 'cluster' – extending west into Soho/Noho and north into Clerkenwell – survey evidence however, highlights infrastructural factors, in terms of high capacity digital links and good access to the major internet 'backbone' networks. As in international surveys, close proximity to others in the sector was the least important of six cited location factors (Jones Lang LaSalle, 2001). For two of our interviewees, concentrations of clients were important. Both were internationally oriented: one had 75 per cent of its business overseas but virtually all of its British clients in the City; the other targeted the 'Big Five' accounting/consultancy firms, while looking for 'scaleable products' that could be rolled out internationally.

Even the most independent of our IT interviewees suggested few benefits from clustering other than access to pools of labour with generic skills. The most conspicuously innovative had emerged from a local (email-based) network among young contractors around Reading, but the major current networks and business linkages of the independents were strongly international. Apart from one spun-off from a City financial service group, none had major finance from UK sources: one relied on a small personal bank loan plus mortgage; two others had Japanese and American finance. Clearly the limited role of local networks reflects the dependent nature of much of the IT activity in the Thames Valley, with recently introduced small business network initiatives in the area being of little use to highly specialist firms.

But as one of the start-ups with strong US links said, there's also 'a certain amount of romanticism to tales of networking in Silicon Valley'. A female interviewee from another Reading IT firm suggested that regional – as well as religious and gender – ties might be stronger in the periphery:

> *That really is a buddy system that operates with the Scottish people. It's a national thing – it's not something you can put down on paper but you know it . . . Being a southern-based company, you're semi-the enemy (and) viewed as a bit flash . . . and when you go up there you definitely have to be one of the boys.*

### Product innovation

In high-cost areas such as the London region competitiveness in most activities depends on successful innovation. The 1996 LES suggests that this was most widely recognized among high-tech services group and in the health sector (by respondents representing 75–80 per cent of employment) – but recognition was also high in general manufacturing, transport, financial services and cultural/recreational services (at 60–65 per cent).

In these terms, however, Greater London itself does not appear to be an especially innovative area, although much of the OMA is, together with adjoining areas in the Greater South East. According to the EU's 1996 Community Innovation Survey just 51 per cent of London manufacturing firms had introduced new products or services in the previous three years. This was around the EU norm and below the UK average of 59 per cent, whereas four of the OMA counties to the north and west of London and three of their neighbours outside the region figured among the top eight counties, while all of the OMA counties (bar one marginal case) were among the top twenty-five (Simmie and Sennett, 1999).

In the case of services, London's performance again appears around the national/EU norm, while three of the OMA counties and two of their neighbours appear among the top eight in the UK. In the case of manufacturing this seems to reflect the distribution of high-tech sectors, though there are no such simple explanations for services. One simple factor seems to be that key economic assets for innovative businesses, including international air services, are at least as accessible from many areas in the OMA as they are from most London locations outside the high-rent central area. Compared with those frequently involved in advisory or deal-making functions, innovators' needs for external face-to-face contacts seem not to be sufficiently frequent to justify a high-rent city location (perhaps one or twice a week rather than several times a day) and satisfiable with rapid rail access to the core. And as Simmie *et al.* (2002) argue, innovators in the London region, like those around Paris, are internationally-oriented. What they require from of their environment is not the tight local linkages found in the more regional production complexes of Lombardy or Baden-Württemberg, but access on a more 'pick and mix' basis to the array of possibilities for connections available across the metropolitan region.

This conclusion is borne out by our own analyses of innovating businesses within Greater London from the 1996 and 1999 LES. These highlighted several distinctive features of such businesses, including a tendency for 'leaders' among them to be substantially larger than either 'followers' or non-innovators. Spatially, leaders (in particular) tended to be concentrated either in parts of Inner London outside the central area, or else around Heathrow in the outer west. Most pertinently, however, it showed that innovating businesses in London were externally oriented, and with no particular interest in local clustering. Joint ventures and strong customer/supplier links were important, but their value did not seem to be significantly affected by physical separation (Gordon and McCann, 2000*b*). What the region offered was talent.

## Cultural Services

The cultural or creative industries are a category of activity with a small, clear core and a large fuzzy edge. There is a quite uncertain boundary with the knowledge industries, and on almost all definitions the relevant activities include a mix of manufacturing and service industries. We follow Pratt (1997) in taking music, film, radio/television, publishing and advertising, together with art and theatre, as the key elements, and in distinguishing between sets of activities associated with production, distribution, consumption and the supply of inputs. Among these sets of activities it is the first – more fully defined in terms of original production, commissioning and directing – which is distinctively concentrated in the London region. On our estimates, which include artistic and literary creation, film/video production, radio/television, advertising and all forms of publishing, this production set directly employed 204,000 workers in the region, to which should be added 65,000 or so self-employed. There are a further 138,000 involved in the distribution, consumption and supply sets. Unlike the production set, where the region has twice its share, none of the others is heavily over-represented, and the (manufacturing-based) supply activities, which were once important, are now substantially under-represented in the region. There is a concentration of production jobs within Inner London, which had 60 per cent of the regional total and 28 per cent of that for the country as a whole in 2000. Within Greater London at least there is a particularly well-qualified workforce, with 52 per cent having degrees (against 29 per cent) elsewhere, and half of all graduates in these activities working within London, according to the LFS. As Pratt (1997) points out, this sort of concentration is peculiar to London, cultural production not being significantly over-represented in any other conurbation. Despite some much higher costs in operating from London, it clearly has major competitive advantages within the UK. In terms of its share of national employment it has held its own both through the fairly static years of the 1980s (Pratt, 1997) and in the growth period of the 1990s (when employment increased by about a third). Average pay in the region's cultural production sector is estimated (from the 2000 LFS) to be 60 per cent above that in the rest of the country, suggesting that the region's share of national value-added is about 56 per cent.

The main markets for Greater London's cultural production activities tend to be national (39 per cent according to the 1999 LES) but for a quarter of jobs the main markets were international (including 20 per cent outside Europe). The proportion of export-dependent employment in 1996 is estimated at 24 per cent, with higher proportions in non-newspaper publishing. Comparisons with other global cities (Llewelyn-Davies et al., 1996) suggest that cultural service employment in London in the early 1990s was substantially more than in Paris, but somewhat less than in New York or Tokyo. London publishing activities were larger than those in any of the other three cities, while film/TV/multi-media was reported to be twice the scale in New York, but only one-fifth of the Tokyo figure. For fashion/clothes, employment was seen as comparable with Paris but only a third of that in New York, while for music and dance London employment was slightly more than Paris but eight times the New York figure. Even allowing for likely data inconsistencies, this suggests a pattern of comparative advantage. Other indicators point to the competitive strength of London music, theatre, and art auctions (though its prestige is falling here), while in film/TV where the balance of trade is heavily negative a concentration of craft skills attracts US directors to use facilities both in the OMA and Soho. Despite such niches in the international division of labour, globalization has had a negative effect on this sector, due to the sheer scale of the US industry, and cultural preference for American products in the global market – not offset by any effective government support for the (once successful) industry. In publishing too there are threats to London's previously strong international role, due to the entry of new publishers into the English language market from non-English speaking countries, foreign takeovers removing strategic control of British publishers from London and the growth of IT, threatening the whole industry (Llewelyn-Davies et al., 1996).

## The Local Economies

Within the region the two obvious patterns of economic differentiation are between inner and outer areas, and between east and west. The inner/outer dimension is the simpler, reflecting a basic trade-off between accessibility to key agglomeration economies and affordable space. This encourages a pattern of specialization in which those functions with the greatest need for frequent face to face interaction with influential people tend to be centralized while those with less pressing or frequent needs of this kind locate further out in the region. But it also means that growth, especially in space-extensive activities, tends to occur a long way from the core (actually reaching a peak during the last cycle some 75–90 miles out, beyond the northern and western boundaries of our region). Because of this there is a tendency for newer activities to be relatively dispersed.

The east-west dimension is a bit more complex. For businesses selling goods on the national market there is the simple geographic fact that road access is much better from the northern and western sides of the OMA – though worst of all from many sites within congested parts of Greater London. For those with strong international connections, another key factor is the location of Heathrow airport, on the western edge of Greater London, and (secondarily) of Gatwick, in the south-western part of the OMA. But there is also a historic social dimension with the traditionally higher status of west London getting translated to the OMA through typically radial patterns of population decentralization. This means that areas, particularly in the OMA, have access to a better qualified labour force, attracting businesses in the knowledge-industries seeking this kind of labour, which further reinforces the difference. By most measures then, the strongest parts of the regional economy outside central London (which boasts high productivity and exports, if not growth) are to be found in the western crescent of the OMA, with a spur into the Heathrow area of south-west London. Correspondingly, the weakest areas appear to lie in outer east and north London (beyond the influence of Docklands development) where the density of private business is low, particularly in terms of enterprises with substantial markets outside London (whether national or international), and LES evidence suggests significant constraints on their competitiveness.

In relation to these patterns, the nine areas chosen for our case studies of local businesses (the eight introduced in Chapter 2 plus the City of London) occupy distinctive locations. Some of the broader regional patterns are clearly evident across this sub-set of areas (see Table 3.5). For example rent levels are highest in the centre and fall away less to the west than to the east, with Reading rent levels actually not far below those in City fringe areas of Southwark. Earnings follow a similar pattern, with the lowest levels in the outer east areas (Redbridge, Greenwich and especially Dartford), though in the west Wandsworth earnings are below those further out. In terms of employment growth rates over the last cycle, however, the pattern is clearly one of stronger performance in the outer areas, and to the west. The proportion of higher grade workers naturally peaks in the City followed by the two inner areas (Wandsworth and Southwark, both with significant overspills of CBD activities) and Reading. Among the seven areas inside Greater London (for which data are available), the City also tops the list in terms of orientation to national and international markets, followed by Hounslow and Southwark, with each of the others being more oriented to the regional market. This may reflect either lack of competitiveness or simply comparative advantage for different functions. In terms both of subjective evaluations from firms we interviewed, and LES data on the numbers of constraints to business expansion noted by firms, and their perception of growth/decline in the markets they were involved in,[5] the two weakest areas appeared to be Newham and Redbridge with twice the incidence of constraints reported in the City or Southwark, and none of the self-confidence expressed in the City, or Reading.

While these are the general patterns at district level, however, the local employment centres, whose employment structure is summarized in the last two columns of Table 3.5, are not in every case typical of the district. In particular, the selected employment centre in Dartford/Gravesham – identified here as Kent Thames-side – has a particularly strong representation of transport activities, giving it a much higher proportion of manual jobs than the two districts as a whole. These local employment centres were briefly described in the 'localities' section of Chapter 2. In some cases they are very close to, and share an area identifier with, the residential neighbourhoods to be discussed in chapter 9. In other cases, though quite nearby the centres have distinct local identities, by which we refer to them here (cf. Table 2.1). The following observations about these areas – presented in a sequence from west to east – combine results from the LES with our own firm interviews

**Table 3.5.** Economic characteristics of the case study areas as workplaces.

| | Employment change 1987–2000 % | % Professional, managerial, technical workers 1999 | Estimated prime office rent levels (£ per ft²) 2000 | Average full-time earnings (£s per week) 2000 | Market orientation (% of employment by main market areas served by establishments) 1999 | | | % Employment in manual sectors 2000 | Leading activities 2000 |
|---|---|---|---|---|---|---|---|---|---|
| | | | | | Local | Regional | National/International | | |
| Reading/Wokingham | 35 | (51%) | £30 | 424 | – | – | – | 16 | Insurance / IT / Engin. / Consultancy |
| Hounslow | 30 | 34% | £24 | 465 | 23% | 31% | 46% | 33 | IT / Chemicals / Broadcasting |
| Wandsworth | 14 | 54% | £22 | 398 | 49% | 32% | 19% | 34 | Food wholesale / Postal service |
| City of London | 5 | 73% | £60 | 744 | 8% | 23% | 69% | 5 | Finance / Law / Accountancy |
| Southwark | 14 | 52% | £40 | 454 | 24% | 40% | 36% | 29 | Rail / Finance/business / TV |
| Newham | -1 | 37% | £13 | 393 | 48% | 34% | 18% | 25 | Finance/business / Public services |
| Greenwich | 7 | 46% | (£18) | 364 | 17% | 66% | 17% | 29 | Printing/publishing / Public services |
| Redbridge | 21 | 45% | £12 | 340 | 48% | 29% | 22% | 15 | Retail / Public services |
| Dartford/Gravesham | 20 | (37%) | (£18) | 313 | – | – | – | 55 | Pharmaceuticals / Road freight / Health |

*Sources*: columns 1, 8, 9 Census of Employment; columns 2, 5–7 LFS (bracketed figures from LFS); column 3 summary of surveyors' reports; column 4 NES.
*Notes*:
All data relate to boroughs/districts except for columns 8 and 9 which refer to the chosen employment centres.

## Reading (Centre and East)

In this area the leading activities are insurance and engineering consultancy, both decentralizing from London before the 1980s, together with IT including the main UK bases for many major multi-nationals. The crucial location factors reported by business here are proximity to Heathrow and rapid rail access to central London decision-makers and meetings. Secondary factors include the local concentration of IT skills (though pressure on these was recognized to be very high) and external perceptions that this was the right area for IT operations. The principal disadvantages were very high house prices (by national standards, not London's), a very tight local labour market (where anyone unemployed was perceived to be unemployable), and relatively high rent levels. An effect has been to displace operations which do not really need the locational advantages, which would include most actual manufacturing of electronic equipment. More qualitative aspects of the local business environment were rarely mentioned, partly because of a wide commuting field, and because some firms in business parks felt they were not in Reading in any meaningful way. It may also have been that they had little to complain about, and the employment growth record of the 1990s supports a 'boom town' image. Direct linkages between local businesses seemed weak and one Dutch interviewee commented that there was 'no real business community'. Opinions about local agencies were rather muted: despite some friction over attempts to restrict car traffic in the CBD, several businesses indicated that communications with the council had started to improve and recent town centre initiatives were welcomed.

## Hounslow (Great West Road)

The local economy here is somewhat more heterogeneous, with the legacy of inter-war industrial expansion, though again most production has been displaced. Of those firms taking an active decision to locate in the area, proximity to Heathrow tended to be the key location factor – particularly for the many foreign-owned multi-nationals – followed by accessibility to central London. A secondary factor for several firms was the existence of nearby ethnic or expatriate concentrations – the South Asian community in Southall and smaller Japanese and American communities (in Ealing and Surrey respectively) each with their own schools – offering particular support for key staff. This is a high-rent area and suffers from traffic congestion (as does Reading), particularly generated by car commuting and the inconvenience of public transport. The only out-movement under consideration was short distance and for premises reasons, with a side benefit in reducing commuting distances for many workers. The physical and social image of the area was not thought to be good, but the concentration of blue-chip companies still made areas such as the Great West Road competitive work locations for office-workers. The local labour market is clearly tight (with above average turnover and reported recruitment difficulties) and there were some particular complaints about the quality of local recruits (e.g. in relation to communication skills) – but there are large numbers of highly skilled workers within commuting range. Despite differences of view about the appropriateness of workplace parking restrictions, businesses appeared satisfied with local authority relations. Though the council was not proactive, this was the one area where substantial collective action was evident among major local businesses to improve their operating environment.

## Wandsworth (Battersea and Clapham)

Many of the businesses here are heavily transport dependent (including firms trading in New Covent Garden produce market), and key advantages were the combination of centrality and relative space availability (plus low parking charges). Two interviewees described the area as 'the middle of nowhere' and 'London's best kept secret'. Traffic congestion is a substantial problem, however; some firms saw no opportunity for physical expansion, and rent levels were rising, all of which may account for only modest employment growth. But many firms saw themselves as in high growth sectors, the level of reported constraints was the lowest for any of the case study areas in Greater London, and none of the firms interviewed were considering moves elsewhere. The major perceived threat lay in the swing of major customers to centralized purchasing of foods rather than purchases through the Market. Many of the firms had high turnover rates, but (perhaps for this reason) labour quality and recruitment were not seen as major issues, except in relation to irregular hours. The only significant involvement with business organizations involved two recruitment agencies, who used them as a means of marketing. Wandsworth Council was seen as having a hands-off, business-like attitude – offering basic services, attracting in new firms to enlarge the rate base, and keeping rates down – which seemed to command approval.

## The City of London

For our City interviewees, the key advantages of their location were the high level of contact potential and simple time-savings in organizing meetings, the central position in relation to rail termini, the presence of key institutions such as Lloyds, the prestige value of a London address (particularly internationally) and 'the buzz'. Foreign clients were also said to enjoy coming to London. Very few disadvantages were mentioned (except the fact of high rent levels), with one respondent saying he had never really thought of any, apart from crowded trains and rush hour traffic. Others recognized that these transport problems could be extremely stressful, however. Rent levels *could* be reduced by moving out to the edge of the City, but at a cost in centrality. Other firms were moving out to cheaper Docklands locations, but our interviewees saw higher costs as an acceptable trade-off for the City's international 'pull' – and Docklands transport connections as still inadequate. There was some consciousness, however, that these arguments became less powerful as more potential contacts moved to Docklands (or from the West End to Paddington

Basin), out of easy lunching reach. Self-confidence was high among our interviewees, and the level of perceived constraints low (in the 1999 LES), though the growth record of the 1990s has to be set against sharp job losses in the last 'bust' phase, and some more are now in prospect. The one more serious issue mentioned by interviewees was that of the City's potential as a terrorist target (following the Bishopsgate bombing in 1993), seen by one respondent as 'a big thing from our point of view', in contrast to May Day riots or street crime. Recruitment was not seen as a problematic issue, since the business/social environment and City salaries give them extensive choice in the London, national and international labour markets. For an area with a high degree of collective consciousness and an ethic of co-operation, local business organizations (and the Corporation of London) were seen as remarkably unimportant. But the counterpart to this was a high degree of involvement with national business organizations – which just happened to be dominated by City members. The exception was the effort by City-based insurers to create a united image of London insurance around reformed London Market Principles, to counter external perceptions of inefficiency (LIBC, 2000).

## Southwark (Bankside and Bermondsey)

The recent attractions of this area for business have stemmed largely from the fact that it is within walking distance of the City, but has had very much lower rent levels, reflecting its position on the 'wrong side' of the river. For older firms in the area, in activities such as printing, proximity mattered primarily in terms of contact with and actual deliveries to clients. For the newer business service activities, many of whom have less localized markets, it is primarily in terms of networking. (One French firm actually highlighted the value of access to Paris via Eurostar, rather than to the City.) For years, during which the area was blighted by redevelopment plans, rents fell even lower, but this ended with gentrification and the development of Bankside as a cultural service/tourist area (focused on the Globe Theatre and Tate Modern). One of the features of the area continues to be the close juxtaposition of residential and productive activities. But with some of the older, noisier activities this has become an increasing source of friction with the new middle-class residents, adding to pressure for change in the economic base. An above average proportion of businesses report growth prospects as being constrained by operating in too narrow a market. Older activities may mostly go, though as a small local businessman put it:

> The poor businesses were not pushed out; the poor businesses sold out when profit margins were at their strongest . . . took the money and ran like hell.

A distinctive element in this 'City fringe' area has been the growth of live-and-work developments. For various reasons – including the mixed character of development – local recruitment seems to be more significant than elsewhere for new businesses as well as old, partly it seems as a way of managing potential tensions with residents. For office activities, however, attraction of commuters through London Bridge station was a very important asset. Judgements about local labour were mixed, although few of the criticisms, such as those about difficulties in recruiting into craft jobs, actually seemed area-specific, and there were positive comments about willingness to work and enthusiasm to learn from firms offering training opportunities. Partly because of the level of regeneration activity in the area, more businesses than elsewhere had some involvement in partnerships of various kinds. One old established business maintained a very high level of engagement with all sorts of public activity (including Masonry and the Chamber of Commerce) for a combination of social and business generating reasons. Comments about the local authority were generally rather neutral, apart from frustrations over particular issues such as failure to be offered contracts.

## Newham (Stratford)

Though it has been a more significant economic centre (and now has one of the oldest sets of businesses in London), Stratford now has a rather weak economic base, reflected in substantial reliance both on local markets and on public sector employment. However, there are some significant non-local business service functions and expectations of more substantial office growth (although nearer parts of the City fringe are competing for this). The level of reported constraints here was close to that in Ilford, with a particular emphasis on local transport problems, employee resistance to change, and health/safety legislation (though there was the least concern over management quality). Our Newham interviewees were generally unable to think of advantages of their location, beyond the fact noted by one that it was 'convenient' and cheap, and its relative proximity to City business contacts noted by another. Virtually all were critical of the poor quality of the environment (conveying a bad image both to clients and potential recruits) and of locally recruitable labour. Inertia seemed to be the major factor keeping businesses there, though one firm, which would prefer to be in Milton Keynes, felt constrained to stay in London because its provincial clients expected to come up and be entertained. For businesses with little commercial reason to stay, environment seemed to be an important consideration. One firm was spinning off its IT operations to a West Country site largely because the Director was moving for personal reasons; another considering a shorter move (to Redbridge) said that he 'might as well be somewhere pleasant . . . where perhaps there is more of a community'. Another firm which felt tied to the area because of its specialized manual labour force was now facing compulsory purchase for redevelopment, and feared that without financial help for a move it would have to close and sell on its respected brand name.

In the LES, firms reported substantially more problems with recruitment and high turnover than in other areas, and one of the highest skills gaps among existing workers. Interviewees expressed slightly more mixed views, with some firms recognizing a traditional strength of character in East End workers which was now being lost, while others could only see the difficulty of recruiting reliable workers with adequate numeracy and literacy to cope with (for example) the safety requirement of manual jobs. There was a similarly negative array of comments about local agencies, ranging between complaints about poor communication, failure to deal with transport and environmental problems, irrelevance to the needs of business, and over-emphasis on potential inward investors rather than support for established businesses. One respondent at least conceded that gentrification and major transport investment in Stratford would bring economic improvements, but more for consumer service activities than other elements of the existing economic base.

### Redbridge (Ilford)

The borough as a whole is primarily residential, housing many commuters to Inner London. As such it has a rather thin economic base, signalled by the fact that half of employment is serving a local market. Ilford, the employment area on which we focused, has fulfilled a more sub-regional role as a retail and service centre, with a little bit of manufacturing and a few specialist services. But the nature of its role is conveyed in the fact that retailing and public administration are its leading activities. Firms here reported a very high level of constraint on their growth prospects due to operating in too narrow a market. As in the local centre at Gants Hill, while there were recognized advantages in terms of transport links, there were also concerns about roads, traffic and environmental quality, with a perception that the area had gone downhill both socially and physically. Amongst firms serving the sub-regional market these were linked to worries about competition, not only from the new regional shopping centres at Lakeside and Bluewater, but also from an upgrading of Stratford. Current proposals to respond to these challenges include a long-term scheme to develop a distinctive image as a Cosmopolitan Centre, including a purpose-built Asian Shopping Centre – though currently ethnic minority business in the borough is on a very small scale. Two business service firms among our interviewees highlighted different reactions to the current local situation. One, a law firm, targeted the local market through adoption of low fee rates, but was worried about provincial competition from firms with a lower cost base. The second, in financial services, had more upmarket ambitions, but was proposing to move to the City primarily in pursuit of a better image – 'solid, robust and all that' – but also to recruit more ambitious staff.

### Greenwich (Charlton)

The Greenwich economy shares the apparent weakness of the other two east London areas in terms of its lack of orientation to national/international markets, but has a much stronger regional role. A number of our Greenwich interviewees had previously moved out from areas of inner east London, and some were now contemplating moves further out. These included one freight forwarder considering Dartford as a site offering less congested road access. For other local firms an important attraction was the combination of affordable space with speedy access to central London customers. One paper distributor noted that increasing emphasis on JIT in printing was giving them a competitive advantage over rivals who had moved warehouses out to cheaper Midland locations. The JIT factor also underlay expected inward investment by companies storing documents for City firms. For a few the Millennium Dome had provided a more short-term locational advantage. The principal disadvantages were seen in terms of transport, particularly the need for another Thames crossing, though it was recognized that new underground links had improved the area's connectedness. Despite an actual shrinkage of employment in the 1990s, reported recruitment difficulties were on a par with those in Hounslow, while the perceived skills gap among existing workers was matched only in Stratford. Interviewees' opinions about the local labour market varied, however, according to their particular needs: for some, its relative slackness was an advantage, with local availability of packing skills as one particular asset; others were vociferous about the shortcomings of local workers, particularly in terms of poor attitude, which was ascribed to high levels of deprivation in some local estates. As elsewhere views about the effectiveness of local economic agencies (including Chambers) were rather sceptical, and there was criticism of fragmentation in public sector business service provision. Small business also seemed to feel discriminated against. But there were also complimentary remarks about local authority efficiency, understanding and help in developing training from the local Training and Enterprise Council.

## Dartford (Thames-side)

In discussing reasons for being in Dartford, local firms tended to emphasize a combination of historic considerations and classic location factors. For many the key was proximity to the motorway network, the Channel ports and/or the Channel Tunnel. This was particularly so for goods transport, but the motorways were also seen to extend the hinterlands for retail custom (at Bluewater) and commuting. The town's position at the edge of London was another positive factor in terms of easier property rents and availability. It also allowed access to exurban labour pools, which were seen as better for some office functions. However, one firm was planning to move further out for the same reasons. Access to the region's customer base was clearly important for many activities, but there was little sense that proximity to London provided other advantages – beyond its interest for overseas clients and appeal for skilled professionals reluctant to live in more remote locations. More generally the region was felt (particularly by one firm which had moved all its production to the North) to have major advantages as a source of sales, marketing and similar skills. Culturally, a number of the freight operators in particular gave the impression that the area was rather rough and ready – with a need to keep tight control to avoid internal crime – though perhaps less so than in areas further in. Sensitivity to crime risks seemed rather industry specific, however, and one business mentioned the rapid international connections as adding to the risks of cargo and vehicle theft. In the transport industry at least there were indications of rather tight local networks of contractors, with local knowledge and favours being crucial to maintaining connections. The competitiveness of local haulage firms here was recognized by one of our Greenwich interviewees as an attraction of the area. Public agencies were rarely seen as a significant local feature, with limited capacity to deal with firms' problems in tight labour and property markets. By comparison with town centre sites, a major advantage of Bluewater was seen as its private management, removing the need to deal with local government in getting problems resolved.

## Social Influences on Business Performance

A central question for this book is the degree to which social characteristics of the region, and of localities within it, affect competitive performance, in the context of a literature which has increasingly emphasized 'soft' location factors. This view is also underwritten by business magazines' global league tables of the 'best cities to do business in', which presumably contribute to their images among inward investors. However, as we saw earlier in the chapter, direct questioning of businesses tends to provide only weak evidence for their role. Two possible reasons for this are: that businesses may take their current environment for granted unless they actively have to consider a move; and that social aspects of this environment only impact on them indirectly through mediating processes affecting factors of more direct relevance to business. So, we shall start off here by reviewing some of the more direct influences on competitiveness which may be affected by one of the aspects of social cohesion in an area – leaving it to later chapters to identify how and how far local social factors actually affect them.

From this perspective, there seem to be four main, tangible routes through which the social or natural environment might exert a significant influence on business competitiveness:

- the availability of relevant types of *'skilled'* (and co-operative) *labour*, both:
  - mobile labour attracted to, and retained in, the area; and
  - locally trained and recruited labour of less mobile kinds;

- the level of *entrepreneurship*, reflected in the generation and survival of new businesses, both from the population at large, and from minority communities who may have new and distinctive products and skills to offer;

- the existence of *supportive networks and institutions* facilitating co-operative developments and ventures between local businesses and/or other local institutions;

- freedom from *significant threats* to business operation and viability as a result of crime, civil disorder or the expectation of these.

### Labour Supply

The current pressure of demand for labour in the region is very tight, especially in the outer west where unemployment is extremely low. As in the 1980s boom, the region's ability to attract labour from elsewhere in the UK has been constrained by an inelastic land and housing supply, leading to a widening house price gap between the London region and elsewhere. Unsurprisingly, there are frequent reports from firms of recruitment difficulties and/or problems in retaining workers, particularly skilled ones, both in the public sector and in some multi-plant companies with rigid pay policies. In London a new 'Keep London Working' partnership is pursuing non-market provision of key worker housing for groups such as teachers, nurses and bus drivers, with encouragement from an Assembly report on the issue (Greater London Assembly, 2001).

These are cyclical problems, equally evident in the last boom, but there could also be more structural difficulties in meeting employers' needs, linked to social cohesion issues. One issue is about the attraction and retention of talent, which Florida (2002) has emphasized as key to competitive success for US cities, and how this is influenced by their perceptions of the quality of life. A second issue is about the adequacy of the local supply of workers with required skills and other qualities, for those jobs filled within the more local labour market. Both issues will be considered further, in relation to the educational system and the dynamics of the regional labour market (Chapters 5 and 6 respectively). Here, it is appropriate to ask whether employers see them as significant.

In relation to the first issue, our business interviews suggested that there was no general problem in attracting and retaining highly skilled workers, and certainly not one related to negative perceptions of the social environment in residential areas. In Reading/Wokingham private employers were having some difficulties in meeting a rapidly expanding demand for high-level IT-related skills, but the issue was simply one of widening house price differentials relative to competing regions The only other locality in which such problems were reported was Stratford, where the problem was one of competition for business service professionals against (nearby) City jobs seen as offering greater challenges and prospects of rapid advancement. Although the City is an extreme case, these attractions, together with a positive evaluation of London's social life – including its openness, an influence highlighted by Florida (2002) – substantially explain why talented people are attracted to jobs in dynamic parts of the region, despite the attendant stresses.

For more routine, locally recruited positions, the picture is different. Whether in sales, production, or servicing, a common set of concerns were reported about labour quality, in relation to basic and/or 'soft skills' rather than formal qualification or specific training. In East London, particularly, these included complaints about levels of literacy, numeracy and communicative skills, while in the Thames Valley the emphasis was on securing the social and presentational skills required to sell services and/or maintain good relations with customers and collaborators. Across the case study areas, there were worries about job-seekers' capacity for teamwork and self-motivation. More quantitative survey evidence from the LES similarly suggests that employers find substantial 'skill deficiencies' across a range of rather routine jobs (including large numbers of clerical and sales jobs). Some judgements may reflect unrealistic expectations, while others reflect boom conditions; Greenwich interviewees, speaking from an area with more employment slack, were more positive. But, however good or bad London's human capital resources, this appears to be one area with substantial scope to improve the city's competitiveness.

### Entrepreneurship

Because modern London is not a particularly small-firm economy (with a slight bias in employment towards big establishments, especially in the centre), the proportion of residents involved in running significant businesses is fairly average, ahead of the North but below the rural South. It does, however, have very high rates both of business formation and business closure (above those in any other region). Through the 1980s/90s the annual VAT registration rate for businesses averaged 14.8 per cent of the stock compared with 12.6 per cent nationally, while the corresponding deregistration rates were 12.8 per cent and 11.4 per cent. This sort of dynamism was most evident within Inner London and least in the OMA, only being approached elsewhere by the North West and West Midlands (which also include major conurbations). The high deregistration rate may be a mark of competitive pressure, but primarily reflects the fact that new businesses always have high failure rates. In terms of the ratio of registrations to deregistrations, survival prospects actually seem significantly better in the London region – as in the adjoining Outer South East area – giving it the highest rate of net business formation. Overall the pattern seems to be one in which entrepreneurship is strongly associated with urban agglomeration, while survival rates are highest in core southern regions. The London region then enjoys the double benefit of agglomeration and southern location.

Another, more qualitative indicator of entrepreneurial success, rather than of the flow of small business start-ups, is provided by the Fast Track's league table of the country's fastest growing unquoted companies (*Sunday Times*, 9 December 2001). Of the top 100, 48 appear to be based in the London region as we define it: 33 in Greater London, and 15 in the OMA, compared with expectations of 15 and 12 respectively given the areas' shares of all businesses. Within the region two more particular concentrations are in central London and the western side of the OMA (each with 12 firms in the top 100), while there are conspicuously few on the eastern side of the OMA.

This picture is consistent with other indicators of relative dynamism, and the role of agglomeration economies, but tells us nothing directly about the social bases of entrepreneurship and how these may vary between areas. One case where social variables have been thought to be significant is that of immigrant groups (and their descendants) with particularly strong communal networks – for example the South Asian and Chinese communities in London, which are known to have higher rates of self-employment. It is not clear, however, to what degree this self-employment reflects particular resources of entrepreneurship which can be combined with the distinctive skills, energies and connections of immigrant groups, rather than a defensive response to discrimination in the open labour market.

Clearly there are success stories, but the general picture presented by responses to the 1999 LES is that a preponderance of businesses run by members of non-white groups are very small enterprises, oriented to limited local markets and facing particular problems in growing. This is particularly true of those groups (blacks, Pakistanis and Bangladeshis) in the weakest position in the general labour market. But even for Indians and Chinese, who are more successful, employment in minority-owned businesses (totalling 10 per cent for all non-white groups) is clearly below their share in the population. Managers seemed generally optimistic about growth prospects, but reported particular constraints both in relation to finance and the competitiveness of their products (reflecting low rates of product innovation in the case of black and Pakistani/Bangladeshi businesses). Orientation to the national market is generally weak, and though there are some significant examples of businesses serving overseas markets (notably South Asian-owned hotels), the main bias is still toward direct sales functions in local or London-wide markets. The one significant advantage evident in the survey was that Asian-owned businesses were less likely to perceive skill shortages as a constraint, perhaps because they have access to under-employed skills from within their own communities. Business success could offer much to these communities, but this will require stronger connections to the external market, and at present intra-communal networks are inadequate as a means of overcoming constraints.

## Local Networks

Networking – building and using relatively informal channels of communication as an aid to recruiting customers or sub-contractors, developing collaborative relationships, and extending market or technical information – is clearly important for small and medium-sized firms in particular, and could be especially valuable in times of rapid change. Many firms we interviewed recognized this; others took it for granted. But we found big differences both in the degree to which firms saw networks as central to competitive advantage, and in the importance they accorded to local networks. The 1996 LES showed that the great majority of London businesses saw no significant advantage in being close to related businesses, save for City-based financial services who valued access to market intelligence, and West End-based consumer services whose concentration brought customers. Some mentioned the advantages, and others the disadvantages, of local labour-pooling and proximity to competitors. A mere 5 per cent – rising to about 12 per cent in financial and cultural services – saw potential for active networking. Smaller firms were no more interested than bigger ones; they seemed to distinguish themselves only by their belief that speed of response (rather than quality or design) was critical to success. Though many London firms had built up significant relations with customers and/or suppliers, location did not play much role. And, though London firms were rather more likely to form joint ventures with other London firms than with those elsewhere, 70 per cent of partners were outside London, and these were just as likely to stimulate significant innovation as London partnerships (Gordon and McCann, 2000*a* and *b*).

In Chapter 8 we shall discuss further what efforts firms made to develop forms of local social capital. But for the great majority of businesses in all areas, including the most innovative and internationally oriented sectors, the key opportunity London offers is not for building enduring strategic relations with local firms, but the opportunity to exploit a much greater variety of linkages (and connections to external partners), as and when required. With very few exceptions – one establishment which had just transferred to the City, and freight forwarders reliant on local transport contractors – our interviewees told us that local networks played at best a supportive role, mainly as a source of clients for those supplying local markets. Even in the high-tech Thames Valley 'cluster', respondents pointed to regional (or international) linkages and synergies as critical, rather than local ones; the nearby area served primarily as a specialized labour pool. This, of course, is quite at variance with much of the academic theory with which this chapter opened.

### Crime and Other Threats

Many businesses we interviewed had been victims of some form of crime, most commonly theft of computers/chips and cargo in transit, or damage to vehicles, while in a number of areas staff were reported fearful in returning home through isolated or decaying areas – or unwilling to be sent to some other 'inner city' areas. Without exception, however, firms reported these risks either to have been brought under control by appropriate security measures on the site, or to be marginal. Inter-area comparisons suggest more variability in the types of criminal risk than in the overall level of risk. Thus high-tech firms in the affluent Thames Valley area seem to have experienced some of the highest value losses, through targeted thefts of computing equipment; distributors in Thames Gateway have also faced highly professional thefts of cargo (sometimes for export), and the risk of involvement in illegal immigration. Here, as in Southwark, victims were inclined to link the hazards to local culture. In no area, however, did our interviewees suggest either that the costs seriously affected their viability/growth potential or that it would induce them to locate elsewhere.[6] This is supported by survey evidence (from the 1996 and 1999 LES): very few firms – 1 per cent in Wandsworth, zero in Kingston and Merton – saw high crime rates as significant; and it failed to appear on a list of twenty-four reasons cited by businesses across London for potential relocation. The clear implication seems to be that crime does not significantly affect the ability of London business to compete successfully. More speculatively, it seems that if crime or other disorder were to impact, it would more likely do so via perceived personal risks outside the immediate business environment, affecting the willingness of key personnel to live in the city, rather than through direct threats to profitability.

## Conclusion: Is London Competitive?

In this chapter we have tried to get behind simple generalizations about the competitiveness of the London economy, its size and variety, its global city status, its post-industrial character, and its remarkable growth during the greater part of the 1990s – and the less simple suggestion that all of these are characteristics of the new flexible internationalized economy.

We have found it by no means easy to arrive at simple criteria for assessing how competitive London is, or is becoming. But on three partial criteria – growth, productivity and export performance – we found evidence that London has performed well relative at least to other parts of the UK, and that its performance has significantly improved over some portions of the last two decades. In part it has clearly done this by attracting and mobilizing high-level human capital, from across the UK, as well as locally-grown talent. By the standards of major European cities, however, London's performance is only average.

Though some boosts to London's growth have come from seemingly unrelated sources (notably from new flows of international migrants, which we discuss in the next chapter), there is clearly some connection between the city's current affluence, productivity and dynamism and the great liberalization of markets that occurred in the 1980s – as well as some connection with internationalization. But there is a question about market liberalization and its effect in boosting income productivity: how far does this change reflect real increases in productivity, achieved in more competitive *product markets*, or how far does it merely signify a redistribution of purchasing power to the region, through greatly widened earnings differentials in deregulated, winner-takes-all *labour markets*?

In relation to the second process, we have amassed much evidence that this is a very international economy, in terms of exports, ownership, capital flows, communications and labour migration. But it is too simplistic – and a great exaggeration – to see it as primarily an international city, particularly if that implies that its economy is (and has to be) driven by an identifiable core of truly 'global' activities (notably in City financial services). This is one of the London economies, but not the only one, nor is it necessarily the dominant source of growth. Periods of the recent past do seem to have been dominated by the impact of swings in this sector and associated speculative activities, but over the medium term the much larger nationally-oriented segments of the service base seem to have grown as fast. The combined effect of recent changes – including internationalization, the financial market deregulation which has accompanied it, and the shift to a post-industrial economy – has been to make the London economy substantially less stable. A side-effect is to make it much harder to establish how far underlying employment trends have shifted for the better.

Spatial as well as sectoral diversity has been a theme of this chapter, both in terms of the substantial differences in economic performance evident between east and west, and the existence of poles or sub-regions of substantial strength away from the traditional CBD (notably in the Western Crescent and the 'western wedge' within London) which are quite as integral to the way the modern city operates. Differentials in growth between the core and faster growing periphery (inside and outside the metropolitan region) have narrowed within the past 20 years. But those between an economically strong west and a less competitive east persist, and may have increased during this period.

A second aim of the chapter has been to start the process of linking (or rather searching for causal links between) competitiveness and cohesion. Six or seven plausible routes have been identified, though some – such as vulnerability to crime and insecurity – appear less significant than those that come through education (or perhaps area image). We have also found almost no confirmation for the social network model of clustering, based on cohesion among businesses, in London. The real strength of the London agglomeration effect, now as in the past, seems to consist in the more random possibilities for connections and stimuli made possible by its sheer scale and diversity. The competitiveness of the London economy is rooted in its complexity as well as its strong international connections, and its ability to attract and sustain a pool of advanced skills in the city. Recognizing this complexity should be fundamental to strategies to promote the city's competitiveness, but there are strong temptations to simplify the issues by identifying a single set of activities and markets as crucial to success.

## NOTES

1. These estimates relate ONS workplace-based local GDP estimates to LFS workplace employment data for Greater London as a whole, and residence-based data for other areas adjusted to a workplace basis, using 1991 Census ratios.

2. Estimates of earnings change in the OMA are based on data for the four counties (Berkshire, Essex, Hertfordshire and Surrey) wholly or preponderantly included in the OMA, together including three-quarters of its workforce.

3. This interpretation of the reasons for widening differentials in the UK is preferred to ones based on technological change on the grounds that actual changes were concentrated in the Thatcher years of labour market liberalization, and that among major industrial countries only the UK and (to a lesser extent) the US experienced sharp increases in differentials.

4. These come from the SEEDA's South East Competitiveness Survey (2000) and simply record numbers of establishments by banded values of export propensities, disaggregated (separately) by sub-region, sector and size.

5. These data are not available for Reading or Dartford.

6. The closest exception was the report that another (Brixton-based) branch of a financial services firm had been closed due to repeated robberies.

Chapter 4

# More Opportunity, More Inequality: Social Structure and Economic Change in London

For who would leave unbrib'd, Hibernia's land,
Or change the rocks of Scotland for the Strand?
There none are swept by sudden fate away,
But all whom hunger spares, with age decay:
Here malice, rapine, accident, conspire,
And now a rabble rages, now a fire;
Their ambush here relentless ruffians lay,
And here the fell attorney prowls for prey;

Samuel Johnson, *London: A Poem in Imitation of the Third Satire of Juvenal*

Is it nice to win 20 grand? Definitely – but after spending time in this city, I can tell you it won't last very long.

Madonna, *Presenting the Turner Prize, London, 10 December 2001*

The interactions between social structure and spatial structure are extremely complex. A core theme of this book is to explore the relationship between economic competitiveness or economic performance on the one hand and social cohesion and social exclusion on the other. One view of such a link is to see the social structure as being a simple product of economic structure. So London, with concentrations of higher level control functions, will contain high proportions of employers, managers and professional workers, and similarly the share of other occupational groups may be 'read-off' from other aspects of the industrial structure. In this view, shifts in the industrial structure, or the pattern of labour demand, will lead via various adjustment processes to shifts in the social structure. Economic change drives social (and spatial) change.

One popular version of this economically determinist hypothesis is the view that new processes of globalization in the world economy are leading to increasing inequalities, even a polarization, in the social structures of cities. In fact we can distinguish two variants of this view. The first focuses on occupational processes in cities at the top of the urban hierarchy, and with the most international orientation, leading to growth at the top and bottom of the occupational hierarchy at the expense of the middle. This would follow from the growth of central functions in finance and business services, and the routine service industries which support them, at the expense of goods production industries. The second focuses on wage effects, resulting either from changed patterns of trade or changes in technology, which, it is argued, increase sharply overall earnings inequality. This latter is not specifically urban in its focus, but it might be expected to have particular effects in large cities. We discuss this view of social change in London below.

A less determinist view focuses on incomplete or lagged adjustment between industrial change and social change. Here the processes involved include migration, both domestic and international, changes in commuting patterns, occupational change and career mobility, movements in and out of unemployment and in and out of the labour market, acquisition of human capital through education and training. If some of these processes work more efficiently than others, industrial change might lead to increasing unemployment. In this chapter we discuss the operation of some of these processes, though the discussion of their impacts on London's unemployment is reserved for Chapter 6.

Two other positions are possible, however, which give greater weight, or even primacy, to *social* change, as a driver of economic change. Here the starting point is microeconomic – rational decisions by individuals or households – rather than macroeconomic – the overall pattern of structural economic change. Most migration follows from households attempting to improve their housing, or because of changes in their family circumstances, rather than to find better jobs. Even in the case of long-distance movement, which typically responds to labour market signals, other factors such as education, consumption and lifestyle choice and refugee movements play a particularly significant role for London. Education and training are likely to be acquired with a view to long-term opportunities, rather than in response to short-term changes, in the labour market, insofar as labour market opportunities are taken into account at all. Even most moves into unemployment will be a consequence of turbulence in individual firms, or difficulties in the match between workers and firms, rather than trend change in an industry. The cumulative impact of all these processes on how the social structure of individual places and of the London region as a whole are shaped is rather indeterminate. Given that these processes are themselves partly independent of labour market change, this gives the social structure a degree of autonomy. In addition, other institutions and market processes will exert an independent influence – the housing market, the education system and, not least, the built form of London.

Finally, there is a stronger version of the 'primacy of the social' in which changes in social/occupational structure drive changes in the economic structure. The argument is that cities which have the right kind of labour supply in terms either of occupational categories or, more broadly, in terms of human capital, will be more 'competitive', both in terms of their ability to attract new investment, and in their capacity to generate new businesses and endogenous growth. Thus there are reasons for thinking that social structure and the processes through which it changes may have influences on economic competitiveness.

However describing the social structure is problematic. Even if we focus on a single dimension, such as socio-economic status or class, categorization is highly contested. We have already referred in Chapter 1 to the contrast between dualistic views of society implied by some approaches to social exclusion and more structured views of social class or social position. We return to this in Chapter 7.

Moreover, we need to recognize that the social structure cannot be entirely described in terms of labour market situation and social class. The division into households of different types itself has consequences for inequality, related in part to gender inequalities, and also perhaps to age inequalities. It also has consequences for the pattern of social relations. In the London region there are major variations in the ethnic composition of areas, and to the extent that different ethnic groups face very different social and economic opportunities, this also contributes to the overall pattern of inequality. There may be further bases for social divisions including, for example, health and disability.

There are important spatial aspects to this too. First the interaction between social structure and labour demand raises policy issues – for example, whether new needs for high-skilled labour can be accommodated by the development of brownfield sites. More generally, changes in occupational structure may have particularly marked consequences for social composition in particular parts of the region. Secondly, in order to understand the dynamics and functioning of neighbourhoods we need to understand local social structures, including social class composition, household structure, and ethnic mix. Thirdly, there are questions at the London region level about whether patterns of social or ethnic segregation are becoming more intense, which might serve to compound the patterns of inequality at the individual level. The spatial pattern of deprivation is left to Chapter 7, where it is discussed in the context of social exclusion.

We now turn to social structural processes at the broadest spatial scale, dividing the London region into Inner London, Outer London and the Outer Metropolitan Area (or the Rest of the South East), discussing population change and its major components, especially migration, including international migration. From here we consider the demographic consequences of these processes, especially for household structure, and for the ethnic composition of the population. We then look at aspects of social structure associated with the labour market, including occupational class structure, patterns of inequality of rewards, and variations in unemployment and labour market participation. We move on to the housing market and commuting patterns. In the remainder of the chapter we examine some of these dimensions at finer spatial scales, and especially patterns of segregation and changes in social structures at the neighbourhood level. And in the final section we set out our conclusions.

## Population Change and Its Consequences

Throughout the last century, the South East region has been the most dynamic part of the British economy, although for the last quarter of the century growth rates in population and employment have fallen behind those in the less developed adjoining regions, namely the South West, East Anglia and the East Midlands. In recent decades the region and London in particular has attracted a disproportionate share of net immigration into the UK from overseas. In population terms, above average growth in the South East (or more recently the Greater South East) has clearly also been due to net migration attracted from other parts of the UK, although London itself has lost population to other parts of the region throughout the post-war period.

Within the region the pattern of movement has varied greatly between different lifecycle stages. For British migrants, as well as those from overseas, (Inner) London has long had a particular attraction for young, single people, drawn to the city by a combination of employment and social opportunities. At the later stages of family formation, however, the search by those with the necessary resources for larger but affordable owner-occupied dwellings, coupled with more staid tastes about suitable areas in which to live and bring up children, has tended to mean outward movement. This may be just into the Outer London suburbs, or right out of Greater London, into the commuter belt, which now extends beyond the boundary of the South East region. At least until recently, these moves produced a continuous gradation from high rates of population loss in the inner areas through to substantial gains at the edge of the region. As with other types of housing and labour market adjustments, however, this overall pattern was much less the result of long distance moves from the centre than the cumulative (rippling) effect of many shorter distance moves responding to quite local variations in the distribution of opportunities.

It is important to draw a distinction between the reasons why individuals at particular lifecycle stages are moving outwards, and the causes of overall population decentralization. On its own, the lifecycle pattern of movement would simply produce differences in population mix and household structure between inner and outer areas. Aggregate population changes, on the other hand, depend on changes over time in residential preferences and the distribution of opportunities. In particular, rising income levels lead to increased demand for housing space which can only be met by a displacement of demand toward less developed areas. For a given population mix this would lead to falling population densities within London, though this tendency could be countered if there was substantial immigration into the city of groups with a weaker demand for residential space, for economic and/or cultural reasons. Population decentralization tends to lead to increased employment decentralization, both indirectly through increased demand for private and public services in these growing residential areas, and directly through firm decentralization in pursuit of available skilled labour.

The outcome of these forces was a more or less continuous decline in Greater London's population from a peak level of 8.6 million recorded in 1939 until the mid-1980s, when growth resumed from a low figure of 6.7 million. For Inner London the period of decline was longer, its peak population being in 1911. Rates of population loss were substantially faster in Inner London through the 1970s.

From around the beginning of the 1980s there was a significant change in trend. Between 1981 and 2000, Greater London's population grew by 569,000 or

8.4 per cent, to reach nearly 7.4 million. Most of this growth, 485,000, has occurred since 1991. Over the 1990s, growth in London and especially Inner London has been more rapid than in the OMA. The growth in Inner London did not simply occur because of the major injection of housing into the former Docklands area. Indeed during the 1990s only two boroughs, both in the outermost east, have experienced reductions in population levels. Particularly rapid growth has been experienced in a line of boroughs running south-west from the City to Richmond (London Research Centre, Government Office for London and Office of National Statistics, 2000). Population growth of all parts of the region has been more rapid than in the UK as a whole, where it averaged 0.4 per cent per annum.

The net change in the 1990s, as shown in Table 4.1, is the outcome of both natural increase and net migration. Natural increase has been relatively strong, especially in Inner London reflecting a relatively young population. Total migration again shows significant gains in all parts of the region. However this disguises significant variations by migration origin and destination and also substantial changes over time. Greater London, and to a lesser degree the London region, tends to experience net population losses through migration within the UK. London however gains substantially through net immigration from abroad.

Total population increase has depended on the last of these components, where London has absorbed about 55 per cent of the national inflow. Net gains from international migration were averaging around 30,000 per annum in the early part of the 1990s, to be set against a net loss of around 42,000 per annum through domestic migration. In the mid-1990s gains from international migration rose to around 65,000 per annum and by the end of the decade to over 100,000 per annum. Over the 1990s international migration flows are estimated to have added more than half a million to the population of London. It has clearly become a major node in global population flows.

However, it should be noted that even without such immigration, population levels in London would have more or less stabilized – a significant change from previous trends. As compared with the period of most rapid population loss, in the

**Table 4.1.** Components of population change: London region 1991–2000 (populations expressed in thousands).

|  | Inner London | Outer London | Greater London | OMA | London Region |
|---|---|---|---|---|---|
| Population 1991 | 2627.4 | 4262.6 | 6890.0 | 5542.9 | 12432.9 |
| Natural change | 179.9 | 179.2 | 359.1 | 176.1 | 535.2 |
| Net migration | 67.0 | 58.9 | 125.9 | 72.5 | 198.4 |
| Of which: Domestic migration and other changes International migration |  |  | -434.2 560.1 |  |  |
| Total change | 246.9 | 238.2 | 485.1 | 248.4 | 733.5 |
| % change per annum | 1.04 | 0.62 | 0.78 | 0.50 | 0.66 |

*Source:* Mid-year population estimates and international migration statistics.

decade from the mid-1960s, this reflects both a cut-back in the scale of net out-migration to other parts of southern England and a faster rate of natural increase. This is also against the national trend, as London birth rates have been held up by the indirect effects of earlier waves of immigration.

Some elements of international migration, notably the moves of highly skilled professionals from other advanced economies, can be linked quite directly to developments in the London economy. A key factor here has probably been the growth of foreign owned businesses in international traded sectors, especially in central London. Nationally there is evidence of pro-cyclical fluctuations in migration from both the EU and the 'Old' (White) Commonwealth, which may well account for an upturn since the early 1990s recession in the element of net migration to London as recorded by the International Passenger Survey count (which excludes both asylum seekers/visitor switchers, and exchanges with the Republic of Ireland).

The majority of net international migration during the 1990s has, however, clearly been in the asylum seeker and visitor switcher (i.e. those who arrive as visitors but later become classified as immigrants) categories. Sixty-six per cent of those in the first group arriving in the UK since 1991 are estimated to have come to London. In 1996–1997 these two categories accounted for 22,000 and 7,000 respectively of London's estimated 53,000 gains from net international migration (Hollis, 1999, London Research Centre, 1999). The level of these flows increased during the 1990s, but there is no evidence of a cyclical pattern, and it is reasonable to assume that push factors have been largely responsible for their growth since the early 1980s, rather than developments in the UK or London economies.

For internal UK flows, the balance of movements into and out of London reflects a combination of labour and housing market factors, with the relative strength of the South East economy, including London, a key factor. Typically, London has gained migrants from areas outside the Greater South East, but lost to other areas within. Shifts in the overall balance of moves between London and the rest of the UK are strongly influenced by fluctuations in differential house prices as between London and its hinterland (Gordon, 1996b).

The age profile of migrants to the city is skewed toward the younger working age groups, while out-migrants tend to be either slightly older, or else, in the case of moves within the UK, the dependent children of these out-movers. Net migrational gains are effectively confined to the 16–24 age range, both for domestic and international moves. For domestic moves there are clear losses in every other age group, while for international moves, in- and out-flows balance outside this age group. The youth of these migrants has implications both for employability and also for future fertility (hence the link between past immigration and current birth rates).

The pattern of population movement within the region has been selective in social as well as lifecycle terms. In particular, outward movement in the family stages of the lifecycle has increasingly become limited to those able to buy into owner-occupation. Suburban council estates and New Towns provided some support for outward movement by the skilled working class in the first three decades after the war. However, more recently, a substantial proportion of working-class Londoners dependent on public sector tenancies that were not readily transferable between areas, particularly in the inner boroughs, were excluded from such movement.

Unlike migration from other British conurbations, migration from London to the rest of the UK no longer comprises only more affluent, white-collar workers, but shows more differentiation within both manual and non-manual groups (Champion, 1999). In particular, London emerges as relatively more attractive to professional and technical workers than to managers, and less attractive to skilled manual workers than junior non-manual groups, or personal service workers. Much of London's special appeal as a destination for employment-motivated migrants seems to relate to the opportunities which it offers for human capital and career development on its 'escalator' (Fielding, 1991). Location within the region may be partly explained by differences in the extent to which career advancement in different occupational groups depends on internal organizational progression, or external interactions and mobility within a metropolitan economy, the latter leading to a stronger preference for a more central location. Alternatively, it may be a matter of tastes and lifestyle difference reflected in residential preferences between city and suburb.

Population flows also have direct consequences for the social structure. In the first place they reproduce a rather distinctive population in terms of age and household composition. Table 4.2 shows age structures and differences from the UK age structure for parts of the London region in 1979 and 2000, using the Labour Force Survey for an up-to-date estimate. While there have been demographic shifts affecting the whole country, parts of London have diverged from these in important ways. First, there are considerable differences between Inner and Outer London and the OMA. Inner London has tended to be the main destination for inter-regional flows into London, especially for younger people, while Outer London has also been a destination for outflows from Inner London. The OMA has tended to gain from outflows from both other parts of the region. Thus we expect to find a somewhat older population structure in Outer London than in Inner London. In practice, the 1979 figures do not precisely conform to this expectation. There is a small over-representation of young adults in Inner London (up to age 35), and a greater over-representation of older adults in Outer London. However, the main divergences are a substantial under-representation of children in Inner London, and a substantial over-representation of people over 65. The former is consistent with the tendency for people to move out in search of more space (and better schools) when they have children. The latter probably reflects the residual consequences of the substantial and socially selective outflows from London in the 1960s and 1970s. The less affluent older population were one group unlikely to be able to leave. The OMA age structure reflects its tendency to gain from the outflow of families with children from London. However in 1979, the region taken as a whole had an age structure relatively close to the national average, except for a shortfall in the number of children.

The change over the next 20 years is substantial. The over-representation of the elderly in both Inner and Outer London disappears, replaced by an even greater under-representation. By contrast the young adult age groups (aged 20 to 44) are now substantially over-represented in Inner London, and modestly over-represented in Outer London. Interestingly, while Outer London by this stage still has an older

**Table 4.2.** Age structure of parts of the London region.

| | | 1979 | | | | 2000 | | |
|---|---|---|---|---|---|---|---|---|
| | | Inner London | Outer London | OMA | London Region | Inner London | Outer London | OMA | London Region |
| 0–15 | % Share | 20.01 | 21.70 | 23.42 | 22.11 | 21.08 | 20.94 | 20.71 | 20.87 |
| | Diff UK | −3.41 | −1.73 | +0.00 | −1.31 | +0.50 | +0.36 | +0.13 | +0.29 |
| 16–19 | % Share | 6.40 | 6.06 | 6.47 | 6.30 | 4.82 | 4.82 | 5.00 | 4.90 |
| | Diff UK | +0.08 | −0.25 | +0.15 | −0.01 | −0.13 | −0.13 | +0.05 | −0.05 |
| 20–24 | % Share | 8.05 | 6.39 | 7.50 | 7.19 | 8.02 | 6.89 | 5.61 | 6.56 |
| | Diff UK | +0.87 | −0.79 | +0.32 | +0.01 | +2.10 | +0.97 | −0.31 | +0.64 |
| 25–34 | % Share | 14.60 | 13.92 | 15.08 | 14.55 | 18.66 | 16.04 | 15.62 | 16.41 |
| | Diff UK | +0.39 | −0.29 | +0.86 | +0.34 | +3.76 | +1.14 | +0.71 | +1.51 |
| 35–44 | % Share | 11.70 | 12.28 | 12.17 | 12.12 | 18.26 | 16.15 | 15.29 | 16.22 |
| | Diff UK | −0.06 | +0.53 | +0.41 | +0.36 | +3.17 | +1.07 | +0.21 | +1.13 |
| 45–54 | % Share | 11.57 | 11.95 | 11.59 | 11.72 | 10.81 | 12.69 | 13.82 | 12.79 |
| | Diff UK | +0.11 | +0.49 | +0.13 | +0.26 | −2.41 | −0.53 | +0.60 | −0.43 |
| 55–64 | % Share | 11.37 | 12.14 | 10.91 | 11.46 | 7.83 | 9.21 | 10.33 | 9.41 |
| | Diff UK | +0.17 | +0.95 | −0.28 | +0.27 | −2.49 | −1.11 | +0.01 | −0.91 |
| 65+ | % Share | 16.29 | 15.56 | 12.85 | 14.54 | 10.52 | 13.26 | 13.51 | 12.79 |
| | Diff UK | +1.84 | +1.11 | −1.59 | +0.09 | −4.50 | −1.77 | −1.52 | −2.24 |

*Source:* Labour Force Survey micro-data sets. The OMA and London Region estimates for 2000 are based on the assumption that the relative share of each age group in OMA and the Outer South East are the same as in 1979.

age profile than Inner London, it is younger than that for the country as a whole. Children are also by this stage slightly over-represented in both parts of London. This is less likely to represent any increased attractiveness of London for bringing up children than the age profile of the adult population, and perhaps especially the ethnic minority population with fewer opportunities to move outwards. The OMA age structure has changed rather less than the other parts of the region, but the combined impact of the changes is that the region as a whole had a relatively younger age structure than it did in 1979.

Younger people are not only more likely to be in London, but they are also less likely to live in traditional family households. When they do form such households they are then likely to move outwards. Table 4.3 shows the distribution of the population by the type of household in which they live. Some of the changes in the age structure are reflected here, such as the shrinkage of elderly households in London. However what is most striking is the strong and increasing concentration of non-standard household types in Inner London, as well as some tendency for their share to increase in Outer London.

We can divide households into types more associated with a traditional life course (i.e. couple households, with and without children, and single elderly households), and those which reflect non-traditional forms (i.e. single young people, lone parents, and other mixed households). In 1979, 13 per cent of the UK population lived in such non-traditional households, but 24 per cent of the Inner London population. Outer London was similar to the national average population, and in the OMA fewer people lived in such households (11 per cent). By 2000, the UK share had risen substantially, to 20 per cent, but Inner London's share had risen even more rapidly, to 39 per cent. Outer London was also diverging more from the UK pattern, with 23 per cent living in non-traditional households, while the OMA fell further behind national trends, with a share of 16 per cent. For the region as a whole the over-representation of these groups increased over the period.

This simple separation of household types somewhat understates the distinctiveness of London, since the above average share of younger couples without children reflects in part the preference to pursue careers and postpone child-bearing. It is also notable that the substantial over-representation of lone parents, at least in Inner London, means that by 2000, the combined share of households with children under 16 in Inner London is above the national average. However one-third are lone parent households, compared with under a fifth nationally. As we shall see later, this is important because household structure is an important factor mediating life chances, inequality and social exclusion. It is however worth noting that couple households with children were less under-represented in Inner London by 2000 than they were in 1979. This reflects in part the growth of family households in the ethnic minority communities.

## The Changing Ethnic Composition

The ethnic mix of the London population reflects several different waves of

**Table 4.3.** Household structures, 1979–2000.

| | | 1979 | | | | 2000 | | | |
|---|---|---|---|---|---|---|---|---|---|
| | | Inner London | Outer London | OMA | London Region | Inner London | Outer London | OMA | London Region |
| Single non-pensioner | % share | 9.40 | 4.02 | 2.97 | 4.61 | 11.79 | 6.35 | 4.92 | 6.87 |
| | Diff from UK | +6.03 | +0.65 | -0.40 | +1.24 | +6.06 | +0.62 | -0.81 | +1.14 |
| Single pensioner age | % share | 8.03 | 6.18 | 5.25 | 6.14 | 5.98 | 5.79 | 5.55 | 5.72 |
| | Diff from UK | +2.13 | +0.27 | -0.65 | +0.23 | -0.40 | -0.59 | -0.83 | -0.66 |
| Couple no children <45 | % share | 5.40 | 5.47 | 5.68 | 5.55 | 8.28 | 7.06 | 7.28 | 7.42 |
| | Diff from UK | +0.60 | +0.67 | +0.88 | +0.75 | +2.08 | +0.86 | +1.08 | +1.22 |
| Couple no children 45–64 | % share | 6.53 | 8.27 | 8.73 | 8.13 | 4.76 | 6.66 | 9.96 | 7.72 |
| | Diff from UK | -1.86 | -0.13 | +0.33 | -0.27 | -4.76 | -2.86 | +0.44 | -1.80 |
| Couple 65+ | % share | 6.73 | 7.97 | 6.74 | 7.20 | 3.99 | 6.61 | 7.93 | 6.64 |
| | Diff from UK | -0.59 | +0.65 | -0.58 | -0.12 | -4.48 | -1.87 | -0.54 | -1.84 |
| Couple with children <16 | % share | 37.95 | 44.97 | 49.37 | 45.50 | 31.11 | 39.10 | 39.88 | 37.74 |
| | Diff from UK | -10.67 | -3.64 | +0.75 | -3.11 | -6.37 | +1.62 | +2.40 | +0.27 |
| Couple with children >16 | % share | 11.01 | 13.86 | 13.13 | 12.99 | 6.62 | 11.53 | 12.45 | 10.89 |
| | Diff from UK | -1.02 | +1.83 | +1.10 | +0.96 | -4.82 | +0.09 | +1.01 | -0.54 |
| Lone Parent | % share | 7.44 | 4.09 | 3.92 | 4.67 | 15.48 | 9.21 | 6.01 | 9.13 |
| | Diff from UK | +2.86 | -0.49 | -0.67 | +0.08 | +6.86 | +0.59 | -2.62 | +0.50 |
| Other | % share | 7.51 | 5.17 | 4.22 | 5.21 | 11.98 | 7.70 | 5.42 | 7.60 |
| | Diff from UK | +2.53 | +0.19 | -0.76 | +0.24 | +5.83 | +1.54 | -0.73 | +1.44 |

*Source:* Labour Force Survey micro-data sets. The OMA and London Region estimates for 2000 are based on the assumption that the relative share of each household type in the OMA and the Outer South East are the same as in 1979.

immigration during the post-war period. The Afro-Caribbean population is the longest established of the minority groups, followed by the Indian and Pakistani communities. In the case of all three groups the majority of the current population is likely to have been born in London. The smaller Bangladeshi community is rather more recent in arrival, while the African community, now approaching the scale of the Afro-Caribbean group, is largely a product of immigration during the last two decades.

By 2000, 29 per cent of the Greater London population was estimated to come from non-white ethnic minorities, including 10 per cent each identified as black and South Asian, compared with just 7 per cent in the rest of the country. Whether immigrant or British-born, these groups face particular difficulties in access to good jobs in the London economy, though this is less true among the Indian community, many of whom arrived with more human capital. The latest waves of migrants also include many Central/Eastern Europeans whose prospects are uncertain. The consequences of this are explored in Chapters 6 and 7.

The size of the ethnic minority population in London and its spatial distribution has also been changing over the last two decades, as Table 4.4 shows. Both Inner and Outer London have experienced a substantial increase in their ethnic minority population (an 18 percentage point growth in Inner London and a 15 percentage point growth in Outer London). By contrast growth in the rest of the South East was very weak. There appears to be a widening gap between London and its hinterland. The ratio of the London non-white share to that in the rest of the South East was 4.33 to 1 in 1979, rising to 7.31 to 1 in 2000. This cannot be explained by increasing international migration alone, and must reflect in large part relatively low rates of outward movement within the region. There are a number of possible reasons for this low rate of ethnic minority decentralization, but no very clear basis for choosing between them. It could reflect the effects of relatively low incomes and large family sizes in restricting housing choices in the suburbs. It could reflect a (more or less well-founded) fear of racial harassment there.

Within London there do appear to be distinct areas of concentration for different ethnic groups. These are, of course, also evident at smaller spatial scales. There is also some evidence of decentralization within London. The black Caribbean group is mainly concentrated in Inner London, where it has been growing gradually (the black 'other' group, introduced during the 1990s is almost certainly mainly composed of British born people of Caribbean origin). This group is also increasing significantly in Outer London. The Indian origin population, the other group which settled relatively early has always been more likely to be found in Outer London, and this tendency is clearly increasing. The rather smaller Pakistani group has a basically similar trajectory. Taken together these three groups account for around a tenth of the growth in the share of the non-white population in Inner London, but nearly half of the growth in Outer London. It is the newer groups who account for the great majority of change in Inner London, and the remaining half in Outer London. Bangladeshis are almost entirely concentrated in Inner London, while the black African group is largely concentrated there. On the other hand the 'other' group is located in both, and accounts for the largest part of the non-white growth

**Table 4.4.** Percentage population distribution by ethnic group, 1979–2000.

|  | Inner London | | | Outer London | | | Rest of South East | | |
|---|---|---|---|---|---|---|---|---|---|
|  | 1979 | 1991 | 2000 | 1979 | 1991 | 2000 | 1979 | 1991 | 2000 |
| White | 82.8 | 73.9 | 64.5 | 91.1 | 83.8 | 75.8 | 97.3 | 96.9 | 96.1 |
| Black – Caribbean | 6.9 | 7.3 | 6.4 | 1.5 | 2.3 | 2.6 | 0.4 | 0.2 | 0.5 |
| Black – African | 2.3 | 3.8 | 7.1 | 0.6 | 0.9 | 2.5 | 0.2 | 0.0 | 0.2 |
| Black – other |  |  | 1.9 |  |  | 0.7 |  |  | 0.1 |
| Indian | 3.5 | 3.3 | 3.0 | 3.8 | 6.6 | 7.7 | 0.9 | 0.8 | 1.0 |
| Pakistani | 0.6 | 2.1 | 1.4 | 0.8 | 1.8 | 2.4 | 0.3 | 0.6 | 0.5 |
| Bangladeshi | 0.2 | 2.4 | 4.7 | 0.1 | 0.1 | 0.5 | 0.1 | 0.2 | 0.2 |
| Other | 3.6 | 7.3 | 11.0 | 2.2 | 4.4 | 7.8 | 0.8 | 1.2 | 1.3 |
| Total | 100.0 | 100.0 | 100.0 | 100.0 | 100.0 | 100.0 | 100.0 | 100.0 | 100.0 |

*Source:* Labour Force Survey micro-data sets.

in both. This group is extremely heterogeneous, containing a number of substantial minorities, including Chinese, other East Asian, Turkish, Arab and Iranian. Between a quarter and a third of this group are mixed race.

In contrast to earlier waves of immigration, most of the present asylum seekers come from outside the Commonwealth, and from a wide range of countries. Projections suggest that population growth in London up to 2011 will be accounted for entirely by growth in non-white ethnic groups amongst which black Africans are projected to increase in numbers most rapidly, although their share of the population would only rise by 2–3 per cent (London Research Centre, 1999).

One consequence of London's focal role in the current pattern of international migration flows is that it also concentrates those people who do not have full British citizenship. Once again it is important to stress that this group is extremely heterogeneous. It includes a range from both EU and other foreign citizens working in high status jobs in the financial and business services, to asylum seekers. Estimates from the Labour Force Survey suggest that 22 per cent of the Inner London population and 13 per cent of the Outer London population are not UK nationals. The figure for the rest of Great Britain is 2.5 per cent and for the rest of the South only 3.7 per cent.

The interaction of citizenship and ethnicity is complex. Firstly, only a narrow majority of the non-citizen population is non-white. Five hundred and forty-six thousand out of 1.1 million are white. Secondly, almost three-quarters of the non-white population are UK citizens, 1.44 million out of 2.03 million. UK Citizenship rates are particularly high amongst black Caribbean, black other, and to a lesser degree south Asian groups. They are low amongst black African and other groups.

Analysis by the year in which people came to the UK suggests some significant changes in the pattern of origins. White ethnic origins make up the largest share for each period of arrival, and are increasingly dominant in the late 1990s. This is in part because this group includes more people likely to stay short periods, who will necessarily figure more prominently in current population estimates of recent arrival cohorts – since their equivalents from earlier cohorts are more likely to have returned. However it also reflects the substantial refugee flows from Eastern Europe over this period. The traditional sources of New Commonwealth migration – India, Pakistan,

Bangladesh and the Caribbean – comprise a relatively small share of flows during the 1990s, but black Africans were a substantial component in the early 1990s, less so in the latter part of the decade. The 'other' group contributed around 20 per cent of movements throughout the decade.

The demographic shifts discussed in this section have suggested three key features of social change in London over the last two decades:

◆ a population turnaround for London, with a movement from long-term decline to some significant growth. This has been driven by a growth in international migration.

◆ the consolidation of London, and especially Inner London, as a centre for non-family or non-standard family types, and as a relatively young city.

◆ the acceleration of the trend towards London becoming a very heterogeneous multi-ethnic city. This was shared by both Inner and Outer London.

The area beyond London continued with its rather higher rate of population growth, and did not share in the other two trends. One important consequence of this was to increase the differences in social structure between London and its surrounding region.

## Occupation and Social Class: Is London a 'Global City'?

In this section, we look at how London is structured by class, income and occupation. There are at least two important recent attempts at theorizing the relationship of social structure to economic change that have particular relevance for large cities such as London. The first focuses particularly on global cities and their special features. It is associated most closely with the work of Sassen (1991). This work has been subject to considerable discussion and criticism, and this discussion is only summarized here very briefly (Hamnett 1994a, 1996). Sassen argues that global cities experience a polarization of their occupational structures, both because of a concentration of growing industries which themselves have a highly polarized occupational structure, and because the demands for consumer services from the high earners generate a stratum of low-wage service workers. This polarization is intensified by the global roles of these cities, since international capital flows lead to concentrations of finance and business service industries, and international labour flows are argued to increase the concentration of low-wage workers. However, as Hamnett (1994b) has shown, the evidence on occupational change in London actually suggests a professionalization of the labour market – that is a general upgrading of skills. Moreover, 'Global Cities' and other dualist accounts grossly over-simplify the class structure of large cities, and in particular neglect the experience of economic and social change of the large middle strata in these cities, as well as their important role in political change (Harloe and Fainstein, 1992).

A second, more general explanation focuses on long-term changes in the way goods and services are produced. Aspects of these changes might be variously labelled de-industrialization, post-industrialization, and the shift to the new service economy (Gershuny and Miles, 1983). Rapid rises in productivity in goods producing industries, slow growing productivity in services, and perhaps some shift in final consumption towards services have led to substantial occupational and industrial changes with, in particular, declining employment in goods producing sectors. Productivity changes have also had particularly negative effects on less skilled and more routine jobs. These changes have very uneven effects spatially. They lead potentially to substantial changes in the social structure of places. Some aspects of 'globalization' also influence these trends. There has been a lengthy debate as to the relative strength of trade and technology factors in increasing the wage differential between skilled and unskilled workers in advanced countries. But the key point for us is that whether one identifies changes in the pattern and scale of trade or technological change in the production of commodities as the driving force, both theories imply a stretching of wage differentials. Coupled with the spread of deregulatory government policies and weakened state intervention in labour markets, the implication is a growing polarization between groups of workers, not so much in terms of the numbers of workers in each group, but rather in terms of the growing distance between groups, whether measured by wages or by income more generally.

The last chapter documented changes in the industrial structure of London. Occupational change cannot simply be 'read-off' from the growth and decline of industries, since the occupational structure of individual industries themselves change. This may be because of differing rates of productivity change for different occupations, or deliberate organizational change. This can include, for example, contracting out of services which were previously produced within the organization. It is possible then that some large industrial changes (the growth of business services, for example) would lead to only modest occupational changes, if the pattern of real activity was essentially unchanged.

It may therefore be useful to separate occupational change from class and status issues. Esping-Andersen (1993) has proposed an occupational model based on two distinct hierarchies. Both are divided by skill level, but one contains jobs predominantly found in traditional goods processing and distribution industries, as well as larger bureaucracies, while the other contains those predominantly found in newer service and knowledge based industries. The model aims to illuminate the impact of two changes: a tendency towards the upgrading of skill levels, and shift between the industry groups. The first hierarchy, which Esping-Andersen labels Fordist occupations, comprises managers, clerical and sales workers, skilled manual workers, and unskilled manual workers. The second is labelled post-industrial occupations, comprising professional workers, semi-professional and technical workers, skilled service workers and unskilled service workers.

This occupational model is useful since it allows us to advance a number of hypotheses about the pattern of change in social structure, given de-industrialization, and a 'Global Cities' view. In fact Esping-Andersen himself suggests a number of alternative hypotheses about likely directions of change in the composition of the labour force on the basis of this structure, mainly from a post-industrial perspective. He suggests five likely directions of change:

1. A stagnation in the relative number of managers, and a sharp decline in unskilled manual workers with the decline in goods industries.

2. The growth of professional and semi-professional groups will depend on the vitality of business and social services, and hence in part on the strength of the welfare state.

3. The growth of the service proletariat will depend on two factors – the extent of growth of low-wage consumer services, and hence on the growth of private demand and perhaps on the flexibility of wages in these industries, and secondly, the scale of social service growth, and hence again the strength of the welfare state.

4. The growth of what Esping-Andersen labels the 'outsider surplus population' will be large under conditions of jobless growth, that is low welfare state growth and/or barriers to the creation of lower wage jobs.

5. Finally, compared to their 'Fordist' forebears, 'post-industrial societies will exhibit a considerably more positive occupational structure. But since they face a naked trade-off between accepting a large outsider population or, alternatively, a large service proletariat, they may produce two alternative kinds of polarization. In one case, the polarization will be between a small, but highly upgraded insider structure and a large outsider surplus population. In the other case, a large service proletariat will constitute the pivotal source of polarization' (Esping-Andersen, 1993, 27–28).

The 'Global Cities' perspective suggests strong support for substantial growth in professional workers and in the service proletariat, based on business and private demand (variants of hypotheses 2 and 3 above), and polarization of the second sort indicated under hypothesis 5. It would support the view of a decline in much of the Fordist hierarchy. Here though it might suggest that the occupational model was too coarse, since there would be no reason to expect a decline in the concentration of the most senior managers in large cities. Sassen has also suggested that some forms of low-wage manufacturing activity have persisting advantage.

Table 4.5 shows changes in the occupational structure of London between 1979 and 2000 based on these categories. The marked concentration of higher skilled (especially professional and managerial) workers can be seen, as can also the concentration of service industries in London, including headquarter operations in public and private sectors, accounting for the large share of managerial workers.

The evidence for London (and the UK) suggests growth at the top of both hierarchies and hence that Esping-Andersen's hypothesis of a stagnant share of managers is not confirmed. The growth of the share of managers reflects in part a tendency for an increasing role of managerial structures in predominantly professional organizations in both public and private sectors. It is also likely to arise from another factor he neglects – the growth of self-employment. Growth in the share of managers in London is in fact somewhat slower than for the UK as a whole. The remaining 'industrial' occupations display declining shares, especially so amongst manual workers. Within this hierarchy then there is a marked growth at the top, and a decline at the bottom, though in total this segment is declining. Within the 'post-industrial'

**Table 4.5.** The changing occupational structure of London.

|  | 1979 Place of residence | | | 2000 Place of residence | | | 2000 Place of work | |
|---|---|---|---|---|---|---|---|---|
|  | London | ROSE | GB | London | ROSE | GB | London | ROSE |
| **Industrial Occupations:** |  |  |  |  |  |  |  |  |
| Managers | 12.6 | 11.5 | 10.6 | 20.1 | 18.8 | 16.3 | 22.4 | 17.3 |
| Clerical and sales | 28.0 | 23.9 | 22.2 | 23.0 | 23.4 | 23.0 | 22.3 | 24.0 |
| Skilled manual | 16.2 | 19.0 | 19.7 | 7.3 | 10.9 | 11.8 | 7.3 | 11.0 |
| Unskilled manual | 13.9 | 17.1 | 20.3 | 6.5 | 8.3 | 10.9 | 6.1 | 8.9 |
| **Post-Industrial Occupations:** |  |  |  |  |  |  |  |  |
| Professional | 6.6 | 6.3 | 4.8 | 10.1 | 8.0 | 7.2 | 9.9 | 8.1 |
| Semi-professional | 9.3 | 9.5 | 8.5 | 18.1 | 14.8 | 14.2 | 17.9 | 14.4 |
| Skilled service | 3.3 | 3.5 | 3.5 | 5.8 | 6.7 | 6.8 | 5.6 | 6.9 |
| Unskilled service | 10.1 | 9.2 | 10.3 | 9.3 | 9.1 | 9.7 | 8.5 | 9.6 |

*Note:*
Data are based on the Labour Force Surveys micro-data sets and so are subject to some sampling error. An important caveat is that the underlying classifications of occupations have changed. Efforts have been made to ensure consistent recoding.

hierarchy, growth is again concentrated at the top, and is particularly strong amongst semi-professional workers.

But most notably, there is no growth in the share of 'unskilled service workers' – the service proletariat, which both Sassen and (more tentatively) Esping-Andersen lead one to expect. In summary neither hierarchy shows polarization, in the sense of growth of top and bottom at the expense of the middle. The pattern of change in the rest of the South East is rather similar to that in London, except that clerical and sales workers retain their share of employment, and the growth of higher level 'post-industrial' occupations is rather weaker.

Comparing London with the UK suggests that the main relative losers in London have been the middle strata of the 'industrial' hierarchy: clerical, sales and skilled manual workers, reflecting declining production industries and the decentralization of routine activities. In the 'post-industrial' hierarchy there was a rising concentration of semi-professional workers and a modest fall in the share of skilled service workers. The share of unskilled service workers was static. It is also worth noting that within each industry the service proletariat is less well represented in London than in the UK as a whole.

In summary this analysis does suggest a series of impacts on the London labour market following from a decline in employment in the production industries, which both mirrors national decline and reflects relative decentralization. The consequence has been a decline in the lower part of the overall occupational hierarchy. The relative growth of the service sectors has led to an expansion of the upper sections of the hierarchies, including managers. Unskilled service workers have retained their share, in contrast to unskilled manual workers. However, contrary to the 'Global Cities' hypothesis, they have not expanded, either absolutely or relative to the national economy.

With the exception of the category of managers, these findings tend to support a view of de-industrialization of the occupational hierarchy, but one in which the role of public service and welfare state growth is at least as important as private consumption growth. These findings tend also to support those of Hamnett (1994*a*), which use class rather than occupational classifications, and confirm that there is no occupational polarization in the sense of growth at both top and bottom of the hierarchy, but rather something closer to professionalization. There is some room for argument (see Bruegel, 1996) about how genuine some of the skill upgrading really is, and how far it reflects a redefinition of some occupations, and may be undermined by a downgrading of employment conditions associated with the feminization of occupations.

What does this imply about social class? Here we use something closer to a class classification, which takes account of employment status and the employment relations of workers. Table 4.6, shows the pattern of social change between 1979 and 1991 and between 1991 and 2000.

The table illustrates two major processes, one well known, the other perhaps less so. The first is the sharp upward shift in the class structure in all regions, in line with the occupation based analysis above. In the UK the percentage share of employers, managers, professionals and intermediate non-manual workers increased from 24 per cent to 41 per cent between 1979 and 2000. The second aspect of change was the particularly sharp upward shift of Inner London. Its share in these groups rose from 26 per cent to over 50 per cent. On this measure it moved from being the lowest status part of the region to the highest status. Outer London, by contrast, which enjoyed rather slow growth in these groups moved from highest status to lowest. As far as all parts of the region were concerned, the most substantial shifts occurred in the period before 1991, and the contrast with the rest of the UK is most striking in this period.

## Earnings and Incomes in London

Earnings in London have always been substantially above the national average in money terms. Some of the higher level is necessary to compensate for additional costs, particularly in relation to housing and transport. Recent estimates suggest that the cost of living in London is around 11–12 per cent higher than the average for the UK (Centre for Economics and Business Research, 2001, Baran and Donoghue, 2002). Table 4.7 shows summary earnings data for Greater London and Great Britain for male and female workers separately, for 1979 and 2000. Unfortunately these data relate to full-time workers only.

The first point to note is that there is a substantial and rising London premium, which is somewhat greater for women than for men. Thus London median male earnings were 14 per cent above the national level in 1979, rising to 24 per cent in 2000, while median female earnings were 16 per cent higher in 1979, rising to 31 per cent higher in 2000. For men the distribution is also somewhat more unequal in London than in the country as a whole, reflecting the larger number of high-income earners in London. Pay inequality for men increased substantially over this period in

**Table 4.6.** Class change, 1979–1991 and 1991–2000.

### Class change 1979–1991

| | 1979 Percentage shares | | | | 1979–1991 Percentage point change | | | |
|---|---|---|---|---|---|---|---|---|
| | Inner London | Outer London | Rest of South East | UK | Inner London | Outer London | Rest of South East | UK |
| Employers and managers | 10.88 | 14.39 | 12.44 | 10.80 | 8.65 | 3.34 | 6.33 | 4.57 |
| Professional | 4.14 | 4.71 | 4.24 | 3.34 | 4.12 | 1.77 | 2.68 | 2.25 |
| Intermediate non-manual | 11.20 | 11.36 | 11.06 | 9.76 | 6.33 | 4.98 | 3.97 | 4.01 |
| Junior non-manual | 24.92 | 28.65 | 23.86 | 21.92 | -5.16 | -4.77 | -3.56 | -2.66 |
| Personal service | 6.56 | 4.43 | 5.34 | 5.75 | -0.97 | -0.40 | -0.74 | -0.67 |
| Skilled manual | 18.21 | 17.18 | 19.94 | 22.45 | -8.31 | -4.49 | -7.15 | -6.21 |
| Semi-skilled manual | 13.12 | 10.25 | 13.35 | 15.39 | -6.25 | -2.90 | -4.85 | -4.06 |
| Unskilled manual | 7.04 | 4.31 | 5.07 | 6.45 | -1.32 | -0.41 | -0.59 | -0.68 |
| Own-account workers | 3.63 | 4.42 | 4.11 | 3.68 | 3.15 | 3.05 | 4.06 | 3.38 |

### Class change 1991–2000

| | 1991 Percentage shares | | | | 1991–2000 Percentage point change | | | |
|---|---|---|---|---|---|---|---|---|
| | Inner London | Outer London | Rest of South East | UK | Inner London | Outer London | Rest of South East | UK |
| Employers and managers – large establishments | 11.02 | 9.91 | 10.47 | 7.91 | 3.35 | 3.08 | 2.57 | 2.18 |
| Employers and managers – small establishments | 8.51 | 7.82 | 8.29 | 7.46 | -1.11 | 0.26 | -0.23 | -0.06 |
| Professional | 8.26 | 6.48 | 6.92 | 5.59 | 1.33 | 0.29 | -0.11 | 0.21 |
| Intermediate non-manual | 17.54 | 16.33 | 15.03 | 13.77 | 2.07 | 0.71 | 0.92 | 1.38 |
| Junior non-manual | 19.76 | 23.88 | 20.30 | 19.26 | -2.40 | -1.43 | -0.43 | 0.06 |
| Personal service | 5.59 | 4.03 | 4.60 | 5.07 | 1.73 | 1.78 | 1.07 | 1.12 |
| Skilled manual | 9.89 | 12.69 | 12.80 | 16.25 | -2.88 | -2.37 | -1.91 | -2.50 |
| Semi-skilled manual | 6.87 | 7.35 | 8.51 | 11.33 | 0.18 | -0.81 | 0.20 | -0.45 |
| Unskilled manual | 5.72 | 3.90 | 4.48 | 5.76 | -0.94 | -0.46 | -0.36 | -0.68 |
| Own-account workers | 6.78 | 7.47 | 8.17 | 7.06 | -1.29 | -1.13 | -1.71 | -1.26 |

*Source:* Labour Force Survey.

**Table 4.7.** Earnings inequality measures: Greater London and Great Britain, 1979 and 2000.

| | Lowest Decile | Median | Highest Decile | Inter-Decile Ratios: | | |
|---|---|---|---|---|---|---|
| | | | | Median/ lowest | Highest/ lowest | Highest/ median |
| **Full-Time Male Workers** | | | | | | |
| 1979 Greater London | £67.2 | £115.5 | £174.9 | 1.72 | 2.60 | 1.51 |
| United Kingdom | £61.9 | £101.4 | £147.3 | 1.64 | 2.38 | 1.45 |
| Ratio GL/GB | 1.09 | 1.14 | 1.19 | 1.05 | 1.09 | 1.04 |
| 2000 Greater London | £242.3 | £465.3 | £1008.6 | 1.92 | 4.16 | 2.17 |
| United Kingdom | £211.1 | £374.3 | £711.6 | 1.77 | 3.37 | 1.90 |
| Ratio GL/GB | 1.15 | 1.24 | 1.42 | 1.08 | 1.23 | 1.15 |
| **Full-Time Female Workers** | | | | | | |
| 1979 Greater London | £46.7 | £73.3 | £105.5 | 1.57 | 2.26 | 1.44 |
| United Kingdom | £40.6 | £63.0 | £92.6 | 1.55 | 2.28 | 1.47 |
| Ratio GL/GB | 1.15 | 1.16 | 1.14 | 1.01 | 0.99 | 0.98 |
| 2000 Greater London | £212.3 | £373.2 | £665.6 | 1.76 | 3.14 | 1.78 |
| United Kingdom | £169.5 | £284.0 | £521.2 | 1.68 | 3.07 | 1.84 |
| Ratio GL/GB | 1.25 | 1.31 | 1.28 | 1.05 | 1.02 | 0.98 |

*Source:* New Earnings Survey.

London, the ratio of highest decile to lowest increasing by 60 per cent. This was a significantly higher rate of increase than for the country as a whole (41 per cent). For women the pattern is different, with London having rather lower inequality than the country as a whole, and with inequality growing only marginally faster than in the country as a whole. The inclusion of part-time workers would increase both the inequality in women's earnings, and also the rise in inequality, since these workers tend to be placed towards the bottom of the earnings distribution. However it would be more likely to reduce further London's inequality level relative to the country as a whole, given that London has fewer part-time workers.

Are changes in earnings inequality driven by what is happening to lower wages or to higher wages? The ratio of median to lowest earnings in Table 4.7 shows the former, while the ratio of highest decile to median shows the latter. This evidence suggests that for men, while there was growing inequality in both parts of the distribution, inequality grew both absolutely and relative to the UK more rapidly in the top half of the distribution. On the other hand, for women it appears that while absolutely inequality increased more in the top half of the distribution, relative to the UK it was increasing inequality in the lower half which was more exceptional. While there is thus some support for 'Global Cities' polarization, a large part of the change in earnings inequality was shared with the whole UK economy, so more general explanations must also play a part.

Next we consider household income data. Labour market earnings are only one component here, and so our analysis includes other sources of income too, such as social welfare benefits. Table 4.8 shows simple measures of household income distribution for London and for the UK, drawn from the Family Expenditure Survey, and the Family Resources Survey (for 1999). In order to reach an adequate sample size for London using the former source, two sets of three consecutive years (1978–1980 and 1989–1991) are pooled. The table shows the ratio of the weekly income of the highest decile to the lowest decile for all households and as in the previous table the ratios of median to lowest decile, and of highest decile to median. It shows very starkly an enormous increase in inequality in the UK, and an even more substantial increase in London in the period up to 1990. In the late 1970s the inter-decile ratio in London was only marginally greater than that for the UK as a whole. By the early 1990s, it was nearly 40 per cent greater. Thus there was clearly something distinctive going on in London. However, during the 1990s inequality in London appears to have narrowed slightly, whilst that in the UK continued to increase. Nevertheless London remains very much more unequal than the UK at the household income level.

Over the 1980s, rising UK inequality was mainly caused by change in the lower part of the distribution – i.e. the poor fell further below the median. This was especially true in London. There was also some 'stretching' there at the top end of the distribution in London as the incomes of the richest groups accelerated ahead of the rest. Other analysis shows that the increase in inequality was driven by increases in the number of people unemployed or inactive, and by a growing gap in incomes between those in work and those not in work (Buck, 1997). It also showed that occupational change contributed relatively little to increasing inequality in the 1980s. This suggests that for working households, the change in inequality in London was very close to the national change – refuting the 'Global Cities' hypothesis that greater polarization in London has been caused by a shift to an 'hourglass' earnings distribution.

During the 1990s, a time of economic upturn, there was an increase in inequality in the UK, as measured by all three inter-decile ratios. In London there was increased inequality at the top end, but a sharp narrowing of income inequality in the lower half of the distribution. As a result, London's relative inequality fell at the lower end, but rose at the top end.

Over the period as a whole, whose start and end points are at similar stages in the economic cycle, London's relative inequality on all three measures has increased. This provides some support for 'Global Cities' polarization, but within a context where the dominant effects are major national changes, especially in the changing patterns of inequality between the employed population on the one hand and the unemployed and those outside the labour market on the other.

Whatever the source of these changes, the fact remains that over the last two decades London has become significantly more unequal. Although the lower end of the employed labour market has not expanded, the number of unemployed people and people outside the labour market has increased. The causes of this and the situation of these groups are discussed in Chapters 6 and 7, but it is worth pointing out here that the size of these groups has been surprisingly little reduced by the improving macro-economic situation of the late 1990s. This is particularly true of Inner London. For example, in 2000, 38 per cent of children in Inner London lived in households containing no workers, compared with 22 per cent in Outer London and 12 per cent in the rest of the South East. Social changes of this sort do not happen as a result of changes in the situation of a fixed group of people. They also arise from differential patterns of migration. As the more routine jobs are increasingly created

**Table 4.8.** Income distribution measures: Greater London and UK 1978–1981, 1989–1991 and 1999.

| | Lowest Decile | Median | Highest Decile | Inter-Decile Ratios: | | |
|---|---|---|---|---|---|---|
| | | | | Median/ lowest | Highest/ lowest | Highest/ median |
| All Households | | | | | | |
| 1979–1980 | | | | | | |
| Greater London | £50.53 | £107.78 | £194.33 | 2.13 | 3.85 | 1.80 |
| United Kingdom | £45.07 | £93.50 | £168.98 | 2.07 | 3.75 | 1.81 |
| GL/UK | 1.12 | 1.15 | 1.15 | 1.03 | 1.03 | 1.00 |
| 1989–1991 | | | | | | |
| Greater London | £88.21 | £322.36 | £720.56 | 3.65 | 8.17 | 2.24 |
| United Kingdom | £91.31 | £256.40 | £541.99 | 2.81 | 5.94 | 2.11 |
| GL/UK | 0.97 | 1.26 | 1.33 | 1.30 | 1.37 | 1.06 |
| 1999 | | | | | | |
| Greater London | £161.49 | £486.07 | £1278.77 | 3.01 | 7.92 | 2.63 |
| United Kingdom | £154.59 | £434.64 | £1028.35 | 2.81 | 6.65 | 2.37 |
| GL/UK | 1.04 | 1.12 | 1.24 | 1.08 | 1.19 | 1.11 |

*Source:* Family Expenditure Survey micro-data sets. Money amounts are weekly equivalent income adjusted for household size and composition, and inflation adjusted to the central year in each period grouping.

outside London this will lead the holders of these types of jobs to leave the region. At the same time, the concentration of social housing in Inner London will lead those with limited earnings opportunities to remain concentrated there.

Thus we have two apparently contradictory social changes emerging from the evidence presented here – both an increasing professionalization of the London labour market, especially in Inner London, and an increasing polarization of the social structure, with persistent, or even increasing levels of deprivation and exclusion. There is in fact no essential contradiction, and this pattern is consistent with the hypotheses advanced by Esping-Andersen above. However it does raise additional questions. For example, at what spatial scale do the processes operate? Is there an increase in residential segregation between social classes, or between employed and unemployed? We address these questions later in the chapter, but first we need to say a little about the housing market and the residential location of London workers.

## The Role of the Housing Market

London's housing market has undergone major transformations over the last three or four decades. In large part this reflects a response to the changing social and economic structure of London, described in the previous sections. Historically, Inner London has had very high shares of rented housing, both public and private, and correspondingly low shares of owner occupied housing. The same was true to a lesser degree of Outer London. The concentration of social housing was a response to the housing needs of a largely working-class population in a period when many boroughs in Outer London were able to resist the construction of local authority housing. The scale of private renting reflected both a survival from the period when this was the dominant tenure, and the continuing demand for such housing from younger people moving into London. New housing construction was relatively limited.

Two factors changed this situation, and resulted in a substantial decline in the share of social housing throughout the region, some decline in other housing for rent in Inner London, and a corresponding growth in owner-occupation. The first and probably less significant factor was the sale of part of the council housing stock to tenants following Conservative legislation at the beginning of the 1980s. This was rather more important in Outer London, where the council stock was of a higher quality than in Inner London. The second process, gentrification, followed from the continuing growth of professional and managerial jobs, especially in central London, along with a growing popularity of London residence. Gentrification involved a number of distinct processes, including the transfer of property from renting to owner-occupation, and also the conversion of multi-occupied housing into single-family housing (and paradoxically as prices rose, also the reverse process). It spread spatially from a number of key areas of Inner London in the 1960s and early 1970s, to affect most of Inner London and parts of the inner fringes of Outer London. This process underpinned the transformation of the social structure of Inner London described in the last section. There was also a modest increase in the level of new private house construction in London in the 1990s compared with the 1980s. Total construction was however at a lower level than at the beginning of the 1980s, given the sharp fall in the construction of social housing.

However it is through price rather than quantity that most of the potential housing market effects on the competitiveness of the London economy and the evolution of its social structure are likely to be occurring currently. In 2001, average prices in London were around 80 per cent above the UK average. We saw earlier that earnings were around 25 per cent higher. Evidence on mortgage advances suggests that first time buyers in London in 2000 had average recorded incomes of £37,642, compared with a national average of £26,259, or 43 per cent higher in London. This suggests that fewer workers in London had access to owner-occupation.

It should be noted that the London house price premium is highly cyclical. Figure 4.1, based on Nationwide Building Society data, shows the ratio of London, OMA and Outer South East house prices to the UK average over the period 1973–2001. It suggests relative stability in this ratio, at around 1.3 over the period from 1973 up to the mid-1980s, above the relative earnings ratio for this period (1.15), but not as dramatically so as later. There are then two peaks, one in the late 1980s, and one in the late 1990s, reaching about the same level, and in between, the ratio fell back to close to its earlier level.

This raises a set of issues for the competitiveness of the London economy. London depends on inward migration flows to meet its need for high-skilled labour. Since these flows mainly involve younger people near the start of their careers, the people coming in are likely to be in a relatively weak position in the housing market. Prices and rents may act as a deterrent to such flows. Housing costs may also have impacts on the availability of middle level skills. People on middle incomes may need to move out of London as their space needs increase (e.g. with children), since larger housing will not be affordable. The evidence of Figure 4.1 suggests extreme house price variation is not necessarily a permanent condition. It leaves open the question whether current conditions represent a new structural threat to London's competitiveness, or another example of its increased volatility.

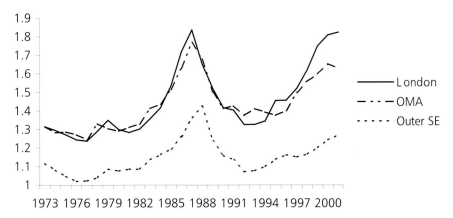

Figure 4.1  London region: UK house price ratios.

## Commuting

Spatial dimensions of the social structure of London depend not only on local economic structures but also on the pattern of commuting. As Chapter 6 will show London is a very open economy, with a complex interaction of commuting patterns. An analysis of net flows by social class suggests some significant differences between parts of the London region.

Not surprisingly, central London experienced substantial net inflow rates from all social classes, and these were highest for large employers and managers and routine non-manual workers, who are particularly unlikely to live in central London. Interestingly the semi- and unskilled manual population of this area remains significant, and the net inflow is relatively low compared with other classes. Both eastern and western parts of the remainder of Inner London experiences net inflows, with a rather higher inflow rate to the inner east. However here social structure differences do emerge. Inner east London is a substantial net importer of employers and managers (though the inflow rate for professional workers is about average), while it is a net exporter of semi- and unskilled manual workers. By contrast the inner west is a substantial net exporter of professional workers, and importer of skilled manual workers. In other words in inner east London, workers are generally of higher status than residents, while the reverse is true in inner west London.

All the other parts of the region have positive net outflows. These tend to be higher in the eastern parts of the region, which have lower employment concentrations. Not surprisingly, the outflow rates tend to be higher for employers and managers, professional workers and other non-manual workers than for manual workers. Outflow rates for all social classes tend to be higher in the eastern zones than in the equivalent western zone. Indeed, for example, outer west London has a net inflow of skilled manual workers. However the divergences in the higher status social classes are perhaps more notable, given that the eastern areas have lower residential concentrations of such groups. It reflects the even lower concentration of such jobs in the eastern zones.

## Neighbourhood Change and Social Segregation

How have these changes impacted at the more local scale? Principally we address this question through our qualitative work in the neighbourhoods. However, there is something to be said from an overview across the whole of the London region. Here we are somewhat hampered by the absence at the time of writing of small area data from the 2001 Census. However we can say something about trajectories between 1981 and 1991, and also have some indication of whether they continue from borough level data in the 2000 Labour Force Survey.

The first question we need to address is whether spatial segregation has been increasing alongside the increasing inequality. If, for example, social classes were becoming more spatially separated from one another it could have wider consequences for social cohesion. In terms of social class the answer seems fairly clearly to be that segregation has not been increasing. Table 4.9 shows indices of dissimilarity for 1981 and 1991 between the main SEGs. The indices show the percentage of the population which would need to move for two groups to have the same spatial distribution.

It is clear that with the exception of skilled manual workers each class is becoming relatively less segregated from other groups. In particular there is no tendency for employers, managers and professionals to become more segregated from unskilled and semi-skilled manual workers. Indeed some of the sharpest falls in segregation are between these groups at the different ends of the distribution. This reflects in part the impacts of gentrification, and the growing tendency for higher status workers to live in Inner London. However even if we carry out the analysis for Inner London alone, segregation is still tending to fall. Of course this is what we might expect to find in early stages of gentrification, when housing in basically working-class areas is being taken over by more middle-class households. We would need more detailed analysis and a longer time series of data to establish whether segregation tended to rise again as the gentrification process matured.

More recent data at the borough level from the 2000 Labour Force Survey suggest that while there remain considerable variations in the class structure of London boroughs, there is not an increasing concentration of particular social classes at borough level. The broad pattern of social mix found in 1991 is still found in these later data. They also suggest that to the extent that there is a spatial structuring to the class composition of London it cannot be described in simple inner-outer terms, or indeed simple east-west terms, though the lowest status boroughs of all are to be found in an eastward arm along the river Thames. If we take the share of the employed population who are employers, managers, professional workers and intermediate non-manual workers, it ranges from 28 per cent in Barking to 62 per cent in Westminster. Eight of the ten lowest status boroughs are in outer London (the exceptions being Newham and Hackney). The outer London boroughs lie to the west, north and east in the 'cross' identified by Young and Willmott (1973). In spite of the changes identified above, there are historical continuities in the spatial structure. The change has been the relative rise of Inner London. Thus, by contrast, seven of the ten highest status boroughs are in Inner London, making up much of the centre, north and west of that area. The three exceptions are all in the south-west (Richmond, Merton and Kingston).

On the other hand there is evidence that segregation by employment status has been increasing. Thus the index of dissimilarity between the employed and the unemployed increased from 21.5 to 23.1 between 1981 and 1991. In fact it appears to be the segregation of the unemployed and economically inactive combined which is increasing most rapidly, rather than of the unemployed on their own. Thus the index of dissimilarity between the employed and all those of working age not in employment increased at a rather greater rate from 7.3 to 12.2, while that between the unemployed and everyone else did not increase substantially. This is one indication that in terms of area deprivation there may be a tendency for segregation to increase. A number of other changes confirm this. Thus the index contrasting households with no car with other households increased from 28.7 to 29.8, that for living at high housing densities increased from 29.5 to 31.7. Lone parents appeared to become more segregated, the index increasing from 22.8 to 27.2. However housing tenures were becoming less segregated, with the index contrasting social housing with owner-occupation falling from 47.9 to 43.3. This presumably reflects in part the sales of council housing under right to buy legislation of the early 1980s.

Unfortunately substantial changes in the way data about ethnicity were collected and reported in the Census means that it is impossible to compute strictly equivalent indices. Here we compare the segregation indices for two different definitions of a part of the minority ethnic population. In 1981 we contrast the population in households whose head was born in the New Commonwealth or Pakistan with all others. In 1991 we contrast those who defined their ethnicity as black, Indian, Pakistani or Bangladeshi. For this comparison to be valid we do not require the groups to be identical, we simply require that they are spatially distributed in the same way as the comparison group. The index for the whole London region is 47.9 in 1981 and 52.4 in 1991. This change appears sufficiently large that it probably reflects some real increase in ethnic segregation, and not simply differences in the measure. However, we have already observed a tendency for a greater relative concentration of the minority ethnic population within Greater London in contrast to the OMA. An index of segregation calculated only for Greater London suggests a smaller increase, from 38.3 to 39.9. There is probably then some tendency for ethnic segregation to increase at smaller spatial scales, but it is not on a scale to suggest intensified formation of ethnic ghettos.

**Table 4.9.** Ward level social segregation, London region, 1981, and 1981–1991 changes.

| 1981 Indices of Dissimilarity | Employer/ manager Small | Employer/ manager Large | Professional | Intermediate non-manual | Junior non-manual | Skilled manual | Semi-skilled manual | Unskilled manual | All |
|---|---|---|---|---|---|---|---|---|---|
| Employer/manager Large | 16.98 | | | | | | | | 22.08 |
| Employer/manager Small | | | | | | | | | 21.79 |
| Professional | 17.70 | 17.56 | | | | | | | 26.26 |
| Intermediate non-manual | 17.23 | 17.24 | 18.45 | | | | | | 15.40 |
| Junior non-manual | 20.43 | 20.34 | 25.39 | 14.73 | | | | | 9.93 |
| Skilled manual | 32.35 | 31.67 | 37.14 | 25.84 | 17.42 | | | | 17.26 |
| Semi-skilled manual | 32.85 | 31.28 | 36.41 | 25.46 | 19.23 | 12.81 | | | 17.03 |
| Unskilled manual | 40.69 | 39.86 | 44.10 | 33.42 | 26.90 | 19.71 | 16.37 | | 24.70 |
| Own-account | 25.16 | 21.96 | 28.69 | 19.86 | 15.41 | 20.47 | 21.01 | 28.89 | 14.48 |
| **1981–1991 Change in Indices of Dissimilarity** | | | | | | | | | |
| Employer/manager Large | -1.79 | | | | | | | -3.13 | -3.71 |
| Employer/manager Small | 0.76 | -0.75 | | | | | | | -2.04 |
| Professional | -2.35 | -3.56 | -1.38 | | | | | | 0.00 |
| Intermediate non-manual | -2.62 | -3.19 | -1.36 | 0.02 | | | | | 0.02 |
| Junior non-manual | -1.99 | -1.81 | -0.23 | 1.28 | 0.89 | | | | 1.25 |
| Skilled manual | -3.75 | -3.69 | -2.94 | -0.18 | -0.75 | 1.13 | | | -0.90 |
| Semi-skilled manual | -5.36 | -5.97 | -4.89 | -2.05 | -2.20 | -0.88 | -0.64 | | -2.45 |
| Unskilled manual | | | | | | | | | |
| Own-account | -2.49 | -1.88 | -0.11 | 0.23 | -2.09 | -2.39 | -2.00 | -3.57 | -1.12 |

*Source:* 1981 and 1991 Population Census Small Area Statistics.

We can go beyond an analysis of segregation between small areas, to compare small area social structures, in order to produce a typology of areas, and then investigate how this has changed. The same socio-economic group data can be clustered. This analysis reinforces some of the conclusions of the segregation analysis but suggests some nuances. Cluster analysis was undertaken for both 1981 and 1991, using common ward boundaries, and for the changes between these years.

The typologies in 1981 and 1991 were not quite identical, but they had broad similarities. Numbers of wards and distribution between parts of London are shown in the first two panels of table 4.10. There was a group of lower status wards, with an above average share of semi- and unskilled manual workers. This cluster was significantly over-represented in Inner London at both years, but the total number of wards in this group fell by around a quarter. A second pair of clusters, again falling in number, had above average shares of skilled manual workers. This cluster was more evenly distributed across the region, but with under-representation in Inner London, and over-representation in Outer London. The next pair of clusters were characterized by large shares of more routine non-manual workers, a group whose pay levels are rather similar to those of skilled manual, but where status differences and differences in the industry in which they worked lead to different spatial distributions. This cluster is particularly prevalent in Outer London, but the share in the OMA has been rising. The pair of clusters below labelled as 'petite bourgeoisie' are characterized by large shares of employers and managers in small establishments and also in 1981 at least, by agricultural workers. They are heavily concentrated in the OMA. The highest status cluster, particularly over-representing professional workers and large employers and managers, has shifted its distribution. In 1981 it was rather over-represented in the OMA. However by 1991 the most substantial over-representation was in Inner London. The mixed clusters had a ward social profile similar to the overall regional distribution, and thus contained significant numbers of both manual and non-manual workers. The number of such clusters increased marginally over the period. At the beginning they were over-represented in both Inner London and the OMA, but later they tended to grow relatively in Outer London.

Of course since the clustering for each of these years was different, there were substantial moves between groups, and for example a significant number of the 1981 high status wards were classified as petit-bourgeois in 1991. Similarly there were large exchanges between the two working-class clusters. An alternative way of looking at the pattern of change is to cluster the percentage changes themselves. Four clusters are shown in the last panel of Table 4.10. Here the changes are relative to overall change rather than absolute changes. So, for example, the cluster labelled 'growing routine non-manual' really means growing relative to an absolute decline in the share of this group across the whole region. Two of the clusters are particularly notable. The first is the gentrification cluster, with increasing shares in large (but not small) employers and managers, professional workers and intermediate non-manual workers. This cluster was strongly concentrated in Inner London, but with a significant representation in Outer London. By contrast the declining status cluster, with manual workers and routine non-manual workers growing relatively, is barely represented in Inner London.

**Table 4.10.** Social class cluster of London region wards.

| 1981 Clusters – Location quotients by region | | | | |
|---|---|---|---|---|
| | Inner | Outer | OMA | Number of Wards |
| Semi & unskilled manual workers | 2.27 | 0.90 | 0.69 | 323 |
| Skilled manual workers | 0.66 | 1.16 | 1.02 | 379 |
| Routine non-manual | 0.43 | 1.99 | 0.74 | 316 |
| Petite bourgeoisie | 0.27 | 0.03 | 1.62 | 138 |
| High status | 0.83 | 0.88 | 1.10 | 333 |
| Mixed | 1.18 | 0.49 | 1.17 | 327 |
| **1991 Clusters – Location quotients by region** | | | | |
| | Inner | Outer | OMA | Number of Wards |
| Semi and unskilled workers | 2.51 | 0.46 | 0.81 | 253 |
| Working class, especially skilled | 0.71 | 1.23 | 0.98 | 336 |
| Routine non-manual | 0.14 | 1.69 | 0.94 | 397 |
| Petite bourgeoisie | 0.52 | 0.30 | 1.44 | 212 |
| High status | 1.34 | 1.13 | 0.85 | 247 |
| Mixed | 1.20 | 0.74 | 1.06 | 371 |
| **1981–1991 Change Clusters – Location quotients by region** | | | | |
| | Inner | Outer | OMA | Number of Wards |
| Shrinking middle | 0.94 | 1.17 | 0.94 | 395 |
| Declining status | 0.26 | 1.09 | 1.17 | 494 |
| Growth of routine non-manual | 0.52 | 0.84 | 1.21 | 508 |
| Gentrification | 2.51 | 0.93 | 0.61 | 419 |
| Number of Wards | 297 | 457 | 1062 | 1816 |

*Source:* 1981 and 1991 Population Census Small Area Statistics.

Similar analyses of dimensions of the demographic structure were also carried out, though detailed results are not shown here. The analyses in both 1981 and 1991 tend to show concentrations of two types of area in Inner London, one characterized by single person households, young adults and high migration rates, the other characterized more by families, especially those with lone parents, but still with rather high turnover rates. Outer London has some of these latter type of areas, but was more dominated by two other types, one with families with children, but with a rather average age profile, the other concentrating older people. The OMA, while containing some of the older clusters, had three types of family area, distinguished by life stage, the first over-representing families with very young children, the second more mature families, and the third older pre-retirement families.

The expected patterns of change in local area demographic structure are somewhat different from those in the analysis of local area social class structure where areas may remain stable, or be transformed through migration patterns. In the absence of migration the demographic structure of areas will change as the population ages, and areas mature from one lifecycle stage to another. In practice the Inner London areas appeared to be reproducing their characteristics through migration processes, though there was some tendency, consistent with Table 4.2, for the proportions of children to increase. In Outer London there was a tendency in some areas for a movement towards the Inner London demographic pattern. There was also some tendency for a transformation of areas which previously had a rather elderly population as younger people moved in to replace them. However for a significant proportion of areas, the pattern of change was a maturing of the demographic structure of each area, rather than a succession tending to reproduce a continuity of structure. In the OMA this pattern of maturing *in situ* was dominant.

## Conclusion: Social and Neighbourhood Change in London

There has been an historic shift in the population trend in London with a move from long-term decline to significant growth. London, Inner London particularly, has become strongly associated with non-family or non-standard family types. At the same time London is becoming a very heterogeneous multi-ethnic city. Continuing international migration is very much concentrated on London, and this includes a wide group, ranging from highly skilled and high-income workers through to asylum seekers and clandestine migrants.

Over the last 20 years London has undoubtedly become a much more unequal place. However, in contrast to explanations which tend to highlight London's global city status, this increased inequality has come about through a combination of national and local factors – with national change being the dominant factor. Moreover, the key drivers relate to the size and relative incomes of the in-work and non-working population, rather than to the stretching of the earnings distribution – although that too, has occurred.

The analysis at neighbourhood level suggested an extremely complex and varied pattern of change in London's neighbourhoods, but certain themes do emerge, and these tend to reinforce some of the earlier conclusions of the chapter. In the first place they suggest a geography of change in London, with the most intense and substantial change amounting to a transformation of social structure occurring in Inner London. Outer London has experienced a rather mixed pattern of change, with some encroachments of Inner London patterns of social structure, and certainly a weakening of the sense that Outer London was the secure and stable hinterland to the turbulent core of the city. That role is more clearly reserved for the OMA, and the evidence would tend to suggest sharper differentiation between London and its surrounding region. Another conclusion is that the social transformation of London has not generated a substantial increase in social segregation. This is suggested both by the direct evidence on segregation and by the growth of more socially mixed class clusters in Inner London, and to a degree outer London. This must remain a somewhat tentative conclusion, since there is some evidence of increasing concentration of deprivation, and later chapters will suggest that the historical pattern of deprivation in London (i.e. its concentration in a horseshoe around the eastern side of the central area) has persisted.

Chapter 5

# 'Education, Education, Education': The Role of Schooling in London

Successive Governments have failed to resolve the educational problems of the major cities. Standards have been too low for too long. Raising standards in order to lift opportunities for our children is the key priority for the Government.

Department for Education and Employment, *Excellence in Cities,* 1999

How important is education to competitiveness and cohesion? It has become a truism that economic success – for individuals, for cities, for nations – rests on improving educational outputs and raising investment in human capital. But some analysts have always been sceptical of such claims. Some suggest that education qualifications merely act as a 'screening' device by which individuals can signal their possession of abilities that are in fact intrinsic, rather than the result of education (Spence, 1973). In this account, individuals differ in their initial endowments, the richness of their social background and in their abilities to learn – all of which are more relevant to productive capacities than are higher levels of formal education, but hard for employers to detect except via the evidence of qualifications.

The screening paradigm is a plausible alternative explanation for the observed fact that those with higher qualifications tend to earn more and run less risk of unemployment than those without. But it cannot so readily account for macro-economic evidence of a real link between formal education and competitiveness. Cross-national studies suggest that increasing school enrolment rates (a *flow* measure) by one percentage point leads to increases in per capita GDP of between one and three percentage points, while an additional year of secondary education in the population (a *stock* measure) leads to more than one percentage point faster growth each year (Sianesi and van Reenan, 2000) A recent OECD report finds similarly significant effects on cohesion as well as competitiveness:

> *Education, training and learning can play important roles in providing the basis for economic growth, social cohesion and personal development. Investment in human capital takes time to develop and yield benefits. In so far as impacts can be measured and compared, some studies suggest that the social impacts of learning (health, crime, social cohesion) could be as large as the impacts on economic productivity, if not larger.* (OECD, 2001, 35)

In economics the newer endogenous growth theories highlight the significance of educational attainment to competitiveness. Education not only delivers tangible benefits to the individual, but there are also wider economic effects on productivity growth, through stimulation of research activity, technology diffusion, and capital investment (Lucas, 1988; Romer, 1990). And, whereas in neo-classical models, a simple increase in human capital stock (for example, from additional years of education) was only expected to produce a once-for-all increase in productivity, in the new growth theories it can induce continuing faster growth (Sianesi and Van Reenan, 2000). These theoretical arguments are now fairly well supported by macro evidence, with Levine and Renelt (1992), for example, identifying education as a key determinant of differences in growth rates across countries.

At the level of an individual city one might expect human capital availability to have similarly positive effects on business competitiveness, incomes and growth – although economically successful cities may also be able to draw in highly skilled workers from elsewhere – both as commuters and as migrants. In an American context, Glaeser *et al*. (1995) have found strong supporting evidence for the impact of local schooling from an econometric analysis of 30-year growth rates across 203 cities:

> *Initial median years of schooling exert a positive and significant influence on the subsequent population growth . . . A closer inspection . . . shows that the percentage of the population with 12 to 15 years (high-school graduates or some college) is more important than the percentage of the population with over 16 years (college graduates). This result suggests the importance of a well-educated labour force, not just of the top of the education distribution.* (Glaeser *et al.*, 1995, 131–132)

The emphasis here on general levels of education seems particularly relevant to London where it is frequently complained that the city's pre-16 education system does not deliver workers with the appropriate skills to enable businesses to compete successfully – i.e. that London's economic competitiveness is threatened by the poor performance of its education system. We examine the evidence for this below.

In policy terms, education is also seen as being important to social cohesion, particularly as a basis for securing waged work, which New Labour sees as the key to social inclusion. More generally, it is argued that education and knowledge have become pre-requisites for citizenship and social participation. The core of this argument is well founded. In a post-industrial economy, the importance of formal qualifications is rising, and the lack of them increasingly implies higher risks of unemployment (Arulampamlam and Stewart, 1995). Educational failure is also linked to other indicators of social exclusion. For example, evidence from the UK National Child Development Study shows that poor educational test scores in childhood are associated with much higher risks, as an adult, of early parenthood, mental illness and living in social housing (Hobcraft, 1998).

Moreover, there appear to be clear benefits to additional educational inputs later on. Both men and women who upgrade initial educational qualifications during their 20s and early 30s add significantly to their earning power, while women can also increase their probability of employment. The gains seem to be less for men, however, while those with problematic backgrounds, such as contact with the police in childhood, fail to benefit significantly (Gregg and Machin, 1997). Hence for some groups getting education right the first time around is crucial.

Recent American research has also rebutted long-standing scepticism about the potential of educational initiatives to reduce inequality, by demonstrating that schools do have the capacity to improve skills and earning capacity – in other words, schools *do* matter. In particular, studies of intra-family variation have shown that 'the return to schooling is not caused by an omitted correlation between ability and schooling . . . the school is a promising place to increase the skills and incomes of individuals' (Ashenfelter and Rouse, 1999). Moreover the benefits of schooling seem to be greatest for children of parents with the least education (Dearden, 1998).

For two other dimensions of social cohesion – connectedness/social order and inequality – there are also potentially strong links with the education system. This is particularly true of schools which can play a key role in the construction of communities and social linkages, as well as being key sites in which individuals either learn how to be a citizen, or fail to. This is obviously more than a simple matter of acquiring qualifications, but (as the OECD report indicated) achieving these does tend to be correlated with more active social participation, formation of more stable partnerships, and lower levels of criminality. The links here may well be indirect (e.g. via labour market experiences) or reflect a common cause (e.g. truancy and/or school exclusion), but schooling experiences are potentially critical.

Some of these tasks may be particularly hard to achieve in London, which has (as we saw in the last chapter) a particularly heterogeneous population, wide economic divisions, and quite strong social segregation – and is also suspected of being an especially individualistic place (an issue which we take up in Chapter 8). The burden imposed on the education system must be correspondingly greater than elsewhere. But there are still questions to be asked as to whether – as many in the region suspect – failures of the education system are holding back London's competitiveness, and exacerbating problems of social cohesion. In this chapter we explore these issues, both in relation to the region as a whole and in relation to particular sub-regions where there seem to be special difficulties. We also address the question as to how far the metropolitan setting, and the institutional arrangements of education in the region significantly affect the way in which the school system operates, and thus its impact on competitiveness, inequality, connectedness and social order.

## Skills and Human Capital

The London region as a whole has one of the best qualified labour forces in the UK with 29 per cent of working age residents having higher education qualifications in 2001, compared with 24 per cent nationally. In terms of the three main 'rings' of the region, this proportion is highest in Inner London, at 36 per cent, compared with 28 per cent in Outer London and 29 per cent in the OMA. Among those actually in work, the proportions qualified at this level are even higher, especially in Inner London (47 per cent), where the gap reflects a particularly high incidence of unemployment and inactivity among those who are less qualified. At the other end of the achievement spectrum, the proportion of residents without any qualification is lower than for the UK as a whole in *all* parts of the London region (Table 5.1). Greater London (and Inner London in particular) does have many more people with unrecognized qualifications, but this is simply due to the capital's much higher proportion of foreign born residents.

**Table 5.1.** Highest qualifications of working age residents, Spring 2001.

|  | Inner London | Outer London | Greater London | Rest of the South East | United Kingdom |
|---|---|---|---|---|---|
| Degree or equivalent | 30.5% | 19.6% | 23.6% | 16.5% | 14.7% |
| Other higher education | 5.6% | 6.8% | 6.4% | 8.3% | 8.6% |
| GCE A level or equivalent | 14.8% | 20.9% | 18.6% | 24.7% | 23.9% |
| GCSE grades A* to C or equivalent | 13.6% | 21.2% | 18.4% | 24.0% | 22.3% |
| Other qualifications (low and/or unrecognized) | 20.2% | 18.0% | 18.8% | 13.3% | 13.9% |
| No qualifications | 15.3% | 13.5% | 14.2% | 12.5% | 16.6% |

*Source:* Labour Force Survey, Office for National Statistics.

On the other hand, there are indications that the current stock and flow of human capital are failing to meet the needs of the city's economy. Reported skill shortages and skill gaps among existing workers are each particularly large in the London region, especially in west London and the 'Western Crescent' of the OMA – as well as in two adjoining areas to the north and west (Green and Owen, 2001). Within Greater London, the 1998 London Employer Survey recorded 40,000 vacancies (36 per cent of all those current) as being difficult to fill, including 16,000 where employers identified the problem as one of skill shortage. Difficulties were greatest in higher occupational groupings, particularly for associate professional/ technical jobs – but half of the reported skill shortages actually involved occupations with much lower typical entry requirements (Table 5.2).

In the same survey, 10 per cent of London employers identified a gap between the skills of their existing workforce and those required to meet their business objectives, with a particular emphasis on shortcomings in respect of computer literacy and technical abilities, together with a range of interpersonal skills. Five per cent of employers thought that a quarter or more of their staff was affected by this gap. Skill gaps were most frequently reported by manufacturing employers. In terms of the occupational structure, skills gaps were more marked in lower than in higher occupational groupings and highest for clerical and secretarial occupations – which are very largely staffed by products of the region's own education system.

**Table 5.2.** Current vacancies difficult to fill because of skill shortages, Greater London, 1998.

|  | Vacancies difficult to fill because of skills shortages (000s) | Proportion of total vacancies that were difficult to fill due to skill shortages | Occupational distribution of difficult to fill vacancies |
|---|---|---|---|
| Managers and administrators | 2.0 | 73% | 12% |
| Professionals | 2.4 | 73% | 15% |
| Associate professional & technical occupations | 4.2 | 76% | 26% |
| Clerical and secretarial | 1.7 | 34% | 10% |
| Craft and related | 1.9 | 31% | 12% |
| Personal and protective services | 1.8 | 37% | 11% |
| Sales | 0.4 | 11% | 3% |
| Plant and machine operators | 1.3 | 21% | 8% |
| Other occupations | 0.2 | 15% | 2% |
| All occupations | 15.9 | 41% | 100% |

*Source:* London Employer Survey.

Lack of formal qualifications may not be the critical issue, however. Employers stated that no qualifications were required for 40 per cent of their vacancies in 1998 – including 25 per cent of those identified as hard to fill. The main exception was in occupations where degrees were the normal requirement. Overall, only 15 per cent of vacancies had a requirement pitched in terms of school level qualifications. Much more emphasis was placed on attributes such as relevant experiences, positive motivation and basic literacy/numeracy. Schooling is, however, clearly relevant to the last of these, and probably also to the 'soft skills' and attitudes to which employers give increasing weight:

> *Youngsters coming in are invariably unqualified . . . (but we're) usually looking for literacy, personality and the correct attitude – probably more important than a formal education. If they've got enthusiasm you can normally channel that and develop the person.*
>
> Insurance brokers, Reading

These skill shortages and deficiencies clearly matter to business competitiveness. Fifteen per cent of businesses in 1999 reported direct effects on sales levels or output quality. But there are also indirect effects, through slowing adoption of new technologies, and (for manufacturing firms at least) discouraging investment in physical capital (Nickell and Nicolitsas, 1997). The region's education system clearly has some role to play in meeting the skill gaps. However, it is far from clear that the regional skills gap reflects particularly worse performance in the education, training or socialization of workers in the region, at least by UK standards. Skill shortages in London intensified during the boom years of the late 1990s (London Skills Forecasting Unit, 2000) and there are strong spatial differences in skill gaps within

**Table 5.3.** Occupational breakdown of employees reported to lack skills, Greater London, 1998.

|  | Number | Percentage of employees |
|---|---|---|
| Managers and administrators | 7943 | 10 |
| Professionals | 8253 | 10 |
| Associate professional & technical occupations | 5077 | 16 |
| Clerical and secretarial | 15922 | 19 |
| Craft and related | 8069 | 10 |
| Personal and protective services | 11126 | 13 |
| Sales | 15228 | 18 |
| Plant and machine operators | 4175 | 5 |
| Other occupations | 2998 | 4 |
| No occupation info provided | 4175 | 5 |
| Total | 82966 | 10 |

*Source:* London Employer Survey.

the region – with Berkshire topping the national list on almost all measures and East London below the national average. This suggests that the size of skill gaps in the region is primarily a reflection of strong demand and healthy rates of technological/ organizational change.

In our face-to-face interviews with London firms there were common complaints about the quality and attitudes of (at least some) school leavers and even graduates, seen explicitly or implicitly as reflecting shortcomings in educational preparation for the world of work:

> *There are still an awful lot of kids who don't have any understanding of what work is all about – you are selling your time, you do a job for somebody and they pay you for it and that's the deal. I think a lot of young people are still expecting to come to work and not do anything*
>
> Printing firm, Woolwich

> *Socially [school leavers] aren't trained for work. At work you have to work with people who maybe you don't like, at school they only work with their friends, so it's alien to them . . . [also, universities] build graduates up too much . . . they think they will come in and run the company. We have to take them down and they have to learn the basics which they aren't always willing to do.*
>
> Biotech firm, Dartford

In some cases, the criticisms involved an over-emphasis on academic skills and new technologies:

> *I am a Londoner, I love London, and my grandfather was a carpenter at Woolwich Docks. My heart is in this part of London . . . but it needs some extra work, and we need to start by talking to schools about the benefit of having a manufacturing base . . . Sitting in front of a PC is the only thing [teachers] seem to think is valuable and the only way to make any money . . . yet there are some good livings to be made in printing . . . just because you aren't doing A level maths doesn't mean that you haven't got a lot to contribute.*
>
> Printing firm, Woolwich

But how much of this is specific to London? Hard-working (and often middle-aged) employers have been complaining about the attitudes and behaviour of young people since time immemorial. Are there any characteristics of the London education system, the London labour market or London employers, which make this issue particularly acute? Four possibilities present themselves.

*First,* it might be the case that the upgrading and professionalization of the London labour market, described in Chapters 3 and 4, makes young people more likely to reject routine and more mundane job opportunities. In addition, upgrading may remove some of the available intermediate job slots, thus giving young people a stark choice between high-status, high-paying jobs (for which many are not qualified) and others, which while not necessarily badly paid initially are still dead-end jobs, offering weak prospects of security or advancement.

*Secondly,* and more directly, the buoyant London economy and its high turnover labour market mean that there are attractive alternatives to school or further training:

> *A lot of kids work on building sites cash in hand. They get lots more than they would get by going on some training course where they get £30 or £40 a week. 'If I go on a building site 3 or 4 days I will get 200 pounds' . . . a lot of them wouldn't get support at home, a lot of parents might like to but they can't afford it.*
>
> Careers Adviser, Inner London

*Thirdly,* where – as in the business services of central London or the western 'wedge' and 'crescent' – firms' key labour force is one of nationally-recruited graduates, they may have less effective concern about the quality of local school leavers.

*Fourthly,* there may be a particular problem in some parts of the region with higher numbers of young people who have dropped out entirely from the system – that is, who are neither working nor in any form of education or training. This 'status zero' group was highlighted as a strategic issue by one respondent to the Mayor's draft Economic Development Strategy who argued that:

> *It is this group who bounce back into regeneration schemes when they reach age 25, often with few skills, and additional baggage in the form of criminal records.*

This seems to be an issue primarily in Inner and East London where unemployment is relatively high and educational participation rates are among the lowest in the country. Elsewhere in the region an above average proportion of this group tend to be in education (particularly) or training.

London's economic success has always rested in part on its ability to draw in skills, talent, energy and entrepreneurship from elsewhere – a function of its regional, national, imperial, and now global position. The London region acts as 'a kind of escalator for those who wanted to "get on" in life' (Fielding, 1989, 35). That is, the region attracts many of the most highly qualified people from Britain and beyond; it trains, develops and promotes them; and finally (in their middle age) exports some of these professionals and managers to other regions in the UK – along with part of its entrepreneurial culture. We discuss this phenomenon further in Chapter 6. But its immediate significance is that, in relation to jobs demanding the highest levels of human capital, the competitiveness of businesses in the region is unlikely to be very dependent on the performance of local educational institutions. This is less true, however, of the large number of jobs requiring intermediate levels of human capital, where local recruitment is much more common. This would include the clerical and secretarial occupational group, where London employers report the greatest number of hard to fill vacancies, and also the broader range of clerical, sales, and managerial workers who are the focus for particular dissatisfaction about both basic and 'soft' skills (unpublished tabulations from the 1999 London Employment Survey).

At the extreme, it might be argued therefore that any skills gap in the resident population, and any under-performance in the London education system, are in practice irrelevant to the performance of the London economy and to the maintenance of London's 'competitiveness'. Suitable skilled labour can simply be drawn in from elsewhere: commuters from Braintree and Bracknell, EU migrants from Bilbao and Bremen, clandestine workers from Burkina Faso and Belarus. However, this ignores several disadvantages of relying entirely on migration as a solution to an under-supply of skilled and trained workers. First, in an era when endogenous factors are identified as the key long-term causes of sustainable economic growth, it is short-sighted to ignore deficiencies in the local education system and skills base. Secondly, there are human and social costs to increased commuting times, and to temporary and permanent short- and long-term migration. The London region has high proportions of two-earner households and long journey to work times. This clearly places strains on family and other relationships, as shown by some of our household interviews in the OMA, with impacts on quality of life and perhaps social cohesion in the region. Thirdly, there will be significant social and economic consequences if a proportion of London residents remain in effect permanently excluded from many of the job opportunities in the region.

## Educational Outcomes and School Performance in the London Region

In addressing these issues we must start by asking how true it is that London schools 'under-perform'. Once again, the answer seems to depend on how we define 'London'. In discussions of school performance, much of the focus has actually been on Inner London, which from 1965 to 1990 had a single education authority, the Inner London Education Authority (ILEA). Even then, Outer London boroughs each ran their own system, and since ILEA abolition in 1990 (in the wake of the GLC's demise), all boroughs have been separate education authorities. In the OMA, all state schools used to be run by the shire counties, but with local government reforms in the late 1990s, control in several areas has been passed to local 'unitary' authorities, notably in Berkshire where the county was voluntarily dissolved. Perceptions about the 'performance' of London schools in examination terms still tend to be focused on the former ILEA area, however. And, Inner London state schools do (still) have well below national average success rates in the GCSE exams (taken by 16 year olds in their last year of compulsory schooling). This is offset, however, by slightly above-average performance in Outer London. Because there are many more pupils in Outer compared with Inner London, success rates for Greater London as a whole are around the national average – a bit above or below on different indicators. In the OMA results are better still, so the region as a whole emerges as performing at or above the national average on all measures, and clearly so in relation to 'good passes' (Table 5.4). This is true even in relation to the state sector on its own, despite independent schools (where the average 'good pass' rate is twice as high) 'creaming off' many more of the potential high flyers in the London region than they do nationally: in the London region 14 per cent of secondary school pupils are in the independent sector, compared with 8 per cent nationally.

In terms of the most basic levels of achievement (pupils with at least one pass), London results had been especially poor up to the mid-1990s. Since then there have been substantial improvements within Inner London: the numbers with no passes fell by 40 per cent over 5 years, against about 10 per cent nationally, bringing this area close to the national average. Furthermore, a comparison of Greater London results with those for the rest of England in the Department for Education and Employment's (DFEE's) 1998 value-added pilot study (which assessed individuals' progress between age-14 tests and age-16 exam results) showed that while London schools were four points behind on the raw exam scores, in terms of value-added they were actually three points ahead. This suggests that London secondary schools are actually performing above the national average once intake characteristics are taken into account.

As well as the inner-outer variations in exam results highlighted in this table, there are also marked east-west differences within each of the 'rings', with the west doing consistently better. In inner East London, just 32 per cent of pupils in state schools gained five good passes, 14 per cent below the English average, while in the western part of the OMA the figure was 58 per cent – 12 per cent above. At local education authority level, variations are even greater, with the region including both 11 of the 25 worst performing LEAs nationally on this indicator (mostly in Inner London with none in the OMA) and 12 of the 25 best performing (6 each in Outer

**Table 5.4.** GCSE examination results by area and school type, 1999.

| Area | School Type | % of pupils gaining | | |
| | | 5 grades A*–C | 5 passes (A*–G) | At least 1 pass (A*–G) |
|---|---|---|---|---|
| England | All | 49.0% | 90.2% | 95.3% |
| | Independent | 84.7% | 90.6% | 94.6% |
| | Maintained | 46.2% | 90.1% | 95.3% |
| London Region | All | 52.7% | 90.9% | 95.7% |
| | Independent | 87.6% | 92.2% | 95.7% |
| | Maintained | 48.9% | 90.7% | 95.7% |
| Inner London | Maintained | 35.0% | 85.8% | 94.6% |
| Outer London | Maintained | 48.5% | 90.7% | 95.5% |
| OMA | Maintained | 53.8% | 92.4% | 96.2% |

*Source:* Department of Education and Employment.

London and the OMA). Among our case study districts, Southwark, Greenwich, Newham and Wandsworth figured in the 'worst' list. Redbridge was among the best, and Hounslow was above the national average. Wokingham was above average while Reading was just outside the 'worst'. Results were relatively good in both Dartford and Gravesham.

The picture then seems to be not that schools in the London region generally do poorly, but that there is an unusually large variance in exam results between parts of the region. In part this is an artefact of there now being so many separate education authorities in the region, especially within Greater London. This exaggerates the degree of real variation relative to other parts of the country where often education authorities are larger and hence cover more heterogeneous areas. But even if we compare at the level of local authority districts, wards or even single schools, it remains true that there are substantially greater variations in performance within the London region than in other city regions.

## Socio-economic Influences on School Performance

A likely explanation starts from the premise that exam results are substantially affected by the social mix of the pupils. A second important factor (as discussed in Chapters 2 and 4) is the sheer scale of the London region which allows residential segregation of various kinds to operate across broader spatial scales than elsewhere. Segregation may therefore be operating not only at the level of school catchment areas, but also across wider areas, including whole LEAs. The first part of this argument is supported by the fact that the sub-regional pattern of inner-outer and east-west differentials in exam results parallels those for many of the broad indicators of social differentiation, described in Chapter 2 and subsequently. More detailed geographic comparisons can be made at ward level using measures from the educational 'domain' of DTLR's IMD2000 deprivation index which combines indicators from primary and secondary school tests, university admission rates and adult qualification levels. Even at this level of geographical detail, some very strong spatial patterns are evident, particularly in the concentration of poor scores throughout East London, south Essex and Kent Thames-side, in the Lea Valley and in some outlying industrial centres and new towns (Figure 5.1). This is also very much the pattern emerging from a map at local authority level of the proportion of students gaining five good GCSEs (Figure 5.2), indicating that these exam results form part of much broader patterns of strength and weakness in human capital development. It also bears a very strong similarity to maps of each of the other domains of socio-economic disadvantage identified by DTLR (except for that of service access), suggesting a strong likelihood of causal relationship between these and educational performance (see for example Figures 2.15, 6.2, and 7.1 in chapters 2, 6 and 7). Where there are differences these are principally that Kent Thames-side, the upper Lea Valley and, in general, the old industrial areas in the region perform even worse in education than in other domains of deprivation.

An obvious question then is how far the spatial disparities in education

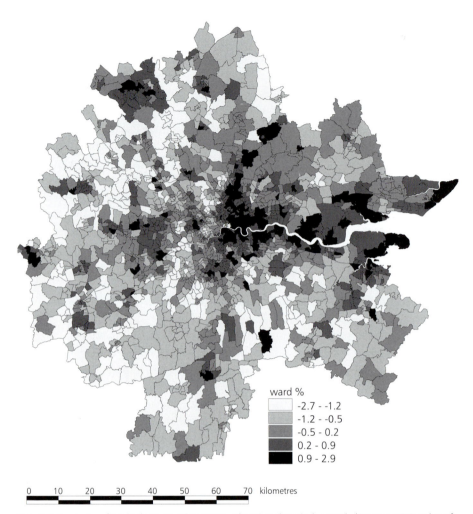

ward %

| | |
|---|---|
| ☐ | -2.7 - -1.2 |
| ▨ | -1.2 - -0.5 |
| ▦ | -0.5 - 0.2 |
| ▩ | 0.2 - 0.9 |
| ■ | 0.9 - 2.9 |

0    10    20    30    40    50    60    70   kilometres

**Figure 5.1.** Index of Multiple Deprivation 2000: education domain by ward. (*Source:* DTLR Index of Multiple Deprivation 2000)

performance across the region simply reflect more or less advantaged social backgrounds of the children going through local schools, given the scale at which social segregation operates in this region. Some strong associations between non-school factors and low levels of educational attainment have long been recognized in the educational and sociological literature, particularly in relation to the effects of low family income. In terms of spatial variation, recent research has shown that the proportion of children dependent on income support could account for two-thirds of variance in educational attainment at the local authority level (West *et al.*, 2001). This factor is closely reflected in the proportion of pupils known to be eligible for free school meals – which was 44 per cent in Inner London secondary schools in 2000, compared with 19 per cent in Outer London, 17 per cent nationally and just 10 per cent in ROSE. Other area-based research emphasizes the association between exam results and the distribution of one of the particular groups receiving income support, namely non-employed lone parents, which Gordon (1996c) claims to account for between two-thirds and four-fifths of variation between education authorities.

Such ecological correlations might be spurious, but similarly strong associations have been found at the individual level also. For example, Thomas and Smees (1997) report pupil intake factors as accounting for up to 59 per cent of variance in pupils' academic test scores. In terms of social class variations, national data for 1997 showed that children from the most advantaged backgrounds were more than three times as likely to attain five or more higher grade GCSEs as their peers at the other end of the spectrum. Moreover, social class gaps in educational attainment seem to be growing. Between 1988 and 1997, the difference in the success rates, in terms

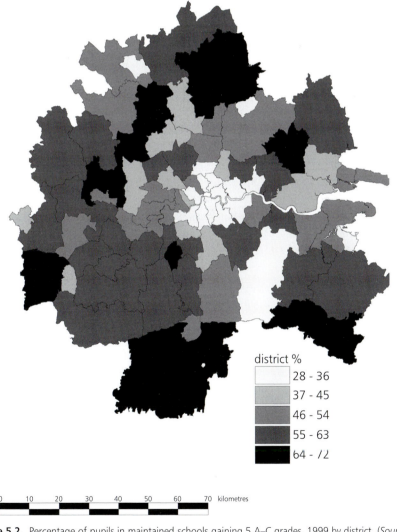

district %

28 - 36
37 - 45
46 - 54
55 - 63
64 - 72

0   10   20   30   40   50   60   70 kilometres

**Figure 5.2.** Percentage of pupils in maintained schools gaining 5 A–C grades, 1999 by district. (*Source*: Department of Education and Employment)

of five 'good' GCSEs, between children from 'managerial/professional' and 'unskilled manual' backgrounds widened from 40 to 49 percentage points (Gillborn and Mirza, 2000). Other evidence shows that not only poverty/class factors but also parental education and single parenthood have major effects on success rates (Ermisch and Francesconi, 2001).

There are also significant differences in educational attainment by ethnic group, which might contribute to the observed spatial variations within the region, although they do not follow a simple white/non-white pattern. Nationally in 2000, according to evidence from the Youth Cohort Study, the ethnic group with the highest proportion achieving five or more 'good' GCSE passes was Chinese/other Asian (70 per cent), followed by Indian (62 per cent), then white (50 per cent), black (37 per cent) and Pakistanis/Bangladeshis (30 per cent) (Cabinet Office Performance and Innovation Unit, 2002). These differentials substantially exceed the more publicized 'gender gap' of 9 percentage points (in favour of girls), though they are still much smaller than the social class differential cited above. Indeed, some of the gross variation across ethnic groups might well reflect the impact of different distributions between class positions, not purely 'ethnic' differences. National analyses of school level variations in exam results actually suggest that, after control for socio-economic disadvantage, the only significant effects of schools' ethnic (or linguistic) composition involved *positive* associations with proportions of pupils from some of the newer immigrant groups (Bangladeshis, black Africans and Chinese) (GB Department for Education and Employment, 1999).

To see how far differences in local population mix on these dimensions could account for the wide variations in attainment within the London region, we undertook a series of regression analyses relating the GCSE results of individual secondary schools within the maintained sector to characteristics of these schools and of the population of surrounding areas (defined both narrowly and more broadly). The results highlighted a number of very strong effects of school characteristics, including its position in relation to pupil selection, its degree of autonomy from local authority control (which may also permit selective recruitment), gender mix and size (with clear returns to scale). But there was also a number of evidently important relations with populations in surrounding areas, in terms particularly of social class, the incidence of single parenthood, ethnic composition, and unemployment. The negative effects associated with concentrations of deprived groups (single parent families and the unemployed) tended to be localized, whereas the positive impact of more professional and managerial families was diffused over a wider area – as was the negative (creaming) effect from the presence of selective schools. This clearly reflects differential abilities to take advantage of choice in the system, and implies a very limited impact from gentrification on school results in the immediate vicinity. The one more localized positive effect was from concentrations of South Asian (and/or immigrant) families, which were associated with better GCSE results in local schools.

At school level it is clear that a key factor in exam performance is the rate of pupil absenteeism, especially through truancy which is particularly significant in Inner London schools where the rate is three times that in the OMA. A strongly non-linear relationship with exam results implies something beyond a simple effect of missing classes, perhaps in terms of the disciplinary climate and sense of order in particular schools. Among schools in the region truancy rates were found to be clearly higher among smaller, coeducational schools and those under direct local authority control (as distinct from grant maintained or voluntary aided schools) – but also in areas with more children from lone parent families. This last relationship is also a non-linear one, implying that it is not simply a matter of *these* children being more prone to truancy. But it is a very strong association and clearly a major route through which concentrations of this group, especially within Inner London, are associated with poorer exam results (Gordon and Monastiriotis, 2001).

## The School Quality Factor

Even after these factors are controlled for, there remains substantial variance in results between schools, and also between local education authority areas. Clearly there are good and bad schools – a fact attested to by national research (Thomas and Mortimore, 1996), and also probably better and worse LEAs. But, once allowance is made for the socio-economic context, wider differences in performance between Inner London schools/LEAs and those elsewhere are very largely accounted for. The only LEA in which results now appear significantly worse than expected is the outer borough of Merton, rather than any of the inner boroughs normally labelled as 'under-performing' – though most of the 'over-performers' emerging from this analysis are found in the 'western crescent' of the OMA, the exceptions being Haringey and Redbridge.

Although the major influences on achievement and outcomes for children are factors from outside school, such as family background, social class, and poverty, this does not mean that schools have *no* impact on attainment. Schools *do* make a difference, and this was reflected in our interviews with parents and teachers in the case study areas. In some schools there was a particularly strong commitment to raising pupils' expectations and achievements:

> We have a *relentless emphasis upon improving ourselves as teachers and improving the circumstances in which children can learn. So unremitting attention to the trade of teaching and learning. You have got to get the culture right. A sense of we can do and we will do it. That sounds a bit clichéd but it's true.*

Head, City Technology College

This requires high-quality teaching, but major difficulties were reported in recruiting and retaining good staff, not just in Inner London but across the whole region:

> It's not so much recruitment that's a problem, it's retention is the problem. Now part of it in this area is about housing . . . people can't afford to step up from a rented or a shared flat to a two or three bedroom . . . also, teachers are getting fed up with the abuse they get, usually verbal but also sometimes physical, from a minority of pupils and parents.

Director of Education, Inner London

Teacher vacancy rates have been rising generally during the economic upswing but are especially high in Greater London, with a peak figure of 8 per cent in Hackney in summer 2001 (*Education Guardian*, 30 August 2001). This is partly because of higher turnover rates in London and the South East, and the net drift of teachers from London to other regions (Employers Organisation for Local Government, 2001), but largely because of simple recruitment problems, affecting all parts of the region. Two common responses have been to recruit from overseas and to rely increasingly on long-term supply teachers. This is a complicated problem, in which there is an interaction between: teachers' pay, conditions and status; specific London issues of housing affordability and quality of life (which have become more pressing during the 1980s and 1990s); and the particular stresses of teaching in the more 'challenging' schools within the London system.

A second key variable influencing the effectiveness of learning in particular schools – which some schools have sought to alter as part of an attainment-raising strategy – is the social, cultural and ability mix of the intake group. Changes in intake have a two-fold effect. As well as the direct effects of pupil characteristics on their own performance, national studies have shown important peer group effects, such that all pupils' performance (and subsequent earning capacity) tends to be raised by the presence of a high performing peer group (Robertson and Symons, 1996; Willms and Echols, 1992). Any tendency for more able pupils to be clustered in particular schools is then likely to lead to a polarization of outcomes – with positive peer group effects going disproportionately to this group (and *vice versa*) – which in Feinstein and Symons' study (1999) emerges as a main route for the passing on of parental social advantage.

In principle, one can distinguish between the effects of 'better teaching' and the effects of 'changed intake'. But in practice, these processes may go together. In seeking to change their intake, schools may tighten up disciplinary as well as academic standards, perhaps with a rise in exclusions, as a means of turning around their reputation to achieve a broader range of applications. This is part of the competitive London schools market which we shall discuss in the next section. But it also highlights questions about the ways in which pupil attainment is influenced by different parental and community attitudes. Some parents in particular communities clearly see education as the key route to improved life chances for their children. This was especially true of many minority ethnic parents, notably those from South Asian and African backgrounds. Where such values are widely shared within a community, they operate as a form of social capital (Coleman, 1988), reinforcing family attitudes and producing effects on educational outcomes independent of both financial capital and human (individual) capital:

> [In my class] there were lots of people who went to university . . . more because they come from Asian families and their parents expect them to go to university rather than the fact that the schools are very good here . . . going to university is definitely the norm in this area . . . it's just because it's expected.
>
> Single woman, employed, Sikh, homeowner (living at home)

> Pupils at this school have a more realistic view than the pupils at the previous school I was at, which was predominantly white. They all felt that it didn't matter how they worked at school or didn't work at school, because they deserved a job. Whereas I think here the perception is

*– you only get the job if you work for it . . . and that's why education is important, because you can't expect to get a job if you haven't got decent education.*

Deputy Head, secondary school, Outer London

In many cases this meant exit to the private sector or use of tutoring to supplement state education:

*Southwark has the highest numbers of supplementary type schools which is mostly black, also Asian, Bangladeshis, Vietnamese . . . they push their kids.*

Careers Adviser, Inner London

*I'm actually paying for [my daughter] to be in a nice, friendly environment, you know, where the parents are concerned about their children and their progress . . . everyone's motivated, all the parents have the same goals for their children and so she'll just be in a very sort of motivated environment. And that's what I'm paying for.*

Married mother, employed, Indian, owner occupier (lives with in laws)

Nevertheless, there were also some 'cultural' factors at work in particular minority communities that are less conducive to educational attainment. Head teachers referred to extended visits to the Indian sub-continent and the low level of literacy among mothers in some communities as barriers to educational achievement.

Teachers and other professionals – particularly in inner-city areas – also identified some very important negative parental and community influences. These included both long-standing local cultures, and newer social trends – particularly the fragility of marriages and family relationships, and the impact of more generally chaotic lives. In outer areas as well as in Inner London, conflicts between families brought tensions and disorder into the school. Teachers often felt they were being asked not just to teach children, but to try to repair damaged families and communities:

*The responsibilities placed on schools are growing – schools now have to do the parenting and parent the parents – this is difficult when the most important issue is to change parental attitudes.*

Head Teacher, primary school, Outer London

*A lot of [the children's] lives aren't consistent and the only thing that they do do every single week is go to school. But a lot of them stay at their Dad's one day or stay with their Mum and some of them don't have fixed addresses so school means a lot to them. And they do react and may be terrible in a group of twenty-five but you take each as an individual and they are lovely.*

Head Teacher, secondary school, Inner London

At the extreme, social and personal disadvantage can seriously damage any kind of learning:

*Sometimes in the project we got to the stage where we were saying there is a whole piece of work that has to be done with these young people before we even get into teaching. And if you haven't got those foundations you can forget about the teaching no matter how brilliant you are as a teacher – for some of them it's just not going to work.*

Outreach worker, secondary school, Inner London

Another common problem in (mostly white) working-class areas was that of narrow horizons, both socially and spatially, restricting aspirations and career prospects:

> *Pupils and their families have very low expectations and motivations in relation to education . . . A significant minority of pupils are from families where there is third generation unemployment. The achievement of white boys at the school is particularly low . . . Pupils in the school are in desperate need of successful role models, a lot of them just don't know what's out there. Many would not have been into central London.*
>
> Head Teacher, secondary school Outer London

> *For girls . . . it was about having babies, having them quite young that's what their mum did. If you said childcare is a really good profession to get into but if you are going to go into the nursery are you going to be a child psychologist? 'No no I'm going to be a Nanny'. . . It is very much a pattern within families, this is how my family is so this is how I am.*
>
> Project worker, voluntary agency, Inner London

## The Competitive London Schools Market

The school system in the London region reflects the social and spatial structure of the city and region. Parents compete to place their children in 'good' schools, but also schools compete for pupils, especially those who will enhance a school's reputation. In effect a 'quasi-market' operates (Le Grand and Bartlett,1993) – but with particular competitive pressures reflecting the greater variety of kinds and qualities of schools in London, together with the fact that there tend to be more alternative schools within reasonable travelling range. As a result, London parents have responded more strongly to the enhanced opportunities for parental choice following from the 1988 Education Reform Act and the publication of school league tables. One clear indicator of this is a substantially higher rate of parental appeals against non-admission of their children to first-choice schools, especially in the secondary sector, where fewer children simply go to the nearest school. Across the region as a whole, 14 per cent of these admissions decisions were taken to appeal in 1999/2000, against 10 per cent nationally. But the proportion was 19 per cent in Inner London, and 21per cent in Outer London. The extreme cases were Enfield, where 66 per cent of decisions were appealed, and Westminster, with 33 per cent. Among our case study districts, the highest proportions were in Hounslow and Wandsworth, with 27 per cent and 22 per cent respectively, while the lowest were in Reading/Wokingham and Southwark, with 9 per cent and 12 per cent. Some other major cities had appeal rates matching those in London (notably Birmingham and Liverpool), while in others (notably Newcastle and Sheffield) it was only a third as high.

On the supply side of this quasi-market, there is a considerable range of provision over and above the mainstream coeducational local authority comprehensives. Firstly, there are independent schools, which have always been disproportionately represented in both Greater London and the OMA because of the relative affluence of their population. Two other major elements are the voluntary-aided sector (mostly denominational) and the 'grant-maintained' schools which were allowed to opt out of LEA control under Conservative governments in the 1980s/90s. Both of these are more significant in London than elsewhere – the voluntary sector particularly in inner areas and the GM sector in outer areas. Together they account for 40 per cent of places in the maintained sector, leaving barely half of pupils in mainstream LEA schools. Most of these are non-selective comprehensives, but in seven of the outer boroughs (including Redbridge), and in four of the eight contiguous OMA counties (including our Reading and Dartford study areas) both the LEA and GM sectors include selective grammar schools, which are mostly single sex and draw from wider catchment areas. Within each of these categories, individual schools have differentiated reputations, and distinctive features including religious affiliation and the sex of pupils admitted. In pursuing the school of their choice, parents are no longer constrained (since the Education Reform Act) by LEA boundaries, nor in most boroughs (Greenwich being an exception) by the banding system which ILEA used to balance the intake to comprehensive schools. One effect is that those middle-class gentrifiers, in places such as our Wandsworth and Southwark study areas, who are unhappy with the quality of local schools can opt for comprehensives in neighbouring boroughs with a better intake, as an alternative to exiting to the independent sector. Overall, some 14 per cent of London secondary school pupils were attending school in another borough in 1998, with some boroughs experiencing major net gains or losses of pupils. From Brent, Haringey, Hackney, Southwark and Lambeth the net outflow was over 10 per cent of resident pupil numbers, while Bromley, Sutton, Richmond, Hounslow, Barnet, Camden and Westminster had net inflows of this scale. As this suggests, the larger flows were outwards and/or westwards. Statistical analyses suggest no evident links with the mix of school types or secondary school performance in the boroughs involved, but there do seem to be links both with the ethnic composition of the school population (involving a drift away from boroughs with more Afro-Caribbean pupils than their neighbours) and the local ability mix (as represented by primary school Key Stage Two results).

In this competitive situation, there was a general perception among residents that schools are better in LEAs further out. Within our case study areas, recognized hierarchies of secondary schools have emerged. This process has been aided by the league tables which the government introduced to put pressure on weak performers.

> 50 per cent of children get 5+ A–C [grades], which is the figure the Government is using . . . If you [send] the top 25 per cent to grammar schools, then you only have 25 per cent left, and if you have a hierarchy of schools which is what you have got here, with Grammar schools at the top, then CTC, then the denominational schools . . . as you go down the line, someone has to be at the bottom.
>
> Head Teacher, Outer Metropolitan Area

> it's dog eat dog . . . it's very competitive . . . only one person can be bottom of the league tables. Now I am and the only way I get off is to put someone else there and that's the bottom line. You have to become ruthless and a 110 per cent champion of your own school.
>
> Head Teacher, Outer London

The popularity or unpopularity of particular schools seems to rest on a combination of quantitative information on academic attainment and more general behaviour, reputation and social factors – what Bernstein (1975) called the 'expressive order' of the school. This pattern of assessment of schools seemed to be common across our study areas, and across social classes of parents:

> I'm going to sound terribly snobbish and stuck up and I really don't mean to. S-town isn't a particular nice area. And we went over to the meetings at the school and the head was speaking and the parents were talking amongst themselves and getting up and walking out. And when you've got the parents with that attitude, obviously the children, it's just the same. I didn't like it at all.
>
> Separated mother, employed, white, homeowner

> School P is an unsuitable school because all the kids were locked in . . . You had to sign in and out. There was a security guard on the door. I thought this is ridiculous. And there's a bunch of tarts hanging outside the pub . . . hanging around a lamppost, so, it didn't seem very suitable or good environment to be for [my daughter] to go to.
>
> Divorced mother (living with partner), employed, white, homeowner

Exclusion of pupils threatening the disciplinary order of the school has been one possible response to this situation, and there was a clear upward trend in permanent exclusion rates during the early/mid-1990s. The numbers involved have never been very large, peaking at about 0.3 per cent for Greater London secondary school pupils. Evidence on the risk of more general social exclusion for those involved led to a policy change in the late 1990s, with the Social Exclusion Unit pursuing initiatives to reduce both exclusions and truancy. Nevertheless, schools face pressures from parents seeking firmer discipline:

> There is a little bit of a not-on-my-back-doorstep syndrome . . . we have had a pressure group from a set of parents who when we tried to work with a child who was . . . a sort of an exclusion child, a difficult child who didn't want to come to school and was hell when he did come to school, we took him on because he came from another school and wouldn't go to school there. We had a band of parents who quite frankly shocked me to the core, their attitude was 'We don't want him here, why do we have to have him, he's upsetting our children's education' . . . They're not as for inclusion as we have to be.
>
> Head, primary school, Outer Metropolitan Area

The existence of spare capacity in the system creates the conditions through which a hierarchy can be strengthened, leading to decline of the weaker schools. In some terms this might be seen as an efficient outcome, but it raises major questions about what becomes of the schools, and the pupils within them, who end up at the bottom of the hierarchy. This has been especially so, since spare capacity has been most evident in areas with the most severe problems both of deprivation and of school discipline. Following recent action to remove surplus places this pattern is much less evident. But it remains true that a system in which large numbers of children are categorized as failures and – even worse – perceive themselves to be failures has very destructive consequences:

They walk in the door defeated. The first assembly I run is telling them that *x* number of you will go to university . . . after three years of constantly telling them . . . they start to believe you.

Head Teacher, Outer Metropolitan Area

## Parents' Educational Strategies

With widening choice, and institutional fragmentation in the system, the process of getting children into an appropriate secondary school has become very complex for London parents. One aspect of this is the need felt by many mothers (in particular) to undertake considerable research with both published 'League Table' data and more informal word-of-mouth sources. But for the more ambitious parents there are also opportunities to adopt a more strategic approach, through choosing a residential location or some other affiliation which offers access to better schools.

Traditionally this has been seen as the province of 'middle-class cosmopolitans', in contrast to working-class groups whose approach to choice is often defined as being more practical and limited to the here and now. This view is rather supported by Butler and Robson's (2002) study of gentrifying households in several London neighbourhoods. They showed that education was one of the key variables in the gentrification process – alongside employment and housing considerations – and that the gentrifiers tended to pursue cohesive and exclusive educational strategies. There were, however, some significant differences between areas, particularly in the extent to which gentrifiers relied on economic, social or cultural capital, and in their degree of commitment to the area – itself partly dependent on the availability of a satisfactory educational infrastructure. In Battersea, they found that a more privatized middle class, prioritizing economic capital, naturally relied on private schooling. In Telegraph Hill (in Lewisham), where social capital is relied on to a greater extent, 'the "adoption" of the local primary school . . . over a period of ten years was one of the key factors in building it as a middle class enclave' (Robson and Butler, 2001, 81). However, none of the parents sent their children to a local secondary school:

> Children are pointed towards 'the most appropriate' schools, whether in the private or the state selective sector [accounting for 45 per cent and 27 per cent of children respectively], taking into account their individual needs and this is squared with ideological and often professional commitments to state provision in a common narrative with other parents. (Butler and Robson, 2002)

In Brixton, where both economic and social capital were lower among gentrifiers, there had been less success in colonizing a local primary, and with less inclination (or capacity) to pursue private or non-local secondaries, those gentrifiers with children (the minority here) were more worried about education, and likely to be considering a move away, even out of London.

In our research, looking at a broader range of areas, we found evidence both of other strategies, and of other groups with a strategic approach to the education of their children. In particular, families from various ethnic minorities emerged as particularly alert to these possibilities, since they saw education as the key to upward mobility. Like the white middle class they were able to 'envisage their children in yet to be realized contexts' (Ball *et al.*, 1995 quoted in Robson and Butler, 2001), and their particular concerns appear at various points through this chapter. The widespread awareness among parents of differences in school quality and the implications of school choice contradicts the notion that only a few groups were active choosers. However, limits on the resources available to working-class families naturally (and rationally) affected the choices which they made, and so the overall effect is for choice to operate in class-bound ways. At secondary transfer stage in London middle-class parents identified as their first choice schools averaging 53 per cent five or more A*–C grades at GCSE, whilst working class parents chose schools averaging 40 per cent (Noden *et al.*, 1998).

For those in the owner-occupied sector, choice of a residential location near good schools is a key element in educational strategies. This was one factor encouraging outward moves:

> *What I've found out around here, that the schools are not that good . . . I get the impression that the further out of central London the better the schools.*
>
> Single father, employed, black British, council tenant

> *The lady that I bought this house from had only been here about four years before she moved and it was because of schools . . . All of them are moving out for schools . . . going up to Egham, Staines, Ashford, there are better schools up there.*
>
> Married mother, part-time employed, North African origins, homeowner

At a more local level there is evidence of the importance attached by movers to school quality in the house price differentials associated with proximity to schools with better records of exam success. As we have seen, a large part of such variations actually reflects differences in pupil intake, linked to the social mix of the local population, and not simply school quality – though if peer groups matter, pupils themselves contribute to school quality. But in any case, house purchasers behave as if school will have an independent effect on the educational outcomes their children will achieve. And, the rationing impact of house prices means that 'good schools' are likely to attract a catchment area population which is both more socially advantaged (i.e. affluent) and more strongly motivated toward educational achievement.

There is considerable research evidence for the existence of school catchment effects on house prices. Cheshire and Sheppard (1998) found the price differential between similar houses in the catchment areas of the lowest- and highest-performing secondary schools in the Greater Reading area to be around 15 per cent. In Coventry the differential for the catchment areas for two popular schools were estimated at 15 per cent and 19 per cent. For primary schools, households in London and the South East appear to be willing to pay a premium of between 5 per cent and 8 per cent on property prices for each 10 percentage point improvement in the performance score of local schools (Gibbons and Machin, 2001).

Another important strategy – particularly in suburban areas such as Gants Hill and Hounslow – was to use (or find) a religious affiliation as a way of gaining access to schools with conditions more conducive to educational success. A quarter of all maintained secondary schools in Greater London are denominational, two-thirds of them Roman Catholic and the rest mostly Church of England. Because pupils are generally admitted on religious criteria, catchment areas tend to be larger – with the Jewish Free School in Camden as an extreme case, drawing pupils from sixteen London boroughs. This is obviously important for those with strong religious concerns for their children. But since these schools generally also have positive educational reputations, the denominational route is also a means of avoiding poor local schools, at least for those who are able to gain access, as many of our interviewees emphasized:

> *When my eldest was ready to go to school . . . I didn't want him to go [to school X], so that's why we decided he should go to Ilford Jewish. But you had to have an interview and they were slightly oversubscribed and we were lucky we got in because we fitted into the criteria . . . you had to go to synagogue . . . and show you were quite religious.*
>
> Married mother, part-time employed, homeowner

> *My daughter changed her religion to get [her son] into the only school what's worth sending a child to in Hounslow . . . she changed to a Catholic . . . so that he could go to the local Catholic school, because it's very good.*
>
> Married mother, employed, white, homeowner

In general we found that London parents seeking to exercise choice had to be well informed, determined, flexible in their spiritual orientation – and if necessary be prepared to cheat, for example in relation to their true home address.

## Effects of the Quasi-Market

One expected effect of the educational quasi-market is increased segregation. Households and teachers that we interviewed did strongly perceive an increase in social segregation across schools, an impression supported by Noden's (2000) research on recent changes in the segregation of those entitled to free school meals. He found that between 1994 and 1999 schools in twenty London boroughs experienced an increase in segregation, with only six showing a decrease, while five of the twelve LEAs across the whole country which showed sharp increases in segregation were within London. However, in the early 1990s trends appear to have been moving in the reverse direction, so that Gorard and Fitz (2000) find, for London as for the country as a whole, that segregation between schools, in terms of poverty, ethnicity and special needs, showed no increases over the period since 1988 when market principles were introduced to the sector. There is a suggestion that school segregation levels may vary cyclically (Noden, 2001), but the straightforward effect of increased freedom of school choice on segregation of the economically disadvantaged seems to be rather small by comparison with migration patterns and other factors only indirectly linked to the educational system.

Survey evidence indicates that in Inner London at least actual freedom of choice is more constrained than in other areas (including another large city), with 32 per cent of parents failing to get their first choice, compared with 9 per cent across all areas (Audit Commission, 1996). This could be because, with stronger residential segregation, London parents are more likely to be making choices between what everyone would agree were better and worse schools, rather than on the basis of more particular preferences, which could more easily be satisfied within the constraints of capacity. Whatever the reason for this, Inner London respondents proved much less satisfied with the working of the transfer system than those in any of the other four area types surveyed – the most satisfied being those in a small city within a semi-rural region. There is clearly a great deal of frustration with the working of the quasi-market system, though the real test of this will be whether the competitive pressures which it applies have led to better performance among the weaker London schools.

## Further and Higher Education in the Competitive City

The influence of educational institutions in the region on competitiveness and cohesion does not end with schooling, but assessment of the contribution of post-school education is complicated by the fact that students in higher and further education may be only temporary residents in the region. Many come from other parts of the UK or from abroad: some of these remain in London, adding to the stock of human capital in the regional labour force, while others return home or move on elsewhere. Institutions within the sector vary greatly in the degree to which they are oriented to local, regional, national or international markets. At one extreme, the three elite institutions – LSE, University College London, and Imperial College – together draw 30 per cent of their students from abroad. In the case of home students, the wider group of research-oriented universities in the region – those with good scores in the 1996 'research assessment exercise' – draw two-thirds of their intake from outside the region, while among other universities the proportions are reversed. In the further education sector the orientation to local demand is likely to be stronger. The other side of this picture is that the elite institutions have narrower patterns of recruitment in social terms. Just 6 per cent of students at the elite institutions come from neighbourhoods with a historically low level of participation in Higher Education, compared with 15 per cent at the University of East London. It is still mostly the former polytechnics, together with further education (FE) colleges, that provide opportunities for less advantaged sectors of the London population to gain higher qualifications.

The rate of university participation among young people originating from the region is a little above the national average. In 1997/98 successful university applicants represented about 28 per cent of the age cohort in the region compared with 26 per cent for England as a whole. Higher Education Statistics Agency (HESA) data on those actually graduating in 1995/96 suggest a slightly wider gap, with students from the region accounting for 24 per cent of the UK total, compared with its 20 per cent of residents in the main student age group. A majority of these graduates actually attended institutions outside the region, so there is a substantial net outflow of students at this stage. However, this is greatly exceeded by the inflow of graduates coming to work in the region, especially those with good degrees and from the higher status institutions. Of those graduating from British universities in

1995/96 30 per cent had their first job in the London region, a net gain of 5 per cent as compared with the numbers originating from the region. This represents a very important addition to the region's human capital stock – reflecting the attraction both of London jobs and London lifestyles – but it still means that a high proportion of graduates working in the region actually came through its school system.

This is a significant point since there are still very great social disparities in access to higher education within the region. As a proportion of the 18 year old age cohort, local success rates in admission to universities (in 1997/98) show a particularly strong inverse association with the child poverty indicator from the IMD2000 deprivation indices. In fact, rates of university entry in the worst areas on this measure were four times lower than in the best (14 per cent compared with 58 per cent). Interestingly, there was a much larger difference between the most affluent areas and the median than between the median and the poorest. In part the sharp disparities may reflect the deterrent effect of the current costs of higher education for those with no parental support to fall back on. But to a very large extent it must represent wide differences in the proportions achieving appropriately high levels of school qualification, as between those from the most and least advantaged segments of the regional population.

The less elite part of the university system and the FE colleges provide opportunities for re-skilling and career change. There is a relatively dense infrastructure of FE and other colleges, vocational and private training which can provide opportunities for highly individualized mixes of working and studying. This yields opportunities for education, skills acquisition and improved job prospects for Londoners who can commit the personal and financial resources to them. Further education plays a major role for example in providing basic skills to asylum seekers and refugees.

We found numerous examples of individuals devising re-skilling and education strategies to enable them to change their fortunes. Many were women and many from minority ethnic groups. The paths could hardly be described as easy: in most cases there was a daunting mix of education, work and family responsibilities. Nevertheless, it is *possible* in London to re-make yourself this way.

> I did a typing course, I did a secretarial course, I did a business and admin course, did a computer course . . . So I thought right I've done all these things, I've worked in the office for about eight years, and I've done that and I've done this, so I've worked in a solicitors, I've been a legal executive for about two years and so I thought I'll just have a go at working with the elderly and mentally handicapped and I just got in to that and it's different . . . I thought I'd give that a go, and it's okay, I'm enjoying it . . . if you make up your mind to do something you have to do it, you don't need somebody to say 'Go to school'.
>
> Single mother, employed, Afro-Caribbean, council tenant

> At the moment I'm a cashier but I'm doing it part-time because I'm studying full-time . . . I'm studying to become an accountant so hopefully to get a good job.
>
> Married, employed, African, living with council tenants

However, acquiring further qualifications and skills does not automatically mean a better job. For many, particularly minority ethnic and recent arrivals, the only employment they can obtain is well below their skills and education. This respondent was working as a porter and studying:

*I've finished [training as a housing officer] at North West College . . . where I work now, I've stayed there for seven years . . . it is really boring doing one thing every day repeatedly, just like cleaning or . . . answering the phone, coming to take boxes or whatever upstairs, that's why I have to do these courses, it's better . . . I've got some teaching qualifications, but . . . I didn't want to go into that.*

Married father, employed, African, council tenant

This is not to suggest it is easy to upgrade skills in this way: it is hard to do, but it can be done. But the London labour market does not necessarily reward determination or qualifications appropriately. Gender, ethnicity and class still matter.

## Ethnicity, Immigration and Schooling in London

At all levels the region's education system is distinguished by its very high degree of ethnic diversity. This is much more marked than in most other activities because of the relatively young age distribution of all of the minority ethnic communities, especially those with large numbers of more recent immigrants. Thus Table 5.5, relating to primary school pupils, provides a much more heterogeneous picture of the region's ethnic mix than emerged from the overall population figures discussed in the last chapter.

In England as a whole, around 12 per cent of primary school pupils are non-white, and in OMA the proportion is 8 per cent. But in Outer London, 30 per cent of pupils are from minority ethnic groups, while in Inner London, there is now a 'majority minority' population in state primary schools. At borough level, in Newham, Tower Hamlets, Hackney and Brent two-thirds or more of primary pupils are non-white, implying that in particular schools the white 'host' population is likely

**Table 5.5.** Percentages of pupils in maintained primary schools by ethnic group and mother tongue, 1999.

|  | Inner London | Outer London | OMA | London Region | England |
|---|---|---|---|---|---|
| White | 43.5 | 69.8 | 92.3 | 75.7 | 88.2 |
| Black Caribbean | 11.9 | 4.1 | 0.7 | 3.9 | 1.6 |
| Black African | 14.0 | 4.2 | 0.3 | 4.1 | 1.2 |
| Black Other | 5.1 | 2.5 | 0.4 | 2.0 | 0.9 |
| Indian | 3.5 | 8.3 | 1.4 | 4.1 | 2.3 |
| Pakistani | 2.7 | 3.4 | 2.3 | 2.7 | 2.5 |
| Bangladeshi | 9.0 | 0.8 | 0.6 | 2.2 | 1.0 |
| Chinese | 1.0 | 0.7 | 0.3 | 0.6 | 0.3 |
| Other minority ethnic group | 9.3 | 6.2 | 1.7 | 4.6 | 2.1 |
| Mother tongue not English | 43.0 | 21.9 | 5.2 | 18.1 | 8.4 |

*Source:* DfES SFR 15/1999 Minority Ethnic Pupils in Maintained Schools by Local Education Authority in England – January 1999 (Provisional).

to be in a very small minority. There is considerable geographical diversity within the minority ethnic population, with black Caribbean, black African, black other and Bangladeshi pupils concentrated in Inner London, and Indians and (to a lesser extent) Pakistanis in Outer London. Across Greater London a third of all schoolchildren have a mother tongue other than English, though no other language is used by more than 5 per cent of pupils, while overall some 300 different languages are spoken by London schoolchildren (Baker and Eversley, 2000). There is little sign of this diversity in the OMA, however, where the (preponderantly white) ethnic mix is very similar to that in the rest of England, outside the London region.

The position and experience of ethnic and linguistic minorities within the educational system is significant from several different perspectives, such as: relative levels of achievement and their knock-on effects in the labour market; the experiences of particular groups within schools and through the educational process; the impact on the system of recent waves of refugees; and finally the more general quality of inter-group relations within schools and the communities associated with them. As we have seen earlier in this chapter, there are substantial differences in school attainment by pupils from different ethnic groups, though these are not simply between whites and non-whites – or between natal and non-natal English speakers – and are on a smaller scale than differences between social class groups. Indeed, much of the inter-ethnic variation in exam results does appear to be a reflection of differing degrees of (dis)advantage associated with parents' socio-economic and family status, rather than something peculiarly 'ethnic'. Of course, this observation begs the question as to why there should be such variations in status. And it is the simple (unfair) fact of difference in outcomes along ethnic lines which is most readily noted, by the pupils involved and their families, as well as outside observers. While Indians and some others have fared relatively well, national studies point to increasing disparities between the attainments of white pupils and those from lower status minority groups, both over time and during their own passage through the system:

> African-Caribbean and Pakistani pupils have drawn least benefit from the rising levels of attainment: the gap between them and their white peers is bigger now than a decade ago . . . (and) the inequalities of attainment for African-Caribbean pupils become progressively greater as they move through the school system; such differences become more pronounced between the end of primary school and the end of secondary education. (Gillborn and Mirza, 2000, 14, 17)

In our interviews with minority ethnic parents, several expressed concern about their children's treatment within the school system, although usually in the context of a particularly strong motivation toward education on the part of immigrants, and more general disapproval of lax standards:

> I don't know how to describe it but it is really disgraceful that the teachers are not . . . taking the full potential of the people from the sub-continent . . . They are not being encouraged and this education is going down the drains . . . My daughter was given CCC/CCB [as an assessment] . . . she got three A's, almost . . . she [eventually] went to Cambridge, she did LLM [Masters in Law] and she . . . won some award as well.
>
> Married father, retired, Asian, homeowner

*When the girls came here they were intelligent . . . and when they got into this country . . . all that intelligence deteriorated, they didn't seem clever at school. They used to get As and Bs – their grades dropped down to really Es and Fs, so I couldn't understand whether was it the school, or was it them children just changed – I didn't know. But I think it was more to the environment, the fact that they changed from the lifestyles that they used to be to this type of lifestyle where people can be in control of theirself and say: 'Yes, I'm all right, if I don't want to do something, I don't have to do it'.*

Single mother, part-time employed/student, African, HA tenant

In the case of pupils from Afro-Caribbean origins – who are mostly British born – a more specific source of concern is their disproportionate rate of exclusion from schools on grounds of poor behaviour. Nationally, Afro-Caribbean pupils are four times as likely to get permanently excluded from school as their white counterparts – while those from the 'black other' group are three times as likely to be. Among black Africans exclusion rates are much closer to those for whites, while among Asian groups they are significantly lower. Similar differentials (and rates for particular groups) seem to apply in London, although published figures only distinguish a combined 'black' group. What is different in London (particularly Inner London) is the relative size of the Afro-Caribbean (and 'black other') community. Following initiatives by the current government, which substantially reduced exclusion rates in all communities over a couple of years, the 1999/2000 exclusion rate for black pupils in London was just 0.3 per cent, probably implying 0.5 per cent among Afro-Caribbeans. Since 84 per cent of all excluded pupils are male, the rate among Afro-Caribbean boys is likely to be about 0.8 per cent. This is still a low figure (though long-term consequences can be severe for the excluded) but it is an indicator of a more widespread problem which schools seem to have in resolving disciplinary problems among this group – and a sensitive issue within the community.

This issue was rarely mentioned, in our interviews either with schools – where ethnicity was discussed mostly in relation to groups with more obviously different cultures – or with Afro-Caribbean residents. One teacher did, however, say that:

*I would think it's probably because . . . a black Caribbean child is much more prepared to stand and argue the case than another child (who) – if they're rebuked by a teacher and told off for doing something wrong, even if the teacher may be inaccurate in their diagnosis of the situation – will to a certain extent accept it, whereas a black Caribbean child won't. They will stand and . . . argue the case, and very often what happens then is what started off as a fairly minor offence inflames itself into a much greater one, (so) that then steps have to be taken.*

Deputy Head, Outer London comprehensive

Since parents tended to be supportive of the school's approach, he suggested that this assertiveness had its roots in 'the community', rather than home or school.

Relations between ethnic groups in schools and elsewhere are complex. In some cases there are white/black issues, particularly in regard to choice of schools:

*School A is our catchment area and I actually know a teacher that teaches there. She said 'don't let [your son] go there . . . and School B had so many Indians in, the Asians, and I mean let's be honest we are white, I want him with the majority . . . [the area] definitely has changed, they're moving in . . . and they're such big families this is the thing. They don't have one or two they have four or five or six . . . the Asians don't want to give anything back to schools . . . they don't go in and help.*

Married mother, employed, white, homeowner

*Some . . . kids are being held back because the others have got to learn the basic English before they can pick up the general education . . . it's not only Asian . . . it's Eastern European as well now . . . that will hold back the others.*

Married father, employed, white, homeowner

But the picture is not straightforward, and relations between and within ethnic groups can be complex:

*[bullying] usually it is among, it is more so . . . between . . . blacks and Asians.*

Married father, retired, Asian, homeowner

*there are more upsets between Muslims, the strict Muslim and the non-strict Muslim, a girl who feels, or the mother of a girl who feels those Muslims are being far too western in putting on lipstick and showing their legs and 'We are following the hard line' . . . They get angry and they get up fights between them, not black white fights much, but inter-Muslim.*

Deputy Head, Secondary School, Outer Metropolitan Area

Clearly there is racism and racial tension within London schools, as in other institutions in the city – and we found some direct expressions of racism by white parents. But it would be misleading to ignore the strong elements of integration and racial harmony also, as indicated by comments from students:

*I think there's a mixture, total mixture . . . I can't see racism going on at all, but I mean it does exist obviously . . . but . . . in our school there's a total mixture of people [who] . . . just hang around in any type of group, no matter what colour . . . most of my mates are white and black . . . there's a couple of Asian friends as well.*

British-born Asian male, A-level student

*The group of [my] friends was . . . so diverse, we've got Moroccan, Ethiopian, Indian, Pakistani, Lebanese, English . . . no-one grouped themselves in terms of race or things like that.*

Single man, employed, Lebanese, homeowner (living at home)

Typically, parents were at least accepting, and often positive, about multi-culturalism in schools – reflecting opinion poll results in which 83 per cent of respondents said they enjoyed the cultural diversity of London (MORI, 2002):

*It's important as far as we are concerned that, that [our son is] educated in an environment that has a diversity of cultures, and I think that's the best way to bring kids up, and of course this part of London is one of the best areas, because it is so cosmopolitan.*

Married father, employed, white, homeowner

Domination of a school by any single ethnic group was perceived to present problems, however. In Greenwich and Dartford teachers reported obstacles to countering racist attitudes in largely white schools serving a local working-class community. And, in Hounslow particularly we found anxieties about effectively monocultural, Asian schools:

*I took [my daughter] out of that school and moved her to another school . . . I don't want you to think I'm a racist if I say it, but it was because in the morning, instead of going in and saying 'Good morning' to the teacher, they had to say '??' or whatever it was . . . There's been Indian children at school in Hounslow with me and my children, so please don't think it's because I'm a racist – I'm not that way. But culturally it's changed completely in the space of two or three years. It went from being a school in England where a lot of Asian children went, to a school in England that was like an Asian school.*

Married mother, employed, white, homeowner

*I would like [my son] to go to a school where it's multiracial, so there's Asian, black, Chinese . . . But the school round the corner . . . there was one Western name and they were all Asian . . . I don't want him to be the only white child in an Asian class . . . When we were at school . . . we had an Asian girl come to the school and it's not very nice, whatever culture you come from, to be the only one.*

Female cohabitee, mother, employed, white, private tenant

A complicating factor has been the recent arrival of large numbers of refugee children. In 1997, the Refugee Council estimated that refugee children in London represented around 4 per cent of the school population in Greater London, and about 90 per cent of refugee chilren in school. They are very unevenly distributed, owing to a combination of housing factors, the location of existing communities from particular origins, and allocation to (the less popular) schools which have spare places (Rutter and Jones, 1998). This concentration intensifies the costs of absorbing new arrivals – including many unaccompanied children – often likely to be disturbed by experience of war, famine or torture, as well as uncertainties about settlement:

*I've got 1,300 asylum seekers and refugees at my schools . . . I've got a very high proportion in a low number of schools . . . [in one school] about 60 per cent of its cohort, be it asylum seekers or refugees – so you have all the issues about language and culture, and added to this is the issue of trauma . . . the recent refugees coming in from Sierra Leone and some from South America have quite high levels of trauma.*

Director of Education, Inner London

In fact schools can have to deal with a series of waves of needy new arrivals, since as families and communities become more settled, they are likely to ripple out to other areas, being replaced by a new cohort of entrants. This imposes particular stresses on particular schools, which may contribute to the persistently low attainment recorded for some – although we cannot yet assess how great this effect is, nor how successful schools are actually being in easing refugee children's adjustment into the system. Once this has been accomplished, however, there are reasons to expect this group to perform well – and add to the city's human assets – since refugees tend to be drawn from relatively highly skilled and educated groups, with a resilience and resourcefulness attested to by their success in getting to the UK.

## Conclusion: Education, Economy and Society in London

Education matters especially in London, because of the swing in its occupational structure toward jobs in which mental skills are a prime requirement. At the top of the distribution many of these are filled by graduates attracted from other areas, both home and abroad. Such mobility is normal for specialized, high-status jobs, and sustained both by the opportunities for upward mobility that many London jobs offer and by the attractions of London life for educated young people. And it serves to fill the gap between the number of suitably qualified graduates coming out of the region's own school system, which is only modestly above the national average, and the larger numbers required by the London economy. The gap is not itself a measure of failure for the regional education system, by the standards of other regions of the UK, nor a real problem for the London economy. It should go without saying, however, that the system as a whole 'could do better', particularly as there are great variations in standards of achievement within the region. A little lower down the occupational hierarchy, where London demands are less disproportionate, the gap is less marked. But here London employers rely more on the output of London schools and report skill shortages that are of some significance in relation to competitiveness. At this level, the argument that London could do better applies more strongly, and there is obvious value in broadening the base of attainment – as policy-makers clearly recognize. Perhaps surprisingly, education is not especially rewarded in the London labour market, but the higher status jobs for which qualifications are a necessary condition are rewarded (Duranton and Monastiriotis, 2000), and it is only by getting into these better jobs that many Londoners are going to be able to cope with the city's housing and living costs.

By national standards educational attainment is poor in Inner London and on Thames-side, but this is driven more by deprivation and other social problems than by under-performing schools. The limited evidence on value-added suggests that typical schools in this area are doing quite a good job. But they are faced with particular problems (including high absence rates) associated with local concentrations of unemployment and (especially) lone parenthood. Cohesive communities and parental attitudes are also important, and while there are some highly motivated groups in inner areas, notably among some immigrants and some ethnic minorities, several communities still appear to be very isolated in social and educational attitudes. Some schools are also under great stress as a result of pressures in the local community being imported into school.

The London schools market is complex and highly competitive, with many parents adopting sophisticated strategies to get the best possible education for their children. This is not confined to middle-class cosmopolitans, although they do have the resources to work the system more effectively. This can make schools even more socially or ethnically segregated than naturally tends to be the case in London with its more broadly defined social areas – although it is not clear that the removal of constraints on inter-borough transfer has had much effect on this. Increasingly clear pecking-orders among local schools in terms of results and parental demand do, however, worsen the problems of schools in deprived areas which can attain the status of sink schools, with a concentration of pupils with particular problems – now including refugees.

Ethnicity and race are important issues in London schools, especially in those areas where white, English pupils are now in the minority. This is not, however, because any of the minorities do particularly poorly in school relative to their social background, while several groups clearly achieve better results than the average white pupil. Class is still the major differentiating factor, and both white and Afro-Caribbean boys in working-class areas seem to present schools with particular problems and end up underachieving. In these situations schools stand in the front-line of urban life, especially in London's more deprived areas where they have to work both with and against local cultures in order to promote opportunities for pupils and to advance inclusion.

Chapter 6

# Climbing Up, Bumping Down and Flitting Around: London's Dynamic Labour Market

Contrary to popular belief, Dick Whittington was not a poor, ill-treated orphan who managed against all the odds to work his way up to Lord Mayor. Coming from a wealthy family, Richard Whittington had a successful business and civic career before he became Lord Mayor. [and] carved out a successful business career in a very practical way as a mercer (dealer in costly fabrics such as silk), wool merchant and royal financier.

Corporation of London website

In the last three chapters we have looked in turn at changing patterns of employment in London, the making of the London labour force, and its skilling. Here we focus on the processes through which these demands and supplies for labour get matched, and perhaps mismatched, in the region's labour markets. This is a central issue both for competitiveness and cohesion, and a crucial link therefore between the achievement of economic and social objectives in the region. Indeed concerns with competitiveness and cohesion may be most strongly interrelated around the question of whether London labour markets succeed in making the fullest and most productive use of the human capacities available in the region. If they fail to achieve this there will be economic waste, a lower quality of life for at least part of the labour force, and more serious risks of various forms of social exclusion. And, as we shall show, meeting these objectives is not simply a matter of the aggregate balance and composition of labour demands relative to supplies, but depends to a substantial degree on *how* a range of labour market processes actually operate.

Issues and problems in relation to these processes arise because labour is a strange sort of 'commodity' – heterogeneous, subjective and potentially recalcitrant, in ways which introduce a whole series of social judgements, strategies and risks into the operation of the market and individuals' career prospects within it. Thus the operation of this market involves both many externalities – wider consequences of individual actions – and power relations. What appears best and most economic for individual actors does not necessarily result in the best use being made of the potential labour force, either socially or economically. Some of these conflicts can be seen in relation to the emphasis on labour market 'flexibility' which emerged in the 1980s/90s which, as we show later, has a particular salience to London. One agent's 'flexibility' may be another's 'insecurity' – most often the flexibility of the employer and the insecurity of the worker in a short-term (or casual) job. Admittedly, there are groups, among both established London workers and migrants to the city – including young single workers with strong desires for variety and mobility – who find their freedom increased by the new array of short-term opportunities for bar, shop or office 'temp' work. But even these cases raise potential problems with labour market externalities, for example over whether anyone assumes responsibility for skill development, or for reintegrating older workers who have lost their foothold in work.

Labour market performance may be especially important for London's capacity to secure competitiveness and social cohesion, particularly because of the scale of economic and demographic changes which have to be dealt with. Though not experiencing the economic devastation of a number of older industrial areas, the London region has undergone an extended process of structural change over the past 40 years involving a shift from manual to non-manual sectors of employment beyond anything experienced in other British cities. Internationalization and the shift to a post-Fordist economy have also brought a greater degree of cyclical instability to the London economy than it had encountered within the last century. London has passed from being one of the most stable economies in the UK, as it was up to the early 1980s, into the most volatile. The city region also faces some of the greatest issues in the achievement of equal opportunities, since it houses a large share of Britain's ethnic minorities, and has been overwhelmingly the destination of choice for asylum seekers arriving since the late 1980s. Within the British Isles, it has long attracted not only highly qualified, economically ambitious migrants but also large numbers of unattached young people, in search of freedom or in flight from difficult family situations, who may also present particular problems of labour market integration. And there is a longstanding suspicion (endorsed by some Durkheimian social theorists) that the city itself encourages forms of individualism that inhibit establishment of durable employment relations and social capital formation, with a consequent risk (for some) of exclusion from the mainstream labour market.

A major concern of this chapter is to consider how successful the labour markets of the London region are in responding to these challenges. Potentially these markets are among the city region's key economic assets, offering major economies of scale and scope that reflect both sheer numbers and a range of specialisms unrivalled among British cities. And, though official statistics treat the region as an amalgam of fifteen separate Travel To Work Areas, dense overlaps and interactions among these fields enable the whole area to function as a single metropolitan labour market. Despite these strengths there are, however, some strong indications of market failure, which justify investigation of the way that labour market processes operate in the region, and how these have been affected by developments within the last two decades.

On the one hand there is evidence, discussed in the last chapter, of London employers facing substantial problems of skill shortage, both in terms of their ability to fill vacancies in a range of occupations, and their perception of skill deficiencies among those they do employ. This seems mainly to be a side effect of economic dynamism. National comparisons locate the highest incidence of both kinds of shortage in west London, the 'Western Crescent' of the OMA and its extensions north-east into Cambridgeshire and west into Wiltshire. On the other hand skill shortages in East London were actually below the national average (Green and Owen, 2001). There are special cases within the public sector, where the London weighting is about 10 per cent below what is required to compete effectively with the private sector, leading to particular recruitment problems such as that for teachers noted in the previous chapter. For example, 20 per cent of the secondary school posts in London advertised during summer 2001 remained unfilled, compared with 12 per cent elsewhere in the UK (*Guardian*, 31 August 2001). There may also be a tier of semi-skilled service work (e.g. in clerical jobs) which cannot be adequately filled from local sources, but attract fewer migrants than do jobs requiring higher levels of qualification. In general, however, it is not clear that reported skill shortages are anything more than a symptom of strong demand and healthy rates of technological/ organizational change.

A less problematic indicator of labour market failure is the level of unemployment in some core areas of this otherwise successful regional economy (notably inner East London), and among disadvantaged groups. For example, 10 of the 14 inner boroughs figured among the 20 districts with the highest unemployment rates in Britain in mid-1998 – whereas none had done at the start of the 1980s. Most of the areas involved were in inner East London, where there is a history of under-employment stretching back into the nineteenth century. But the current pattern of very highly concentrated unemployment in this area only seems to have emerged during the last 20 years, against a background of relatively strong performance in the regional economy – whereas the other high unemployment areas were all in declining regions. Given the centrality of unemployment to many other forms of deprivation, one key concern of this chapter has to be with understanding the role of labour market processes in producing this outcome.

We address this question, and the broader issues about how labour market processes in the region contribute to competitiveness and cohesion, in three stages. First, we discuss imbalances arising from the aggregate supply and demand trends discussed in Chapters 3 and 4, and the adequacy of labour market adjustment processes in responding to these. Central here is the question of whether concentrations of unemployment simply reflect the inability of such processes to cope with the scale of structural change experienced in parts of London.

The second stage pursues a micro-approach, focusing on processes of recruitment, turnover and the matching of requirements, aspirations and assets.

Labour market flexibility is a central issue here, both in the way that it is facilitated, for good and ill, by distinctive features of the metropolitan labour market (including its sheer scale), and in the degree to which it has been affected by structural change and a more intensely competitive environment during the past 20 years. Two key hypotheses here (signalled in the chapter title) are that, on the one hand, these may have heightened the opportunities for upward movement in this 'escalator region' while, on the other hand, higher rates of job turnover may have generated new risks of falling off.

Finally, we look at the implications of a second distinctive characteristic of much of this period – namely chronically high absolute levels of unemployment in the wider southern and UK economies – for job competition between groups within the regional labour market, and its legacy in terms of concentrated unemployment. The argument here is that, far from the problem simply being one of inertia, some of the forms of flexibility and adjustment prevailing in this context actually contributed to the increasing concentration of unemployment and under-employment within the city (partly through a bumping down process). Indeed, in some ways the 'global city' era seems to have brought back not only a pattern of inner-city unemployment reminiscent of the pre-Fordist 'imperial city', but also new versions of the processes of casualization, demoralization and residualization invoked to account for London unemployment in that earlier period (Stedman Jones, 1971).

## Aggregate Imbalances and Adjustment Processes

The obvious starting points for analyses of the regional labour market and its problems are the overall relation of supply to demand, and variations in this between different parts of the labour market. In a closed labour market, where no-one had the option of finding work or potential workers externally, under-employment at any point in time could be accounted for simply in terms of the level some years earlier and subsequent changes in the balance between jobs and potential workers. In real spatial labour markets the situation is more complicated because of opportunities for migration and commuting across their borders in response to a shifting distribution of opportunities. Gordon (2002a) presents the theoretical background to this account, and rather more evidence than we have space for here.

In common with most of our analyses, we take as a baseline the situation around the start of the 1980s (in this case 1978/79 as years of high demand analogous to the time of writing). As Figure 6.1 shows, the level of unemployment in the region as a whole at that time was relatively modest (3.6 per cent in claimant count terms), both absolutely and relative to the national average (then standing at 3.9 per cent). The official rate for Greater London was the same as for the region, but after correction for the inconsistent way in which commuters are treated statistically it would have been about 0.5 per cent higher. Soon after this, the rate rose sharply across the metropolitan region, though much less than in more industrial regions, and gaps in unemployment rates started opening up between the core and the OMA. Through the 1980s and 1990s, swings in unemployment continued to follow

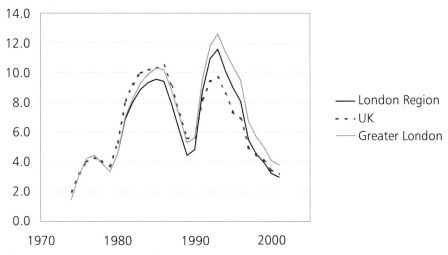

**Figure 6.1.** Unemployment rates for region, Greater London and UK, 1974–2001.

those in the country as a whole, but whereas in the 1980s recession the regional rate was clearly below that in the country as a whole, in the early 1990s recession the reverse was true. Only at the end of the decade did unemployment fall back below the national rate. Within the region a gap opened up between Greater London and the OMA in the early 1980s which has yet to close, and since the start of the 1990s its official rate has remained above the national average. Thus, while the UK unemployment rate fell between 1979 and 2000 (from 3.8 per cent to 3.6 per cent on a claimant count basis), in London the rate, corrected for commuting flows, actually grew markedly (from 4.0 per cent to 4.8 per cent). Fluctuations in between these points have something to do with the contrasting character of the two recessions. Focusing on change over the two decades effectively neutralizes these short-term influences, but even on this basis it is evident that the relative position of Greater London has substantially deteriorated, while that of the OMA has substantially improved. Including various categories of hidden unemployment, among people who want a job, but are not currently in the labour market (for one reason or another) would substantially increase all these figures (doubling them on some estimates). But the broad patterns and trends would remain the same.

In terms of employment, however, we have already seen (in Chapter 3) that this was a period of overall stabilization within Greater London, while across the region as a whole there was clear net job growth at a rate above the national one (see Table 3.2). Most of the growth was, of course, in business services, where at least higher status jobs may be filled on a national basis. Arguably then, trends in the preponderantly manual sectors (i.e. production and transport industries) are more relevant, and there large-scale job losses continued during the 1980s and 1990s, with the rate of decline in Greater London well above that in the rest of the country. In this part of the economy there was no real improvement in trends over those exhibited in the 1960s and 1970s. But this in itself represented a *relative* improvement, since industrial decline in other parts of the country clearly sharpened after 1979. Even in these sectors then, employment trends fail to explain why relative levels of unemployment in Greater London worsened so clearly in the 1980s and 1990s.

Another route to explaining this development is in terms of population trends, and the turnaround from decline to growth in London's working age population, especially within Greater London (see Chapter 4). This is a plausible line of argument but, like those linking London unemployment to job loss, it suffers from treating labour supply and demand as though they were independent of each other. This is particularly unrealistic in relation to the flows of young people into the region from elsewhere in the UK and now also from the continent, which seem to be strongly dependent on job opportunities. And, at least at the Greater London level (if less so for the wider region), there is a strong potential for adjustments in commuting patterns to absorb the effects of shifts in the geography of job opportunities. In fact such adjustments in migration and commuting are a major reason why London unemployment rates move in sympathy with the national average – though other factors cause the gap between them to widen or narrow over time. In particular, they account both for the fact that London unemployment increased sharply during the 1979–1982 recession despite its own rate of job loss accelerating only slightly, and for the failure of the London-focused boom of the mid-late 1980s to bring about a noticeably greater reduction in its unemployment rate than occurred elsewhere in southern England.

At the Greater London level, adjustment processes involving commuting, migration, employment and unemployment changes have been investigated more thoroughly using time series statistical analyses, over the period 1977–1994. These show that commuting flows are very sensitive to differential employment trends, especially for non-manual sectors of work. In fact, it appears that during this period 90 per cent of differences in rates of male employment changes outside manufacturing, between London and the ROSE, were absorbed by commuting changes, as was 50 per cent of the differential for female employment change. There was also evidence of higher national unemployment rates stimulating longer distance commuting into London (Gordon, 1996*b*).

Other evidence from time series analyses of unemployment rates for Greater London over the years 1972–1994 indicated that employment and population trends within London itself were largely irrelevant to its level of unemployment. The possible exception was change in manufacturing (accounting over this period for a minor and diminishing part of total employment). The loss of 1000 manufacturing jobs in London, over and above that expected from changes elsewhere in the South East, was estimated to add around 100 to unemployment during the year in which it occurred, though the relationship was not statistically significant. Otherwise, unemployment changes in London seemed solely to reflect unemployment trends across the South East (standard) region as a whole, if in a somewhat complicated fashion (as we shall see later in this chapter). At this wider scale, similar analyses showed a much clearer impact of employment changes, and also of international migration, with half of the (differential) regional changes in manufacturing employment being translated into changing unemployment levels across the region. But for jobs outside manufacturing the proportion was still only one-sixth, indicating that the great bulk of the effects of faster or slower service employment growth in London and its hinterland actually leak right out of the South East (Gordon, 1996b). At a more local scale within the region, variations in unemployment have been shown to have very little to do with local or sub-regional patterns of employment change – and this is true not only for localities, but also more widely in relation to the broad inner and outer rings (Gordon, 1989; Gordon, 2002a).

Thus the London labour market appears to respond very flexibly and efficiently to differential shifts in the balance of regional labour demand/supply. This is most conspicuously true locally, and for changes affecting the non-manual segment of the market. But it is also largely true at a regional scale for shifts in the manual sectors, except where these involve redundancies. There are two major implications of the strength of these adjustment mechanisms. First, they mean that at a sub-regional level, and even for areas as broad as Greater London, there is likely to be only a weak connection between local employment or population changes (past or future) and the incidence of unemployment. This finding is reinforced by evidence for the period 1981–1991 discussed in the fourth section of this chapter. Hence we very largely reject claims that concentrations of unemployment in the inner city reflect a spatial mismatch between demand and supply, despite the popularity of this notion as an explanation of high unemployment among young Afro-Americans in US inner-city areas. A second implication is that that we must look elsewhere for explanations both of the established concentration of unemployment within inner areas, and of its marked intensification since the early 1980s. A crucial starting point is the fact that local residents have to compete for jobs with commuters (or migrants) from other areas, and that their competitive position can vary greatly, in terms of how their human and social assets are valued in the labour market.

Apart from the evidence of intensified concentration, little of what emerges from these aggregate level analyses is surprising or really novel. Though more evidence is now available, the qualitative conclusions are much in line with earlier work on the London labour market (Buck et al., 1986; Gordon and Sassen, 1992). They remain at variance, however, with the sort of commonsense judgements underpinning much policy discussion about the need for job creation in London and specific targeting on areas of manual job loss. These arguments have been reinforced recently by Turok and Edge's (1999) work on the continuing scale of 'the jobs gap' in British cities implied by the combination of substantial job losses in the main conurbations between 1981 and 1996 with growth in less urban areas. However, comparison of labour market trends in different cities within this data set makes it clear that most of the consequences of differential employment changes were experienced in terms of changes in the balance of commuting and migration, with much smaller effects on unemployment (cf. Bailey and Turok, 1999). In any case, among the cities recorded as experiencing substantial job losses, London is unique in doing so within the context of a region with overall employment growth, which should produce much more favourable outcomes. In Glasgow or Merseyside, on the other hand, a large part of the problem is attributable to the weakness of their regional economies, which is much less readily coped with through supply adjustments than is localized decline within a core city.

# Flexibility and Turbulence
# in the Metropolitan Labour Market

Underlying the adjustment processes discussed in the previous section are decisions which individual workers and firms make about mobility, recruitment and retention, and which reflect their particular current needs and ambitions. The scale of the metropolitan labour market increases the range of options available both to workers and employers, and makes it more attractive for them to use the external labour market (outside the firm) as a flexible way of achieving their goals. Indeed a basic effect of agglomeration on labour market processes is to reduce the risks of labour market flexibility, since new jobs and workers can be found more easily as and when they are required, through the external labour market. Hence metropolitan labour markets are likely to be characterized by higher turnover rates, both (directly) because given firms or workers have less incentive to commit to a long-term relationship, and (indirectly) through 'natural selection' of firms and workers needing or wanting such flexibility (Gordon, 1987; Scott, 1988). This can be one of the major competitive advantages of the metropoles, but there may be important side effects, both in terms of under-investment in skills by free-riding firms, and of unforeseen risks falling on individuals with little organizational support.

A second key aspect of big city labour markets, especially those with concentrations of advanced service functions, is that they provide increased opportunities for ambitious workers to develop their skills – and other kinds of marketable human capital including contacts and reputations – through face to face interaction with workers in other enterprises. This is in contrast to other types of locales in which such individual development is more likely to be achieved within an organizational setting, and hence rather less likely to have marketable value outside that setting. Indeed Glaeser argues, using earnings data for workers in US cities, that it is this opportunity for learning, and being able to appropriate its value in an urban wage premium growing with time spent in the city – rather than any initial advantage in real wages – which attracts a certain sort of worker to city jobs, specifically those who are not too risk averse and have the capacity to benefit from such opportunities (Glaeser, 1999; Glaeser and Marc, 2001). This is consistent with Fielding's (1991) 'escalator region' thesis that residence in core regions provides substantially enhanced prospects of upward occupational mobility. In the London case we might expect part of this simply to reflect the greater quantitative potential for interaction. But the career value of these interactions can also be enhanced (in key parts of the London economy) through readier access to new developments, international experience and the opinions of powerful groups – and potential involvement in the collective activity of interpreting these (Amin and Thrift, 1992).

These arguments clearly complement the simpler propositions about urban scale effects on mobility rates and reliance on the external labour market, since it is the potential for mobility which allows workers to appropriate more of the productivity gains associated with their growing human capital. However, the processes have different incidence. A reduction in the risks associated with job mobility and hiring/firing employment strategies is liable to have effects right across the labour market. But both the opportunities and the capacity to add significantly to earning capacity through interactions outside an employing organization are going to be very unequally distributed. In part this must be a matter of personality, including sheer ambition. Generally, however, the more serious gains are likely to accrue to those in higher level positions and the least routinized activities, and to those whose learning skills have been developed through higher education. Hence, it is these groups who are likely to respond more strongly to, and gain most from, the learning potential of the metropolitan economy. Their representation among London workers has been growing for a long time as a consequence of the dispersal of more routine functions from London and a rapidly growing proportion of graduates in the labour market. But internationalization and increasingly competitive forms of economic organization have probably had even greater effects over the last couple of decades.

The expectation that contemporary metropolitan labour markets will be substantially more 'flexible' than those of other areas, or than they themselves previously were, has both negative and positive implications. Money wages (at least) should be higher but earnings disparities are also likely to be greater, implying greater individual inequality. Risks are also greater, with less protection for those experiencing bad luck and spells of unemployment, particularly if they fail to make a transition to secure jobs in their middle years. And, though workers in advantaged positions have more opportunity here to acquire transferable human capital through their personal interactions, employers will generally have less incentive to invest in (non-firm specific) skills which can be purchased in the open market. Hence there is liable to be some shortfall in training provision, especially where a sector lacks core employers who are willing to accept some leakage of the skill stock which they develop. This may have implications both for competitiveness and for inequality. And, London's own experience of casualized labour markets more than a century ago as a competitive international (imperial) city, as depicted by Stedman Jones (1971), suggests that flexibility/insecurity can also have serious negative effects on the other dimensions of social cohesion, i.e. connectedness and social order.

## Flexibility and Job Changing in the London Labour Market

In order to see how far the London labour market is actually characterized by a higher degree of flexibility in terms of the potential for mobility between jobs, we need to focus on rates of job turnover. In doing this we shall ignore some other aspects of flexibility less directly related to the urban setting, including employers' efforts to match hours of work to peak periods of customer demand. On the other hand, we shall look beyond the limited number of formally temporary or casual jobs, since most mobility actually occurs from jobs with open-ended contracts of employment. In such 'standard' jobs there are in practice highly variable expectations, both about the likelihood and the desirability of extended employment relations, as between different firms, different types of job, different groups of workers, and potentially also between areas.

As direct indicators of labour market flexibility (or job instability) we use three measures of job turnover – based on individual data from the Labour Force Survey (LFS) over the years 1986–1996 – distinguishing probabilities of having started a job, left a job, or having made a job-to-job move over a 12 month period (Buck and Gordon, 1998).

Although there is a general tendency for mobility rates to be higher in contexts of strong economic performance, in a typical year some 10–11 per cent of both men and women made a job-to-job move, while a further 5 per cent of men and 10 per cent of women moved into or out of employment. Comparing these rates for Inner London, Outer London and ROSE we find that each is clearly above the national average, and especially so in Inner London. Here the higher rate of mobility is partly attributable to having more young unmarried residents. But after controlling for demographic, socio-economic and industrial characteristics, the probabilities of job changes remain around 40 per cent higher in Inner London, and between 15 per cent and 30 per cent higher in the other areas, depending on the measure. Treating ROSE rates as an approximation to those prevailing in the OMA, these imply standardized job change rates in the London region 20 per cent above those in other parts of the UK in terms of overall start and quit rates, and 30 per cent higher in terms of job-to-job moves. By contrast, in each of the other British conurbations turnover rates are only around the national average, or in the case of Clydeside and Merseyside clearly below it (Buck and Gordon, 1998). In terms of the job-to-job moves, which are the most direct indicator of flexibility, this pattern of differentials is consistent with an earlier finding that turnover rates are higher both in areas with denser labour markets and in those with lower rates of unemployment (Gordon, 1987).

From the worker's point of view the relatively unstable, dynamic and turbulent character of the London labour market has both positive and negative consequences. For some workers it provides a context for greater choice between jobs and more rapid career advancement, while for others it may lead to weak human capital formation, insecurity and ultimately a restricted range of job choices. This is likely to depend in part on the occupations and activities in which workers are involved, and how turnover rates vary between these. In fact, virtually all sectors and socio-economic groups exhibit higher turnover rates in London, but the differential is most marked in those activities where turnover rates generally tend to be low. Thus although personal service and unskilled manual workers clearly have the highest turnover rates in London, as they do elsewhere, those for professionals and managers are not far behind them (Table 6.1). Similarly, in industrial terms London has unusually high rates of turnover in sectors such as finance, education, health and public administration. In relation to age, however, the normal steep decline of mobility rates with age is strongly exaggerated in London, with the tendency to greater instability being concentrated among young workers, and more or less disappearing by the age of 40. By that time it is likely that most of those involved will have successfully made the transition to an established job, rather later than their peers in the provinces though possibly at a higher level. Both in terms of age and activities, these patterns seem to be consistent with our development of the Glaeser argument about the impact of learning opportunities in cities. Specifically they lend support to the view that higher turnover rates in the London region are not just a response to scale, but also reflect the particular opportunities in this urban environment for well qualified young people to advance their careers through movement between firms.

How far this has actually been affected by changing economic processes over the past 20 years is much less clear, however. Comparing 1979 with 2000 we actually find no change in national turnover rates, despite temporarily higher rates during the late 1980s boom. Within Inner London we do find an increase of about 10 per cent over this period, but this was off-set by lower rates in both Outer London and the OMA. Since LFS data reported only region of residence, it is quite possible that these changes simply reflect changing patterns of residential segregation in the city, and in particular the increased concentration of non-couple-based households (whose members have less stable patterns of employment) in inner areas – rather than any significant changes in either employer or worker behaviour. Neither at the regional scale nor nationally, however, do we find general evidence of an upward trend in turnover rates, of the kind implied by propositions about increasingly flexible employment relations: this is consistent with Doogan's (2001) findings of stability in tenure lengths.

As the statistics imply, turbulent career patterns are particularly an Inner (and especially Central) London phenomenon, notably in City financial services where, staff are now expected to be:

> *Negotiating with at least one other if they were any good, to see if they could get a better position elsewhere . . . A year's good experience, with the right education and the right attitudes and the right skill sets, within a year if you come in on a junior level you could be negotiating a very substantial increase.*

Fund and asset management business, City of London

**Table 6.1.** Annual rate of mobility between jobs by socio-economic group.

|  | UK | Inner London | Outer London | Ratio Inner London: UK | Ratio Outer London: UK |
|---|---|---|---|---|---|
|  | % | % | % |  |  |
| Employer/manager large | 14.2 | 19.1 | 16.4 | 1.35 | 1.15 |
| Employer/manager small | 13.4 | 18.0 | 15.2 | 1.34 | 1.13 |
| Professional self-employed | 12.2 | 21.5 | 14.5 | 1.76 | 1.19 |
| Professional employee | 13.1 | 18.5 | 15.4 | 1.41 | 1.17 |
| Intermediate non-manual | 11.4 | 17.8 | 13.3 | 1.56 | 1.16 |
| Junior non-manual | 15.2 | 20.2 | 16.2 | 1.33 | 1.07 |
| Personal service | 19.1 | 22.2 | 22.0 | 1.16 | 1.15 |
| Foreman,supervisor | 12.7 | 12.8 | 14.4 | 1.01 | 1.14 |
| Skilled manual | 14.6 | 18.3 | 15.5 | 1.26 | 1.07 |
| Semi-skilled manual | 14.7 | 16.8 | 15.8 | 1.14 | 1.07 |
| Unskilled manual | 18.2 | 21.5 | 20.3 | 1.18 | 1.11 |
| Own account | 14.4 | 17.8 | 15.1 | 1.23 | 1.05 |

*Note:*
These estimates derive from a model incorporating demographic controls, and represent expected rates for a married man aged 30, in a particular SEG at the start of the year concerned.

In commenting critically on the attitudes of prospective recruits from an outer suburb, a second interviewee from this firm expressed a preference for those from 'within the tube map' who 'based living around work' and wanted to live within London because of the excitement and opportunities for career advancement available. The clear assumption here that mobility and a strong sense of 'market worth' are evidence of 'the right attitudes' well represents the particularly sharp change in City attitudes to loyalty and appropriate career paths since the early 1980s, and especially during the 1990s (cf. Augar, 2000).

## Upward Mobility

In relation to this role of the region as an 'escalator' for middle-class careers, the major evidence so far comes from Fielding's (1989, 1995) studies of how regional context affected occupational mobility during the 1970s and the 1980s. For an extended London city region represented by the South East standard region he showed that there was:

- a higher rate of movement into professional and managerial jobs from lower classes;

- a higher rate of movement from education into managerial posts (implying a faster track than the normal progression via time served in subordinate jobs); and also

- a higher degree of churning between professional, managerial and self-employed positions (Savage et al., 1992).

These patterns predate the main onset of internationalization and flexibilization in the London economy in the 1980s, and the follow-up study of upward mobility in that decade found it proceeding much as in the 1970s:

> Not significantly more so as one might have thought, given the 'serious money' that was offered by City of London employers to capable and ambitious young people in the heady days of the late 1980s' boom. (Fielding, 1995, 186)

For the 1990s, although end of decade Census data are not yet available, patterns of mobility can be assessed through the first nine waves of the British Household Panel Survey (covering the years 1991–1999). To examine the quantitative significance of the escalator function in this decade, and to allow some control of relevant factors other than regional location, we have used continuous measures of occupational standing (reflecting relative pay, status and risks of unemployment) rather than the broad classes employed by Fielding. On these measures we also find quite clear evidence that younger workers with good educational qualifications do progress more rapidly if they are based in the London region. However, the margin of difference is relatively modest, especially when we control for youth, educational qualification and a measure of personal ambition. Each of these factors exerts an independent, positive effect on occupational progression, and (partly because of selective in-migration) each is more characteristic of this region's workforce than of those elsewhere in the UK. In terms of the additional income which might be expected as a result of upward occupational mobility, the London region escalator itself seems to have been worth about 0.75 per cent per annum to the average young, qualified worker. We find no evidence that those (among this group) with higher levels of personal ambition benefited especially from being in the region (Gordon, 2002*b*). Though we cannot directly compare these results with those for earlier decades, it does not appear that changes in the regional economy's functioning since the 1980s can have greatly increased the significance of the region's 'up-escalator' function.

## The Role of Agencies

One factor contributing to labour market flexibility has been the growing role of employment agencies. These formed one of the recurring themes of our business interviews, with very mixed judgements about their value and the side effects of their role. Employers in the Thames Valley (Hounslow and Greater Reading), who were especially keen to retain staff, were particularly sensitive about their head-hunting activities, going as far as to impose switchboard bars against calls to their staff from identified agency numbers, or concluding non-aggression pacts with some friendly local firms. Other complaints included agencies touting for business when vacancies had been publicly advertised, and completely inappropriate candidates being submitted for jobs involving scarce skills. But employers in many activities clearly relied heavily on them – and one at least of our household interviewees had gained substantially from a head-hunting phone approach at work.

Agencies who we interviewed ranged from specialist firms for computer and legal staff, through mainstream office temp agencies, to one operating at the 'lower end of hotel catering', with a largely immigrant workforce (currently 50 per cent East European). None was actually involved in head-hunting, although the computer agency was clear that the recruits it wanted were people in secure, well-paid jobs, ready to move on after a year or two in post. Even in the office temp business it was reported that clients' demands had become much more specialized:

> Gone are the days when they were simply looking for arms and legs . . . If they want cover they want someone to do almost the same job as a full-time person. So that's it – more specific and higher specification.
>
> Battersea branch of multinational employment agency

It was clear that there had been a lot of recent growth in the business, with one manager seeing 'flexible employment' as an idea of the late 1990s (rather than the 1980s). Between 1991 and 1999 total employment of recruitment agencies (i.e. their temps) grew by 200 per cent in the London region. This was actually below the national growth rate (of 250 per cent), though still representing a higher proportion of jobs (3.6 per cent compared with 2.5 per cent nationally). These numbers do not, however, reflect the full impact of agencies' operations. Agencies also play an important role in recruitment to more permanent jobs. And for many employees (according to a Battersea agency) they have become a way of securing job offers with substantially higher pay, which are then used to extract pay increases from existing employers.

## The Costs and Benefits of Flexibility

Much of this evidence is consistent with a positive view of the role of job turnover in career progression and the accumulation of human capital. While some career progression takes place within the internal labour markets of large organizations, many other occupational career paths, particular in professional and related occupations depend on accumulating experience across a variety of employers. It is also likely that there has been some shift towards the latter form of career progression, for which metropolitan labour markets play especially important roles.

However, there are potentially two negative effects from this kind of flexibility. The first could be a greater reluctance on the part of employers in high turnover areas and employment sectors to invest in staff development, given both the risk that trained staff will move on, and the potential to free-ride on others' training activities. This expectation is only partially supported by available evidence for London, however. Percentages of workers reporting training during the last three months in the LFS are slightly above the national average. However, after controlling for age, sex, industry sector and broad occupational group, workers in central London are around 20 per cent less likely to report training. For other parts of the region there is no significant difference. And, within London, although types of job associated with high turnover – including those in small, recently established businesses, and the entertainment, leisure and catering industries – displayed notably lower levels of training effort (in the 1999 LES), there was no evident link with establishments' own turnover rates.

Secondly, there are real risks associated with a high turnover labour market, which can have very serious consequences for some of those involved. Involuntary job losses, or the failure of some speculative moves mean a greater risk of spells of unemployment, which though typically short are liable to leave people in a lower quality job than would otherwise have been expected. This is a particular risk for those in the type of job where short-term experience gives the worker little human capital that can be taken on to future jobs. Thus, although the differential in mobility rates between London and other parts of the UK is most marked for skilled workers, it is those in the lower reaches of the labour market who run the greatest risks of entering downward career paths as a result of the unstable character of the metropolitan labour market. As White and Forth (1997) have shown, there is a strong tendency for the unemployed to cycle through more unstable or downgraded parts of the labour market. Indeed even the evidence of stabilization among older workers has ambiguous implications, since it can reflect not only many people finding more stable jobs, with some sort of career prospect, but also longer spells of unemployment among those who fail to achieve this by middle age. And, significantly, it is in these middle-age ranges that London exhibits the highest unemployment rates, relative to the national average. For some people at least, youthful turbulence seems to be followed by a form of sedimentation. Along with other forms of sedimentation this seems to have become increasingly important during the 1980s/90s, contributing to the increased concentration of unemployment within London, an issue to which we now turn.

## Concentrated Unemployment and Its Causes: Discrimination, Recession and Sedimentation

We have already observed that unemployment in the wider London region is remarkably concentrated in particular parts of the region. We can also show that it is concentrated on particular types of people, and that the residential concentration of these people is the main explanatory factor behind spatial concentration. We present more evidence on these patterns of concentration, and then review the question of why the labour market works in such a selective way. As in the accounts of unemployment trends for the whole region, the traditional interpretation of urban employment problems as simply reflecting an inability of a spatially and occupationally constrained labour force to adjust in the face of major structural shocks is rejected. But experience in the past two decades raises new issues about how major increases in concentration are to be explained.

Figure 6.2 shows the distribution at ward level of scores on the employment domain of the IMD2000 deprivation index, discussed in more detail in Chapter 2. These are effectively non-employment rates, including some categories of the inactive as well as the unemployed. In the west of London it shows a concentration around Brent. But most prominent is the East London horseshoe of highly deprived wards around the City of London, in the boroughs of Islington, Hackney, Tower Hamlets and Southwark, extending northwards into Haringey, and eastward into Newham. Beyond this area there are moderately high levels of employment deprivation stretching eastwards along both sides of the Thames, and in other more working-class parts of outer London. This is a pattern, which as Figure 2.8 in Chapter 2 showed, became more sharply defined between the 1981 and 1991 Censuses.

The extent of variation at an individual level between people with different characteristics is shown in Table 6.2, based on the1998–2000 LFS, for London, ROSE and an average of the two, weighted to approximate our London region, as well as for the UK. Overall London unemployment is around 30 per cent higher than UK unemployment, but this essentially reflects the concentration in London of some groups with a generally higher incidence of unemployment.

The table reveals substantial variations in unemployment rates on each of the dimensions distinguished. Men, non-white ethnic groups (especially blacks, Pakistanis and Bangladeshis), non-UK citizens, more recent migrants (though not the most recent group, including more students and ex-pat workers), the young, renters (especially from social housing) and the poorly qualified all show significantly higher rates of unemployment. There are also evident differences between groups in terms of whether their members seem more vulnerable to unemployment in London than elsewhere. These include the fact that people in their twenties do relatively better than other age groups in London, perhaps related to their also being especially mobile between jobs in London (as we have seen), whereas older workers may be

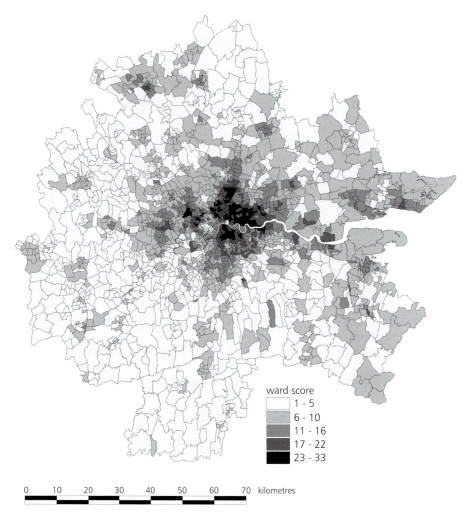

ward score
1 - 5
6 - 10
11 - 16
17 - 22
23 - 33

0    10    20    30    40    50    60    70  kilometres

**Figure 6.2.** Index of Multiple Deprivation 2000: employment domain by ward. (*Source:* DTLR Index of Multiple Deprivation 2000)

less able to exploit the flexibility of the London labour market. Interestingly, no ethnic groups, apart from the (very small) Chinese community, seems to do much worse in London – suggesting that apparently worse performance on other dimensions may reflect the ethnic mix of the London population. Uniquely Indians and Pakistanis have lower unemployment rates in London.

In order to control for such mix effects and identify which factors independently affect individuals' chances of being unemployed we undertook some regression analyses within the London and South East sample of the LFS. This identified five particularly important factors: age, marital status, ethnicity, lack of qualifications, and living in rented (especially social) housing. The odds of being unemployed were found to be at least twice as great for young people, the unmarried, some ethnic minorities (particularly Africans, Pakistanis and Bangladeshis), those without recognized educational qualifications, and social housing tenants. For each of these groups there seems to be a 'social mismatch' in the labour market, in that (at the wages people are prepared to work for) there is less demand than supply for these characteristics – whether because of real or imagined associations with lower levels of productivity and reliability. And these disadvantaging factors multiply together – so that someone who is (say) unqualified, living in a council house and of African ethnic origin may be 21 times as likely to be out of work. A similar picture of inequalities in the distribution of unemployment emerges from repeating this analysis in other parts of the country. Essentially differences are limited to variations in the base probabilities of being out of work (for those with none of

**Table 6.2.** Percentage unemployed by individual characteristics, 1998–2000.

|  | London | ROSE | London Region | UK | London: UK ratio |
|---|---|---|---|---|---|
| **By Sex:** |  |  |  |  |  |
| Male | 8.2 | 3.8 | 6.2 | 6.5 | 1.26 |
| Female | 6.6 | 3.8 | 5.3 | 5.0 | 1.32 |
| **By Ethnicity:** |  |  |  |  |  |
| White | 5.6 | 3.7 | 4.6 | 5.4 | 1.03 |
| Black – Caribbean | 14.8 | 6.0 | 14.2 | 13.0 | 1.14 |
| Black – African | 16.2 | 4.5 | 15.8 | 15.4 | 1.05 |
| Black – Other Black groups | 23.0 | 20.2 | 22.8 | 21.1 | 1.09 |
| Indian | 7.9 | 5.8 | 7.6 | 8.4 | 0.94 |
| Pakistani | 16.7 | 10.9 | 15.7 | 17.4 | 0.96 |
| Bangladeshi | 25.7 | 13.3 | 24.9 | 22.2 | 1.16 |
| Chinese | 10.5 | 5.4 | 9.7 | 7.4 | 1.42 |
| Other | 14.4 | 5.5 | 13.5 | 12.9 | 1.11 |
| **By Nationality:** |  |  |  |  |  |
| British | 6.8 | 3.7 | 5.3 | 5.7 | 1.20 |
| Other | 11.1 | 5.2 | 10.2 | 9.5 | 1.17 |
| **Year came to UK:** |  |  |  |  |  |
| British born | 6.4 | 3.7 | 5.0 | 5.5 | 1.16 |
| Before 1980 | 8.6 | 3.6 | 7.5 | 6.6 | 1.31 |
| 1980–1989 | 10.0 | 5.8 | 9.4 | 10.1 | 0.99 |
| 1990–1994 | 12.8 | 7.2 | 12.1 | 11.0 | 1.17 |
| 1995–2000 | 12.9 | 5.5 | 11.8 | 11.6 | 1.11 |
| **By Age:** |  |  |  |  |  |
| 16–19 | 21.9 | 10.0 | 15.9 | 15.5 | 1.41 |
| 20–24 | 11.4 | 6.3 | 9.4 | 9.7 | 1.18 |
| 25–29 | 7.0 | 4.1 | 5.8 | 6.2 | 1.12 |
| 30–39 | 6.4 | 3.2 | 5.1 | 4.9 | 1.30 |
| 40-49 | 5.5 | 2.6 | 4.1 | 4.0 | 1.37 |
| 50–54 | 5.8 | 2.5 | 4.1 | 4.1 | 1.41 |
| 55–59 | 5.8 | 3.7 | 4.7 | 4.9 | 1.18 |
| **By Tenure:** |  |  |  |  |  |
| Owner Occupiers | 3.9 | 2.5 | 3.0 | 3.3 | 1.20 |
| Social housing | 20.3 | 12.2 | 21.6 | 19.2 | 1.05 |
| Private renting | 9.3 | 6.8 | 8.5 | 9.5 | 0.98 |
| **Qualifications:** |  |  |  |  |  |
| Quals > NVQ1 | 5.6 | 2.9 | 4.4 | 4.5 | 1.27 |
| Low qualifications | 10.1 | 5.6 | 8.4 | 7.6 | 1.32 |
| No qualifications | 13.4 | 6.7 | 10.4 | 10.6 | 1.26 |

*Source:* Labour Force Surveys.

these characteristics) between high unemployment and low unemployment regions. Differences in rates of unemployment (between social and demographic groups) tend to be proportionately larger in the high unemployment regions. And they will similarly tend to be wider in times of high unemployment than they would be in the context of full employment. Controlling for the effects of nationality, ethnicity, age, marital status and qualifications, we find that chances of unemployment in Greater London are very close to the national average, but are significantly less in ROSE (and hence we expect in the OMA also).

These findings put in some perspective explanations of urban unemployment in terms of a skills mismatch, since so many factors other than direct indicators of ability evidently make a difference to the risks of unemployment facing individuals. Typically 'skills mismatch' arguments simply record the imbalance between the sets of occupations in which most unfilled vacancies exist and those with which the unemployed are identified. At best this is a snapshot, saying nothing about the processes through which these distributions arise, and assuming a fixity about skill requirements and capacities which is quite unrealistic. We need to look a bit more closely at some of these processes in order to understand why and how personal characteristics make such a difference, and how concentrations of urban unemployment are produced and reproduced.

## Discrimination

Prejudice – in the sense of subjective assessments of people's likely performance beyond what the available evidence directly conveys – is an inescapable element in all labour market processes, from decisions about who to hire, through the allocation of training, to promotion and decisions about retention or 'release'. The pursuit of equality of opportunity is partly about trying to reduce this subjective element and make fuller use of objective forms of information. However, it is also about reducing systematic sources of bias in the way that subjective judgements are made so as to minimize the chances that individuals repeatedly face the same sets of prejudices. Studies of recruitment processes (such as Jenkins, 1986) show that decisions commonly depend not only on the 'gut feeling' of those making decisions, but also a set of stereotypes. These involve some common prejudices in relation to age, family status and housing tenure as well as particular assumptions about the suitability for particular roles of different gender groups and ethnic minorities. On the other side, with varying degrees of sophistication and willingness to compromise their own sense of identity, both job applicants and those in work 'signal' to employers their possession of the competences and character traits which they see as required for the positions on offer.

As Duster (1995) argues in relation to young Afro-Americans, the subjective aspects of this interaction have become an increasingly important and sensitive matter with de-industrialization. The perceived quality of personal interactions with colleagues, customers and gatekeepers (often from the white, middle-aged, middle classes) appears much more critical to an organization's successful performance than was the case in Fordist production industries. Clearly these could present particular issues in cities such as London with ethnically diverse populations and large numbers of immigrants. However, as Duster points out, the areas of conflict between the cultures of job applicants and employers may be as much ones of youth and class as (solely) of ethnic identity. Moves towards more 'flexible' employment relations, discouraging employers from making serious investment in recruitment and personnel functions, could also substantially exacerbate the difficulties for those lacking formal qualifications or fitting negative stereotypes. But the effects on these groups are probably much less invidious than those arising from situations of recession, when employers enjoy an embarrassment of choice and do not have to look beyond 'risk-free' categories of applicant.

Objectively there is still strong evidence of discrimination in the labour market on ethnic lines. Nationally, Blackaby et al.(2002) find that, even among the UK-born male population, chances of employment (in the mid-1990s) were 10 per cent lower for Indians, 12 per cent lower for blacks and 24 per cent lower for Pakistanis than for comparable whites. Among those in work they found a similar pattern of differentials affecting earnings, with UK-born blacks having earnings 5 per cent, Indians 8 per cent and Pakistanis 13 per cent lower than comparable whites. Direct wage discrimination thus appears less significant than that in access to employment. However, some of the characteristics which have been controlled for in deriving these estimates – notably shorter current job tenures and employment in lower wage sectors – may well themselves be partly the product of barriers to entering sectors offering longer attachments and higher pay. All of the disadvantaged groups are strongly represented in the London region, where a majority of the country's employed blacks and Indians work. And there is no evidence that any of these groups fare significantly better (relative to their white counterparts) in the London region than elsewhere. Indeed for the (small) Bangladeshi community the gap in both employment rate and earnings differentials appears significantly wider in London than elsewhere.

On the other hand, in our household interviews, while there was evidence of a great deal of racial stereotyping, it seemed to be mixed in a strange way with class prejudice. Very few respondents identified themselves as direct victims of discrimination. Responses from others suggested that people simply do not like acknowledging or talking about the discrimination they have experienced. Some, who strongly denied experience of discrimination, later gave clear examples of it without apparently being aware of any contradiction. On the whole, racial discrimination is something which its victims prefer to ignore or not attach importance to and therefore the amount of discrimination may be underestimated. It is also likely that people who do not want to confront discrimination modify their aspirations and behaviour to avoid it.

The one clear allegation of (indirect) discrimination in employment came from a man who believed that he was rejected by the army on racist grounds, through the way in which the army (in common with the police) applied their physical criteria:

> (In) all the establishment, the fire service, the police, racism it is strong, strong, strong, strong, strong. Still very, very strong.

Employed Afro-Caribbean male in his 50s, Battersea

More common attitudes were reflected by the following responses, the first from someone whose current job did not appear to reflect his level of qualifications.

> *If you see any other Asian young guy round my age, they'll probably tell you that there is a lot of racism and stuff. But I don't see that.*
>
> Teenage Asian male, Heston

> *There are times when I have gone for a job and I don't get it and maybe I would have felt that I'd done better, but I would think that maybe I didn't do – it's just to console myself, I say I didn't do well . . . So I always find an excuse that will make me feel comfortable and kind of consolation, if you like.*
>
> African woman, working part-time, Upton Park

> *The only way I impose myself on them is that I have to be better than all of them, you understand? Wear better clothes, buy a better car, . . . you know, I have to do that extra effort, you know . . . Sometimes you just get fed up saying, 'Bugger them, you know, I've got my own community here . . .'.*
>
> Employed African male, Battersea

In employer interviews, there was (unsurprisingly) even less hint of racial discrimination. At one extreme, around the IT industry, several interviewees offered forceful comments on how they would react to hints of racial discrimination, or racism in working relations, while others made the point that:

> *When you're in a tight talent pool any discrimination seems to me to be myopic at best.*
>
> Large US computer firm, Thames Valley

Formal equal opportunities policies were rare, however, and there were some issues about language with South Asian workers, both in terms of competence and a disciplinary insistence on English being spoken in the workplace. In one case also there was a notable discrepancy between a reported lack of ethnic minority workers and acknowledgment that most of the CVs seen for high-level jobs were from people with Asian backgrounds. One employer noted that employment agencies were used as a means of imposing selection criteria which they could not have applied directly. On the other hand, the legal recruitment agency mentioned above explicitly vetted clients to ensure they were equal opportunity employers.

Among interviewees in manual-employing sectors, ethnicity was much less often addressed. In Reading, having a majority of non-white (predominantly South Asian males) workers was said to be normal for local manufacturing, while an engineering employer noted that aspirations had risen, with an increasing proportion of supervisors and graduate engineers now coming from Asian backgrounds. A manager in a large private postal business in Hounslow noted as an issue an unexplained shortfall in South Asian job applicants, relative to the communities' share in the local population. However, another similar firm in the same area, with a formal equal opportunities policy (including a realistic recognition of Muslim religious obligations) reported equal shares of South Asians, Afro-Caribbean and white workers. A Post Office manager noted that some ethnic groups were reluctant to accept delivery jobs on status grounds, but were heavily represented in sorting offices. A Battersea courier company (with a 90 per cent white labour force) said that 'because of quotas' they might look more sympathetically at ethnic minorities. And a senior executive of a Stratford-based freight company expressed several concerns about the work ethic of 'ethnic minority' office staff in terms of uncertified sick leave and an unwillingness to follow traditional 'staff loyalty' by doing unpaid overtime to finish a job – as well as issues about their communication skills.

In general, however, it must be noted that stronger prejudices were displayed about work attitudes, motivation and competences of *local* residents in several inner areas, usually with predominantly white populations. These included references to the 'tribalism' of East Enders (e.g. the 'Isle of Dogites'!), and the increasing difficulty, in Battersea, of finding people who appreciated that the 'world didn't owe them a living'. A Woolwich fruit importer noted that they deliberately chose a more suburban (Bexleyheath) employment agency for non-manual jobs, because they produced 'a better class of person'. Most forcefully, a printing firm MD from Charlton (Greenwich) said:

> *If you employ people in walking distance from here, you can bet your bottom dollar they are going to be unreliable. They are going to have high absenteeism records. It's a generalization of course, but this is how you get to feel. One of our directors said 'if I could formulate a policy it would be not to employ anyone who lives within a five mile radius of the factory'. This is a dumping ground for families with problems. It's a deprived area . . . it just perpetuates itself; you can see it going through the generations, and it's sad . . . It's social deprivation and it's not easy to take on board when you are an employer.*
>
> Medium-sized independent printers, Greenwich

Communication skills were sometimes an issue, but formal qualifications rarely seemed to be required, except at the highest level. One small food distributor operating in New Covent Garden (Battersea) – described as 'not the most salubrious location' – spoke about their successes in training-up unqualified workers with basic literacy, loyalty and a willingness to learn who revealed administrative skills while on the job. Reliability and 'common sense' were commonly cited concerns, with implications for age as well as area of recruitment: a Stratford (Newham) chemical firm handling dangerous goods noted that it targeted 25–40 year olds, partly because 17–18 year olds 'want to act the goat all the time'.

## Segregation and Unemployment

Given normal patterns of residential segregation within city regions in relation to such personal characteristics, it follows that there can be substantial spatial variations in unemployment rates, even if where people lived, within such regions, made no difference at all to their chances of being in or out of work. And, since spatial segregation operates over larger scale units in larger city regions, with London as the extreme case, variations in unemployment rates will be more conspicuous at larger spatial scales, including districts or parliamentary constituencies – and even across the administrative divide between Greater London and the Eastern/South Eastern Government Office regions.

This is a very familiar line of argument (if not consistently reflected in urban policy initiatives) and empirical studies from the 1971 and 1981 Censuses have shown that variations in unemployment rates across areas within Greater London (at least) can be accounted for almost entirely by varying proportions of the local population with those characteristics known to be associated with higher risks of unemployment at the individual level (Metcalf and Richardson, 1976; Gordon and Lamont, 1982; Gordon, 1989). This is the other side of the coin to the observation (made earlier in this chapter) that variations in rates of population and employment change make very little difference to rates of unemployment across an integrated set of metropolitan labour markets.

These findings still broadly applied at the time of the last Census in 1991, when the inter-district variation, and even more the inter-ward variation, in unemployment rates could very largely be accounted for through regressions with a standard set of social, demographic and housing tenure measures for the local population. However, neither these population mix factors, nor measures of local job loss, could adequately explain why unemployment was quite so high in a number of areas on the eastern side of Inner London. In fact, there were then a dozen wards in the region with unemployment rates over 25 per cent (about five times the modal value), all lying in an arc in the inner east, between North Hackney and Brixton. These areas (and the boroughs within which they lie) had all been areas of high unemployment 10 years previously, at the top of the regional league table. But for some reason the gap between them and averagely bad parts of the region had very substantially widened during the course of the previous decade, even though the overall unemployment rate was much the same as it had been 10 years previously. At the borough level there were four areas – Hackney, Haringey, Newham and Tower Hamlets – where unemployment rates had increased by 6–7 per cent between the 1981 and 1991 Censuses, compared with about 2 per cent in the typical London borough and 1 per cent in the Outer Metropolitan Area. Increases in the numbers 'permanently sick' or on government schemes suggest a further growth of 2–3 per cent or so in concealed unemployment in the first group of areas, against apparent reductions of 1–2 per cent elsewhere in the region. And statistical analyses suggested that only about 1 per cent of this differentially higher unemployment could be accounted for by the worse employment trends for semi/unskilled workers across inner East London (Buck and Gordon, 1998).

There is a link to changes at a broader scale, discussed in the first section of this chapter, which have seen a widening gap in unemployment rates between Greater London and the OMA. Throughout periods when unemployment in the hinterland (taken as the indicator of demand-deficiency in the regional market) is above the traditional 'full-employment' benchmark of 3 per cent – as it was for most of the 1980s and 1990s – the gap between London and OMA unemployment has widened. However, during the (shorter) periods of peak demand, when at least the OMA has attained full employment, the unemployment differential has narrowed (Figure 6.3). This is not simply a matter of changing terms of competition between Londoners and those living in its commuter hinterland, as comparisons with developments in neighbouring regions make clear. Rather (as we can see from comparisons with neighbouring regions) it involves a progressive accumulation of structural unemployment within the urban core,

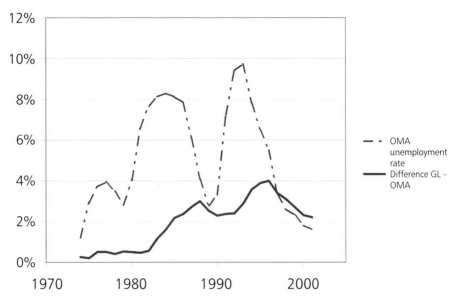

**Figure 6.3.** Difference between Greater London and OMA unemployment rates, 1974–2001. (*Source:* Original claimant count data from NOMIS adjusted to comparable basis)

raising the aggregate rate of unemployment across wider areas, including the South East as a whole (Buck and Gordon, 1998). The implication is that an extended period of deficient demand has both led to a spatial polarization of unemployment within the South East (notably within parts of inner East London) and also induced an upward shift in the region's overall level of unemployment – a regional version of what macroeconomists call unemployment hysteresis.

As far as the spatial polarization of unemployment is concerned, there are three possible sorts of explanation to be considered. One is that the spatial segregation between groups in stronger or weaker labour market positions has increased, leading to more of the unemployed being concentrated in a smaller number of areas. Indeed it is argued that increased individual inequality during the 1980s is likely to have led to intensified segregation within the region (Cheshire *et al.*, 2002). However, as we have seen in Chapter 4 there is actually no evidence of increasing social segregation within the London region between the 1981 and 1991 censuses – *except* in relation to the spatial concentration of unemployment. Nevertheless, it is possible that markedly higher levels of unemployment during this decade did provide an especially strong incentive to higher levels of segregation, between those experiencing repeated or extended spells of unemployment and those in more continuous employment. In the case of the inner East London boroughs there is actually evidence of population shifts which could have raised unemployment rates by 1 per cent or so between 1981 and 1991, but that is a marginal factor in relation to the overall deterioration which they experienced (Buck and Gordon, 1998). And (for the following decade) there is evidence from the British Household Panel Study (BHPS) of high rates of out-migration by employed residents from inner East London. Indeed between 1991 and 1999 over 40 per cent of those in paid employment seem to have moved out of this area (though the self-employed remained, and there was some in-movement by new entrants to the labour market). If this were the main factor, geographical concentration of unemployment need imply nothing about its social concentration or any processes of exclusion. But it would not explain why there was no evident fall in OMA unemployment to balance increases within London.

A second line of explanation focuses on the greater difficulties that individual residents of high unemployment areas may experience in gaining employment, simply because of where they live. This might be because employers use postcodes as a basis of discrimination in seeking to identify potentially more reliable recruits. Or it might be because area-based information networks become ineffective as a means of finding jobs when fewer locals have contacts with stable jobs (Buck, 2001). In this case, spatial concentration of unemployment *might* conceivably lead to social concentration as well, with a smaller group of people bearing more of the brunt of unemployment, and in the process becoming more marginalized from the mainstream labour market, and a less effective source of labour supply. For the 1991–1999 period, however, the BHPS provides no evidence, once economic status at the start of the period is controlled for, as well as relevant personal characteristics, that Inner London or inner East London residents were less likely to be employed.

A third possibility is that slack labour markets lead more directly to marginalization of this kind, with spatial concentration of unemployment serving purely as a symptom of its social concentration. One mechanism which could produce this effect is the 'bumping down' process, whereby with an inflexible wage structure, individuals respond to demand-deficient unemployment by lowering their sights and taking a job one tier down in the occupational hierarchy. In this position they can out-compete others previously linked to these jobs, who are then displaced to the tier below, and so on. Analyses of London labour market flows (using the LFS) indicate that people are substantially more likely to enter unemployment from higher non-manual or supervisory jobs than they are to return there. Experience of unemployment causes a net shift downward particularly into personal service and less skilled manual jobs. A consequence is that the unemployed always include disproportionate numbers from the lowest tiers (the 'unskilled'), even when falls in demand are equally spread across all types of job. This can give a misleading impression about the causes of unemployment. But it would not matter too much if cyclical upturns and a relaxation of hiring standards could be counted on to restore everyone (including the unemployed) to their previous position within the labour market.

However, particularly if recession has been prolonged, there may be several brakes on this process. Those who, under pressure of redundancy, secured permanent jobs at a lower position in the occupational hierarchy may not feel the same pressure to start searching again for a better paid job, particularly if they are middle-aged or older workers. In any case, they (like the unemployed) may now be judged less employable, whether on the basis of their current occupation or a lower valuation of 'experience' in the open labour market, and are particularly liable to be over-taken by younger workers on an upward trajectory. Those who have had spells of unemployment are also rather likely to have been forced to take less permanent jobs (White and Forth, 1998), thus acquiring an unstable work history which further reduces their chances of regaining stable jobs commensurate with their previous standing and talents (Norris, 1978). Their marginalization may be increased through deteriorating health or the acquisition of alienated attitudes which can be both effect and cause of repeated unemployment spells. Periods of continuing demand-deficiency are thus likely to induce a process of sedimentation in the labour market with the accumulation of growing numbers of structurally unemployed people, many of them inner-city residents, reversible only through extended periods of full employment, rather than simply by an up-turn in labour demand.

Our analyses of occupational mobility during the 1990s using the BHPS (discussed above in relation to the up-escalator) substantiate a version of the bumping-down model, both in relation to the UK as a whole and the London region. Specifically they suggest that it applies to people who start off above the lower quartile of occupational positions, where the higher risks of unemployment are concentrated, and generates downward movement into this quartile. In the London region we find that among those starting off in the more secure sector of the labour market (above this lower quartile) 24 per cent actually experienced some unemployment between 1990 and 1999. This compares with 34 per cent among those starting off in the bottom quartile, while the average time unemployed for those affected was significantly lower (at five weeks per year for those affected, compared with nine for those from the bottom quartile). But for those from the higher groups, this experience of unemployment typically led to a downward occupational shift, representing about an 8 per cent reduction in likely earnings, controlling for other influences on occupational mobility. For a proportion there were further knock-on effects taking them down into the riskier, and increasingly over-crowded, regions of the labour market. Short-term effects were even greater, with evidence of some successful bounce-backs being achieved in the following year, but not apparently after that (Gordon, 2002b). The picture is not one of spiralling falls down the occupational hierarchy, but of relatively modest downward movement among many of those in the middle and upper ranges of the occupational distribution. The overall effect during periods of higher unemployment is to push larger numbers into lower segments of the labour market, where the risks of unemployment get concentrated.

Alongside the up-escalators of the flexible and dynamic metropolitan labour market, we can see then that there are also a set of down-escalators leading those on them to positions well below their capacities – and in extreme cases past long-term unemployment into effective disengagement from the labour market, in some form of concealed unemployment. From these positions there may be only limited chances of movement across to an up-escalator, while those who are moving up can make recovery even harder by blocking spaces on the higher floors. As we envisage it, two sorts of circumstance lead people on to this downward escalator. One is a set of risks particularly associated with less stable labour markets, which will always produce a minority of casualties among those who fail to establish a more secure position for themselves by their middle years. The other set of factors is more structural, involving various forms of rigidity in mainstream labour markets which are benign in their effects so long as there is an adequate pressure of demand in the labour market, but which lead to sedimentation, marginalization and concentrated unemployment in circumstances of prolonged recession, such as the UK experienced from the late 1970s to the early 1990s.

These processes are not peculiar either to major cities or their inner areas, but they are especially relevant to them, because these are likely to include extensive areas with concentrations of those individuals most likely to be 'bumped' out of regular, secure and reasonably rewarded employment, and because some area specific processes may exacerbate sedimentation there. We have referred already to one such process, involving the deterioration in the networks of informal job information when there are fewer local people in such regular employment. Others operating over more extended timescales include the impact of (male) unemployment rates on family structures (including higher rates of lone parenthood), with knock-on effects on educational achievement (Gordon, 1996c) – and hence on the future incidence of unemployment. And all of these have a particular salience for the larger metropolitan areas where the scale of residential segregation increases the likelihood that the personal networks of those at risk of unemployment will be localized within relatively homogeneous areas. How important these area effects may be in quantitative terms is by no means clear, but qualitatively they reinforce the simple expectation, based on individual level processes and housing market geography, that there will be growing differentials in unemployment rates between inner and outer areas so long as conditions of deficient demand persist in the regional labour market.

Our discussion here has focused on the processes underlying an increasing concentration of unemployment within the last 20 years, but (as Figure 6.3 shows for the two main components of the region) recent experience since 1996 has been of a reversal of this process. This we attribute primarily to a healthy pressure of demand in the region, reflected by effective full employment in the OMA. However, another relevant factor in this period has been the Blair government's pursuit since mid-1998 of a range of 'welfare to work' programmes (the New Deals), targeted first at youth unemployment and long-term adult unemployment, and since at several other groups including lone parents. The diagnoses underlying these are consistent with our arguments about the factors involved in the persistence and concentration of unemployment. They are generally seen as having greater prospects of success in the South East, because of a relatively strong pressure of demand, more capable of absorbing an enhanced supply of employable 'graduates' from the programmes. But, on the other hand, in these circumstances it is more likely that those who are unemployed have substantial personal disadvantages to overcome (in the jargon they may be least job-ready). By the end of 2001 New Deal for Young People had got 350,000 young people nationally into jobs, just under half the number who had started the scheme. But there were large local variations in success rates, with London areas concentrated at the bottom of the list, with success rates as low as 33 per cent, only half that in the best areas. Inner parts of other major cities also figured near the bottom of the list. The average for Greater London is around 40 per cent, compared with 50 per cent in the OMA. This suggests that, whatever its absolute achievements in getting people back into work, New Deal is unlikely to have contributed anything much to the narrowing of the unemployment gap between these areas. And time series analyses with a dummy variable for the New Deal period also suggest that there has been no significant effect. What is critical does seem to be the broad pressure of demand for labour across the region – depending very much on macro-economic management, and the general competitive strength of the (southern) UK economy.

The extreme concentration of unemployment in inner East London, in areas with a very long history of deprivation, owes much to supply side factors, some of which are related to that 'demoralization' which was supposed to be the bane of late Victorian London. However, their force reflects two demand-side factors: the employment practices of individual employers, and overall weakness of demand in the regional labour market during most of the last two decades. The improvement in London's relative position in unemployment terms over the past few years of stronger demand shows that such sedimentation is reversible. But these conditions will have to persist for longer than currently seems likely in order for the bulk of those representing the accumulated sediment to be brought back into circulation simply through pressure of demand.

## Conclusion: London's Distinctive Labour Market

Our starting point in this chapter was the distinctiveness, on several dimensions, of the London region's labour market in relation to those of other British cities. Several of these distinctive characteristics – including its sheer scale (in area and numbers), the flexibility offered by its incorporation of many overlapping local labour areas, the range and diversity of skills on offer within it, and the ability to draw in young migrants on the Whittington trail – suggested that it could be key economic asset underpinning competitiveness. Some others, however – notably the inclusion within a diverse population of some groups with weak labour market positions, and the speed of the shift away from manual jobs (especially skilled jobs) toward higher status non-manual jobs – suggested problems for cohesion. Both of these sets of expected effects seemed likely to be heightened by shifts towards more 'flexible' and less durable employment relations since the 1980s. And many of the key features of the London labour market seemed likely to be double-edged. For example, scale could imply either spatial mismatch or flexibility and positive external economies; diversity could be a resource or a basis for exclusion; occupational change might cause unemployment through skills mismatch or enable upward movement; dynamism may mean flexibility or insecurity and under-investment etc.

Against this ambiguous set of expectations, several of our main findings emphasize the more positive aspects. Thus we find that adjustment processes have generally worked well in the face of major structural changes, with little evidence of serious spatial or skills mismatch: there is spatially concentrated unemployment but not for these reasons. The up-escalator function works for ambitious and qualified young people, but can be credited with too much, since a high-status labour force very largely reflects a combination of inherited social/human capital with selective inmigration of talented and motivated groups. There is substantial turbulence in the labour market, and it has risks, but there is no very strong evidence of its downside and none that overall turbulence has actually increased over the past two decades.

However, the overall position of the region, and particularly of inner areas, has clearly worsened in terms of unemployment over this period. In particular, concentrations in various parts of eastern inner London have markedly intensified. This does not, however, appear to be substantially due either to the structural shifts in employment or increasingly 'flexible' relations in the economy and labour market. The main factors that we identify are a combination of prolonged national recessions with established forms both of discrimination and of residential segregation. Residential segregation of the non-employed from the employed has grown, partly at least because of responses to higher background levels of unemployment. But an increased spatial concentration also reflects increased concentration of risks of unemployment among vulnerable and marginalized groups during the periods of generally slack demand (prior to the mid-1990s). A series of potential feedback processes have also been identified, operating through health, family formation, and educational factors as well as the labour market itself, which serve to reproduce and/ or intensify concentrations of non-employment, especially in these conditions. These contribute to wider processes of exclusion to which we turn in the next chapter.

Chapter 7

# Down But Not Out in London: Marginality and Social Exclusion

Erst kommt das Fressen, dann kommt die Moral.

Bertolt Brecht, *Die Dreigroschenoper*

All happy families resemble one another, but each unhappy family is unhappy in its own way.

Leo Tolstoy, *Anna Karenina*

In this chapter we analyse the patterns of poverty and disadvantage in London; the factors which impact negatively on the life chances of Londoners; and why, given the city's economic dynamism, levels of disadvantage are so high. The purpose is not just to describe the patterns but to explain them in terms of structural features of London's economy and society.

Chapter 6 showed that London, especially Inner London, experienced exceptionally high levels of unemployment and that its unemployment levels had generally been deteriorating compared with national averages. However, this could not be explained on the basis of a 'jobs gap', caused either by a general failure to adjust to declining employment levels, or by emerging spatial or occupational mismatches. Rather, this unemployment problem followed from the residential concentration in London of those who were in the weakest position in the competition for jobs. The chapter also suggested some intensification of this concentration over time, and some processes by which the spatial concentration of unemployment might be self-reinforcing. All this means that when in this chapter we look at patterns of deprivation and disadvantage we must be aware of potential influences from the labour market. However, these are rather complex and depend on interactions with other factors.

As Chapter 1 indicated, theories of social exclusion are the currently favoured approach to addressing deprivation. However, some of these theories have serious flaws. A key issue is whether, given high levels of disadvantage, it is helpful to see the social structure in terms of a division between 'insiders' and 'outsiders'. In this chapter, we do not adopt any single approach from the variety available in the social exclusion literature but draw on some of the debates that this work has generated to address disadvantage in London. Since the concept of social exclusion is so contested we use 'disadvantage' when we need a more theoretically neutral word to refer to the substantive social and economic experiences of individuals. As we also indicated in Chapter 1, social exclusion has a problematic relationship to the idea of social cohesion. We preferred to see the latter as referring to a complex interaction between social order, social inequality and social connectedness. Social exclusion draws on ideas of inequality and connectedness. We return to these issues in Chapter 11.

However, there is one clear potential advantage of social exclusion, identified in Chapter 1: its multi-dimensionality. Frequently though this has led to a definition of exclusion in terms of an eclectic melange of forms of disadvantage with no underlying conceptual basis. This is a typical example from the Social Exclusion Unit:

> Social exclusion is a shorthand term for what can happen when people or areas suffer from a combination of linked problems such as unemployment, poor skills, low incomes, poor housing, high crime environments, bad health and family breakdown. (Social Exclusion Unit, 1998).

Kesteloot (1997) has provided a more organized way of approaching this multi-dimensionality which applies Polanyi's (1944) concepts of modes of social integration: the market, redistribution, and reciprocity to the understanding of deprivation and social exclusion. Kesteloot argues that all three modes of integration shape individual life chances (though their impact varies cross-nationally). Corresponding to each mode of integration is a form of social exclusion. So there are three modes of exclusion based on:

◆ The market, where economic restructuring leads to certain groups suffering a loss of market integration, with limited access to the labour market.

◆ Citizenship, or access to state redistribution, where declining quality and levels of services and benefits and increasing difficulties of access and/or access on stigmatized terms act as exclusionary processes for those who are reliant on the state.

◆ Community or reciprocity, where changes in households and in social networks, as well as processes affecting groups defined by race, gender or disability increase exclusion through social isolation.

Of course, not all these modes of social exclusion affect the same people. Kesteloot depicts them by means of a Venn diagram in which three intersecting circles overlap. There are then three distinct situations. First, where all three circles overlap, here fall those groups that are jointly affected by all three forms of exclusion. Second, where two circles overlap, and groups suffer from two of the three forms.

Third is the area where groups experience only one form of exclusion; for them especially, other forms of integration may provide some compensation.

The processes that create these modes of exclusion work in complex and contradictory ways. Thus, for some labour market exclusion is experienced as long-term unemployment, while for others it involves a series of temporary, insecure jobs. For some, exclusion from citizenship takes the form of welfare benefits which constitute a poverty trap, while for others it takes the form of exclusion from all benefits (e.g. the homeless or asylum seekers). For some, community exclusion takes the form of weak individual ties (the disabled, many single person/single parent households), while for others, especially some of the ethnic minorities, it takes the form of poor links between the minority community and the wider society.

This framework can be seen in two ways. First, it suggests that the intensity of disadvantage will be greatest where more than one mode of exclusion is operating – for example, suggesting that it is where a benefits poverty trap exists, exacerbated perhaps by childcare needs or high housing costs, that labour market exclusion is likely to be most extreme. Such effects will be strongest where individual or community networks are weakest. Conversely, the experience of prolonged labour market exclusion will deplete a community's resources with effects seen in lack of motivation and self-esteem. Second, it also emphasizes the diversity of experiences of exclusion, and suggests that we should not treat all forms of exclusion as if they were the same. We use both these aspects of the framework to organize some of our evidence on patterns of disadvantage and exclusion.

We also draw on recent international debates on urban poverty, which work within a variety of theoretical frameworks. We return, for example, to the issues raised in Chapter 4 on global city polarization. In the recent literature there is a set of hypothesized changes in large metropolitan areas leading to:

(a) Increasing inequalities in occupational structure, labour market opportunities and household income distribution,

(b) Increases in the size of the group experiencing poverty and other social and economic disadvantage.

(c) Increases in residential segregation between classes and ethnic groups.

(d) Increasing separation of the group experiencing poverty and disadvantage from mainstream society to form an outsider population, variously labelled as the underclass, socially excluded, marginal etc.

(e) In the context of long-term de-industrialization, where employment opportunities for communities are disappearing, an increasing social disorganization of those communities with consequences for a range of other outcomes, including family life, childhood socialization, crime and social disorder (see especially Wilson 1987, 1997).

It is important to separate out these different components of change, which are often confused with one another, because there is no *necessary* relationship between any of them. There can, for instance, be increasing inequality without any increase in the size of the group experiencing disadvantage, unless there is a definitional link between, for example, poverty and place in the income distribution. It is equally possible that either inequality or the size of the group in poverty may increase, or both, without increasing residential segregation or the social disconnection of such groups. It is likely that there will be some causal relationships between one or more of these outcomes, but these must be established empirically – not just assumed to exist. One of the sources of confusion is that these different outcomes tend to be the concerns of different social science disciplines, each working in isolation from the others.

The issue of global cities polarization, discussed in Chapter 4, concerns how (a) and (b) above should be conceptualized. In that chapter we concluded that inequality in London had grown. Recently this was more due to rising incomes at the top of the distribution than to a growing gap between poor and middle-income households, though that continued too. It provided some evidence of increasing labour market marginality and more will be presented here. Chapter 4 also provided some mixed evidence on (c), with declining class segregation, but modest increases in spatial segregation based on deprivation indicators. None of these findings necessarily implied that (d) or (e) was also occurring. So this chapter preserves the distinction between these various strands of argument.

## The Analytical Framework

Our analysis employs four useful themes or questions drawn from the relevant literature. The first of these, drawing on one of the conceptual advances linked to social exclusion, is a concern with the persistence of individual states of disadvantage. Leisering and Leibfried (1999) define and describe a variety of time-based trajectories of poverty and disadvantage, showing that these are extremely diverse and concluding that long-term exclusion is not the large-scale phenomenon that many have held it to be. Their qualitative analysis of German social assistance claimants shows that there is a division between those who are simply enduring poverty, and those who are actively coping with it. The latter group then divide into those who find a way out of poverty after a relatively short time and those who manage it over the long term. Those who are coping number significantly more than those who are passively enduring. Such findings are of considerable importance, both in formulating and targeting policy, and for what they reveal about the connectedness of the disadvantaged to the wider society. Later we draw on panel study evidence concerning the persistence of forms of disadvantage in London.

The temporal dimension to disadvantage also suggests a need to consider its association with different life stages. This is not a new idea; in 1899 Rowntree identified periods of relative poverty (such as old age and when children were being raised) and plenty in the typical working class life course. Leisering and Leibfried also identify some poverty careers associated with life stages and family circumstances and such a focus is explicit in the analyses of exclusion by Kesteloot (1997) and Castel (1998) referred to in Chapter 1. One implication is that since many family situations are transient, so is the associated exclusion.

However, even transient exclusion may have deleterious future consequences, especially when life chances depend on accumulated assets such as education qualifications and other forms of human capital. Chapter 6 has already discussed how bumping down the occupational hierarchy occurs following unemployment and there is other evidence showing the later effects of previous experiences. Some also argue that there are inter-generational effects beyond the normal transmission of social class advantage and disadvantage – for example that children brought up in lone parent families do less well in life than those brought up by two parents, although the real cause here may be the experience of frequent family disruption.

Our second theme concerns the idea of agency implicit in exclusion. Thus exclusion is a process which results to some degree from the action of others – people are, partly at least, excluded by other individuals or institutions. So to understand exclusion requires a focus on the operations of the gatekeepers to social and economic resources. This is not to imply that all exclusion is based on conscious or unfair discrimination. Some selection practices may be entirely fair. Others may not be, but as the discussion of institutional racism indicates, that need not imply conscious discrimination. In addition, individuals' own actions may contribute to their disadvantage. Some of these have already been discussed – in relation to the education system in Chapter 5, and in relation to discrimination and selection processes in the labour market in Chapter 6. Here we shall focus on the operation of welfare and housing policies and their exclusionary effects. One of the difficulties in investigating this theme, however, is that those subject to exclusionary processes may not also be aware of it.

Our third theme concerns the validity of the insider/outsider model. How far is disadvantage so cumulative and so persistent that one can identify the excluded as a distinct social group? And if identifiable, should this group be the primary focus of policy? Or might this be at the cost of ignoring much more prevalent states of disadvantage? Adopting an insider/outsider model is not a necessary element in the analysis of exclusion (as it was in analyses of the 'underclass'), especially if the focus is on exclusion as a process, not a state. However, such a model is often adopted in practice and then underlies the concern that social exclusion may threaten cohesion and social order.

This issue also engages with the arguments in Chapters 1 and 4 over conceptualizations of the social structure. There we listed three approaches: a theorized structure of social classes based on underlying regularities (employment relations in the case of the Erikson and Goldthorpe (1993) schema); a view in which it was not possible to identify categorical class groups, especially classes-for-themselves, but where there was a pattern of structured inequality based on a range of resources and attributes; and one based on the insider/outsider dichotomy in which differences within the insider group were held to be of less significance than those between this group and the 'outsider' population. This marginalization is seen as extremely undesirable and public policy is focused on mitigating the division. However, in this analysis of marginality and social exclusion in London we need to consider how far this view of the social structure is consistent with other accounts of social divisions and with the empirical evidence.

This leads to our fourth theme, indicating the need to distinguish between, first, the processes that change the size and composition of the population at *risk* of exclusion and potentially subject to exclusionary processes, and, second, the *actual* existence and causes of more extreme forms of exclusion which may have wider social consequences. We have already introduced the idea of unemployment risk in Chapter 6. Other individual risk factors might include a low level of education and human capital, poor physical or mental health, a vulnerable family situation, weak social ties or problems of legal status. In particular contexts these risks are more or less likely to be converted into actual disadvantage. Such disadvantage, especially if severe, may then increase levels of further risk.

A more general point concerns the need, in analysis and in policy responses, to avoid confusing risk states with outcomes. First, there are groups who are at greater risk of disadvantage, for example lone parents and international migrants. Second, there are mediating individual circumstances which may make disadvantage more likely, for example poor health, lack of work experience or lack of qualifications accepted in the UK. Third, there are the types of disadvantage actually experienced, such as poverty, homelessness or unemployment. Fourth are the proximate causes, or exclusionary processes which generate those disadvantages, such as employment selection practices, housing allocation rules, welfare benefit regulations and individuals' own beliefs about the opportunities available to them. Finally, there are the 'social problems' which are associated by policy-makers and others with these forms of disadvantage. It is important to distinguish the last from the third of these matters, since they may be very different. For example, reliance on welfare benefits may be individually perceived as a practical way of coping with the high costs of London living for those without well paid jobs but policy-makers may be concerned about this generating a culture of dependency which undermines the incentives on which the labour market works.

Geographical indicators have played a prominent role in the discussion of exclusion and we next examine the spatial pattern of disadvantage in the London region. However, our main focus is on individual and family level patterns of disadvantage, and for this we need individual level evidence. So in the following section we draw on such evidence to outline some major dimensions of disadvantage, including issues of persistence. We then develop the discussion begun in Chapter 6, to identify populations at risk of exclusion. The final main section uses the life stories of our respondents to explore the processes which may lead to exclusion. The significance of welfare systems and housing markets in reinforcing deprivation clearly emerges from this account.

## The Spatial Pattern of Disadvantage

Recently there has been much interest in mapping patterns of disadvantage, particularly stimulated by the work of the Social Exclusion Unit in developing a National Strategy for Neighbourhood Renewal (Social Exclusion Unit, 2001) and the general interest in area regeneration policies. There have been several attempts to develop new deprivation indicators, as noted below. Given that one of our main interests is in the persistence of and continuities in the spatial pattern of deprivation, it is frustrating that we cannot easily use these indices to measure temporal changes in deprivation. The major problem is the discontinuities in the data used. However, current developments should allow for better measurement in the future.

Chapter 4 showed that there was some evidence of an intensification of segregation in London as measured by indicators of disadvantage. Chapter 6 also suggested that there are significant continuities in the spatial pattern of deprivation. The continuities in the high levels of Inner London unemployment are reinforced by evidence from deprivation indicators. Inner London has typically scored extremely high on local deprivation indicators at ward or borough level. One explanation may lie in overall city size (Gordon, 2002c). This picture is repeated in the more recent DTLR index of multiple deprivation (IMD), which was presented in Chapter 2. Inner London areas rank rather less high in this set of indicators than in earlier ones (such as the DoE Index of Local Conditions). The IMD is based on much more recent data than other indicators. However, Inner London's 'improvement' does not reflect much real improvement in the indicators but rather the changing weights attached to the components of the index – in particular the lower weighting of housing conditions, such as overcrowding and lacking amenities, gives this area lower scores, though inner east London boroughs such as Newham or Hackney continue to display extremely high levels of deprivation.

The IMD was constructed as a single index based on a number of domains, including deprivation in housing, health and income. The pattern of income related deprivation in the late 1990s is shown in Figure 7.1. It is not dissimilar to the overall index, shown in Figure 2.15. The top category corresponds broadly to the worst decile of wards in England, and the second category to the next decile. The figure highlights the concentration in the inner East End. This is not unlike the pattern in the late nineteenth century, with a horseshoe around the Cities of London and Westminster, though the outer edge of area has expanded somewhat, particularly east and north-east up the Lea valley. There is also a substantial pocket of deprivation to the north-west, across the northern parts of Westminster and Kensington and into the southern part of Brent, and one in west London around Southall in the Borough of Ealing. Almost all the areas in the highest deprivation category are within Greater London. However, there are some smaller concentrations in OMA centres including Luton, Slough, Reading, Thurrock and Chatham, and in some of the New Towns, such as Stevenage, Harlow and Basildon.

Figure 7.2 shows the housing index. This shows much more extensive deprivation than does the overall IMD, stretching across Inner London, though it still has some of the same spatial structure of the general index, with a large cluster in inner east and inner south-east London and further ones in north-west and west London. These are all larger areas than those shown by the overall indicator; in particular a large area of Outer London to the west is shown as experiencing housing deprivation. This reflects in part the location of the Asian origin population with larger family sizes.

The health domain, shown in Figure 7.3, has a somewhat different pattern,

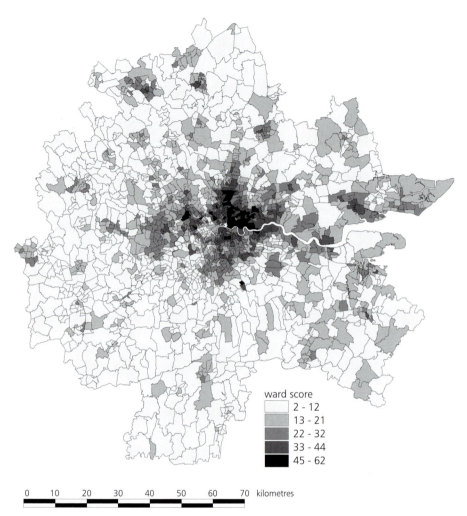

ward score
2 - 12
13 - 21
22 - 32
33 - 44
45 - 62

0    10    20    30    40    50    60    70   kilometres

**Figure 7.1.** Index of Multiple Deprivation 2000: income domain by ward. (*Source:* DTLR Index of Multiple Deprivation 2000)

with a much clearer eastward bias and an extension to outer east London and the OMA. This pattern is more strongly associated than the other indicators with the geographical distribution of manual working-class occupations. A similar pattern is shown in the distribution of the education deprivation indicator presented in Chapter 5. The child poverty indicators have a rather similar pattern to the general indicator and the employment indicator has been discussed in Chapter 6. The remaining indicator concerns accessibility; unsurprisingly, this shows the reverse pattern to that of the general indicator but it is questionable how far this really mitigates the other dimensions. The fact that the various maps do produce significantly different distributions does confirm the point made earlier about the importance of seeing disadvantage and exclusion as multi-dimensional.

All this evidence begs the question of how spatially concentrated deprivation relates to social exclusion. One issue is whether there are genuine area effects:

whether, if we control for individual characteristics, living in a deprived area has an additional negative effect on life chances. Buck (2001) concludes that this is so but the scale of these effects is not very large in comparison with the effects of personal characteristics. Nevertheless, there may be some important consequences of this factor; for example, there may be effects on social networks, the degree to which people have contacts with others who can provide support or information. Such possibilities, which may have small but cumulative effects on life chances, are discussed in the next chapter.

However, our central concern here is to understand individual and family problems of disadvantage and exclusion, rather than neighbourhood problems. The indices that have been discussed in this section are no more than useful indicators of underlying individual problems. In order to understand disadvantage and exclusion we now need to draw on evidence about individual behaviour and circumstances.

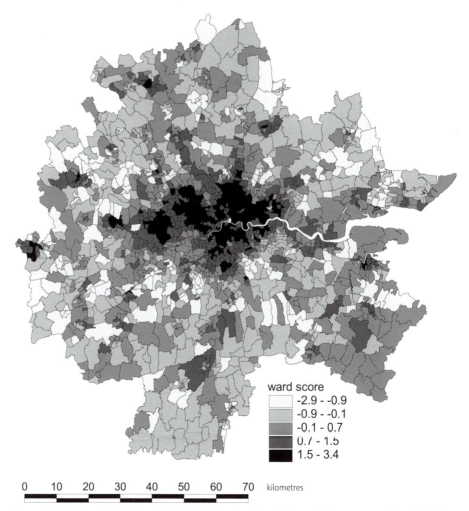

ward score

| | |
|---|---|
| | -2.9 - -0.9 |
| | -0.9 - -0.1 |
| | -0.1 - 0.7 |
| | 0.7 - 1.5 |
| | 1.5 - 3.4 |

0    10    20    30    40    50    60    70    kilometres

**Figure 7.2.** Index of Multiple Deprivation 2000: housing domain by ward. (*Source:* DTLR Index of Multiple Deprivation 2000)

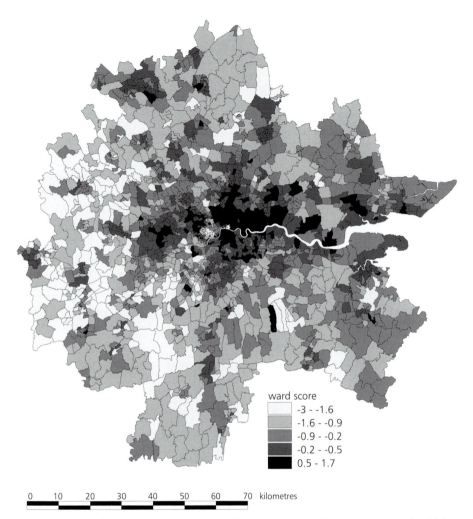

ward score

| | |
|---|---|
| | -3 - -1.6 |
| | -1.6 - -0.9 |
| | -0.9 - -0.2 |
| | -0.2 - -0.5 |
| | 0.5 - 1.7 |

0    10    20    30    40    50    60    70   kilometres

**Figure 7.3.** Index of Multiple Deprivation 2000: health domain by ward. (*Source:* DTLR Index of Multiple Deprivation 2000)

## Forms of Poverty and Disadvantage in London

In this section we document the extent and nature of poverty and disadvantage in the wider London region, although here and throughout the chapter we shall focus most attention on those areas of the regional core, Greater London and especially Inner London, where, as the analysis in the last section demonstrated, poverty is most concentrated and risk of exclusion is most evident. Our indicators include labour market marginality, poverty, claimant numbers, subjective disadvantage, social isolation and stress. Here we shall not use the language of social exclusion or seek some aggregate measure of it. However, we do consider evidence on the persistence of poverty and disadvantage for individuals. Much of our evidence comes from large surveys, but our interviews add to this with information about how poverty is experienced and how people strive to cope with it. We start with some of this material.

Many of our respondents, and not just those in poverty, had great difficulties in coping with the costs of living in London. Two incomes were frequently seen as essential.

> . . . together we pull in a pretty decent amount of money . . . but we're still struggling . . . to, you know, meet the mortgage, which is just crazy because it just shouldn't be like that.
>
> Female cohabitee, employed, white, homeowner

> . . . it's very hard in this day and age unless somebody's got a fantastic job to live on one income . . . you need two incomes, you know to afford holidays but I think one income you literally you sort of cope . . .
>
> Divorced mother, part-time employed, white, homeowner

This often made the work/family balance particularly difficult, especially where both partners worked and had children. Many had to juggle child care between them or used informal carers' care to avoid the high cost of registered child care services. Long commuting times added to the pressures, especially in Dartford and Earley. Some were conscious of the risks of needing to rely on two jobs. One respondent told us that while currently she didn't feel that there were things she had to go without, if she or her partner lost their jobs 'it would be a nightmare' as they needed two jobs to pay their mortgage and 'for the whole thing' (Married mother, employed, Asian, homeowner).

Many older people living on the basic pension or facing retirement on inadequate means had a sense of slipping downwards:

> . . . we as a couple we don't go without at the moment but our savings are dwindling . . . you are not putting nothing away but you are taking out all the time. So sooner or later we'll have to be looked after.
>
> Married mother, retired, white, council tenant

Many spoke of a constant struggle to make ends meet – the nightmare that some key support – a car, a second job – would be lost or their inability to afford the little luxuries that would give them pleasure. Here is a recent graduate:

> I left in '96 and (am) still paying off big debts. I got so financially unstable that I ended up taking out a bank loan to try and consolidate some debts . . . but now I'm paying off the bank loan which is a big chunk of my wages every month . . .
>
> Single woman, employed, Asian, private tenant

And here is a working woman who lost a vital second job:

> . . . financially, I am struggling . . . I used to have two jobs and I've lost one of them. So . . . financially things are very tight . . . I live from day to day basically.
>
> Divorced mother, employed, Jewish, homeowner

The result is that many struggle just to feed and clothe their families, especially those largely dependent on benefits, or a mix of benefits and some 'casual' income:

> . . . it's adequate to . . . feed and clothe everybody, but it's not adequate for over and above the basic necessities . . . they never stop needing things, they never stop needing finance . . . I haven't asked * * * * [elder son] to contribute to his food . . . I can't believe the amount he eats . . . So the shopping bill in Sainsbury's this week shot up from about forty six, when it's just * * * * [younger son] and me, to eighty five . . .
>
> Divorced mother, unemployed, white, private tenant

> . . . I can only afford to give them a certain amount of clothes once a year . . . right now, my daughter's in need of trainers, and I've just said she's got to wait until I can actually afford to get it for her . . .
>
> Single mother, 30s, unemployed, black British, council tenant

After food, clothes and housing, possession of a car – however old – was seen as a necessity by many and the lack of one a severe deprivation by others.

> . . . my car's absolutely ancient, it's eighteen years old . . . so I always dread it when it comes up for its MOT . . .
>
> Divorced mother, unemployed, white, private tenant

In this situation, managing expenditures and 'getting by' was an endless battle:

> . . . your main priority is your rent and your Council tax. Now even if you're working . . . if you're on a low income you can claim Housing Benefit to help with your rent, 'cos very few people can afford the full rent as well as the full Council tax but because of the slowness and the incompetency in the Housing Benefit system, if you miss a week you then get an eviction notice or a possession order so your first priority is that, so all your money goes to making sure you have your home, your gas, your electricity, your home. After that, your main priority is the children, if you have children, if you're a working mother for instance or even a working couple, your next priority is you getting to work and your children getting to their school.
>
> Single mother, unemployed, white, homeless

Many respondents felt demoralized by this endless struggle or saw others in this state. The effects of this on the neighbourhood and its children were also noted:

> I would love to drive a car, I can't afford a car, I'm so old now – I'm 48 and it's this buses, get up in the morning – I wish I could drive my nice car. And I wish I could eat out, and really . . . [be living] somewhere where . . . you don't have to fear anything . . . but people are – they respect themselves . . . they respect other people's private lives . . . and they eat out and go on holiday. I never go on holiday – I'm so stressed out as it is, I feel like – I was itching the other day, I thought maybe I need the sun. I need a holiday and I need a lot of things . . .
>
> Single mother, part-time employed/student, African, HA tenant

> Because once you're poor, you just don't want to care . . . you say: 'After all this rubbish, why should I clean, it's dirty anyway'. So everything is like I don't care – once it's I don't care, it just becomes rough [the neighbourhood] and it will just drown. Whereas if people care for

*whatever they have, they will improve it, so children would improve from that point of view, they would sort of, you know, everybody go on the same line.*

Single mother, part-time employed/student, African, HA tenant

The worst off were those substantially dependent on state welfare. In extreme cases it put at risk their physical or mental health as these two interviews illustrate. The first is a homeless family man who was moved to bed and breakfast accommodation in a town distant from the dialysis that kept him alive:

*And homeless that time, I'd been there since 9 O'clock they call me, I am waiting, waiting, waiting, you know, all day. The evening, 6 O'clock, they called my name – yes, yes . . . before I explain everything and letter, everything, and then one day, you know, 24th, move the house, you come there early morning, 9 O'clock there. OK, hand over key . . . This is on the day we vacated the house, 9 O'clock in the morning we had to go . . . All things I put in my son house . . . I went to there – went to there, me and my son. All day I wait there – so many people . . . And the evening, 6 O'clock only the officer call me: 'we've got a hotel arranged'. So I said: 'Where – hotel', I say, 'is it somewhere here – we want to live here', you know. [Makes groaning noise] '[town 30 miles from London]' . . . So I say – I explain my dialysis say: 'I'm going weekly three days dialysis \* \* \* \* Hospital - how can I come – without dialysis be dead'. 'I don't know – you want take this or not?' . . . I come back home . . . Next Monday, 6 o'clock – September . . . the landlord say: 'You have to move, please' . . . Life better – I get the Council house, I'm quite happy until I'm dead – that's all I say . . . Anywhere – I don't bother – \* \* \* \* or \* \* \* \*, anywhere – if we've got the Council house I can settle one place . . . But nobody help me.*

Married father, unemployed, Asian, private tenant

The second was driven near to suicide:

*I rang them, I said: 'I am on the beach front with my children in my car and I have enough petrol to gas us all'. And they said: 'Well there's nothing we can do about it'. But even the number for the Samaritans, nothing . . . I was, and I kept thinking, all I kept thinking to myself was, I can go to my mum, I've got my daughters and my mum and my family, if I had nobody, I would have been dead that night, I would have killed myself.*

Single mother, unemployed, white, homeless

## Labour Market Marginality

Critical indices of labour market exclusion include unemployment, particularly long-term unemployment, and various forms of labour market inactivity. Chapter 6 showed that unemployment rates have fluctuated substantially, nationally and in London, and that unemployment in London rose relative to the national average in each recession, and only fell back in prolonged periods of economic growth. So in the 1990s London unemployment was on average at much higher levels than before 1980. It also suggested that unemployment was strongly concentrated within parts of the region, and especially Inner London. However, there have been two other prominent trends.

First, there has been a substantial rise in labour market inactivity among people of working age. There have been continual increases in early retirement, in long-term sickness, in the numbers of people who – while they may be registered as unemployed – are not seeking work because they believe no jobs are available ('discouraged workers'), and in lone parents who are not seeking work, in part because of the unaffordability of child care on low wages.

Second, there has been a growing divide between work-rich and work-poor households, with a strong tendency in those where at least one member is unemployed or inactive for other members also to be inactive. This tendency is reinforced by welfare benefit rules which mean that when the partners of unemployed people work, the latter's benefit is reduced. This growing polarization is reinforced by the increase in single-person and lone-parent households.

Chapter 6 presented the evidence on unemployment. Basically similar findings exist if we look at other measures. For example, Figure 7.4 shows trends in the percentage of the population aged under 60 living in households with no one in employment, for different parts of the London region. This may be compared with figure 6.1, which showed unemployment rates. The relative positions of different parts of the region are rather similar. For example, the Inner London to UK ratio for these data averages around 1.76 for the second half of the 1990s compared with 1.79 for the unemployment series. However, a significant difference between the series is that in all areas the jobless household rate has declined much less in periods of economic growth in the late 1990s than has the unemployment rate. The 2000 level in all areas is around 80 per cent of the peak 1993/94 level for household joblessness, compared with around 50 per cent for unemployment. Figure 7.4 also indicates a significant relative deterioration of the position of both parts of Greater London in the 1990s compared with the 1980s. In the period 1986–1989, the proportion in jobless households in Greater London as a whole was just about the same as the national average. In the period 1998–2000 it was 28 per cent higher. The change is particularly striking in Outer London, which has moved from being significantly better than the national average to around that level.

In 2000, just under a quarter of all children in London lived in a household with no-one in employment. For lone parent families, this proportion was 60 per cent,

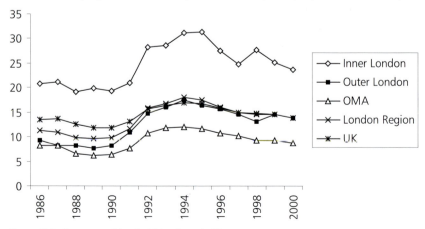

**Figure 7.4.** Percentage living in jobless households.

and such families accounted for 64 per cent of the children living in households with no-one in employment. Couples with children accounted for the remaining 36 per cent of these 'excluded' children.

To summarize, this evidence and that discussed in Chapter 4, indicates that, to the extent that change in inequality and social divisions over the last two decades in London has been different from that in the country as a whole, it is a result of the growth of unemployment and inactivity, rather than of marked changes in the occupational hierarchy. However, this pattern is less clearly evident now, at the beginning of the current decade, than a decade earlier, given the prolonged phase of national economic growth that has occurred.

Our neighbourhood interviews reinforce this conclusion, as few respondents felt that there was a gross shortage of available jobs. We did not find people saying, in effect, 'there are no jobs around here to be had', as we would have in the early 1980s in London and more recently in still depressed regions. Instead, many, especially those with children, said that the sorts of jobs which they could get paid too little to make it worth working. Some questioned whether it was worth working at all:

> Well, a lot of people gave themselves that question, didn't they. And they're using that as an excuse . . . Well, I'm better off not working, because I can't find a thing that'll pay the actual . . . a living fucking wage, you know . . . And basically, I was clearing, after tax, after I'd paid me fares as well, I was clearing 23 quid a day. And that's 8–5 . . . it was basically treading water . . . I weren't getting no further forward, but . . . I had the choice. I could've done that, or I could've gone, 'No, I'll go on the dole', and waited six weeks with no money . . . Anyway, I went to work as a road sweeper, I was getting up at half past four in the morning . . . So anyway, I ended up in court over that, because of non-payment of rent, and all that shit.
>
> Single male, unemployed/employed, white, council tenant

There were two problems in taking low wage jobs. The first was the high costs of travel to work in London and of other costs associated with working such as childcare. The second was the potential loss of state benefits, in particular Housing Benefit which is very important in London, given its very high housing costs. This problem was compounded by the major inefficiencies in benefits administration in some boroughs (see the discussion in Chapter 10). If taking low paid work meant losing some benefits – especially where the job might be short term and then there could be major problems in promptly re-establishing benefits – this became a significant disincentive to becoming employed. Inefficiencies of the benefit system also exacerbated problems associated with family break-up or re-formation.

More generally, the difficulties of coping on a low income that we have already referred to are made worse by the vagaries of the welfare system and the ever-increasing intrusions of officialdom.

> I was trying to help my son . . . off of the Social, so he had nowhere to live so I said: 'Well stay with me'. They took forty-six pounds away from me and he was only earning thirty pounds and I said he wasn't giving me any rent but they took no notice. As a result of that, I got into rent arrears . . . and I had a letter of eviction and I was really quite panicked . . .
>
> Single mother, unemployed, white, homeless

One respondent's daughter had continually had her Housing Benefit claims 'mixed up' by the local authority and had been threatened with eviction for arrears, so she had taken several days off work to go to its offices to try and sort this out, eventually giving up her job under this pressure:

> . . . she kept getting eviction notices, you can't go to work when you're worried that your house is going to be taken away so you have to sort that out . . . which got to the point where she took a video in, you know like to prove I'm here and it got to the point where the stress of that and the stress of going to work and not seeing her son, he was only little, and she see him for what, twenty minutes when she picked him, take him home, go to bed. It just got too much for her and she became very depressed and ill and had to give it up.
>
> Single mother, unemployed, white, homeless

And those who tried not just to cope but to get better qualified for employment through education also felt frustrated by the benefits system:

> . . . you're on benefit yeah? And you go . . . to say I'm gonna go to college . . . now you go into full time education, they're telling you that they're going to take your benefit away from you because you're in full time education, and if you're gonna be in full time education you can go and work full time. Now that is stupid, init? But that's how they work.
>
> Divorced mother, part-time employed, black British, council tenant

## Poverty

When we consider direct measures of monetary poverty a slight puzzle emerges. The recent evidence suggests that poverty rates in London are quite close to the national average, being nothing like as high relatively as unemployment or inactivity rates. In Table 7.1, based on the Family Resources Survey, the poverty rate is defined as the proportion of the population living in households whose income, adjusted for size and composition, is below a poverty line set at 60 per cent of the median income. It shows that the basic poverty rate in London, without any adjustment for housing costs, is 17 per cent: identical to the national rate. There is some evidence of higher rates for children but pensioner poverty is rather lower. As may be expected from other evidence in this book, poverty rates in the London region outside Greater London are significantly below the national average.

How can the apparent contradiction between this result and the concentration

**Table 7.1.** Poverty rates in London 1999/2000 (percentage below 60 per cent of median).

|  | Before Housing Costs | | | After Housing Costs | | |
|---|---|---|---|---|---|---|
|  | Greater London | Rest of South East | Great Britain | Greater London | Rest of South East | Great Britain |
| All individuals | 17 | 12 | 17 | 29 | 18 | 23 |
| Children | 24 | 15 | 22 | 43 | 25 | 32 |
| Working age adults | 14 | 9 | 13 | 24 | 15 | 19 |
| Pensioners | 19 | 19 | 21 | 30 | 23 | 25 |

*Source:* Households Below Average Income, Department of Social Security, 2001.

of jobless households be explained? An obvious possibility is that poverty data do not take into account the high costs of living in London. The second part of Table 7.1 shows that 'after housing cost' poverty rates are significantly higher overall and now there is a significantly worse situation in London than in the nation as a whole.

In general, the demographic characteristics of London, with the concentration there of several high risk groups, make it particularly prone to having high levels of disadvantage. However, there is one major exception to this concentration, and a second more tentative one. London, as we saw in Chapter 4, has relatively few elderly households, including single elderly, compared with the UK. Such households have a particularly high poverty rate. Couple households with large numbers of children are another group with relatively high poverty rates. Overall, London has relatively few such households, though there are concentrations within certain ethnic minorities. It is also possible that the fact that London has smaller than average households may mean that its poverty rate is biased downwards, because of the way the data are adjusted for household size.

Another partial explanation could be that large numbers of people who are marginal to the formal labour market are relying on earnings from the informal economy. Without wanting to dismiss the importance of the informal economy in London, it seems unlikely to explain this discrepancy, since it implies that people are prepared to declare informal earnings in one government survey, while in another such survey they are concealing informal work activity. A possible explanation for the fact that London poverty is not higher involves the composition of the poverty population amongst those of working age. This consists of both jobless households and households containing the working poor. Nationally, 55 per cent of working age poor are in jobless households and 45 per cent in households containing at least one worker. However, London wage rates are relatively higher than elsewhere. So it may be that relatively fewer households containing members with jobs count as poor in London compared with other areas. This would tend to depress the poverty rate and (statistically) compensate for the rather high share of jobless households in London, even though these do have a high risk of poverty.

Further evidence comes from data on social security claimants. Table 7.2 shows that within the working age population, the proportion of claimants in London is not especially high. However, it differs from the national distribution. In particular, the proportion of sick and disabled people is rather low in London. The proportion of working families receiving income supplements is also rather low, consistent with the point about London's relatively high wages made above. In contrast, the shares of unemployed and lone parent recipients are particularly high. In parts of the region outside Greater London overall claimant rates are very much lower, and working families, the sick and disabled make up a larger share than they do in Greater London.

## Subjective Poverty and Stress Indicators

This last discussion concerned monetary poverty. However, there are alternative and

**Table 7.2.** Social security benefit claimants, August 1998.

|  | London | ROSE | Great Britain |
|---|---|---|---|
| Thousands | 830 | 753 | 6,100 |
| % of working age population | 18% | 11% | 17% |
| % of claimants who are: |  |  |  |
| Working family | 7% | 13% | 12% |
| Unemployed | 28% | 21% | 22% |
| Sick and disabled | 37% | 45% | 47% |
| Lone parents | 21% | 17% | 15% |
| Others | 7% | 4% | 4% |

*Source:* Social Security Statistics, Department of Social Security, 1999.
*Note:* ROSE figures estimated from South East and East Regions.

additional poverty indicators, including measures of consumption and expenditure and more subjective measures of how people feel they are getting by, or indicators of what they must do without. One reason for wanting to look at other indicators is that income measures do not fully take into account variations in the costs of living. The housing cost adjustment made above may be only a part of the variation between areas. However, another reason is that the monetary measures are rather crude and are not particularly sensitive to variations between families and in the pressures on them.

The neighbourhood interviews that we quoted from earlier sharply outlined these more subjective aspects of poverty and the everyday pressures of making ends meet for sections of the population in London that extend well beyond those who might formally be defined as being in poverty. We can support some of this evidence from analysis of quantitative social surveys. The British Household Panel Survey (BHPS), covering the period since 1991, and containing sufficient London respondents to identify differences from other areas, has a number of relevant indicators. We have carried out some regression analyses, to establish how far parts of the London region differ from other parts of the country, after controlling for individual characteristics, including age, sex, household type, income level and tenure. We also contrasted London with other large conurbations in Britain that have a similar and in some cases a more acute range of social problems.

Our first indicator is a score based on six non-monetary poverty indicators. These are having a holiday; keeping the home warm; replacing furniture; buying new clothes; having meat or fish every other day; and providing meals for visitors. Respondents were asked whether they did these things and, if not, whether this was because they could not afford to do so. The data show that, after controlling for income and personal characteristics but not tenure, Londoners are more likely to report having to do without than the UK sample as a whole. This is also true for people in the rest of the South East and these differences are rather greater than the relevant differentials in other conurbations. It does seem then that high living costs do intensify poverty in the London region. However in absolute terms this differential is relatively modest. For example being in a lone parent household raises this measure by eight times as much as being a resident of Inner London. Interestingly, when analyses are carried for those in social housing and other tenures separately, the pattern changes somewhat. Amongst tenants in social housing, those in Inner London report lower levels of going without than the similar group in other parts of the country, while in the rest of the region there is no significant difference from the national level. However, for those in private renting or owner occupation, where housing costs are greater, people throughout the region are more likely to report having to do without than the matched national sample.

A second indicator is based on responses to the question 'How well would you say you yourself are managing financially these days?' Even after controlling for income, people in Inner London were around 52 per cent more likely to respond 'finding it quite difficult' or 'finding it very difficult' than for the rest of the UK. In Outer London the difference was 26 per cent and for the Rest of the South East, 27 per cent. No such differentials existed in the case of other conurbations.

## Housing

As already indicated the housing market plays a particular role in exacerbating disadvantage in London. On the demand side, this is a consequence of the social mix of its population, identified in Chapter 4. The high demand for professional, managerial and related workers in London drives up housing costs generally and supply constraints increase this effect. Low-income households are then faced with either paying high prices, even for poor properties, or trying to gain access to that part of the housing system which is relatively sheltered from these effects. However, in the past 20 years this protection has been weakened by social housing sales which have also led to the marginalization of much of the remaining council housing – frequently this is now some of the worst housing. Some respondents spoke particularly of how undesirable it now was to live on 'the estates'.

BHPS evidence indicates two aspects of the housing problem. Londoners were much more likely to report having experienced difficulties over meeting housing costs than people elsewhere. Controlling for personal circumstances, including income and tenure, the relative odds of reporting such difficulties were around 80 per cent higher in Inner London, 14 per cent higher in Outer London, and interestingly as much as 55 per cent higher in the Rest of the South East. In the other conurbations, with rather higher levels of poverty, but fewer equivalent housing market pressures, the degree of difficulty was the same as in the remainder of the country.

Problems with the physical fabric of the house and with its immediate environment were also particularly acute in London. BHPS contains eleven housing problem indicators. If these are scored one if the respondent reports the problem and zero otherwise and summed, the overall score has a mean of 1.4, and a standard deviation of 1.6. The score for Inner London, controlling for personal characteristics and tenure, is about 0.8 above the level in the remainder of the UK outside the London region. For comparison, this is also about the scale of the difference between renters and owners nationally in this score. In Outer London the score is about 0.3

higher and in the Rest of the South East 0.2. However, if we separate the index into the four items which relate to the local neighbourhood environment and the seven items relating to the house itself, the former dominate the Inner London result. For these the score is 0.5 above the rest of the UK, for the property items it is 0.3 above. In Outer London and the Rest of the South East the score divides more evenly.

The evidence on housing stress contained in our interviews shows that there is a fundamental distinction between council tenants, dependent on officialdom, and owner-occupiers who are able to exercise some freedom of choice – albeit a constrained one. Some tenants in public housing tell stories of lives that are constrained by the arbitrary boundaries of the local authorities in which they happen to live – and in some cases in which they were born – and many in social housing more generally are constrained by their dependent status.

> It [the location] was chosen by the Council.
>> Married mother, employed, white, council tenant

> Yeah they just gave me a transfer and I had to come down and view it and I had to say I liked it, otherwise I don't know what would have happened but I had to take this one so . . .
>> Single father, unemployed, white, council tenant

> . . . when you are on the Peabody list [a housing association] you do not have much option, well . . . you can circle preferable areas where they might offer you somewhere, and the more areas you circle the more chance you will have a quicker offer of a flat . . .
>> Gay cohabitee, self-employed, white, housing association tenant

Some experienced endless years on the waiting list and many spoke about the compromises that had to be made and the lack of choice.

> Eleven years . . . on the list to get a one bedroomed flat . . . and they said 'Take it or leave it, you won't get another one'. So that's how I moved to Battersea.
>> Married man, employed, white, council tenant

Many respondents dreamed of escape, like this Peckham resident who wanted to get away to a leafy suburb like Kingston:

> . . . I don't know . . . just to get away from this place . . . this place they call a ghetto . . . really . . . I can't really explain it . . . It's just what people say . . . I feel it is the wrong impression really . . . but . . . you know . . .
>> Single man, student, African, lives with family (council tenants)

Many of those we interviewed told us stories of quiet and not-so-quiet desperation: the struggle to live on low – or, in some areas, moderate – incomes; their sheer inability to find any alternative housing; and the inexorable operation of points systems that left them for years on the waiting list, or even permanently excluded. Their incomes made it inconceivable that they would ever graduate into owner-occupation or reasonable quality private rental housing, in any location in our region:

> . . . financially . . . even for a minimum rate flat, it would cost me a thousand pound to begin with because they want four weeks rent in advance and four weeks' deposit, so if it's a

*hundred pound a week that's four hundred pound, that's eight hundred pound I'd have to pay before I even moved in.*

Single mother, unemployed, white, homeless

Another respondent stressed that it was not just a matter of income: with children, one was at a permanent disadvantage in the housing market, especially if dependent on welfare benefits:

*. . . apart from the financial aspect, it's very hard to find someone who will take someone who's on Housing Benefit or on Social Security, Income Support and difficult to find somewhere that will take children, even though mine are twelve and fourteen at the moment, they . . . they prefer professional people because obviously there's, there's less risk of them having noise in the place or anything broken and usually because they're worried that if you're a mother with children, you might end up not being able to pay them, so it's almost impossible.*

Single mother, unemployed, white, homeless

Others talked about the severe lack of council accommodation and the endless arguments about the rules.

*. . . the big problem in Reading is the lack of council accommodation as well . . . I mean, my sister got a council flat after I think she'd been on the list for, well, probably since she was eighteen and she moved into that flat three years ago . . . And the only reason she got that was 'cos she had two kids and was living in a converted garage that was damp.*

Married man, employed, white, homeowner

*. . . because I was in a bit of arrears, so they wouldn't move me on that ground. Then . . . my son's the eldest of them all, then I had a girl, and then I went back to them, and I said, 'Well, look, I've got a daughter'. And they said, 'Oh, not till when she was five'. And when she got to five years old, they measured up the flat, and told me . . . because I had a kitchen and a dining room, they told me I could make my dining room into a bedroom, which was totally stupid! And after that, I had two more. And it was only until . . . when my other daughter, my last one was born, when they decided that I was [eligible to move to a larger property].*

Single mother, unemployed, black British, council tenant

Nonetheless, council housing frequently represents security. This respondent, a single mother of four, was highly dissatisfied with her location in Eltham, largely because of her experience as a victim of crime and her fears of repeat victimization. Although she was clear that moving house was the change that would most improve the quality of her life, she was not prepared to trade the security of her social housing tenancy for the risks of the private rented sector in her preferred West London location:

*I've been trying to move over to my dad at Hounslow 'cos he's really . . . and my sister's really ill. And she's got the only kid, so I'm always quite a lot up there . . . I've been trying for four years now but no other council will accept me. I've tried [to get a transfer with another council tenant] . . . like I buy the Loot [free newspaper] and all that and whatever, as soon as you say Eltham, people don't want it . . . It's to do with that Stephen Lawrence in't it? . . . people say the only way I'm going to get up there is by going private but I don't really want to. I want to stay on council really. I haven't got that sort of money to put down for private . . . My brother, he offered me eight hundred pound . . . two hundred pound deposit and six hundred pound for the first month. And, 'cos I'm not working now, I said yeah it ain't only the deposit I need. I need to like . . . for a van and you know, all different things and like when you're moving, it is costly and all that . . . he said, I don't want it back . . . No, I'd rather sort of wait to do a council exchange. At least that way, you know you're still on the council and you ain't going to be chucked out at the end of the month. I mean going private is too much of a risk.*

Separated mother, unemployed, council tenant

One effect of borough based systems of social housing allocation could be to weaken family ties. This couple, who had moved out to Gants Hill, told us of the problems of their aged parents left behind in Islington:

*I don't know how we're going to get on with my mum and dad when they, because being in Islington's going to be a bit awkward. We really wanted to try and move 'em this way. It's not an easy job though . . . we've been up to the Town Hall and asked and they said that they'd have to come down and put their name down. Em, but they have to sort of literally be thrown out of their house I think to be able to get a council place . . . they're actually in a tenants association house, so literally to get a council place they have to be thrown out physically . . . they was in a position where they was frightened. I mean my dad's what he's 78, 77 and my mum is 67. And they was petrified . . .*

Married mother, white, homeowner

## Stress and Isolation

More light is thrown on aspects of poverty in London by a mental health index (scaled from 1 to 12) taken from the General Health Questionnaire, which is also sometimes used as an indicator of stress. High levels are clearly related to poverty and to life events such as job loss. Controlling for personal circumstances, the index is higher in Inner London than in the nation as a whole, with an average differential of about 0.3, equivalent to that linked to living in social housing. There are also significant and positive effects from living in Outer London (0.2) and the Rest of the South East (0.1). However, most of the effect in Inner London is for men, where the score is increased by 0.45, while for women it increases by only 0.15. Differences are not so great in other parts of the region. London living is clearly relatively stressful and this will tend to compound other disadvantages.

We also have some evidence from the BHPS on lack of social support, using a number of questions about whether people have access to someone who can help in a crisis. Once again we find evidence of higher levels of social isolation in both Inner and Outer London, though the differences are not enormous, around a third of the effect linked to living alone, or to living in social housing. Again we find that it is men in particular who lack social support in Inner London, though in Outer London, women are at somewhat greater risk.

## The Persistence of Poverty and Other Measures of Disadvantage

In the introduction to this chapter we suggested that persistence was one important dimension of social exclusion. In spite of assumptions that poverty is substantially a long-term phenomenon, much international evidence has shown that there are considerable volumes of movement in and out of poverty. So, while considerably more people will be affected by poverty over say a 5 or 10 year period than are implied by a single year's measure, the proportion that are poor for the whole of such a period is very small. Evidence for Great Britain, based on the BHPS, suggests that at the poverty rate of around 17 per cent referred to earlier, around 32 per cent experienced some poverty over a 7 year period, but only 2 per cent were poor throughout this period (Devicienti, 2001). However, this research also shows that people who leave poverty have a relatively high chance of re-entering poverty later. The best way of analysing geographical differences in poverty turnover and persistence is to examine poverty exit and re-entry rates.

It is not entirely clear what we should expect in London in relation to exit and re-entry rates. One the one hand, high levels of exclusion and separation of the poor from the non-poor population would imply high levels of persistence and therefore low exit rates. On the other hand, the fact that London has a rather turbulent labour market, with large numbers of poor-quality and short-term job opportunities might imply relatively high exit and entry rates but low persistence. In fact, after controlling for personal characteristics, income and tenure, we find a tendency for the relative odds of poverty exit in Inner London to be around 10 per cent lower than in the comparison area (Britain outside the South East, and excluding the other conurbations), but the difference is not statistically significant. Outer London is not at all different from the comparison area, but exit rates in the Rest of the South East are much higher (odds around 26 per cent higher). In other conurbations there is statistically significant evidence of low exit rates, around 14 per cent below the comparison. Thus poverty is more persistent in London than in its economically affluent hinterland, but is not exceptionally so in comparison with the rest of the country.

Poverty re-entry rates in London are rather below average. In Inner London the difference is not statistically significant, but in Outer London the rate is substantially and significantly lower. The two parts of London combined have re-entry rates around 23 per cent below the comparison area, while the rest of the South East has rates 21 per cent lower. The reference period for this analysis is 1992 to 1999 and this low tendency to re-enter poverty may reflect the relative prosperity of the region.

We have undertaken a parallel analysis on the probabilities of leaving and re-entering, living in a jobless household. This is a direct measure of household labour market marginality and it tells a rather similar story to that for poverty. London as a whole has significantly lower exit rates from the jobless household situation, around 16 per cent below the comparison area, while the Rest of the South East has exit rates 30 per cent above the comparison area. Exit rates in other conurbations are even lower than London, around 22 per cent below the rest of Great Britain. There is no clear, statistically significant pattern for re-entry rates to jobless households.

This evidence does point to rather higher persistence of disadvantaging states in London compared with elsewhere, though for poverty at least the differences are not substantial, and in neither case are they as great as those in other UK conurbations.

This persistence may have consequences for the social connections between groups in poverty and the rest of the population. We will suggest, from evidence presented later, that this situation is mainly a consequence of the intensity of the poverty trap in London caused by the high costs of living there.

## Populations at Risk

In the previous section we presented evidence on the extent and nature of disadvantage in London. Here we discuss how it is distributed between population groups. In part we focus on this issue because it gives some insight into the causes of the disadvantage. For example, if minority ethnic groups experience particularly high levels of disadvantage, then we should expect to find some part of the explanation in the social situation of such groups or the discrimination processes they face. In Chapter 4 we identified some demographic patterns in London, especially its distinctive age and household structure, its large ethnic minority population, and the migration processes it experiences, which have implications for the size and composition of the population at risk of social exclusion. Evidence in that chapter provided a first indication of the processes which can lead to changes in this at risk population. While in the previous section, evidence was presented on several dimensions of disadvantage, here we mainly focus on the characteristics of those at risk of labour market marginality because the evidence from social surveys on distribution at the household level is much better for this indicator than for any others.

The main aim is to indicate how far levels of risk in London linked to the unemployment and inactivity levels reflect a concentration of the generally most vulnerable groups there and how far they reflect higher levels of unemployment and inactivity for all workers or for particular groups who experience exceptional exposure to risk in London. Chapter 6 discussed unemployment risk in some detail. When unemployment in London is compared with the situation nationally, the conclusion at the individual level is, with some exceptions, that the same sorts of people have higher risks in London as elsewhere, but the overall level of risk in London is rather higher for everyone. In addition, there is a substantial compositional effect: London has a higher share of the sort of people who are more generally exposed to greatest risk. However, it is important to stress that the effect is not entirely compositional. So an individual with a given set of characteristics – including age, gender, race and qualifications – is more likely to be in a marginal labour market position in London than elsewhere. Analysis of other forms of labour market marginality suggests essentially similar conclusions about its distribution.

This chapter has identified the importance of the household and family dimensions in the analysis of deprivation and exclusion. The family situation of those experiencing unemployment and inactivity is particularly important, given the polarization of work between work-rich and work-poor households. There are six clusters of family situations that together cover around 98 per cent of those of working age who are experiencing some form of labour market exclusion:

• young single people still living in the parental home;

• young singles (under 30) who have left home and who are living alone or with unrelated singles;

• lone parents;

• couples with children under 16;

• older singles, divorced and widowed, without children;

• older couples over 45, childless or with adult children only.

The distribution of those excluded from the labour market in the period 1998–2000 is shown in Table 7.3. This distinguishes between those unemployed or inactive for less than one year ('short term') and those in these states for more than a year ('long term'). Young single people are more heavily represented in the short-term than in the longer group category, reflecting their greater involvement in unstable labour markets. Other groups, and especially lone parents, are more strongly represented in the long-term category. Comparing London with the UK, there are differences in the composition of the excluded category. Some of these follow directly from the differences in the population structure discussed above. So there are fewer young single people living with their parents and couple households. Interestingly, even though there are more lone parents in London than elsewhere, they do not figure more strongly amongst the excluded. The prominent groups in London are young single people who have left home and older single, widowed and divorced people. This reinforces the point made earlier that people over the age of about 30 are relatively more disadvantaged in London than elsewhere in the UK.

**Table 7.3.** Distribution of short- and long-term labour market exclusion by life stage.

|  | London | | ROSE | | UK | |
|---|---|---|---|---|---|---|
|  | Short term % | Long term % | Short term % | Long term % | Short term % | Long term % |
| Young single with parents | 21.2 | 7.2 | 22.2 | 7.8 | 22.7 | 7.5 |
| Young single left home | 16.2 | 6.0 | 11.8 | 4.7 | 12.6 | 5.1 |
| Lone parents | 10.5 | 32.5 | 10.8 | 31.8 | 11.3 | 29.6 |
| Younger couples with children | 19.5 | 22.7 | 23.8 | 19.9 | 22.8 | 23.6 |
| Older single widowed and divorced | 17.0 | 18.7 | 12.9 | 16.2 | 14.0 | 16.5 |
| Older couples | 7.7 | 8.6 | 12.4 | 16.2 | 10.8 | 14.2 |

*Source:* Labour Force Survey micro-data sets, 1998–2000.

The interaction of household circumstances with other key indicators amongst those in marginal labour market positions is shown in Table 7.4. The key indicators, which are also identified in our analyses of unemployment risk, are ethnicity, housing tenure, and qualification level. Young single people, whether living with their parents or elsewhere, as well as younger couples with children, who are in a marginal labour market position, are especially likely to come from the ethnic minority communities.

Lone parents are more likely to come from the white and the black population, but not other ethnic minority groups. However, non-married groups aged over 30, and older couples are substantially more likely to be white.

All groups, except for the older couples, are more likely to be living in social housing than any other tenure but in the case of both groups of single people (and especially the young) there is a substantial representation in the private rented sector. The household types with children are especially likely to be in social housing, reflecting allocation policies in that tenure. Across all household types, more than half have no qualifications or only minimal qualifications.

**Table 7.4.** Characteristics of long-term labour market excluded in London, by life stage, 1998–2000.

| | Young single living with parent | Young single left parental home | Lone parents with children | Younger couples widowed divorce | Older single, | Older couples | Total |
|---|---|---|---|---|---|---|---|
| **Percentage:** | | | | | | | |
| White | 51.4 | 52.8 | 62.9 | 51.6 | 66.0 | 70.6 | 59.0 |
| Black – Caribbean | 11.5 | 17.5 | 12.2 | 2.5 | 9.0 | 2.2 | 8.4 |
| Black – African | 3.9 | 12.8 | 12.5 | 7.4 | 7.1 | 0.5 | 8.3 |
| Indian | 6.3 | 2.4 | 0.9 | 5.3 | 4.4 | 12.4 | 4.8 |
| Pakistani/Bangladeshi | 11.4 | 0.8 | 3.4 | 16.1 | 2.8 | 5.0 | 7.6 |
| Other | 15.5 | 13.6 | 8.2 | 17.0 | 10.8 | 9.3 | 11.9 |
| Owner occupier | 46.1 | 18.6 | 8.4 | 18.5 | 35.6 | 55.9 | 24.9 |
| Social housing | 49.9 | 42.0 | 77.2 | 66.3 | 43.3 | 34.2 | 58.2 |
| Private renting | 4.0 | 39.3 | 14.4 | 15.2 | 20.8 | 9.9 | 16.9 |
| No qualifications | 30.1 | 28.7 | 39.2 | 41.9 | 30.2 | 43.4 | 36.5 |
| Low qualifications (NVQ 1) | 14.2 | 28.6 | 23.0 | 34.4 | 25.2 | 23.4 | 26.6 |

*Source:* Labour Force Survey micro-data sets, first quarters 1998–2000.

## Processes and Trajectories of Social Exclusion

Earlier we drew on our interview material to describe the sorts of disadvantage experienced by Londoners, extracting specific examples from the responses of a considerable number of people. However, theories of social exclusion focus our attention on the need to understand the interaction between different areas of deprivation and their combined impact on individual lives. Such an approach also accords well with the longitudinal focus implied by social exclusion – we are interested in trajectories of inclusion or exclusion. The detailed analysis of the life stories that were revealed by our interviews is beyond the scope of this book, so here we can only summarize the material and draw on a small number of examples.

We can approach the interview material in two ways, either for its evidence on material and behavioural aspects of exclusion, or for what it can reveal about more subjective expressions of exclusion. In practice we must do both but there is then a question about just what is to count as a subjective expression of exclusion. This could concern, for example, hopelessness, alienation or resentment – but such views are rare and are not necessarily associated with poverty. For example, at several points in this book we refer to an interview with a female lone parent in Battersea that contains some of the clearest expressions of resentment against the 'system' and occasional desperation in the face of events. However, it would be difficult to conclude that this person was 'excluded' because of her continued willingness to struggle to improve her situation. By contrast, another interviewee, also a single parent from Battersea, while she had rather better material circumstances than the first interviewee and had a substantial resource in her social networks, nevertheless expressed a deep sense of alienation from her neighbourhood.

However, having reviewed our resident interviews, whose selection was biased towards lower-income Londoners, with the exception of one important group, none of them presents a pattern and combination of individual circumstances which would lead us to conclude that that individual was truly excluded on all dimensions of Kesteloot's (1997) typology, i.e. in relation to the market, to family and social networks, and to the state. The exception concerns some of the recent asylum seekers whom we interviewed. We cannot claim that these findings can be generalized across London's population as a whole because the number of interviews is too small for that and there were some biases in our sampling, other than that already mentioned. We did not try to interview those sleeping rough, and, generally, we can expect that the most alienated individuals will also be the ones most reluctant to take part in interviews. Nevertheless, we can say that there is not a large group of low-income Londoners who are alienated from the wider society and who, to coin a phrase, might be dubbed 'the truly excluded'. The fear frequently expressed in public debate that such a group exists and is growing has, on the evidence of our research, little empirical foundation.

It has already been suggested in the earlier discussion of labour market marginality that we did not have any clear evidence from our interviews of people for whom labour market exclusion was a matter of having no access to jobs. Rather it was the interaction of the limited types of jobs that were available with other aspects of their situation which led to problems. One more direct form of labour market exclusion affected those immigrants whose qualifications were not recognized within the British system and who were therefore working in jobs substantially below their capacities. In general the main group of 'risk of exclusion' cases in our interviews consisted of people whose material conditions were poor because of family circumstances or ill-health and whose capacity to get by was limited or undermined because of weak social networks and/or problems in the operation of state services or benefits. However, difficulties in finding and retaining jobs could exacerbate other situations. There are those who face potential problems because they are in rent arrears and may also have other debts, are unemployed and who have a largely passive approach to their situation, relying on the social welfare system to prevent destitution. All respondents appeared to have some knowledge of and capacity to access the welfare system, although some had more difficulty than others in making the system work effectively for them. Amongst the overall group at risk of exclusion, recent immigrants and asylum seekers stood out as having particular problems. However, individual variations in the capacity to cope with and manage their situation made a huge difference, and some who apparently had the least resources were still making a success of life in London. Five examples illustrate some of this variety.

The first case involves a combination of family breakdown, mental health problems and weak labour market position. The interviewee is a separated white woman living in a council house. She has four children, one of whom has left school, though all the children still live with her. She has had employment in the past but has remained in each job for only a short time. Before she was married, she worked in shops and when the children were small, she did seasonal agricultural work and cleaning. After having been in a care centre herself, she worked in an old people's home/day centre as a care assistant. She got this job through a friend. She left after a staff disagreement. Her last job was caring for an elderly woman with cancer (she knew the woman's daughter). She is no longer actively seeking work, although she would like a job. She also has had rent arrears. She said that she had been a victim of stalking and became agoraphobic for a period afterwards. It also appears that she gets on extremely badly with her neighbours and there have been some violent confrontations. However, in spite of these problems she does have some resources as she is part of a large family. While her brothers and sisters live elsewhere in the region, they maintain contact and she has had an offer of financial support from a brother.

The second case is similar in some respects but with differences partly due to a more active use of support. This is a lone parent with five children, who has had two marriages. She was evicted from her previous house for rent arrears, because of problems with her housing benefit and could no longer get on to a council housing list. This eviction was just one of many: 'I've been evicted so many times I can't remember now'. Her two youngest children now live with her mother and her son in his late teens lives with her older daughter. Her son is wearing a tag after release from prison/young offenders' institution. She had lived in squats when the children were young. She also associates the current loss of accommodation with her divorce three years ago and subsequent nervous breakdown. At the time of the divorce she had been working in the same firm as her husband, a job she left after one year. She heard of the job through a friend. Previously she had had a number of jobs – these may have been of a 'cash in hand' nature. She believes that she cannot afford to work because of the loss of benefits that this would incur. She is an articulate woman and has used Citizens Advice Bureaux (CAB), law centres, Women's Aid, and the Church for advice and help on a number of occasions. Her mother lives in a housing association property that she got through Women's Aid. The mother has also been in arrears with rent and used the Citizens Advice Bureau and Law Centre for help to prevent eviction. Mother and daughter complain that both the local CAB and the law centre have closed down and there is nowhere to turn to other than the Church, which neither currently attends.

There are other lone parents who can cope more successfully, perhaps because they have stronger social networks. For example, one respondent in Bermondsey made a conscious decision not to work while bringing up children. She could rely on a very strong, family based social network. She has ten brothers and sisters, some of whom are well off and still live in the London area. In other cases the out-migration flows of the more successful family members may mean that poorer siblings are left behind, and have fewer family networks on which to draw.

As we have already suggested, migrants may face particular problems, since there may be no family nearby on which to rely and their social support networks may be very fragile. Of course, the great majority of migrants, including those who come from other parts of Britain, assimilate successfully. Here the focus is on those in a weak economic position, or with relatively weak social ties, or dependent on failing public services, or with problematic citizenship status. Our interviews suggest some considerable variation in the ability of these groups to get adequate support from the public services. Sometimes this reflects a preference for using private services (for example, in housing), but in other instances it suggests that services are over-stretched, or insufficiently responsive to the needs of this group. However, some of these respondents were able to draw on informal systems of support.

Our third example concerns an Indian unemployed man living in private rented accommodation. He has children from two marriages. After marrying his second wife, he moved to the UK in the early 1970s, with a British passport, and got a job in a local factory. He owned a house. Following a heart attack, he decided to take his four children from his current marriage back to India to give them an understanding of their background and language. He sold his house to finance the trip in the late 1980s. He was unable to stay longer than three years in India because his visa ran out and returned to the UK, when he applied for a council house. He has been living in private rented accommodation since then. He has lived in a number of properties; the longest was for three years. He was evicted from his previous house the year before we interviewed him. Earlier in this chapter we referred to the offer of unsuitable (because of his continuous medical needs) bed and breakfast accommodation that was made to him. The council offered no alternative accommodation and the family stayed temporarily with the eldest of their children and put their belongings into a council store. He has not paid the storage bill. Although he receives housing benefit, he has not been paying the shortfall between the benefit and monthly rent of his current accommodation so is now under threat of eviction again. He is on Income Support and receives a small monthly occupational pension. Three children still live with him. The eldest son is unable to provide any financial support. A community association has provided support and advice. He has been trying to persuade the council to recognize the implication of his health problems for his housing need but it will only help after he has actually been made homeless. This example illustrates the importance of accidents and misfortune in leading people onto downward trajectories. The critical differences are in the degree of vulnerability of different people. Arguably some migrant groups are more vulnerable when they lack networks with significant resources and are unfamiliar with benefit systems.

While there was a number of first generation immigrants who seemed to be at risk of exclusion on one or more fronts, the refugees and asylum seekers interviewed were a clearly identifiable group who appeared to be excluded on multiple grounds. From the sample of households across the eight boroughs only five included refugees and asylum seekers. Of these five, two refused to be interviewed. The experiences of three refugees and asylum seekers can by no means be taken as representative. However, they shared a number of factors in common, including difficulties in understanding how services such as education and welfare benefits operate; problems in gaining access to services such as banks; relatively poor housing conditions; a lack of recognition of their previous skills and qualifications; and a lack of social networks.

Our first case here concerns a Middle Eastern man who arrived in the UK in the late 1990s. In the year after his arrival, he and his family were given indefinite leave to remain. He left his native country because of political persecution, and his father had been killed there. He has relatively few social contacts, in part because of fear of contact with people from home. Other relatives are also in London. His brother lived with them at first, but has mental health problems, a result of having watched his father being killed and he now lives with a cousin. They rarely see one another as they cannot afford the cost of the bus fares, but they do speak on the telephone occasionally. He said he preferred to see only his wife and children but he was glad that his children had made friends with the neighbours' children. He said that he was 'very tired' and felt 'finished with life', but 'if I am not here safe where I be safe?'. He was clearly still scared and this affected his ability to make friends or have contact with people outside his family. He talked quite a lot about not being able to trust people and was obviously frightened when discussing his past. However, he also said that in the last two or three months things felt better. He thought now he had an ability to speak English he had the confidence to improve his life and that of his family.

One of his major problems was difficulty in dealing with various government bureaucracies, in part because of a lack of a passport or other identification documents, but also because of his own and his wife's poor English. The administration of housing benefit and council tax allowances had involved numerous forms which they found difficult to fill out, and visits which had left them confused. Whenever he was asked for proof of his identity, for example when he tried to set up a bank account and when he applied to sit the driving test, his letter from the Home Office granting him indefinite leave to remain was not accepted as sufficient.

However, he did not like having to accept benefits and had been undertaking training for work. He has recently finished a government-funded course in English and had just started another course in IT. He could not get onto a course to develop his previous trade as an electrician. He has already tried to find work, but:

> because I have no connection with other people . . . I've tried many times . . . anywhere I go they say OK leave your name, if you leave your telephone number if we need you we will phone you.
>
> Married man, unemployed, Middle Eastern, private tenant

He has had no calls; he thinks 'they make judge for me because they think my English not so good'. He also thought that his lack of ID was preventing him from gaining employment and that until he got the necessary documentation he would be unable to find work. However, he thought that having finished his English course this would eventually help him to find a job. Before he started the course, he said that he could not write a letter or fill in an application form and that he could not cope with answering the telephone as he did not have enough English to make himself understood. He also said that finishing the language course had given him more confidence.

Another respondent does suggest that in time it is possible to overcome lack of material or network resources. Our final example concerns a black African woman in her forties, a lone parent who came to Britain in the early 1990s, as an asylum seeker, after separating from her husband and with few resources. She had been an accounts clerk in her country of origin, but had limited qualifications, and came to London with little money (£50) and apparently few social contacts. This would seem to be a person at very high risk of social exclusion on all dimensions. However, by 2000 she was clearly not socially excluded on any basis. She had built a new career as a care assistant, and was near completion of a social work course. She had achieved sufficient financial security to bring her three teenage daughters from Africa and had more or less successfully seen them through into further and higher education. She was living in a shared-equity housing association house. She has sorted out her own and her daughters' legal residency status. It is not all positive – she does not like the area she is living in, she is stressed by the amount of work she has to do and the lack of money for a holiday or other leisure consumption. She may technically be in poverty. She claims to be rather socially isolated, though this is belied by what seems to be rather a high level of social activism. In some ways she sees herself as downwardly mobile compared with her position before coming to the UK. However she remains optimistic about the future and what she can achieve when she has finished her current course.

While this case is heavily influenced by personal capacities and motivation, it relates to a more general point: many migrants are highly motivated and migration is often accompanied by a long-term commitment to saving and investment in human capital for the future. However, this story also suggests two other conclusions. First, this woman made substantial use of state agencies and voluntary organizations in obtaining training and regularizing her legal position. It is possible that she would have found it much more difficult to establish herself successfully under the current more punitive asylum regime and would therefore have been more dependent on state support. Second, there is a more London specific conclusion. A crucial factor in her success was the interviewee's ability to draw on the city's rich range of training opportunities, support services, and agency type jobs that allowed her to combine work with study.

Indeed, this point illustrates our conclusion that, for all the problems experienced by our respondents, it is difficult to see how most of them would be any better off outside London. While there are many problems with public services in London, they are more fully geared to dealing with a diverse population than those of most other areas, and they are supported by a relatively rich environment of voluntary services. Moreover London is in effect a relatively socially tolerant environment for diversity and failure. It is probably easier to get by in such a situation.

## Conclusion: Deprivation and Social Exclusion in London

So we conclude this chapter by confirming the hypothesis we posed at the start: deprivation and social exclusion are much more complex than they seem – or than they have been presented in recent accounts that have powerfully influenced government policy.

Deprivation in the London region is largely (though not entirely) concentrated within the Greater London boundary, and indeed within a horseshoe-shaped group of inner East London boroughs, plus two smaller areas west and north-west of the centre. When we decompose the deprivation index into its components, there are some variations – albeit less significant.

But the housing deprivation index shows a much wider spread, almost the inverse of the others, reaching its highest intensity at the region's periphery: a graphic indicator of a special dimension to the general problem. And our interviews showed that throughout our area, high housing costs and the resulting problems – locational constraints, commuting, financial strain, childcare problems, poor quality accommodation – mean that many groups, who could never be described as deprived on other dimensions, are struggling to survive. They also add greatly to the problems of those who are disadvantaged in other ways. Their only feasible option is social housing. And they thus find themselves deprived on multiple fronts – lack of choice of location, life on 'problem estates', the operation of the benefits system – which seriously diminish their quality of life.

In Chapter 6, looking at labour market exclusion, we found that London's special labour markets produce both a high concentration of groups 'at risk' (ethnic minorities, young single people) and a higher set of risks for all groups. Labour market exclusion has risen over time (and across economic cycles), with a growing divide into work-rich and work-poor households. It has been concentrated in Greater London – especially parts of Inner London – not in the outer parts of the region. And this, not changes in the occupational hierarchy, has been the main cause of rising inequality and social divisions. London does not suffer from the absolute lack of jobs that has produced the 'jobless ghetto' described by William Julius Wilson in Chicago. But, as our interviews show, a combination of low wages and perverse welfare benefit rules can produce significant disincentives to seeking any work that may be available. And this will not be solved by attempts to put unemployed people back into the labour market, as much recent policy assumes.

Thus parts of London suffer from real deprivation, worse than the UK average. But this does not simply translate into monetary terms. London's higher wage rates mean that fewer fall below a fixed national poverty datum. But these higher wages do not completely compensate for higher housing, travel and other costs – yet, perversely, they can make people ineligible for benefits, so increasing their deprivation.

The paradox is that in London, such high levels of deprivation exist side by side with the highest concentrations of the least deprived citizens in the country. And this is highlighted by the fact that poverty persists longer in Inner London than nationally – and stays at about the national level in Outer London – though it persists much less in the Rest of the South East. A similar pattern exists in relation to exiting from a jobless household. The position in other conurbations is even worse – but there, an absolute shortage of jobs may be a salient factor.

London's at-risk population shows the importance of household and family structures that powerfully influence the basic division into work-rich and work-poor households, in turn linking to many aspects of deprivation. But other factors – ethnicity, citizenship, housing tenure, qualification levels, access to benefits – also enter in, to produce concentrations of deprivation (and the risk of deprivation) among non-white minorities, non-citizens, those caught in benefit traps, those who live in social housing, and those who lack qualifications. And many of these factors are of course themselves related, thus reinforcing each other.

In consequence, we found that some parts of our region and some groups of its population experience high levels of deprivation – and even, on some dimensions, of exclusion. But we did not find a major growth of the 'truly excluded' in London, as hypothesized by Kesteloot or as found by Wilson in Chicago. He found that in large areas of the city there were very high concentrations of exclusion with all that that implied socially and economically. We did not find this, either from our statistical analyses of segregation or from our interviews. To be sure, the 'truly excluded' do exist in London – but on nothing like the scale that some imagine.

One reason is the relatively wide welfare 'safety net', including the stock of social housing. True, in comparison with some Western European welfare systems, Britain's has done less to combat deprivation and exclusion. Moreover, as we have seen, its effects are contradictory: it can prove to be both inclusionary and exclusionary. Such effects occur nationwide, but London's relatively high wage rates and high costs reduce the eligibility there of the 'working poor'; a telling example of a negative relationship between economic dynamism and social cohesion.

In consequence, deprivation in London takes a different pattern from Chicago: a concentration of deprived households – but, even here, only a small proportion of those who could be regarded as 'truly excluded' – on some social housing estates, especially in the eastern Inner London boroughs and the two western enclaves that we identified. This is a consequence of selective in- and out-migration of people and units from this stock, highly influenced by government policies, over the last two decades – together with the wider factors and processes that have led to the growth of deprivation in the city, analysed earlier. In Chapter 9 we will show in greater detail that in small parts of our eight localities, there were indeed high levels of deprivation, considerable conflict and insecurity and so on. But London is unlike Chicago: here, neither housing nor job markets are so divided (primarily by 'race'), nor is the welfare state so reduced or family and social networks so broken, as to extend this limited area-based deprivation and exclusion across large parts of the inner city – or even to suggest that this process is underway. Of course, London's high levels of deprivation, and their concentration among certain groups and on certain social housing estates, represent a pressing problem for public policy. But they need to be seen as problems in themselves, not as the harbingers of large-scale threats to social cohesion, social order or even competitiveness.

Our selection of interviewees under-represented some minorities most likely to be so excluded – such as young men, including ethnic minorities, with few qualifications – but one group, asylum seekers and recent migrants, did stand out as at notably high risk. However, as the last section showed, London exhibits the same pattern as Leisering and Leibfried (1999) found in their study of German cities: personal capabilities and opportunities (some of which may be greater in London than elsewhere) meant that risk did not always translate into reality; some were successfully making their exit from exclusion, some were not.

Finally we return to the five hypotheses about changes in the social structure of large metropolitan areas, outlined at the start of the chapter. The first of these, increasing inequalities in occupational and income distributions, has already been supported by the evidence in Chapter 4. The second hypothesis, an increase in the size of the disadvantaged group – the group at risk of exclusion – is also generally supported by the evidence on trends in unemployment and household labour market marginality, though short-term cyclical trends in the late 1990s mitigated this somewhat. For the third hypothesis, our evidence in Chapter 4 suggested conflicting evidence on social segregation, with declining segregation by social class, but some increase in segregation between those with and without jobs. Chapter 6 has also suggested some intensification of the concentration of unemployment in eastern parts of Inner London.

All of this could provide preconditions for our fourth and fifth hypotheses: a growing separation of those in poverty and disadvantage from mainstream society, and increasing social disorganization. However, this chapter has found no strong evidence for the existence of a distinct outsider group, who might for example be alienated from the norms and values of the wider society. Indeed, if there is a wider message for policy, it is to reinforce Peter Townsend's (1979) view of poverty as a material problem of participating in the wider society. The most acute problem of the poor and disadvantaged in London may be simply that they do not have enough money – and this has a specific dimension in London, because of the relationship between the high cost of living in London, and the low level of wages at the bottom end of the labour market.

However, another feature of life in London, which was also brought out in Chapter 6, is its instability and riskiness. For people with relatively low levels of material resources, or weak social networks, physical or social or economic accidents can have particularly severe consequences, substantially exacerbating disadvantage. But, to underline the point, this does not translate into the large-scale and area-wide social isolation and social pathologies that some have predicted – to which we return in the next chapter. There has been a smaller-scale tendency in some groups and some neighbourhoods – mainly within Greater and especially Inner London – for greater concentration of those suffering longer-term and more complex forms of exclusion. Policy cannot ignore this – but it needs to be seen as just one extreme manifestation of the growth of inequality and deprivation which affects many more Londoners.

Chapter 4 pointed to the growing gap between Greater London and the outer parts of the region. This chapter has further demonstrated a marked concentration of disadvantage in London, in part because of the housing system, and the money costs of moving outward. It is unclear whether there are also less tangible factors creating this concentration, what we might term *cultural walls*. Factors deterring movement to the outer suburbs might include racism, an absence of community institutions of support for disadvantaged living and greater problems of relative deprivation in people comparing themselves with their neighbours than in London. Generally it is not clear that the disadvantaged would find any advantage in moving out of London to accessible places with lower concentrations of disadvantage. For all the significant problems of over-stretch in London's public services, they are more adjusted to dealing with the problems of highly diverse, disadvantaged populations. There is also a dense network of voluntary organizations, which we found particularly important in supporting immigrants and asylum seekers. Beyond this, informal social support networks are likely to be stronger than in areas where there are fewer disadvantaged people.

More than most places, it may be that London provides the resources for the most disadvantaged people to get by. In terms of getting ahead, we saw in the last chapter that for those whose qualifications and experience gave them access to the high-skilled, high-paid part of the labour market, London gave exceptional opportunities. However, at the other extreme, for those without such qualifications and experience, London imposes particularly high hurdles.

Chapter 8

# How Social is the Capital?
# Getting By and
# Getting On in London

People of the same trade seldom meet together, even for merriment and
diversion, but the conversation ends in a conspiracy against the public.
Adam Smith, *The Wealth of Nations*, 1776

So far, we have looked at London's economy, its social structure and its labour
market; at how its workforce and residents are trained and educated, and at
some of the material problems of securing an adequate income. But in order to
understand how people live and work in London, we need to extend our analysis
from these structural factors to include also the nature and quality of social relations
between Londoners. This affects not only Londoners' daily experience – their 'quality
of life' – but also their economic circumstances. Social relations – and social capital
– influence individuals' abilities to 'get ahead' through finding a job or advancing
their career, or simply to 'get by', coping with economic and social disadvantage. By
adding the analysis of social relations to our picture of London we can try and form
a clearer impression of that shadowy creature 'social capital'.

Here we also get to the heart of what people mean when they refer to
social cohesion. In Chapter 1 we distinguished social connectedness, social order
and social inequality as dimensions of social cohesion. Social capital, as Chapter 1
also indicated, is the currently favoured term for discussing the patterns of social
relations, and is clearly most concerned with social connectedness. However, many
proponents of social capital suggest that it has consequences for social order. There
are also reasons for thinking that social order, as well as social inequality, will have
consequences for the development of social capital. We are thus also concerned in
this chapter with issues associated with crime and disorder.

Social capital was discussed critically in Chapter 1, and we do not repeat this discussion here, though it is important to reiterate certain points. Social capital can be defined in terms of community characteristics or in terms of individual assets. Indeed, the recent work on social capital has drawn a link from social cohesion to the effective functioning of political and social institutions, and to economic consequences (Putnam, 2000). This causal link is perhaps the most difficult one to establish in a satisfactory way, particularly in a single case study. However, if we are to understand the dynamics between social cohesion and economic competitiveness, then a first step involves understanding the role of social support networks, trust, norms of co-operation and patterns of social interaction, within and between communities, as either cohesive or divisive agents.

In terms of individual assets, de Souza Briggs (1998, 178) makes a useful distinction between social support and social leverage – or 'get by' and 'get ahead' social capital. Social support consists of social capital that helps people get by, or cope. It includes having someone to turn to for help with practical things, like lending a bowl of sugar or keeping an eye on the kids, emotional things, like a shoulder to cry on, and financial things, like lending a small amount of money to help in a crisis. Social leverage consists of social capital that helps people get ahead. It includes such things as networks to jobs, information about new opportunities, and putting in a good word for someone. Both types of capital are necessary, but some people need one more than another at different times of their lives. This distinction relates to Granovetter's (1973) discussion of the relationship between strong and weak ties, and the functions they perform. The two types also clearly relate in different ways to two of the key debates: the relationship of social capital to social exclusion, and the relationship of social capital to economic competitiveness.

Social capital remains a rather ill-defined concept. This is, in some ways, its strength, leaving researchers to explore the actual existing relationships between networks, trust and communities, and diverse outcomes linked to health and wealth. As a result, agreeing on a set of indicators of social capital is similarly difficult, and different authors have focused on different areas. For Coleman (1990), social capital can be any of the following: shared norms and values, close-knit community relations, parental and sibling expectations, parent/child relations, embeddedness in the community. For Putnam (2000) social capital is civic engagement, or the extent to which we engage in the lives of our communities, and is best identified in indicators of trust, joining, voting activity, and newspaper readership. Temkin and Rohe (1998), in their research on the effects of social capital on neighbourhood stability focused on civic engagement, and specifically examined formal political activity plus other forms of public participation among neighbourhood residents, while Hall (1999), making an assessment of changing levels of social capital in Britain, examined both formal and informal patterns of sociability and involvement in voluntary associations.

In the end the main conclusion is that we should avoid using the term *social capital* generically as some single property of inherent value and should rather, as Portes (1998) suggests, explore separately the manifestations and implications of its many constituent parts.

The literature on social capital has said rather less about how social capital might be built and maintained than about its consequences. However the tendency of the argument is that the regular patterns of social and economic interactions by individuals within families, neighbourhoods, workplaces, markets etc. are critical to building the norms, trust and networks which underlie forms of social capital. The building of social capital also implies something about the resources individuals bring to these interactions and about their contexts: building relationships requires time and money, and insofar as relationships are based on exchange, they require present or future resources to put into those exchanges. The security of the environment will affect the nature of interactions, as will expectations of their future longevity. Patterns of interaction will also be affected substantially by class, gender and ethnicity.

There is a clear urban dimension to this discussion, which makes it particularly relevant for a book on London. There is a now-traditional hypothesis, dating back from Tönnies (1955) and Simmel (1936), through Wirth (1939), reflected to some degree in current communitarianism, that city life represents the worst aspects of social change. In this hypothesis, cities are anomic places populated by large numbers of individuals engaged in impersonal and calculative exchanges. And this is in contrast to past societies (or rural, village areas) which are characterized in terms of strong, cohesive communities, familiarity, personal face-to-face contact, and strong traditions. For Simmel, urban evils included impersonality, isolation and alienation. For Wirth, urban culture *is* the modern culture, which in turn is superficial, transitory and heterogeneous. Similar arguments and fears are promulgated by contemporary communitarians who are drawing on the idea of (shrinking) social capital to depict modern lifestyles as individualistic, competitive and atomistic (e.g. Etzioni, 1995). Even a positive perspective on the dynamism of city economies tends to suggest features inimical to the building of long-term stable relationships. On this thesis, inner-city neighbourhoods will be weakest in terms of neighbourliness and community.

Thus in this chapter we need to ask how effectively social capital can be built in London, and about variation between different parts of London, and between different social groups. Is London a place in which there are particular obstacles in the way of building and maintaining social capital? Are there major differences between different individuals and social groups? Are there some for whom it will be difficult to build even 'get-by' social capital while for others what they crucially lack is 'get-ahead' social capital? We can suggest a number of possible influences on the building of social capital in London.

For example it has been suggested that social and economic segregation in London is strong and growing, though our evidence in Chapter 4 was somewhat equivocal on this point. However, there are some areas with high concentrations of disadvantaged people. If such people are living in close proximity to other excluded groups, they are more likely to mix with these people. People who are long-term unemployed might spend more of their time with others who are in similar positions or who are networked only to people in insecure jobs. In Wilson's account (1997) of the US inner-city ghettos, problems of spatial mismatch are aggravated by the lack of informal information networks. Individuals in jobless ghettos (and perhaps jobless areas of London) are less likely to gain employment through the crucial channels of information leading from working partners, relatives and friends. They are also less likely to benefit from recommendations for jobs from people they know. Such networks are beneficial both to the individual in need of a job and the employer in need of a good worker. The lack of such networks is potentially damaging to both. There are a number of other possible effects. Concentrations of high crime and disorder themselves generate secondary effects on the building of social relations. To the extent that people are afraid to go out on streets and do not mix with neighbours, fear of crime leads to low social capital.

Residential mobility in London is high, and a high proportion of the population are in-migrants from other regions, and likely to leave. Moreover the distance from home to workplace for many Londoners is relatively long. This might leave Londoners with less time or incentive to invest in the building of neighbourhood based social capital. On the other hand, some types of migration flows do depend on already existing networks, so we should not necessarily assume that in-migrants lack London based social capital. Mobility may also generate a countervailing tendency, since links with extended family are likely to be more distant than elsewhere, and people may therefore substitute relationships with friends.

As we showed in Chapter 4, London contains low proportions of couple families with children, and relatively high proportions of single people, and people who have experienced partnership break-up, including lone parents. High mobility might also lead to a relatively low level of extended family networks. On the one hand this is likely to imply a more intense effort on the part of individuals to build non-family networks of friends, but it may also lead to a weaker establishment of networks which can provide social support, and for some particular groups it may lead to more extreme social isolation.

Chapter 6 also showed that job turnover in the London labour market is particularly high, as firms and individuals take advantage of some of the characteristics of large-scale agglomeration. This gives rise to a number of questions: how far does this instability imply greater reliance on informal networks than elsewhere? How far are these networks closed or open? How far does this instability make it easier or more difficult for individuals to build networks? Are there structural differences between different types of worker? Are there negative consequences for reliable labour supply for employers?

Finally, urban patterns of consumption and social life may create countervailing tendencies. Chapter 4 identified a concentration of non-family households in London. More out-of-home sociability may generate a greater density of weak ties. Moreover, the relative anonymity of urban life, which we might conceptualize as the absence of repressive social capital, may actively encourage the development of strong communities of those whose lifestyles do not conform to social norms.

We consider evidence for these arguments at a number of levels. The first level concerns the patterns of social support found within families, and family like groups. The second level concerns the somewhat more distant patterns of association found amongst friends and neighbours, which can provide forms of support to get by or get ahead, but which quite apart from this are an important contribution to personal well-being. Thirdly, there are somewhat more generalized patterns of trust and association within neighbourhoods and other communities, which may contribute to social cohesion, and perhaps also contribute to civic effectiveness. We also then consider some of these same issues from the point of view of businesses, to explore how far they rely on social capital. All this is from the perspective of individual actors. In the final part of the chapter we focus on possible system-wide consequences, using evidence on crime, and from the education system.

## Families in London

As we saw in Chapter 4, residents of Greater London, but not the surrounding region, are particularly unlikely to be living with other adult family members. BHPS data also suggest that Londoners are somewhat unlikely to mention family members living outside their household as being among their three closest friends. However this does not mean that families are unimportant. Indeed traditionally family networks have been seen as a most important part of people's lives in London, as Young and Willmott's classic work on family and kinship in East London showed (Young and Willmott, 1957). And we still do find evidence of dense working-class family networks:

> *I've got eight sisters and seven brothers . . . Yes, I see 'em . . . we're always there every Saturday . . . Over the East End. Most of 'em live in the East End, yeah . . . Mile End . . . Stepney Green, Bow, yeah, they all live along that way, yeah . . . mean, we're all going away, there's, I'm showing off, no I'm not showing off, there's only weekends, only cheap weekends, fifty-four of us . . . We're going . . . to a hotel in Brighton . . . We've been there before. We've been there, I think there was about thirty, thirty of us before, but now there's fifty.*
>
> Divorced mother, unemployed, white, council tenant

More generally, the continued importance of family links, and their role in providing support was an important theme in our interviews. Families freely help each other; the need is not questioned, and takes many different forms. Sometimes, it is helping a son or daughter with furniture, or with basic services.

> *She was moving and she was moving to a smaller house and she knew I needed a couple of beds so she gave me some beds. She gave me my fridge cos she was getting brand new . . . So my family's always there for me, yeah.*
>
> Single mother, unemployed, white, council tenant, referring to his mother

Sometimes, a mother will help her daughter who falls sick and has to juggle work and child-rearing:

> *I was very, very ill and she didn't know what was wrong with me and she goes 'I thought I'd have to take a week off work' and things like this. So she is there for me yeah, so yeah I know my mum would be there, she would be.*
>
> Single mother, unemployed, white, council tenant

Often it is the reverse, when adults help older parents with heavier chores:

*You do practical things I suppose. That's what it is. Washing, drying, ironing, cleaning. Practical things . . . I know for a fact that if I asked my mother for every penny she's got, she would give it to me. Whether it be for a pound or thirty thousand, she would let me have it. She wouldn't ask me necessarily why I wanted it, she would give it to me. And I know that . . . I think that sums it up.*

Married man, employed, white, homeowner

Many respondents were quite clear that they would first turn to their families for material help or with other problems, in preference to friends. Many families have close ties reinforced by proximity with very regular personal contact, on at least a weekly basis. They offer a close support system:

*I come in they phone me, my kids phone every night and say 'Are you home?', cos they know what time I get in . . . they really care about you, it's really nice. It makes me feel good . . . we discuss everything, we talk together, discuss things. Usually we have family meetings and things like that . . . and we discuss, they say 'No, you shouldn't do that'. 'No, I don't think you should do that'. 'Try it this way, don't do it that way'.*

Single mother, employed, Afro-Caribbean, council tenant

Family ties can of course also be perceived as a constraint – for example, the need to look after ageing relatives, especially parents. This was a theme that emerged from many interviews:

*I don't know – I'd have to keep within a radius of where my daughters were because I rely on them a lot, very much I rely on them.*

Widowed mother, retired, white, homeowner

There are disadvantages, too, in being close:

*you've got your family there. You can go to them if you need anything. But the disadvantages are, you don't really never get no peace. You've got them all round you all the time, you know. They just come to you if they want anything.*

Married mother, employed, white, council tenant

However the decades of outward migration from London, and patterns of social mobility, will mean that the siblings of many current Inner London residents have moved outwards, and patterns of linkage will be weakened:

*We're a small family. There was only me and my brother you know and I only had the one daughter and my brothers moved out to Kent so we've got no one what you'd call really close in family.*

Married mother, retired, white, council tenant

*My eldest brother has just moved to Watford. My middle brother, cause I'm the baby, he lives in Welwyn Garden City. My mum lives in Brighton, my dad lives in Neasden. But we do try . . . My mother I speak to a lot. She comes up whenever she can. Especially over holidays.*

Divorced mother, employed, Jewish, homeowner

Clearly, with international migration links may be stretched. This woman of

West Indian origin had evidently lost touch with her extended family:

> I haven't been back . . . cos I wanna take, I want all of us to go, I will cost me like about £500
> each for them and plus spending money . . . my uncles, I've got uncles and aunts over there.
> Do they ever come over here to visit?
> I don't know, I don't know most of them.
>
> Divorced mother, part-time employed, black British, council tenant

## Friends

Survey data on friends, neighbours and informal association show that London does
not turn out to be so different from other places, and in particular the differences
do not suggest that life in London is more anomic. We saw in Chapter 7 that there
is some evidence from the BHPS for higher levels of social isolation and lack of social
support in London. However, this problem concerns a relatively small group and
average levels of social support for the majority of Londoners are no different from
the national average. This measure includes both support from people living with the
respondent, and those living elsewhere.

An alternative measure from the BHPS focuses on support from people outside
the household. This suggests that the level of external support is above the national
level. Eighty-four per cent of Inner Londoners and 85 per cent of Outer Londoners
have someone outside the household they can rely on when depressed, compared
with 82 per cent nationally. Sixty-one per cent of Inner Londoners and 56 per cent
of Outer Londoners said there is someone outside the household they can rely on
to help find a job for self or family member, compared with 55 per cent nationally;
and 78 per cent of Inner Londoners and 77 per cent of Outer Londoners said there is
someone outside the household they can rely on to help when they need to borrow
money for urgent bills, compared with 72 per cent nationally.

There are significant differences between social groups. In London, the long-
term sick or disabled and the retired are the groups most likely to say they have no
one to rely on outside the household for help when depressed, when they or a family
member needs to find a job, or when they need to borrow money for urgent needs.
Full-time students are the least likely to have no one to turn to on these occasions
(see Table 8.1). The unemployed are similar to those whose main activity is looking
after their family and the self-employed in terms of social support although they are
less likely to have someone to help them find a job.

Contrary to implications in much of the social capital literature, moving house
does not seem to make Londoners more likely to feel isolated. Four per cent of those
who have moved in the last year have no one to turn to when depressed compared
with 10 per cent of those who have not moved. Eleven per cent of those who have
moved in the past year have no one to turn to when looking for a job, compared
with 23 per cent of those who have not moved. Six per cent of those who have
moved have no one to turn to lend them money, compared with 15 per cent of
those who have not moved. These differences partly reflect age differences, but if we
control for age there is no evidence that movers are more isolated.

**Table 8.1.** Social support by job status.

| Percentage of Londoners with no one outside the household to turn to when: | | | |
|---|---|---|---|
| | Depressed | Looking for a job | Need to borrow money |
| Self-employed | 13 | 19 | 12 |
| Employed | 7 | 18 | 10 |
| Unemployed | 11 | 28 | 14 |
| Retired | 15 | 38 | 28 |
| Looking after family | 11 | 18 | 16 |
| Full-time student | 2 | 13 | 6 |
| Long-term sick or disabled | 22 | 43 | 26 |

*Source:* BHPS.

There is some evidence that some people, for whom friends play a major role, have weaker contact with their family, while conversely those who have strong family connections tend to have fewer friends and less contact with them. As we have just seen, family ties are often very close and they provide extremely strong forms of support which are not found often in other social relationships. Further, these ties appear to become more important once children are involved. Thus, in the course of life one may turn from friends to family.

Where there are high levels of geographical mobility (for example as a result of moving location in order to work or study), family connections become weaker and friendship-based social networks take their place. These friendship-based networks perform many of the functions which family networks do for others. There is perhaps less emphasis on childcare as geographical mobility of this kind often (but not always) coincides with childlessness. Also, as with the archetypal extended family, the friendship networks may be built around people who live fairly locally. This may happen partly as people get to know their neighbours through sharing the same geographical space; but there is also evidence to suggest that those who are geographically mobile may act as magnets, attracting to the area other geographically-mobile people they knew before. However geographical mobility also means that friendship networks may be rather stretched, and many friendships will be maintained over long distances. Moreover those who have always lived in the same place may have a more dispersed friendship network as their friends migrate away.

National data from the BHPS on whether individuals have 'family-focused', 'friends-focused' or mixed networks show that those with family-focused networks tend to be more working class, on lower incomes, and in social housing. On average, such people are under-represented in all parts of the London region, but after controlling for social class and other demographic characteristics, there does seem to be some tendency for more family-focussed networks in Inner London. Non-family networks are over-represented in Inner London and the OMA. However, after controlling for class and demographic characteristics, these two parts of the region are not significantly different from the national average, whilst Outer London tends to under-represent non-family networks. We can conclude that, while London's demographic and social characteristics tend to imply weaker extended family networks, and stronger non-family networks, once we take account of these differences, there is no evidence that extended family networks are weaker in London.

Friendship networks in all parts of the London region are less geographically compact than elsewhere. Not having close friends living within 5 miles is associated positively with having a degree, a higher income, being in higher social classes – i.e. the factors which influence long-term career mobility. Similar factors influence being in contact with friends less than once a week. It is clear that even after controlling for these sorts of factors, Londoners are particularly unlikely to have all of their three best friends living within 5 miles, and this tendency is strongest in the OMA. This presumably reflects the consequences of outward migration within the London region and inter-regional migration to the London area. The measure of frequency of contact with friends also suggests that networks are somewhat weaker in London. After controlling for other influences, people in Inner London are around 42 per cent more likely to say that they do not contact any of their three best friends at least once a week. Outer London is no different from the national average, but in the OMA the non-contact rate is around 32 per cent higher.

Friends are generally seen as different from family, but people also see a clear distinction between friends and neighbours or other acquaintances. There was a perception that you cannot have many real friends. The social network hierarchy seems to go: family, friends, then neighbours; but this is a generalization rather than a rule, and as we shall see there were people for whom friends were more important than family. The contrast between friends and neighbours is captured by the following respondent:

> Our friends before we moved here, put it that way, are pretty scattered aren't they all over? . . . they're spread around but not . . . no-one's that far away are they? . . . You know, 20 minutes in the car at the most . . . Your friendship is different because they're sort of like close friends, you know, your friend type thing . . . Whereas your neighbours . . . you may not tell them your closest secrets or you know your problems. I don't know about that, I don't know. It's a different sort of thing isn't it?
>
> Married woman, employed, white, homeowner

It appears that men may be more selective about who they regard as friends; only males made these kinds of observations about friends and acquaintances:

> In your life you have a lot of acquaintances, but you only have half a dozen real friends that are real mates, you know, but you have a lot of people who you get on with, you know, you enjoy their company, but they aren't real mates that you would trust implicitly.
>
> Married man, employed, white, homeowner

Women told us that they made friends locally through their children:

> Strangely enough, the closest friends I've got came about through the parents of the children that my children played with . . . You meet the other parents and you become friends. And some of those friends are really close and others you see them now and again. But they do

*become good friends . . . Friends acquired by your sons' and your daughters' friends, yeah, they're local. Yeah, there are mainly around, yes.*

Divorced mother, employed, white, private tenant

On council estates the distinction between friends and neighbours seems to blur: neighbours help out with child care where necessary. One interviewee told us that she knew about 40 people on this estate:

*There's . . . all in all, on this estate, I think there's 113 flats.*
So you know about one-third of the people.
*Your closest friends tend to be your neighbours, or the people that you've grown up with.*
How many people are close friends that you've got, in general?
*I would say about six.*

Divorced mother, unemployed, council tenant

It seems that people on council estates are more likely to have friends who live locally, sometimes neighbours. They are also well linked in with their families:

*I've got two sisters and two brothers, like, and their friends are my friends, and my friends are their friends.*

Married mother, employed, white, council tenant

But often, we found, friends have moved away, and so are spread over a wide area:

*All of them are scattered about actually . . . some in Sussex, one in Lincolnshire, Yorkshire . . . Everyone's sort of moved on and . . . so yeah, but they're all close friends. But we don't see them as much, but they're still very good friends.*

Married mother, part-time employed, white, homeowner

That is true for this respondent, who continues to live in the same area where she grew up, while her friends have left. As with family, distance is relative: if you are a not particularly well-off single mother Battersea, Tooting and Streatham become far away, while if you are more affluent with one child a similar area becomes 'just down the road':

*I had school friends and I don't know they've all just, they've just disappeared like that but . . . I've got a friend who lives in Tooting, another lives in Streatham. So they're all, live everywhere . . . It's hard because they've got children and I've got children, so it's hard. Yeah it is hard really.*

Single mother, unemployed, white, council tenant

Mothers with many children, or single parents, also often find it more difficult to keep in touch with friends unless they are those at the school gate. This respondent's circle of friends changed after she had a child. She developed a local network of friends rather than one based around work. Things changed yet again after she got divorced:

*Before I had [child] I had my own circle of friends. We were all married. We were all working . . . If it hadn't been for **** [friend] I don't know what I would have done. We got very, very* *friendly. Very close. The kids are best friends. They're in the same school, they've been in the same class since they started . . . But it's not the same, not having her over there.*

Divorced mother, employed, Jewish, homeowner

For some people work relationships tended to dominate over friendships based on the local area. Work also caused problems for friendship networks. Some said that long hours at work made it difficult to keep friends:

*You know travelling and stuff it's like by the weekend I just wanna sit at home and do nothing . . . you're just mentally tired by the end of the week, I'm just shattered you know.*

Single woman, employed, Asian, private tenant

## Neighbours

Relations with neighbours are different from those with family or friends, and seem governed by a system of strong but implicit rules. Among neighbours almost everywhere, there is a very general and widespread system of reciprocity: people watch each other's houses and perform small errands for them if they fall ill. This is a very general system of informal social capital. But it seems to be governed by informal rules and has some kind of informal limits.

BHPS evidence suggests that around 73 per cent of Londoners talk to their neighbours at least once or twice a week. There are no differences between men and women, but as age increases so does the chance of talking to neighbours regularly, tailing off at around pension age. Moving within the last year is significant. Movers are half as likely to talk to their neighbours as non-movers. Interestingly, the economically inactive (who are not unemployed) are one and a half times more likely to talk to their neighbours regularly, while the unemployed are less likely to talk to their neighbours than are working people (though the difference in this case is insignificant).

Most people seem to have approachable neighbours. People perform a variety of conventional services: turn lights on when neighbours are away, take in their post, open a neighbour's door for a repair or maintenance person, and – perhaps most crucially – notice if something is amiss:

*I say perhaps the immediate neighbours, one each side. As I say things like you know when they go on holiday, perhaps going in to switch a light on every now and again and putting rubbish out for them.*

Divorced man, employed, white, homeowner

*I could probably trust \*\*\*\*, \*\*\*\*, \*\*\*\* [names] any of them, to hand over my keys, and say to them, 'Can you let so and so in?'*

Divorced mother, unemployed, council tenant

But respondents were inclined to put a limit to this: it was 'neighbourly', nothing more. However, in some cases it seemed to go rather further. Especially, many neighbours would act as a kind of informal social service for ill or elderly people:

*Like the old man when he was sickly and ill over there. You would all pop over there, you know. I would bake pies and I would go over and take him a pie. He would grow tomatoes and he would give me a punnet of tomatoes. And he would say, put it under your shirt, he would say, I don't want her in the corner . . .*

Divorced mother, employed, white, private tenant

*I would know without any hesitation if I was in trouble then **** [name] the young fellow from next door would help me out. I know this, but I wouldn't call him my friend in any sense.*

Married man, retired, white, homeowner

Local frictions do occur, but generally they do not affect neighbourly relations:

*We have had a little bit of friction sometimes, only because they've, they've had a lot of festivals where, one where **** [son], he's only a young baby, ten months now, but he was very young and the music would go on all night 'til the early hours. So, but you could have that anywhere. But no, we chat and I say, 'Hello'. And next door we're very friendly with and they come round and what have you.*

Female cohabitee, mother, employed, white, private tenant

Thus there seems to be a kind of ideal – and very 'English' – relationship with neighbours which is found across all areas, except perhaps on council estates. Crow *et al.* (2002) in their study of a south coast town, found a similar pattern with a careful balance between 'keeping ones distance' and 'being there when needed'. This ideal relationship seems to be typified by knowing your immediate neighbours to say hello to and exchange a few words with, perhaps helping one another out in small but important ways, but with none of the obligations which might come from friendship or any closer kind of socializing. For many, the unspoken distance maintained between neighbours is important to a good quality of life.

*My immediate neighbours that I . . . no, but I don't really have time to speak to them all, you know. If they need anything, I always say like I'm more than happy to help, but I wouldn't . . . not really. I don't belong to any clubs or anything like that to be of help that way.*

Married mother, part-time employed, white, homeowner

## Getting Ahead – Access to Jobs

The literature on social capital points to the role of friendship and neighbour networks in getting people into jobs. Do friendship networks make a 'bridge' between the employed and the non-employed? Using BHPS data, we can examine this in two ways. On the one hand we can see whether non-employed people have employed friends, or whether employed people have non-employed friends. Amongst non-employed people (aged under 60), the main predictors of having no employed friends are low income, being single and living in social housing. In this respect London is just like the rest of the country, with no tendency for non-employed Londoners to be more or less isolated from employment networks than people living elsewhere. Indeed, when we look within the region, the tendency in Inner London and also in the OMA is for a higher probability that the non-employed have employed friends. On the other hand there is some tendency in Outer London and the OMA for employed people to have only employed friends, though this is not so characteristic of Inner London. There is therefore only limited evidence that the spatial segregation of the non-employed, which we observed in Chapter 4, led to a general high level of social segregation between employed and non-employed.

This evidence on friendship relates essentially to 'strong ties' – but what about weak ties? BHPS data suggest that nationally, 50 per cent of the unemployed said that half or more of the people they socialize with are unemployed, compared with 6 per cent of the employed and 8 per cent of the self-employed; while 62 per cent of employed people and 17 per cent of unemployed said none of their friends is unemployed. In a regression controlling for a range of factors we find that the unemployed are *nine times* more likely than employed working-class people, from whom most of the unemployed are drawn, to say that half or more of the people they meet for leisure are unemployed. Those engaged in family care are three and a half times more likely, and students five times more likely to say they mostly associate with unemployed people than employed working-class people, but those employed in the service class are half as likely as to say this.

This still does not quite capture the idea of weak ties, which would include acquaintances with whom one might have chance encounters, and who could provide information and connection to wider networks. There is no good survey evidence on this pattern of weak ties. Our interviews tend to suggest that at least in relation to getting jobs, it is a wide range of informal contacts, including friends, but also people such as previous employers or colleagues and occasionally teachers from school, who are important in providing information. Those that comment on having heard of vacancies or being given contacts through one of these routes are primarily in non-professional employment.

One example concerns a widow, with two children, whose husband was a caretaker. She obtained her current job as an administrator in a primary school, after someone she knew told her the school was looking for short-term maternity cover. She worked there until a full-time permanent post came up in the school a year later, applied and got the job. In another case, a married woman, now in her late fifties, had never applied for a job. Towards the end of her college course, the principal of the college had been asked by the local education department whether he knew of a suitable candidate for a job in administration. He took her to the education department and she got the job. She had worked there until she had children. Some years later, when the children had started school, she was shopping and met her former boss who asked her if she would come back to work for them part-time. She did and the job became full-time. Four years later she met a head teacher who had been at primary school with her and he asked her if she would come to work as his secretary. She worked there for 6 years and when the school was closed, she was transferred to the school in Gravesend where she currently works.

A married man in his fifties also reported that he had never applied for jobs. People have always asked him to come and work for them. Originally from the East End, he started work at 15 because his family needed the money. He got his first job in a clothing factory through the father of a friend from school. He then worked in shops and factories as a buyer, and became friends with a couple of suppliers and through them went into a company they owned as a clothing salesman. He did this for about 3 years, until during the three-day week they stopped paying his salary, although he continued to work for them. This was explained as a measure to prevent the firm going under. He had a friend who was a bailiff and began to do some work with him, continuing both jobs for a while. Eventually, he went into partnership with the bailiff and they set up a company together in Kent.

Such networks may also be of particular value to those from some ethnic minority backgrounds:

> *I got my first job through a friend, when I first came here he took me there, he was working there. My second job another guy that I knew in Ghana told me that he has got a job that is very good, that if I wanted I should give it a try. And then this third job somebody told me that he has been doing it for a while and that the money is good. I have never been to the job centre looking for a job . . . They show you the procedure, I will go and get a form and talk to this man and that . . . the first time I didn't even fill in a form, he came and said you should start this afternoon.*

Male cohabitee, employed, African, council tenant

But our interviews provide only limited evidence of an extensive use of informal networks to get jobs by younger people or those who might otherwise appear at risk of social exclusion.

## Trust, Neighbourhood Affiliation and Communities

There is no clear step from social capital at the individual level to community social capital, and since most of our evidence is at the individual level, we can only make indirect inferences about consequences for the community. Nevertheless we can shift to look at measures which have a more direct bearing on this level, in particular membership and participation in voluntary organizations, trust, and more general perceptions of neighbourhood affiliation.

Londoners are members of, and active in, organizations in much the same way as the rest of the nation (Table 8.2): 54 per cent of Inner Londoners and 49 per cent of Outer Londoners are active in at least one of the organizations listed by the BHPS, compared with 47 per cent nationally. Three per cent of Londoners are members of environmental groups, while just under 2 per cent are active in these groups, the same as the national figures. Trade union membership and activity is as high in London as elsewhere (with membership, at 16 per cent, being far higher than activity, at 4 per cent). Three per cent of Inner Londoners and 4 per cent of Outer Londoners are active in voluntary organizations, compared with 4 per cent nationally. Six per cent of Londoners are active in parents associations, compared with a national average of 5 per cent. Twenty-two per cent are active in sports clubs, 8 per cent in a social group (compared with 20 per cent and 9 per cent respectively). Most interesting are political party membership and activity, religious activity and professional group membership. Inner Londoners are considerably more likely to be involved, and actively, in these organizations than the national average. Some of these organizations are more strongly represented in London because of its functions as a capital city.

Inner Londoners attend religious services relatively frequently. Ten per cent of the national population attends religious services once a week or more, compared with 17 per cent of Inner Londoners and 9 per cent of Outer Londoners. Women's Institutes and women's groups, scouts and guides, pensioners groups and other community groups have very low membership and participation rates both nationally and in London.

**Table 8.2.** Organization membership and activity.

|  | Inner London | Outer London | London | UK |
|---|---|---|---|---|
| Active in at least one organization | 54 | 49 | 50 | 47 |
| Member environmental group | 3 | 3 | 3 | 3 |
| Active environmental group | 1 | 2 | 2 | 2 |
| Member trade union | 16 | 16 | 16 | 16 |
| Active trade union | 5 | 4 | 4 | 4 |
| Active voluntary organization | 3 | 4 | 4 | 4 |
| Active parents association | 6 | 6 | 6 | 5 |
| Active sports club | 22 | 22 | 22 | 20 |
| Active social club | 7 | 9 | 8 | 9 |
| Member of political party | 5 | 2 | 3 | 3 |
| Active in political party | 4 | 1 | 2 | 1 |
| Member of religious group | 15 | 13 | 14 | 11 |
| Active in religious group | 17 | 12 | 13 | 11 |
| Member of professional organization | 13 | 10 | 11 | 9 |
| Active in professional organization | 6 | 4 | 4 | 4 |
| Attends religious service at least once a week | 17 | 9 | 12 | 10 |

*Source:* BHPS.

Organizational activity varies quite dramatically by class (see Table 8.3). Those in the service class, as defined in the Erikson and Goldthorpe (1993) class schema, are active in most organizations. Those in the working class are more likely than those in the intermediate and service classes to be active in a social club or a trade union, whereas those in the service class are more likely than those in the working class to be active in all other mentioned associations. The most common clubs for the service class are sports clubs, professional associations and religious groups, whereas the intermediate class are more likely to be active in sports clubs and then religious groups; and the working class are more likely to be active in sports clubs, social clubs and then religious groups.

Men are more likely than women to be involved in trades unions, social and sports clubs. Women are more likely than men to be active in parents associations, tenants/residents groups and religious groups. Otherwise there is little variation by gender. The economically active are slightly more likely to be active in an organization than the inactive. The economically active are more likely than the inactive to be involved in political associations, parents associations and sports clubs. The

**Table 8.3.** Organization activity by Erikson and Goldthorpe (1993) class.

| Organization in which active | Service | Middle | Working |
|---|---|---|---|
| Professional association | 11.2 | 1.8 | 0 |
| Sports club | 30.0 | 28.8 | 19.4 |
| Social club | 5.8 | 6.1 | 11.9 |
| Religious group | 14.4 | 9.2 | 9.7 |
| Tenants/residents group | 5.1 | 1.8 | 3.7 |
| Parent/school association | 7.9 | 6.1 | 5.2 |
| Environment group | 2.5 | 1.2 | 0.7 |
| Trade union | 6.1 | 3.7 | 9.0 |
| Political party | 3.6 | 1.8 | 0.7 |

*Source:* BHPS.

economically inactive are a little more likely to be involved in residential or tenants associations, religious groups, voluntary associations and social clubs.

A large number of our respondents were members of social clubs and organizations, for example the British Legion, bowling clubs etc. However, other than providing a social/friendship network, very few describe the friends that they rely on as being known from these sources. The most important organizations which provide sources of 'getting on' social capital are religious. This is particularly evident in terms of access to schools for those who are Jewish or Christian. Overall it appeared that the non-conformist Christian churches provided the strongest and most heavily used networks. For example, for one respondent the Baptist Church was a particularly important source of friends, and also contacts through which he found accommodation. The church is also an important source of contact for some refugees.

One of Putnam's (2000) indirect measures of social capital is trust, measured by answers to the question 'generally speaking do you think that most people can be trusted, or that you cannot be too careful in dealing with people?' The basic data from the BHPS in 1998 suggest that trust is lower than the national average in Inner London, but rather higher in Outer London and the OMA. However, this is almost entirely explained by population composition. Trust measured in this way is strongly related to class, income and education. After controlling for these, significant differences disappear, though the Inner London level is still somewhat low. Even this difference disappears when we introduce an area deprivation measure – since there is also a strong negative correlation between area economic deprivation and social trust.

The BHPS also carried a set of measures which form a scale of neighbourhood affiliation (Buckner, 1988). Nationally, neighbourhood affiliation is negatively related to income, education and social class, though it is positively related to owner occupation, and to being married, and in a larger household. It is strongly negatively related to neighbourhood economic deprivation. So, working-class people are likely to express stronger neighbourhood affiliation, but this is undermined if the neighbourhood is particularly poor.

If we do not control for personal characteristics, neighbourhood affiliation is low in all parts of the London region, and especially in Inner London (where the 8 point score, created by adding one for each positive answer, has a mean value of 4.5, compared with 5.2 nationally, the lowest of any region). Table 8.4 shows the regional regression coefficients. After controlling for population composition, the difference between Inner London and the rest of the UK is reduced by about half, while the differences for the other parts of the region are reduced to a lesser degree. When we also control for the degree of area deprivation, the Inner London difference disappears altogether, but the OMA difference is strengthened somewhat. Thus deprivation and other social factors account for much of the lower levels of neighbourhood affiliation in Inner London, but in the rest of the region other factors persist. If we examine the individual items which make up the scale it is clear that in Inner London, the majority of items are no longer significantly different from the national picture after controls, except for questions about whether advice is obtainable locally, or whether people talk to neighbours. On the other hand in Outer London and the OMA most of the items relating to commitment to the area (such as whether people feel they belong to the neighbourhood, or are willing to work to improve it) remain negative after controls. However items relating to neighbourhood resources (e.g. advice obtainable locally, or can borrow things from neighbours) are more positive in these areas.

Speculating somewhat, this suggests that in Inner London lack of neighbourhood identification is a reaction to external circumstances (poverty, deprivation, characteristics of the area) while in suburban areas, there is a positive choice to live in a less 'cohesive', more individualized, and more anonymous area. This is consistent with the analysis of 'moral minimalism' in suburban areas explored by Baumgartner (1988).

**Table 8.4.** Regional differences from rest of UK in neighbourhood affiliation.

|  | No control variables | Controlling for class, tenure and demographic factors | Also controlling for area deprivation |
|---|---|---|---|
| Inner London | -0.76 *** | -0.37 *** | 0.03 |
| Outer London | -0.44 *** | -0.35 *** | -0.31 *** |
| Rest of London region | -0.22 *** | -0.15 *** | -0.25 *** |

*Source:* BHPS

*** significant at 0.1%.

# Social Capital, Civil Society and Governance

People can come together for many different reasons. Sometimes, they associate purely and simply for social purposes. We found one remarkable example in Greenwich:

*Chitagong Association*
What's that?

*It's another town in Bangladesh where my husband is from, it's a port town like your Manchester and is the second largest, yeah he's a member of that.*
And do they do special . . . ?
*They do, like they organize like trips, last week the Redbridge one went to Clacton-on-sea. We went to Cornwall last year with them, you know the bank holiday, August bank holiday end of August. In May we went to Scotland with the group. Two years ago when I first moved here we went to EuroDisney so it's quite good, it's quite active and during Ramadan*

Married mother, Bangladeshi, homeowner

But when we turned to active civic engagement, we found a different story. As a rule, people get involved in civic activity only when they face a change in their local environment which they do not want, or when they want to change something which to some degree affects their quality of life. Further, a small minority may become very active; it may be that these are long-time residents who are more aware of change in their local community and find it unacceptable, and who are better connected politically. Greenhithe, in Dartford, provides a classic example:

*One time, many, many years ago, when we lived in the village of Greenhithe down the hill here, we had a problem with the cement works chucking out the dust at night, you know, when they weren't supposed to . . . In the morning you'd come down and your car would be white and the washing would be white with cement dust and we literally stopped the traffic. We said we was going to stop the traffic and we did stop the traffic. And we got ourselves in the paper. But apart from that, you know, we moved away from there then . . . I think it becomes, you know, you can put up with things for so long and so long and then you say, right, enough's enough and you've got to stand and do something. And I think a lot of people are like that. You know, you put up with things for so long and that's when people get really angry.*

Married couple, employed, white, homeowner

We also found that people – here and elsewhere – are quite cynical, or disillusioned, about their capacity to influence anything in their neighbourhood:

Do you think you have influence over what happens?
*Not really, no. Anybody that says that they do is conning.*

Married father, employed, Sikh, homeowner

This respondent, for instance, knows her ward councillor but does not believe that he has very much power to get things done. So she has a feeling of helplessness:

*You don't change, the only way of changing what's there is by voting differently and bringing in someone else . . . albeit, but it doesn't, it doesn't change, people don't bother any more, we've gone past it in Hounslow.*

Married mother, employed, white, homeowner

*You phone the civic centre, you're put on hold for 15 minutes, and you get through to someone who's actually not their department, and then they take a message and say they'll get someone to call you back within three working days, and a fortnight later, someone who doesn't know what you phoned about in the first place leaves a message on your answerphone while you're out, and then you call back and they say 'Oh sorry, what was that about?' And then you tell them, and they say 'Oh it's not my department, I'll pass it on'. You never ever get to speak to anyone who cares or can do anything.*

Married mother, employed, white, homeowner

Others said frankly that they were not sufficiently concerned to become involved: maybe they might, but not now. Others pleaded family or work commitments; they just lacked the time:

*If I really felt where I am living was deteriorating, you know, really badly, say if I kept coming across people doing, or dealing drugs on the stairs, if I kept walking into people doing that, then I would feel, perhaps, I was in a . . . you know, a harmful situation to my person. So I would make something of that. But, as yet, it hasn't got to that stage.*

Single man, unemployed, white, council tenant

*I, we don't have time for clubs because my oldest got so many after school activities, I haven't got time to paint my nails. As my husband says the other day he goes, 'When do you have time to do anything?' er we're always running around . . .*

Married mother, part-time employed, Egyptian parents, homeowner

People told us of the occasion when they decided they were sufficiently aggrieved to take action, often on the spur of the moment. But we actually found a great deal of local resentment against self-appointed busybody groups:

*They now want to sit on little committees and decide who's eligible to live in them blocks. So you've got to go up before a tribunal of people who know nothing, but have got opinions. I wouldn't do it. I personally wouldn't do it . . . Turn me out, and a few others in here, and just have, like, the whole block of clones of their selves.*

Single+divorced (father) brothers, unemployed/employed, white, council tenant

*I cannot stand [school-name] mothers, they are sort of busy-body types who, I think they're power . . . who actually would love to be back at work, maybe can't afford the child-care, and so they have to find another power role for themselves, and that's actually organizing the fete and bossing the teachers around and bossing other parents around. And I absolutely despise them.*

Divorced mother, unemployed, white, private tenant

Thus, where social networks are very strong, they can paradoxically undermine the capacity for action, because any resulting movement is seen as too 'cliquey'; others will not join.

Overall, the story on social capital and governance is complex. In general, there is not much evidence of civic activism – although, as we saw above, Londoners are rather more likely than other British citizens to join organizations. What seems to be happening is not any sudden disaffection from civic life; rather that the life strategies which Londoners pursue are usually individually based, or at most family based, rather than based on any wider collective identification. Only when major problems present themselves, particularly at neighbourhood level, do wider and more collective strategies become a serious option. However, this may be a partial view, driven by the specific characteristics of our case study areas. Butler and Robson

(2002, 21) find considerable variation in the deployment of social capital among middle-class households in various gentrifying urban neighbourhoods in London, but in one – Telegraph Hill – they find that social capital 'is deployed more broadly and deliberately here . . . and . . . is used to compensate for *relative* lack of economic capital' – for example, in order to secure local environmental improvements.

## Social Capital and the Economy

Ideas about the importance of social capital have played a very important role in the recent discussions on economic development. Commonly this is expressed in terms of a need for trust between businesses, to cover those contingencies which contracts alone cannot cover, with networking and/or institutionalized co-operation as means of securing this trust. More positively, Storper (1995) argues that a key resource for competitive firms is access to sets of 'untraded interdependences', grounded in sets of shared conventions built up through social interaction between networked firms.

This is a powerful set of ideas but, as with writings about the value of social capital to private individuals, there is a whole series of questions to be asked about their application – not least why these concerns have come to the fore during the past decade. Several plausible answers suggest themselves. One cause may simply be that competitive pressures have become more intense, encouraging a more vigorous search for ways of enhancing performance. Or it may be that a more uncertain general economic environment makes it harder to take co-operation for granted as a matter of simple habit, in view of the risks of being let down. Another factor is the tendency towards out-sourcing and vertical disintegration of productive organizations, which means that bureaucratic routines cannot be relied upon to deliver the necessary co-ordination. Another influence, as discussed in Chapter 1, is the recognition (by Porter (1990) and others) that in advanced countries competition has increasingly to be pursued in terms of qualities, rather than simply price. This increases the importance of qualitative aspects of interaction with other firms which are normally outside the scope of formal contracts. A related idea is that securing the positive externalities on which competitive success increasingly depends would require forms of collective action by business. These will rarely emerge spontaneously from calculations of advantage by individual businesses (Cheshire and Gordon, 1996).

This range of explanations for the growing interest in the importance of social capital is critical because each may suggest rather different expectations about forms of trust, networks and social capital – for example about the roles of strong versus weak ties – and what these can deliver. None, however, directly implies anything about geography, though a major theme both in the literature and the lessons drawn by policy-makers (as in current enthusiasms for cluster development) is that social capital and trust can most effectively be developed on a fairly local basis. The basic idea here is that transaction costs will be lower within areas, whether because of higher levels of routine interaction, localist affiliations and the power of tradition, easier recognition of shared interests, or the potential to build on purely social linkages and institutions.

However, we have already seen in Chapter 3 that while agglomeration economies are clearly valuable to London firms they seem to attach little importance to the opportunities which proximity to related kinds of businesses offers for building closer relations. In the particular case of innovating businesses we noted evidence that potential connections at the regional scale seemed to matter more than specific local links, while the value of joint ventures and strategic relations with customers did not seem to be reduced if partners were actually quite far away. In the language of social capital theory the implication is that at an urban scale extensive networks of weak ties were more valued than strong ties, while strong ties did not seem to be particularly distance-sensitive. Here we look at how far these attitudes are reflected in what firms told us about their relations with local institutions and community involvement.

In comparative analyses of local economic development activity, much has been made of the stronger role played by local Chambers of Commerce in continental Europe as a key means of articulating relations among businesses and between them and public authorities. This was one of the spurs in the early 1990s to initiatives to strengthen the role of British Chambers, particularly through sub-regional groupings of local Chambers. One of the major examples then was the creation of a Thames Valley Chamber of Commerce (incorporating former the Reading and Wokingham Chambers among others in Berks and Bucks), which then became one of the key actors in the Thames Valley Economic Partnership. A more recent push towards mergers, including construction of a London-wide Chamber has been catalysed by the pressures around the government's new Small Business Service.

Within Greater London about 15 per cent of workers were in firms belonging to Chambers of Commerce in 1996 (according to the LES), half the proportion for other, national trade associations. Within central London, the rate of Chamber membership was substantially lower. Compared with members of other trade federations, firms belonging to Chambers tended to be rather older, and included fewer of the largest establishments (with over 1000 workers). There are also sectoral biases with more Chamber members among lawyers/accountants and fewer in City financial services, printing/publishing or other business services. Another strong influence on membership was the share of exports in sales, reflecting the Chambers' national role in provision of export advice and formal certification of origin as a reason for joining – quite independent of the value attached to Chambers' local networking and representative functions. The LES suggests that Chamber members might be more 'progressive' in management terms than their counterparts, in so far as they had more active interest in the Investors in People programme, greater use of external consultants, and a stronger tendency to believe that their products had a competitive advantage. But they did not appear to be especially innovative, growth-oriented or productivity-conscious. And there was no evidence that they had particularly strong relations with local suppliers, customers or collaborators, nor more positive attitudes to the advantages of clustering.

Among our business interviewees, very few were interested in membership of the local Chamber of Commerce, and attitudes to its role were frequently negative. As our reviews of the area economies in Chapter 3 indicate, this was a fairly consistent finding across areas, with the case against membership being most strongly put by a medium sized Greenwich firm, serving a mostly regional market:

> I found it a very male-orientated, boring group that seemed much more interested in the drink they were going for afterwards than the content of the meetings.

For a number of firms with local markets, this social element was seen as useful, since it allowed them to network with potential customers. Some respondents noted, however, that functions set up explicitly for this purpose tended not to work. In one case a Newham accountant reported:

> There were about fifteen people there, fourteen of whom were accountants looking for new business, and this one businessman, who had fourteen accountants.

Informal networks seemed more useful, and were also widely used for recruitment. A City insurance broker noted that:

> On the broking side, where people are frequently out of the office those people will know each other simply because they've been doing a job for years. They all talk generally, and then someone will say, 'we need a broker on the North American side, someone with a bit of experience'. Someone will then say 'what about * * * *, he was saying to me the other day that he was a bit fed up. That's the 'people you know' route . . . and you save the agency fees!

More typically such local networks were used for recruiting less skilled workers such as those to work in administration, cleaning, call centres and on night shifts or as temps. In the most significant example we found a firm using local community networks for general recruitment, a long-established Newham manufacturer, which had recruited men through the labour exchange and women through local family networks, had found that by the late 1980s:

> The families were moving away and they wanted their kids to go and be computer specialists or work in the City – it just stopped the flow.

There was also a single example of a firm using a London-based ethnic community network for recruitment, a Southwark office cleaning firm which relied on extended families of their Portuguese workforce.

What we did not find were examples of firms developing other kinds of collaborative relationship, or using local institutional settings to acquire information important to firms' own strategies, or investing significant effort in the hope of doing so. In the case of Chambers of Commerce, and similar local organizations, interest in making contacts with other businesses seemed largely restricted to finding potential customers. Of more interest was making contact with public agencies, either in hopes of getting work from them, or because of future issues where help might be required from them. Nor was there much expectation of Chambers playing a positive representative role in developing local assets, as distinct from responding to negative developments in relation, for example, to roads and traffic. The one significant example of collaborative activity among firms in our areas was among firms on the Great West Road in Hounslow. They established a Golden Mile Integrated Travel Group to campaign for public transport solutions to their workers' travel problems, under the aegis of West London Inward (now West London Business), which has been one of the most proactive business groups in the region. In terms of more general community involvement the main example was of the proprietor of a long-established Bermondsey firm strongly involved in the Masons and high-profile charities, as well as local employer groups. Many other firms contributed to local charitable and educational activities, partly for image-building, partly in support of committed employees, and quite often – it seemed – for straightforwardly altruistic reasons. Rarely did this appear part of a policy of building strategic economic relations.

## Social Disorder

Up to now we have focused largely on social capital from the perspective of individual residents and firms. However we are also interested in community level consequences. It is extremely difficult to observe the causal processes which may lead to community level order and disorder. However, we can observe some of the outcomes. We have two sources of evidence here: our interviews with schools, which are one of the main sites where the consequences of disorder are manifest, and data on crime.

Our research on schools and the communities they serve in our eight case study areas gave us a particular insight into some aspects of how social cohesion and social order is generated within communities and social institutions. Schools both reflect the characteristics and values of their local communities and provide a stimulus or a challenge to them. In Chapter 5 we have already seen how local area characteristics can impact on education and schools as institutions. There was evidence of the middle classes using their social capital to maintain the quality of local schools. More negatively we saw substantial variations in truancy rates associated with area characteristics, and we also saw how teachers perceived their role in repairing damaged communities.

Schools seem to be the institutions where the consequences of social disorder are most apparent. This is obviously most extreme in areas of severe deprivation, but social order and disorder were a constant theme in school interviews across all areas. Schools have to deal not only with the consequences of material poverty and social polarization, but also with a whole raft of personal and family pathologies. Because of this, many tensions and conflicts present in the wider society are played out or imitated within the school perimeter. However, it is of course, just as naïve or fanciful to portray a local school as purely a neighbourhood institution, as it is to pretend there is something straightforward called 'community' which unites all those people living in a defined geographical area. As we saw in Chapter 5, the choice (or lack of choice) of schools by parents is already part of a process of economic, social and ethnic structuring within a local education authority area. Housing mobility and cross-borough movements provide additional complexity, and the option (for those who can afford it) of private education, or partly private education (through tutoring) increases the range of choice and the fragmentation of 'community' still further.

Schools as institutions, and teachers as people, find themselves in the position of trying to instil and maintain social order, not only with the children, but with parents too. Nor surprisingly, this is not a role that in general they wish to perform, but of necessity they have to:

> *How do we tackle attendance? I can say off the top of my head that you can't do it without involving parents because parents are one of the main contributors to kids not coming to school . . . Some work done here, I think it showed 95 per cent parent condoned unattendance. So you know we set up a system which has got to be working with young people and also working with parents.*
>
> Voluntary project worker

> *You're not only a teacher, you're a social worker, you're a psychologist. You get parents in, not worried about their children's achievement, but 'Why did you say this to my little so and so? . . . they're being bullied and there's nothing being done about it' . . . the parents can be quite stressful . . . they can be quite aggressive.*
>
> Female teacher, Outer Metroplitan Area school

What sometimes appears to be happening is that parents are increasingly expecting school to take responsibilities for the behaviour of their children, or simply are not in a position to take these responsibilities. Schools inevitably find themselves therefore taking on a more social role:

> *We are not social workers and that is the problem. Teachers are being expected to take on that role of socializing kids . . . sometimes we do get the feeling that . . . parents have said 'I can't cope, could you do that for me?' or they aren't around enough to be taking on that responsibility. But once they do work experience at 15 and you see them in the workplace, you realize what children they still are. And they are having problems getting involved in an adult world.*
>
> Teacher, secondary school

Indiscipline, incivility and violence are a recurring theme. This is most frequent/ extreme in the more deprived areas, but suburbs and the OMA are not immune. The following comment comes from Outer London:

> *There is an awful lot of argy bargy that goes on in the estate, and that increasingly these days comes into school, we have fighting . . . [for example] a long running feud going on between the two families starting off with the boys . . . these two boys . . . are now at each others throats with a knife. Everything outside the school gates, they all live on the estate as well . . . we have racist name calling and one thing and the other, it doesn't go on in school but parents come in and make complaints about the parents of other children because again it's been happening outside school and will I sort it out please and have a word with this mother or this father. And no matter how hard I explain that really I've got no control and shouldn't have any, they want me to wave my magic wand.*
>
> Head, primary school

Nevertheless, schools remain key institutions in the complex process by which neighbourhoods and communities define themselves, and are defined by others. They can in part define the community and the sense of spatial and temporal continuity, and hence are key generators of 'social capital'. This is not naïve romanticism; we found evidence for this in communities as different as Hounslow, Wandsworth, and Reading and Wokingham:

> We had a nun, who ran the school, who was the headmistress for twenty-five years and she was one of those people who was so kind and so, she just got the respect . . . the children . . . had great time for her, and parents had . . . She was there all those years. In fact, my children went through while she was there and before she left a lot of the children she had taught in the beginning were then back with their children
>
> Female widow, unemployed, white, homeowner

> We had a ten year old when we moved here, she had one year before she went to secondary school and so you didn't want to move her anywhere else. So you had to make roots and by the time she was finished 'A' levels, our second one was just going into secondary school, so that's probably why we stayed.
>
> Married mother, employed, white, homeowner

Our fieldwork revealed a complex relationship between the leadership of the school (particularly the head teacher) and the views of the community, or rather communities which it served. The school, and the Head, play a role in the community which goes beyond the provision of education:

> If [a parent] is cross I know about it because I'll hear somebody out there shouting: 'who the fucking hell is in charge around here'. . . that's the culture, they want it sorted, and they want it sorted then . . . They'll start with that level and you have to talk them down and sort it out . . . The upside to it is the loyalty I get here, from the children and from parents very often. The same parent who one week is 'who the fucking hell is in charge' if I sort something then the next week [will be very helpful] . . . We are sort of family so we have our rows but when outsiders come to criticize us or put us under pressure we will pull together like family . . . I like that, that's a lovely quality around here.
>
> Head teacher, Outer London

# Crime

Crime has always been of particular concern for the media in their reporting of London. At the time of writing the concern is particularly acute, and there is a continuing crisis of confidence in the fairness and competence of the Metropolitan police. There have been a series of killings, in different circumstances, of ethnic minority children over the past decade – these include two notoriously unresolved cases in or close to our south-east London case study areas, apparently involving young gangs, and against a background of racism or inter-ethnic conflict. Quite separately there has been a rapid growth in the use of guns on the streets and in public places, notably by gangsters in the drug industry. And levels of street crime have grown rapidly, including a very recent epidemic of thefts of mobile phones from children. These are real but also highly emotive issues, because of the involvement of young people, public places, racial issues, drugs and firearms. Very unfavourable comparisons have been made with New York City where Mayor Giuliani's anti-crime drive seems to have brought spectacular successes. In autumn 2001, safety and crime rates ranked just behind the cost of living, and well ahead of transport issues, in Londoners' lists of the worst things about living in the city (according to a MORI poll), with 52 per cent seeing this as a key issue. Public confidence in police effectiveness has fallen since the early 1980s, but there also remain great concerns among the young, black people, and those from poor areas about police treatment. Both have been attributed to styles of policing which are insufficiently responsive to local need, partly because of emphases on quantitative targets (Fitzgerald *et al.*, 2002).

Statistics tell a more mixed story. Between 1981 and 2000 (broadly the period covered by this book) victimization statistics from the British Crime Survey show a modest overall growth for the country as a whole (of 17 per cent), although the trend has been sharply downward in recent years (with a 33 per cent fall since 1995). For property crime at least this is believed to reflect the upturn in the economy. Over the period as a whole, several categories of crime have grown particularly strongly: domestic violence, bicycle theft, stealth thefts from the person, *attempted* burglary or car theft, and robbery (though snatch thefts with no threat of force have declined). All categories of crime with identifiable victims appear to have fallen substantially since the mid-1990s apart from stealth thefts, stranger violence and robbery. Recorded crime statistics tell a somewhat different story, partly because rates of reporting have risen substantially for some offences, notably for violent crime, and partly because of changes in police recording practice, with higher recording rates for reported violent crime and lower ones for property crime. Risks of victimization for burglary, vehicle thefts and violent crime are all substantially greater in urban areas, particularly in the inner city.

For Greater London, however, the only substantial excesses over national rates are in respect of mugging (where the rate is between two and three times the national average), thefts from vehicles (a third higher) and burglary (with more actual entries and fewer attempts). For the region as a whole, crime rates are clearly lower as is clear from recorded crime statistics, which indicate much lower crime rates in the OMA than in Greater London – around half for most property crimes (with a smaller difference for thefts from vehicles), about one-third for personal violence, and an eighth for robbery in 1999/2001. Combining these two sources of information, it seems that rates of theft from vehicles in the region are likely to be marginally above the national average, but that the one important difference is in relation to mugging where rates of victimization are probably 60 per cent above the national average. BCS data indicates that half of the victims are young men between 16 and 24 – with significant numbers of younger victims not covered by the survey – but other groups in the population (with victimization rates of 0.5 per cent and below) actually think they are at greater risk. People tend to perceive that crime has been growing (though more outside their own areas), but Londoners are no more fearful of crime than 20 years ago, though concerns have grown about disorderly teenagers, litter, graffiti and drug dealing (Fitzgerald *et al.*, 2002). On the positive side too is that despite the (anti-police) Brixton riot of 1996, London has up to now missed out on the two main waves of rioting in residential areas elsewhere, involving predominantly white youths in deprived council estates across the country in 1991/ 92, and Asian Muslim youths in Yorkshire and Lancashire towns in summer 2001.

There are, however, great disparities in crime risks between areas and population groups within London. In terms of recorded crime, high crime rates in London are essentially an Inner London phenomenon, with Outer London being very close to the national average in almost all respects – though there are, of course exceptions. For property crimes the real difference may well be understated, because better-insured middle-class households are more likely to make reports. For violence against the person and sexual offences recorded rates in Inner London are 2.5 times the national average, while for robbery they are five times as high. Regression analyses across the districts of the region link these higher rates particularly to concentrations of bar/club employment, ethnic minorities, the non-employed and single parents, as well as to urban centrality. One of the mediating factors is a larger drugs industry in Greater London, indicated by rates of cocaine/crack seizure 3.8 times the national average in 1999, and of other drugs which were 60 per cent above that average. Convictions and cautions for drug offences grew by 70 per cent per annum between 1989 and 1999 (with a recent downturn): this is much slower than in the rest of the country, and conviction rates are no longer uniquely high, but still are about 50 per cent above the national average.

Among the groups particularly at risk of victimization nationally, apart from inner-city residents, were those with low incomes and/or no educational qualifications, the over fifties, and (for crimes against the person) non-white ethnic minorities. The higher risks for ethnic minorities reflect rates of racially-motivated crime running at about 2 per cent among blacks and 4 per cent among south Asians in 1999. For these two groups together, the risks of experiencing such crime were similar in London and in the rest of the country, and have shown a similar fall to overall crime since the mid-1990s (Clancy et al., 2001).

In the next chapter we will see that perceptions of crime constitute an important component of people's quality of life in London's neighbourhoods, and most of the evidence from our interviews on area variations is left to that chapter. Here we draw links with the discussion of social capital. With one exception the evidence does not suggest that crime levels are lower in places where community networks are stronger, as Coleman (1990) might suggest, though our study is too small to make this in any way conclusive. On the other hand the strengths of people's links to their neighbourhood had a major bearing on their fear of crime.

We will see that, although crime was clearly an important element in deciding where a person would like, or not like, to live, overall people did not seem worried about it, and that was directly related to the fact that they knew plenty of people in the area and felt there was a good sense of community there. Crime, though, did tend to be a somewhat more prominent concern for women and older interviewees. Most respondents were aware of specific instances of crime in the neighbourhood, and some had experience as a victim. Many took precautionary measures to protect themselves and their property (and frequently that of their neighbours) as part of their daily routines – even where neighbour relations were strained. But only in a very small minority of cases did fear of crime seem to permeate all aspects of life, with major effects on quality of life. More typical was this reaction:

> We've had a stabbing, we've had a murder since we've been down here . . . that's obviously frightening. But . . . it's quiet compared to a lot of other places where you live, you know, I mean, anywhere you live nowadays, let's be honest . . . you take your chances now don't you? I mean we had the car bashed in three weeks ago. Someone come on the drive and done it . . .Yeah. There was a big fight outside. So, you know, I mean, that could happen anywhere, you know . . . But for a village, it's sometimes . . . you think, God I'm living in a village and it shouldn't be happening, but it has and, you know, you just live with it really don't you?
>
> Married man, self-employed, white, homeowner

Surprisingly, perhaps, people affected by crime seem not to worry about it. Generally, fear of crime seems to have little relation to the reality of crime. People who knew their neighbourhoods, who felt they belonged there, had little fear. Contrariwise, when someone did not identify with people in the area, they tended to be more concerned with crime. Where a person felt that there was a strong community, even if they had experienced crime, that experience did not develop into a fear. Alternatively, when a person moved out of an area and had been living somewhere different for a while, they perceived crime in their previous area to have gone up, although the residents who carried on living there did not seem aware of this. Consequently, fear of crime becomes much more a reflection of a person's relationship to the community than a gauge of actual levels of crime:

> I don't really identify with the people in the neighbourhood. I don't know anywhere else at all and don't even know my neighbours . . . I don't really know Peckham at all. I just go into work and come back . . . I don't like the area very much partly because of what I heard before coming to live here and partly what I see myself . . . I see a lot of drug dealers and rowdy behaviour. I don't feel safe here and that affects my sense of freedom. I have seen two yellow police assault signs in the last couple of months and things like that make me feel uncomfortable about going out at night.
>
> Married father, employed, black British, council tenant

While generally interviewees from inner-city council estates were most likely to perceive crime as a major problem that they could not do anything to control, some respondents in Battersea and Bermondsey suggested that a great deal could be achieved through informal social controls: in particular, the degree to which teenagers were socially integrated. In a few places there is a strictly informal and old-fashioned system of crime control, independent of the police, and more reminiscent of a peasant village of old than of a twenty-first century metropolis:

> There was one guy . . . he came out of Wandsworth prison and was living in X Court, he probably done nearly all the flats . . . So some of the lads on the estate had a quiet word with him and then I think there was a fight outside the paper shop, they grabbed him out there one day. He had to run and leave his shoes, he hasn't come back since.
>
> Male cohabitee (father), employed, Afro-Caribbean, homeowner

*We've never had a lot of crime on this estate cos we always knew the families that were crime, but . . . they've all grown up and then their children started it and we started neighbourhood watch, and through neighbourhood watch we watched the crime go down to 1 or 2 per cent . . . we just tell 'em straight: 'If we catch you again we give your name to the police, we know who you are, we know where you live'. We don't know where half of them live but you bluff them and it's stopping them selling drugs on our estate.*

Single mother, unemployed, white, council tenant

## Conclusion: Social Relations in London

In this chapter we have explored the nature of social relations in London, using the concept of social capital. As with social exclusion, discussed in the last chapter, this is not something which can be measured simply and about which we can draw straightforward conclusions. In particular we should again reiterate that it is extremely difficult to find evidence that social capital has the effects which some of its proponents suggest. What we have done here is to provide evidence on a number of dimensions of social connectedness and social order in London.

In the introduction we advanced a number of hypotheses suggesting that London might be a rather anomic place, with low levels of social capital. Our conclusions are rather mixed. Overall, London is not a particularly anomic place. Once we control for population composition, people in London are just as socially connected, in terms of family, friends and neighbours as in any other part of the country. However their pattern of association is somewhat different, with family members playing rather less of a role in networks than elsewhere, and friends playing more of a role. The spatial spread of networks in London also tends to be rather wider. Nevertheless family networks do remain important.

We do find a small minority of people in London, for example amongst the long-term sick and disabled and the retired, who experience much more social isolation. However, in general Londoners do not perceive themselves to be socially isolated. This does not mean that neighbourhood relations are necessarily particularly close. The ideal neighbour relationship is the classic 'English reserve': to be on good terms with one's neighbours but not to be too closely involved.

In relation to membership and activity in organizations, one of the standard measures of social capital, London comes out as an area of high participation, though there are some significant social class variations as well. However, our respondents did not in general see any particular value in collective action, except in rare cases where the neighbourhood was under some clear and direct threat.

Our discussion of the engagement of firms in networking and collective action has some parallels and some contrasts here. In spite of the arguments for the importance of social capital for firms, we find rather weak evidence of firms valuing local linkages particularly highly. While there is some organizational involvement, it does not appear to be orientated either to establishing business linkages or for collective action.

For residents, other measures of social capital related to social trust and neighbourhood affiliation are significantly lower in the London region than in other areas. These differences are largely 'explained' by the social and economic characteristics of the population, and the intensity of neighbourhood deprivation. However this supports our initial hypotheses that these characteristics would be detrimental to the building of some sorts of social capital in London. It is possible that this has wider consequences for maintaining social order, though we have no direct evidence on this.

We do have evidence of higher levels of crime and social disorder. We have seen how schools face pressures to generate and maintain social order, especially in deprived communities. Crime rates in London are significantly higher than in other areas and there are widespread fears about incivility, crime and social disorder. However for most people, crime is not a major issue – rather it is 'factored in' and adjusted to via burglar alarms and general wariness. But for some, crime and the fear of crime has a major impact on quality of life. We shall see in the next chapter that people's perception of crime substantially varies between areas. But as we have seen here it also depends on how people relate to their neighbourhood; in general, where people are strongly integrated into their neighbourhood crime is more manageable. Of course this is a double sided process, and the degree to which people feel part of their neighbourhood will also depend on their perceptions of crime and disorder.

Chapter 9

# Things Endure,
# Things Change:
# London's Neighbourhoods

Things endure, things change: improvement, deterioration, adjustment – all
respond to the deep pulse of the city. And in that respect the south London
community where I grew up forms a cameo of London at large: the physical
fabric engages in endless dialogue with the inhabitants; the townscape shapes
them, while they reconstruct it . . . People make their own cities but never under
conditions of their own choosing.
Roy Porter, Preface to *London. A Social History*, 1994

In the Preface to his social history of London Roy Porter paints a vivid picture of New
Cross Gate, South London just after the Second World War. He depicts a vanished
world: on the one hand, poverty, pollution and poor housing; on the other hand,
the secure employment in the nearby docks and railways, the closeness of family
and neighbours, the freedom from crime and fear. He describes a certain quality
of life with appreciation and affection but without sentimentality. Above all, it was
people and how they lived together that generated what was good for them: the
neighbourhood contained this good life but contributed little to it. Indeed, it had
a 'grimy, dingy feel' and 'people wanted to get out . . . nobody liked living in New
Cross Gate' (Porter, 1994, xiii–xiv). Its main contribution to the residents' quality of
life was its location – close to jobs, parks and playgrounds, cinema and football
and, for a special treat, all that the centre of a great city offers. It was what this
neighbourhood didn't offer that led so many to yearn for a move to suburban
London – good housing, clean air, trees, fields and woods. Like countless others, the
Porter family finally made the dream come true and 'it was heaven'.

We can draw two lessons from this story. First, most people's quality of life is
largely fixed by how they live, not where they live. But, second, where they live still

matters – though more for some than for others, as we shall see. The hundreds of hours of interviews that we taped with the residents of our eight neighbourhoods contain a rich set of materials about individual and household ways of living and quality of life. In the preceding chapters we have used this resource in describing those ways of living and what shapes them. Were we writing principally on social dynamics and divisions, with London as merely a site for their exploration, this chapter would put place in its place and focus upon individual and group variations in quality of life. But this book is about London, so the relationship is reversed. So this chapter focuses on what place contributes to quality of life, or removes from it.

Quality of life is one of those slippery concepts that have social meaning but that defy the best efforts of social or natural scientists to define and measure. Thwarted, they frequently confuse cause and consequence in the search for definable and measurable indicators of quality of life, which are then taken to be valid measures of that which they only indicate. The problems indeed go beyond the sciences: in popular parlance our concern is with 'the good life' and defining what is good takes us directly to the philosopher's world of morals and values. However, it is within studies of the economics of inequality that the greatest effort has been made to define, measure and understand individual levels of quality of life (Sen, 1970, 1999; Nussbaum and Sen, 1993). But none of this valuable work touches on our concerns here. Explaining how the quality of life of London's people is shaped by social and economic forces is, of course, central to our project; and in the preceding chapters we have pursued these questions and given our answers. Our aim here is merely to show some ways in which place contributes its own part to this overall explanation; not to become immersed in another entirely different and non-spatial set of concerns and theories.

Turning to work which focuses on cities, there is an extensive literature which seeks to relate quality of life to measures of city competitiveness – for example the city league tables beloved of city marketers. Frequently, the most unlikely places appear near the top of such tables – Pittsburgh was the classic US example. However, like the economists' studies, these too are based on statistical indicators chosen by those who produce the league tables; for example concerning pollution, the physical environment, crime, education and health. As Rogerson (1999, 979) notes, such 'hard' indicators presume (without any proof) that they do measure the 'reality' of quality of life. This is the approach that the Social Exclusion Unit adopts in developing the indices of local deprivation which we mapped in Chapters 2, 5 and 7 (Social Exclusion Unit, 1998). It ignores work that has centred on 'conceiving of quality of life at the level of the individual' and so has 'focused on how personal characteristics and views shape people's quality of life'. The raw material for this work is social survey research which is based on 'the notion that quality of life expressed the degree of satisfaction or dissatisfaction felt by people with aspects of their lives . . .'.

It is this approach to examining quality of life in our neighbourhoods that we pursue here. Our interviews recorded how the residents viewed where they lived, speaking in their own words and conveying their own meanings, at first hand rather than through any 'translation' into statistical indicators. The results must inevitably, however, be only our own selective interpretation of what we were told. Although we quote directly from some of our respondents, more frequently we shall have to summarize what we were told in our own words, drawing on far more interview material than we could directly reproduce here.

Obviously views vary greatly about what the locality adds to the quality of life of its residents. One problem is that some people's views are less influenced by any intrinsic or more widely perceived characteristic of that locality than by their personal circumstances and to a degree that sets them apart from their neighbour's views. We met one downwardly mobile middle-class single parent living in a pleasant locality who was almost entirely negative about it. It was a gentrifying area, housing the upwardly mobile middle class whose mere presence there, regardless of their behaviour, made her feel inferior. We met several others whose attitudes to their neighbourhood were hostile or fearful to extraordinary degrees. Here too features in their personal lives and psychologies filtered and distorted their vision. In some cases, an almost pathological racism provided this filter, to a degree which went far beyond the much more frequent place that 'race' and racist references took in the wider evaluation of where people lived.

In what follows we have used the well-worn principle of triangulation in the social sciences. Fascinating though they are, we have excluded these 'aberrant' cases and drawn our conclusions on the basis of what we heard from the many rather than the few. However, apart from these few highly individual responses, the degree of significance that residents attached to their locality also varied according to their stage in the lifecycle, their social class and tenure. For example, while the young single professional worker and the council tenant might agree in their evaluation, the importance of this for their own quality of life might differ. So, alongside the variation in quality of life across our neighbourhoods there are differences that cut across the geographical boundaries based on the social and economic circumstances of our respondents.

A useful starting point is evidence on people's own opinions of their neighbourhood taken from the British Household Panel Survey. When asked whether their neighbourhood was 'good', 'bad', or 'mixed', less than three-quarters of those resident in Inner London said 'good', compared with 85 per cent of all UK residents. Satisfaction was higher in Outer London, close to the national level, and well above the national average in the Rest of the South East. Given what we know about these areas, these results are not surprising. It would be interesting to have such comparative data for other UK city regions to see whether Londoners' varying perceptions are typical or unusual.

In fact, for our purposes the most useful responses from this survey are to a question which asked what aspects of their neighbourhood most strongly influenced respondents' overall valuations of their localities (up to six answers allowed). The resulting list contains around ninety items. However, many are little more than different expressions of the same variable, or its negative. Thus we have 'people friendly', 'neighbours friendly'; and 'drugs', 'no drugs'. Summarizing this detail, four clusters of factors mainly shape the views that emerge. These are, first, the quality of social networks and relationships; second, perceptions of how secure the place is to live in; third, its facilities and accessibility; and, finally, aspects of the physical environment. Our interviews confirm that these are central to most people's evaluation of their neighbourhoods, so we concentrate on them in this chapter – although the picture is richer and more nuanced than this limited analysis can completely encompass, as the ninety social survey answers illustrate!

## Six Kinds of Neighbourhood

The neighbourhood portraits that we present here are archetypes. No area corresponds precisely to another, as some of the variations within this classification will show, and, as we mentioned, the significance as well as the valuation of what the locality adds to quality of life varies within each area. But our belief is that they do capture important characteristics of local neighbourhoods at a time when London is moving rapidly away from its past into a new era.

### The New Melting Pots: Battersea and East Reading

The first kind of neighbourhood is exemplified by Battersea and inner East Reading. Both are inner-city neighbourhoods, once predominantly working class, where de-industrialization and gentrification have brought huge changes. Artisan terraces have been bought by the young middle class who have flocked here – in Battersea, from the fashionable area next door; in Reading, because they are or were students at the university. There is also, much more so in Battersea, public housing – now part-privatized. Such areas are mixed in terms of social class and ethnicity. But most respondents felt that in its social dimensions the quality of life there was high. Perhaps this is because many people are young and have grown up in a multi-cultural environment. People know their neighbours and feel on good terms with them. Many have children, and make friends through them. Others have friends they made at university, through work or through a rich social life, quite often in the same locality. They have middle-class jobs, and reasonably high incomes; lifestyles are affluent, Sunday magazine style. That can make them vulnerable to crime, and some certainly feel it.

Turning first to Battersea, of course, not all residents shared in this lifestyle. For a few, as we mentioned, their personal circumstances shut them off from social interaction with their neighbours and their overall evaluation of their neighbourhood was coloured accordingly. Less extreme was the perception that what the locality offered them was diminishing:

> I'd love to be a yuppie! [laughs] I would! No, I don't have a problem with that at all, because it means that there's nice places to go out for a change . . . Lots of . . . places to eat. But I suppose it's getting expensive as well, so maybe that's why people are complaining.
> Single mother, unemployed, white, lives with father's family, council tenant

In Battersea, many working-class residents, who had been decanted from their council estates to make way for the newcomers, felt resentful that they and their children had been deprived of the chance to stay in their area. However, the council estates also showed rich social interaction. Many families have close ties reinforced by proximity. They offer a close support system. But many lack access to a car, and the bus service is not always convenient, so a couple of miles can seem a long way away:

> . . . when I lived in Brixton . . . my mum lived in Brixton, my sister lived in Brixton . . . My sister still lives in Brixton and my mum has moved to north London . . . so I feel even though it is only down the road Brixton, they are all really far away because they were all within quick walking distance. I have nobody to pick Craig up if he falls ill at school. Things like that have been really difficult.
>
> Widowed mother, employed, white, housing association tenant

In fact, it was obvious that these social aspects of neighbourhood life, while noted and appreciated by working class and gentrifiers alike, loomed far larger for the council tenants. For example, the council tenants had patterns of friendships and family links that were far more concentrated in and around their neighbourhoods, while the gentrifiers' networks spread far and wide. Despite such differences, generally, people in Battersea seem on good terms with their neighbours:

> Everybody's very friendly around here . . . If anything happens to anyone everyone's interested to know why, who, and what happened . . . The area in general, cos you're walking up the road and somebody'll just say, 'Hello, good morning, good afternoon'.
>
> Single mother, employed, Afro-Caribbean, council tenant

So although Battersea is divided by class, this does not seem to lead to trench warfare in its neighbourhoods. As we shall see, there are some neighbourhoods where 'race' and class create divisions and contribute to a less happy outcome. However, here, an increasingly culturally and racially heterogeneous area had evidently blunted some of the earlier divisions:

> What's the use of arguing over people who come in here and live with you all their lives yeah? . . . I mean I've got, my cousins are all black and I've got one, two, I can say I've got about three black friends. Most of the rest of them are white . . . Well most of my family were black people, all my brothers and sisters except one, two.
>
> Single mother, unemployed, council tenant.
> She is white and the children appear to be mixed race and white

However, there were some, especially the elderly, for whom 'race' was linked to a perception of neighbourhood decline, socially and in its facilities:

> There's only one doctor here that I go to, I've been going to him for years but they're all Indian now, there aren't any English and I object to going to the Post Office and finding all Indian and Indian music, I don't feel as if I'm in England . . . people are beginning to feel alienated and that they're not in their own country, they can't explain, get what they want or they can't understand what's going on and if they complain or say anything, then they're classed as racist or difficult people.
>
> Single mother, unemployed, white, homeless

There was some evidence more widely that integration was far from complete. Thus a young black woman complained that both blacks and whites segregate themselves, in pubs or in parks, and identify with one community or the other. But another argued that the real discrimination was by class and that nowadays was determined by lifestyle, therefore by income.

On security, the response was mixed. Some felt that crime was rife, partly because pockets of poverty persisted among the affluence, partly because of drugs. They talked about needles on stairwells, of drug-dealing on the estates. The arrival of new tenants on housing estates could trigger anything from noisy parties to a local crime wave, ruining the quality of people's lives overnight. But others felt perfectly safe for themselves and their children, probably because they knew the area and its people well; other places, they suggested, were far worse. In a few places, we found an informal and old-fashioned system of crime control, independent of the police: if someone caused trouble, 'the lads on the estate had a quiet word with him' (*Male cohabitee (father), employed, Afro-Caribbean, homeowner*).

The many enclaves of desirable housing in Battersea (as well as its location) were what attracted gentrification to the area. However, many council tenants also appreciated the good design of some estates, and how the council had improved them in recent years, especially the smaller ones with trees and open spaces. But other amenities were lacking. Some spoke of the lack of space, especially for children's play, and the effect that high housing density had on quality of life.

Despite their generally positive views about the quality of their neighbourhoods, for many one dimension was missing not just from here but from anywhere in London. Frequently both tenants and gentrifiers wanted to leave London for the country and sometimes for the coast. They wanted space, they wanted peace and quiet, for themselves and their families. The city by its very nature could not offer this.

Not surprisingly, given its location, the easy access to facilities and services was seen as a big advantage of their neighbourhood by many residents. Transport links were good too. Above all, here and elsewhere, people most frequently wanted some local 'convenience' stores and chemists, doctors, dentists and post offices, as well as easy access to one of the supermarket chains that suited their budgets and requirements:

> . . . you're in the middle of Battersea . . . there's shops, there's the trains . . . there's everything . . . you don't need to go to the city for anything. It's like the city itself . . . there's a park right across . . . I can see Battersea park . . . they've always got concerts.
>
> Single mother, employed, Afro-Caribbean, council tenant

> Well that's all right cos there's a Somerfield down there which is quite cheap and Asda's is only up at Clapham Junction, that's not too bad.
>
> Single mother, unemployed, white, council tenant

Views about the quality of local government services were remarkably positive, from a high proportion of council tenants as well as other residents. One did say 'Wandsworth Council is pretty good in some ways but they are for the rich and not for the poor' (*single mother, unemployed, white, council tenant*). However, this was an exception. Tenants appreciated the improvements in their estates and how they were managed and were positive about the basics like rubbish collection. Above all, people said that the area was improving and recognized that the council was a strong influence on that. This summed it up:

> Yeah. They're alright. I think, well they're OK for me anyway. I don't know if anybody says there're bad or whatever, but whenever I need something done they do good.
>
> Male cohabitee, self-employed, Jewish, homeowner

Our East Reading neighbourhood included New Town, a late nineteenth century artisan quarter, and some quiet middle-class streets close to the university campus. Many had stayed on there after leaving the university, especially because it was a convenient location to access jobs in London or the Thames Valley and, earlier, because the housing was cheap. This was no longer so and many reported that they were struggling financially, even while earning good salaries.

Many New Town residents appreciated its physical environment, its social life and its security:

> . . . it's near the University, it's relatively nicer aesthetically, and feels safer and has got a lot of people of my kind . . . living around.
>
> Single woman, employed, white, private tenant

However, as in many of our neighbourhoods, some aspects of the physical environment did not contribute to its quality – noise and traffic being regularly mentioned:

> . . . overall the area is not the most . . . exclusive area, there's a lot of noise, a lot of bad driving . . . people speed up and down the roads, they are narrow roads and double parked on some of them. The council put speed bumps in two years ago, and people just seem to accelerate over them . . . It's usually people in cars with . . . really loud bassy stereos on, that just come thumping down the road at two or three o'clock in the morning, and it can be quite annoying . . .
>
> Single woman, employed, white, private tenant

As in Battersea, but here partly because of influence of the university, the locality offered a rich social and cultural milieu. Many residents appreciated the area's ethnic mix; there was little of the resentment at this change that we found elsewhere:

> I really like it. I like the fact that it's multi-cultural, I like the fact that you step out of your door and there's just so many different people, I like the community, the local shops, I've actually got quite a lot of friends that live in this area and towards town as well. I like the fact that it's in walking distance to town.
>
> Single woman, employed, white, private tenant

The area also had good local facilities and the fact that it was only a short walk into the centre of Reading and to the new Oracle shopping centre and the leisure facilities, added to its high rating:

> . . . what I like about it is it's quite close to town. There's plenty of nice local pubs around the area; you've got the river just down the road . . . the Junction is quite good because you've got a lot of shops and . . . restaurants there . . . There's Palmer Park over the road.
>
> Married man, employed, white, homeowner

For most residents, the quality of council services was not a burning issue, though many complained about rubbish and litter. A few commented on the lack of neighbourhood policing but did not see this as a serious concern. On the whole, people felt positively about how the wider area had developed in recent years and, although some had reservations about what had been lost by central area redevelopment, the balance of opinion was favourable.

However, not all residents value equally what the neighbourhood offers. There was a more transient population for whom what it contributed to their quality of life was minimal. Many were young, upwardly mobile professional and managerial workers who worked long hours. We meet them again later in another part of Reading. Frequently they expressed no attachment to – or affection for – the area; they seemed rootless and many wanted to move farther away from London, generally to a town with more architectural or cultural character:

> I would be very happy to live in Oxford. London I wouldn't because I didn't like it at all, I think it's completely different from anywhere else in the country, and the people are strange and I don't feel safe there . . . I don't like the feel of the place, it's so dirty and crowded.
>
> Single woman, employed, white, private tenant

## Proletarian Islands Under Pressure: Bermondsey/Peckham

The second model is in important ways a variant of the first but in others is its diametric opposite. Here, a long-standing white working class, living in a homogeneous housing area with strong family and neighbouring networks, has experienced multi-dimensional change: the loss of traditional jobs in docks or factories, the arrival of newcomers to the public housing estates, the gentrification of working-class streets, and the loss of a tight sense of community. In Bermondsey especially, they desperately try to defend their turf against newcomers, whether these are decanted black and white tenants from neighbouring council estates in Peckham or asylum-seekers. They see rising crime everywhere and they seek to contest it, often by informal means ('The lads will have a word with you'). Their sense of intolerable crisis can reach very high levels on the most problematic estates, where different groups are brought together in layouts which provide little protection against crime or mayhem. These are among the unhappiest neighbourhoods in contemporary London: places where perceptions of the quality of neighbourhood life, especially by contrast to how it once was, are of the lowest.

Nearby, the gentrifiers have colonized certain enclaves, especially in Bankside, where the shopping, culture and entertainment they demand has also developed. Here, in sharp contrast, neighbourhood quality is highly rated and is linked to the availability of facilities that they value and the accessibility to those near by:

> *I love it here. I love getting up and going down for a coffee at the shop and getting the freshly baked bread cause there is a bakery here . . . the All Bar One has made a big difference. You can go round there for a drink, it's a proper bar. I love being near the water . . . coming into all the lovely restaurants . . . and the little shops for gifts . . . and there is always taxis round here . . .*
>
> Single woman, employed, white, private tenant

> *. . . being in the centre of London means you're not far away if you want to go and bungee jump, you can go down to Chelsea Bridge, which is about twenty minutes away, and throw yourself off a crane. If you want to go and blast someone away with a laser gun . . . you can do that at Piccadilly Circus . . . pubs, clubs, everything else, cinemas, pretty much anything you want to do you can get to within half an hour . . .*
>
> Single man, employed, white, private tenant

Meanwhile the white working-class residents here and nearby in Bermondsey are doubly frustrated and very angry: on the one hand housing is disappearing to the gentrifiers, on the other hand they resent the remaining council property going to 'outsiders', especially non-white ones. In Bermondsey such pressures conflict with a very strong sense of locality and community and have provoked an acute reaction.

> *Bermondsey is very close knit because of the old docks and you find people who have been here for years and then they have their children, and their children you find living in the same block and people round the corner marrying each other that sort of thing. So they resent anybody coming in and if you are black it is worse . . .*
>
> Local authority housing officer

Especially for people who spend a lot of time in the area or have a long- term attachment to it, the sense of community is very real. So older people seemed to complain the most bitterly about the loss of it:

> *Well it's like a little village really, you know, everybody comes from Bermondsey, born here, their mums and dads come from here, their grandfathers come from here, so they're all close-knit and you could leave your door open, well I mean you can't do that now because of the way society's changed anyway. So it's really closed in the community, where everyone was more friendly and they're not quite so friendly as they used to be.*
>
> Married parents, employed, white, housing association tenants

The tenants' perceptions of local services and amenities were dominated by their scathing views of their council landlord. Here too references to newcomers linked to 'race' were frequent:

> *The Council are not building any new property, they're getting rid of all their property . . . So you've got a brand new place like this and there's hundreds and hundreds of new houses being built and there's people, can't speak a word of English, and these people are still stuck up in the tower block or some really old block of flats round on Manchester Road or*

*something . . . it makes them resentful, you can't blame them. You can't say 'Oh yeah we're giving them because they deserve' . . . they don't deserve it, they've only just arrived in the country.*

Married parents, employed, white, housing association tenants

They were also extremely sensitive to perceived slights by black officials, especially if they found themselves in a dependent position. Many tenants' perceptions of neighbourhood were dominated by fear of change that they could not control. People were terrified that they would find themselves with bad neighbours, or that people would move out without anybody knowing. As a member of a focus group put it, 'as long as they get the rent they don't care what goes in there'.

Especially, this happened on housing estates where letting policies had changed, bringing in younger people to estates that had previously been reserved for old people, bringing a clash of lifestyles.

*Nine o'clock you said that party was going to be over. I must have looked a right state I 'ad no teeth in my 'ead I had my nightgown on running up and down the stairs telling them to be quiet . . . Anyway they went through a stage slamming and banging the doors. Coming in and everything they dropped you could hear . . . thinks she can do just as she pleases and she mustn't be told. I said it to her in a nice way. And if I say anything, I'm racist. And when that kiddie runs across its as if she's got hob nailed boots on. They must be out at the moment I wish she was in so you could hear it. But I'm not allowed to say anything and its wrong . . . Nothing about when he was nearly murdering her upstairs and she was screaming and shouting and hollering. But that's what you got to live with.*

Married mother, retired, white, council tenant

The feeling that they lived in insecure areas was pervasive. Again, frequently there was a racial divide: whites reported problems with noise and mayhem, blacks reported abuse and harassment. The poor physical environment added to their low perceptions of the locality. A recurrent theme, already noted in Battersea but intensified, particularly in Peckham by the scale of rebuilding and relocation, was a lack of space. This directly affected quality of life, causing individuals to feel claustrophobic, trapped, or cramped. Density also had an impact on many of their other complaints. Limited space amplified the noisiness of a neighbours' music or their playing children, increased the possibility of a football going through a window, the likelihood of children being naughty and the problems of parked cars. It also meant that uncollected rubbish and dog mess were more likely to cause offence.

Unsurprisingly, all but the gentrifying minority frequently wished to move out. Many think the area is going downhill: they fear crime and the impact of conditions on their children and this is frequently seen as a consequence of its changing ethnic composition:

*If you'd asked him five years ago he would have said no wouldn't you? . . . they could take me out of here in a box, but not any more. I've seen too much happen round here . . . We're more worried about the children and the crime and what they can get into, this is the problem.*

Married parents, employed, white, housing association tenants

*What's happened to all the white families is there is a lot of people moving out just because they don't like the blacks.*

                                        Married parents, self-employed, white, council tenants

Although the problems of high-density living were, as already mentioned, present in Peckham too, there was a rather less negative picture of the locality painted by many whom we spoke to there. The familiar combination of sociability, facilities and location was mentioned and here there were at least some who valued the area's ethnic and cultural mix. The following sentiments are not uncommon here, from white and non-white respondents, but never heard by us in Bermondsey:

*Oh, I love Peckham as an area, it's quite a vibrant area, there is lots of facilities, there's a cultural mix of people, black, white . . . it's a nice little area it is, near to the West End and all the other places . . . it's easy to get to.*

                                        Married father, employed, black British, council tenant

However, the council tenants were no more complimentary about council services than their Bermondsey counterparts. They were angry about the lack of environmental maintenance and about housing management failures, especially in relation to vandalism and problem tenants. As in Bermondsey, there was an acute sense that this led to decline in the quality of their neighbourhood and of their lives. The withdrawal of on-the-ground policing from many areas was a part of this change. The loss or deterioration of nearby public facilities such as swimming pools, libraries and parks contributed to the impression of a council whose focus was more on strategic redevelopment than on the quality provision of the basic, neighbourhood level services.

Yet there were some pluses. As in Battersea, new developments in the wider area had bought some welcome changes. While the neighbourhood shopping centres had declined, many mentioned that they now shopped at the large supermarket at the Surrey Quays development and used its leisure facilities. The dense network of bus routes in the area made this accessible. Perhaps the most frequently expressed need was for better provision for children and young people at the neighbourhood level. Finally, while crime and personal security were still a great concern for many, some felt that an improvement had recently occurred, especially in Peckham. However, the link between drugs and crime was mentioned frequently:

*Like everywhere else you do get the crime, but not so much on the ground here now, you do get drugs, people get mugged, but I guess it is just a reflection on South London in general or even the whole country. It's just that it happens . . . although I haven't witnessed much . . .*

                                        Married father, employed, black British, council tenant

## An Area of 'Potential': Upton Park

This part of Newham has a location and transport links that provide it with considerable advantages. Its history means that it still has a good deal of housing which is relatively inexpensive. So, in the language of the estate agents, it is an area with 'great potential'. This has resulted in an influx of white and minority households who, because of their stage in the lifecycle or longer-term level of earnings, are towards the bottom end of the home owner market:

> . . . we were living in a Council property before, and then we wanted to buy our own property and we just found out that it was much cheaper in Newham than Hackney . . . because I work in Hackney and the kids were at school in Hackney, so it was convenient.
>
> Married parents, both employed, African, homeowner

This might be described as a form of gentrification, but it is a world apart from the classic, high-earning professional colonization of more desirable areas such as Battersea and Bankside. Nor does it seem likely to become such, as its physical environment, facilities and infrastructure still bear the heavy imprint of its working-class history. The area had thus become mixed socially and ethnically. What the neighbourhoods offered socially was valued. This could be because certain kinds of people – young, more outgoing and sociable and less fixed in their lifestyles – tend to settle in such areas:

> Everyone's quite nice I think, there's a good mix, it's very racially mixed it's quite cosmopolitan . . . the majority of people round here are black but that includes black West Indian, black African, black Other . . . Newham in general is very mixed.
>
> Single woman, employed, Asian, private tenant

Older residents could find, as in Bermondsey, that a traditional sense of community was eroding. But the loss seemed to be much less catastrophic.

However, other parts are becoming increasingly Bangladeshi and these locales are evolving their own distinctive quality of life:

> Ninety per cent of this people live on this street are Muslim . . . He met me in the launderette and he said to me: 'If you're selling your house, sell it to me' . . . 'I don't even wanna come and have a look at it, I just buy it' . . . 'cos it's near to the, his brother is the owner for the laundry, so he want to live near to his brother . . . on top of the launderette, and it's near to the mosque. That's why most of them buy houses on the street.
>
> Married father, retired, Afro-Caribbean, homeowner

In such areas, some reported a sense of anonymity and that there was little or no social dimension to neighbourhood life. Here and elsewhere, such feelings were also prevalent in areas with much private rented housing where tenants came and went rapidly:

> I think it's cos a lot of people rent as well so . . . people just come in from all over the place . . . People like living near others of a similar ethnic identity to themselves, leading to concentrations of people from particular groups . . . Well, it's all right, you know, because . . . most of the neighbours, my next door neighbour, she's English, and my next door neighbour is . . . Indian, so everybody kind a keep themself to themself, they don't really, you know well, they will say hello . . . if we see them outside I say hello, we have a talk and that sort of thing . . .
>
> Married father, retired, Afro-Caribbean, homeowner

Perceptions of neighbourhood security fell somewhere between those commonly expressed in the two previous case studies. However, most people said that crime was widespread and in some respects (e.g. car crime) getting worse. Several spoke of a past sense of calm and security, recently lost:

> *It's getting worse – this particular road was very quiet, very safe when I came here not so long ago, just 11 years, and there've been a few burglaries on this road in the last year, cars have been stolen – our car got stolen . . . I'd be quite scared to go down to the petrol station at night, after dark.*
>
> Married mother, employed, Indian, lives with in-laws, owner occupiers

Some suggested that their immediate area was safe, but that Stratford centre was dangerous.

> *I wouldn't say it's safe because where I work at the job centre I know there's a lot of nutters that live in Stratford, there's a lot of mad people around in Stratford but you know around here you do feel a bit safe.*
>
> Single woman, employed, Asian, private tenant

However, as in Peckham, the impression we gained was that high crime was seen as an almost inevitable consequence of living in Inner London, another fact of life to be coped with.

Racism, as ever, was present but as in Battersea it was much less dominant and aggressively expressed in our interviews here than in those in Bermondsey:

> *Not really – other things are basically all right. When we first come back to this country we were in East Ham where there was a bit of racism, so we had to move to Camden Road.*
>
> Married father, unemployed, Asian, private tenant

For some in the Asian community feelings about their neighbourhood are affected by the anxiety of an older generation having to come to terms with the very different mores of the host community which their own children were adopting.

As elsewhere, traffic and parking, especially that generated by non-residents, seriously affected neighbourhood quality and people wanted cleaner streets and public areas. Stratford is a major public transport interchange (train, underground, bus and taxi) and the excellent access that this provided to work, shopping and entertainment is a key advantage. Many felt that Stratford town centre itself, though improving, did not offer more than the basics. Those who wished for something different, including minority ethnic residents who needed specialist food and other stores, had to travel out of the area but this was relatively easy for most of them. The continuing lack of neighbourhood and local facilities, especially for children and young people, was often mentioned and the council's poor provision was criticized. The absence of cinemas, good places to eat, gyms and 'places to go out to' sets Stratford apart from Battersea or Bankside.


## The Suburb Challenged: Eltham, Heston

The fourth archetype is a variant on the second, though very different in appearance:

it is a long-stable neighbourhood, which has recently had to face changes and challenges – including the arrival of new ethnic and cultural groups, coupled with the ageing of the built environment and infrastructure. Many interwar London suburbs, which were predominantly white upper working- and middle-class, are now being settled by groups who are following the traditional path out of the inner city, seeking more space, a better suburban environment and better schools for their children. Frequently, this transition is regretted rather than contested, perhaps because the existing community has faced less traumatic changes elsewhere in its life and is less in competition with the newcomers for a wide range of resources, especially those provided by the public sector. But problems can arise when successive waves of movement overlap and come into conflict, for example when middle-class white and recently migrant minority ethnic groups come under challenge from further newcomers whom they perceive as threatening to local social relationships and standards in the schools.

In Eltham, despite its reputation as a racist area following the Stephen Lawrence murder, the transition seemed less fraught than in Heston. Much of it remains a stable and coherent community, settled by people – many from inner-city locations like Bermondsey – who had moved from their parents' homes a short distance down the railway line. Good transport links back to the family were important to enable mutual support to be maintained:

> I originally come from the Elephant & Castle and Nick from Deptford, so our parents are still in that area, so we wanted to move out but we wanted to be close enough to get to them you know.
>
> Married woman, employed, white, homeowner

Some of the new white and minority ethnic households had come seeking better schools for their children. They also valued the physical environment:

> I know the areas around this area. I know Charlton's more expensive, Greenwich is more expensive. I know what Lewisham's like . . . this outer part of Greenwich has got a lot of greenery attached to it . . . I used to live in New Cross for 7–8 years and I wouldn't want to go back there either, because it's too cramped, there's no open spaces for children . . . It's just the road noise.
>
> Divorced mother living with partner, employed, white, homeowner

However, though many people appreciated such assets, the area's location also had a negative effect on the quality of life because of the length, cost and strain of the daily commute to work in the inner city. The poor commuter train service was a very frequent complaint here and in the other suburban and ex-urban locales that we visited:

> For the last five months, it has been absolutely disgraceful . . . normal train home has been cancelled because there's been a landslide at the Strood Tunnel. They've cancelled my train for, I think it's eight weeks out of the last twelve . . . We buy season tickets. I pay over £700 and most mornings you can't get a seat. It's stressful [but] I just couldn't earn the same money locally.
>
> Married woman, employed, white, homeowner

Overall, many residents had a sense that they 'fitted in' to their area and felt psychologically comfortable there. This was equally true of older white and minority ethnic people:

*First of all it's security. You like to know where you are. Again the idea of fitting in. And also just like to feel part of the place, so you like to be recognized and you know say hello . . .*
                                   Divorced mother living with partner, employed, white, homeowner

Yet not all parts of the area provided this quality of life, again especially in the case of some of the council estates. Here the lack of security is paramount and in sharp contrast to other nearby areas – this tenant describes a virtual state of siege:

*. . . well, we think it's going down . . . you are getting groups of youths . . . they're sort of roaming about and creating a nuisance more than anything, but . . . the effect is that you have to be on your guard all the time . . . before we move to that front door, I mean we've got a wide view here across everything. If you see them wandering about you won't go out . . . we don't go on long holidays . . . we have a paper delivered. I'm thinking I'll cancel that paper . . . once you cancel the paper people know you are away . . . on my bottom fence now I've got carpet gripper. I don't know if I'm breaking the law or not . . . If any one grabs the fence they've had it now.*
                                                   Married man, employed, white, homeowner

Often, this seemed to be general hell-raising, resulting from boredom as much as anything. But there were also older children engaged in more systematic crime, in particular drug dealing which could lead to threats and violence. As elsewhere, 'race' played a part in these conflicts and the Stephen Lawrence murder has given Eltham a reputation as a racist area – a reputation which many residents wished to deny. Interestingly, however, one respondent suggested that racism had been imported by those who had moved out from Bermondsey and the Docklands, and was rooted in their belief that much of the new public housing in these inner areas had been allocated to incoming blacks rather than the white sons and daughters of the locals.

But in other areas there was a very different picture:

*No problems at all. We like it here. The neighbours are wonderful and I've never seen any trouble. I accept that there has been trouble, but nothing that I've ever seen.*
                                                   Married man, employed, white, homeowner

Here, we found in operation the system of neighbourly reciprocity that seems to characterize the stable and well-integrated neighbourhood:

*. . . if Ken goes away on holiday or something, I'll have a little look to make sure that papers are gone and all that. Those sort of things. But they're just neighbourly things aren't they.*
                                                   Married man, employed, white, homeowner

As in most areas, noise, pollution, traffic and parking worsened the local environment. However, especially for those near Greenwich Park, the open space and sports facilities were appreciated. Eltham town centre was a place to shop and not much more, however. Most of these suburban households owned a car, so they were less dependent on the quality and range of services and provision in their immediate neighbourhoods and on effective public transport (except for the commute to work) than were many inner-city households. Many were also less dependent on council provided facilities and services and there was none of the bitterly critical responses that we heard, for example, in Southwark.

Like Eltham, Heston has its troubles. Many people from different ethnic and cultural groups said they wanted to move out because it was going downhill and they wanted urgently to realize the equity on their houses. Some who remain saw this as a sign of failure:

> Well, they all moved away cos Hounslow, everyone laughs about it, you know if you're still in Hounslow they think you're either mad or as bad as the ones who live here, all my friends moved away years ago.
>
> Married mother, employed, white, homeowner

> . . . a lot of the changes I've seen I don't like . . . I've been contemplating moving out, 5, 6, 7 years, and every time I've gone to move there's something come up that's blocked it like, kids at school, going to a new school, changing schools and so I've waited till they're . . . finished school, and then I'm sure I'll move out . . .
>
> Married father, employed, white, homeowner

The most commonly cited reason for the exodus is the arrival of asylum seekers. It affects whites and Indians alike, who until now have lived together in a stable, sociable and secure community with an acceptable quality of life. Compare these responses:

> It's predominantly Asian, as opposed to Afro-Caribbean and Asian, they're very family orientated, they are very respectful within their families and I think that rubs off on the general area itself. So we don't really get . . . violence or anything and then, there's a lot of white people who have obviously lived here for about 50 years, a lot of old white people and so really the mix is quite good.
>
> Female cohabitee, mother, employed, white, private tenant

> Everyone wants to move from here now . . . the Asian people like us, I live here 25 years and sometimes we are thinking . . . we should move from here now, it's not a safe area now . . . we go where there are not many refugee people there.
>
> Married mother, part-time employed, Indian, homeowner

The asylum-seekers are frequently blamed for rising crime and for some the impact on their quality of life is extreme:

> It's intimidating there, you get the feeling that you're not safe, I can't explain it, there were a lot of beggars there last year especially, well, we had them knock on our door, you know I think it's scary there, when I see bullet proof glass and everyone's got a video camera on them and things like that, I don't wanna be anywhere like that, scares me a lot.
>
> Married mother, employed, white, homeowner

But perceptions as to who the villains are do vary; some, for example, mentioned Irish travellers as the worst offenders.

As elsewhere, there was anxiety about the impact of all of this on children. Here is an Indian mother whose son's computer was stolen:

> . . . it's not good impression for the children. We understand it's not good future if you're stealing the things but children, they think it's easy . . . My, my son, he work hard in holiday time and collect some money for the computer and later they come . . . they took the computer away and everything is gone. He is a younger brain, he think that's easy way to earn the money . . .
>
> Married mother, part-time employed, Indian, homeowner

One of the main complaints was the poor quality of local schools. Here too, much was laid at the door of the new arrivals. It was a potent reason for choosing the exit option:

> Coming and going because of schools. Yeah, the lady that I bought this house from had only lived here about 4 years before she moved and it was because of schools . . . we were talking to the next door neighbours and she goes 'the people before that, in this house, have only stayed for a while'. And all of them are moving out for schools . . .
>
> Married mother, part-time employed, Egyptian parents, homeowner

Aspects of the physical environment were another minus, especially noise and pollution. Here is a Sikh respondent, whose parents are leaving:

> . . . cos of the main road, airport, it's quite polluted and dirty, isn't it. It's a nice area for other reasons, you know, to get into London and things like that, but it's just . . . it is really polluted.
>
> Single woman, employed, Sikh, living at home

In reality, the picture in Heston is extremely complex; there is an almost bewildering range of different ethnic and cultural mixes in different enclaves, the result of the locality's role as a receiving area for new arrivals, adjacent to Heathrow. And the quality of neighbourhood life was equally varied; some areas were deteriorating, others were holding their own. Compare the following:

> Along here . . . you'll probably see mainly Asians, but down the road, it's really close . . . there's an estate and . . . it's quite rough…it's mainly a mixture . . .
>
> Male teenager, at school, Asian, tenure not stated

> Hounslow as a place for residence is not bad at all . . . some pockets are equally as good as . . . any place in London. Peaceful, nice . . . spacious.
>
> Married father, retired, Asian, homeowner

Apart from the local schooling, views about the performance of the local council were not particularly negative. The town centre shopping and leisure facilities were better than those available to Upton Park residents and, like the latter, the Heston residents benefited from good access to central London.

## The Arcadian Suburb under Shadow: Gants Hill

In the fifth archetype, at least in legend and in fiction, nothing much happens. For much of the last century these areas – semi-detached London and its predecessor, the *'Diary of a Nobody'* rows of late Victorian and Edwardian villas – were inhabited by the white English middle class, in its various stations and degrees, living comfortable lives. They remain rather homogeneous in class terms though less white than before. Families keep themselves to themselves. Some have close family ties; others do not. Yet they like to feel neighbourly and to live alongside like-minded people, but there are well-defined limits to these relationships. They may have local friends, especially if their children are at school here; often, however, their friends have moved away. Most live in streets where they do not feel threatened, either by new groups who might disturb their peace, or by threats of crime. The physical environment and local facilities such as schools and shops make an important contribution to their quality of life.

However, even in some of these places people sense the shadow of change and its effects on those aspects of the locality that they value. In Heston that shadow has lengthened and deepened, so many are now leaving or trying to leave. In others, doubts are just emerging. The perceived threat comes from the physical decay of the area, accompanied by a decline in the quality of its basic facilities, and the arrival of new residents who do not fit in and are seen as compromising the quality of the schools and of social relations.

Gants Hill is such an area. Like Heston, its ethnic mix had changed but not in a disruptive way. Its original Jewish and other white inhabitants, many of whose families moved here from the East End in the 1920s and 1930s when the area was newly-built, were later succeeded by a wave of arrivals from the Indian subcontinent, now in the second or third generation, whose families also started in East End slums but who moved to gain a better quality of life. These groups live the same kinds of family-oriented lives as those who came before them. Many referred to the quiet, the suburban quality and the good schools which had drawn them here and which they cherished. Some linked being here to a move up the social ladder:

> *Quiet, tree-lined, nice style houses – these houses are Smith built and they're nice style houses, near the park . . . where we previously lived wasn't as quiet as this is. It's just like a step upwards, that's what it really was.*
>
> Married mother, part-time employed, Jewish, homeowner

For many, the quality of local schools was critical. They made specific comparisons with the schools in other boroughs, which they perceived to be inner-city in character and so inferior. As we shall see, this concern was also central to some people's perceptions of incipient neighbourhood decline.

Overall, many Gants Hill residents still seemed content and, although as elsewhere some wanted to move out, this was less urgently expressed, being something that might occur 'when the children are grown up' or 'when we retire'. But there were intimations of change, with some worrying about the future of their neighbourhood. One concern, expressed mainly by older residents, was their sense of a physical decline in their area. More than once they told us the story, which attained national fame, of Gants Hill's disappearing shopping centre:

> *I mean years ago Gants Hill was the local – where all the shops were, but now it's changed – now it's dead and it's all gone into Barkingside High Street – that's the area to go.*
>
> Married mother, part-time employed, Jewish, homeowner

Concern about the social changes occurring as a result of new waves of migrants in some parts of the area was also expressed by the upwardly mobile now-established Asian residents as well as by their longer established white counterparts:

> *It's quiet, it is nice area but you're getting a lot of Asian people, Tamil people mainly moving into this area . . . I wouldn't like it to be like a ghetto . . . so far it's alright but, I don't like East London that's just a ghetto . . .*
>
> Married mother, Bangladeshi, homeowner

Some of the tensions were illustrated by this black British professional woman who lived with her white husband in an owner-occupied house, and who felt forced to move out because of noisy neighbours:

> *I think maybe it's because it's a very large extended family when I came here it wasn't so extended and now it's so extended and it's very noisy . . . people live the way they want to live, fine – but there must be consideration for the change of culture, you know – the houses are very close to each other, it's a very small home . . . so many people in it – I can't get the peace . . . it's just impossible to work.*
>
> Married mother, employed, Afro-Caribbean, homeowner

This British Asian described a growing sense of insecurity. She felt safe within the immediate neighbourhood but unsafe further from home – and would not allow her children out:

> *I think it's not fair. Yes, if older one come late, I get worried, and little children they can't play outside, I think, and they don't mix with neighbours, because I don't let them – allow go out.*
>
> Married mother, employed, Asian, homeowner

All this, according to a long-time older resident, represented a sharp decline in the area's quality of life:

> *There are gangs of youths . . . been vandalizing the buses . . . in the evenings the buses won't come down from Hainault – they've diverted down the road as there was so much vandalism.*
> That's not something that used to happen is it?
> *Oh good heavens – well, I was telling you that you could leave the baby in the pram outside.*
>
> Married father, retired, Jewish, homeowner

However, compared with some of the locales we have so far described, the experience of one white resident who did not know of anybody locally who had been burgled or experienced car crime was common; she thought her neighbourhood a low crime area. And the link that we have noted elsewhere between lack of crime, 'peace' and a sense of security was clearly expressed by another resident:

*I have found this is peaceful . . . I feel safer than other areas, I don't know why, maybe I live in this area, I feel more confidence about the area.*

Married mother, employed, Asian, homeowner

Education was a critical point of anxiety, as we mentioned above. Asians were as worried as whites about the implications of neighbourhood social change. Some concerned whites expressed their worry in racist terms:

*I actually know a teacher that teaches there she said don't let Daniel go there [laughter] and * * * * had so many Indians . . . and I mean let's be honest we are white, I want him with the majority of [people like ourselves] . . .*

Married mother, employed, white, homeowner

Compare this with a more class based form of the wish to avoid certain schools expressed by a British Asian of Bangladeshi origin:

*. . . you get too many Bangladeshi children going there it's like a ghetto . . . Here there are a lot of Asian children, lot of Tamil and Indian and Gujaratis you know varieties but they're more from professional classes so they have an incentive to do well, whereas some of those children their parents are not educated and they're not from professional classes they don't really want to work as well, you don't get that incentive from home for them to do well because they've got different ideology as well.*

Married mother, Bangladeshi, homeowner

We have already mentioned the loss of local shopping as one element in a perceived decline in the quality of the neighbourhood. Here car ownership and the Central Line underground helped – many mentioned the need to travel to Ilford (especially for the needs of minority ethnic households), Romford or the Lakeside Centre by the Dartford river crossing. But suburban bus routes are less dense and services less frequent so the lack of accessibility for those without a car was a problem. The most highly valued amenities were the parks and open spaces and their sports facilities. This added a dimension to neighbourhood quality that could not be rivalled closer to the centre of the city and it was a major factor in attracting newcomers to the area.

In home owner suburbs like Gants Hill, people expect the council to provide the 'basics' – public services such as libraries and rubbish collection – to a good standard and at a reasonable cost in terms of local taxation. There is none of the extended and multi-faceted dependence on the council for key aspects of quality of life, including the quality of the locality itself, that is true for the public sector tenant and others in rented housing. In a sense, in Gants Hill the residents were customers of the local authority; in these other areas they were its clients. Because of these less exacting standards most residents felt that the council was doing an adequate job and appreciated its efforts – for example, to keep the streets clean and to promote recycling which helped to maintain the quality of the environment.

### The Dynamic Edge Suburb: Dartford, Earley

The final archetype is best represented by large-scale development outside London, though some similarities might be found in the Docklands developments. It is characterized by very rapid physical change: new housing, new roads and new shopping centres. These are not edge cities proper on the American model (though Dartford may become one with the Thames Gateway developments) – so we have coined the term 'edge suburbs' for them. Here change engulfs smaller settlements and some feel a sense of loss. Disruption, noise, congestion and pollution arise where none previously existed, and there are crowded roads and schools. Many feel that their physical quality of life falls short in some respects of what it ought to be. However, for some their neighbourhood does not add much to the quality of social life because participation is minimized by lack of time, the stress arising from the need to earn two incomes to survive economically, and from the need to juggle the demands of work, commuting and child care. Socially, there can be a sense of impermanence and anonymity: people report that their neighbours change rapidly; they barely know who lives next door. Although a surprising number have older family members nearby, others lack the support of either relatives or neighbours. However, these complaints are relative and there are some compensations.

People living in Dartford, like those in older suburbs, have often moved out from London or from closer by seeking more space, and more peace, at a price they can afford. Many respondents were seeking Arcadian calm. Yet earlier settlers now complained about its loss and wanted to move further out but were constrained by the resulting commute, by family or school ties and by housing costs in better locations. However, this is more typical:

> I mean I like the area, but it wasn't . . . well there's nothing there. There was factories over the road . . . they've pulled them down now to make a Sainsbury's. So, it was just basically, I'd liked the look of the houses and it looked nice and quiet and that was the reason.
>
> Married man, self-employed, white, homeowner

Some valued the location's accessibility to the national motorway system:

> . . . we're handy for the Tunnel, for the motorways, going up to London, that was one of the reasons we chose this area.
>
> Married mother, employed, white, homeowner

However, this location also contributed to a poor quality of life for others, due to the strain and unreliability of their daily commute:

> On a good day, when the wind's in the right direction, I can do it door to door in an hour and twenty minutes. But it can be anything. The worst journey I've ever had, is leaving work at 5 o'clock . . . and walking in here at 10 to 10 in the evening. It's so wearing . . . you're fit for nothing at the end of the week, which is why I don't bother too much about the social side and why peace means a lot to me . . . we've not really got involved in clubs and things like that. In a way, it's a shame. Because it's a sort of a dormitory place for me. Because of working up in London . . . but I know I would only earn half the money, if that, locally.
>
> Married mother, employed, white, homeowner

But local social networks were significant for some, especially those who had only moved a relatively short distance into the area:

> *I'd have to keep within a radius of where my daughters were because I rely on them a lot . . . I see them every week. I saw Mandy yesterday and I saw her a couple of days ago but Tracy I see Fridays if I'm lucky, but Tracy works full time and Tony works full time . . .*
>
> Widowed mother, retired, white, homeowner

And the lack of neighbourhood life and social interaction, even from those who mentioned this, should not be overestimated. Overall, most people liked life here, not only because of the environmental quality but because they lived in a pleasant neighbourhood with decent neighbours, even if they did not really know them:

> *So, it's a nice atmosphere and it's always been that . . . here, you just say good morning and if you wanted anything, you know that they'd be there to help you . . . It's a good environment in that respect.*
>
> Married man, self-employed, white, homeowner

One aspect of this decency was the security that most people felt in the area where they lived. It was the foundation for a kind of informal social control, which helped create a generally crime-free atmosphere. Though some expressed apprehension about rising crime rates generally, even they admitted that they did not sense it here:

> *I wouldn't be overly struck on my wife walking about late at night on her own, but I'd say if she had to I'd think this would a good enough area as any to do that.*
>
> Married man, employed, white, homeowner

> *We've got quite a little cul-de-sac and everybody watches everybody out the lace curtains. It's not an area that attracts crime.*
>
> Divorced mother, employed, white, private tenant

They would compare this area favourably to others they know, often in the inner city, in this case one that we have discussed:

> *I'm not frightened to go out. Whereas I would be if I lived in London. I come from Bermondsey originally . . . If I lived there now, I wouldn't step outside my door after 5 o'clock.*
>
> Married mother, part-time employed, white, homeowner

However, for many of the elderly neighbourhood change had reduced their quality of life:

> *Well if I went down into the pier, the heart of the village, the old pub, there has got to be somebody in there that knows me . . . [but] we don't even know who they are. Where they come from . . . They live their own little lives. They're all new people. They are people that are in new houses, you know?*
>
> Divorced mother, employed, white, private tenant

Many of the old shops and facilities had gone. This was also regretted and seen as a symptom of decline. Such people saw the opening of the Bluewater shopping and entertainment centre entirely negatively, at complete variance with many more who appreciated a massive improvement in the locality's facilities, although regret at the impact of the traffic coming from new developments was widespread. And other places were easily accessible by car; one mentioned 'hopping over' the Dartford crossing to buy fresh produce in Essex farm shops. For those dependent on public transport however, some locations could be problematic. And the cost of bus travel was heavily criticized. For many, even more than in Gants Hill, rather little was expected of the council and there were few complaints.

We found the same sense of change, of mobility, and for some the perception that of growth had damaged the quality of life, in Earley which included an enormous 1970s private housing estate:

> . . . it's grown, no-one seems to be able to stop it . . . we moved to Lower Earley because there was houses available and we wanted to move quickly . . . we had a dog we could walk miles around here, but now there isn't anywhere.
>
> Married mother, employed, white, homeowner

For some, as elsewhere, the neighbourhood contributed little socially. Mobility and other sources of change are blamed:

> In terms of the neighbours, would you know the people either side?
> Sort of either side and probably just to say hello across the road because if someone lives with a two bedroomed house, usually after two years they move on . . . Probably they move to another area, [or] to a bigger house or we seem to have a lot of young couples who are not married and then suddenly they split up and that's it then, yeah that's probably why.
>
> Married mother, employed, white, homeowner

However, as in Dartford, this lack of neighbourhood sociability can be overemphasized. And here, for a new suburban neighbourhood, and in sharp contrast to Dartford, the area was extraordinarily cosmopolitan, because of the close location of the university, the European Medium-Range Weather Forecasting Centre, and major IT multinationals:

> Very cosmopolitan – Japanese, Chinese, Canadians down here, my neighbour is Indian or Pakistani, there's Italians, French.
>
> Married mother, employed, white, homeowner

Unsurprisingly, given this professional element, the quality of the schools was an important and attractive feature of the locality. And some other aspects of the locale contributed to perceptions of a good quality of neighbourhood life. Partly this was based on the camaraderie that usually exists in newly-built residential areas, especially through the children:

> Oh this street's brilliant [though] it's not quite as good as it used to be . . . about 3 or 4 years ago we knew all the neighbours like the neighbours next door were here when we moved in . . . we've been here best part of 10 years. And it's great. It's one of those streets that if you need something you can always go and knock on somebody's door, it's very close knit.
>
> Married father, employed, white, homeowner

However, as in Dartford, the commuters suffered greatly from their location:

*. . . all come back in suits between 7 and 8 . . . I always thought working in London would be really exciting – but it's a pain in the arse! Today on the tube it was so hot and there were so many people. Even in the morning it's hot. You get into work and feel exhausted.*

Married father, employed, white, homeowner

But people felt secure in Earley and compared its situation favourably to that of other areas of Reading. However, although there were some local facilities – a supermarket, petrol station and swimming pool – the quality of life for many was heavily dependent on car ownership, for the journey to work, schools, shops and entertainment. Yet they were also aware that the growing volume of traffic was damaging the quality of their area. It also led to changes that were serious for those without a car, especially the elderly and disabled:

*There was a little parade of shops which, when the estate was built, catered to every need. It was before the days when people had cars, it was before there were supermarkets everywhere. The result now of that is that we have lost our butcher, our greengrocer, our baker . . . when my husband was alive we went to Tesco by car . . . [now] it means two bus journeys . . . there used to be from town three buses an hour which this week was changed to two buses an hour which didn't come today so it took me three hours of waiting before I even did any shopping.*

Widowed stepmother, retired, Australian, homeowner

During our research the poor quality bus service was a burning topic in Reading. However, most people thought that the town centre shopping and leisure facilities were improving considerably, recognized that these could not be supported in a suburban location and were able to drive to them. Also they had access in the other direction to the countryside.

As in other suburbs, Wokingham District Council was expected to supply basic services and there were few complaints about these. A successful campaign for a swimming pool and other responses to resident needs was thought by one respondent to be due to the Liberal Democrat control of the council and the attention that the party paid to the locality.

## Generalities and Commonalities: Dimensions of Neighbourhood Life

Many accounts of London's neighbourhoods divide over-sharply and exaggeratedly into the dystopian and the utopian. Confusingly, the same places may appear under both classifications – the arcadian versus the soulless suburb or the cheery working-class community versus the 'dreadful enclosure'. The reality neither fits the hopes of some nor the worst fears of others.

Earlier we identified four main dimensions to what neighbourhoods contribute to quality of life, based on survey research. These are: sociability, security, facilities and accessibility, and the physical environment. Our interviews confirmed this. However, how these dimensions combined to inform the judgements of our residents was highly variable.

First, what people ask of their neighbourhood socially differs immensely. Compare, for example, the low-income Bermondsey council tenant where local social networks are the cornerstone of getting by in a hostile world (especially for the elderly) with the professional, middle-class residents nearby or the hard pressed young salariat in Earley or Dartford. For many in the latter groups the good neighbourhood is one where other people are 'decent', will 'look out' for one and 'pass the time of day' but no closer link is required. And some areas contain both situations.

There is a more universal wish to live in a secure neighbourhood. Despite the publicity that rising crime and disorder gets and the high concerns expressed about it in surveys of Londoners as a whole (Greater London Authority, 2001) we found that there are areas, including enclaves of the inner city, where people still feel relatively secure. Surprisingly large numbers here – while expressing fear of crime – had not actually experienced much. However, crime and disorder was endemic in some neighbourhoods and could all but destroy any quality of life there. The insecurity expressed by many council tenants was frequently acute and in many more areas crime was an everyday fact of life, if at a somewhat less intense level. The survey mentioned above confirmed our impression about the areas where crime and insecurity are worst: they include Newham and Southwark in the inner city. By contrast people felt far more secure in Wandsworth, Greenwich and Hounslow, though interestingly rather less so in Redbridge. However, even in the worst areas, a form of coping strategy was often expressed – there was a certain inevitability about crime, a risk run in exchange for London's benefits – so it became partially factored out of respondents' judgements about their locality.

In relation to facilities and accessibility, despite detailed variations, there is a clear contrast between the inner-city neighbourhoods (including Upton Park, Heston and East Reading) and the suburban locations (Earley, Gants Hill and Dartford). Even if their local facilities were poor, those in the inner-city areas had good accessibility to shopping centres, leisure and entertainment elsewhere and a dense public transport network to get them there. For the young in particular (of all classes) the proximity to the bright lights of the big city was an important reason to live where they did. However, parents regretted the lack of open space and facilities for children and this, they felt, contributed to crime, vandalism and disorder. In the suburban neighbourhoods the situation was the reverse. Access and facilities were less good, especially for those dependent on public transport, but the open space meant that recreational facilities for children and their parents were better.

The significance attached to the public provision of these services and facilities by the local authorities differed greatly. The tasks that the councils faced were less comprehensive and onerous outside the inner city. Everywhere people wanted to have good local schools; their rubbish collected, the streets, open spaces and shopping centres kept clean; a local library and so on. But in the inner city, alongside this basic service delivery role, the council's remit, especially where it was also the landlord, went much wider. In some areas there was a belief that council policies and poor services had contributed to the declining quality of the neighbourhood, an issue we take up in Chapter 10.

The principal aspects of the physical environment that most felt were important concerned traffic and the attendant noise and pollution; the built environment – its design and layout; and the natural environment – open spaces, trees and so on. It is unnecessary to spell out the salient divisions between inner-city and suburban neighbourhoods here. However, while all residents dislike traffic, noise and pollution (though those in the inner city suffer the most), some find quality in the urban built environment – in the gentrifying terraces and villas of Battersea or in newly constructed and renovated habitats along the river. Others, with traditional middle-class preferences perhaps, want decent, spacious but bland modern housing in (eventually) leafy suburbs close to open space and the countryside. The choices are narrower for public housing tenants; but here too layout, open space and design are all important aspects of neighbourhood quality and, despite their lack all too frequently, some estates scored highly.

In all these respects the quality of life in our neighbourhoods varied greatly and unevenly. Accessibility and good facilities do not necessarily go together with security and a good environment. And what people value most, living brightly but dangerously or in 'peace and quiet', also varies. Some therefore judged the quality of their neighbourhood on one basis and some on another. To some extent also it was recognized that living in a big city involved trade-offs; there were downsides as well as upsides. This was an easier proposition for those that had some real choice in the matter, less so for those that did not.

Of course, these conclusions are based on what we discovered in just eight localities. Not long after our research was completed the GLA (2001) published the survey of Londoners' views about living in the capital that we have already referred to. Eighty-three per cent of those questioned were satisfied with their neighbourhood and 75 per cent with London as a place to live. London's economic and cultural diversity – the range of shops, nightlife, museums and galleries, the good job opportunities and the diversity of the people who live there – were what were most valued. The class and age divisions here were clear – the young especially emphasized London's nightlife, those aged 25–54 the good employment opportunities, and the managerial and professional middle class the cultural facilities and the population mix. What most concerned them was high crime, poor public transport, unaffordable housing and the health services. Traffic congestion and environmental pollution were also mentioned frequently. Attitudes to change varied, with a quarter thinking that their neighbourhood was getting better, a third saying that there was no change and over a third feeling that they were getting worse. Long-term residents were much more likely to be in the last group. These findings indicate that our more limited sample of residents' views, and the conclusions that we draw from them, do reflect a wider reality

## Conclusion: Change and Continuity

London throughout this book has been a city profoundly affected by change and transformation, and clearly these forces have powerfully impacted on London's neighbourhoods and on their residents. But, as we have seen repeatedly in this chapter, amidst all this perturbation people have struggled to maintain a degree of continuity; this, they seem to say, is vital to their quality of life. At one level, the wider changes we have described are affecting all of our localities – through growth in Dartford and Earley, suburban succession in Gants Hill and Eltham, forms of gentrification in Battersea, Bermondsey and Peckham, and Upton Park, or – to use the language of urban ecology – invasion rather than succession in Bermondsey and Peckham and Heston.

However, not all such changes are destructive of neighbourhood quality, and some may improve it. Some may even do both, depending on who gains and who loses. And some may not make much difference. Although it is a massive generalization, our impression is that change is often viewed as enhancing the quality of neighbourhood life – and this seems true of very varied areas, such as Gravesham, East Reading, Upton Park and Battersea. In other areas, change may not, for many at least, have made enough difference to alter their positive neighbourhood evaluations, for example at Gants Hill, Eltham and Earley.

Beyond these divisions, or perhaps beneath them, there is more variation. Change is frequently Janus-faced – Bluewater but more traffic; or, more profoundly, the economic dynamism generated by Heathrow but the crisis caused by its role as the port of entry for migrants. And, even in the areas where most think that change has been for the better, there are some for whom this is not the case. Many council tenants have benefited from the changes in Battersea, except those that were displaced by them. In many areas, it is the newcomers and the young that welcome change the most, the long established and elderly who can only see what has happened to their locality as a loss.

Heston and, above all, Bermondsey were very different; here change went hand in hand with neighbourhood deterioration. Although a lack of investment in facilities and services and poor environmental quality play their parts in what people feel is getting worse in their neighbourhood, above all it is social change that has created a sense of crisis and a feeling of insecurity. In this situation, 'race' is often targeted as a prime cause, especially when connected to a struggle for housing and other resources. But conflict between newcomers and established residents can cut across the more conventional divisions between white and minority ethnic groups. In other areas, where the other grounds for division are less strong, ethnic succession and the multi-cultural locales that it brings about are accommodated somewhat more easily and are seen by some as contributing new dimensions to neighbourhood quality, though not universally.

At the end of his book, Roy Porter's vision of London is one that returns to its neighbourhoods and their qualities. He struggles between optimism and despair, between the utopian and the dystopian – the 'dazzling enclaves' of Belgravia and Hampstead versus the desolation, despair and dereliction close by. But he is also aware that much continues as before – in central, inner and outer suburbs alike, that still have the 'deeply liveable quality' recognized by many past writers. The changes discussed in this book have had palpable effects on the quality of life in London's neighbourhoods. But London is not now, and never was, a city sharply divided into rich and poor neighbourhoods – whether we define riches and poverty in terms of money income, or access to quality of life, or life chances for people or their children. Nor is it changing in a single unilateral or inevitable direction: London's neighbourhoods are not bifurcating into the upwardly mobile and the downward descending, and as a result London is not – yet at any rate – in any danger of becoming a dual city on the American or Brazilian model.

Porter saw the future of this London as under threat and – writing in the early 1990s – he despaired at the inability of London government to cope with the challenge. What is that challenge? He implied in what he wrote that it is the threat to 'the socially redemptive power of its trading position' and the 'cohesiveness of its population' from external and internal change. No longer could these be guaranteed without a more active and effective government to pursue them. Certainly, as this chapter shows, it is where competitiveness and cohesion do not extend their redemptive remit, but their reverse effects, that life in London's neighbourhoods is at its worst. How the systems of governance are coping with Porter's mission is taken up in the next chapter.

Chapter 10

# Steering, Rowing, Drowning or Waving? The Modernization of London's Governance

Nobody heard him, the dead man,
But still he lay moaning:
I was much further out than you thought
And not waving but drowning.
Stevie Smith, *Not Waving But Drowning*, 1957

Central to the much discussed shift from government to governance is a re-focusing of the policy agenda around competitiveness and cohesion. Since 1997 this has been accompanied by a far reaching project to 'modernize' local government, involving new ways of working and organization as well as radical changes in the accountability of local government to its electorate and central government. These changes occurred during our research and affected all councils.

While theoretically there need not be a central role for local councils in a system of urban governance, even the 1980s New Right reforms showed that they remained essential. This was demonstrated in London Docklands, where the relationship between the centrally imposed development corporation and the boroughs moved from hostility through peaceful co-existence to *glasnost* and even *perestroika*. Appointed agencies, however powerful, required the democratic imprimatur of the local authority; while councils were won over to the advantages of focused, professional intervention with ring-fenced funding.

So local government remains at the heart of urban governance. In fact, its remit has been widened by the duty placed on all councils in the Local Government Act 2000 to promote the economic, social and environmental well-being of their areas and to prepare Comprehensive Community Strategies involving key partners and local communities. This formalizes the growing engagement of local authorities with issues of competitiveness and cohesion but the modernization agenda embraces the 'traditional' service provision role too. New Labour shares much of the Conservative governments' distrust of and impatience with local government. But it seeks to *modernize* not replace the councils.

So three functions combine in the emergent system of local governance:

♦ Maintaining and reproducing the conditions of everyday life for the local population as a whole through the provision of public services and goods – the maintenance of highways and public spaces, rubbish collection and waste disposal, environmental regulation, libraries, cultural and sporting facilities etc.

♦ Economic competitiveness – for example, provision of infrastructure, land-use planning, attracting inward investment, business services, and support for SMEs and education and human capital development.

♦ Social cohesion – policies to combat social exclusion and disorder: these have become central to established services, notably education and social housing, but have also taken on new aspects such as crime and disorder (following new legislation), equal opportunities, labour market skills and new forms of community development.

The extension of the local authority remit from the first to the second and third functions poses problems. Issues of competitiveness and cohesion involve strong positive and negative spatial externalities going beyond any local authority area. In London, they require policies and action that minimally operate at the metropolitan level and frequently at the level of the functional urban region or the nation. If competitiveness is the responsibility of lower tier local government then activities with large positive spillovers may be ignored or under-provided and inefficiently organized, while those with negative spillovers such as competitive 'city marketing' at the micro-scale will be over-emphasized. London business, particularly larger and more global business as represented by London First, strongly supported establishing the GLA, primarily to advance the competitiveness agenda.

In relation to cohesion there are similar considerations. Also residential segregation (itself one way of dealing with local cohesion issues) pushes the main cohesion issues up to an inter-area level and frequently requires redistributive action across rather than within each area. The long disputed case for a London metropolitan authority (the LCC, then the GLC, now the Mayor and the GLA) relates fundamentally to this issue of externalities, the inability of borough level governance to encompass them, and its propensity to exacerbate some.

There is less conflict over the spatial scale of the third function, which is generally assumed to be intrinsically local. Such service provision involves fewer and smaller spillovers and addresses needs and preferences that differ across localities. Clearly though, there is ample scope for conflict between metropolitan and local government, each pursuing its own functions, especially in London where the GLA and the boroughs have a remit covering competitiveness and cohesion. In addition, the GLA, while primarily a strategic authority, has some service delivery functions;

and both the current and future Mayors are likely to continue intervening in service areas which are strictly beyond their responsibilities. Moreover, the service delivery function, while intrinsically 'local', is also a focus of the modernization agenda. This entails an extraordinary bombardment of legislation, regulation, inspection, monitoring and micro-management by the centre. Furthermore, when London had no metropolitan government between 1986 and 2000, boroughs collectively played a more strategic role, and individually became more used to the idea at least of deciding their own fate. Post-2000, a neat distinction between a strategic GLA and boroughs focused on service delivery was never a possibility.

A definitive assessment of the performance of London governance on each of these dimensions was beyond the scale of our research. The local authority 'performance indicators' collected by government only cover the more traditional direct and contracted-out services. So they only provide insights into the relative performance of our local authorities concerning the third function. A quantitative approach to measuring the impact of local governance on competitiveness and cohesion will only be possible when more systematic evidence on policy outputs is collected. And more difficult still is assessing the independent impact of these policies on competitiveness and cohesion when this is likely to be minor compared with the market and population driven economic and social changes that earlier chapters have analysed. So here we can only assess the degree to which our local authorities are engaging with the wider agenda of competitiveness and cohesion, show the approaches they are adopting, and draw some tentative conclusions about their consequences. To what extent is London government evolving in the directions set for it by the modernization agenda and by its new remit?

## The Modernization Agenda

By 2000 Labour had put in place its project to 'modernize' local government. While there are important differences with the previous approach of the Conservatives, this development should also be seen in context as the latest phase of an evolution towards a new form of governance in Britain. Conservative reforms, focused around privatization and the introduction of 'new public management', had the unintended consequence of stimulating a 'new vision of the role of local government' (Stoker, 1999, 12). In particular, local authorities began to develop a leadership role in the governance of their communities. As already noted, rather than a narrow focus purely on services, councils took on a wider remit. Service delivery remains important, but this now implies customer focused services, a plurality of providers (not just direct council provision), more 'market discipline' in service provision, partnership working, neighbourhood-based delivery and control, and a requirement for continuous service improvement backed up by an elaborate system of performance indicators and inspection. While the Conservative lineage of some of this is evident, the modernization agenda aims not to reduce the role of the local authorities but to alter it radically and incorporate it more firmly as a delivery mechanism for central government policies and priorities.

A central feature is the replacement of the Conservatives' requirements for the compulsory tendering of certain local services and their control over local taxes (rate capping) by a 'Best Value' system. This requires councils to deliver their services to government established standards of cost and quality, by the most economic, effective and efficient means possible, and continually to improve them. Each local authority now issues an annual Best Value Performance Plan and reviews every service on a five yearly basis. The reviews ask how and why the service is provided, compare performance with outside benchmarks, check that there has been fair competition in choosing the providers, and consult local users and residents. All this is inspected by the Audit Commission, together with other regulators and inspectors, for example OFSTED and the Social Services Inspectorate. It can make strong recommendations to Ministers if it finds adversely, and direct intervention may follow which can involve, for instance, the provision of services by an outside contractor not under local political control.

The modernization agenda also requires local authorities to reorganize and become better able to carry out their new responsibilities and ways of working. The old system of collegial rather than corporate organization with strong functional committees, departmental baronies and in many cases relatively weak political leadership is to be replaced. Under the Local Government Act 2000, councils must consult their communities and adopt a new constitution, taking one of three forms:

◆ a directly elected mayor with a 'cabinet';

◆ a cabinet with a leader elected by the council;

◆ a mayor directly elected by the people with a council manager appointed by the council.

All involve a strengthened political executive and a changed role for 'backbenchers' in scrutinizing the policies and actions of the leadership. The new London authority incorporates the government's favoured plan with an executive mayor and a small group of senior leaders plus an assembly which has a mainly scrutinizing role. As an interim step all the authorities with which we were concerned had opted for the Leader/Cabinet model. However, in early 2002, Newham residents voted for an elected mayor while in Southwark the vote went the other way (only 22 per cent voted in the first case, 11 per cent in the second).

The intended role for councils is to be an 'enabling authority', that 'leads the provision of services – "steering not rowing" – by working with and through a wide range of public, private and voluntary organizations' (Hill, 2000, 180). The image of steering not rowing is taken from theorists of privatization (Savas, 1987) and of 'reinventing government' (Osborne and Gaebler, 1992). This role implies a 'governance' model in which there is a 'network of partnerships, providing a mixed economy of services' (Hill, 2000, 180).

In this chapter we assess whether our local authorities were moving from 'rowing' to 'steering'. Two less optimistic possibilities (with apologies to Stevie Smith) are that some councils (and the GLA/Mayor) were 'waving' – for example multiplying 'strategies' and 'visions' that lacked resources and action; or, worse still, 'drowning' – sinking beneath the weight of local problems. Insofar as the shift from government to governance, and to the social and economic objectives at its core, is being achieved we may expect, according to recent urban political theories outlined in Chapter 1, some association with the emergence of coalition based 'urban regimes' or elements of these (John and Cole, 1998; Dowding et al., 1999). In the conclusion we review whether regime formation was occurring in our localities.

While these changes occurred and the GLA was set up, the government also established Regional Development Agencies covering the rest of the country, including the rest of the London functional region. As we noted in Chapter 1, after the GLC was abolished the lack of a metropolitan authority with functional responsibility for competitiveness, cohesion and environmental sustainability became increasingly evident. From the early 1990s the Conservatives responded to these pressures (notably from the business community) – setting up a Government Office and a Cabinet sub-committee for London and encouraging business led initiatives. But it would not establish a 'new GLC'.

However, the new metropolitan government which New Labour established is no GLC. While the GLC employed several thousand staff, the GLA directly employs only 400. The Mayor oversees London-wide authorities for policing, fire and emergency services, transport and economic development (the last, the London Development Agency, is the equivalent of the Regional Development Agencies outside London). He sets the budget for the GLA and the functional agencies, directs the activities of the economic development and transport agencies and makes key appointments to the other two. The Assembly is weak by comparison, its elected members scrutinize the Mayor's work, consider the budget (but need a two-thirds majority to change it) and can investigate issues of importance to London. We discuss these agencies later. However, our conclusions will be tentative as they had only been in place a year when our research ended.

## The Local Authorities and the Modernization Agenda

As mentioned in Chapter 2 our research focused on six London Boroughs – Wandsworth, Southwark, Greenwich, Redbridge, Newham and Hounslow – two new unitary authorities, Reading and Wokingham, and one district council, Dartford. In order to understand the contexts in which they operated some differences need to be noted in their powers, politics and problems. The London boroughs and unitary authorities are 'all purpose' authorities, responsible for the full range of local government services, including education and social services, housing, highways and planning (though the London boroughs are subject to the Mayor's planning strategy for the metropolis). As a 'lower tier' authority Dartford has fewer responsibilities and resources. It depends on Kent County Council for education, social services, planning strategy and much else. In terms of the remit to promote the well-being of their areas, Dartford has fewer powers and resources to respond than the other authorities.

Politically, there were some important contrasts too. In autumn 2001 Reading, Dartford, Greenwich, Newham and Hounslow all had solid Labour majorities while Wokingham was almost equally split between Conservatives and Liberal Democrats, the latter having one more councillor than the former. While Labour was the largest and controlling party in Redbridge, the Liberals held the balance of power and with Conservatives and Independents could outvote Labour. Southwark was also divided; here Labour was the majority party but there were a large number of Liberal Democrats and some Conservatives and Independents who together could also outvote the leadership. Wandsworth was dominated by the Conservatives. Attitudes to the modernization agenda varied in consequence. The non-Labour authorities were more restrained in their acceptance of the changes and Wandsworth was highly critical of them. Enthusiasm also varied across and within the Labour authorities. Much depended on whether these authorities had 'New Labour' leaderships, able to carry the rest of their party with them.

Finally, the authorities varied according to the problems that they faced. As we saw earlier, in Reading and Wokingham and increasingly in Dartford the local economy was buoyant, inward investment was considerable; most residents were employed and were home owners. Here, problems of competitiveness, exclusion and cohesion did not dominate the political agenda as they did in areas such as Southwark and Newham. In earlier chapters we compared these localities using the government's deprivation indices (G.B. Department of Transport, Local Government and the Regions, 2000). The rank orderings derived from these data highlight key differences. Using an index combining income and employment deprivation, of the 354 local authorities in England and Wales, Newham was the 5th most deprived, Southwark ranked 14th and Greenwich 44th. Here the demands on local services and the salience of the competitiveness and cohesion agenda are the greatest. By contrast, Wandsworth (148th) and Hounslow (153rd) were in an advantageous position, although not without some problems. Reading (188th) and Dartford (193rd) were areas in which deprivation, while not absent, was much more confined. Finally, Wokingham (353rd) was the second least deprived area nationwide. The rapidly improving position of Wandsworth was notable; up to the late 1990s such indices had placed it much higher.

These three factors – powers, politics and position – affected the local government agenda and the response to issues of economic and social development. In broad terms, neither competitiveness nor cohesion was a key political issue in Reading/Wokingham or Dartford. Here the concern was more with striking a balance between economic growth and the preservation of the environment and the quality of life of existing residents. Also in Dartford the council sought to ensure that the local population benefited from the new investment. Economic development and social inclusion were not foreign to the policy agenda in these areas but their significance and resourcing were relatively minor. Instead local government centred on the effective and efficient delivery of the more traditional local authority services, a priority that the modernization agenda served to accentuate.

This picture was not so different in Hounslow and Redbridge. In both these there was some concern about deprivation and social exclusion but these were confined to limited areas and were not yet priorities for local government. In three of the remaining boroughs the competitiveness and cohesion agenda had far greater importance. In Wandsworth it had importance too but that borough had already seen a marked change in its fortunes, as its deprivation score illustrates. Improving service delivery was important everywhere, with variable results.

## The Local Authorities and Service Delivery

By 2001 there were around 190 local authority 'performance indicators' – produced annually and published on the Audit Commission website. These data are not designed for research but for the monitoring of service delivery by government. Also they mainly concern the traditional services, not the newer remit of the councils. Moreover, many indicators – such as number of benefit claimants or the percentage of children in special schools – say more about the socio-economic composition of the locality than about the performance of its council. In addition, some may appear to indicate variations in service performance but interpreting this is fraught with difficulty. Some indicators relate to inputs (e.g. net spending per head), some to outputs (e.g. average relet times), and some to outcomes (e.g. satisfaction levels with specific services). Finally, some are of less relevance to the foci of this book – for example, museum usage, the availability of public conveniences and food inspection.

Nevertheless there are some more useful indicators: these are shown for the year 1999/2000 in Table 10.1. Achieving good service delivery is more difficult in some areas than others, even allowing for genuine variations in efficiency. This is largely why, on all the indicators in Table 10.1, the London figures are inferior to those for England and Wales as a whole. While spending per capita is affected by efficiencies in service delivery, the differences also reflect variations in the scale of need and demand for services. Thus Greenwich, Southwark and Newham – the most deprived boroughs – spent most, well above the Greater London average. Hounslow and Redbridge were much closer to this average – reflecting lower levels of need. The most striking variation was Wandsworth whose spending fell well below the London level. As we discuss later, efficient and cost-effective service delivery was the *leit-motif* of the Wandsworth Conservatives and the socio-economic transformation of the borough – their other key 'project' – enhanced their ability to restrict spending. Outside London, the figures for Wokingham and Reading were typical for large unitary authorities in the more affluent regions of the nation. The very low figure for Dartford was because it is a second tier district council. It was close to the average for such councils.

One indicator of the levels of dissatisfaction with councils is provided by the number of complaints about them determined by an Ombudsman. While not too much can be read into these figures, and they vary from year to year, there were far more cases in London than outside. Within the metropolis levels were highest in Southwark and Newham, plus, interestingly, Wandsworth. Table 10.1 also contains some indicators of service performance which focus on groups

**Table 10.1.** Local authority services: performance indicators 1999/2000.

| | Newham | Southwark | Wandsworth | Greenwich | Hounslow | Redbridge | Dartford | Reading | Wokingham | Greater London | England & Wales |
|---|---|---|---|---|---|---|---|---|---|---|---|
| Percentage of Council Tax collected | 83 | 80 | 93 | 91 | 93 | 96 | 97 | 95 | 99 | 92 | 96 |
| Number of complaints to an Ombudsman | 140 | 191 | 121 | 83 | 93 | 39 | 3 | 14 | 25 | NA | NA |
| Days to accept homeless applicants | 45 | 64 | 65 | 26 | 45 | 67 | 17 | 30 | 16 | 68 | 27 |
| Percentage of clean highways | 86 | 81 | 96 | 92 | 90 | 90 | 95 | 94 | 96 | 89 | 92 |
| Percentage satisfied Housing Benefit/Council Tax claimants | 61 | 36 | 53 | 68 | 67 | 71 | ND | 77 | 95* | 68 | 78 |
| Days to process new Council Tax claims | 169 | 130* | 77 | 80 | 71 | 67 | 29 | 62 | 23 | 80 | 50 |
| Days to process new Housing Benefit claims | 82 | 132* | 72 | 59 | 74 | 46 | 20 | 47 | 22 | 65 | 44 |
| Weeks to relet council housing | 5.8 | 7.3 | 6.5 | 6.9 | 6.3 | 8.5 | 4.3 | 5.9 | 3.6 | 7.1 | 6.0 |
| Council housing repairs by government time limits | 95 | 76 | 89 | 85 | 81 | 96 | 100 | 50 | 95 | 84 | 88 |
| Council rents collected as percentage of rent due | 98 | 93 | 95 | 95 | 100 | 94 | 99 | 96 | 103 | 97 | 98 |
| Serious rent arrears | 14 | 27 | 13 | 15 | 9 | 7 | 3 | 7 | 2 | 11 | 5 |
| Rubbish collections missed per 100,000 collections | 60 | 84 | 264 | 21 | 65 | 37 | 55 | 81 | 17 | 509 | 194 |
| Percent of child protection cases reviewed in time limits | 78 | 62 | 99 | 65 | 76 | 98 | NP | 100 | 89 | 78 | 84 |
| Total net spending per head of the population (£) | 1319 | 1314 | 848 | 1245 | 1003 | 945 | 89 | 783 | 746 | 1026 | NA |

*Source:* Audit Commission.

Notes:
All data rounded up to nearest unit or first decimal place.
NA = not appropriate; NP = not provider; ND = no data, * = doubts expressed about validity of data.

that are most dependent on the authorities' operations. First, the time taken to accept homeless applicants, much longer in London than outside it, but within the city Greenwich (especially), Hounslow and Newham did considerably better than Wandsworth, Southwark or Redbridge. Turning to the time taken to process new claims for council tax and housing benefits again the non-London authorities did better, though Reading less so than Dartford or Wokingham. Within London, Newham was much less effective than the others and possibly Southwark. But there were interesting variations, with Greenwich and Redbridge scoring well, especially in relation to Housing Benefit. The data on the level of satisfaction with the service that claimants received are notable for the very low levels recorded for Wandsworth and Southwark.

In relation to local authority tenants and the efficiency with which the council stock was managed, there are also sharp contrasts. Comparing the time it took to relet vacant property, most performed fairly close to the average levels (for Greater London in the case of the London boroughs, nationally in the case of the other three), although Newham, Wokingham and Dartford did rather better. Most councils did well or very well in completing repairs within nationally set time limits, although Southwark's performance was less strong and Reading's was poor. Rent collection was less efficient, especially in Southwark but to some degree in the other London boroughs except Newham and Hounslow. All councils faced a growing arrears problem, except Hounslow and Wokingham, and only the latter was reducing them. A more potent indicator of boroughs with a severe problem is the proportion of tenants in serious arrears (over 13 weeks due and disregarding amounts of £250 or less). This was extremely high at 27 per cent in Southwark and considerable in Wandsworth, Greenwich and Newham. Even in the outer boroughs of Redbridge and Hounslow, and in Reading, it was clearly above the national average. The other two OMA authorities, Wokingham and Dartford, however, had especially low levels of arrears. These variations do partially reflect the varying levels of deprivation but this is unlikely to be the only explanation.

Although we do not focus on local authority social service provision in this book, it is a major element in expenditure and in the policy response to exclusion by all our councils except Dartford. One indicator of effectiveness is the proportion of cases on the Child Protection Register that are reviewed with the statutory time limits. Here Wandsworth, Redbridge, Reading and Wokingham did well, Hounslow and Newham were average performers (in relation to Greater London) but well over a third of all cases were not reviewed on time in Greenwich and Southwark – a serious level of underperformance. In relation to education, as we showed in Chapter 6, the councils' performance varied widely, for example Southwark had particularly severe problems while Redbridge and Wokingham were high achievers.

Two services that affect the whole population are domestic rubbish collection and the cleanliness of the highways (both frequently commented on by residents). In terms of rubbish collection all authorities seemed to do well. But the Greater London average was inflated by crisis conditions in a few boroughs. Once this is taken account of, the poor performance in Wandsworth becomes clearer. It did, however, keep its highways cleaner than any of the other councils. In sharp contrast

Southwark was the worst performer in this respect; only it and Newham among our case study areas fell below the London average.

A final indicator that reflects the scale of the problems the authorities faced and their effectiveness in responding to them is the percentage of council tax collected. Here, Southwark and Newham did poorly, only collecting about 80 per cent of the tax due. They were also the councils with the highest per capita expenditure and those that ranked lowest on the deprivation index.

Taking these data as a whole, within Greater London, Redbridge appears as a generally effective authority; Wandsworth, Greenwich and Hounslow came some way behind this; Newham seemed to be improving from a low level; Southwark still had severe difficulties. Outside London, Wokingham and Dartford outperformed the national averages on all our selected indicators, while Reading underperformed on most of them.

## The Local Authorities: Their Agenda, Policies and Politics

As we noted, the local authority agenda and performance, while increasingly shaped by central government, is still strongly moulded by local contexts. Having looked at indicators of comparative service performance we now consider in more detail local responses, drawing on our interviews and other information. These accounts are qualitative and to some degree impressionistic. Nevertheless, they shed light on how our local authorities have responded to the competitiveness and cohesion agenda. We start with the most deprived inner boroughs, then the Outer London areas and finally our three OMA authorities.

### Newham

Newham has an enthusiastic and committed New Labour leadership that has fully accepted the modernization agenda and the new remit for local authorities. In 2000 the Council's Leader, Sir Robin Wales (who became the first elected Mayor in May 2002), and Wendy Thompson, its former Chief Executive were listed as two of the fifteen 'most powerful people in local government' (*Guardian*, 15 November). The Leader's vision, as he explained it to us, is for:

> *Newham to be a major business location and a place where people will chose to live and work . . . the key word there is the word 'choose'. We want to get to the position that when people have the economic capacity – jobs – and also the ability to say what they'd like to do and where they'd like to live, they'd choose Newham.*

Interestingly, having transformed the council agenda in conjunction with its New Labour politicians (and seen it become a pilot authority for Best Value) Thompson left in 1999 to be the Audit Commission's first Director of Best Value Inspections and later became head of a new office of public service reform inside the Cabinet Office.

Newham has participated in numerous government policy initiatives and is active in various cross London and East London partnerships. Its engagement with social and economic change is such that two of the Cabinet portfolios concern regeneration and social inclusion. Officers and councillors are committed to innovation and Newham has been successful in tapping additional sources of funding for regeneration and social inclusion.

The importance of strong leadership and a vision for the borough was cited by several interviewees. The Labour group is generally united around a development and regeneration agenda, with the vision noted above of making Newham a place of choice. However, there is an emphasis on regeneration benefiting the existing population alongside changing the population mix by attracting newcomers. The tension between these two aims occurs in several of our areas. It concerns the relationships between competitiveness and cohesion both in reality and in how these are conceived by local leaders:

> *A lot of people coming here . . . don't chose, they come because it's the cheapest place . . . when they have some more money they move out. What we're trying to do is make it a place of choice. And there are some pretty stereotyped images of the East End which we have to . . . work quite hard to change.*
>
> Senior Officer

> *What we are talking about is increasing the life chances of people that live around here, give them a decent place to live, a decent job, and raising their aspirations so they think they can do a lot better than their forefathers did.*
>
> Chief Executive: regeneration organization

This vision is shared by councillors and officers. Cross-departmental working is the norm:

> *It's the most joined up council I've ever worked for in my life . . . we just have corporate projects, corporate initiatives, we work with whichever bit of the council is appropriate . . . No one is a traditional director in their silo.*
>
> Senior Officer

Physical regeneration, inclusion and positive image creation are the key strategies of the council. The strongly pro-development agenda builds on the LDDC achievements, aiming to develop sites in an 'arc of opportunity' through the east and south of the borough. There is an emphasis on employment creation that links new jobs with local people:

> *We need to get [unemployed residents] into jobs. If we want to raise income levels and raise aspirations, one of the first routes out of poverty is to get people into employment.*
>
> Senior Officer

Raising aspirations and changing Newham's image also means improving its education system and skills levels generally and attracting new residents by improving social and leisure facilities and creating a wider range of housing and job opportunities. So the council wants to balance changes that benefit existing residents with those that attract better off newcomers. It sees a strong connection between these, with the second aiding the first. This quote that refers to a possible clash with the Mayor demonstrates the philosophy:

*We don't feel the Mayor understands some of the things [that] have to be in place and some that have to give if you're going to achieve regeneration in an area like this . . . [We] can only sustain a certain level of affordable housing . . . we do already have quite a lot . . . and we don't have too much high value housing. So if we're going to create sustainable communities, we want a mix. So I'm not sure that we're fully in tune with the Mayor's policies.*

Senior Officer

Presentation and image creation is important to change the view of the borough among current and potential residents and investors. On its web site the Leader claimed that previously poor service delivery had been turned around so it was now 'in the top three of the 33 London councils'. However, as we showed, Newham has some way to go with service improvement. Several of our interviewees commented on the closure of local facilities, such as shops and libraries; the problems of access to facilities; the lack of places of entertainment, for eating out and so on. Employers and residents commented on the poor environment, mostly mentioning rubbish and dumping. And while education has begun to improve, employers were very critical of standards of literacy and numeracy.

Newham is an example of the New Labour project: innovative, committed to networking, focused on physical regeneration and image creation but also on social inclusion, linked to increased place-competitiveness and a jobs/investment agenda. There is significant involvement in partnerships such as the Stratford Development Partnership and one that focused on crime reduction (mandated for all authorities under new crime and disorder prevention legislation), as well as more locally based examples. Two problems frequently mentioned, as elsewhere, are the difficulties of building cross-borough partnerships and of bringing together partners locally when they are in competition for scarce resources. There was the beginning of large-scale regeneration, especially in the Stratford and East Ham town centres. There was strong political leadership backed by shared values and vision across key councillors and officers.

So there was a potentially emergent policy regime in Newham. Its activities in regard to competitiveness are a mix of boosterism and interventions to try to improve the local economy through attracting inward investment and attaching conditions about employing local people. Economic regeneration has been more successful in the south of the borough so far. Newham does not aim to change the ethnic composition of the borough and values multi-culturalism. However, an Asian councillor said that there were tensions, for example, over which neighbourhoods got housing grants, and around social events such as festivals. In the longer run Newham's efforts to alter the class mix in the borough may affect its ethnic composition too. Overall, as one councillor suggested, it was 'early days' to tell whether Newham's policies will materially alter its situation.

## Southwark

Southwark faces the most severe difficulties – including high deprivation and weak service delivery – of all our authorities. As we saw in Chapter 9 its approach to regeneration was controversial; many residents gained little benefit and felt disenfranchised. In 2001 an independent commission into the council's organization stated 'what is starkly evident is that the people of Southwark want change and that, for them, an objective of change should be to halt a perceived decline in residents' influence over their Council'.

Unlike Newham or Wandsworth, where strong political leadership is linked to effective and innovative senior officers, Southwark has a history of weak political leadership and dominant officers. In the 1980s the leftist council tried to avoid government controls on its spending, got into serious difficulties and was rescued by its officers. By the time of our research the balance was probably changing, although the following suggest that the politicians were still less in control than elsewhere:

> The role of the [Cabinet] member is stronger; they are far more empowered so decision making is faster. From point of view of officers the fact that you can get a challenging professional debate is a great step forward.
>
> Director of Education

> It is the officers who run the council and . . . set the strategy and . . . the policies . . . they tell the councillors what needs to be done. So you've got officers tell the councillors tell the public rather than public telling councillors telling officers which is the way I always thought government should work.
>
> Liberal Democrat councillor

At the time of our research Labour's grip on the council was shaky; it only retained power by the Mayor's casting vote. So it had to negotiate with the Liberal Democrats. The uncertainty affected the council's ability to negotiate with private developers and led to the abandonment of a plan for the mass transfer of council housing out of local authority ownership and management:

> Officers are making sure that things are done cross party because when Labour is in a weak position it makes developers nervous about co-operating with them unless they know that the possibly future leaders of the council are on board as well. For stock transfer they wanted cross party agreement. The Liberals are not coming on board with stock transfer; Labour felt that they needed the Liberals' support.
>
> Liberal Democrat councillor

Southwark's strategy is determined by its deprivation and by its location. It focuses on redevelopment and area-based regeneration which it believes will eventually help to lift the poor out of poverty and improve the lives of all residents. The idea is that improving the environment and building higher income housing will increase the proportion of better off residents, so reducing the proportion of poor people, if not their number. This will also attract new businesses with new jobs for all. Having a more socially mixed community will, it is hoped, reverse some of the class and ethnic ghettoization of schools. The strategy has certainly had an impact:

> I think we have been successful in physical and economic regeneration. You can see this particularly in the north of the borough where property values have been going up very

*rapidly . . . [it] has exploded in terms of economic activity. The prestige of prominent successes like the Tate has given the whole area a boost.*

Council Leader

However, she added 'we have been successful at bringing in new money but the extent to which this has benefited the existing population is variable'.

As we noted in Chapter 2 the key individual in determining the strategy was Fred Manson, the Director of Planning and Regeneration from 1994 to 2001. The £160m that the borough had received from the Single Regeneration Budget and the New Deal for Communities (plus European and other funding) was used to lever in private investment. The biggest impact has been in the north, close to the river and involving major partnerships which we described in Chapter 2. These are a response to the need for CBD users of land to 'overspill' across the river and associated demands for high-income housing, services and tourism. As we noted, in this part of the borough there have been spectacular changes in the landscape and the Jubilee line extension has improved communications. So the area is being transformed but the benefits accruing to existing residents are uncertain. The council was also spending over £230m to improve the troubled Aylesbury Estate and another very large scheme involved the regeneration of the Elephant and Castle, with 'affordable' private housing and a new commercial centre and transport interchange.

Critics say that this regeneration does not significantly benefit the local population because rather than addressing the root causes of poverty it aims to reduce the numbers of poor:

> *It is trying to do a Wandsworth to deal with its low performance indicators; if you get rid of services then it ceases to be your fault. If you have got poor people you move them out of the borough rather than enabling them to raise themselves out of poverty . . . It is going for these glitzy physical regeneration things . . . It is all physical, design-led. Fred [Manson] sees regeneration as based on trickle-down theory where getting offices in will benefit the local community . . . But there is a gap between getting in lots of offices and businesses and this having a positive effect on the local community and it is a gap which the council hasn't thought how to join up.*
>
> Liberal Democrat councillor

As we saw in Chapter 9, many who felt left out by these developments were among the majority of Southwark's residents who live in council housing. While formally the council had area-based participatory structures in place, as we have seen dissatisfaction with the housing service was high and, one informant suggested, the contracting out of Housing Benefit administration was 'a mess'. There had also been much opposition to the decision to contract out the education service, although the council had been under intense pressure from government to do so, given its failings.

These conflicts between the council and its residents led to quite extensive community organization and protest with some backbench councillors seeing their role primarily as community caseworkers and representatives, rather than formulating policy and strategy.

On a wider scale, territorial divisions bred resentment and conflict. Bermondsey residents often felt that the Labour council took little interest in the Liberal Democrat north of the borough. It spent money in Labour wards while the north was treated as a cash cow and many of its long-term residents were forced out by regeneration and the influx of new residents, not only the high earners but also those who competed with them for inadequate council housing and services.

As elsewhere, while some partnerships were producing results, this feature of the shift from government to governance had its drawbacks. Some officials and councillors believed that Southwark already had quite good structures in place to involve residents and voluntary organizations. They felt that the insistence on partnerships reflected the government's mistrust of local authorities (as did its forced privatizing of the education system). And in practice partnerships complicated everyone's lives:

*The kinds of consultation mechanisms are incredibly tough on local people: huge amounts of time and energy are expected from [them] . . . One should involve local people but they need a huge amount of support and it is very, very costly.*

Council Leader

*Every few months there is another initiative. The government talked about how it was going to join everything up: it has created health action zones, employment zones, sports actions zone, national health trust plans, neighbourhood renewal strategies, New Deal for Communities with specialist straight routes to Ministers at top level so they think they can by pass all sorts of people and do different things . . . The point is there are about forty of them and to me that is not joining up, that is completely separating the initiatives.*

Senior executive, Pool of London Partnership

A senior officer said that the shift to governance was fragmenting the public sector and reducing the capacity to develop strategic and coordinated policies. Others were concerned about the long-term sustainability of initiative funded programmes and one explicitly stated that improving the area's competitiveness did not necessarily have a positive effect on cohesion. The high level of conflict supported this contention.

Southwark has similarities with Newham in its situation and in the council response to it. However, in Southwark there is a more radical attempt to use design-led and market-friendly urban regeneration to change the competitiveness and social composition of the area. It has been loosely planned and coordinated, taking opportunities as they arise. It aimed to reduce the council housing stock thus displacing some poor residents. The programmes that helped residents gain a share of the new jobs coming in were rather modest and geographically limited. And most of the new housing was unaffordable by them. Overall, it was not clear that the 'trickle down' solution was working. Meanwhile, Southwark had severe problems with service delivery, while Newham seemed to be addressing them more effectively.

Like Newham, Southwark had a 'project' to change the fortunes of the area. The 'change coalition' involved powerful officers and the council leaders making agreements with private sector developers with support from the cross-river authorities and heavy government assistance. Its approach to urban regeneration was bold and innovative. However, in the face of political and community opposition, it fell a good way short of a distinctive and dominant governing regime.

## Wandsworth

Wandsworth has the most noteworthy or notorious reputation – depending on one's political persuasion – of all our councils. From 1978, when the Conservatives gained firm control, it became a test bed for Thatcherite policies and its influence on government was considerable. It led the way in competitive tendering, council house sales, school testing, City Technology Colleges and grant-maintained schools. Two of its Leaders became government ministers. It was the first Inner London council to embark on a project of economic and social change with a strong commitment to effective and efficient service delivery. Its aim is to provide 'high quality services at a price people can afford'. While its Thatcherite approach differs from that adopted by Labour's modernization project (of which the Wandsworth politicians are scornful), there are echoes of the former in the latter.

In recent research into urban regime formation in London Dowding *et al.* (1999, 525) conclude that Wandsworth has a 'service delivery regime':

> Wandsworth developed a strong consumer-oriented, low-tax, contracting-out and privatizing council with a developed corporate spirit among its officers and members. Assisted by central government largesse, it also gained the respect, and, more important, votes of the electorate.

The Council was able to take advantage of the borough's physical assets – including many areas of potentially attractive housing and some major open spaces – plus its location to pursue the strategy of social change outlined in Chapter 2. This housing-led strategy would not have been possible in many other areas – location, market forces and political objectives came serendipitously together here. One criticism was that the improved and new housing were unaffordable by key workers such as those employed in the public services.

Wandsworth has reluctantly adopted a Cabinet system, so confirming a senior officer's earlier prediction that 'we are likely to go for the least change and the one which most closely reflects the way we have been doing business for many many years'. Over time the council had attracted a group of able chief officers, sympathetic to its approach. The political leadership set out clear policy guidelines and priorities but encouraged them to innovate in their implementation:

> Over the last 20 years it has been very much a vertically run organization and very much saying 'right you Director of Housing you are responsible for that go and do it. Education get on and do it. Social services get on and do it'. So it is very service and performance orientated and it is only latterly that people are starting to think that more things could be done across the board corporately. That's not to say there is not a very strong corporate ethos at the centre. Half a dozen key people have got their hands very firmly on half a dozen strings. The Chairman's

*group, the Chairs of all the committees, meets with the Director of Finance on a fortnightly basis and that's the core group and they know exactly what is happening in each department and deliver the overall vision which is fairly simple: successful communities, successful economy, value for money, quality services, keep the bloody council tax down.*

Head of Economic Development

There is a large economic development section with a budget of about £10m providing business support. It focuses on small businesses as their growth has been particularly significant. The Head of Economic Development saw a link between this growth and the population change and felt that it provided a secure base for the future:

*It is also a very popular place to live . . . there are a lot of entrepreneurial people so we can encourage them to stay. They can set up a business in the borough and with a lot of small firms you have a hell of a lot of diversity so you are not necessarily depending on a small number of large companies for local jobs . . . if one goes, two goes, one hundred goes or three hundred goes you have got others coming to take their place.*

In the 1990s the borough moved from having an unemployment level above to one that was only half the London average. It supported some programmes to help its less well off residents access the new jobs. The stress that it laid on improving education was also linked to an agenda of providing this population with 'choice and opportunity' for their individual advancement – the Thatcherite credo.

Wandsworth was involved in some partnerships but less enthusiastically and to a lesser degree than were Southwark or Newham. It received far less Single Regeneration Budget (SRB) than Southwark – but had benefited greatly from the Conservative's urban programmes in the 1980s when its level of deprivation was higher – so this reason for the formation of partnerships was less. The most important one was with London Business Link which delivered government-funded services to small business. But the council worked closely with business interests generally and in relation to specific sites. Community engagement in policy formation was limited; perhaps the council's longstanding Conservative domination meant that it simply delivered what its residents wanted – good, cheap services. As we saw, while not totally the case, this claim had considerable justification. A flavour of the relations between the council and its residents is given by its Chief Executive's reference on the council website to an 'experiment' due to run until 2002 in which ward-based 'report back' meetings allow residents to voice their concerns. Early meetings had been 'reasonably' popular with an average attendance of around fifty.

By the time of our research there was broad cross-party agreement about Wandsworth's approach to economic development and urban regeneration, although Labour criticized the scale of housing privatization and the Conservatives' approach to the voluntary sector – contracting out services in a commercial, performance oriented way rather than entering into community based partnerships. Apart from the policies that had led to a reduction in the proportion of lower-income residents in the borough, the council had also responded more directly to potential threats to social cohesion and order. For example, it established a support agency for ethnic minority business and had monitored the ethnic composition of its own workforce for many years. After the Brixton riots in the early 1980s it invested large sums in a predominantly Afro-Caribbean housing estate that was feared to be a possible site for similar conflict.

On its website the council Leader noted that it had a record twenty-three Charter Mark (government) awards for excellent services and had, he claimed, the lowest average Council Tax in the UK. A resident survey indicated that two-thirds were satisfied with the council, the second highest level in London. Small wonder then that he criticized the 'tortuous Best Value process' as costly and inimical to local flexibility (a view discreetly echoed by the Chief Executive on the same web site). The Mayor came in for equal treatment, costing local residents more in tax and failing to deliver. But, it was said, Wandsworth's 'self-confident' local government would continue to defend its residents' interests.

Wandsworth had little time for, to quote its Chief Executive, 'national directives and centrally driven policy agendas' – the modernization project and all that it entailed. He added 'not surprisingly local people are most interested in quality of life issues: clean streets, fly-tipping, car parking, crime, vandalism and anti-social behaviour. Above all people want efficient local services'. But, as we have seen, more than this was involved in the council's agenda. In concluding that Wandsworth was governed by a 'regime' Dowding *et al.* (1999) suggest that its basis was service delivery rather than 'the conventional economic development dynamic'. While this is the view that the council propagates, in our view economic development has been an equal aim. Dowding *et al.* also conclude that Wandsworth's regime differed in form from the US model based on coalitions of public and private sector interests. Rather they saw it as based on one party domination of the council and a coalition of local and national politicians. However, although the national partners lost office in 1997, the local regime persists and, despite its rhetoric, has arguably achieved much of the modernization agenda by a different route.

## Greenwich

Compared with Newham and Southwark, Greenwich has been a less vocal supporter of modernization. However, under a high profile leader, Len Duvall (1992– 2000), it abandoned its 1980s stance of opposition towards partnership with government and business. Working closely with the Chief Executive, new officers were brought in and Greenwich became more outward looking and less isolationist. Duvall became increasingly involved in pan-London partnerships and politics. Until 2000, he chaired the Greenwich Development Partnership, the Thames Gateway London Partnership and was Deputy Chair of the Association of London Government. After his election to the GLA he became Deputy Chair of the LDA:

> Len Duvall was instrumental in Greenwich being more outward looking, in being more pro-business than it was, and it was logical he would go to the GLA because he was increasingly becoming a major player in London terms.
>
> Senior Council Officer

Some informants suggested, however, that the council remained somewhat isolated and insular, though they expected that its new Leader and new Chief Executive would accelerate the process of modernization and building more genuine partnerships. There is now a stronger orientation towards the New Labour agenda and the council's web page lists three main objectives: raising service quality (like Newham it was a pilot Best Value authority); combating poverty; and regeneration.

Regeneration initially became a political priority as a defensive reaction to the threat of the LDDC:

> *The original driver for [waterfront regeneration] was what was happening in Docklands. [We had] this peninsula of 300 acres which was the same size if not bigger than the area that had been handed over to the LDDC and it was in part a defensive mechanism to prevent the LDDC's remit being extended into Greenwich . . . at the end of last year we had Michael Heseltine down here, and he was saying 'I wish we'd put the peninsula in the LDDC' and I said 'we were eight years ahead of you and just as well'.*
>
> Council Leader

Since then the council has successfully bid for public funds, securing seven SRB programmes which are at the core of its partnership activity.

Some in the borough feel that the council is too focused on physical redevelopment at the expense of social and economic regeneration. But the form of regeneration which has been pursued strongly reflects the massive de-industrialization of the north of the borough, which we outlined in Chapter 2. This had major repercussions for social cohesion as well as economic competitiveness. Summarizing the position in the early 1990s, the council's website noted that only 6000 manufacturing jobs remained in an area that had had 150,000 at the turn of the century; that male unemployment rates were up to 60 per cent (in some unspecified localities); 80 per cent of the council housing needed repair; there was widespread fear of crime and violence; a very large amount of contaminated land; and the worst health inequality in London.

This led the council to focus on large-scale regeneration in the north of the borough where most job loss had occurred and where the major development opportunities are located. Creating new jobs for local residents, rather than changing the social mix of the borough was the principal objective, unlike the other boroughs that we have discussed so far. In Chapter 2 we described the major projects and the council's employment objectives.

Given Greenwich's problems and its location (unlike Southwark or Wandsworth it is not a preferred location for business 'overspill' from the CBD or new higher-income housing), much public investment was needed to initiate regeneration. Up to 2001 it had received about £1.4bn, a very high figure, and this has levered about £1bn from the private sector. This is a modest ratio and indicates that 'turning around' Greenwich is likely to be very difficult. However, it has resulted not only in the Dome, but also in a good deal of new residential, business, retail and leisure development close to the river and some new jobs.

Greenwich established a series of development agencies and partnerships to deliver its SRB programmes, mostly close to and along its northern riverside border.

All involve physical renewal and environmental improvements linked to economic revitalization and programmes to provide better services, facilities and opportunities for local residents. While voluntary organizations and business are included in the partnerships the former seem mainly to have been viewed as service deliverers and the latter's involvement, as we discuss below, has been problematic. Less apparent is a major engagement of the local communities in helping to steer and participate in the programmes. Here Greenwich has not yet fully signed up to a key aspect of the modernization agenda.

As we have noted, unlike Southwark, and perhaps reflecting its now fading 'Old Labour' culture and priorities, Greenwich has tried to ensure that some of the new jobs benefit low-income residents, combating poverty and social exclusion. It established the Greenwich Local Labour and Business (GLLaB) which, despite its title, focuses on helping local people to benefit from the opportunities on the development sites. GLLaB offers advice, training, a recruitment service and grants for tools. According to the council's web page 'GLLaB has developed the most sophisticated local labour scheme in the UK. It has filled over 2100 jobs and trained over 3000 people'. Creating new jobs for women and ethnic minorities is an important objective. However, nothing like the transformation in unemployment rates that has occurred in Wandsworth has been seen here. In the economic upturn of the 1990s, as London unemployment rates fell, so did those in Greenwich. But the adverse gap between the two rates remained almost constant.

River crossings were also seen as crucial by the leadership, particularly in the north of the borough. New transport infrastructure is identified as a key driver of economic development, and greater business investment and involvement. It also opens up new job opportunities for residents:

> Some parts of the borough are still struggling; not least places like Woolwich and Plumstead. A lot of that is because it is still comparatively cut off. We hope to bring the Docklands Light Railway to Woolwich, and securing the transport links across the Thames in Greenwich will be the final piece of the jigsaw in the west of the borough. Private sector investment in Greenwich really took off when we got the Docklands Light railway and the Jubilee line – that was essential. There are huge numbers potentially in the East of London and getting people from Woolwich, Plumstead and Eltham is hard if the only route is the Blackwall tunnel.
>
> Council Leader

Thames Gateway, the major sub-regional partnership, has helped shape views about the future of the area, reducing inter-borough competition, and acting as a vehicle for lobbying government:

> There are tensions between the boroughs . . . to some extent they are all in competition with one another. What Thames Gateway partnership has done has allowed those competitive factors to be recognized, but to also allow some recognition that what's good for Stratford is good for Thames Gateway and good for Greenwich and Lewisham and Bexley . . . and that we would achieve more by supporting one another than by trying to compete with Stratford.
>
> Senior Council Officer

Council sources said that until recently, its relationship with business was poor and partnerships were public sector dominated. However, pushing the council towards a more pro-business approach is a key leadership priority:

> In the past 7 years Greenwich has gone from being a business-unfriendly borough to at best a business-neutral borough, and hopefully to a business-friendly borough. That has not just come about by accident, there has been a very clear political desire to achieve that and to listen to business more . . . in the decade before that the wrong signals were sent out to business. Some, who could have been persuaded to stay, left.
>
> Senior Council Officer

It established the Greenwich Business Forum with membership open to all businesses in the borough. This provides the business membership for the partnership boards and is the main business related body with which the council engages. In practice, most members of the Forum come from the Waterfront area and have been involved in the partnerships located there.

However, according to business, the council still has a long way to go. Key concerns include: service delivery issues such as speed of planning applications and business rates; the structure of business support services in the borough; business's lack of real involvement in the regeneration process; and the poor local transport infrastructure and difficulties crossing the river. Business support services were characterized by duplication and ineffectiveness, with a proliferation of agencies that should be rationalized:

> If you are starting up a business, how do you know who these people are, so you really need the one stop shop . . . there must be 23 different organizations all purporting to help local businesses.
>
> Chair, Business Forum

The Chief Executive of the Asian Chamber of Commerce felt that the council's focus on special support for ethnic businesses only exacerbated and politicized racial tensions. Such businesses did not want to be singled out in this way. In some respects, the council had not shaken off its anti-business culture. For example, we were told, the council still preferred to use its own direct labour force on many SRB projects rather than local firms and an informant referred to its 'paternalistic attitude'. One business leader suggested that the Forum was a device to co-opt business into support for the council's policies rather than an 'authentic' partnership and that local authority-business links were 'in disarray'.

As in Southwark, there is a territorial politics, with the southern areas, represented mainly by opposition councillors, feeling ignored:

> We . . . were in despair about the lack of interest in the south amongst the council . . . I've been to meetings where officers have . . . plans for the whole of the borough and I've had two or three local councillors sitting beside me, and I've said where is the south in all of this? And I've had both [Conservative and Labour councillors] saying there are no plans for the south, they don't understand the south and they don't come to the south.
>
> Community Worker

Relative neglect of the south, at least in terms of regeneration funding, was acknowledged by the political leadership:

> *I can understand the sense that more money has been spent in the north, that's where,*
> *according to the indicators, the poverty is. We are investing in the south now – in addition to*
> *the SRB, there's an Education Action Zone and Sure Start.*
>
> Council Leader

The major scheme was an SRB funded partnership to regenerate five large local authority housing estates in Kidbrooke and Eltham that began in 2000. Here the communities were involved through a residents' steering group. These partnerships mainly concern housing, security and environmental improvements – in essence conventional, public funded estate improvement schemes.

Greenwich's conversion to the modernization agenda was partial in several ways. First, although it was a pilot Best Value authority and had had a high profile Leader it was recognizably an authority where the transition from Old Labour culture and ways of working came slowly and was incomplete. Second, its engagement with regeneration linked to social and economic change was confined to the north of the borough. Third, its partnerships, perhaps because they were so heavily dependent on public funding as well as its remaining Old Labour 'paternalism', only engaged with business and the voluntary sector to a limited degree and, except in the estate projects, hardly at all with resident organizations. As we saw Greenwich still fell short of meeting the service delivery goals of the modernization agenda – especially in two crucially related to competitiveness and cohesion: education and social services. While there has been change, driven by key politicians and officers, this falls far short of being 'modernized', regime based network governance. Rather as in Wandsworth, local government adapted to externally imposed change.

## Hounslow

A similar conclusion applies to Hounslow, another but very different Labour borough. As we outlined in Chapter 2, while not without its problems, the Hounslow economy was dynamic and it had not had to face the same long-term problems that Greenwich had incurred when it too lost manufacturing jobs. The economy is now dominated by the presence of Heathrow Airport:

> *Quite clearly this is an airport economy . . . The biggest employer of Hounslow residents is*
> *the airport. We knock it because people are concerned about aircraft noise and stuff like that*
> *and, and politically Terminal Five was a big issue . . . I think the art in West London is to try and*
> *create an economy which benefits from the airport without being totally dependent on it.*
>
> Senior Council Officer

Business development occurs without much need for the council to foster it, nor are there large areas of derelict land which can only be regenerated with public investment.

The priorities were outlined on the council website in its 'Pledges to the People'. These included improving the education system; reducing litter and developing 'green corridors'; working in partnership with the police and local communities to improve public safety; delivering the government's Welfare to Work programme; keeping council rents down and assisting those on low incomes; using public funding to invest across council services; and implementing Best Value and related reforms. There is no mention of a council role in economic development and the section on deprivation mainly concerns the delivery of a major government programme and issues such as keeping rents low which are hardly innovative. There seems little reflection here of the high levels of concern with conditions in some areas that we discovered in our resident interviews.

Therefore the council did not have a strong pro-development stance – despite some major development opportunities in the area. For example, town centre redevelopment proposals have been stalled for some time. The approach is closer to a traditional 'Old Labour' authority than the New Labour ones in Newham and Southwark. The council did support the provision of business services but its economic development section employed only 3.5 staff. Informants said that, given the buoyant local economy, this was not a priority. The borough was represented on two sub-regional partnerships but, we were told, Hounslow had not played a significant role on these bodies and its councillor representatives were 'too parochial'.

So relations with business were less well developed than in the other boroughs discussed so far. According to a senior officer, there was a big gap between councillors' ideas and business ideas. And the council's recent start on building partnerships involving business and the community was only occurring because the government required it (there were area committees linked to tenants and residents associations but these were not partnerships). In these and other ways Hounslow seemed to be a rather reluctantly reforming council. What we were told about its politics reinforced this impression. There is a large Asian caucus that holds the balance of power on the Labour Group. Many key programmes, and the areas and groups that benefit, are affected by the bargains which the rest of the Group has to strike with the caucus to get its support.

Therefore the focus is more on a politics of territory and ethnicity within a rather traditional Labour culture. The council lacked the desire and, we were told, did not have the skills to engage in major development schemes. Anyway, the economy was market driven and there was not much the authority saw for it to do. Also, the area's fortunes were highly dependent on national decisions, notably concerning whether the fifth Heathrow terminal could be built (it was given the go ahead in November 2001). Although the council was being forced to change, its internal organization reflected its dominant culture and the traditional service delivery arrangements – with little evidence of a cross-departmental, fully corporate approach or one clear centre of official or political leadership. As we saw, in terms of service delivery this system performed reasonably well. It seemed likely to change slowly while Hounslow and most of its residents continued to prosper, despite the problems for some that we discussed in Chapter 9.

## Redbridge

Redbridge was Conservative controlled from its formation in 1964 until 1994. This was regime government old style with a deeply conservative (in the more general sense) culture. Since 1994 no party has had overall control, and for most of this period there has been a minority Labour administration.

There have been disputes over running the administration, often over the division of power between the two main parties. There had been critical OFSTED (despite the excellent local education results) and Best Value reports. The principal issues were the lack of accountability of committee chairs and of consultation with service users. The Deputy Leader said that these issues were being addressed by the appointment of a new Director of Education and the change to Cabinet government which should improve accountability and clarify decision-making responsibilities.

Redbridge is characterized by strong localism, with an emphasis on residential issues, environmental protection, and the quality of services, particularly education. This shapes the council agenda and, as we saw, it does deliver most services to some of the best standards in London and, in the case of education, nationwide. As we showed in Chapters 2 and 9 this is an affluent area, with only limited deprivation. There is little out-migration although considerable in-migration of upwardly mobile households. This is a commuter economy, with a well qualified population working elsewhere:

> Redbridge is the quintessential suburban borough . . . the least self-contained of all the London boroughs. We have the largest proportion of our workforce commuting out . . . the Redbridge population looks to the City and is a white collar workforce largely.
>
> Senior Council Officer

The council advertises Redbridge as 'a green and leafy borough' and to some extent does not see it as part of London. So economic development is not a high priority, unlike environmental, service delivery and quality of life issues.

However, Redbridge's current leadership and its senior officers – who are of a modernizing tendency – are concerned about the traditional approach of the council, ignoring pockets of deprivation in the south and the north east of the borough. Some felt that Redbridge's suburban role and the lack of indigenous employment might make it vulnerable. These issues were noted in the borough's Economic Development Strategy 1999–2002. In practice though, Redbridge's main regeneration concerns relate to town centre decline with partnerships to revive Ilford Town Centre and other retail areas. It has established a local business support service and a Business Forum and had two small projects to widen employment opportunities for ethnic minority women and young people. However, an indication of the significance of all this is provided by the size of the budget for the borough's 2.5 strong economic development team in 2001/02 – £136,000 (data from council website).

Given its prosperity, Redbridge does not qualify for large-scale regeneration funding, so was not involved in regeneration partnerships, except as part of the Thames Gateway area and through some other East London bodies. Participation by councillors in these had been marginal. This was ascribed to the previous Conservative administration's insularity, NIMBYism and resistance to change. But such sentiments were not confined to the Conservatives. The current leadership is trying to change the culture, but there is a large measure of cross-party agreement that the key issues still relate to the environmental and resident concerns, rather than economic development.

In this sense the councillors are close to the community. However, active community engagement has not been the norm, although area committees were being established. Indeed, we were told, some councillors still did not hold surgeries and we found that contacting them was difficult. The paternalistic flavour of relations between the local authority and the community that we encountered elsewhere existed here too.

The contrast between the continuing reality of politics and local government in Redbridge and the concern of its current leadership to move forward is reflected in its Economic Development Plan for 2001/02. This refers to the new local authority remit and looks to exploit this opportunity by 'a number of cost-effective proposals that add value to the activities of local businesses and encourage a more coordinated approach' but do not 'involve large revenue or capital spending projects'.

Redbridge remains a typical old-style outer London borough, dominated by suburban interests, a service delivery agenda and a degree of NIMBYism. There is little in the way of a core identity to the borough, a sense that change is needed or a serious engagement with the policy issues relating to competitiveness or cohesion. However, a new leadership is emerging. It remains to be seen whether it will shape a modernizing regime suited to Redbridge's situation.


## Dartford

As we explained in Chapter 2, economic development is not a minor concern for Dartford. However, as a second-tier authority, it lacks the resources, staff, responsibilities and powers to engage fully with the economic, social and environmental agenda. Its basic function is to deliver certain local services which it does effectively. It also strives to support and promote the major developments now occurring, protect its residents from their adverse consequence,s and press for some of the benefits to trickle down to those in need. It contracts its business support service to the Chamber of Commerce. An indication of its limited role is that at the time of our research it had just appointed its first full time Economic Development Officer.

Dartford is dependent on the actions of other private and public organizations that it cannot control and can only weakly influence: major developers of offices, housing and retailing; national government especially through its location in the Thames Gateway area and its accommodation of the Channel Tunnel Rail Link and terminal at Ebbsfleet; and Kent County Council which provides education, social services and strategic planning and is the dominant local authority partner in the economic development of the area.

We outlined Dartford's recent economic history, and the current developments in Chapter 2. These are expected to increase the current population of 140,000 to over 200,000 by 2021. The number of jobs in the area is predicted to double between 1991 and 2021 to 163,000. A consensus among the tiers of government responsible for the area and between the political parties, at the national and local level, has been established around this growth agenda. Within the council there is a high level of agreement between the Labour leaders and the Conservative opposition. This has survived the swings in political control of the council that have occurred periodically. There is substantial collaboration and joint working between the tiers of local government despite differences in political control and tension around Dartford's wish to be a unitary authority:

> There has been a lot of consensus as to where we are going in terms of regeneration policies, not so much at County Hall where there has been a lot of argument about education and social services but when we talk about strategic planning, regeneration and development there is much more consensus . . . We work together because our general direction is the same, some details particularly planning issues on particular bits of land may change and that usually changes for political reasons rather than regeneration reasons . . . It is important, very important because what we don't want is for it all to change if another party comes in.
>
> Council Leader

But the picture of consensus should not be overplayed. Within both parties there is some opposition to the development agenda by those who wish to preserve the area as it is and in the ward that we researched there were four residents' association councillors, elected on such a mandate. Their existence underlines the tensions around economic development with the benefits it brings to some sections of the population and the threat it poses to the quality of life of other groups.

In Chapter 2 we described how the area's current transformation began, the key role in it played by Blue Circle and the important public-private partnership that has developed – the Kent Thames-side Association. Its purpose was 'to help plan and promote the area of Dartford and Gravesham north of the A2' and has now been defined by 'a single agenda to grow the GDP in the region':

> The Association is by far the most successful public-private partnership that I'm involved in and I'm involved in three or four, they are focused, it is there for a specific purpose.
>
> Council Leader

The promotion of the area to inward investors in relation to its proximity to London rather than as part of Kent is an important component of the partnership's work, in particular by Dartford's Chief Executive. So the council's role has been to provide the boosterism that attracting inward investment requires – perhaps a realistic adaption to its limited ability to engage in economic development in other ways:

> If ten years ago we'd said we'd see this area as one of the major new growth points in the South East, we're attracting high quality jobs, an international transport system, that's not the popular image of Dartford at all. We had to win hearts and minds . . . that was something that our Chief Executive was immensely successful at. It was almost a question of belief that we could move from a site for London's rubbish to a site for international investment, it was probably done in a slightly ad hoc way, but getting the message across was important . . . there is still more selling to be done, but now that the private sector is convinced of that case, it's time for the local authority to think about something else.
>
> Economic Development Officer

Blue Circle's recent collaboration with LendLease, the Australian property development company, had strengthened the public-private partnership. The company's distinctive approach to development reassured the key councillors who were concerned about the inclusion of local communities in the new opportunities:

> The impact of LendLease's involvement in the area has been dramatic, the confidence they instilled in us as a developer . . . they didn't just build houses they built community, that's the difference, other developers only build houses, and they only put the other bits in if you force them to, they start from the premise that if they are going to make a site successful they build communities and give the planning authority confidence to negotiate with them on issues . . . its their ethos; I've never come across it before.
>
> Council Leader

Like Redbridge, and with the major exception of the CTRL and its terminal, there is little public regeneration investment involved. Statistics from Kent Training and Enterprise Council showed that average earnings in Thanet, Kent's most deprived authority, are about a quarter of the average in Dartford. Given this, some Dartford officials understood why it was not a priority for the county council services. But this limits their ability to address the small areas of deprivation that do exist in Dartford and the polarization between this community and the newcomers. Even more pressingly, there was a lack of county council investment to meet the basic service needs of the new housing areas and residents.

The social composition of Dartford is changing due to new housing but this is not part of a strategy to reengineer the class basis of the area. The inclusion of existing communities in the new opportunities created by growth is desired by the council though its powers to affect this are very constrained:

> The task of the local authority has to be to ensure that all that new investment and growth in the area benefits the local community, so that's local jobs for local people, it's sustainable environment, it's ensuring the skills and the transport is in place to enable local people to benefit from jobs, ultimately our responsibility is to the community, and economic development has to fit in with that, I know that sounds very grandiose but that's what we have got to do.
>
> Economic Development Officer

Some schemes have addressed social inclusion and opening up the new jobs to residents. But these are small scale and some argue that far more could and should have been done.

Dartford remains in many respects a traditional local authority whose main remit is service delivery. However, its leadership participates in the wider coalition that spearheads regeneration, using what powers and resources it has to support that partnership's objectives. It has worries about the impact of change on the locality and the rising demands on public services. None of this amounts to regime-based network governance, although the authority is a key partner in a successful private sector led growth coalition.


## Reading and Wokingham

Reading and Wokingham became unitary authorities in 1998 when Berkshire County

Council was replaced (at its own suggestion) by six such councils. As Chapter 2 indicated, this is one of the most economically dynamic parts of the country and deprivation is very limited. The main issue is how to absorb the impacts of growth, not actively to promote more of it. Issues such as future housing growth, road and rail congestion, the availability of affordable housing and shortages of skilled workers loom large:

> The economy is thriving and it doesn't need a huge amount of effort by the council to ensure that it thrives. So my job is to identify accurately . . . what the council should be doing without reinventing the wheel, without doing another agency's job for them but positioning itself in the most intelligent way as early as possible to ensure that we contribute . . . I think the council has to be wary of encouraging, of promoting too hard the need for inward investment into an area which is booming and where the infrastructure and the land and everything else can only take so much.
>
> Senior Officer, Reading

The creation of relatively small unitary authorities has increased fragmentation, and made strategic planning for transport, economic development and education more difficult:

> The unitary councils have not got the depth of experience and they're not able to deliver the service which a county council does. It's too small and to make strategic decisions it is far too small. In terms of what of is required by the government, there is a need for a much broader view to be taken by the councillors and by the council. There's no way in which the six unitaries can work together on a proper basis strategically, certainly in terms of education . . . I'm afraid we haven't got the quality of officers that we actually require or the salaries to attract them in, people will come to us and then leave, whereas the county council [had] got experienced officers who stayed.
>
> Councillor, Wokingham

Significantly the active sub-regional Thames Valley Economic Partnership (spanning Buckinghamshire and Oxfordshire as well as Berkshire) is very much business-led. Concerns about social cohesion linked to poverty hardly feature although there are a few pockets of deprivation within Reading. The growth of Reading's '24-hour economy' has increased social disorder and incivility as well as actual crime. A police respondent saw it almost as an inevitable consequence of a growing and dynamic town centre economy, the product of a deliberate council policy to prevent Reading becoming a 'ghost town'.

However, apart from this, there was no need for either council directly to initiate economic developments such as new business parks or new facilities and shopping – for example, the privately funded Oracle Shopping and Leisure complex in Reading town centre. Here though partnership working between the council and retailers had been effective. Elsewhere, private housing developers had contributed to new education and other public service needs. The council's small Regional, Economic and European Development Unit engaged in promotional and advice-giving activities for business, training schemes and community projects as well as bidding for external funding. The council is strongly committed to the modernization agenda, acting as a Best Value pilot authority (like Newham and Greenwich) and now operating a Leader-Cabinet system. It has a vision for Reading to be a 'wired city' and education was, hardly surprisingly, an important concern.

Wokingham Council's key concern, according to its website, is 'to balance the need for housing development against protection of the District's pleasant semi-rural environment' and to cope with the demands new developments made on its services and the infrastructure. In Chapter 2 we examined what these were. The council's statement of its Core Values emphasize its commitment to high quality, cost effective service provision. It aims to support and enhance 'a prosperous and thriving community' especially through its mainstream environmental, education and social services. There are special flavours to this which probably derive from the Liberal Democrat leadership: equality and fairness in service delivery and in access to local authority employment with comprehensive equalities monitoring. Reference is made to developing a Social Inclusion Policy. However, the key issues were expected to be skills and labour shortages, affordable housing and the use of e-technology. In Wokingham, like Reading, partnership working had occurred but only to a very limited degree. In both areas the Best Value and Community Strategy requirements will probably lead to a step change in such engagements.

Meanwhile, both councils remained, just below the surface perhaps, traditional local authority service providers. What shapes this remit is the need to accommodate the pressures of growth while not stifling it. Neither council needs to foster the competitiveness of their areas nor focus heavily on problems of social cohesion. However, growth did impact on their service provision. As we saw this remained excellent in Wokingham but had some weaknesses in Reading. Despite their adoption of the apparatus of the new local government agenda, a major part of its purpose seemed simply irrelevant in these areas.

## New Governance Organizations: the Mayor, the GLA and the RDAs

We have already described the major changes in London and regional government under New Labour. It is too early to evaluate properly the impact that these new organizations will have on the overall system of governance or on competitiveness and cohesion. Nevertheless, we can make some preliminary observations. First, it is clear that very few of the city-wide partnerships that arose between 1986 and 2000 disappeared after 2000. Most survived, by simply continuing their role, by re-inventing themselves, or by making themselves useful to the Mayor. Secondly, the weak powers of the Mayor and the few staff directly working for him mean that he is dependent on other agencies to implement his strategies. A key issue facing this (or any other) Mayor is, as a respondent remarked, 'how do you influence the agenda of others to deliver your policies'. In order to solve it he must engage with partnerships, business organizations, sub-regional entities – but above all the boroughs.

To date, some Mayor/borough relations have been antagonistic, some more harmonious. The Mayor's level of spending, wish for more affordable housing, support for tall buildings and proposals to introduce a congestion charge on cars coming into the inner city in particular and a pro-growth agenda more generally have emerged as areas of conflict. Much less ambiguous is the position of the London Assembly, widely seen as weak and ineffective: as one informant stated, 'you tend to hear about them in negatives rather than positives – when you hear about them at all'. Another referred to the Assembly as 'a reactive scrutiny committee that occasionally makes mischief'. Its major success during our research was in forcing the Mayor to cancel a firework display. In fact, given the growing involvement of the boroughs with cohesion and competitiveness, it is the boroughs rather than the Assembly which provide the 'checks and balances' to the executive power of the Mayor.

Meanwhile the outer part of the London Region has been partitioned between two RDAs – the South East England RDA (SEEDA) and the East of England RDA (EEDA). The latter covers the counties to the north and north-east of Greater London and SEEDA those lying from Buckinghamshire round to Kent, so including Reading/Wokingham and Dartford. The RDAs like the LDA exist to further economic development and regeneration; promote competitiveness and employment; improve the skills of the regional labour force; and contribute to sustainable development. In line with the government's overall approach to social exclusion, RDA concerns here centre on raising employment and skills. By 2000 all RDAs had produced economic strategies. At first their relatively small budgets were taken up by inherited commitments (the SRB and other programmes), though this has now begun to change.

In a survey of its region SEEDA examined the situation in the Thames Valley and in Kent ('State of the Region' on its website). It identified the pressures caused by growth in the former area as the main issue and prioritized the improvement of communications (enabling Reading to develop as a 'European Centre'), initiatives to address skills shortages, to promote lifelong learning, and to develop tourism and leisure. Kent was now growing fast but areas in the north of the county had a poor environment and lacked enough high quality business premises. Overall, government indicators of competitiveness showed that Kent was lagging behind other counties in the region.

Nothing proposed by SEEDA seems likely to impede or seriously change the strategies that have been adopted by our three OMA local authorities. Our interviews outside London contained few comments about the possible effects of SEEDA, which reflected its lack of visible impact so far. Within London, not surprisingly, there was more awareness of the possible significance of the Mayor and the LDA, especially in relation to regeneration and transport. While there were some concerns about possible conflict with borough policies, for example, over affordable housing, it was expected that the new agencies would be supportive rather than obstructive (Wandsworth excepted). Perhaps the more likely source of conflict is between the three regional agencies into which the wider London region had been partitioned, each pursuing strategies for 'their' region competitively with the others. In the statutory guidance that government issued to the LDA on its economic strategy, the Mayor was enjoined to secure 'effective co-operation' with the other RDAs, working together on matters of common interest. The guidance included specific reference to the importance of recognizing the key role of the Thames Gateway Partnership which crosses the boundaries between Greater London, EEDA and SEEDA.

The balkanization of regional government in the South East will make an effective strategy for the functional region hard to achieve. Over the past 25 years governance in this region has been characterized by the politics of growth, with conflicts over where growth should occur (away from the west and to the east) and, in the growth areas, over further housing development. The government's Regional Planning Guidance for the South East aims to provide a co-ordinating framework for the preparation of local plans and the RDA strategies but no single body has responsibility for the whole area and for the wider issues of competitiveness and cohesion whose externalities require regional solutions, as we noted earlier.

In the first two years since the establishment of the new London government the main political event was the Mayor's battle with the government concerning the future arrangements and the financing for the Underground, a battle which the latter finally won. In addition over this period the Mayor was developing a series of strategies, the most important being those for transport, economic development (via the LDA) and spatial development. By late 2001 the first two were completed, while the draft Spatial Development Strategy (SDS) (significantly now called the 'draft London Plan') was published in early summer 2002. The Mayor's vision, set out within the plan, is for a strategy that both accommodates and encourages growth, with projections of large increases in both jobs and population: 'London is to grow within its existing green belt and will be a more dense, compact city with massively improved infrastructure to ensure it is an exemplary, sustainable world city' according to the GLA website. Through his firm support for a growth strategy, orientated mainly around finance and business services, the Mayor set out a vision for London which was in strong contrast, not only with previous national policies of containment and diversion, but also with the policies he had previously pursued at the GLC. We return to the London Plan and the future options for London in chapter 11.

As we noted in Chapter 1, the Economic Development Strategy (EDS) takes a strongly pro-business approach, which places it close to the government's competitiveness and social exclusion agenda. It differs radically from the policies pursued by the Mayor and the Chief Executive of the LDA when they led the GLC in the 1980s. The main concerns include: improving the skills of Londoners – especially school leavers; using regeneration programmes to combat social exclusion; focusing large-scale physical regeneration on certain corridors – Thames Gateway, Lea Valley, West London Approaches and Wandle Valley – through supporting the partnerships already in place there; promoting and supporting business development and growth, with a particular emphasis on minority ethnic business; fostering higher and further education and knowledge transfer; and working with business to help improve London's schools.

In 2001 the London Assembly published a critical response to the draft strategy, stating that it was based on 'existing priorities and patterns of activity, offering a fragmented "pick and mix" approach to economic development'. It lacked an overall vision and a balanced approach to economic development across London. The role of the suburbs and local employment centres needed greater consideration and the principles of sustainable development, health, and equal opportunities were not properly integrated throughout the strategy. The draft EDS – and (even more) the emerging Spatial Development Strategy – focused on developing London as a 'world city' and thus on the inner city and CBD. This is why the Assembly referred to the need to consider the suburbs and the local economic base and stated 'economic development is a means to an end'. It defined this end as sustainable development: social progress that recognizes the needs of everyone, environmental protection, prudent use of natural resources and maintenance of high levels of employment and growth.

This goes to the heart of the problematic relationship between competitiveness and cohesion which, as we saw, influences the policy agenda for local governance to widely varying degrees across the region. However, it seems inevitable that the Mayor's centre of gravity will be these world city concerns. As a key insider put it:

> [Livingstone] is the Mayor over a city with more people than in New York and a greater land area than in Paris – it's hard to be the mayor of a city that's 30 miles by 30 miles, that encompasses everything from the entertainment areas to the industrial areas to the suburbs. Now he doesn't really represent the suburbs – he represents the 'symbols of London' that the rest of the world identifies with. But the suburbs are where the people live.

This may bear out a general observation of the Mayor of Denver at a pre-GLA London seminar that 'elected mayors inevitably come to see their city through the warped crystal of its Central Business District – and airport.'

Whether the Mayor and the Assembly will make an impact in the eyes of London's population remains to be seen. A MORI (2002) poll found that 77 per cent could name the Mayor, and 35 per cent were satisfied with his performance, with only 14 per cent dissatisfied. This yields a net rating of +21 per cent – Peter Kellner commented in the *Evening Standard* 'Most politicians would sell their grandmother for such a rating' (22 January 2002). Knowledge about the Assembly was more limited with less than one-third expressing a view either way. Most respondents had an idea (not always accurate) of what the Mayor's responsibilities are. However, few could even attempt to say what the Assembly did – the proportion saying that they did not know what the Assembly was responsible for actually rose from 42 per cent in 2000 to 59 per cent in 2002 (MORI, 2002).

## Conclusion: From Government to Governance?

This chapter began with a discussion of Labour's modernization agenda and a typology of local and regional functions. The agenda is being implemented across all our authorities. Its objective is not just to improve the traditional services of local government but also to create an effective delivery vehicle for the local aspects of New Labour's core concerns with competitiveness and cohesion, especially through partnerships and network governance. However, in reality this agenda is less relevant in areas where the local economy is dynamic, unemployment is low and deprivation confined to a small minority. Reading/Wokingham, Redbridge and Hounslow fell into this category. Here little seems to be required of local government in relation to competitiveness and cohesion beyond that effected by good basic service provision. As a lower-tier authority, Dartford was anyway confined in what it could do and also benefited from a growing local economy and limited deprivation.

So the principal sites which test the capacity of local government to respond to the competitiveness and cohesion agenda are Wandsworth, Newham, Southwark and Greenwich. From the experience of these boroughs, the key points are: first, the contrast between an approach that involves changing the social mix of the area and relying on the trickle-down effect from growth to open up opportunities and reduce exclusion, and one that wishes to balance economic development and social inclusion by policies to address the tensions between them. The contrast here is between Wandsworth and Southwark, on the one hand, and Newham and Greenwich, on the other. In terms of its impact so far, the first approach had probably achieved more. However, the former boroughs were more advanced with their strategies than the latter two, and both have location and market forces working in their favour while the latter do not.

A second contrast is highlighted by comparing Wandsworth and Southwark. It concerns the possibility that the 'social engineering' approach to competitiveness and cohesion, rather than serving both may improve the first at the expense of the second. In Wandsworth, social change had already been induced, through consistent policies pursued over the last two decades. In Southwark, planned social change was at an early stage and hence more contested. Moreover, whereas in Wandsworth gentrification policies had clear electoral advantages for the Conservative administration, this was not the case in Labour-controlled Southwark. In Wandsworth, an important factor was the improvements that the authority had made in service delivery, including services which serve low-income residents – at least those that still remain in the borough. So far, however, Southwark has been unable to combine its development strategy with delivering satisfactory services to its residents. So the council is accused of turning its back on local communities, fostering conflict and division.

Another contrast concerns the leadership, control and culture of the local authorities. Establishing and implementing the new agenda for local governance requires considerable leadership, strong and stable control of the council and a shared, supportive culture across the local authority. Wandsworth had all these and they seemed to be emerging in Newham, while Greenwich was less far along the path. In Southwark, there was strong corporate leadership at officer level and support for policy innovation and new thinking. But Southwark lacks (for the present at least) secure and sustained long-term leadership linking politicians and officers.

As we explained earlier, is it difficult to come to well-founded conclusions about the overall impact of local programmes to raise competitiveness and address issues of social cohesion. How can the effects of market driven change be separated out from those initiated by the governance system in explaining the causes of economic and social change where it was most evident – in Southwark and Wandsworth?

Certainly, the limitations that a weak market position placed on the efforts in Newham and Greenwich are evident. In these circumstances, one concern is that locally-controlled policies may be powerful levers to 'solve' – i.e. displace – economic and social problems by altering the class and/or ethnic composition of an area – an example of the negative externalities that we mentioned earlier.

Finally, we return to more general questions about governance. Some claim that a transition from government to partnership-based network governance has now occurred (Hill, 2000). Our findings show that this is not so. In the outer areas, while the rhetoric of partnership increased and a small amount of such collaboration actually occurred, local government continued and there were few signs of governance breaking out. In the other areas the degree to which this transition had occurred or would probably occur in future was limited. Business and the community remained largely unengaged and where they were engaged, it was not always to any great effect. To some extent this was linked to local authority culture and attitudes but it was also because the various costs of involvement were prohibitively high for many intended partners. The former obstacle to network governance may be easier to resolve than the latter.

In relation to the three functions of sub-national government outlined in the introduction, service provision is the one being most effectively if unevenly discharged. And, although we have maintained a division between this and wider objectives concerning competitiveness and cohesion for the purposes of analysis, in reality effective service provision, especially in health, education, housing and social services, is the crucial basis on which more specific regeneration related initiatives depend, including ones directly linked to cohesion and competitiveness. It is also the basis on which credibility is established (or not) with residents, communities and businesses.

In pursuing the new objectives there is a danger that some authorities may neglect their traditional functions. In addition, while there are clear possibilities for improving the efficiency and effectiveness of their services in observable and even measurable ways, this is not so for many of the new programmes and policies. Earlier we argued that the effectiveness and efficiency of many local programmes related to competitiveness and cohesion would be poor. In practice, there is little attention paid to assessing how successful or not such policies are. Indeed the bidding and competitive culture for programmes like SRB and for Best Value reviews puts a premium on talking up success backed up by a selective appropriation of supporting evidence.

A further issue concerns the co-ordination of policies and strategies regarded as essential to 'joined up' governance. Here we note that across the region as a whole there is still no means of ensuring that this occurs. Within Greater London it remains to be seen whether the Mayor can provide some integration. Within each local authority the proliferation of government ordained partnerships and specially focused programmes (by service, group and/or locality) is making a co-ordinated approach and 'joined up' governance harder than ever. Many respondents from business, the councils, voluntary organizations and community groups, while recognizing some of the benefits of partnership, were despairing of the fragmentation that it created;

the overload that it placed on the partners and the councils; the lack of long-term sustainability of initiative funded projects; and the sheer organizational costs of the whole system. Our conclusion is that, while partnership has a role to play, its virtues have been overstated and its costs downplayed or unrecognized. All that this involves places a strong obstacle in the way of a full transition from government to governance. There are other reasons too, including accountability and professional organization and skills, why government rather than governance will continue to predominate, even in those areas where the modernization agenda has its greatest impact.

In trying to understand how local government systems have responded most effectively as change agents, especially in relation to economic development, a link has been made to the emergence of network, regime-based governance. With the possible exception of Wandsworth there is little evidence that such regimes yet exist in our areas, nor, we suspect, across the London region. Some of the features that taken together have been held to define a regime (Dowding *et al.*, 1999) were present in some: a distinctive agenda, strong leadership, public/private partnerships and so on. However, nowhere were all these conditions satisfied. It may well be that some of the larger sub-regional and cross-regional partnerships, notably the Thames Gateway and the others referred to in the LDA's draft economic strategy, will provide conditions closer to those necessary for regime formation than anything else.

Earlier we suggested London's local government might be shifting from 'rowing' to 'steering', from government to governance. However, two other possibilities are 'waving' – multiplying 'strategies' and 'visions' in the absence of resources and action; or 'drowning' – sinking beneath the weight of local problems and ineffectiveness in responding to them. This is too polarized a set of distinctions; nevertheless it is worth returning to. First, as we saw, the shift from rowing to steering is limited within each locality and varies across them. Second, while none of the authorities was sinking, in some areas, notably Greenwich, Southwark and Newham, avoiding this fate and its consequences presented the most acute challenge to local government. Third, a degree of waving needs to accompany pro-active local government. It should not always be dismissed as evidence of failure. Indeed at the metro scale, a form of waving – that is, the politics of presentation, publicity and promotion – may be a key to achieving policy goals.

Within Greater London, while the Mayoralty has relatively weak formal and fiscal powers, it is possible that a focus for new urban leadership and a new vision for the capital may emerge. If the Mayor can articulate the concerns of London and in doing so frame the debate, he may be able to advance his cause and so create the conditions for some extension of his currently somewhat meagre powers. Successful policy initiatives will however continue to require co-ordinated action from different actors in London's complex system of multi-level governance. A directly elected Mayor provides a focus and a fulcrum for the system, but implementation remains mainly with the boroughs and other service agencies, while finance and (ultimately) legitimacy rests with the government of the day. It remains to be seen whether the new governance of Greater London will be more or less successful than previous arrangements in balancing London's local, regional and national roles.

Perhaps the main question mark concerns the future of the new sub-regional institutions more generally. They have significant funding but are expected to achieve much with it, to shape the impact of markets and market-based agents of change on the region, and in this region especially, to balance the interests of local and globally organized business, local residents and newcomers, in a situation where the inherent conflict between these and other interests is clear. In Greater London, given that the Mayor has to work through other agencies, there will be pressure to move to a situation where he interacts with a smaller number of bodies than the thirty-three lower-tier authorities. A more general question is whether these new agencies can wave, row and steer at the same time – and avoid drowning in the process.

Chapter 11

# The Name of Action: Ideas, Commitment and the Agenda for Cities

And thus the native hue of resolution
Is sicklied o'er with the pale cast of thought,
And enterprises of great pith and moment
With this regard their currents turn awry,
And lose the name of action.
Shakespeare, *Hamlet*, Act 3 Scene 1

The best lack all conviction, while the worst
Are full of passionate intensity.
Yeats, *The Second Coming*

This has been an academic study, which has sought to do what any such study should do: to question simplistic theories and superficial explanations, to dig deeper beneath the surface of things, in order to provide a better approximation to the true state of affairs. That has necessarily meant making qualifications and reservations and casting doubts: this was not a simple tale to tell. But, from the start, it also had a practical purpose. As Keynes once memorably said, 'Madmen in authority, who hear voices in the air, are distilling their frenzy from some academic scribbler of a few years back' (Keynes, 1936, 383). Out of inadequate scholarship can come misguided policy. Passionate intensity, compounded of impatience and intuitive reason, can impel charges into the valley of death – though more often against quixotic targets, or in pursuit of shortcuts. But 'resolution', combining seriousness and persistence, is as important as science in securing comprehension and effective action. Our aim throughout has been to distil our findings in order to help policy-makers do better.

The largest general conclusion of this book is that things are not always as simple as they seem: many of the comfortable generalizations about London – that it is the most globalized city on earth, that in consequence it is one of the world's most economically competitive cities, that as a result it is a deeply polarized city with a growing underclass, that a collapsing social fabric threatens the entire future of the city – prove to be quite massive oversimplifications, or even to be plain wrong. True, there are elements of all these features, but they often prove to be quite minor and relatively unimportant. Reality, as often, is more complex – as we try to explain below. In essence: London has changed, but not always as the conventional theory suggests. It has become highly entrepreneurial and highly competitive. It has become a more unequal city. But it is not – at least so far – a polarized or segregated, still less a ghettoized, city. It has become a multi-ethnic and multi-cultural city of an American kind, but without many of concomitant problems of American cities.

So, in this final chapter, we first perform the necessary work of distillation: we try to summarize the conclusions from our research for the five key questions that were set out at the start, in Chapter 1 – together with a consideration of their relevance to other cities. From that, we go on to suggest some implications for future academic research on the contemporary city: in particular, we suggest some ideas we think may prove fruitful for the future development of urban sociology. Then, we similarly attempt a reformulation of key urban policy priorities – which, paradoxically, prove to be some very old priorities, in a new guise. As a postscript we look at key elements and assumptions of the Mayor's recently published *London Plan* in the light of these arguments and our research findings.

## Answering the Five Key Questions

First, then, we turn to the central questions we posed at the outset of our study.

### 1. What do competitiveness, social cohesion and social exclusion actually mean for London's residential and business communities?

Competitiveness, cohesion, and exclusion – together with governance and social capital – have become key terms in the policy discourse about processes of change in advanced capitalist societies – the new conventional wisdom, or 'liberal formulation', as we have described it elsewhere (Harloe, 2001; Gordon and Buck, 2003). But, as we signalled in Chapter 1, each of these ideas contains substantial ambiguities, with elements in each that are not necessarily very closely associated. This presents problems in mobilizing evidence to assess how areas are performing in terms of each of them, or how they affect an area's development. And there is another difficulty in applying these concepts to London: the great diversity and complexity of the London city region, two characteristics that we see as quite fundamental to the way in which it operates – for better and for worse.

In this study we have approached these difficulties in two ways. First, we have sought to clarify the ideas underlying these concepts and the distinctions which need to be made in operationalizing them. Sometimes it appears that the language of competitiveness, cohesion and governance is little more than an updated, but still very broad, rewriting of traditional ideas of economic, social and political performance – updated because in 'new times' old terms go out of fashion (Hall and Jacques, 1989). Some of the particular fuzziness around the words 'cohesion' and 'governance' seems to reflect their secondary status: they tend to be employed as convenient shorthands for any social and political conditions that might appear necessary for achieving and sustaining competitiveness. To help clarify, we have found a need to disaggregate each of these concepts. Thus, within the blanket term 'social cohesion', we distinguish aspects of inequality, connectedness and order; under the umbrella of 'competition' we likewise distinguish different kinds of markets – for products, inward investment, desirable residents and governmental favours.

Second, we have sought to combine region-wide analyses of aggregate or standardized indicators with more qualitative and localized investigations of the factors that firms, households and other actors find to be significant at a more practical level in their own particular contexts. This dual approach reflects two key facts about urban life, particularly in major cities. On the one hand, people and organizations operate in very different kinds of niches and circumstances across the city region, about each of which they may have varying perceptions, with many of them exercising some choice over the location(s) in which they operate. On the other hand, these locales are far from isolated, but rather experience a high degree of interdependence and interaction with other locales. This operates both directly through flows – of information, services, migrants, commuters, school-goers and shoppers – between them, and indirectly through the mediation of property, labour and other markets (including quasi-markets for public services). Hence life in all areas and sectors is affected in some way by various aggregate characteristics, potentials and constraints of the metropolitan region, lying outside the immediate experience of individual firms, people or local public actors, as well as by those immediate connections which they recognize.

In the case of *competitiveness*, we find that the most important issue concerns the ability of London-based firms to sell their products in open, contested markets, and the characteristics of the city's economic and social environment which help or hinder them in this task. In the literature there is still some ambiguity about whether the value of such urban assets accrues basically to firms with their 'home bases' in the region, even if their main production occurs elsewhere – Porter's (1990) position – or is of comparable benefit to all businesses operating in the area, irrespective of where their home base may be. In practice, we have focused on the performance of establishments operating in the region, which connects more closely with the second interpretation, but also bears more directly on issues of social and policy concern in the region. For these businesses we have taken growth, productivity and export success as the key indicators of product market competitiveness.  In these terms, the region's performance is somewhat mixed: distinctly strong by British standards on the second and third criteria, but only average in terms of growth over the last couple of decades. Productivity and earnings levels are substantially higher than in any other UK city-region, while across the range of service trades, plus publishing/printing, export propensities are double those in the rest of the UK.

In terms of product innovation London also scores well, though the real areas of strength are outside Greater London – and a number of the most innovative areas are actually beyond the boundary of our region, in the fringes of the Greater South East. The region's growth record is held back by an inelastic supply of space, rather than weak demand, partly reflecting the maturity of core areas, but also planning constraints, which bite especially strongly in the OMA. Within the region there seem to be substantial differences in competitiveness, with the eastern half clearly doing worse on all criteria. By European standards, London's overall economic performance has been on a par with the group of leading cities, but not generally ahead of them, despite its position as the most internationally oriented of these cities (and arguably of all major cities).

What is not quite so clear is precisely how a London location contributes to this competitive success. For most individual firms, the key factors affecting performance are almost inevitably bound up with their specific company strengths, including the technologies they can access, with the strength of the market sector in which they operate, and also with much wider economic factors. This does not mean that regional factors are unimportant; as we aggregate across the London economy, many firm-specific influences will cancel out, while the wider influences can be seen as just defining the playing field on which firms and city regions compete. Making such allowances, some of the relevant regional influences are very clear – deteriorating public transport, for example. But for others, including many broad agglomeration economies, this is not the case: firms only have to take notice of them if and when they consider relocation out of the region, which very few ever do (see Chapter 3). Nevertheless, the fact that market rents are so high – particularly in central areas of the region – and that firms thrive despite such higher costs, suggests that agglomeration economies are really important, even if London firms habitually take them for granted.

Urban competitiveness involves more than successfully producing and selling goods or services; it is also a matter of developing, or somehow securing, both the high quality human assets and the more routine skills necessary to sustain a successful service economy. Resident Londoners compete too: against other Londoners, and new arrivals, for worthwhile jobs in this economy. At graduate level the region is currently very successful in attracting well-qualified and ambitious candidates from both home and abroad, even though the high cost of living absorbs much of the nominal difference in earnings compared with the rest of the country. In part this clearly reflects the opportunities for personal development (building both human and social capital) in the responsible leading-edge jobs which the city offers, together with the strong prospects for advancement through inter-firm movement in a flexible, high-turnover labour market. This 'up-escalator' is one key aspect of the region's competitive performance. But it is clear that the city also attracts talent for other reasons, including the vibrancy of its cultural life (of all kinds) and a level of tolerance and open-mindedness – in social as well as economic settings – which is particularly valued by a more highly-educated workforce, as well as by migrants and minorities.

In terms of the education of its own young residents, London's performance appears more ambivalent. Overall school results for the region are a little above average by British standards. But this is probably not good enough for a region specializing in service functions where the great majority of jobs require at least a basic level of academic and interpersonal skills, including those jobs filled almost entirely from within the local population. In much of Inner London and Thames-side school-level performance actually looks very poor. Basically this reflects concentrations of disadvantaged groups within catchment area populations, including relatively high proportions of lone parent families. In value-added terms the average school does not seem to be doing a bad job, in difficult circumstances. But the degree of variation between schools points to clear room for improvement, both in achievement levels and in behavioural factors such as truancy rates which mediate the effects of social disadvantage. There has been progress in reducing actual failure rates, but this remains one of the weak areas in the region's competitive performance and in the assets it has to offer.

As for social cohesion, social exclusion and social capital, we have redrawn the conventional distinctions (which tend to overlap) in terms of dimensions of inequality, connectedness and social order. Within each of these there are other distinctions to be made: notably, for inequality between characteristics of the top and the bottom ends of the distribution, as well as (at the bottom end) between relative and absolute deprivation. Nevertheless, on this dimension it is clear that the London region is one of particularly sharp inequality, with much more than its share of the really affluent, and rather more than its share of the poor. Poverty here, in real income terms, is particularly associated with a high cost of living (especially for housing and transport). But it also reflects an above-average concentration of many vulnerable groups – together with unemployment rates which have tended to remain somewhat above the national average. All of these characteristics are exaggerated if we focus on Greater London alone, and still more so in the case of Inner London. This is principally because of the way that the region's housing market (or the quasi-market that characterizes today's social housing sector) generates patterns of residential segregation. To this extent, like the overall concentration of vulnerable groups in this region, their spatial concentration cannot be seen as simply reflecting local factors which exacerbate poverty and inequality. But there are clearly processes operating within the region which do tend both to reproduce and to magnify the scale of such outcomes, particularly for vulnerable groups and for residents of some of the inner areas – just as others tend to increase the rewards for those who have the assets, determination and luck to succeed in this competitive environment.

For connectedness, the second dimension of cohesion, we have focused on a number of particular aspects: 'getting on' and 'getting by' forms of social capital, the effects of London's relatively fragmented family structures, and the question of how far individuals suffering from various forms of material deprivation are effectively 'excluded' from participation in normal social relations. We found that Londoners, in the main, get about as much social connectedness as they want. Against many expectations, Londoners are just as connected in terms of friends, family, organizations or trust, as similar sorts of people in any other part of the country, although physical distances separating people from family and friends are much greater. Because the population composition is different in London, average levels of connectedness are actually lower on some indicators of social capital, which may have some broader consequences for the community. Some groups – such as the long-term sick and disabled and the retired – clearly do experience substantial social isolation, while those lacking qualifications, income or networks perceive themselves to be (and are) isolated and remote in the midst of a successful, global city. But we found few people who were 'truly excluded', in the sense that they concurrently experience all forms of exclusion: from the labour market, from communal support, and from citizenship entitlements, as hypothesized by Kesteloot (1997) and found in Wilson's (1987, 1997) studies of Afro-American ghettos.

On the third dimension of cohesion, namely order, Londoners report many worries – about incivility, crime and social disorder. For most this is an inconvenience, but for some it is a major blight on their lives. Across the entire region general crime rates are actually close to the national average – except for mugging, which is much more common – but, as elsewhere, there are great variations, and the risks of crime are clearly greater in inner areas. Maintaining social order is an issue that increasingly impinges on local institutions – particularly schools in socially stressed areas, where it can form one of the key constraints on raising performance.

Generally, most Londoners felt comfortable where they were. An appreciable minority did not: in some inner areas, in particular, they felt a general sense of menace and fear. Here, many reported that they wanted to move away, and that others had already gone. And this was reinforced by some of those living more comfortable lives in quieter and more secure areas, who told us that they had moved from places they regarded as distinctly less secure. But the comfortable ones were the great majority, and we were struck by the large numbers who liked not merely the physical qualities of their neighbourhoods but also the social relationships: the small courtesies done by or for neighbours, the sense that help would be at hand in a sudden emergency, the general sense of security that all this brought. This was not a city where anomie or alienation loomed very large.

All the same, the exceptions were important, and they seemed to fit one principal stereotype: they occurred in places of transition, where a settled order was being disturbed by new residents with different ways of life. There was sometimes a racial (or racist) component here, as in Bermondsey, but it was confusingly mixed with other elements like age (the old people's block invaded by young people with different lifestyles) and economic status (a settled Indian population facing an influx of refugees). Yet sometimes these transitions seemed to work quite satisfactorily for almost everyone, as in Battersea. Generally, London does not seem to be a city with very high tension levels; people of different ages, different incomes and lifestyles, different races live well together, and even celebrate the fact.

London is a very competitive place, not only in the sense that it is a place where businesses of many kinds thrive, and many people make successful careers, but also in the sense that for businesses, and (more pertinently) for workers and residents it is a harder place to be than many other places, with more challenges and rather less security. Connectedness, order and a sense of belonging are important – and people find ways to try and create such qualities, even where inequality is high and other external circumstances do not foster them. The region is a place of choice, opportunities and risks. Trade-offs are continually being made, from the OMA commuters grudgingly accepting delays for the sake of better salaries, or the inner-city residents accepting disorder and stress for the sake of proximity to jobs and social life, to the 'escalator' professionals and home-owners calculating when it is time to cash in and step off. That is the kind of place London is – and indeed Paris or New York or any great metropolitan city. In them, such features come with the territory.

## 2. How substantially have these processes changed as a result of internationalization and intensified competition since the early 1980s?

There are really two questions here: one asking how far outcomes in terms of aspects of competitiveness and cohesion have altered for London and Londoners over this period; the other about the respects in which such changes may be attributable to these two 'global' processes, rather than to some other factors. For the first, the picture is fairly clear: much does seem to have changed in the patterns of social and economic outcome. Among our three competitiveness indicators we lack any measure as to how the export performance of London businesses may have changed. But there have been markedly positive developments in relation both to growth and productivity. For growth, the extent to which the region's economic progress has improved is somewhat obscured by a very marked increase in the volatility of the regional economy, both absolutely and relative to other parts of the UK. So far this has involved two unprecedentedly strong 'boom' phases – in the late 1980s and 1990s – separated by a 'bust' phase, also (for London) of unprecedented strength. So any interpretation of the degree to which underlying trends have changed for the better would depend to some degree on a judgement as to whether the recent, extended upswing is likely, soon, to be succeeded by another 'bust' phase. In our view, this is more probable than not, quite irrespective of whether the events of September 11th 2001 turn out to have provoked an international recession – or a net diversion of activity away from vulnerable major cities. On this basis, comparisons with earlier peaks in London employment levels indicate that within Greater London the downward trend which marked the 1960s and 1970s has been replaced by effective stability in levels of employment. In the OMA an established growth trend has been given a further boost – though the change in trends is somewhat more modest here. Assessments underlying the Mayor's *London Plan* take a more bullish view, however, of the extent of turnaround in Greater London's employment trends during this period (Greater London Authority, 2002).

In terms of productivity levels, evidence of an upward shift is also clear, and much easier to quantify, at least in terms of earnings differentials – with which they are strongly associated. Basically the gap between Greater London and national performance doubled during this period (in the case of earnings moving from a differential of around 15 per cent to about 30 per cent): the OMA's gap is smaller but also more or less doubled. However, virtually all of the shifts seem to have occurred in the earlier part of the period (in fact between 1979 and 1990), effectively representing a step change in relative performance, rather than a shift to a higher (per capita) growth path.

For inequality, also, there is clear evidence of a change. At the top end of the income distribution, this involved an exaggerated version of the rapid growth rate of earnings among top groups evident nationally during the 1980s. At the bottom end, it took the form of increased proportions of the population, especially within Greater London, who did not enjoy any earnings from employment – including growing numbers both of formally unemployed people and of other non-employed groups within the working age population, notably many lone parents. At a domestic level, there has been an increasing polarization between fully-employed households and those with no workers. Over the past two decades these are very clear tendencies, but they have not operated consistently through the period. Absolute levels of non-employment have, of course, shown a strong cyclical pattern, with very substantial improvements occurring during the years of strong demand since 1996. Indeed much of the region, outside Inner London, is now clearly enjoying something like full employment. But overall levels of non-employment are still well above those at the start of the period.

The other major social change has been a great increase in the ethnic and cultural diversity of the city since the late 1980s, highlighted in Inner London schools where a majority of children are now from non-white ethnic origins, including many immigrants from non-English speaking backgrounds. This has not, however, been accompanied by further spatial separation, though other trends have brought some increase in segregation of the employed from the non-employed and of couple-based from non-couple-based households. In terms of social order, there have been short- and medium-term swings in both actual crime rates and perceptions of insecurity, but though concerns over incivilities and drug dealing have risen, Londoners are no more worried about crime than they were 20 years ago.

Turning to the processes underlying these changes, the evidence is, naturally, less easy to interpret. In part this reflects some conceptual complications. Thus, 'internationalization' – which we cited at the outset as one of the possible explanations of change over this period – involves at least three distinguishable elements through which the London economy might have been affected. The first of these is simply that of increased levels of trade and factor mobility – though what is notable in economic terms about the last two decades is the growth of trade in services and of capital mobility, particularly related to the growth of multi-national corporations, rather than trade in goods (which has not conspicuously accelerated) or labour mobility (which has increased, but largely for non-economic reasons). The second path of potential impacts is via policy adjustments which governments have made in response to the new opportunities and challenges which these developments present, notably in London's case through deregulation of financial markets and capital mobility – but also the 'rolling-back' of state activity. Finally, there is the emergence or intensification of a specialized set of global/continental urban functions, both in relation to directly traded services and in support of other forms and agencies of internationalization – which Gordon (2002*d*) labels 'global-cityization' to distinguish it from more diffuse aspects of globalization.

In this last, most specialized, respect London has clearly gained from both globalization and European integration over the past two decades. By most criteria it is one of the most 'global' of the major cities of the world, with advanced services that are only comparable in their international orientation with those of New York (Sassen, 2002). But whereas New York (and to a still greater extent Tokyo) functions very largely as the interface between national (American or Japanese) business and the rest of the world, London has a wider range of third-party functions, operating (as in the foreign exchange market) in support of activities and transactions in which UK firms are not directly involved. In this respect it may only be paralleled by some city-states (such as Singapore or Dubai) which fulfil similar roles for particular regions of the world. Growing internationalization of business since the early 1980s has thus provided a significant boost to the London economy.

But it is important not to exaggerate the extent to which 'global city' functions are responsible for the upturn in the city's economic performance over this period, or represent the real 'drivers' of the city economy. In terms of their contribution to the economic base of the city, they are obviously important, but the global and European roles together are still clearly much less significant for London than its continuing role as a national centre. In relation to changes in levels of activity, the international sector does seem to have played a considerable role in the boom and bust cycles of the 1980s and 1990s. But over the longer run, it is not clear that it has grown much faster than comparable nationally-oriented activities. Two reasons are the continuing shift of British comparative (and competitive) advantage away from goods-related sectors, and policy responses to internationalization, in the form of privatization and deregulation, both of which have boosted demand for financial and business services. Among British cities London has gained most from this, at least partly because it started from a larger and stronger service base than any other centre.

For increased inequality in the city, 'global-cityization' must bear some responsibility, both through the boost which it has provided (together with privatization and related processes) to demand for the most highly-paid types of business professional, and through a certain levelling-up of salaries toward American norms in the most internationally mobile job categories. But at the bottom end, as we have seen, it is unemployment rather than lower wages which kept personal incomes down. This cannot be directly blamed on globalization, either in terms of Sassen's (1991) thesis about global cities' burgeoning demand for low-paid service activities, or in terms of a 'race to the bottom' driven by competition from new producers in cheap-labour economies. In the 1980s, at any rate, the difference may reflect the fact that London (unlike New York, which seems to have been Sassen's main source of evidence) lacked an elastic supply of cheap immigrant labour to meet the latent demand for affordable consumer services. In the 1990s there has been a remarkable change in the picture, with the emergence of comparably high rates of international immigration into London from a range of poor countries, a large part of it in the form of asylum seekers rather than economic migrants. The economic implications of this are not yet clear, since many of the recent arrivals have yet to be absorbed in the mainstream labour market, but they may have contributed to a faster rate of consumer service employment growth during this decade.

Overall, we can see that internationalization has intensified the processes discussed in answer to question 1 above. It has created more opportunities for talents of all kinds, more spaces and opportunities, and it has added both to the city's diversity and to recognition that this is an asset. But it has also helped to make it a more volatile city, with more risks, larger gaps, and bigger tumbles for firms and individuals that fail. These outcomes reflect a variety of processes, however, both direct and indirect, and are not simply a reflection of the growth of command and control, or finance and business service functions. Nor are all of them peculiar to London, since they also reflect ways in which the country as a whole has accommodated to internationalization.

The impact of intensified competition on London's performance is also somewhat complex to untangle. The main hypotheses here were that vertical disintegration and more 'flexible' forms of business organization should work to London's advantage in terms of its competitive performance, but that these were likely to create new kinds of insecurity, turbulence and volatility in the city's economy and labour market which would be inimical to social cohesion. On the two indicators of competitiveness for which we have change data (i.e. growth and earnings/productivity), there is some evidence that the new competitive environment has had an effect. In the case of growth, it is mostly in terms of the boost to demand for business services of many kinds stimulated both by out-sourcing and by the active encouragement to 'self-provision' in relation to pensions, health insurance and other personal financial arrangements, as expectations of state provision were cut back during the 1980s. This would have affected all regions, but with more benefit to London, because of its greater concentration of these activities.

For earnings and productivity, the sharp widening of London's differential which we have noted was clearly associated with the Thatcher era of deregulation in both labour and product markets, which seems to have worked to the competitive advantage of residents and/or businesses in the region. We are unable clearly to separate the relative contributions of changes in the functioning of these two markets. However, a major part at least must reflect the impact of widening earning differentials, passed on via prices to measured productivity – as distinct from those gains which more productive London businesses may have achieved in more open markets, and passed on in higher earnings to their key workers. The other point to make about the concentration of change in this decade is that it reflects responses to exogenous shifts not simply in competitive pressures, since these were not neatly confined to this period, but also to the competitively motivated responses of the British government.

In relation to social cohesion, the sharp widening of earnings differentials in the region, associated with increasingly competitive labour market behaviour during the 1980s, clearly contributed to the observed increase in inequality. But it is less clear that intensified competition was responsible for the higher levels of unemployment experienced during the 1980s and 1990s, which were the other major factor in rising inequality. Certainly these increases owed rather little to casualties among the region's own businesses in this period – in contrast to the situation in other, more industrial British cities. A more plausible link is in terms of increased turbulence in the labour market making more people in the region vulnerable to the risks of long-term under-employment. But while we do find a generally higher level of turbulence in the region's labour market (as compared with those in other areas) to be a significant risk factor, we have no evidence of an upward shift in turnover rates during this period, either in the region or nationally.

Rather, we find that the rising levels of unemployment, which particularly affected Inner London during this period, were primarily a consequence of national recessions and industrial restructuring, associated particularly with a loss of competitive advantage in older manufacturing activities mostly located in other regions. Their impact on the London region reflects the openness of the regional economy and labour market more than competitive forces acting directly on the region – even if the 1990s recession was experienced more severely because of the puncturing of the region's earlier 'bubble economy'. The effects were both prolonged and concentrated on particular areas and social groups through a set of processes of downward mobility and marginalization associated (until the boom of the late 1990s) with generally slack demand in the labour market. This served to exacerbate the effects of long-established sources of labour market inequality, and induce important knock-on effects on other components of deprivation, notably sickness and lone parenthood. Similar factors would have operated in most other parts of the country, and continued beyond the mid-1990s in regions of weaker demand. But the scale and structure of the London region meant that the pattern of deprivation has been particularly concentrated and statistically visible. These developments are likely to have had substantial implications both for connectedness and order, though the major changes here appear to be those associated with shifting family and household structures, rather than direct repercussions of deprivation or rising inequality.

### 3. Which processes within the city are key to the achievement of a more economically competitive and socially cohesive future? Which processes may work against either or both of these?

Though these are questions about the future, our understanding of key future processes is clearly based on evidence from the past and present. We couple this with some speculation about the implications of a continuation of present trends, and about what may be key opportunities and threats facing the city-region.

Starting with trends, a crucial point is that they are surrounded by a very high level of uncertainty. This is most obvious in relation to demography, where the turnaround in population trends, particularly in Greater London, reflects in large part the upsurge of migration from poor countries since the late 1980s, much of it in the form of asylum seekers for whom London is one of the preferred destinations. These processes are largely driven by forces outside the country, rather than either local economic developments or British immigration policy, and it is not clear what influence either admissions controls or recent dispersal policies will have on numbers eventually settling in London. GLA forecasts are for continued rapid growth (Greater London Authority, 2002). But the implications for future population size are also unclear, especially for Greater London: other groups might be predicted to move out in search of space, but they have not done so to any great extent, perhaps because migrants have been too poor to form households. Yet this should not last. But in any case, the share of ethnic minorities in the population (both white and non-white) is expected to grow substantially.

As we have seen already, even ignoring the effects of uncertain population growth, there are major uncertainties also about the scale of employment change to be expected over the medium and long term – and even the direction as far as Greater London is concerned. We have taken a view earlier about what can be inferred from past trends in terms of a 'most likely' outcome, but the fact is that internationalization and the new 'flexible economy' together have brought a volatility to the region's economy, which makes quite different outcomes very possible, and mean that it is very unlikely to be 'on trend' in any given year. Strategies for the city have to be flexible enough to cope with substantial uncertainty and variability, which will not be resolved simply by better research or a few more years' experience. In relation to competitiveness, the key processes are those promoting and sustaining the city's diversity, openness and adaptability, both in terms of the existing broad base of firms and people and talent, and the continuing massive import of human capital, ideas and skills from all over the world as well as all over the UK.

It is the city's ability to make the most of these rich resources, which makes it a major national and European asset, rather than the 'great wen' which Cobbett perceived as draining strength from the rest of the system. The main threats to its continued success would lie in deterioration in the UK economy as a whole or in global economic activity, further neglect of basic infrastructure and public service provision, and over-restrictive planning policies across the region. Such policy failures are more likely if governance of the region continues to be fragmented. External challenges may come from several directions: from other contenders for 'European city' status (though that is the least likely); from more dynamic second- and third-tier European centres successfully developing competitive advantages in niche specializations which eat away at London's hegemony; and/or from increased dominance of US multi-nationals in sectors such as finance and the media, drawing away strategic functions and taking a more dispassionate view about the need for support operations to be undertaken in a high-cost location, rather than in (say) India or China.

In relation to cohesion, we start from a position of high earnings inequality and a pattern of joblessness which is still unusually concentrated, despite the positive effects of 5 years or so of strong demand. The second of these is particularly important, since – as we have seen – there is a series of circular processes linked with unemployment which tend to perpetuate and reinforce deprivation, at the level of individuals, households, and neighbourhoods or sub-regions. We have seen this in the cases of education, family fragmentation, and information networks – and it is obviously true in relation to health as well, although that is not a field with which we have dealt explicitly in this study. Current problems are the cumulative product of processes operating over decades, and reversible only gradually in the context of sustained support, particularly in the form of a strong pressure of demand for labour.

This persistence is partly a matter of deprived groups acquiring further characteristics which reinforce initial disadvantages. But, as the example of 'bumping down' in the labour market illustrates, it is also a reflection of the fact that marginalization is often only a symptom of misadjustments and unevenesses among core groups which also need to be reversed and remedied if the marginalized are to be effectively reintegrated. In other words, although problems are concentrated at the margins – in terms of individuals, population groups and areas – that is rarely where they originate, or where solutions (as distinct from palliatives) are to be found. At worst, if another prolonged period of slack demand were to return, it could well produce levels of concentrated disadvantage worse than those experienced in the early 1990s. One aspect would be a widening of gaps in achievement, between areas, social classes and ethnic groups, all of which show a disturbing persistence and a liability to widen substantially in periods of slack demand, when employers have an embarrassment of choice. But it needs to be emphasized that the lines of division which emerge are by no means simple, as for example between all white and all non-white ethnic groups. Thus in the case of schooling we found that there were high levels of motivation, support and achievement among some groups in inner areas, including some immigrant and ethnic minorities, while other communities (white and non-white) appeared very isolated in social and educational attitudes.

Overall, however, the combination of background circumstances, less supportive communities and over-stressed schools does mean that too many young people emerge into the new London economy with few of the necessary resources to perform a responsible or satisfying role in it. At best, they will occupy a series of temporary roles, in casual jobs requiring little or no training, and even there they may find themselves competing with a far better-qualified labour pool – of schoolchildren looking for supplementary pocket money, of Europeans or Australians seeing the world – which will bring more resources to the job. In these circumstances, the temptations of the alternative economy and of alternative lifestyles may be all too great. Petty crime may offer its attractions to some, hard drugs – with the obvious dangers of falling into crime – for others, early pregnancy for many of the girls. And with the mounting costs of housing, residential choices for under-achievers are few. Often this will involve the least habitable housing in the least accessible or attractive locales, with the poorest shops and public services, and above all the poorest-performing schools from which the other parents have withdrawn their children – thus perpetuating the cycle of deprivation.

However, one outcome which we do not envisage for London is the emergence of the ghetto poverty which Wilson (1987, 1997) has so powerfully portrayed in Chicago. One reason is that both disadvantage and segregation are much more multi-dimensional in London. The broadest spatial divisions are actually between coupled and non-coupled households, irrespective of class or ethnicity, with the latter predominating in inner areas. Ethnic concentrations exist, but (as we saw in Chapter 2) these are among the most localized – partly reflecting the fact that no particular minority has a large share of the population, or is ever likely to do so. But the second reason is gentrification, which after 40 years of progress has now made a very real mark on the social geography of London, and seems likely soon to involve virtually all the inner boroughs. A paradoxical effect, as we have seen, is that Inner London is now simultaneously the highest status of the 'rings' of the region, and the one with the greatest concentration of disadvantaged groups. Within this area segregation is increasingly localized, reducing the risks of a complete separation from mainstream society. This may be one reason why London experienced none of the large-scale inter-ethnic conflict that affected some northern industrial towns in 2001. In London schools, however, there can be considerable segregation, with some primary schools already having very largely South Asian pupils, because their catchment areas are localized, because the age composition of ethnic minorities can be very different – and because some other parents exit in the face of a potentially monocultural situation.

For somewhat similar reasons, we do not envisage any part of London experiencing the large-scale residential abandonments which have marked, for example, east Manchester as well as many American cities. But in this case the key factor is clearly that the level of housing demand in London as a whole is extremely high. This alone is sufficient to distinguish the character of neighbourhood regeneration issues in London from those customarily identified in the north. As we have seen, London has its share (or something like it) of areas of poverty, crime, educational disadvantage and housing stress, but none of these is directly related to the economic weakness of parts of the city – and neither local job creation, nor policies to stop population decentralization, are of direct relevance to addressing them.

## 4. How important are different aspects of social cohesion, social exclusion and social capital (and policies for these) for sustaining economic success in this new context? And are there causal links in the other direction too?

In this book we have given considerable emphasis to investigating ways in which one or other dimension of social cohesion might feed back into economic success or failure. In this we were motivated both by an academic literature which suggested an increasing dependence of the economy on social relations, and a policy literature which questioned whether neo-liberal policies promoting increasingly individualistic and deregulated forms of behaviour were compatible with sustained economic success. To some degree this policy literature (to which academics contributed) might be seen as looking for an alternative justification for welfarist policies when their normative basis seemed to have lost legitimacy.

But in searching for evidence of such links we encountered two main difficulties. The first is that connections between aspects of social cohesion and economic performance are likely to be quite indirect, rather than things which would be directly recognized either subjectively by economic actors or objectively through analyses of statistical data. To investigate these, we need to identify key variables and processes through which connections might plausibly be mediated. The second difficulty is that some of the more powerful arguments for the importance of social conditions and relationships imply thresholds beyond which some key processes or sources of order start to break down, while available evidence tends to relate to conditions inside these thresholds where little evidence of such potential breakdowns is likely to be found.

To deal with the first of these difficulties, our approach was to start from the economic 'end' and to identify possibly significant influences on business competitiveness for which there was a plausible link back to some aspect of social cohesion (as we did in Chapter 3). We then sought to work our way back through the analysis of mediating processes (in schools and/or labour markets, for example) to find evidence of links back to inequality, connectedness or order. There were, however, some limits to our ability to follow this through – notably where this involved actors outside the region who might have been discouraged from coming to London, opening up businesses, or buying services here – and our final judgements about the potential significance of links are inevitably subjective.

We identified a number of paths through which cohesion (or its absence) might plausibly be seen as impacting on competitiveness within a city or region. Though we actually found little strong evidence that most were operationally significant in the London region, it is worth listing them to indicate the sort of connections through which one or more versions of cohesion might in principle exert an influence on an area's competitiveness:

1. Aspects of connectedness or order affecting the willingness of mobile individuals with desirable characteristics (human capital and/or spending power) to live in the area.

2. Aspects of inequality, disconnectedness and/or disorder affecting the supply of middle-range skills (typically recruited within the city region) via under-achievement in the local school system.

3. Aspects of order, in particular, affecting the image of an area in the eyes of prospective inward investors – or tourists – and in extreme cases outward investors too.

4. Aspects of inequality, connectedness and order affecting competitiveness through levels of crime to which businesses are subjected.

5. Aspects of connectedness within a business (or business-related) community affecting levels of trust, and thereby willingness to participate in collaborative ventures with uncertain pay-offs, both in relation to innovation and to collective action in support of local economic development.

6. Aspects of connectedness within a workforce and between workforce and employers affecting levels of productivity and the development of human capital.

In addition, there are some potential negative paths – for example, mirroring 'path' 5: tighter cohesion among residential communities may well facilitate collective action against local (physical) development, or NIMBYism. Here, however, we concentrate on the positive aspects.

In each case, the plausibility of the various linkages postulated could be grounded in some sorts of empirical evidence, as well as *a priori* argument – and the intuitions of 'common sense'. How significant they may be in practice also depends, however, on the real strength of some of the connections, on whether all necessary conditions are likely to be met in the same situations, on whether there are countervailing forces, and on the range of situations to which they apply (Gordon, 2003).

For various reasons, few of these arguments seemed very convincing in the London case. Both because of the opportunities on offer, and the insulation afforded by large-scale residential segregation in the region, fear of crime and disorder did not currently appear to be a significant factor affecting the willingness of mobile, highly-skilled groups to live and work in the region. There are currently serious problems of recruitment and retention to 'key worker' jobs in the public sector (as there were in the last boom). But these reflect a failure of wages there to adjust to exceptionally high housing costs and the unusual demands faced by those working in over-stretched services, rather than the city's unattractiveness to such workers (Greater London Assembly, 2001). Other aspects of social connectedness and order, namely diversity and tolerance, seemed potentially at least as significant, and to be positively valued features of the London scene. In relation to area image, we lack direct evidence from potential inward investors, or discouraged tourists, but we could find no indications that fear of disorder or other forms of social conflict in London are liable to exert significant negative effects, and they do not feature among the reasons cited by the small minority of businesses potentially moving out of London. It is conceivable that current publicity about levels of street crime in the city might have some effect on tourist demand: it is too soon to assess this, but we should not expect any effect to be more than very short term. These are issues, however, where thresholds are clearly important, and problems can be triggered by quite specific incidents. Hence we cannot know reliably how far social inequality and connectedness would need to deteriorate in order to have major negative impacts on London's image as a business centre, as occurred to New York in the late 1960s. Our judgement, however, is that the city is not approaching any of these thresholds.

Many businesses had experienced repeated crime, but surprisingly rarely was this seen as a major problem, since to a considerable extent it could be dealt with by effective and affordable security measures. There was more concern about the vulnerability of staff travelling to and from work, but again this did not seem to be a major factor affecting the operations of the firms. Nor, though its form varied, was crime a risk peculiar to areas of deprivation. As a motive for relocation it was clearly much less important than traditional concerns with premises, transport links and, perhaps, labour supply.

In relation to potential gains from local social networks, involvement in local institutions and the development of relations of trust within spatial clusters of businesses, London businesses generally appeared sceptical. The main exception was the City financial services cluster, though here the key issue was one of access to current intelligence rather than a greater potential for collaboration. There were two key reasons why local social capital of this kind was not more highly valued. On the one hand, London's value as a location is predominantly in the array of possible business links that can be pursued to cope with shifting market circumstances, rather than in building more restricted and durable partnerships: agglomeration promotes weak rather than strong ties. On the other hand, London firms are outward looking and where stronger relations with customers or partners were critical to successful innovation, these were as likely to be with non-local (including international) businesses as with those based in the city – as in Amin and Graham's (1997) model of the multiplex city.

Finally, in this set of negative findings, we came across very little evidence that London businesses felt constrained by local labour cultures of opposition or non-co-operation connected with forms of local social cohesion or lack of cohesion, as might be the case elsewhere. There was considerable dissatisfaction in relation to some areas (particularly in East London) and some groups (particularly the young) about the available quality of labour, including their 'soft skills' in team work and customer relations. But this rarely seemed to be a direct expression of social incohesion or disorder.

Rather it seemed to be part of a broader problem: though London can easily fill high-status jobs from a national pool, which generates a ready flow of well-qualified and ambitious young workers, it has more difficulty in filling jobs that demand basic and middle-range skills, where the pool is more local or at most regional. Formal qualifications do not appear to be the issue here, though they are among the few signals available to employers, and schooling is clearly relevant to both the basic and soft skills with which employers are concerned. Such complaints are not new and some of the issues seem to reflect sub-cultural differences along age and class lines more than conventional notions of skill. But these are much more salient issues in a post-industrial economy where workers' performance is much more directly relevant to competitiveness. In part they need to be addressed through employers' personnel practices, but they are at root issues of social cohesion, since sub-cultural differentiation among young people in particular seems to be largely about means of achieving and sustaining 'respect'. And it is an educational issue, since achievement of formal qualifications is – together with equal opportunities policies – a critical route for reconciling these aspirations with those of employers. However the reasons why achievement levels in parts of Inner London, in particular, are poor, are not simply to be found in what happens in school, and or in poor attendance; they also reflect background social factors, notably the impact of family fragmentation, both on those directly affected and at neighbourhood level.

Gentrification, which initially at least involves a reduction in social segregation, could in principle put some of these processes into reverse and raise local school quality for the benefit of all. But experience suggests that actual gains are limited, since at secondary level, where catchment areas are more socially mixed, a large proportion of incoming middle-class families opt out of the local school system. And, in any case local gains accrue only to those who have not been displaced, with the others possibly ending up in new one-class areas, e.g. in the least desirable housing in the middle ring of London, potentially reproducing the pattern created (through rather deliberate policy) around Paris.

The fact that we have not been able to trace more clear effects of cohesion on competitiveness does not decisively prove that these do not exist, or that levels of inequality, disconnectedness and disorder can be allowed to drift without any regard for possible economic consequences and thresholds which may be crossed. But it should redirect attention to the basic point that poverty, isolation and insecurity are bad in themselves. Our findings suggest that it is quite easy to over-dramatize both the possibility and the implications of social exclusion, and particularly the extent to which these are tied to specific neighbourhoods in urgent need of targeted 'regeneration'. But there is a very great deal of old-fashioned poverty and poor housing conditions, together with newer problems of racism and family fragmentation – and a lot of Londoners who simply have difficulty getting by or exerting much control over their situation. Some, but by no means all, of the victims are concentrated in poor neighbourhoods, which makes some problems worse, but most of their difficulties relate to who they are, and what their past experiences have been, rather than where they are within the region.

Connections in the reverse direction, running from economic competitiveness to social cohesion, are rather more obvious. We have found much evidence of the negative impacts of economic deprivation on social relations, while in the medium term, at least, economic growth does seem to lower the incidence of many kinds of crime. However, there are two important qualifications to be made. One is that what is likely to be critical is the economic position of the bottom quartile or so of the population, who have clearly not benefited to the same degree from the generally rising prosperity and economic success of the region over the past couple of decades, when a very large share of the gains have accrued to those with access to high-status jobs. The second qualification is that, even for this disadvantaged group, the spatial scale at which economic competitiveness matters is not local, nor even sub-regional, but closer to that of the Greater South East, since labour markets are so strongly interconnected across this region. Thus while neighbourhood level unemployment rates have a strong bearing on (for example) rates of single parenthood, these unemployment rates are much less sensitive to whether employment in surrounding areas has been growing than to growth and the pressure of demand across the extended region. From a social as well as economic perspective therefore it is appropriate to address issues of competitiveness in a regional rather than local context. And, though the vast majority of Londoners are better off as a result of living in an economically successful region, rather than one struggling with the legacy of declining heavy industry, it also means that their welfare is heavily dependent on the competitive success and economic management of the national UK economy. Inner Londoners suffered heavily from national recessions and weak demand during much of the last 20 years – though less than those living in inner Strathclyde or Merseyside – and they have clearly benefited from the more sustained growth achieved over the past 8 or 9 years.

**5. What role does urban governance play in relation to achieving competitiveness, reducing exclusion, fostering social capital or, to put it more generally, economic progress, social integration and an enhanced quality of life for London's workers and residents?**

If we interpret this question narrowly (urban 'governance' rather than 'government'), our conclusions are that so far the role is weak and limited. In a large part of the London region this is likely to remain so. In the inner city (and adjacent areas) this may change, but it has not yet done so. But the substantive issue is what difference local government is making/can make. In relation to the three main areas of public policy noted above, effective urban government could be very important. However, in the past 20 years its potential capacity to respond has been reduced, not enhanced: both by its loss of powers and responsibilities to other bodies (market and non-market) and by reduced resources. Insofar as some authorities (those that really need to) are developing such a capacity, it requires internal changes – which, so far, some are better at than others – and two changes which can only come from central government: adequate powers and resources. Labour's modernization agenda so far seems to be providing mixed signals on all of this. On the one hand, there are new policies which aim to address the key issues and to provide some resources for them, plus efforts to improve the performance levels of local services. On the other hand, such policies are still too 'provisional' (in various ways: coverage, resources, time-limited) and while some aspects of the required move to network governance have positive effects, there are significant ways in which this reduces – not enhances – the capacity of the local authorities, without effectively bringing in other partners and their resources.

There is a further key weakness of urban governance in the London region which can only be changed by government, and which recent changes may not effectively address. In a huge, complex, polycentric place like London, governance will always be fragmented. The establishment of the GLA and its agencies represented the beginnings of a seriously flawed new system of sub-regional 'regional' authorities. It remains to be seen whether they can achieve much in the way of redistribution and building positive externalities, or whether their competitive instincts may generate new negative externalities. Early signs are not encouraging. The Mayor's strategies assume that 'London' ends at the GLA boundary, which (we have shown) is far from the case – while those for the South East and Eastern regions turn their back on London. The fact that both central and decentralized government operate at the Greater London level (through GOL and the GLA) exacerbates this situation and also leads to a confusion of roles at this level – especially when the GLA's major 'diplomatic' concerns are either with 'ministries' which are not themselves regionalized (i.e. the Treasury) or with ministers personally.

So these new institutions of sub-regional governance are unlikely to provide all the strategic capacity and political leadership that is required in relation to major issues such as planning, housing, transport, and major public investments. This concerns the need for some single unit of governance at the level of the Functional Urban Region, essentially in relation to the issues of intra-regional externalities discussed in Chapter 10. At the most general level this involves intervention to influence the cross-regional distribution of economic activity, to address the infrastructural and environmental needs and pressures consequent upon this, and generally to enhance the possibilities that the benefits of a dynamic and competitive economy are shared more widely by the region's population and its localities.

However, in London, the creation of a political authority to correspond to the true functional urban region is almost impossible to imagine, given both its scale relative to the UK, in terms of population, area and share of national GDP, and the sensitivity of national governments to developments in their capital city region. What is needed, rather, is an effective form of governance for the London region. We return to this question in the final section of this chapter.

At the local authority level, a key issue is whether some local authorities – by virtue of their inherited assets, political directions, and geographical location – may not increasingly be able to operate a form of urban government which 'purchases' competitiveness and social cohesion, by working with the grain of the more powerful market-based forces which favour closure and exclusion. In such a situation, as Wandsworth illustrates, some real benefits may in fact trickle down to those less advantaged groups that survive the exclusionary phase of this change process. Whether this is so or not does to a considerable degree also depend on locally-determined political choices – Southwark, at least so far and in a way rather strangely, being a counter-example which substantiates the point. The pursuit of more desirable residents is, however, one of those forms of territorial competition which is liable to have negative consequences for neighbouring areas, especially where limited capacity means that it displaces poorer population groups from the area.

For such local authorities, in areas where the issue of competitiveness and cohesion is particularly problematic, there is an overwhelming imperative: they cannot avoid trying to enhance local competitiveness, and they certainly must not impede it. This was the strategy adopted by most Labour local authorities in the 1980s, with no positive outcomes either in economic or in social terms. So the unresolved issue is whether – as Newham and Greenwich are attempting – local policies can enhance competitiveness and cohesion, rather than the first at the expense of the second. Our research indicates that so far at least, the exclusionary route seems to be an easier path for some areas to follow, though these will be limited in number. It cannot however provide a solution everywhere where one is needed, and in fact its externalities are likely to increase the difficulties of such areas. An important point emerging from our work, however, is that actual service delivery remains the central element in what is expected and required of local authorities. Efficiency and responsiveness of performance remain highly variable, but this (rather than strategizing) proves to be the key not only to quality of life for residents, but also to both competitiveness and cohesion.

## Is London Special?

There is a sixth question; not one we posed in Chapter 1, and therefore not one that informed our research; but one that we find ourselves asking – and others will doubtless be asking – as we end: how peculiar is London, and how relevant are findings about it, to other cities, within Britain or worldwide? This arises since many of the things which make it a fascinating and important case to study – not least its scale, complexity and high status as a service centre – also mark it out as untypical.

In a UK context London is distinguished not only by its size, but also by its specialization in a wide range of advanced services, by its internationalism, by its location in what has long been the more successful half of the country, and by being the national capital. In terms of its specialization and its cosmopolitan population, at least – together with its affluence and its unusual degree of inequality – it has clearly moved further from the national norm over the past two decades. In an international context, clearly, it has more peers – though few even of these are both capitals of significant economies and international centres – but it is differentiated from them by peculiarities of history, institutions, state policies, and national economic performance.

So there is an important question: how far are these differences simply ones of degree, or are they differences of kind? This is difficult to answer, particularly because London offers much more information to analyse key processes and outcomes than do other smaller cities. In this study we have had the benefit of 'regional' level statistics for Greater London, useable-sized sub-samples from national surveys, a broader array of district-level statistics for the region's fragmented administrative units – and a much stronger body of past and current research (both academic and governmental) than is available for any other British city. London's complexity also offers a perverse advantage: it makes it clear that it cannot be understood simply bottom-up, in terms of decisions taken by a few key actors, firms or sectors. The same applies to all cities, but is harder to identify there. So we need to ask how far our findings might apply to these other places.

Some of our key findings support the view that London is different from other British cities only in degree. This applies particularly to the question of whether London has become an essentially 'global city' whose attributes are largely shaped by the peculiarities of international financial functions and the distinctive rhythms of an offshore economy. This we find a much exaggerated picture, in respect both of London businesses which remain preponderantly geared to serving the UK market (in their capital city role) and of a labour market which has been very strongly affected by national performance and shocks originating in other regions. But it also applies to our findings about social capital: that Londoners are neither peculiarly isolated, nor particularly anomic, despite a raft of characteristics which might seem to make enduring attachments and mutual support much less likely. Looking at the London economy, where we find London firms distinctly unenthusiastic about the benefits of clustering, we do not know how odd or special these attitudes may be; nor will we, until comparative data are gathered for businesses in other cities. True, London firms find themselves in special positions, notably their ability to pursue opportunistic patterns of collaboration in a rich economic environment; but we nonetheless believe that our findings may have wider relevance in casting doubt on strong models of clustering.

Two special aspects of the complexity of the London region have been highlighted in this book: its continuing governmental fragmentation and its relatively high degree of social segregation, which operates across the region, rather than purely locally as elsewhere. These are related, since both result from geographical scale and from tensions between the forces of regional-scale economic/strategic integration and of local social integration/distinctiveness. Neither is unique to London, though less escapable here; in both respects, London does seem simply to be at the end of a continuum. A similar conclusion applies to labour market organization and outcomes, though here the relations which we have found in London are likely to operate even more strongly elsewhere. The wider London region is very much larger than the commuting fields of any but the highest status groups, and this suggests that the continuing deprivation of inner area residents is a function of their weaker economic performance in more routine economic functions, for which labour markets tend to be quite local. But, even in this extensive region, that is a very small part of the explanation; regional labour markets are very strongly integrated. The clear implication is that in smaller city regions – including those experiencing a much weaker overall pressure of demand – small-area concentrations of deprivation are even less likely to be explained by sub-regional variations in demand. Among the major British cities (though not compared to smaller ones), London is also at one extreme in terms of generally strong demand for labour. During the two decades 1981–2001 this meant that London experienced periods of both above and below full employment demand levels, allowing us to see very clearly the differing social impacts, particularly in processes which lead to a concentration of unemployment during weak demand periods. In northern cities this has been a more permanent state of affairs, and we would expect these processes to have operated more continuously there, with more damaging long-term consequences.

Perhaps, following a recent analysis of long-term trends in UK cities, we can distinguish a three-level hierarchy. London has remained in its unique position at the top, but it has progressively decentralized to produce rings of smaller urban centres at increasing distances from it, which have ascended the hierarchy. The major provincial centres seem to have strengthened their relative position at a second level of the hierarchy, but they tend to be surrounded by single-industry towns that are relatively falling, not rising in the hierarchy. In consequence, there is a third level of medium-sized towns which displays contradictory patterns: northern members, and coastal towns generally, have been declining while their southern counterparts have shown major gains (Hall, Marshall and Lowe 2001). How the features and trends we have identified for London would apply – or not apply – to these other places we must leave to others to elucidate. But there is one point which could prove significant. Some of London's strengths – including those which may appear surprising, such as its relatively strong social cohesion – appear to arise from its very diversity and from the huge range of opportunities this offers to most, though not all, of its people: few people are trapped in London. The contrast with many declining northern one-industry towns could not be more obvious or more stark. But it is arguable that if we disaggregate London, then parts of it – especially on its less economically successful, less affluent eastern side – might demonstrate some similarities with such places. The difference, again, is that they are part of a much wider whole which offers ways of escape. In this regard, the major provincial cities may be more like London than to their single-industry near neighbours.

Other examples could be developed of the ways in which London findings could be translated into different contexts, including more complicated ones for cities elsewhere in the world, where key differences are likely to be more qualitative in character. But our general conclusion is that though London displays a series of distinctive characteristics, it is far from being unique: processes operating in the London economy also operate elsewhere, with differences which are both intelligible and in many cases quite predictable. The reverse also applies, as in the case of internationalization or globalization, which affects London not only, or mainly, through 'global-cityization' but also through relations of competition and institutional change which affect all other places, often through national economic and political adjustments. Amin and Graham (1997) make the point that not only are there current dangers of over-generalizing from the examples of one or a few cities (Los Angeles, 'global cities'), but that even within any one city there are dangers in taking some partial characteristics as representative of the whole. For London we have tried hard to avoid the latter failing – and, having done so, we believe there are fewer dangers in suggesting that processes observed in London are also likely to operate (with more or less importance, and with some variants) in many other places.

## Work in Progress: A New Society, A New Sociology

Throughout this book we have worked with concepts currently in vogue for understanding the relationship between economic and social processes in cities: competitiveness, social cohesion, social exclusion, social capital. We have explored and deconstructed them, and in doing so have established some valuable insights into them. But this leaves a final question: do they in fact provide the best basis for understanding social and economic change in cities today?

That there has been substantial social and economic change there can be no doubt. Early in this book, in Chapter 2, we sought to show how fundamentally London has been transformed in the second half of the twentieth century – economically, socially, politically. In the economic sphere, an entire mode of production, based on mass production for mass home and imperial markets and sheltered behind protective tariff walls, has been shattered. Globalization and global competition have not only removed manufacturing from cities like London, but have helped profoundly to change working conditions for those who work in the all-dominant service industries. Entry into these industries has more and more depended on advanced education and training. Work has become more and more feminized, as women have entered the labour force and moved into more responsible jobs in the advanced service sector. Careers have become less linear and jobs less secure; there is a new insecurity in the workforce.

Socially, a traditional working-class culture has very largely disappeared, to be replaced by middle-class patterns of living. Even more profoundly, not only has the old working-class extended family gone from the scene; the nuclear family too has come under threat, as it is progressively replaced by new styles of living. Marriage rates have drastically fallen, and there are new patterns of living: extended cohabitation, the live-alone single-never-married, the partnerships that form and reform, the complex patterns of family relationship that inevitably result. London's population, once largely British-born and white and sharing strong cultural norms, has become a multi-ethnic, multi-cultural mosaic.

How far do the ideas of competitiveness and cohesion provide any solid basis for understanding these changes? Here we find simply a gap. The motor of change in these accounts is either absent or it is a system-wide process – globalization, individualization, technological change – which is not itself explained in any way. Thus cohesion and competitiveness provide some basis for understanding the comparative successes and failures of cities, but not some of the deeper processes of change that underlie them, and that have profound consequences for the everyday lives of the people who live in those cities.

We also need to ask, more generally: how adequately have these huge transformations been reflected in the development of urban sociological theory? The library shelves are still lined with the classics of the 1950s and 1960s, and indeed of earlier decades going back to founding fathers like Durkheim or Weber or Simmel, Park or Burgess or Wirth. But they describe and analyse a world which is now an historic memory. Young and Willmott's richly interconnected extended families were already disappearing as their respondents left Bethnal Green for new homes in the satellite estates and new towns. Not long after, the suburban nuclear family with its new joint work-home roles, described in their *The Symmetrical Family*, began to go the same way. The same could be said of classics from the other side of the Atlantic like *The Organization Man* or *The Levittowners* (Young and Willmott, 1957, 1973; Whyte, 1957; Gans, 1967).

The transformation of urban sociology in the 1970s recognized the limitations of this earlier tradition: that it gave no clear account of the processes which led to change in cities, had no very clear model of the relationship between the social structure of cities and the processes which drove their economies, and saw individual places as abstracted from the wider society. The tripartite model of competitiveness, cohesion and governance is a recognizable descendant of this turn in urban sociology, largely Marxist-inspired, though one which its progenitors might now want to disavow.

One of the strengths of the new urban sociology has been that it at least tried to understand the interrelationship between economic and social processes. However, capitalist economic relations in the end provided the central driving force of change. Indeed, understanding the space remaining for social and political action, given the critical role of economic processes in shaping cities, has been a problem with which urban sociology has struggled since the 1970s. Sometimes this has had a political motivation: to understand the possibility of resistance to these forces. Sometimes it reflected a refusal to accept that a purely economic determination could alone explain the processes of change in cities.

The new conventional wisdom, with its focus on both competitiveness and cohesion, appears at first sight to be a potential solution to this. But we are still left with a problem. To the extent that we can adequately make a distinction between the social and the economic, the social is defined in a rather one-sided way. While it accepts the embeddedness of economic processes in social structures, it is still an economically-driven theory. The model of the social structure of cities in this current paradigm tends to privilege elements which have the clearest demonstrable relationship (in either direction) with economic performance. It is thus close to a tautological system in which social cohesion is that which promotes competitiveness. If we want an adequate model of how the social structure of cities is now changing, it may involve shaking free from this paradigm.

We need to recognize that in developing an adequate account of social change in cities there are two questions. First, do we currently have an adequate general sociology of the development of modern societies, and in particular of the processes which lead to social divisions, to variations in life chances and in access to power? Secondly, do we have an adequate model of how urban life and spatial variations – both within and outside cities – might introduce specific autonomous effects on these general processes?

Of course, one can point to some current urban sociological research which provides insights into the new social relations that are emerging in cities in consequence of these processes of change. Many Londoners, especially young Londoners, seem to have patterns of living that are as flexible and provisional as their working lives: living alone, with relationships that may be conducted over a distance and without much certainty of permanence, or perhaps in patterns of serial monogamy that may produce complex patterns of stepchildren and half-siblings. And, from some fragmentary research work, this seems to be accompanied by social attitudes among younger people that are very different from anything before, and certainly very different from the rest of the UK (Wilkinson and Mulgan, 1995; Jupp and Lawson, 1997).

> The picture which emerges . . . is of a city at the leading edge of national and international trends in values. Londoners are becoming more tolerant and less puritanical, they seek more excitement and are less authoritarian or worried about economic security. Similar values are emerging throughout the Western world. As a nation, Britons hold these values more than any other except the Dutch. Our analysis shows that Londoners hold these values more than the rest of Britain. (Jupp and Lawson, 1997, 16)

This sort of approach falls squarely within the line of work developed by sociologists such as Beck and Giddens, which rejects the continued salience of class, and focuses instead on individualization. Individuals, freed from the traditional identities of class, respond more flexibly and reflexively to their social world. For Giddens traditional emancipatory politics are replaced by life politics:

> . . . while emancipatory politics is a politics of life chances, life politics is a politics of lifestyle . . . Life politics is a politics of self actualization in a reflexively ordered environment, where that reflexivity links self and body to systems of global scope. (Giddens, 1991, 214)

Beck (1992), in discussing risk society, places more emphasis on the darker aspects of this new world, and both writers see individuals as responding to system processes which are largely beyond their control. But neither author gives a central place to the social structural regularities that can lead to inequalities in life chances. In this book we have seen that these have persisted and deepened, in spite of the alleged end of class society.

If we do need to understand structural regularities and social divisions, then we need to see how social structures get reproduced. The answer lies in the behaviour of individuals and families, deploying various resources – financial, skills, social networks, attitudes and values – which they acquire from their family as children, and then over their life course. This has been the traditional terrain of class analysis. However in twenty-first century Britain class analysis is in something of a crisis, unable fully to respond to the profound changes which are evidently occurring to social structure.

Historically, too, British analysis of social class, social mobility and related issues has been notably aspatial, or even anti-spatial: it denied that there was any major basis for spatial variation in class processes, or that spatially differentiated resources had any role in class formation. This has contributed to a rather low salience of class analysis in urban sociology. But recent developments provide more basis for linkage to the study of cities. One approach focuses on the range of assets which underlie social divisions. Savage *et al.* (1992) distinguished between property assets, organizational assets and cultural assets. In their original formulation they suggested an emergent division between professional and managerial groups, which the authors noted had some particular spatial manifestations. But in a more recent contribution Savage (2000) has sought a broader reformulation of class analysis which rejects the centrality of class consciousness, no longer tenable given the profound change which has occurred in the manual working class, but does see class cultural values as central to class definition. He draws on Bourdieu (1984) to point to the way in which culture is used as a resource in the formation of class, by establishing distinctions and boundaries with other classes. He also points to a changing of role of organizational assets, sometimes also described as organization-specific human capital, as the middle classes, in particular, are expected to behave in an entrepreneurial fashion in building their careers. He distances himself from the sharp differentiation between managers and professionals in the earlier work, and aims for a broader view of the sources of social divisions. He also argues for the centrality of class in the analysis of social change, in contrast to Beck and Giddens:

> Their main problem is that they locate the springs of change away from the proximate worlds of everyday life and over-stress the systemic logic of social change. A reformulated class analysis, I argue, offers a means of understanding social change in a more mediated fashion, as a particular articulation of local and global, individual and social dynamics, as a phenomenon that is attuned to continuity and change and recognizes our complicity in the social world we inhabit. (Savage, 2000, 151)

This approach surely provides a valuable starting point for an urban sociology of London. There are four respects in which we would want to endorse, modify or extend it, and which we believe provide the basis for further lines of research.

In the first place, changes in the role of organizational assets are clearly critical to cities like London. They are clearly the places where the breakdown of organizational affiliation in favour of entrepreneurial careers has gone furthest. However, they also contain many individuals occupying niches characterized by what Savage describes as organizational centrality. This idea goes beyond organization-specific human capital, to convey the capacity to shape the development of organizations, and to benefit from organizational change. Thus the most successful social groups in London are characterized by a mixture of people who have exploited their human capital through careers of considerable mobility, and those who can extract a rent from organizational centrality. This underlies the notion of London as an escalator region (Savage *et al.*, 1992). Other social groups manage this volatile environment with more difficulty. Indeed one of the important things we need to know rather more about is the social distribution of risk. This clearly links to Beck's (1992) work on 'Risk Society' but the concern is much more with the structural regularities which differentiate groups in their exposure to risk, and to its consequences. It also links to Sennett's insights: that the new focus on entrepreneurial careers may well have negative consequences for people's identities and character (Sennett, 1999).

We have already seen that there is a cultural distinctiveness to London. It is probably the place where traditional class identities are weakest, and in which new identities, which may be most divergent from mainstream values, arise most rapidly. This in part reflects its character, which it shares with other big cities, as a tolerant environment. But that does not make it less class-divided, and some cultural forms play precisely the roles of exclusion and distinction that Bourdieu posited. For example Savage (2000) suggests that globalization is in part something that is constructed by the culturally privileged to deny responsibility for their local social activities. Bourdieu and Wacquant (1999) more generally discuss the patterns of dominance resulting from the internationalization of ideas and cultures. Global cities such as London play a key role in these processes.

There is also the question of whether these class perspectives leave gaps in terms of other actual and potential lines of social division, and especially ethnicity, gender and household structure. Here we go back to an old, and unresolved, argument: whether these form genuinely independent bases for social divisions, or are merely modifiers – important but essentially dependent – of a class perspective. Ethnicity and gender do clearly produce systematically unequal outcomes and life chances. In the case of gender these link rather closely to household structure issues, but there have also been differences in the way male and female careers have been structured and opportunities are presented. McDowell (1997) presents a particularly relevant case study, on the gendering of work roles in the City of London.

Ethnicity clearly provides a source of cultural identity separate from class. There is therefore a question of how far processes related to ethnic identity, manifested for example in residential segregation, openness or closure of social networks, employment discrimination, school segregation, in a multi-ethnic city such as London, serve to consolidate social divisions which are of greater significance than those associated with class. This is generally perceived to be the case in US cities. It is much less clear in London.

Our account of London tends to suggest that household structure and family formation might be a rather important factor underlying social change, and cannot simply be dismissed as Savage suggests. Household structures clearly have direct effects on income and well-being, but they also have impacts on future life chances, and potentially at least on inter-generational transmission of resources and values.

This raises an important issue in examining social processes in sub-national units. At the national level it appears possible to ignore migration processes in the reproduction of the population. Inter-generational social mobility is treated as non-spatial, though space clearly plays a role in life course mobility. If residence in non-family households in London was a purely transitory phase in the life course, then it would not be necessary to modify this view. However, if it is more than this, then it could modify the processes of social mobility in London compared with other areas. That this may be happening in relation to more disadvantaged lone parents is already a matter of policy concern. If however other social groups in big cities show distinctively different choices over the timing of childbearing, and over the ways in which children are brought up, the implications are less clear.

Finally, Savage tends to suggest that property assets do not form a major independent line of social cleavage, except in separating off the very rich, since the level of assets tends to follow directly from labour market careers. This was also the response to ideas in the 1960s and 1970s about housing classes as a new basis for social and political alignment (Rex and Moore, 1967). We would not wish to resurrect these arguments – but nevertheless, in a spatial context, property assets do take on an additional force. Chapter 9 has shown the concern which residents feel as neighbourhoods change, and how the behaviour of other residents, and visitors from other areas, spills over on to them. Neighbourhoods constitute resources which may have positive or negative consequences for life chances, and which residents will seek to protect and enhance. We have mentioned in Chapters 5 and 8 Butler and Robson's (2002) work on London neighbourhoods, and the use of social and cultural capital to protect them. Other examples concern NIMBYism in suburban areas, to protect privileged environments from new developments. The protection and enhancement of neighbourhoods is clearly a basis for urban conflict. Such conflicts may be between residents and state institutions, one of the main themes of the urban movements literature of the 1970s and 1980s (Castells, 1983). It may also, implicitly or explicitly, be a struggle for resources between different groups of residents. The capacity of people to pursue these strategies depends very heavily on their own resources. It therefore tends to constitute another way in which social divisions become intensified.

These themes – the role of organizations and careers, cultures as social resources, divisions around household structure and around race, and the role of urban assets in social conflict – emerge for us, concluding our work, as particularly important for the future development of urban sociology. We suspect that a similar agenda would arise from the study of other cities, though the different components would undoubtedly have different priorities.

## The Role of Policy: Obstacles and Opportunities

This book has not been a piece of policy research in any conventional sense; we have neither focused on specific problems in great depth, nor evaluated the impacts of particular public policy initiatives. The aims have been much broader: to try to understand the major forces and processes affecting social and economic outcomes in the city, and do so in a way which treats government as part of the urban system, rather than something standing outside ready to intervene in it. True, there are implications that emerge from this analysis for approaches to public action in the city which are more likely to enhance competitiveness and cohesion – in some of their various forms – but these are necessarily broad. And by no means all of them are very novel, for two related reasons. First because, despite our focus on how things have changed over the past two decades, many of the critical processes underlying problematic or unsatisfactory outcomes in the city actually turn out to be quite old ones. Secondly because, where problems are deeply entrenched, as often they are, a key need is to maintain commitment to lines of remedial policy which cannot be expected to provide actual 'solutions' within the short to medium term. Because this is difficult, both politically and psychologically, the temptation is always to find some new diagnosis promising easier and faster responses. Nor are the prescriptions all specific to the London case, or even specifically 'urban', since quite a few of the capital's problems are just particular versions of more widespread ones – and because the national context, and mainstream national programmes, matter a great deal to London and to some of its most disadvantaged communities.

This is particularly true in relation to some of the key issues of cohesion – inequality, disconnectedness and disorder – where national welfare, employment and macro-economic management policies continue to have the most crucial influences on outcomes in the London region. Despite devolution and administrative decentralization, the basic lines of urban policy are also still produced nationally. Under the Blair government these have been marked by a very strong emphasis on problems of exclusion, and on 'joining-up', both in thought and action, rather than focusing on a single key set of causes as responsible for urban problems. From the perspective of our analyses, which have highlighted the interactions among many social, economic, and political factors in generating and maintaining disadvantage, this seems a very positive development.

However, there are two problematic aspects to the strategy. One is the emphasis on small area-based initiatives as the focus for joining up, given the differing spatial scales over which various processes operate. Combining economic, social and physical regeneration at a local scale misses the point, emerging clearly from our analyses, that the social impacts of economic development get very widely diffused, with little remaining in the target area. This is especially likely when local residents occupy poor competitive positions in the labour market. In the context of a strong regional labour market such economic development is almost irrelevant to the problems of deprived groups and areas. But even in worse circumstances, where an economic boost is clearly required, concentrating this boost on particularly poor localities is likely to be unnecessarily inefficient, and can too easily distract attention from the real sources of disadvantage faced by their residents. Within London, the Mayor and LDA's 2001 Economic Development Strategy does seem to recognize this argument, and gives substantial weight to tackling the social dimensions of disadvantage. But there remains a general danger with area-based strategies: that thinking gets short-circuited (rather than properly joined up) through property-based initiatives whose social benefits rest simply on the physical accessibility of additional jobs. And, though we have earlier presented some evidence of ways in which neighbourhood effects lead to further concentration of deprivation (through attenuating job information networks, and peer group effects within schools), these remain very much less important than the sources of disadvantage which are directly attached to individuals and households (Buck, 2001).

A second problematic feature is the policy's more general reliance on 'targeting' of various kinds as a means of maximizing the impact of resources allocated to tackling deprivation. On the face of it, this is a wholly sensible approach which recognizes the need to secure policy benefits for the most deprived and deserving groups. The problem is that in practice, whether targeting is done by area or by population group, it is almost impossible to ensure that ultimate benefits are actually concentrated there, even where the targeted group seems effectively disconnected from those markets through which leakages might occur. (The exception is where opportunities are of such low quality, e.g. in terms of very low wage jobs, as to be of no interest to any but the very poorest.)

From our perspective, the point about disadvantaged or marginalized groups is not that they operate in a separate world disconnected from the mainstream, but rather that while they are required to compete for opportunities with other groups they do so from a substantially weaker position. One implication of this view is that the scale of action (for example of job creation) required to resolve the problems of a particular targeted group or area is never nearly as limited as it may appear when they are looked at in isolation. A large proportion of the targeted opportunities (whether in terms of jobs, housing or environmental improvement) actually leaks out to the benefit of others, who are not necessarily much less deserving but who start from a slightly stronger competitive position. The real point here is that the scale of the problems to be resolved, typically accumulated over long periods, is much greater than appears when a few priority targets are identified for intervention. And setting aspiration levels beyond what is achievable with the scale of resources allocated is a recipe for frustration and policy abandonment. As an example we may take one of the recently set government targets for the London Development Agency: that it should (by 2004/05) reduce the number of deprived residents by 10 per cent in a set of 'most deprived' wards including almost 40 per cent of its population. This is a scale of change only achievable, if at all, through the government's own macro-economic policy, not with the limited resources available to a regional development agency.

In the context of supply-side initiatives to boost the competitive position of individuals from targeted disadvantaged groups, there is a different version of this problem. This is that the people with whom they will be in most direct competition are those with rather similar levels of disadvantage, whether these are inside the currently targeted group or not. In the case of the labour market, as a key instance, most will realistically be competing for jobs in the lower strata of the market, which are over-congested, not simply because of some natural excess of people with limited abilities, but because in periods of slack demand many have been 'bumped down' from more central parts of the labour market. As with the analogous problem of getting more people from the platform into underground trains at times of high demand, what is required is not more vigorous competition to get through the doors, but encouragement for those already on board to 'move on up the car'. This means promotion of training, career development, and equal opportunities (in terms of class and age as well as race and gender) in mainstream segments of the labour market and not solely at the margins, if currently deprived groups are to be effectively reintegrated. Similar arguments apply in other fields, where the constraints facing disadvantaged groups cannot simply be relieved by action at the margins – since they did not actually originate there.

Despite this scepticism about the virtues of area-based approaches and of concentrating remedial action on marginal situations, our analyses do underwrite the need for joined-up approaches in addressing problems of social cohesion. In particular, we have identified a number of circular relations through which aspects of deprivation (including unemployment) tend to get reproduced and even further concentrated within particular population groups and areas. In the case of unemployment these include two-way relations with health problems and with poorer job information, and more complex ones involving job instability/career advancement and family fragmentation/educational achievement (Gordon, 2003). Given that there will be diminishing returns to any specific form of remedial action, a reasonable response to evidence of such relations is to try to ameliorate outcomes at each point of linkage, rather than to identify one or two of these as critical.

Turning to policies for promotion of competitiveness, three important broad arguments emerge from our analysis. The first of these is that the region's success or failure is very largely an issue of how effectively it can develop assets which support established firms' efforts to compete in product markets – *and* avoid frustrating these – rather than one of attracting or holding on to potentially mobile businesses. The second is that, although (like all places) the region needs to build on its distinctive sources of competitive advantage, in London's case diversity is one of its key advantages, which needs to be maintained – rather than policy identifying and selectively promoting a few core activities. In particular, while London's capacity to carry out various 'global' business functions is among its most distinctive strengths, their economic role has to be kept in proportion, and not seen as *the* fundamental base of the city region's economic prospects. The third point, also relating to the essential diversity and complexity of the region's economy, is that fashionable concerns with active promotion of locally networked economic clusters are rather irrelevant to the London region, including its outer metropolitan parts. Arguably, indeed, the point of cluster policies is to use some form of indicative planning to emulate on a smaller, more specialized basis the very types of positive spatial externality which emerge spontaneously in the major agglomerations. This may or may not be a realistic aspiration for smaller centres or peripheral regions, but it is mostly going to be irrelevant to the requirements of the London economy.

In relation to issues of cohesion and competitiveness, our work has tended both to cast doubts on the efficacy of special programmes, and to underline the importance of a number of mainstream policy areas. In the first case, New Labour's pursuit of 'joined-up' action seems quite perversely to have brought ever more complex arrays of 'initiatives' which are short-term, unsustainable, unco-ordinated and even contradictory. This approach is undoubtedly meant to be flexible, catalytic and subject to continual review – in tune with the times – rather than bureaucratic or supportive of dependency cultures. But it is often confusing and misses the point about the need for persistence (and 'resolution') in dealing with what are typically chronic problems, rather than sudden crises. In particular, hard questions need to be asked about reliance on area-based approaches which have been the staple of urban policy for the past 35 years, but rarely matched their promises with sustainable achievements. The current National Strategy for Neighbourhood Renewal does seem to be based on a more sophisticated understanding of the scope and limits of local initiatives, though still giving too much weight to the role of neighbourhood effects. We are sceptical, however, about what has been achieved through the proliferation of health, education and other action zones. Indeed, rather than assuming that joining-up is something to be accomplished locally at the implementation stage, there is a case for pursuing it through a broadly based audit, encompassing the indirect effects of 'non-urban' policies on competitiveness and cohesion in cities. For example, what are the social costs of London's quasi-market in education, and how do nationally determined levels of welfare eligibility and benefits impact on poverty and deprivation in this high-cost region?

Against such doubts about special initiatives, there are several mainstream programmes where additional resources could more obviously yield significant pay-offs for the region in terms of equality, order, connectedness and/or competitiveness. The prime examples emerging from our interviews with households and businesses involve housing, public transport, and education, although health, land-use planning, and policing are clearly relevant too. More specifically the examples are:

• improving the supply of low- and moderate-income housing – and conditions in the existing stock of social housing – in ways that prevent this stock from being subsequently 'captured' by other groups;

• improving public transport provision while restricting the costs of such travel, so as to enhance particularly the mobility of disadvantaged groups; and

• raising performance in those state schools at the bottom of current league tables, in order to weaken the redistributive effects of the quasi-market and to reduce risks of social exclusion through educational failure among those groups most at risk, including both white and Afro-Caribbean boys in working-class areas.

These are neither very original nor fully worked-out pieces of policy analysis, but rather illustrate how mainstream programmes continue to be of central importance to issues of cohesion and competitiveness in the city. And whether the system generates virtuous or vicious circles of urban change depends, in London as in other cities, to a large extent on how these programmes operate. On the one hand, successful encouragement of business competitiveness, could be reinforced by housing and transport policies which ensured supplies of labour to fill the new jobs, and improving education to ensure that a significant proportion are filled by young Londoners. On the other hand, failure to secure affordable housing, or required transport links, could mean that London cannot find the workers to staff the basic public services on which everyone depends; while misguided land-use planning, or failures in preparation of brownfield land, could severely constrain housing supplies; or without adequate support the educational system could conceivably buckle under the strain of dealing with an unprecedentedly diverse intake of pupils.

The need for better policies in these areas follows directly from our analysis of life and labour in early twenty-first century London. But these social ills – shortages of housing, obsolete infrastructure, and unequal educational opportunities – would be familiar to twentieth century and indeed nineteenth century reformers. This is not solely – or even mainly – because of government failure in these areas. Rather, in each century the nature of the problem changes, but the difficulties of balancing economic growth with social justice – of reconciling competitiveness with cohesion – remain.

## Governance: Structures, Operations, Collaboration

Turning to issues of governance, there are questions about institutional structures and operational and collaborative potential which are more special to the London situation. There are three points of entry into thinking about these. One is that the effective urban system which needs to be managed in order to secure competitiveness, cohesion, and related goals such as environmental sustainability, is substantially larger than the Greater London area for which the Mayor, GLA and LDA are now responsible. And in some ways creation of the new regional agencies – two or three of which are involved in each of the two key economic development areas, in the Thames Valley and in Thames Gateway – seems likely to make problems of competition and co-ordination worse.

The second point is that even the GLA area is too diverse and complex to be managed in an integrated way from a single authority. Boroughs will continue to be important in promoting the broad strategic goals, as well as in sustaining the quality of life of their residents. But interfacing directly with 33 local governments is beyond the capacity of a single Mayor and his slimline organization.

The third point of entry is that the London region is simply too huge, and of too much symbolic significance, for the central state ever to allow it an autonomous unit of government. This is particularly so, given the considerable differences in social interests, values and political attachments between London and its exurban hinterland, which national government can scarcely avoid arbitrating.

So far the sole, timid step toward a more regional capacity for governance has been the signing of a strategic planning 'protocol' between the GLA and regional assemblies for the South East and Eastern regions, creating a Pan-Regional Advisory Forum on Regional Planning, inaugurated in March 2001. Currently strategic regional issues are rather in abeyance since all parties agree, for their own reasons, that London should 'accommodate its own growth' through high-density brownfield development, particularly in outer East London. The realism of this is in doubt, however, in relation both to the residential choices which individuals are actually likely to make, and to the delay before adequate transport links will actually be available to the eastern sites – in particular east-west Crossrail, which may never reach many of them at all. When difficult decisions are to be reached, central government is almost bound to take the leadership role in relation to the wider functional urban region. There is a need now to recognize that this is the case and strengthen the capacity of government to act, in relation to a whole range of pan-regional issues, not just those of physical planning. Given the uncertain present role of the Government Office for London in 'co-habiting' with the GLA, one obvious option would involve a merged Super-Regional Office for the whole of South East England with a Prefectoral or Ministerial director with the political weight to arbitrate between, co-ordinate, and allocate resources to the Mayor and the RDAs.

How the relationships develop will depend to a considerable degree on what sources of authority the Mayor can build up to bolster his very limited set of formal powers and responsibilities. In the first three years, progress in this regard has been hampered because of his need to combat central government's insistence on a private partnership approach to upgrading of the Underground, and his continuing exclusion from the Labour party. This situation could change if the Mayor can successfully articulate a vision of London's future that embodies the concerns both of London electors and of key economic interests, entitling him to make political claims in relation to issues beyond his formal brief. However, the one way in which we can envisage a real challenge from London to the hegemonic role of central government would be if the burgeoning alliance between the political authority of the Mayor, in his glass eyrie on the South Bank, and the financial and economic power of the City across the river was consolidated in a 'global city'-oriented regime. If so, the scene would be set for a further chapter in the long tradition of struggle between state authority in Westminster and the dynamic – and international – municipal power a mile or so to the east.

Within Greater London also there are issues of strategic capacity, given the effective responsibility of the boroughs for implementation of the bulk of the Mayor's strategies, and the extent of the GLA's reliance on a single person executive backed up by a small personal cabinet and a modest bureaucracy. One important step toward more reliable implementation would be the creation of a non-statutory sub-regional structure, through which the GLA could communicate with groups of boroughs, and they could resolve the major issues of competition and co-operation among neighbouring areas. This is crucial since successful policy initiatives will continue to require co-ordinated action from different actors within a complex system of multi-level governance.

In cities, policy challenges have always had two basic aspects. One involves the management of externalities in situations where proximity makes them much more important, for good and bad. The other is dealing with social inequality and its consequences in situations which tend to make these more visible. As the scale of urban government has grown, a third challenge has been to limit the unintentionally negative consequences of existing regulatory interventions. We have found various important examples of all three of these in the current environment of the London region, some of which reflect the changed conditions of the past 20 years, though many others have a long history. Important examples involving externalities within the private sector include the questions of who takes responsibility for human capital development and worker socialization in high turnover labour markets such as those of the London hospitality industry. Within the public sector a new example involves the knock-on effects of some boroughs seeking to upgrade their resident population and their image, while effectively exporting problems to their neighbours. Across the region as a whole, there is a key example of the unintended consequences of regulatory policies, highly topical in 2002: the impact of restrictive planning policies on the supply of new housing, and thus on the supply of key workers needed to operate the region's economy. But the set of policy challenges that seems to have grown most over this period involves those of straightforward social inequality, which seem not to have altered much in kind, but which grew substantially in scale, at least up to the early 1990s. More than the others it is these which call for a combination of 'thought' with 'resolution' rather than the pursuit of quick fixes.

## Postcript: The Mayor's London Plan

As we went to press in June 2002, the draft *London Plan* was published by the GLA (Mayor of London, 2002). It is a major event: this is only the third official plan to have been produced for Greater London, following the 1944 *Greater London Plan* and the 1969 *Greater London Development Plan*. In tone and content it differs greatly from both of these earlier models, reflecting major differences both in authorship, and in the situation which it addresses. The 1944 Plan bore the stamp of a visionary professional planner, Patrick Abercrombie, while the GLDP (as its successor was appropriately known) was the product of County Hall bureaucracy and political compromise; in contrast to both, the new *London Plan* appears in the name of the first directly-elected Mayor and clearly represents his personal aspirations for the capital. In terms of situation, the Abercrombie Plan foresaw strong post-war growth pressures on available space in London, to be dealt with via planned decentralization into the OMA; by the time of the GLDP, however, planned dispersal had been greatly overtaken by voluntary out-movements into a booming OMA, and people were starting to get worried about the effects of unbalanced population and job loss within London. Again in sharp contrast, the Livingstone Plan (or Ken's Plan as it is already being called) appears at a time of substantial growth in London's population and employment, and enthusiastically adopts growth as its key theme. Further decentralization or expansion into the surrounding region, which it identifies as the chosen path during much of the nineteenth and twentieth centuries, is rejected as an option to be considered, because it would be both environmentally unacceptable (particularly in that region) and contrary to central government policy.

A key theme of the Plan is the inevitability of large-scale growth: 700,000 additional residents and 636,000 extra jobs are forecast for 2016. The issue, the Plan argues, is simply whether this is specifically planned for and supported by appropriate infrastructure provision, *or else* allowed to overtake the city, which would entail 'a deepening of the many adverse economic, social and environmental problems already facing London' (Mayor of London, 2002, 35). Thus the Plan is driven by a strong determinism about the scale of growth – which it justifies by projections based 'on long run and deeply rooted trends' (in the case of population, *Ibid.*, 17) and the 'persistence of strong structural trends over a period of three decades . . . driven by deeply rooted changes in the international and UK economies and society' (in the case of employment, *Ibid.*, 23).

In our view, such determinism is misplaced, for several reasons. In the case of employment, the record has been highly volatile over the past 20 years – with two booms, one bust and another bust quite possibly on the way – making trend spotting a very uncertain business. Our guess is both that the trend is flatter than the Plan assumes, and that it should be applied to a lower base position than the current exceptionally high level of demand, which can hardly be expected to prevail through the 15 years over which the Plan looks ahead. But whatever is technically the best forecast now should be regarded as having a very large margin of error attached, rather than as representing a pre-set growth path.

In the case of population growth, there is a more specific source of uncertainty, because of the degree to which the rapid growth of very recent years has been influenced by the influx of asylum seekers (a factor not mentioned in the Plan). This flow to London could well shrink in an economic downturn, or in the face of strong diversionary policies – though it could also conceivably grow. A slowing of current high rates of natural increase is also possible, as immigrants became more like established Londoners – though potential householders and job-seekers in 2016 have already been born. And there is also a very important question about the extent to which other Londoners will choose to live within the more densely developed city which is envisaged, rather than move out in much larger numbers into less dense developments in the OMA. If that is their preference, then there may be little that planners can do to prevent it happening, since out-movers do not have to go into newly constructed dwellings requiring planning permission. Within the draft Plan's framework of thought, however, this possibility is simply unthinkable. One reason for this, as well as the Plan's commitment to the 'compact city' ideal, is clearly that it is the prospect of very large-scale growth which underpins the claim for much higher investment in London infrastructure, implicit in the draft Plan.

This relates to the Plan's basic objectives. Though several are stressed – economic, social, environmental – the central concerns really seem to be three: first, to ensure London's economic competitiveness; second, to find ways to realize the growth targets; and third, to secure for London residents and businesses some of the resources and infrastructure required to make the city function more smoothly. From our perspective, the economic analysis offered by the Plan in support of this case is too one-eyed in its focus on the role of global financial services – which, as we saw in Chapter 3, are not the sole driver of the urban economy. But it is not quite clear how significantly this analysis affects the core strategy, which is to go for growth in order to secure public and private investment for the city.

The Plan's basic strategy for accommodating this growth can be summed up in two injunctions: 'go east' and 'raise densities'. In pursuit of the first, the Plan's East sub-region is supposed to take 142,000 new homes, nearly one-third of the

London total; Central London will take as many, with little more than 10 per cent each in the other three sub-regions. And the same with jobs, but more so: Central and East have three-quarters of the planned growth, East alone has 40 per cent. There is some statistical sleight of hand here: the City of London and the City fringe (with two of the 'major opportunity areas') are counted in the East. But the main thrust of development is to be in the real east of London: 100,000 new jobs in the Isle of Dogs, 30,000 at Stratford (with a European business quarter around the new Eurostar station), another 20,000 in the Lower Lee Valley and the Royal Docks: 150,000 in all, nearly one-quarter of the London total, in what amounts to a huge eastward extension of London's central business district. Likewise with the new homes, most of which are planned to be even farther east, at Barking Reach and on the Greenwich Peninsula.

This would represent a dramatic reversal of the westward bias to growth which – as we have seen – has prevailed over the past 20 years. It is justified on two grounds: physically, because the east is where the major areas of under-used space are to be found; and socially, because it is also where the major concentrations of deprivation are located – though, if our analysis is correct, growth in itself would have only a marginal impact in mitigating them. But the big question is how is this redirection of the city to be accomplished, given the strong natural advantages, and also the prejudices, that favour the west. More affordable space alone is not the answer, since many residents and employers wanting such space would still prefer to be right outside Greater London than in East London. The key in the Plan's approach is a fundamental improvement in levels of physical accessibility from the east, particularly into Central London, through a series of major pieces of new transport infrastructure. These include three very expensive express transit lines across London – two of them, Crossrail One and Crossrail Two, completely new – and three new East London river crossings, as well as two new bus transit schemes for East London.

But there are two problems with this strategy. Firstly, the planned transport links are not closely tied to the major opportunity areas – suggesting poor co-ordination between GLA planners and Transport for London, a point to which we return. For example, Crossrail One will not serve Barking, one of the key sites for large-scale new housing, while the route of Crossrail Two is not even closely specified. Secondly, there is no guarantee that the links will be built in time to attract the expected new residents and employers – since the necessary statutory procedures make it unlikely that either Crossrail could be completed before 2012 – or indeed that the finance for them (and other projects in the Plan) will actually be forthcoming. Some schemes – Thameslink 2000, the East London Line extension (making possible an outer circle or Orbirail), extensions of the Docklands Light Railway, the East London busways – do have a good chance of being realized in time. But these will not produce the necessary capacity to the east of London to make major new development happen there.

At the Plan's launch, the Mayor claimed the private sector was ready and eager to invest in such projects, and for such new projects he is happy to encourage private investment. But private money will come only in expectation of profit, which depends on a sufficient cash flow from the farebox, developer contributions, and/or subventions from Londoners' payments of community charge. The treatment of public investment is in fact one of the general weaknesses of the Plan, partly because of the GLA's lack of control over it. There is no explicit costing, though a London First estimate of £100 billion as a measure of need over the period is quoted. This would require more or less a doubling of the current rate of public investment in the city (Gordon *et al*., 2002), a sum which projected revenue of £1.5 billion from congestion charging barely starts to scratch. Whether the 'go east' strategy is at all feasible in practice therefore depends greatly on recognition by central government that national interests are at stake, which is far from evident at present.

The other key ingredient of a growth strategy for London based on resisting further overspill into the OMA or beyond is increasing density of land use. For job growth most of the extra land estimated to be required has been found in 28 so-called opportunity areas, with about a quarter in Docklands, though this seems to assume that there will be no further increases in space per worker. There is also explicit provision for more tall buildings in key areas such as the fringes of the City of London. For housing, however, two-thirds of the extra capacity is going to have to be found outside the opportunity areas – meaning a very rapid and sharp increase in densities right across London. It is unclear how this can be achieved, given the current pattern of housing preferences and planning machinery. The Plan talks of reducing the numbers of empty dwellings – but exactly how, short of officially-encouraged squatting, remains likewise unclear.

One specific idea is to enhance the role of town centres in Outer London with better access to public transport, and use these as foci for residential densification. But this is dependent on the willingness of the boroughs to make this happen, in a context where electorates may well be uneasy, and there are many conservation areas. Improving the orbital accessibility of these centres, currently dependent on slow and often unreliable bus services, is also problematic since major investment is required in new links. But no provision for this had been made in the GLA's 2001 transport strategy. Orbirail, which would link many of the key sites in London's middle ring, was dismissed as a long-term project, and new road-building has also been firmly eschewed, save for the new river crossings in the east. It looks very much as if one piece of the Mayor's empire, Transport for London, has been proceeding independently of the others.

There are uncertainties also in relation to housing, where the stress on growth presents an almost impossible equation. The overall targets set in the Plan for accommodating the additional population are hugely ambitious, even without any provision for further reductions in household size: a minimum of 458,000 new homes from 1997 to 2016, 23,000 a year. The problem is that this figure is well below estimates of the actual need, but also well above the rate of construction that has recently been achieved. As the Plan admits, over recent years house building in London has failed to catch up with demand. The Mayor's Housing Commission, on whose work the Plan depends, calculated the need at 40,000 units per year up to 2016, of which 28,000 a year should be 'affordable housing'; the actual figures for the year 2000 were 12,000 in total, a mere 30 per cent of target, of which a minuscule 2,743 were affordable (Joseph Rowntree Foundation, 2002, 20).

Raising the overall rate of construction is critical to achieving the Plan's overall growth targets, but securing a much faster building rate for 'affordable housing' is of more specific importance in relation to its social inclusion goals – which are otherwise only uncertainly addressed through the 'go east' strategy. In the context of both a hugely shrunk stock of social housing and cyclically high London house prices, the affordability crisis (which the government was promising to address as this book went to press) involves both traditional social housing needs and intermediate housing for key public service workers, including low cost owner-occupation. The Plan estimates the total need for affordable housing at 25,700 dwellings per year – but, considering capacity and economics, then reduces this to an annual target of just 10,000 affordable homes. This is close to the Plan's goal that 50 per cent of all new housing should be affordable – not quite, since the target is reduced to 35 per cent for thirteen of the boroughs, a variation that seems inspired by a political decision to avoid trouble with some outer boroughs. But even this represents nearly four times the estimated rate of construction in 2000 and would require huge subsidies from central government: an estimated £6 billion, which again cannot be counted on.

In summary, then, the Plan is vulnerable to changes – especially to a prolonged economic downturn. Its determination to accommodate much more growth within its boundaries reflects something of a 'Little London' attitude to the wider region, but also a drive to secure needed investment in infrastructure. Its eastern strategy is admirable, but will need resources on a scale that is far from guaranteed. And there is a sense that its development proposals and its transport proposals do not entirely hang together. The big question is whether the Plan can be implemented, when crucial levers are in the hands of central government, the boroughs and the private market.

That will take 20 years to answer. And over that time, London will continue to change. London is an unpredictable city: many times in its long history, it has surprised both those who wanted to understand it, and those who sought to plan it. We too shall doubtless be surprised. Our analysis, like those of the framers of the London Plan, may prove in some respects ephemeral. In closing, we would only counsel that understanding of London, that most complex of urban organisms, does not yield to simple theses or simplistic prescriptions.

# Bibliography

Abu-Lughod, J. (1999) *New York, Chicago, Los Angeles: America's Global Cities.* Minneapolis: University of Minnesota Press.

Amin, A. (ed.) (1994) *Post-Fordism. A Reader.* Cambridge MA and Oxford: Blackwell.

Amin, A. and Graham, S. (1997) The ordinary city. *Transactions of the Institute of British Geographers,* **22**, 411–429.

Amin, A. and Thrift, N. (1992) Neo-Marshallian nodes in global networks. *International Journal of Urban and Regional Research,* **16**, 571–587.

Arulampamlam, W. and Stewart, M. (1995) The determinants of individual unemployment duration in an era of high unemployment. *Economic Journal,* **105,** 321–332.

Arup Economics and Planning (1996) *London in the UK Economy – A Planning Perspective.* London: Government Office for London.

Ashenfelter, O. and Rouse, C. (1999) Schooling, Intelligence and Income in America. Unpublished working paper. Cambridge MA, National Bureau of Economic Research.

Association of London Government (1997) *The London Study. A Socio-Economic Assessment of London.* London: Association of London Government.

Atkinson, A. (1998) Social exclusion, poverty and unemployment, in Atkinson A. and Hills J. (eds.) *Exclusion, Employment and Opportunity.* CASE paper 4, LSE, London.

Audit Commission (1996) *Trading Places: the Supply and Allocation of School Places.* London: Audit Commission.

Augar, P. (2000) *The Death of Gentlemanly Capitalism.* London: Penguin.

Bailey, N. and Turok, I. (1999) Adjustment to job loss in Britain's cities. *Regional Studies,* **34**, 631–653.

Baker, P. and Eversley, J. (2000) *Multilingual Capital: the Languages of London's Schoolchildren and their Relevance to Economic, Social and Educational Policies.* London: Battlebridge.

Ball, M., Bowe, R. and Gewirtz, S. (1995) Circuits of schooling: a sociological exploration of parental choice of school in social class contexts. *Sociological Review,* **43**, 52–78.

Baran, D. and Donoghue, J. (2002) Price levels in 2000 for London and the regions compared with the national average. *Economic Trends,* **578**, 28–38.

Barker, T. (1990) *Moving Millions: A Pictorial History of London Transport.* London: London Transport Museum.

Barker, T. and Robbins, M. (1974) *A History of London Transport*. Vol. II. *The Twentieth Century to 1970*. London: George Allen and Unwin.

Baumgartner, M. (1988) *The Moral Order of a Suburb*. New York: Oxford University Press.

Beck, U. (1992) *Risk Society*. London: Sage.

Beresford, P. and Beresford, S. (1978) *A Say in the Future: Planning, Participation and Meeting Social Need. A New Approach: North Battersea: A Case Study*. (Battersea Community Action Reports 1). London: no publisher stated.

Bernstein, B. (1975) *Class, Codes and Control, Volume 3*. London: Routledge.

Blackaby, D., Leslie, D., Murphy, P. and O'Leary, N. (2002) White/ethnic minority earnings and employment differentials in Britain: evidence from the LFS. *Oxford Economic Papers, **54***, 270–297.

Blair, T. (1997a) Speech by the Prime Minister on 2nd June at the Aylesbury Estate Southwark. Social Exclusion Unit Homepage at www.gov.uk.

Blair, T. (1997b) Speech on 8th December at Stockwell Park School Lambeth to launch the Social Exclusion Unit. Social Exclusion Unit Homepage at www.gov.uk.

Blatt, P. and Gollain, V. (2000) *Les grands régions scientifiques et technologiques dans le monde*. Paris: Institut d'Aménagement et d'Urbanisme de la Région d'Île-de-France.

Body-Gendrot, S. (2000) *The Social Control of Cities. A Comparative Perspective*. Oxford and Cambridge MA: Blackwell.

Booth, C. (ed.) (1902–1903) *Life and Labour of the People in London*. 17 volumes in 3 series. London: Macmillan.

Bourdieu P. (1984) *Distinction*. London: Routledge.

Bourdieu, P. (1985) The forms of capital, in Richardson, J. (ed) *Handbook of Theory and Research for the Sociology of Education.* New York: Greenwood.

Bourdieu, P. and Wacquant, J. (1999) On the cunning of imperialist reason. *Theory Culture and Society*, **16**, 41–58.

Breheny, M. (1990) Strategic Planning and Urban Sustainability, in *Proceedings of TCPA Annual Conference, Planning for Sustainable Development*. London: Town and Country Planning Association.

Bruegel, I. (1996) Gendering the polarisation debate, a comment on Hamnett's: 'Social polarisation, economic restructuring and welfare state regimes'. *Urban Studies*, **33**, 469–490.

Buck, N. (1997) Social Divisions and Labour Market Change in London. Working Paper of the Institute for Social and Economic Research, Paper 97–25. University of Essex, Colchester.

Buck, N. (2001) Identifying neighbourhood effects on social exclusion. *Urban Studies, **38***, 2251–2275.

Buck, N. and Drennan, M. (1992) The dynamics of the metropolitan economy, in Fainstein, S., Gordon, I, and Harloe, M. (eds.) *Divided Cities: New York and London in the Contemporary World*. Oxford: Blackwell.

Buck, N. and Gordon, I. (1998) Turbulence and sedimentation in the labour markets of late 20th century London. Paper presented to the Conference on Cities at the Millennium, RIBA, London.

Buck, N. Gordon, I. and Young, K. (1986) *The London Employment Problem*. Oxford: Oxford University Press.

Buckner, J. (1988) The development of an instrument to measure neighbourhood cohesion. *American Journal of Community Psychology*, **16**, 771–791.

Butler, T. and Robson, G. (2002) Middle-class Households and the Remaking of Urban Neighbourhoods in London. Unpublished MS, University of East London, London.

Cabinet Office Performance and Innovation Unit (2002) *Ethnic Minorities and Labour Markets – Interim Analysis Report*. London: Cabinet Office.

Cameron, G. and Muellbauer (2000) Earnings biases in the United Kingdom Regional Accounts: some economic policy and research implications. *Economic Journal*, **110**, F412–F429.

Castel, R. (1998) *Les métamorphoses de la question sociale*. Paris: Fayard.

Castells, M. (1983) *The City and The Grassroots*. London: Edward Arnold.

Cathcart, B. (1999) *The Case of Stephen Lawrence*. London: Penguin.

Centre for Economics and Business Research (2001) *London's Contribution to the UK Economy*. London: Centre for Econoomics and Business Research.

Chambers, D., Forrester, P. and Williams, E. (1999) *Social Inclusion – A Study of Kent Thameside*. London: Centre for Public Policy Studies, University of Greenwich.

Champion, A. (1999) Migration and British cities in the 1990s. *National Institute Economic Review*, **170**, 60–77.

Cherry, B. and Pevsner, N. (1983) *The Buildings of England: London 2: South*. London: Penguin.

Cheshire, P. and Gordon, I. (1995) Change and spatial specialisation within the South East's economy, in Cheshire, P. and Gordon, I. (eds.) *Territorial Competition in an Integrating Europe*. Aldershot: Avebury.

Cheshire, P. and Gordon, I. (1996) Territorial competition and the predictability of collective (in)action. *International Journal of Urban and Regional Research*, **20**, 383–399.

Cheshire, P. and Gordon, I. (1998) Territorial competition: some lessons for policy. *Annals of Regional Science*, **32**, 1–26.

Cheshire, P. and Gornostaeva, G. (2001) More useful Londons: the comparative development of alternative concepts of London. *Geographica Helvetica*, **56**, 179–192.

Cheshire, P., Monastiriotis, V. and Sheppard, S. (2002) Income inequality and residential segregation: labour market sorting and the demand for positional goods, in Martin, R. and Morrison, P. (eds.) *Geographies of Labour Market Inequality*. London: Routledge.

Cheshire, P. and Sheppard, S. (1998) Estimating the demand for housing, land and neighbourhood characteristics. Oxford Bulletin of Economics and Statistics, **60**, 357–382.

City Research Project (1995) *The Competitive Position of London's Financial Services: Final Report*. London: Corporation of London.

Clancy, A., Hough, M., Aust, R. and Kershaw, C. (2001) *Crime, Policing and Justice, the Experience of Ethnic Minorities: Evidence from the 2000 Crime Survey*. Home Office Research Study 223. London: Home Office.

Cluttons/Kent County Council (2000) *Kent Property Market 2000*. http://www.kentpropertymarket.co.uk.

Cohen, R. (1981) The new international division of labour, multinational corporations and urban hierarchy, in Dear, M. and Scott, A. (eds.) *Urbanization and Urban Planning in Capitalist Society*. London: Methuen.

Coleman, J. (1988) Social capital in the creation of human capital. *American Journal of Sociology*, **94**, S95–S120.

Coleman, J. (1990) *Foundations of Social Theory*. Cambridge: Belknap Press.

Coopers and Lybrand Deloitte (1991) *London: World City, Moving into the 21st Century*. London: HMSO.

Coser, L. (1976) *The Functions of Social Conflict*. New York: Free Press.

Crow, G., Allan, G. and Summers, M. (2002) Neither busybodies nor nobodies: managing proximity and distance in neighbourly relations. *Sociology*, **36**, 127–146.

Daffin, C. (2001) Introducing new and improved productivity data. *Economic Trends*, **570**, 47–62.

de Souza Briggs, X. (1998) Brown kids in white suburbs: housing mobility and the many faces of social capital. *Housing Policy Debate*, **9**, 177–221.

Dearden, L. (1998), Ability, Family, Education and Earnings. Unpublished paper, Institute of Fiscal Studies, London.

Devicienti, F. (2001) Poverty Persistence in Britain: a Multivariate Analysis Using the BHPS, 1991–1997. Working Paper of the Institute for Social and Economic Research, Paper 2001–2. University of Essex, Colchester.

Dignan, T., Gordon, I. and Gudgin, G (1996) *Forecasting Employment in London and the South East, Report to the Government Office for London*. Belfast: Northern Ireland Research Centre.

Donnison, D. and Eversley, D.E.C. (1973) *London: Urban Patterns, Problems and Policies*. London: Heinemann.

Doogan, K. (2001) Insecurity and long term employment. *Work, Employment and Society*, **15**, 419–441.

Dorling, D., Martin, M. and Mitchell, R. (2001) *Linking Censuses Through Time*. http://census.ac.uk/cdu/lct/.

Dowding, K. et al. (1999) Regime politics in London local government. *Urban Affairs Review*, **34**, 515–545.

Drennan, M. (1996) The dominance of international finance by London, New York and Tokyo, in Daniels, P. and Lever, W. (eds.) *The Global Economy in Transition*. London: Longman.

Duranton G. and Monastiriotis V. (2000) Mind the Gaps: The Evolution of Regional Inequalities in the UK 1982–1997. Discussion Paper 485. LSE Centre for Economic Performance, London.

Duster, T. (1995) Postindustrialization and youth unemployment: African Americans as Harbingers, in

McFate, K., Lawson, R. and Wilson, W. (eds.) *Poverty, Inequality and the Future of Social Policy*. New York: Russell Sage Foundation.

Elkin, S. (1987) *City and Regime in the American Republic*. Chicago: University of Chicago Press.

Employers Organisation for Local Government (2001) *Teacher Resignations and Recruitments 2001*. London: EOLG.

Erikson, R. and Goldthorpe, J. (1993) *The Constant Flux – A Study of Class Mobility in Industrial Societies*. Oxford: Clarendon Press.

Ermisch, J., and Francesconi, M. (2001) Family matters: impacts of family background on educational attainments. *Economica*, **68**, 137–156.

Esping-Andersen, G. (1993) *Changing Classes: Stratification and Mobility in Post-Industrial Societies*. London: Sage.

Etzioni, A. (1995) *The Spirit of Community. Rights, Responsibilities and the Communitarian Agenda*. London: Fontana Press.

Etzioni, A. (1997) *The New Golden Rule: Community and Morality in a Democratic Society*. London: Profile Books.

Etzioni, A. (2000) *The Third Way to a Good Society*. London: Demos.

Fainstein, S., Gordon, I. and Harloe, M. (eds.) (1992) *Divided Cities. New York and London in the Contemporary World*. Oxford and Cambridge MA: Blackwell.

Feinstein, L. and Symons, J. (1999) Attainment in secondary school. *Oxford Economic Papers*, **51**, 300–321.

Fielding, A. (1989) Inter-regional migration and social change: a study of South East England based upon data from the Longitudinal Study. *Institute of British Geographers Transactions New Series*, **14**, 24–36.

Fielding, A. (1991) Migration and social mobility: South East England as an escalator region. *Regional Studies*, **26**, 1–15.

Fielding, A. (1995) Migration and middle-class formation in England and Wales 1981–91, in Butler, T. and Savage, M. (eds.) *Social Change and the Middle Classes*. London: UCL Press.

Fitzgerald, M., Hough, M, Joseph and Qureshi, T. (2002) *Policing for London*. Uffculme: Willan Publishing.

Florida, R. (2002) Bohemia and economic geography. *Journal of Economic Geography*, **2**, 55–71.

Foley, M. and Edwards, B. (1999) Time to disinvest in social capital? *Journal of Public Policy*, **19**, 141–173.

Fothergill, S., Gudgin, G., Kitson, M. and Monk, S. (1988) The deindustrialisation of the city, in Massey, D and Allen, J. (eds.) *Uneven Re-development: Cities and Regions in Transition*. London: Hodder and Stoughton.

Friedmann, J. (1995) Where we stand: a decade of world city research, in Knox, P. and Taylor, P. (eds.) (1995) *World Cities in a World System*. Cambridge: Cambridge University Press.

Friedmann, J. and Wolff, G. (1982) World city formation: an agenda for research and action. *International Journal of Urban and Regional Research*, **6**, 309–344.

Fujita, M. and Krugman, P. (1995) When is the economy monocentric? Von Thünen and Chamberlain unified. *Regional Science and Urban Economics*, **25**, 505–528.

Gans, H. (1967) *The Levittowners: Ways of Life and Politics in a New Suburban Community*. London: Allen Lane.

G.B. Department for Education and Employment (1999) *Ethnic Minority Pupils and Pupils for whom English is an Additional Language 1996/7*. Statistical Bulletin 3/99. London: DfEE.

G.B. Department of the Environment (1977) *Policy for the Inner Cities*. Cmnd. 6845. London: HMSO.

G.B. Department of Environment, Transport and the Regions (2000) *Our Towns and Cities: the Future – Delivering an Urban Renaissance*. Cm. 4912. London: Stationery Office.

G.B. Department of Transport, Local Government and the Regions (2000) *Measuring Multiple Deprivation at the Small Area Level: The Indices of Deprivation 2000*. London: Department of the Environment, Transport and the Regions.

G.B. South East Joint Planning Team (1970) *Strategic Plan for the South East: A Framework. Report by the South East Joint Planning Team*. London: HMSO.

G.B. Thames Gateway Task Force (1995) *The Thames Gateway Planning Framework*. (RPG 9a). London: Department of the Environment.

Gershuny, J. and Miles, I. (1983) *The New Service Economy*. London: Frances Pinter.

Gibbons S. and Machin S. (2001) Valuing Primary Schools. Centre for Economics of Education Discussion Paper 15. LSE, London.

Giddens, A. (1991) *Modernity and Self-Identity*. Cambridge: Polity Press.

Giddens, A. (2000) *The Third Way and its Critics*. Cambridge: Polity Press.

Gillborn D. and Mirza H. (2000) *Educational Inequality: Mapping Race, Class and Gender – a Synthesis of Research Evidence*. London: Office of Standards in Education.

Glaeser E., Scheinkman, J. and Shleifer, A. (1995) Economic growth in a cross-section of cities. *Journal of Monetary Economics*, **36**, 117–143.

Glaeser, E. (1999) Learning in cities. *Journal of Urban Economics*, **46**, 254–277.

Glaeser, E. and Marc, D. (2001) Cities and skills. *Journal of Labor Economics*, **19**, 316–342.

Gorard, S. and Fitz, J. (2000) Markets and stratification: A view from England and Wales. *Educational Policy*, **14**, 405–428.

Gordon, I. (1987) Unstable People, Unstable Jobs and Unstable Places. Paper presented at the Institute of British Geographers/Regional Science Association Conference on Geography of Labour Markets, London.

Gordon, I. (1989) Urban unemployment, in Herbert, D. and Smith, D. (eds.) *Social Problems and the City: New Perspectives*. Oxford: Oxford University Press.

Gordon, I. (1995) London World City: political and organisational constraints on territorial competition, in Cheshire, P. and Gordon, I. (eds.) *Territorial Competition in an Integrating Europe*. Aldershot: Avebury.

Gordon, I. (1996a) Territorial Competition and Locational Advantage in the London Region. Paper presented at the ESRC London Seminar series, LSE, London.

Gordon, I. (1996b) Developing a sub-regional forecasting model for London and the South East: the supply side of the labour market, in *Proceedings of the NOMIS Conference on Labour Market Research*. Durham: NOMIS.

Gordon, I. (1996c) Family structure, educational achievement and the inner city. *Urban Studies*, **33**, 407–423.

Gordon, I. (1999a) Internationalisation and urban competition. *Urban Studies,* **36**, 1001–1016.

Gordon, I. (1999b) London and the South East, in Breheny, M. (ed.) *The People: Where Will They Work?* London: Town and Country Planning Association.

Gordon, I. (2000) The Role of Internationalisation in Economic Change in London Over the Past 25 Years. Geographical Paper 152, University of Reading, Reading.

Gordon, I. (2002a) Unemployment and spatial labour markets: strong adjustment and persistent concentration, in Martin, R. and Morrison, P. (eds.) *Geographies of Labour Market Inequality*. London: Routledge.

Gordon, I. (2002b) Moving up and bumping down in urban labour markets: evidence from the British Household Panel Survey. Working Paper. LSE Department of Geography, London.

Gordon, I. (2002c) Urban Size, Spatial Segregation and Educational Outcomes. Working Paper. LSE Department of Geography, London.

Gordon, I. (2002d) Global cities, internationalisation and urban systems, in McCann, P. (ed.) *Industrial Location Economics*. Cheltenham: Edward Elgar.

Gordon, I. (2003) Integrated cities, in Buck, N., Gordon, I., Harding, A., Turok, I. (eds.) *Changing Cities: Urban Competitiveness, Cohesion and Governance*. Basingstoke: Palgrave.

Gordon, I. and Buck, N. (2003) The new conventional wisdom: city competitiveness, cohesion and governance, in Buck, N., Gordon, I., Harding, A., Turok, I. (eds.) *Changing Cities: Urban Competitiveness, Cohesion and Governance.* Basingstoke: Palgrave.

Gordon, I. and Lamont, D. (1982) A model of interdependencies in the labour markets of the London region. *Environment and Planning A*, **14**, 237–264.

Gordon, I. and McCann, P. (2000a) Industrial clusters: complexes, agglomeration and/or social networks? *Urban Studies*, **37**, 513–532.

Gordon, I. and McCann, P. (2000b) Innovation, Agglomeration and Regional Development. Paper presented to the Regional Science Association, British and Irish Section Conference, Bath.

Gordon, I. and Monastiriotis, V. (2001) Spatial Analyses of Neighbourhood Influences on Examination Performance. Unpublished paper, LSE Department of Geography, London.

Gordon, I. and Sassen, S. (1992) Restructuring the urban labour markets, in Fainstein, S., Gordon, I. and Harloe, M. (eds.) *Divided Cities: New York and London in the Contemporary World*. Cambridge MA and Oxford: Blackwell.

Gordon, I., Travers, T. and Whitehead, C. (2002) *London's Place in the UK Economy*. London: City Corporation.

Gosling, A. and Lemieux, T. (2002) Labour market reforms and changes in wage inequalities in the United Kingdom and the United States, in Blundell, R., Card, D. and Freeman, R. (eds.) *The UK: Seeking a Premier League Economy*. London: Chicago University Press.

Graham. D and Spence. N (1997) Competition for metropolitan resources: the 'crowding out' of London's manufacturing industry? *Environment and Planning A*, **29**, 459–484.

Granovetter, M. (1973) The strength of weak ties. *American Journal of Sociology,* **78**, 1360–1380.

Granovetter, M. (1985) Economic action and social structure: the problem of embeddedness. *American Journal of Sociology*, **91**, 481–510.

Granovetter, M. (1995) The economic sociology of firms and entrepreneurs, in Portes, A. (ed.) *The Economic Sociology of Immigration*. New York: Russell Sage.

Greater London Assembly (2001) *Key Issues for Key Workers*. London: GLA.

Greater London Authority (2001) *State of London 2000. Final Report.* London: GLA.

Greater London Authority (2002) *Planning for London's Growth*. London: GLA.

Green, A. and Owen, A. (2001) *Skills, Local Areas and Unemployment*. Nottingham: DfEE publications.

Gregg, P. and Machin, S. (1997), Blighted lives. *Centre Piece*, LSE Centre for Economic Performance, 15–17.

Gripaios, P. (1977) Industrial decline in London: an examination of its causes. *Urban Studies,* **14**, 181–189.

Gwilliam, M., Bourne, C., Swain, C., Pratt, A. (1998) *Sustainable Renewal of Suburban Areas*. York: Joseph Rowntree Foundation.

Hall, P. (1962) *The Industries of London Since 1861*. London: Hutchinson.

Hall, P. (1963) *London 2000*. London: Faber and Faber.

Hall, P. (1989) *London 2001*. London: Unwin Hyman.

Hall, P. (1998) *Cities in Civilization*. London: Weidenfeld and Nicolson.

Hall, P., Breheny, M., McQuaid, R. and Hart, D. (1987) *Western Sunrise: The Genesis of Britain's Major High Tech Corridor*. London: Allen and Unwin.

Hall, P., Marshall, S. and Lowe, M. (2001) The changing urban hierarchy in England and Wales, 1913–1998. *Regional Studies,* **35**, 775–807.

Hall, P.A. (1999) Social capital in Britain. *British Journal of Political Science*, **29**, 417–461.

Hall, S. and Jacques, M. (eds.) (1989) *New Times*. London: Lawrence and Wishart.

Hamnett, C. (1994a) Social polarisation in global cities: theory and evidence. *Urban Studies,* **31**, 401–424.

Hamnett, C. (1994b) Socio-economic change in London: professionalisation not polarisation. *Built Environment*, **20**, 192–203

Hamnett, C. (1996) Social polarisation, economic restructuring and welfare state regimes. *Urban Studies*, **33**, 1407–1430.

Harding, A. (1994) Urban regimes and growth machines: towards a cross-national research agenda. *Urban Affairs Quarterly,* **29**, 356–382.

Harding, A. (1997) Urban regimes in a Europe of the cities? *European Urban and Regional Studies,* **4**, 291–314.

Harding, A. et al. (1998) *Building Partnerships in the English Regions: A Study Report of Regional and Sub-Regional Partnerships in England.* London: Department of Environment, Transport and the Regions.

Harloe, M. (2001) Social justice and the city: the new 'liberal formulation'. *International Journal of Urban and Regional Research*, **25**, 889–897.

Harloe, M. and Fainstein, S. (1992) The divided cities, in Fainstein, S., Gordon, I. and Harloe, M. (eds.) *Divided Cities: New York and London in the Contemporary World*. Cambridge MA and Oxford: Blackwell.

Hewitt, R. (1997) *Routes of Racism*. Stoke-on-Trent: Trentham Books.

Hill, D. (2000) *Urban Policy and Politics in Britain*. Basingstoke: Macmillan.

Hitchens, D., O'Farrell, P. and Moffat, L. (1992) The competitiveness of business service firms: a matched comparison between Scotland and the South East of England. *Regional Studies*, **26**, 519–533.

Hobcraft, J. (1998), Intergenerational and Life Course Transmission of Social Exclusion: Influences of Child Poverty, Family Disruption and Contact with the Police. CASE paper 15, LSE Centre for Analysis of Social Exclusion, London.

Hollis, J. (1999) Mid-year Estimate Change Analysis: 1991–97, a Report for the London Boroughs. DSS Technical Paper 99/1. London Research Centre, London.

Hutton, W. (1996) *The State We're In.* London: Vintage.

International Financial Services London (2001) *International Financial Markets in the UK*. London: IFSL.

Jackson, A. (1991) *Semi-Detached London: Suburban Development, Life and Transport, 1900–39.* Second Edition. Didcot: Wild Swan Publications.

Jenkins, R. (1986) *Racism and Recruitment*. Cambridge: Cambridge University. Press.

Jessop, B. (1994) Post-Fordism and the state, in Amin, A. (ed.) *Post-Fordism: A Reader.* Oxford and Cambridge MA: Blackwell.

John, P. and Cole, A. (1998) Urban regimes and local governance in Britain and France: policy adoption and coordination in Leeds and Lille. *Urban Affairs Review,* **33**, 382–404.

Jones Lang LaSalle (2001) *London: the New Economy and the 'Dot.Com' – Time for Perspective*. London: JLL.

Joseph Rowntree Foundation (2002) *Britain's Housing in 2022: More Shortages and Homelessness?* York: JRF.

Jupp, B. and Lawson, G. (1997) *Values Added: How Emerging Values Could Influence the Development of London*. London: London Planning Advisory Committee and London Arts Board.

Kent Thames-Side (1999) *Looking to an Integrated Future: Land Use and Transport Planning in Kent Thames-Side*. Gravesend: Kent Thames-Side Strategy, Transport and SRB Groups.

Kesteloot, C. (1997) The geography of deprivation in Brussels and local development strategies, in Musterd, S. and Ostendorf, W. (eds.) *Urban Segregation and the Welfare State*. London: Routledge.

Keynes, J.M. (1936) *The General Theory of Employment, Interest, and Money*. London: Macmillan.

King A.D. (1990) *Global Cities: Post-imperialism and the Internationalization of London.* London and New York: Routledge.

Krugman, P. (1995) *Development, Geography and Economic Theory.* Cambridge MA: MIT Press.

Krugman, P. (1996) *Pop Internationalism.* Cambridge MA: MIT Press.

Kynaston, D. (2001) *The City of London: a Club No More 1945–2000.* London: Chatto and Windus.

Le Gales, P. (1998) Regulations and governance in European cities. *International Journal of Urban and Regional Research*, **22**, 482–506.

Le Grand J. and Bartlett W. (eds.) (1993) *Quasi-Markets and Social Policy*. Basingstoke: Macmillan.

Learning and Business Link Company (1998) *Kent Annual Business Survey 1998*. West Malling, Kent: LBL Company.

Leisering, L. and Leibfried, S. (1999) *Time and Poverty in Western Welfare States.* Cambridge: Cambridge University Press.

Levine R and Renelt D (1992) A sensitivity analysis of cross-country growth regressions. *American Economic Review*, **82**, 942–963.

Levitas, R. (1998) *The Inclusive Society? Social Exclusion and New Labour.* Basingstoke and London: Macmillan.

Llewelyn Davies, Bartlett School of Planning and Comedia (1996) *Four World Cities: a Comparative Study of London, Paris, New York and Tokyo*. London: Llewelyn Davies.

Lloyd's Insurance Brokers Committee (2000) *London Market Principles 2001*. London: Lloyd's.

Logan, J. and Molotch, H. (1987) *Urban Fortunes: The Political Economy of Place.* Berkeley: University of California Press.

London Development Partnership (1998) *Preparing for the Mayor and the London Development Agency.* London: London Development Partnership.

London Economics Limited (1994) The Competitive Advantage of Law and Accountancy in the City of London. Subject Report XIX City Research Project. Corporation of the City of London, London.

London Research Centre (1999) Population Advice Note. PAN 98–5. London Research Centre, London.

London Research Centre, Government Office for London and Office for National Statistics (2000) *Focus on London 2000*. London: Stationery Office.

London Skills Forecasting Unit (2000) *Dynamic London: the Capital's Economy in the Year 2000*. London: LSFU.

Lucas R E (1988) On the mechanics of economic development. *Journal of Monetary Economics*, **22**, 3–42.

Machin, S. (1999) Wage inequalities in the 1970s, 1980s and 1990s, in Gregg, P. and Wadsworth, J. (eds.) *The State of Working Britain*. Manchester: Manchester University Press.

Martin, J. (1966) *Greater London: An Industrial Geography*. London: Bell.

Marshall, A. (1920, 1890) *Principles of Economics*. London: Macmillan.

McDowell, L. (1997) *Capital Culture: Gender at Work in the City*. Oxford: Blackwell.

Mayhew, H. (1862) *London and the London Poor: A Cyclopedia of the Conditions and Earnings of Those that* Will *Work, those that* Cannot *Work, and those that* Will Not *Work*. London: Griffin.

Mayor of London (2002) *The Draft London Plan: Draft Spatial Development Strategy for London*. London: GLA.

Metcalf, D. and Richardson, R. (1976) Unemployment in London, in Worswick, G. (ed.) *The Concept and Measurement of Unemployment*. London: Allen and Unwin.

Mingione, E. (ed.) *Urban Poverty and the Underclass*. Oxford and Cambridge MA: Blackwell.

MORI (2002) *Annual London Survey 2001: Londoners' Views on Life in the Capital*. London: MORI.

Netherlands Economic Institute with Ernst and Young (1992) *New Location Factors for Mobile Investment in Europe*. Brussels: Commission of the European Communities.

Nickell, S. and Nicolitsas, D. (1997) Human Capital, Investment and Innovation: What are the Connections? Discussion Paper 370. LSE Centre for Economic Performance, London.

Noden, P. (2000) Rediscovering the Impact of marketisation: dimensions of social segregation in England's secondary schools, 1994-99. *British Journal of Sociology of Education*, **21**, 371–390.

Noden, P. (2001) School choice and polarisation: any evidence for increased segregation? *New Economy*, **8**, 199–202.

Noden, P., West, A., David, M. and Edge, A. (1998) Choices and destinations at secondary schools in London. *Journal of Educational Policy*, **13**, 221–236.

Norris, G. (1978) Unemployment, subemployment and personal characteristics: job separation and work histories: the alternative approach. *Sociological Review*, **25**, 327–347.

Nussbaum, M. and Sen, A. (eds.) (1993) *The Quality of Life*. Oxford: Clarendon Press.

OECD (2001) *The Well-being of Nations*. Paris: OECD.

Osborne, D. and Gaebler, T. (1992) *Reinventing Government*. Reading, MA: Addison-Wesley.

Peach, C. (1996) Does Britain have ghettos? *Transactions of The Institute of British Geographers*, **21**, 216–235.

Pencavel, J. (2002) The surprising retreat of Union Britain, in Blundell, R., Card, D. and Freeman, R. (eds.) *The UK: Seeking a Premier League Economy*. London: Chicago University Press.

Polanyi, K. (1944) *The Great Transformation*. New York: Rinehart.

Porter, M. (1990) *The Competitive Advantage of Nations*. New York: Free Press.

Porter, M. (1995) The competitive advantage of the inner city. *Harvard Business Review,* **73**, 55–71.

Porter, R. (1994) *London. A Social History*. London: Hamish Hamilton (paperback edition, Harmondsworth: Penguin, 2000).

Portes, A. (1998) Social capital: its origins and applications in modern sociology. *Annual Review of Sociology,* **24**, 1–24.

Pratt, A. (1997) The Cultural Industries Sector: its Definition and Character from Secondary Sources on Employment and Trade, Britain 1984–91. Research Papers in Environmental and Spatial Analysis 41, LSE, London.

Putnam, R. (1993) *Making Democracy Work. Civic Traditions in Modern Italy*. Princeton NJ: Princeton University Press.

Putnam, R. (1995) Bowling alone: America's declining social capital. *Journal of Democracy,* **6**, 65–78.

Putnam, R. (2000) *Bowling Alone: The Collapse and Revival of American Community.* New York: Simon & Schuster.

Rex, J. and Moore, R. (1967) *Race, Class and Conflict*. Oxford: Oxford University Press.

Robertson, D. and Symons, J. (1996) Do Peer Groups Matter? Peer Group Versus Schooling Effects on Academic Attainment. Paper 311. LSE Centre for Economic Performance, London.

Robson, G. and Butler, T. (2001) Coming to terms with London: middle class communities in a global city. *International Journal of Urban and Regional Research*, **25**, 70–86.

Rogerson, R. (1999) Quality of life and city competitiveness. *Urban Studies*, **36**, 969–985.

Romer P. (1990) Endogenous technical change. *Journal of Political Economy*, **98**, S71–S102.

Rudder, B. (1993) *Builders of the Borough: A Century of Achievement by Battersea and Wandsworth Trades Union Council from 1894 to 1994.* London: Battersea & Wandsworth Trades Union Council.

Rutter J. and Jones C. (1998) *Refugee Education: Mapping the Field.* London: Trentham Books.

Sassen, S. (1991) *The Global City: New York, London and Tokyo*. Princeton NJ: Princeton University Press.

Sassen, S. (ed.) (2002) *Global Networks, Linked Cities.* New York: Routledge.

Savage, M. (2000) *Class Analysis and Social Transformation*. Buckingham: Open University Press.

Savage, M., Barlow, J., Dickens, P. and Fielding, A. (1992) *Property, Bureaucracy and Culture: Middle Class Formation in Contemporary Britain*. London: Routledge.

Savas, E. (1987) *Privatization: The Key to Better Government.* New York and London: Chatham House Publishers.

Scholte J. (2000) *Globalisation: a Critical Introduction.* Basingstoke: Palgrave.

Scott, A. (1988) *Metropolis: from the Division of Labor to Urban Form*. Berkeley CA: University of California Press.

Sen, A. (1970) *Collective Choice and Social Welfare*. San Francisco: Holden-Day.

Sen, A. (1999) *Development as Freedom*. Oxford: Oxford University Press.

Sennett, R. (1999) *The Corrosion of Character*. New York and London: W.W. Norton & Company.

Sianesi, B. and van Reenan, J. (2000) The Returns to Education: a Review of the Macroeconomic Literature. DP6, LSE Centre for the Economics of Education, London.

Silver, H. (1996) Culture, politics and national discourses of the new urban poverty, in Mingione, E. (ed) *Urban Poverty and the Underclass.* Cambridge MA and Oxford: Blackwell.

Simmel, G. (1936) The metropolis and mental life, in *The Sociology of George Simmel,* translated by K. Woolf. Glencoe IL: The Free Press.

Simmie, J. and Sennett, J. (1999) Innovative clusters: global or local linkages? *National Institute Economic Review*, **170**, 87–98.

Simmie, J., Sennett, J., Wood, P. and Hart, D. (2002) Innovation in Europe: a tale of networks, knowledge and trade in five cities. *Regional Studies*, **36**, 47–64.

Simmons, M. (1987) The impact of the Channel Tunnel. *The Planner,* **73**, 16–18.

Social Exclusion Unit. (1998) *Bringing Britain Together: A National Strategy for Neighbourhood Renewal.* Cm. 4045. London: Stationery Office

Social Exclusion Unit. (2001) *A New Commitment to Neighbourhood Renewal: National Strategy Action Plan*. London: Cabinet Office.

Soja, E. (2000) *Postmetropolis. Critical Studies of Cities and Regions.* Oxford and Cambridge MA: Blackwell.

Spence M. (1973) Job market signalling. *Quarterly Journal of Economics,* **87**, 355–374.

Stedman Jones, G. (1971) *Outcast London*. Oxford: Oxford University Press.

Stewart, J. and Stoker, G. (eds.) (1994) *Local Government in the 1990s.* London: Macmillan.

Stoker, G. (1999) Introduction, in Stoker, G. (ed.) *The New Management of British Local Governance.* Basingstoke: Palgrave.

Stoker, G. and Mossberger, K. (1994) The Post-Fordist local state: the dynamics of its development, in Stewart, J. and Stoker, G. (eds.) *Local Government in the 1990s.* London: Macmillan.

Stone, C. (1989) *Regime Politics: Governing Atlanta 1946–1988.* Lawrence: University of Kansas Press.

Storper, M. (1995) The resurgence of regional economies, ten years later: the region as a nexus of untraded interdependencies. *European Urban and Regional Studies*, **2**, 191–221

Taylor, P. and Walker, D. (2001) World cities: a first multivariate analysis of their service complexes. *Urban Studies*, **38**, 23–47.

Temkin, K and Rohe, W. (1998) Social capital and neighbourhood stability: an empirical investigation. *Housing Policy Debate*, **9**, 61–88.

Thomas, S. and Mortimore, P. (1996) Comparison of value added models for secondary school effectiveness. *Research Papers in Education*, **11**, 279–295.

Thomas, S. and Smees, R. (1997), Dimensions of School Effectiveness: Comparative Analyses Across Regions. Paper presented at the Tenth International Congress for School Effectiveness, Memphis, Tennessee.

Tiebout, C. (1956) A pure theory of local expenditures. *Journal of Public Economy,* **64**, 416–424.

Tonnies, F. (1955) *Community and Association*, London: Routledge and Kegan Paul.

Townsend, P. (1979) *Poverty in the United Kingdom*. Harmondsworth: Penguin.

Trends Business Research (2001) *Business Clusters in the UK: a First Assessment*. London: Department of Trade and Industry.

Turok, I. and Edge, N. (1999) *The Jobs Gap in Britain's Cities*. Bristol: Policy Press.

Venables, A. (1995) Economic integration and the location of firms. *Quarterly Journal of Economics,* **80**, 190–207.

Vertovec, S. (1997) Social Cohesion and Tolerance. Discussion paper prepared for the Second International Metropolis Conference, Copenhagen.

Wadsworth, J. (eds.) *The State of Working Britain*. Manchester: Manchester University Press.

Weightman, G. and Humphries, S. (1983) *The Making of Modern London, 1815–1914*. London: Sidgwick & Jackson.

West A., Pennell H., Travers T., West R. (2001) Financing school-based education in England: poverty, examination results, and expenditure. *Environment and Planning C – Government and Policy*, **19**, 461–471.

White, H. (1963) *A Regional History of the Railways of Great Britain*. Volume 3, *Greater London*. London: Phoenix House.

White, M. and Forth, J. (1998) *Pathways Through Unemployment: the Effects of a Flexible Labour Market*. York: Joseph Rowntree Foundation.

Whyte, W.H. (1957) *The Organization Man*. London: Jonathan Cape.

Wilkinson, H., Mulgan, G. (1995) *Freedom's Children: Work, Relationships and Politics for 18–34 Year Olds in Britain Today*. London: Demos.

Willmott, P. and Young, M. (1973) Social class and geography, in Donnison, D. and Eversley, D. *London: Urban Patterns, Problems and Policies*. London: Heinemann.

Willms, J. and Echols, F. (1992) Alert and inert clients: the Scottish experience of parental choice of schools. *Economics of Education Review,* **11**, 339–350.

Wilson, W. (1987) *The Truly Disadvantaged*. Chicago: University of Chicago Press.

Wilson, W. (1997) *When Work Disappears*. New York: Vintage Books.

Wirth, L. (1939) Urbanism as a way of life. *American Journal of Sociology*, **44**, 1–24.

World Federation of Exchanges (2002) Exchange statistics: time series 1990–2000. www.world-exchanges.org.

Young, M. and Willmott, P. (1957) *Family and Kinship in East London.* London: Routledge & Kegan Paul.

Young, M. and Willmott, P. (1973) *The Symmetrical Family: A Study of Work and Leisure in the London Region*. London: Routledge & Kegan Paul.

# Index